For the Sake of Present and Future Generations

Roger Clark (right) with Roger Baldwin (left), founder of the American Civil Liberties Union, speaking at the UN Trusteeship Council on behalf of the International League for Human Rights in 1977. Roger Clark was advocating for the independence of the Trust Territory of the Pacific Islands and for an adequate cleanup of the waste from the 67 nuclear tests carried out in the Marshall Islands by the United States.

For the Sake of Present and Future Generations

*Essays on International Law, Crime and Justice
in Honour of Roger S. Clark*

Edited by

Suzannah Linton
Gerry Simpson
William A. Schabas

BRILL
NIJHOFF

LEIDEN | BOSTON

Cover illustration: Undocumented *tapa* from the personal collection of David King.

Library of Congress Cataloging-in-Publication Data

For the sake of present and future generations : essays on international law, crime and justice in honour of Roger S. Clark / edited by Suzannah Linton, Gerry Simpson, William A. Schabas.
  pages cm
 Includes index.
 ISBN 978-90-04-27071-8 (hardback : alk. paper) -- ISBN 978-90-04-27072-5 (e-book) 1. International law. 2. Clark, Roger S. (Roger Stenson) I. Clark, Roger S. (Roger Stenson), honouree. II. Linton, Suzannah, editor. III. Simpson, Gerry, editor. IV. Schabas, William, 1950- editor.

KZ3410.F67 2015
341--dc23

2015014835

This publication has been typeset in the multilingual "Brill" typeface. With over 5,100 characters covering Latin, IPA, Greek, and Cyrillic, this typeface is especially suitable for use in the humanities.
For more information, please see www.brill.com/brill-typeface.

ISBN 978-90-04-27071-8 (hardback)
ISBN 978-90-04-27072-5 (e-book)

Copyright 2015 by Koninklijke Brill NV, Leiden, The Netherlands.
Koninklijke Brill NV incorporates the imprints Brill, Brill Hes & De Graaf, Brill Nijhoff, Brill Rodopi and Hotei Publishing.
All rights reserved. No part of this publication may be reproduced, translated, stored in a retrieval system, or transmitted in any form or by any means, electronic, mechanical, photocopying, recording or otherwise, without prior written permission from the publisher.
Authorization to photocopy items for internal or personal use is granted by Koninklijke Brill NV provided that the appropriate fees are paid directly to The Copyright Clearance Center, 222 Rosewood Drive, Suite 910, Danvers, MA 01923, USA.
Fees are subject to change.

This book is printed on acid-free paper.

Contents

Preface & Acknowledgements   XI
List of Contributors   XIII

PART 1
Roger S. Clark

1. Appreciation   3
   José Ramos-Horta

2. Tribute   6
   Tuiloma Neroni Slade

3. *Laudatio:* In Honour of Roger S. Clark   10
   M. Cherif Bassiouni

4. Roger Clark: A Personal Tribute   12
   William A. Schabas

5. Roger *Avant-Garde*   21
   Gerry Simpson

PART 2
Essays on Peace, War and Global Security

6. Germany and the Crime of Aggression   31
   Claus Kreß

7. Mobilising Law on the Side of Peace: Security Council Reform and the Crime of Aggression   52
   Brian J. Foley

8. From the Shoulders of Giants: Harold Nicolson's Peacemaking 1919 and the Congress of Vienna   72
   Pam Jenoff

9   The Rule of Law, the International Justice System and Africa   82
     Daniel David Ntanda Nsereko

10   Global Citizenship   101
     Kennedy Graham

11   From Dr Strangelove to Dr Suess: Contributions of Professor Roger Clark on the Legal Norm against Nuclear Weapons   119
     Alyn Ware

PART 3
Essays on Human Rights

12   Updating the Standard Minimum Rules for the Treatment of Prisoners   135
     Nigel S. Rodley, Andrea Huber and Lorna McGregor

13   The High Commissioner for Human Rights on the Legal Obligation of Corporations to Respect International Human Rights Norms   153
     Chile Eboe-Osuji

14   Human Rights as International Constitutional Law   204
     Bertrand G. Ramcharan

15   Human Rights in Foreign Policy: Can Realism be Liberalized?   220
     David P. Forsythe

PART 4
Essays on Self-Determination

16   West Papuan Self-determination New Indigenous Rights or Old-fashioned Genocide?   237
     Catherine J. Iorns Magallanes

17   'Professor Clark, What Can We *Do* about the Western Sahara?'   260
     Suzannah Linton

PART 5
Essays on International, Transnational and Comparative Criminal Law

18 Forks in the Road: Personal Reflections on Negotiating the Kampala Amendments on the Crime of Aggression 283
Christian Wenaweser and Stefan Barriga

19 The Elusive Essence of Crimes against Humanity 298
Margaret M. deGuzman

20 Towards a New Global Treaty on Crimes Against Humanity 311
Leila Nadya Sadat

21 Challenges in Applying Article 8 of the Rome Statute 333
Tim McCormack

22 Perpetrators (Article 25 (3) of the ICC Statute) 356
Thomas Weigend

23 The Limited Reach of Superior Responsibility 374
Shane Darcy

24 Possession as a Criminal Offence and the Function of the Mental Element: Reflections from a Comparative Perspective 391
Kai Ambos

25 Of War-Councils and War-Mongering: Considering the Viability of Incitement to Aggression 409
Gregory S. Gordon

26 Individual Criminal Responsibility: Of 'Dog's Law', Offending against Sound Popular Feeling, Semi-colons and Commas 429
Kenneth J. Keith

27 The 2012 Protocol on the Illicit Trade in Tobacco: Signpost to the Future of Transnational Criminal Law? 445
Neil Boister

PART 6
Essays on and from North America

28 Roger Clark's Role in the Removal of Capital Punishment from the American Law Institute's Model Penal Code 461
   Ellen S. Podgor

29 Customary International Law as the Rule of Decision in Human Rights Litigation in the US Courts 473
   Joseph W. Dellapenna

30 Human Rights Treaties in and beyond the Senate: The Spirit of Senator Proxmire 507
   Jean Galbraith

31 Judicial Review of Decision-Making Engaging Public Practices and Other Manifestations of Faith: Lessons from Roger Clark and *Beatty v. Gillbanks* 519
   David J. Mullan

32 The Alien Tort Statute, *Kiobel*, and the Struggle for Human Rights Accountability 533
   Beth Stephens

33 Dynamics of International Legal Systems and State Regulatory Autonomy 548
   Ari Afilalo

34 Practicing E-Legally: The United Nations Convention on the Use of Electronic Communications in International Commerce 555
   Amelia H. Boss

PART 7
Essays on New Zealand

35 Foreign Cultural Heritage Claims: *New Zealand v. Ortiz* Thirty Years Later 577
   Robert K. Paterson and James A.R. Nafziger

PART 8
Essays from the Field

36 Reform of UN Inquiries   597
    Geoffrey Palmer

37 'Knocked over by a Pile of Bombs. Hasn't Felt Well since':
    Nuclear Test Veterans and the UK Ministry of Defence Pensions
    System   617
    Sue Rabbitt Roff

38 Overcoming Implementation Issues of the Victims' Law in
    Colombia   633
    Ashley Clark

    Curriculum Vitae of Roger S. Clark   649
    Index   665

Preface & Acknowledgements

. . . For The Sake Of Present and Future Generations

These words, from the preamble of the Rome Statute of the International Criminal Court that was negotiated by Slade-Clark team on behalf of Samoa, encapsulate our honoree's remarkable journey as a lawyer and academic. It is a voyage that has taken Roger from New Zealand to America, and to many, many, countries all over the world. They also capture something of the warm sentiment that motivates the contribution to this forty-one-person-strong compilation of essays in tribute to an extraordinary man who has been a precious friend to all of us. Forty-one made it to the finishing line, and there were many others who were not able to join us in the book but nevertheless will share in this tribute. We appreciate the support and goodwill of the many Friends of Roger, to borrow from Ari Afilalo's phrase, and especially thank the forty-one who were able to participate in this collection.

Readers who are familiar with Roger will see that the essays in this *Festschrift* span the wide range of issues that have been dear to Roger's heart, and which have formed important phases of his life, many of which have continued to engross him to this day. There are many Roger anecdotes in these pages. Those who are not familiar with Roger will find an abundance of richness in the contributions ranging from essays in peace and global security to essays in self-determination to essays in international criminal law to essays on North American issues, and more. The authors are some of the world's greatest experts and game-changers, and their contributions are authoritative and, often, deeply personal.

Enormous thanks are due to Damian Etone from Adelaide Law School, for his cheerful and able editorial assistance from the very start. Thanks also to Hannah Douglas from Melbourne Law School for ably assisting with editing, and to Guilia Pecorella for assistance with indexing. Robert Paterson was very helpful with the search for a suitably unique textile for the book cover; through Bob, we met David King, who has kindly let us use a photograph of a *tapa* from his personal collection (the sample is undocumented, but it is very close in style, scale, and technique to a number of specimens of *tapa* cloth brought back from Hawaii on Cook's third voyage in 1778). We also thank the Werner Forman Archive Ltd, and Barbara Heller, for generously allowing us to reproduce a photograph of the Ortiz Panels, and for waiving the fee. Finally, we are grateful to our publishers, for patience and perseverance.

Roger, dear friend who has worked so hard for the sake of present and future generations, we hope you will like our tribute to an intellectual and political life led with vim and intelligence.

    1 February 2015
    The Editors: SL, GS, WS

List of Contributors

Professor Ari Afilalo
is a Professor of Law at the Rutgers-Camden School of Law, where his research interests include intellectual property in international trade law and international business transactions. He previously worked as a practitioner on cross-border commercial and financial transactions, and intellectual property matters. Professor Afilalo has also taught at Suffolk Law School in Boston and the University of Mississippi School of Law, and holds an LLM from Harvard University, where he concentrated on international law.

Professor Kai Ambos
is a Professor of Criminal Law, Comparative Law and International Criminal Law at the University of Göttingen and a Judge of the Appeals Court (Oberlandesgericht) of Braunschweig. From 1991 to 2003 he was senior research fellow at the Max Planck Institute for Foreign and International Criminal Law, overseeing the International Criminal Law and Latin America departments. Professor Ambos has been member of the German delegation in the negotiations on the International Criminal Court at the 1998 Rome Conference, and assisted in the drafting of the German Code of Crimes under International Law. He has served as Expert for different International Criminal Tribunals, including as Defence Counsel. He has worked extensively in Latin America on human rights and criminal law reform. He has widely published in the areas of criminal law and procedure as well as international criminal law. He is the author of the three-volume work, *Treatise on International Criminal Law* (OUP 2013) and the co-editor of the *Commentary of the Rome Statute of the International Criminal Court* (Beck/Hart, 3rd edn 2015).

Dr Stefan Barriga
is the Deputy Permanent Representative of the Liechtenstein to the United Nations in New York. He served as the principal legal adviser to the chief negotiators in the Special Working Group on the Crime of Aggression from 2003 to 2010, and led the drafting of the group's proposals. He is the co-editor of the book *The Travaux Préparatoires of the Crime of Aggression* (CUP 2011).

Professor M. Cherif Bassiouni
is a leading authority on international criminal law, human rights and humanitarian law. He is a prolific writer and editor and is widely published in the fields of international criminal law, comparative criminal law, human rights and US

criminal law. Professor Bassiouni is, *inter alia*, Emeritus Professor of Law at DePaul University, Chicago, and he was nominated for the 1999 Nobel Peace Prize. In 2011 Prof Bassiouni chaired the United Nations Independent International Commission of Inquiry for Libya. He is also President of the International Institute of Higher Studies in Criminal Sciences (Siracusa, Italy) and Honorary President of the International Association of Penal Law (Paris, France).

Professor Neil Boister
is a Professor in the Te Piringa Faculty of Law, University of Waikato, New Zealand. His research interests lie in the intersection between the fields of criminal law and international law, particularly the developing notion of transnational criminal law. Professor Boister has previously taught criminal law and international law at the University of Canterbury, the University of Nottingham and the University of Natal.

Professor Amelia H. Boss
is a Trustee Professor at the Thomas R. Kline School of Law, Drexel University. She is a commercial law scholar and an expert on electronic commerce and codifying international commercial law through treaty. Professor Boss was previously the director of the Institute for International Law and Public Policy at the Temple University Beasley School of Law. She is a member of the Council of the American Law Institute and sits on the Permanent Editorial Board of the Uniform Commercial Code.

Ashley Clark
is currently a Fulbright-Clinton Fellow working in the Cabinet of Advisors for the Secretary of State for Youth and Sport in Timor-Leste. Ms. Clark holds a dual Masters in Public Policy and International and Area Studies from the University of California, Berkeley. She has focused on post-conflict reconstruction efforts, leading her to work on projects in Colombia, Sierra Leone, Northern India and Afghanistan. She has worked for various governmental and non-governmental entities, including the World Bank, USAID, and Innovations for Poverty Action. Furthermore, she has accompanied her father Professor Roger Clark as part of the Samoan delegation to ICC negotiations in 2008 and 2010. For the first time in her life, she can outrun Professor Roger Clark, but does not expect this to last long.

Dr Shane Darcy
is a lecturer at the Irish Centre for Human Rights, National University of Ireland, Galway, where he teaches international criminal law. He has

been a visiting fellow at the Human Rights Program at Harvard Law School, and a visiting scholar at the Centre for Public, International and Comparative Law at the University of Queensland. Dr Darcy is the author of *Judges, Law and War: The Judicial Development of International Humanitarian Law* (CUP 2014).

Professor Joseph W. Dellapenna
is a Professor of Law at Villanova University School of Law, where his scholarly interests focus on water management and international and comparative law. He holds an LLM in International and Comparative Law from George Washington University and an LLM in Environmental Law from Columbia University. Professor Dellapenna is the author of numerous books on water rights, and his book *Suing Foreign Governments and Their Corporations* (Martinus Nijhoff 2003) was cited by both the majority and the dissent in *Saudi Arabia v. Nelson*.

Hon Justice Chile Eboe-Osuji
has been a Judge of the International Criminal Court since 2012. From 1997 to 2005 Justice Eboe-Osuji was prosecution counsel and senior legal officer to the judges of the International Criminal Tribunal for Rwanda, and from 2008 to 2010 was the senior prosecution appeals counsel in the Special Court for Sierra Leone. He has also served as legal adviser to the United Nations High Commission on Human Rights and is widely published in the area of international criminal law. Justice Eboe-Osuji has practised as a barrister in Nigeria and Canada.

Professor Brian J. Foley
is a Professor of Law at Florida Coastal School of Law, where he focuses on criminal law, criminal procedure, and evidence. He has worked in private practice in civil and criminal litigation and has been a visiting associate professor at Thomas R. Kline School of Law at Drexel University and Boston University School of Law. He is one of the founders and organizers of the biennial Applied Legal Storytelling Conference series.

Professor David P. Forsythe
is a scholar of international human rights and the Charles J. Mach Professor of Political Science, Emeritus, at the University of Nebraska-Lincoln. He has been a consultant to the International Red Cross and Red Crescent movement, as well as to the United Nations Office of the High Commissioner for Refugees. He has been named a Distinguished Scholar by the International Studies

Association-Midwest, the American Political Science Association and the International Studies Association.

Professor Jean Galbraith
is an Assistant Professor at the University of Pennsylvania Law School. Her research focuses on U.S. foreign relations law, especially as it relates to international law. She is a graduate of Harvard University and the University of California Berkeley Law School, where she was editor-in-chief of the *California Law Review*. In the past, she has served as an Assistant Professor at Rutgers-Camden School of Law, as an Associate Legal Officer for Hon Justice Theodor Meron at the International Criminal Tribunal for the former Yugoslavia, and as a law clerk for U.S. Supreme Court Justice John Paul Stevens.

Dr Kennedy Graham
has been a Member of Parliament in New Zealand since 2008, for the Green Party for whom he is spokesperson for the 'global affairs' portfolio. He is a member of the Foreign Affairs and Defence and Trade Committee. Dr Graham holds a B. Com (Auckland), MA in International Relations (Fletcher School of Law & Diplomacy, Boston), and a PhD (Victoria University, Wellington). He received Fulbright and Fletcher scholarships and a McCarthy Fellowship (1986), and was Quartercentenary Fellow at Emmanuel College, University of Cambridge, UK (1995). Dr Graham served in the NZ foreign service for 16 years, specializing in global security and the United Nations, his last diplomatic assignment being counsellor in the NZ Mission to the UN in Geneva. He has lived and worked in nine countries in Asia, Pacific, Europe, Middle East and North America. From 1999 to 2004, he worked for the UN University, as Director of its Leadership Academy (Amman, Jordan; 1999–2002); and its Regional Security & Global Governance Project (Bruges, Belgium; 2002–4). He has served as consultant for the UN Secretary-General's High-Level Commission on Threats, Challenges and Change (2004), and as Senior Consultant to the UN's Dept. of Political Affairs in New York (2005–6), assisting with the Secretary-General's meetings and the Security Council's meetings with regional organizations. Dr Graham has taught international law as a Senior Adjunct Fellow at the School of Law, University of Canterbury (2008–9). He is a member of the NZ Institute for International Affairs and is the founding Director of the NZ Centre for Global Studies.

Professor Gregory S. Gordon
is an Associate Professor and Director of the PhD-MPhil Programme at the Chinese University of Hong Kong Faculty of Law. He is regularly consulted as a

LIST OF CONTRIBUTORS   XVII

war crimes expert and was formerly Legal Officer and Deputy Team Leader at the Office of the Prosecutor for the International Criminal Tribunal for Rwanda. Professor Gordon was previously a tenured faculty member at the University of North Dakota School of Law, where he also served as Director of UND's Centre for Human Rights and Genocide Studies. He has also worked as a white-collar criminal prosecutor with the United States Department of Justice, and a Special Assistant U.S. Attorney for the District of Columbia.

Professor Margaret M. deGuzman
is an Associate Professor at the Temple University Beasley School of Law in Philadelphia, where she teaches criminal law, international criminal law and transitional justice. In 2014, Dr deGuzman completed a PhD on the gravity of crimes in international criminal law at the Irish Centre for Human Rights, National University of Ireland, Galway. She is a Fulbright Scholar and was an editor of the Yale Law Journal and the Yale Journal of International Law.

Andrea Huber
is Policy Director at Penal Reform International in London since 2011, responsible for the development of policy and for advocacy at an international and regional level. A lawyer by training, she started as a legal counsellor for asylum seekers, headed the migration department of Caritas Austria, and worked as a legal assistant at the Regional Higher Court Vienna. From 2003 to 2011 she joined Amnesty International fulfilling differing functions in Vienna, Brussels and London headquarters. Andrea Huber published two books, contributed to various reports and comparative analyses and participated in a number of field missions.

Catherine J. Iorns Magallanes
is a Senior Lecturer in the School of Law at Victoria University of Wellington, where her research areas include indigenous rights in international and domestic law, statutory interpretation and environmental law. Ms. Iorns is also a national board member of Amnesty International Aotearoa New Zealand, of 350 Aotearoa, and of Environment and Conservation Organisations of New Zealand; she is a member of the International Law Association Committee on the Rights of Indigenous Peoples, a member of the IUCN Commission on Environmental Law, and an Indigenous Research Officer with the Global Network for the Study of Human Rights and the Environment; and she holds an LLM from Yale University.

Professor Pam Jenoff
is a Clinical Professor of Law at the Rutgers-Camden School of Law, where she teaches employment law, evidence and legal writing. Ms. Jenoff was previously in private practice in the field of employment law and she also served as Special Assistant to the Secretary of the United States Army at the Pentagon, and as a Foreign Service Office with the State Department in Krakow. She is also the author of eight works of fiction.

Professor Claus Kreß
is a Professor of Criminal Law and Public International Law at the University of Cologne, the Director of the Institute of International Peace and Security Law, and Chair of German and International Criminal Law. Professor Kreß has been member of the German delegation in the negotiations on the International Criminal Court since the 1998 Rome Conference. He assisted in the drafting of the German Code of Crimes under International Law and has served as War Crimes Expert for the Prosecutor General for East Timor. Professor Kreß was a sub-coordinator within the Special Working Group on the Crime of Aggression.

Sir Kenneth J. Keith ONZ KBE QC
was a Judge at the International Court of Justice from 2006–2015. A barrister and solicitor of the High Court of New Zealand, he was a law faculty member, Victoria University of Wellington (1962–1964, 1966–1991); Dean (1977–1981), now Professor Emeritus; also Visiting Professor at Osgoode Hall Law School, Toronto (1981–1982), a member of the Legal Division, New Zealand Department of External Affairs (1960–1962); member of the Office of Legal Affairs (Codification Division) of the United Nations (1968–1970) primarily undertaking research for the International Law Commission and working with the Sixth Committee of the General Assembly, including the Committee on Friendly Relations and is a member of the New Zealand Law Commission (1986–1996, President 1991–1996). Sir Kenneth was a judge of the New Zealand Court of Appeal (1996–2003), and of the Supreme Court of New Zealand (2004–2006); at various times Judge of Appeal in Samoa, the Cook Islands, Niue and Fiji; member of the Judicial Committee of the Privy Council, London He has published extensively on international law.

Dr Suzannah Linton
has been, *inter alia*, Chair of International Law at Bangor University in the UK, Associate Professor of Law at the University of Hong Kong, a UN prosecutor for Serious Crimes in East Timor, served at the International Criminal Tribunal for the former Yugoslavia and the Claims Resolution Tribunal for Dormant Accounts in Switzerland, and worked in the field in Cambodia, Indonesia, East

Timor, Bosnia-Herzegovina, Croatia and elsewhere. During her time in Hong Kong, she uncovered war crimes trials held in the territory from 1946–1948 and brought them to global prominence through a database at the University of Hong Kong, and academic publications such as *Hong Kong's War Crimes Trials* (OUP 2013). She is a founding member of the Antonio Cassese Initiative for Peace, Justice and Humanity.

Professor Tim McCormack
is a Professor of Law at the Melbourne Law School and an Adjunct Professor of Law at the University of Tasmania Law School. He is also the Special Adviser on International Humanitarian Law to the Prosecutor of the International Criminal Court in The Hague. Professor McCormack is also the Law of Armed Conflict expert adviser to the Australian Defence Force Director of Military Prosecutions, and a Director of World Vision Australia.

Lorna McGregor
is a Reader in Law and Director of the Human Rights Centre. She researches and teaches in the areas of public international law, particularly international human rights law, international criminal law and transitional justice. Her work has appeared in journals such as the American Journal of International Law, the European Journal of International Law, the International and Comparative Law Quarterly, the Journal of International Criminal Justice and the International Journal of Transitional Justice and has been cited by the UK House of Lords and International Court of Justice.

Professor David J. Mullan
is an administrative law scholar, consultant and researcher, and a professor emeritus of the Faculty of Law at Queen's University, Ontario. Professor Mullan held the Osler, Hoskin and Harcourt Professorship in Constitutional and Administrative Law at Queen's University, and also taught at Dalhousie University and Victoria University of Wellington. From 2004 to 2008 Professor Mullan was the first Integrity Commissioner for the City of Toronto, and is a former long-standing member of the Human Rights Tribunal of Ontario. He is a co-editor of *Administrative Law: Cases, Text and Materials* (Emond Montgomery 2003), now in its seventh edition, and is the former editor of the Canadian Administrative Law Reports.

Professor James A.R. Nafziger
is the Thomas B. Stoel Professor of Law and Director of International Programs at Willamette University College of Law, where he writes and teaches in

many areas including international law, comparative law and international dispute resolution. Professor Nafziger also chairs the Cultural Heritage Committee of the International Law Association, of whose American Branch he has been the former president and chair of its executive committee, and currently serves as the Secretary of the American Society of International Law. He is a member of the United States State Department's Advisory Committee on International Law and an Honorary Professor of the East China University of Politics and Law.

Hon Justice Daniel David Ntanda Nsereko

is a former Judge of the Appeals Chamber of the International Criminal Court and a Professor of Law at the University of Botswana. He is currently a member of the Appeals Chamber of the Special Tribunal for Lebanon, and a member of the Advisory Committee on the Nomination of International Criminal Court Justices. Judge Nsereko was a Fellow of The Hague Academy of International Law and has twice been a visiting scholar at the Max Planck Institute for Foreign and International Criminal Law in Freiburg. He has carried on an active legal practice as an Advocate of the High Court of Uganda.

Rt Hon Sir Geoffrey Palmer KCMG AC QC

is a barrister, former Prime Minister of New Zealand and Distinguished Fellow at the Victoria University of Wellington Law Faculty and Centre for Public Law. Prior to entering politics in 1979, Sir Geoffrey was a law professor in the United States and New Zealand, teaching at the University of Iowa, the University of Virginia and Victoria University of Wellington. Sir Geoffrey was appointed Prime Minister in 1989, having served as Deputy Prime Minister, Attorney-General, Minister for Justice and Minister for the Environment. He returned to private practice and teaching in 1990 and since then has served as an *ad hoc* Judge on the International Court of Justice, President of the New Zealand Law Commission, and Chair of the United Nations Inquiry into the 2010 Gaza Flotilla Incident.

Professor Robert K. Paterson

is a Professor of Law in the Faculty of Law, University of British Columbia. His research interests focus on international trade law, cultural heritage and art law. Professor Paterson is currently the Rapporteur of the Cultural Heritage Committee of the International Law Association and associate editor of the *International Journal of Cultural Property*. He is a member of the bar associations of New Zealand and British Columbia. Professor Paterson is a member of the External Advisory Board of the UBC Museum of Anthropology. He is co-author of *Cultural Law: International, Comparative, and Indigenous* (CUP 2014).

Professor Ellen Podgor
is a Professor of Law at Stetson University School of Law, and the Gary R. Trombley Family White-Collar Crime Research Professor. She teaches criminal law and international criminal law, and is a white-collar crime specialist and former deputy prosecutor and criminal defense attorney. Professor Podgor is a recipient of the Robert C. Heeney Award, the highest honour given by the National Association of Criminal Defense Attorneys. Professor Podgor has authored and co-authored numerous books, including *Understanding International Criminal Law* which is now in its third edition (LexisNexis).

Dr Bertrand G. Ramcharan
is a former United Nations official who served in the position of Deputy and then Acting UN High Commissioner for Human Rights from 1998 to 2004. He is a former Director of the Universal Periodic Review, which reviews the human rights situation of each of the UN member states, and Special Adviser of the UN Secretary-General on the peace process in Georgia. Dr Ramcharan has been Chancellor of the University of Guyana, Professor of Human Rights at the Geneva Graduate Institute of International and Development Studies, UN Fellow at the Kennedy School of Government, Harvard University, and Fellow at the London School of Economics. He is the author or editor of numerous books on international law and human rights and the Director of the Guyana Institute of Public Policy. Dr Ramcharan is also a barrister of Lincoln's Inn, London.

Hon José Ramos-Horta GCL AC
served as President of East Timor from 2007 to 2012. In 1975, he co-founded FRETILIN, the Revolutionary Front for the Independence of East Timor, and served as the spokesperson in exile of the Timorese resistance until the country gained independence in 1999. Dr Ramos-Horta is the co-recipient of the 1996 Nobel Peace Prize, awarded for his work towards a peaceful solution to the conflict in East Timor. He is currently the Chair of the UN High Level Panel on Peace Operations.

Professor Sir Nigel Rodley KBE
is a Professor of Law and Chair of the Human Rights Centre at the University of Essex, and served as Dean of Law from 1992 to 1995. Since 2001 he has been a member of the United Nations Human Rights Committee (Chairperson 2013–2014), prior to which he served as a Special Rapporteur on Torture of the United Nations Commission on Human Rights. Sir Nigel is also President of the International Commission of Jurists, and was knighted in 1998 for services to

Human Rights and International Law. In 2005 he was awarded the American Society of International Law Goler T Butcher Medal for distinguished work in International Human Rights Law.

Sue Rabbitt Roff
grew up in Australia during the UK atomic weapons tests of the 1950s. She was New York Information Officer for the FRETILIN delegation to the United Nations from the Democratic Republic of East Timor in the mid-1970s and subsequently Director of the Minority Rights Group office in New York and its Non-governmental Representative to the United Nations in the 1980s. When she moved to Scotland in 1991 and began teaching in a Scottish medical school, she was able to research the long term health effects of participation in UK atomic and nuclear weapons testing of nuclear veterans from the UK, Australia, New Zealand, and Fiji and submit findings to the military pensions processes of several countries.

Professor Leila Nadya Sadat
is the Henry H. Oberschelp Professor of Law and Israel Treiman Faculty Fellow at Washington University School of law and Director of the Whitney R. Harris World Law Institute at Washington University School of Law. She is the Special Adviser to the International Criminal Court Prosecutor on Crimes Against Humanity and Director of the Crimes Against Humanity Initiative, a multi-year project aimed at the adoption of a new global treaty. Professor Sadat was a delegate to the 1998 Rome Diplomatic Conference and the 2010 ICC Review Conference in Kampala, Uganda.

Professor William A. Schabas
is a Canadian international law and human rights scholar. He is a professor of international law at Middlesex University a professor of international humanitarian law and human rights at Leiden University, and a widely published scholar on subjects including genocide and international criminal tribunals. In 2014 Professor Schabas was appointed to the United Nations Human Rights Council's Commission of Inquiry into the 2014 Israel-Gaza conflict. He is an Officer of the Order of Canada and a member of the Royal Irish Academy.

Hon Justice Tuiloma Neroni Slade
is a Samoan lawyer and diplomat, who from 2008 to 2014 served two terms as the Secretary-General of the Pacific Islands Forum Secretariat. In 2003 he

was elected to a three-year term as a Justice of the International Criminal Court in The Hague, where he served as Presiding Judge in Pre-Trial Chamber II. Justice Slade's earlier diplomatic career included roles as Samoan Ambassador to the United Nations, Ambassador to the United States and High Commissioner to Canada. He has also worked as the Assistant Director of the Legal Division of the Commonwealth Secretariat in London, and was the Attorney-General of Samoa from 1976 to 1982.

Professor Gerry Simpson
holds the Kenneth Bailey Chair of International Law at the University of Melbourne. He is also a visiting professor of Public International Law at the London School of Economics and a Soros Fellow, based in Tbilisi, Georgia. Professor Simpson has been an adviser on matters of international law to the Australian Department of Foreign Affairs and Trade and to the Foreign and Commonwealth Office of the United Kingdom. His book *Great Powers and Outlaw States* (CUP 2004) was awarded the 2005 American Society of International Law's Prize for Pre-Eminent Contribution to Creative Legal Scholarship.

Professor Beth Stephens
is a Professor of Law at Rutgers-Camden School of Law with expertise in public international law, human rights law and transnational litigation. She has published a variety of articles focusing on the enforcement of international human rights norms, and co-authored the book, *International Human Rights Litigation in US Courts*, now in its second edition (Martinus Nijhoff). Professor Stephens has been involved in human rights legal advocacy for over 30 years as an activist, plaintiff, investigator, litigator, professor, and scholar. From 1990 to 1995, she was in charge of the international human rights docket at the Center for Constitutional Rights in New York, and she continues to litigate human rights cases.

Alyn Ware
is a New Zealand-born disarmament and security analyst and peace educator. Since 2002 he has served as the Global Coordinator for Paliamentarians for Nuclear Non-Proliferation, and he is the current International Coordinator for the Lawyers Committee on Nuclear Policy. Mr. Ware has previously served as the United Nations-based coordinator for the World Court Project, Drafting Coordinator for the Model Nuclear Weapons Convention, and Coordinator of the Weapons Systems Caucus of the Coalition for an International Criminal Court. He is the recipient of the 2009 Right Livelihood Award.

Professor Thomas Weigend
is a Professor of Criminal Law and Criminal Procedure at the University of Cologne, Germany. Professor Weigend has taught criminal law in China, Japan, Israel and the United States. He is a widely published scholar in the areas of comparative criminal procedure and international criminal law. Professor Weigend is a co-editor of the criminal law journal *Zeitschrift für die gesamte Strafrechtswissenschaft* and since 2008 has been a member of the Advisory Board of the *Journal of International Criminal Justice*.

Ambassador Christian Wenaweser
is the Permanent Representative of Liechtenstein to the United Nations. He chaired the Special Working Group on the Crime of Aggression from 2003 to 2009 and from 2008 to 2011served a term as President of the Assembly of State Parties of the International Criminal Court. Ambassador Wenaweser has also served as Chairman of the Third Committee of the General Assembly of the United Nations and as a facilitator in numerous negotiation processes at the United Nations.

PART 1

Roger S. Clark

∴

CHAPTER 1

Appreciation

José Ramos-Horta

The first time that I set foot in the big famed city—New York—was one day in December 1975, to plead the case of my country and people before the United Nations, or I should say the (Dis) United Nations? And a few years later, some time in the late 70's, I met Roger S. Clark.

It was winter in December 1975, there was much snow on the ground, and I had never seen real snow in my whole life. I stayed in that cheap Tudor Hotel; I paid $20 per night for a basic room. That rat hole has been refurbished since, and now is grandly called Hilton. But the same tiny room, with no complimentry bottled water and fruits, with all-American TV channels (no BBC or Al Jazeera), now costs about $400 a night.

I do not recall exactly when I met Roger but it was some 40 years ago, when he was Vice-President of the New York-based International League for Human Rights ('ILHR'), the very first human rights advocacy group that cared about Timor-Leste. Through ILHR, I met other great human rights specialists like Michael Posner and Maureen Berman, and Margo Picken and Sidney Jones of Amnesty International. They were the very few who patiently and consistently exposed the unfolding human rights tragedy in my country, in eloquent testimonies before the United Nations, US Congress and academic circles. Of course, Noam Chomsky among them, was the most notable with his devastating and unapologetic exposure of US complicity in the then on-going tragedy in Timor-Leste, particularly in the years 1975–1978.

Roger was the first NGO 'petitioner' to speak on Timor-Leste at the Fourth Committee of the UN General Assembly; he also addressed the United Nations' Special Committee on Decolonization (commonly known also as the Committee of 24), always presenting an irreproachable and eloquent defence of the rights of the people of Timor-Leste to self-determination, solidly grounding his arguments on his unparalleled knowledge of International Law and Human Rights Law. While less known that Noam Chomsky, Roger nevertheless was very effective in his clear and robust legal arguments on the question of self-determination. One of the best papers ever written by any scholar anywhere was his paper on 'The "Decolonization" of East Timor and the United Nations Norms on Self-Determination and Aggression', published in 1980 in Volume 7 of the Yale Journal of World Public Order. Over the years, I myself photocopied hundreds of copies of this brilliant essay and widely circulated it to UN diplomatic community. It was my main support document.

On occasion, I would ask Roger to travel with me outside New York area to appear with me on a campus or at a conference. He never said no, paying his own airfare, flying economy and staying in modest hotel rooms or in someone's home. A most memorable (and useless) trip we made was sometime in 1977 to some conference in Chicago, held at the Governors State University. Roger and I ended up speaking at a workshop, one hot afternoon, having 6 very lovely elderly Afro-American school teachers as our audience. Four of whom were asleep. Obviously, those poor old grandmas were dragged from a bus tour into our workshop because no one had signed up to listen to us.

Roger is a great speaker with a loud voice, and he seemed irritated that the ladies were mostly asleep. So, he would raise his voice even louder and the poor grandmas kept waking up. I was more sensitive and when it was my turn to speak, I spoke more softly so as not to wake up the old ladies. Embarrassingly, the other two who were still awake also fell asleep.

Later Roger told me, 'Jose, this was a real fiasco.' I agreed.

Sometime in the 80's, Roger ran for a vacant position on the UN Committee on Crime Prevention and Control. I remember actively lobbying for Roger with African and Soviet bloc countries. I did not remember in full detail my part in helping but Roger said in a kind email to me:

> You were my lifesaver and, far from going easily, the election went three ballots. The CV was irrelevant and NZ was, at the time, far from harmless! I was running for a WEOG seat at a time when NZ had two of the French government terrorists who blew up the *Rainbow Warrior* in prison. For good measure, the US was mad at NZ over the nuclear ship policy which kept US nuclear-armed and powered ships out of NZ waters. And the UK was supporting the US. The US was also displeased that I was agitating at the Trusteeship Council about nukes in Palau and other aspects of the ending of the trusteeship in the Pacific.

Roger continued recalling that most interesting episode. It must have been his first real life experience in international diplomacy and horse-trading, away from academic life at Rutgers where everything is black and rigid, legal and illegal, right and wrong. Well, not so in the real life outside academia. He continued:

> The only firm WEOG votes we had on the first ballot were Iceland (trade for vote on ILC) and Australia (basic solidarity). PNG lined up some of the

Non-Aligned, but that was dodgy because the NZ rugby team turned up (as 'individuals') in South Africa at just the wrong time. You got the Lusophones and the Soviets delivered most of their bloc. After the first ballot, I was tied with an Austrian and a Canadian for the last available seat. After the second, I was tied with the Austrian; and the Canadian, having been defeated, managed to persuade enough of his votes to go for me. There was no way to win without your help on the first and second ballots.

Thank you for remembering this. Good old Roger. Roger was not, is not, a George Clooney look-alike. Slim, tall, not the greatest looking face around, with a silly mustache to make things worse, but what a lovely, great human being. Great soul. No wonder his wife Amy and daughter Ashley adore him in spite of his disavantaged looks. It gives me some hope that in spite of my own disadvantaged looks I will eventually find a loving wife.

In 2002, I was very pleased to welcome Roger in my home in Dili as a guest to attend our independence celebration. Roger played a part in it. A great scholar, a great human being. Thank you, my friend.

CHAPTER 2

Tribute

Tuiloma Neroni Slade

The offerings in this *Festschrift* combine in warm salutation to Professor Roger Clark and his exceptional service to law and humanity. In range and distinction they represent perspectives typical of the elevated reach of Roger's own life and work, and of the interests and concerns he has inspired in so many. It is the measure of this collective tribute and admiration for an esteemed colleague and friend, especially on the occasion of this his 50th year of service as a teacher of law and his acclaimed standing as an international legal scholar.

Over forty of these years have been spent in distinguished service at Rutgers University School of Law-Camden, where Roger is held in high affection by staff and students and in the community. Deservedly, as Board of Governors Professor, he commands the University's highest acknowledgement for substantial contributions to teaching and research. A great many of his former students occupy today, in widest array and in far-flung corners, positions of responsibility and distinction. Roger will have left with them the marks of his convictions and scholarship as, indeed, his personality and friendship.

As a number of contributing authors have noted, Roger's distinctive sound and mannerisms remain uppermost, irrefutably of *Aotearoa*,[1] he is a *Kiwi*. Not of mean talent and of marathon endurance, Roger's running career is as long as his teaching. During my last visit to Rutgers, I managed to avoid a road race, and was much happier to watch Roger and the other runners and to be at the tail-end to hand out the prizes.

Though at different times, Roger and I attended the same high school in New Zealand, as we did Victoria University of Wellington. I have read that Roger was the first member of his family to attend university. He took his first degree at Victoria University, and commenced his teaching career there at the Law Faculty in 1964. I was privileged to be among his early crop of students. Of course there have been a host of other academic achievements and distinctions, from Victoria University (B.A., LL.B., LL.M., LL.D), from Columbia Law School, New York (LL.M., J.S.D.) and from other institutions elsewhere. Earlier in 2014, Roger was conferred an honorary Doctor of Laws at Victoria University in acknowledgement of his outstanding work and achievements in New

---

[1] Māori: for New Zealand, land of the long white cloud.

Zealand and abroad and for his extraordinary commitment to teaching, international public service and scholarly research during his long stellar career.

By any standard, Roger's expertise and field of teaching is extensive: courses in international law; international protection of human rights; international organisations; international criminal law and criminal justice policy; torts; insurance law; foreign relations and national security law; and criminal law. Others I will have missed, I'm sure. He has taught in numerous institutions around the world, including in my country, Samoa, and my region (University of the South Pacific); and he has served as general editor or editorial board member of various legal publications, and also as a member of several international non-governmental organisations. He gives unstintingly of what he has. Roger's equally extensive writings (13 books and hundreds of articles and other pieces) and ideas are well canvassed in the pages of this collection. His interests and activities range well beyond the lecture halls.

In November 1998, I was among Roger's friends who had come to Rutgers from many parts of the world for his Inaugural Lecture as the first Board of Governors Professor. These occasions serve for deep reflection on one's life and work; and at the appointed hour Roger did not miss it for a performance *par excellence*, and movingly personal. I think it was his first public oration I had witnessed. It was mesmerising, in depth of detail and the intensity of feeling. True to form, Roger had called his lecture *Steven Spielberg's* Amistad *and Other Things I Have Thought About In The Past Forty Years: International (Criminal) Law, Conflict of Laws, Insurance and Slavery*.[2] As he noted, he had come to realise that slavery is a metaphor for much of his life's work as a scholar and an activist. We also know, as attested to by these essays, that for much of his life Roger had agitated against assorted colonial situations (Timor Leste, Pacific islands trust territories, Western Sahara) and other human rights violations, against nuclear weapons and used his influential and prominent roles in shaping international criminal law. A (whimsical) feature of the published lecture is the remarkable number of footnotes—224! Fascinating in detail and learning, and the extraordinary research effort involved. The man himself confessed to an orgy of footnote-citation.

As a Pacific country, Samoa has always felt strongly about nuclear weapons. In just the past century, the Pacific has known the 'scourge of war'; the only region ever to experience nuclear weapons used in anger, and in succeedingly more disastrous ways to become the testing ground for weapons of mass

---

2   Roger S Clark, 'Steven Spielberg's Amistad and Other Things I Have Thought About in the Past Forty Years: International (Criminal) Law, Conflict of Laws, Insurance and Slavery' (1999) 30 Rutgers LJ 371.

destruction. In my associations with Roger, he has taught me that substantively these weapons are bad for the environment and for humanity; and that, ultimately, it is the rule of law which offers protection for us all.

In 1995, the International Court of Justice declined to hear our request to intervene in support of New Zealand's proceedings to block the resumption of French nuclear testing in the Pacific.[3] But, we were to return to the Court later that year, in the context of the advisory proceedings on the *Legality of the Threat or Use of Nuclear Weapons*, this time with Roger leading as Counsel for Samoa. Samoa could not have hoped to be involved in a matter of such importance, without Roger's expert counsel and assistance so generously given. Roger's writings and the book produced about these proceedings[4] are referenced widely and discussed in the essays herein. Preparing for the case and appearing before the Court was a high-point professional experience. Roger had always talked about the *Lotus* case.[5] To watch him expound on it before the ICJ Judges was a treat.

About this time, the UN General Assembly had created the Preparatory Committee to work on a consolidated text for the establishment of an international criminal court. From the ICJ advisory proceedings, it was a natural step to engagement in the work of the Committee and subsequent processes; for Roger in particular, with so many of the issues in his *forte*. For the ensuing years, as is well known, Roger represented Samoa in the international work and negotiations for the development of the International Criminal Court and in the operations of the Court since then, and continues to do so with prominence and distinction.

Working together in the coordination of the negotiations in the Rome Conference in 1998 (on the *Preamble* and the *Final Clauses*), we were able to make a substantive contribution to the making of the *Rome Statute of the International Criminal Court*.[6] Roger was on hand throughout an especially

---

[3] Applications Submitted by the Governments of Samoa, Solomon Islands, Marshall Islands and Federated States of Micronesia (on file with the author); *see also* NZ Ministry of Foreign Affairs (Manatu Aorere), New Zealand at the International Court of Justice: French Nuclear Testing in the Pacific, at <http://www.mfat.govt.nz/Treaties-and-International-Law/06-International-Courts-and-Tribunals/2-NZ-at-the-International-Court-of-Justice.php> accessed 29 September 2014.

[4] Roger S Clark & Madeleine Sann (eds), *The Case Against The Bomb: Marshall Islands, Samoa and Solomon Islands Before the International Court of Justice in Advisory Proceedings on the Legality of the Threat or Use of Nuclear Weapons* (Rutgers University School of Law 1996).

[5] SS Lotus case (France v Turkey) (1927) PCIJ Rep (Ser A, No 10) 28.

[6] Tuiloma Neroni Slade & Roger S Clark, 'Preamble and Final Clauses' in Roy S Lee (ed), *The International Criminal Court: The Making of the Rome Statute, Issues, Negotiations, Results* (Kluwer 1999).

grueling election process in 2003 and was next to me when I was elected among the first Judges of the Court. His long struggle with the issue of aggression, the unfinished business of Rome, his vast insights and the enormous efforts he and others brought to bear, eventually yielded results with the adoption in 2010 of the Kampala Amendments on the Crime of Aggression. Roger's singular contribution to the development and enunciation of law and principle in this area of international endeavour is warmly and widely celebrated, as reflected in these essays.

This, then, is a collection which tells the stories of many important journeys in a life and career of sustained excellence. By his work and example, Roger has touched and inspired women and men, children and policy-makers across many lands and cultures in the respect for the human person and human values and in the service of each other to stand up to the forces of injustice and inequality.

Our tribute, true to Professor Roger Clark, is to the purpose of his life and high calling as a teacher of law and so, as it is written, 'to act, that each tomorrow/Find us farther than today.'[7]

Soifua.[8]

---

[7] Henry Wadsworth Longfellow, A Psalm of Life (1838) reprinted in (JD McClatchy (ed), *Henry Wadsworth Longfellow: Poems and Other Writings* (Library of America 2000)).

[8] Samoan: in wellbeing and peace.

CHAPTER 3

Laudatio: In Honor of Roger S. Clark

M. Cherif Bassiouni

For the past fifty years of his academic career, Roger S. Clark has made a difference and he continues to make a difference.

Making a difference in life is what counts. And it is not how much or how significant a change you can accomplish—it is all in the trying, and Roger has always been trying and has always managed through his teachings as well as his own direct work in the international arena. And that is not to diminish the fact that he has been a law professor, and more importantly a teacher for more than 50 years. Over these years, he taught in his native New Zealand, Austria, China, France, Greece, Italy, Japan, the UK and the US. The cumulative numbers of students who have been exposed to his teachings and views exceeds 5,000. Among them several have in turn made a difference. They include Nobel Prize Winner José Ramos-Horta, who became President of Timor-Leste. Roger was an early advocate for Timorese independence and a major law review article he wrote, entitled 'The "Decolonization" of East Timor and the United Nations Norms on Self-Determination and Aggression' in 1980 in the Yale Journal of World Public Order, articulated the legal case for Timorese self-determination.

Roger is also a lifelong advocate of the elimination of nuclear weapons, writing numerous articles on the topic and speaking about it. More importantly he represented Samoa before the International Court of Justice in the *Advisory Proceeding on the Legality of the Threat or Use of Nuclear Weapons* in 1995. In 2014, he joined the legal team of the Marshall Islands in its cases regarding *Obligations Concerning Negotiations Relating to Cessation of the Nuclear Arms Race and to Nuclear Disarmament* against the United Kingdom, India and Pakistan, which are currently before the ICJ.

In 1972, he was also a trailblazer for the establishment of a United Nations High Commissioner for Human Rights. His book of the same name surely must have had an impact on the decision adopted in Vienna in 1995.

He has been active with the UN Crime Prevention and Criminal Justice Program as a consultant. In 1985, he also served as a consultant to the Crime Prevention and Criminal Justice Division at the time that the United Nations Declaration of Basic Principles of Justice for Victims of Crime and Abuse of Power was being adopted by the Seventh United Nations Congress on the Prevention of Crime and the Treatment of Offenders which was held in Milan, Italy. As chair of the Drafting Committee on that subject, which met in

Ottawa, Canada, in preparation for the Seventh UN Congress, in Milan, and subsequently it was my pleasure to have worked with him. Subsequently, during the UN Diplomatic Conference held in Rome in 1998 for the establishment of the ICC, when I served as chair of the Drafting Committee, Roger represented the government of Samoa along with a former student, Tuiloma Neroni Slade, who was former ambassador of Samoa to the UN and was elected as one of the first judges of the ICC.

Roger has also been a professor for many other students that have gone on to have notable achievements: he has taught numerous academics, several Federal District Court Judges, the Chief Justice of Palau and a member of the US House of Representatives for the state of New Jersey, Frank Pallone. He has also taught several Cabinet Ministers, Judges and Ambassadors in Samoa and his native New Zealand.

His students and others know him for his strong presence, his assertive tone and his uncompromising principles. Many, like myself, remember him at various UN meetings and international conferences speaking up forcefully with a stentorian voice on matters he strongly believes in. He is never gun-shy; no matter what the venue or the audience may be. When Roger speaks, you can always tell that he believes in what he is saying.

All of this having been said, he manages to reconcile his principled positions with his outgoing personality, an easygoing informality and a pleasant way of interacting with others. I am tempted to add that notwithstanding his extraordinary accomplishments, which are self evident in his CV as well as in what Bill Schabas wrote in this book and what others have also written about him, that he is a down to earth man who exudes a simple humility and human kindness.

The fact that so many have contributed to this book is also evidence of where he stands among his peers and his friends—no more than that is needed to express our admiration, appreciation and affection for our friend and colleague.

Suzannah Linton deserves our appreciation for having spearheaded this effort to honor Roger. And to her and all who contributed to this book, I can only say that those who honor others, honor themselves.

CHAPTER 4

Roger Clark: A Personal Tribute

William A. Schabas

Roger Clark has described his participation in the *Nuclear Weapons* Case at the International Court of Justice as a highlight of his career. He is listed in the report of the Advisory Opinion as one of the representatives of Samoa, along with Laurence Boisson de Chazournes and the head of delegation, Ambassador Neroni Slade. Roger had been active in the area since the very beginning of his scholarly career. He published a short article in 1964 exploring legal strategies for preventing French nuclear tests then planned for the Pacific.[1] When the advisory opinion of the International Court of Justice was published, in 1996, Roger and Madeleine Sann of Rutgers University published the materials developed for the proceedings by Samoa and other Pacific Island States in *The Case Against the Bomb*. He also spoke frequently about the case at conferences.

I recall one occasion, at the International Law Weekend that is held in New York every autumn, where Roger began by distributing a photocopied map of the Pacific Ocean. He identified several locations on the map—Hiroshima, Nagasaki, Bikini Atoll, Moruroa, Kiribati, and others—where nuclear weapons had been used, as well as Auckland, in his native New Zealand, where French agents sank the *Rainbow Warrior* as it prepared to interrupt a nuclear test in the Pacific. He was confronting our Atlanto-centric vision of the world of most of his audience with a vision from the other side of the planet. There, he explained, nuclear weapons were real, not virtual. Roger reminded the audience of the participation of the mayors of Hiroshima and Nagasaki at the hearing in The Hague on the request for an advisory opinion. Fundamentally optimistic in his perspective, Roger was not disappointed by the advisory opinion, although he was well aware of its mixed message and its latent ambiguities. Two decades later, he is back in The Hague as a member of the team representing the Marshall Islands in its applications against the nuclear powers alleging that they have failed to bargain in good faith in order to rid the world of nuclear weapons.[2]

---

1 Roger S Clark, 'French Tests and International Law' (1964) 52 New Zealand Monthly Review 5. See also his memoir on anti-nuclear activities: Roger S Clark, 'Is the *Butter Battle Book*'s Bitsy Big Boy Boomeroo Banned? What has International Law to Say About Weapons of Mass Destruction?' (2013–14) 58 NYL Sch L Rev 655, 659–65.

2 *Obligations concerning Negotiations relating to Cessation of the Nuclear Arms Race and to Nuclear Disarmament* (*Marshall Islands* v. *India*), Application instituting proceedings against

During a long conversation held in the summer of 2014 in north London, I asked Roger if he was a pacifist. He shrugged, managing 'no, not really' in a Kiwi accent that must be as strong today as when he left his native New Zealand nearly half a century ago. It seemed an equivocal answer from a scholar *engagé*, someone who has spent much of his life bringing legal expertise to bear on problems of peace, aggression and militarism yet unwilling to rule out the use of armed force in certain circumstances. Speaking of his days as a student in New Zealand in the 1960s, he explained his involvement in the great causes of the day, United States involvement in Viet Nam and South African apartheid. Probably the energy and commitment of that work has never left him.

In the interview, he told me that his interest in human rights was sparked by reading Alan Paton's classic on race in South Africa, *Cry the Beloved Country* in an English class ('beautiful, poetic, prose'). Many years later, Bert Lockwood, Editor-in-Chief of *Human Rights Quarterly*, persuaded him to review it for an issue devoted to books that most influenced the authors.[3] Roger later met Paton in the 1970s at a function in New York organised by the International League for Human Rights. An anti-apartheid advocate who financed a lifetime of activism on the royalties from the book, Paton passed away in the late 1980s.

Roger Stenson Clark was born in 1940, in Wanganui, New Zealand, then a city of about 30,000, the fifth largest in New Zealand. Wanganui is located on the south-western coast of the North Island, about 200 kilometres from the capital, Wellington. He thrived at school and finished at the top of his class. He was also—and still is—a pretty good runner. He was cross-country champion in his final year at high school. An aptitude test suggested that he should become either a minister of religion or a lawyer. He knew some ministers and was sure that was not a career for him. He did not know any lawyers but decided to move to the capital and enter Victoria University of Wellington in a joint history and law programme. Roger was the first person in his family to go to university.

Law was (and still is) an undergraduate programme in New Zealand. It is now very common for New Zealand students to do joint degree programmes, but Roger was the only one in his law school class to complete one. He spent three years as a full–time student while completing the arts requirements and

---

the Republic of India, 24 April 2014; *Obligations concerning Negotiations relating to Cessation of the Nuclear Arms Race and to Nuclear Disarmament (Marshall Islands v. Pakistan), Application instituting proceedings against the Islamic Republic of Pakistan*, 24 April 2014; *Obligations concerning Negotiations relating to Cessation of the Nuclear Arms Race and to Nuclear Disarmament (Marshall Islands v. United Kingdom), Application instituting proceedings against the United Kingdom of Great Britain and Northern Ireland*, 24 April 2014.

3 Roger S Clark, 'Book review of Alan Paton, *Cry the Beloved Country*' (1992) 14 HRQ 653.

most of the basic law subjects. He then, as was common in New Zealand at the time, went part-time for the other three years that it took to complete the programme. He spent the three years working in government, the first two in the New Zealand Justice Department and the final year in what was then known as the 'Department of External Affairs' (later re-named the Ministry of Foreign Affairs). The work at External Affairs included involvement in two areas that were to influence his later career significantly, human rights and extradition.

In his final year of law studies, Roger became a Vice-President of the New Zealand University Students' Association, a body representative of the students in the six New Zealand Universities. He also joined the Board of the New Zealand Council for Civil Liberties. He was one of the founders (and first President) of the New Zealand chapter of a fledgling human rights organisation called Amnesty International. New Zealand was being drawn deeper into the Vietnam War and Roger was an active opponent of that involvement. He told me that while he found the work at External Affairs enormously engaging, he felt privileged to be out of government service so that he did not have to defend the Government's Vietnam policy, and on the contrary, could oppose it.[4] As an academic he felt it an obligation to address the issues of policy, and especially of international law, that were raised by that conflict.

In law school, he again finished at the top of his class and was invited to join the teaching faculty at Victoria as a junior lecturer, beginning in January 1964. The idea was that he would do an LL.M, teach a few years, and then go overseas for graduate study. His teaching commitments were in the areas of legal process, constitutional and administrative law and some criminal law. While at University, he fell under the spell of Colin Aikman, a professor of jurisprudence and constitutional law at Victoria University as well one of the country's most distinguished public servants. While a junior diplomat in 1948, Aikman had participated actively in the drafting of the Universal Declaration of Human Rights and had the honour of addressing the General Assembly when it was adopted on 10 December.[5] Roger studied international law with the late George Barton (who had been a doctoral student at Cambridge under the great Hersch Lauterpacht)[6] and with a young scholar, Ken Keith, later to become Sir

---

4 His second publication was the text of an address he gave at Teach-Ins on the Vietnam War at Victoria University and the University of Auckland: Roger S Clark, 'The Geneva Accords and the Two Vietnams', in Michael Bassett (ed), *New Zealand and South East Asia* (Committee on *South-East Asia* 1966).

5 UN Doc A/PV.181.

6 See Roger's tribute to him, echoing the topic of Barton's doctorate, Roger S Clark, 'Peacekeeping forces, jurisdiction and immunity: A tribute to George Barton' (2012) 43 VUWLR 77.

Kenneth, a member of the International Court of Justice and a contributor to this volume.

Roger Clark received his LL.M from Victoria University in 1967. His thesis was on defences to offences of strict liability in criminal law. It was supervised by Ian Campbell of whom Roger said he 'communicated a joy for teaching and was the first to encourage me to one day be a teacher of the law'.[7] According to plan, he headed off to Columbia Law School in New York in September of that year, encouraged by the great Walter Gellhorn. There he completed a second LL.M as well as a JSD. During the summer of 1968, he interned in the Human Rights Division of the United Nations, then located in New York. There, he worked closely with the Deputy Director of the Division, Kamleshwar Das, another Lauterpacht protégé with whom he formed a lifetime friendship.[8]

Roger returned to teach at Victoria in 1969 and resumed his anti-war and civil liberties activities. He had a small ('and entirely unprofitable', he says) practice as a barrister, mostly representing demonstrators arrested in protests against the Vietnam War or New Zealand sport contacts (primarily rugby) with *apartheid*-era South Africa. Early in 1971, a surprise telephone call from Geoffrey Palmer, who was then teaching at the University of Iowa, led to his return to the United States on a one-year contract. There he taught human rights, a subject that had yet to become the mainstay of legal education that it is today.

The plan was to return to Wellington after the year in Iowa. But two friends from the Columbia period who had joined the Rutgers faculty, Tom Farer and Hunter Taylor, persuaded him otherwise. He joined the Rutgers University faculty on a three-year contract in 1972 and never left. He is now Board of Governors Professor at Rutgers, the University's highest rank. From the beginning of his tenure at Rutgers, he taught international human rights law and criminal law. In the early 1980s, Roger added a course on international criminal law to his repertoire.

Roger Clark's doctoral dissertation, *A United Nations High Commissioner for Human Rights*, was published by Martinus Nijhoff in 1972. The book solidified his position as a serious scholar in the area of human rights. It was one of the early works to offer concrete proposals for strengthening in a structural way the burgeoning United Nations Human Rights Programme. The idea was for a high level official who would be a major catalyst for an ambitious international system. He was ahead of his time. Two decades passed before the UN General

---

7 Roger S Clark, 'Steven Spielberg's Amistad and Other Things I Have Thought about in the Past Forty Years: International (Criminal) Law, Conflict of Laws, Insurance and Slavery' (1998–99) 30 Rutgers LJ 371, 372 note 2.

8 Roger S Clark, 'Human Rights Strategies of the 1960s Within the United Nations: A Tribute to the Late Kamleshwar Das' (1999) 21 HRQ 308.

Assembly created the Office of High Commissioner. Roger's subsequent work on human rights included studies on religious freedom[9] and on the role of non-governmental organizations in the protection of human rights.

While studying at Columbia, he had formed a relationship with the New York-based International League for Human Rights, one of the first human rights NGOs in the United States.[10] Roger worked with the League in an effort to make the nascent United Nations human rights procedures work effectively. The system was very much in its infancy, confined essentially to the '1503 procedure' and those of the Human Rights Committee, namely periodic reporting and individual petitions. He was also very active on behalf of the League at the United Nations in decolonisation matters—East Timor, Namibia, the Trust Territory of the Pacific Islands and the French Territories in the Pacific.[11] He intervened regularly in sessions of the Trusteeship Council, the Special Committee on the Situation with regard to the Implementation of the Declaration on the Granting of Independence to Colonial Countries and Peoples ('the Committee of 24') and the Fourth Committee of the General Assembly.[12]

Important scholarly contributions accompanied this activity. He wrote several major articles dealing with efforts towards decolonisation in the Trust Territory of the Pacific Islands[13] and in South West Africa/Namibia.[14] His 1980 article on East Timor,[15] also translated into Bahasa Indonesia as a monograph, was widely regarded as making the seminal legal case for East Timor's independence. With respect to East Timor, Roger participated regularly in public presentations, academic seminars and debates. He often shared a platform with Jose Ramos Horta, a former student of his who went on to win the Nobel Peace Prize in 1996. Roger was Horta's houseguest for the Timorese independence celebrations in 2002. His daughter Ashley is currently serving as an adviser to the Minister of Youth and Sport in an independent Timor-Leste.

---

9   Roger S Clark, 'The United Nations and Religious Freedom' (1978–79) 11 NYU J L & Pol'y 197.
10 On the League, see: Jan Eckel, 'The International League for the Rights of Man, Amnesty International, and the Changing Fate of Human Rights Activism from the 1940s through the 1970s' (2013) 4 Humanity: An International Journal of Human Rights, Humanitarianism, and Development 183.
11 Much of that involvement is reflected in his scholarly writings.
12 For example, UN Doc A/C.4/35/SR.9.
13 Roger S Clark, 'Self-Determination and Free Association-Should the United Nations Terminate the Pacific Islands Trust?' (1980) 21 Harv Int'l LJ 1.
14 Roger S Clark, 'The International League for Human Rights and South-West Africa 1947–1957: The Human Rights NGO as Catalyst in the International Legal Process' (1981) 3 HRQ 101.
15 Roger S Clark, 'Decolonization of East Timor and the United Nations Norms on Self-Determination and Aggression' (1980–81) 7 Yale J World Pub Ord 2.

In the early 1980s, New Zealand considered nominating him for a seat on the Human Rights Committee but dropped the idea when it judged that it could not muster the votes. Instead, in 1985, Geoffrey Palmer, who was by then Deputy Prime Minister of New Zealand,[16] arranged for New Zealand to support Roger's candidacy for election to the United Nations Committee on Crime Prevention and Control. This was an expert group that supervised United Nations work on criminal justice issues at its office in Vienna. The election in the Economic and Social Council was a hard-fought affair. The seat on the Committee that was in contention was one to the West European and Other Group (WEOG). There were two other WEOG candidates, from Austria and Canada.

Even in the best of times, New Zealand has trouble competing with other WEOG members for positions on international bodies. But on this occasion, there was an added level of complexity. New Zealand was in deep strife with the United States (and to a lesser extent the United Kingdom) over its policy of not allowing port visits by nuclear-armed or nuclear-powered vessels. Roger had himself offended the Americans by complaining at the Trusteeship Council about their stewardship in the Trust Territory of the Pacific Islands, where they had detonated 67 nuclear weapons. For good measure, two French government terrorists who had been involved in blowing up the Greenpeace anti-nuclear vessel *Rainbow Warrior* in Auckland harbour were in a New Zealand jail. *The Warrior*, after moving a number of Marshall Islanders from their radiation-contaminated atoll, had been on its way to try to interfere with the French nuclear tests at Mururoa. In sum, there were few European votes available.

Fortunately, José Ramos-Horta, the independence representative from East Timor, was able to line up some votes from Portuguese-speaking countries. Papua New Guinea, which chaired the Committee of 24 and was appreciative of his anti-colonial work, campaigned hard among the Non-Aligned States. Its efforts nearly came unstuck when the members of the New Zealand rugby team (as 'individuals') turned up in South Africa at just the wrong moment, an official tour having been enjoined in the High Court. Papua New Guinea was able to explain that Roger was on the other side of that issue. He was ultimately elected on the third round of voting.

---

16 Palmer, who Roger credits with 'provoking' what turned out to be a permanent move to the United States, also commissioned Roger in the late 1980s to do a 'peer review' of an (unsuccessful) attempt to revise the New Zealand Crimes Act of 1961. The Act is still substantially based on work done for England by Sir James Fitzjames Stephen (the conservative protagonist of John Stuart Mill) in 1879 (and not adopted there). See his satirical account of this effort: Roger S Clark, 'Criminal Code Reform in New Zealand? A Martian's view of the Erewhon Crimes Act 1961 with some footnotes to the 1989 Bill' (1991) 21 VUWLR 1.

Elected to a four-year term on the Committee, Roger was one of a small group that worked hard to raise the visibility of the programme and to obtain more resources for it. For better or for worse, the result of their efforts was the replacement of the expert Committee by a Commission composed of governmental representatives. More resources were obtained, even at the price of the life of the Committee. Roger had also worked as a consultant to the United Nations Secretariat in the drafting of what became the General Assembly's 1985 Declaration of Basic Principles of Justice for Victims of Crime and Abuse of Power.[17] The Declaration was part of a worldwide effort to make sure that victims are treated with dignity in the criminal process and are not victimised a second time by the ways in which the criminal justice system deals with them. All of this is described in his 1994 book, *The United Nations Crime Prevention and Criminal Justice Program: Formulation of Standards and Efforts at their Implementation*. It is the definitive study of the very significant criminal justice work done by the UN in the first fifty years of the organization's existence.[18]

During the mid-1980s, Roger was active in the creation of the International Society for the Reform of Criminal Law. It brings together academics, practising lawyers and judges, largely but not exclusively from common law jurisdictions. There is an annual conference at which Roger regularly attends and participates. When the new Society decided to launch an academic journal, the *Criminal Law Forum*, Roger was its founding editor. It was the first journal in English dedicated to issues of international and comparative criminal law.

In the early 1990s, the project of international criminal justice that had lain largely dormant since the 1940s began to revive. Already, Roger had made important contributions to the framing of the field through his teaching and scholarly publishing. His 1988 article in the *Nordic Journal of International Law* on 'Offenses of International Concern' was a seminal study of state practice since the Nuremberg trials in the drafting of multilateral treaties on crime, especially in the area of terrorism.[19] In that respect, the book of cases and materials on International Criminal Law, written with Ellen Podgor and the late Edward Wise,[20] is one of the leading teaching books in that area in American law schools.

---

17 UN Doc A/RES/40/34.
18 Roger S Clark, *The United Nations Crime Prevention and Criminal Justice Program: Formulation of Standards and Efforts at their Implementation* (University of Pennsylvania Press 1994).
19 Roger S Clark, 'Offenses of International Concern: Multilateral State Treaty Practice in the Forty Years since Nuremberg' (1988) 57 Nordic J Int'l L 49.
20 Edward M Wise, Ellen S Podgor & Roger S Clark, *International Criminal Law; Cases and Materials* (3rd edn., LexisNexis 2011).

Roger quickly embraced the new international justice movement, participating in the preparatory meetings of the International Criminal Court not only as an academic observer and NGO activist but also as a representative of Samoa. A small island State that punched well above its weight in the legal and policy debates about the Rome Statute, its delegation was headed by Neroni Slade, a former student of Roger's who went on to become a judge at the International Criminal Court. Roger was seated at the Samoa table in the main chamber of the United Nations Food and Agriculture Organisation, in Rome, on 17 July 1998 (really, it was a bit after midnight on 18 July) when the decisive vote was taken to adopt the Rome Statute.

Roger's fingerprints are visible throughout the *travaux préparatoires* of the Rome Statute. In a report on the December 1997 session of the Preparatory Committee, we read: 'Samoa, speaking to a paper circulated in conjunction with Marshall Islands and Solomon Islands, noted that it would be ludicrous if the killing of one person with a poison arrow or expanding bullet could be tried by the court, but not the killing of hundreds of thousands of people with nuclear weapons. Samoa asked whether 'The Law is like a spider's web which catches the little flies but lets the big ones break through?."[21] Or: 'There were very different approaches to the notion of "life imprisonment" as a penalty. Samoa insisted that this should be clarified noting that life imprisonment as imprisonment until the person dies, was debatable since international human rights law may not accept this penalty any more.'[22] Samoa made important proposals reflecting a deep-seated commitment to human rights. For example: 'The Prosecutor may: (d) take necessary measures to ensure the confidentiality of information or the protection of any person, *including victims*.'[23] At the Rome Conference, Samoa's head of delegation, Neroni Slade, took on responsibility for coordinating the negotiation of the preamble and the final clauses. Roger helped to keep mixed metaphors out of the preambular imagery, replacing early references to a 'delicate tapestry that may at any time be rent asunder'[24] with the 'delicate mosaic [that] may be shattered at any time' in the final text.[25] After the Statute was adopted, Roger brought his huge intellect to bear

---

[21] Initial Summary Reports on December 1–12 Meetings of the United Nations Preparatory Committee on the Establishment of an International Criminal Court, Coalition for an International Criminal Court, 18 December 1997.
[22] *Ibid.*
[23] Proposal by the Delegation of Samoa, Non-Paper [WG 4] No. 18.
[24] UN Doc A/CONF.183/C.1/L.61.
[25] Tuiloma Neroni Slade & Roger S Clark 'Preamble and Final Clauses', in Roy S Lee, *The Making of the Rome Statute* (Martinus Nijhoff 1999) 421–50.

on some of the very difficult legal problems involved in crafting the Elements of Crimes.[26] Then he turned to the crime of aggression, participating in the work of the Special Working Group on the Crime of Aggression and the Kampala Review Conference.[27]

Taking up his chair as Board of Governors Professor in 1998, Roger reflected on the past 40 years. He dated the beginning from his first course in Roman Law, in 1958, where he was 'puzzled by the dissonance in the Institutes of Justinian (the basic text for the course) between protestations about justice on the one hand, and the legitimation of the ownership of other humans on the other'. Speaking of 'the four wonderful decades since', Roger listed the activities of his career: 'teaching an assortment of subjects (including criminal law, international law, international criminal law and criminal justice policy, foreign relations law, torts, and insurance law), agitating against assorted colonial situations and other human rights violations, litigating the illegality of nuclear weapons, representing a small state (Samoa) in negotiations to create an international criminal court, writing about structural issues in international organization, and trying to help shape the emerging discipline of 'International Criminal Law', a discipline that includes both public international law and comparative law aspects'.[28] An initial impression might suggest that his tastes are eclectic but closer examination reveals a profound unity—dare I call it a 'policy element'—of these different themes. The list was prepared in 1998 and therefore did not refer to one of Roger's preoccupations during the decade that was to follow, the development of a legal framework for prosecuting the crime of aggression. I recall chatting with him at Kampala in June 2010 after the amendments to the Rome Statute on the crime of aggression had been adopted. He talked of a mission accomplished, saying it as probably time to move on to other issues. It seemed clear to me that there is still more to come, and to surprise us, from this astonishing scholar.

---

26 For example: Delegation of Samoa, Some Suggestions on how the Elements of Genocide and Crimes against Humanity might be Re-worked in the Light of Paragraphs 5 and 6 of the Report of the Informal Inter-sessional Meeting in Siracusa, 31 January-6 February 2000, 13 March 2000. See also: Roger S Clark, 'The Mental Element in International Criminal Law: The Rome Statute of the International Criminal Court and the Elements of Offences' (2001) 12 Crim LF 291.

27 For example, Elements of the Crime of Aggression, Proposal submitted by Samoa, PCNICC/2002/WGCA/DP.2 had a significant effect in shaping the agenda for the subsequent negotiations.

28 Roger S Clark, 'Steven Spielberg's Amistad and Other Things I Have Thought about in the Past Forty Years: International (Criminal) Law, Conflict of Laws, Insurance and Slavery' (1998–99) 30 Rutgers LJ 371, 372–74 (internal references omitted).

CHAPTER 5

Roger *Avant Garde*

Gerry Simpson

I had a discouraging period as a scholar when I repeatedly had the experience of alighting on a brand new topic just a year or two after someone else had already written on it. Not uncommonly, the 'someone else' was Roger Clark. When I went to Vancouver to study secession, I discovered that Roger had already written on decolonisation. Turning quickly to aggression, I hoped to find out that little had been written on this since the salad days of the Nuremberg and Tokyo Trials. No such luck, Roger had been writing on the subject since 1974. Maybe the thing to do was to look for a very small place and write about self-determination in the context of the practice around that place. Western Sahara, perhaps? Roger had been there, too. East Timor seemed promising. After Vancouver, I arrived in Australia, and Hilary Charlesworth asked me if I would like to be involved in IPJET, a group of jurists dedicated to promoting self-rule in Timor Léste. I began doing some preliminary research. There was Roger, again, popping up with one of the earliest essays on East Timor and decolonisation. What about an international criminal court? Roger had written on this as well, and was developing a whole field around it before just about anyone bar a handful of other North-American based scholars. Humanitarian intervention was the coming thing in the early 2000s. There were books (Murphy, Chesterman, Wheeler) and there was an enormous amount of institutional energy (the High-Level Panel, the ISSS). Roger was ahead of the curve. In 1982, he had published a short essay on 'helping friends'. Many of the arguments so ornately presented in later reports are laid out here with precision and a prudent sense of the possible. When I began writing recently on sentiment, I noticed that a Roger Clark had written in the *Colorado Lawyer* in 2005 on 'sadness'. Surely Roger hadn't beaten me to this punch as well? I was enormously relieved to read that this Roger Clark was Roger E. Clark and not our very own Roger S. Clark.

I once not-very-innocently asked him if he had any tips for 'emerging areas'. He rattled off twelve topics, of course. Some of them seemed outlandish to me then. Most of them are now mainstream. Roger's fearless humanitarianism and his intellectual appetites took him into such interesting territories. He arrived as a scholar at a moment of tremendous ferment in the mid-70s, when international law was opening up into the sorts of sub-fields that now appear almost over-familiar. It is easy to forget just how novel all of this was back then.

At Rutgers in 1972, Roger arrives to find that there is no course on international human rights law. This is not so unusual in that there were few such courses anywhere in the world. Roger insists on developing and teaching such a course. By the mid-80's, Roger is introducing international criminal law into the Rutgers curriculum (again, about ten years before courses such as this are being taught regularly in law schools around the world). What is this new thing called international criminal law? Roger, in plain-spoken New Zealandese, once offered as clear a definition as I have heard: 'We have to make a statement that certain things are bad, and we're not tolerating them'.[1]

Perpetually *avant moi*, Roger was also in a broader sense *avant-garde*. My various experiences of having arrived *Midnight in Paris*-like just after the golden period of Rogerish scholarship made me glad I had never taken an interest in the Delaware rules on compensation for road accidents. Because Roger had made an early career intervention into this subject, too. A few years ago, I introduced Roger as a key-note speaker at a conference on war crimes trials. I facetiously referred to his 1974 article on 'No Fault in Delaware' published in the *Rutgers Camden Law Journal* (in order to demonstrate range of overall interests, or narrowness of early interests). I imagined this as a short comment on some minor provision in the Delaware Road Traffic legislation. How wrong. Going back to this article and actually reading it, we find the same attention to detail and interest in reform that is a mark of Roger's scholarship. Indeed, it turns out that 'No Fault in Delaware' is a minor classic of considered and exact socio-legal scholarship. There are cross-tabulations, surveys, questionnaires—the whole gamut of law-in-action techniques. But, there is also a moment of distinctive Clarkish humour. On page 257, after the tables and the statistics, we are told that 'it is all very mysterious'.[2]

But Roger's best work was to come. His work on the crime of aggression is, of course, seminal. Recently, he has written on the *Sakai* Trial in China, possibly the earliest criminal trial involving the crime of aggression.[3] This was unusual, archival work. But even when writing in a more traditional field, Roger manages to tell us things we didn't know about things we thought we knew a lot about. One of his finest works and the one that introduced him to me was a long essay on East Timor and the application of norms of self-determination and aggression to the Indonesian occupation of East

---

1 Kevin Riordan, 'Celebrating a rights champion at Rutgers-Camden', *Philly.com*, 2 May 2012.
2 Roger Clark & Gerald Waterson, ' "No-Fault" in Delaware' (1974–1975) 6 Rutgers Law J 225.
3 Roger Clark, 'The Crime of Aggression: From the Trial of Takashi Sakai, August 1946, to the Kampala Review Conference on the ICC in 2010' in Kevin Jon Heller & Gerry Simpson (eds), *The Hidden Histories of War Crimes Trials* (OUP 2013).

Timor.[4] Here, Roger introduced a generation of international lawyers to the history of that occupation (and the previous Portuguese colonisation and then subsequent abandonment of East Timor) and illuminated our understanding of international legal norms of aggression and self-determination at the same time. The essay begins on an unambiguous note. The invasion and occupation of East Timor has violated two fundamental norms of international law, namely the principle of self-determination and the norm prohibiting aggression. But the application of self-determination was complicated here by several claims. It was argued that the East Timorese had expressed a wish to integrate with Indonesia, that entities such as East Timor were too small to be economically and politically viable, and that East Timor belonged to Indonesia by virtue of long-standing historical and territorial ties.

Roger made a series of powerful arguments against each of these positions. In the case of the popularly expressed will of the East Timorese, the essay pointed out that while there had been some enthusiasm for integration among sections of the East Timorese population, there had not been anything like the level of political development required for the 'responsible choice' envisaged by the United Nations General Assembly in its 1960 Resolution 1541. There was a lack of universal adult suffrage, an absence of impartially conducted democratic process and no third party procedural supervision. These various defects meant that it was impossible to assert with any confidence that the East Timorese people had made a responsible choice with full knowledge of the change in their status. Roger is equally dismissive of the claims made that East Timor's close ties with Indonesia means that integration is permissible under international law. What is most impressive about the analysis here is the amount of research found in the footnotes. Roger really reads around the history of Timor and the Indonesian archipelago with enormous care and skill. The case is compelling especially combined both with the ICJ's opinion in the *Western Sahara* case where historical ties were asserted by Morocco but found lacking (and, arguably, not particularly relevant) by the Court, and with Roger's technically adroit reading of paragraph 6 of G.A. Resolution 1514 of 1960 (compulsory study for students of self-determination). Finally, there was the question of economic viability. I once joked that East Timor was not economically viable enough for independence in 1974 but too economically viable in 1999 (by which time it had become clear that there were considerable oil reserves off the coast of Timor and in the Timor Gap (of which more later). Roger has

---

4 'The "Decolonization" of East Timor and the United Nations Norms on Self-Determination and Aggression' (1980) 7(2) Yale J World Pub Ord 2 ('Clark, 'The "Decolonization" of East Timor and the United Nations Norms on Self-Determination and Aggression").

no time for the economic viability arguments. As paragraph 3 of 1514 puts it 'inadequacy of political, economic, social and educational preparedness should never serve as a pretext for delaying independence'.

Was the Indonesian invasion an act of aggression? Here, I think Roger is less convincing. Of course, there are compelling policy grounds for treating the invasion as an act of aggression. And yet, there is something to the argument that aggression is an inter-state crime or wrong. Article 2(4) does, after all, refer to the political independence and territorial integrity of a 'state' (is 'state' really a 'broader term' than 'nation', as Roger claims (at 36)? In one sense, yes, in another no. Nations both transcend and are enclosed in states). And the differing responses to the Iraqi invasion of Kuwait and the Indonesian invasion of East Timor might have had something to do with the different status of each entity. Kuwait's 'statehood' seemed worth preserving in a way that East Timor's nationhood (embryonic, contested) did not.[5]

What is not in doubt, though, is the weakness of the Indonesian justifications for using force. Roger knocks them off one by one, and with complete confidence. The so-called use of force in self-defence relies on unreliable facts and would have been grossly disproportionate in any case; the 'invitation' issued by four parties in East Timor did not come from a 'recognised government' (but what if Fretilin had invited the Soviets or Portuguese to help them?), there is no right to prophylactic self-defence (i.e. self-defence in the name of long-term regional stability). The argument based on humanitarian intervention was spurious, and to the extent that the East Timorese people suffered under inhuman conditions of life, the invasion 'aggravated, prolonged, and probably created these conditions'.[6]

I have spent a fair bit of time on this essay of Roger's because I regard it as a classic of its kind and one of his finest pieces of work, because it brings together so many of Roger's interests in a meticulous and not dispassionate legal and political analysis, and because it continued for many years to be a foundational work in scholarship about East Timor. I also found myself strangely encouraged by its ending. In 1980, Roger is refusing pessimism. He ends the essay by saying:

---

5 Of course, this does not deny the effect of the general prohibition found in the later clauses of Art 2(4) or Art 1's more expansive prohibition of 'all acts of aggression or other breaches of the peace', *ibid* 36. Nor does it deny that the response to the Kuwait invasion may have had less to do with international law and more to do with oil or the character of the Baathist regime in Iraq or the Cold War requirement to support authoritarian anti-communists in South-East Asia following the 'loss' of Vietnam.

6 Clark, 'The "Decolonization" of East Timor and the United Nations Norms on Self-Determination and Aggression' (n 4) 41.

> The United Nations has shown some capacity to stick with intractable hard cases. One is reminded of the fact that the organisation persisted with the question of the Portuguese territories and with the racist Rhodesian regime for nearly two decades, in situations where it appeared that nothing would be done about either of these two matters. The organisation has persisted with the Southwest Africa/Namibia question for three and one-half decades, with the end still not in sight. East Timor seems destined to join Namibia as an issue that simply refuses to go away.[7]

It is true that East Timor (and Namibia) refused to go away and the result was independence for both these countries. The birth pains in the Timor case were severe (especially around the time of the referendum) but Timor Léste is now recognisably a nation-state undergoing a process of 'development'.[8] For those who despair of international law and its capacity to bring about change, this must be encouraging. Indeed, we can think of the institutional attention of the UN as a sort of place-holder while a political movement begins to take shape or a geopolitical context is transformed.

---

7 *Ibid* 44.
8 Roger continued to write on Timor and to participate in the work of the International Platform of Jurists for East Timor. In 'Timor Gap: The Legality of the "Treaty on the Zone of Cooperation in an Area between the Indonesian Province of East Timor and Northern Australia"' ((1992) Pace YB Int'l Law 69), Roger turned his forensic attention to the (in)famous agreement between Indonesia and Australia to exploit hydrocarbons in the Timor Sea between Australian and East Timor. This case, of course, ended up in the Australian Federal Court, and in the ICJ where Australia won a pyrrhic victory but East Timor's right to self-determination was affirmed by the Court. Roger makes it very clear in this article that Australia's decision to enter into the Timor Gap Treaty with Indonesia breached the duty not to recognise the acquisition of territory through unlawful force and rendered the Treaty null (by operation of *ius cogens* rules and the *nemo dat quod non habet* principle). I had not noticed either that the original Timor Gap Treaty concerned an area between the *Indonesian Province of East Timor* and Northern Australia. This says something about the attitude of the Australian Government at this time. The Timor Gap (now Timor Sea) dispute, of course, trundles on with further proceedings in the Permanent Court of Arbitration and in the ICJ again between Timor Léste and Australia. See *Arbitration under the Timor Sea Treaty* (PCA, 23 April, 2013). Some of these proceedings turn on allegations of espionage on the part of Australia and the effects of this espionage on the validity of the treaty entered into by Timor Léste and Australia (fraud, breach of good faith and intervention without consent). See Donald K Anton, 'The Timor Sea Treaty Arbitration: Timor-Leste Challenges Australian Espionage and Seizure of Documents' (2014) 18(6) ASIL Insights at <http://www.asil.org/insights/volume/18/issue/6/timor-sea-treaty-arbitration-timor-leste-challenges-australian-espionage> accessed 27 January 2015.

It hardly needs stating, too, that this sort of rigorous, informed and textually sensitive analysis is a model for the sort of work scholars can engage in today when studying the effect of referenda in the Crimea or the character of Russian interventions in Ukraine and Georgia or Western interventions in Libya and Iraq. It was a pleasure to go back to this essay.

Roger, of course, has had many other interests. His long-standing concern about weapons of mass destruction resulted in a 30 minute encapsulation before the International Court of Justice of his (and Samoa's) views on the Legality of Nuclear Weapons, but his interests have persisted through the decades. Just last year, Roger wrote, for the *New York Law School Law Review*, on weapons of mass destruction. The article, 'Is the Butter Battle Book's Bitsy Big-Boy Boomeroo Banned?' took the alliterative law review title to new heights (or depths). Inspired by Dr Seuss, Roger explores the madness of the arms race and the development of WMDs more generally. But this does not occasion, for Roger, a disconsolate throwing up of arms. Instead, Roger does what he always does and applies international law to the problem:

> The law is a great engine, in some situations, for promoting dialogue, and this one—with such high stakes—must be one of these situations. International law has a role in matters of war and peace, and in mitigating the worst effects of war should efforts to prevent it fail.[9]

This has been his capstone since the early 1960s. In 1964, he leads a group of young New Zealand lawyers who are trying to encourage the Government to bring a case against France over French nuclear tests in the Pacific. These young lawyers marshal the very latest arguments on environmental law and state responsibility, some derived from the famous *Trail Smelter Case*. The Minister of Foreign Affairs is unimpressed calling it 'one of the dumbest, stupidest ideas he had ever heard....'.[10] Today's dumb, stupid ideas are tomorrow's procedural innovations, though, and a later New Zealand government takes up the idea with some vigour. The result is the *Nuclear Weapons Case* at the ICJ where New Zealand's arguments meet with some success. This story, told in the Dr Seuss article, continues with Roger representing Samoa in the Nuclear Weapons Case. Here, there is an exchange between Roger and Judge Schwebel on the contours of the NPT (does it, in effect, legitimise the possession and use of nuclear weapons? No, certainly not the latter, argued Roger)). The result in the case is famously equivocal. The use of nuclear weapons would *generally* be

---

9   (2014) 58 New York L Sch L Rev 655, 658.
10   *Ibid* 664.

illegal (such a small word, as Roger puts it). At the end of this essay, Roger reminds his readers of the old (perhaps even shop-worn) paradox in international law. How can it be that poisoned arrows are unlawful but nuclear weapons (or the 'Bitsy Big-Boy Boomeroo') are not?[11] The New York Law School essay ends with some thoughts on the Rome Statute and its failure to criminalise weapons of mass destruction. As Roger points out there is no express prohibition. The Great Powers would not tolerate it. However, the provisions on war crimes and genocide leave plenty of scope for asserting a strongly implied prohibition. In particular, it is a war crime to

> ...intentionally direct(ing) attacks against the civilian population as such or against individual civilians not taking direct part in hostilities' or to 'intentionally launch(ing) an attack in the knowledge that such an attack will cause incidental loss of life or injury to civilians or damage to civilian objects, or widespread, long-term and severe damage to the natural environment that would be clearly excessive in relation to the concrete and direct military advantage anticipated.[12]

Roger, of course, has maintained a watchful eye over international legal developments in the Pacific. I witnessed Roger last year in Auckland wow a group of diplomats from the region with a fiery and apparently *ex tempore* presentation on the ICC and the crime of aggression. What had been a very useful, if occasionally sleepy, inter-governmental meeting was transformed into a theatrical performance. Roger's presentation to the American Society of International Law in 1973 was presumably a more sedate affair. Here, he offers his predominantly American audience some thoughts on the varying statuses of the former Strategic Trust Territories in the Pacific. Again, there is the focus on self-determination, a willingness to take seriously the freely-expressed wishes of the people involved, an acceptance that these freely expressed wishes might result in free association (The Cook Islands) as well as independence (Tonga, Nauru), a recognition that UN membership need not be the final destination for all aspiring nations, and a scepticism concerning Great Power (in this case the United States) intentions and prerogatives in the South Pacific.[13]

There is more, of course. I have said nothing about Roger's substantial and influential work on human rights, where he has written on the role of the High

---

11   *Ibid* 669.
12   Arts 8(2)(b)(i) and 8(2)(b)(iv).
13   'The Trust Territories of the Pacific Islands: Some Perspectives' (1973) Proc Am Soc'y Int'l L 17.

Commissioner for Refugees, the UN Declaration on the Elimination of Intolerance and of Discrimination Based on Religious Belief, and the Universal Declaration on Human Rights. His *Human Rights Quarterly* essays on the way in which an early human rights NGO, the International League for Human Rights, shaped the outcome of the dispute over South-West Africa (in 1981) and on human rights strategies (1999) are required reading for those interested in the precursors to Human Rights Watch and Amnesty on one hand, and on the way in which human rights norms and, more particularly, processes developed—sometimes in unexpected ways—throughout the 1960s on the other (the latter article includes a pointed quote from a fellow New Zealander, Professor Quentin-Baxter). The essay on strategies is an homage to Kamleshwar Das, the former Deputy Director of the UN Division of Human Rights. At the end of this essay, Roger describes Das as the '...model of the anonymous British Commonwealth civil servant...his delicate hand touched somewhere on each of the topics I have discussed...'.[14] Whether Roger's hand could be described as delicate is for others to decide but he has touched many topics and always with robustness and intelligence, and with a fierce commitment to the virtues of legality.

---

14   'Human Rights Strategies of the 1960s within the United Nations: A Tribute to the Late Kamleshwar Das' (1999) 21 HRQ 308, 341.

PART 2

Essays on Peace, War and Global Security

∴

CHAPTER 6

Germany and the Crime of Aggression*

Claus Kreß†

My friendship with Roger Clark is a most pleasant collateral advantage of the negotiations on the Statute of the International Criminal Court ('ICC') since the 1998 Rome Conference. While Samoa is perhaps not considered as a global power in military or economic terms, Samoa's delegates, and not least Roger, made a very significant contribution to the establishment of the ICC in intellectual terms. The latter is also true with respect to the negotiations on the crime of aggression that continued after the Rome conference and that culminated in the 2010 diplomatic breakthrough in Kampala. Like Samoa, Germany invested considerable efforts in making the negotiations on the crime of aggression a success. Perhaps it is of some interest to give an account of this active role and to place that role within the broader perspective of Germany's history since 1914. It is my sincere hope that Roger will derive some pleasure from reading such a German perspective, written by a German friend and admirer of his.

1   Introduction

In 1919, the former German Emperor William II and his role in the outbreak of the First World War were at the heart of the first attempt made in modern times to conduct an international trial for the decision of a State to go to war. In 1946, Germany's wars of aggression under the Nazi regime formed the object of the 'creative precedent' set in Nuremberg. In 2010, Germany was widely seen as one of the more important players when a diplomatic breakthrough was achieved in Kampala on the definition of the crime of aggression and on the activation of the ICC's jurisdiction over that crime. This should suffice to indicate a 'special connection' between Germany's history and that of the crime of aggression.

Let me begin with two citations in support of my suggestion that there is quite a rich and eventful story to be told. In 1953, the American State Department commented on that policy as follows:

---

*   The essay is based on a lecture given by the author to the Japanese Society of International Law at its 2014 session in Niigata.
†   The opinions stated in this article are the author's own and do not necessarily represent the official German view.

(The) German position on the trials of war criminals is a problem which has continued to trouble us ever since the trials were held. The Germans have failed to accept the principles on which the trials were based and do not believe that those convicted were guilty. Their attitude is very much sentimental and can not be influenced by arguments or an objective statement of the facts. They adhere to the view that the majority of the war criminals were soldiers who were punished for doing what all soldiers do in war, or indeed were ordered to do.[1]

Forty-five years later in 1998, William R. Pace, the American convenor of the global coalition of non-governmental organizations for an international criminal court passed the following judgment on Germany's international criminal law policy:

(No) country can be prouder than Germany of their participation and support for the (International Criminal Court) (...). The German refusal to accept what they called an 'alibi court', and their resistance to the highly publicized United States threats to the German leaders during the Rome Conference deserves great appreciation by the world community.[2]

These two citations, of course, refer to the German approach to international criminal law in general, but they can be applied to Germany's attitude towards the crime of aggression as well, as I hope the story that follows will show.

2 Versailles, Nuremberg and the Prevailing Scepticism until the End of the Cold War[3]

1 *Versailles*

At the end of the First World War, the British Prime Minister David Lloyd George, declared: 'The (German) Kaiser must be prosecuted. The war was a

---

1 Cited in Jörg Friedrich, 'Kein in Nürnberg Verurteilter kam in das Strafregister' Süddeutsche Zeitung (1 October 1996) 10.
2 William R Pace, 'The Relationship between the International Criminal Court and Non-Governmental Organizations' in Herman A M von Hebel and others (eds), *Reflections on the International Criminal Court* (TMC Asser Press 1999) 197.
3 This part of the essay is a much condensed version of Claus Kreß, 'Versailles-Nürnberg-Den Haag: Deutschland und das Völkerstrafrecht' in Verein zur Förderung der Rechtswissenschaft (ed), *Fakultätsspiegel* (Carl Heymanns Verlag 2006) ('Kreß', Versailles-Nürnberg-Den Haag: Deutschland und das Völkerstrafrecht') 14–37; for an English version, see Claus Kreß,

crime. Who doubts that?'[4] This set the stage for the first attempt made in modern times to conduct international criminal proceedings to determine individual criminal responsibility for going to war.[5] The attempt proved unsuccessful, probably for a mixture of political and legal reasons. The fundamental legal obstacle to which the United States of America, in particular, referred was the novelty of the crime in question. Art. 227 of the Versailles Treaty implicitly went a long way to endorse the sceptical position taken by the United States in that it declared to 'arraign William II of Hohenzollern, formerly German Emperor' *not* for a crime under international *law*, but 'for a supreme offence against international *morality* and the sanctity of treaties'. The Government of the Netherlands, where the German Emperor had taken domicile, declared that State was unable and unwilling to surrender William II to a 'special tribunal' for want of a sufficiently solid legal basis. While the Treaty of Versailles did therefore not result in international criminal proceedings against the German Emperor for waging a war of aggression, the historic fact remained that the idea of criminalizing the waging of a war of aggression under international law had been connected, in Art. 231 of the Treaty of Versailles, with the attribution to 'Germany and its allies' of the responsibility for the outbreak of the First World War—an attribution of responsibility which, at the time, proved extremely controversial in Germany, to put it mildly. As one consequence of this broader historical context, there was little German involvement in the inter-War debates on international criminal justice. As Hellmuth von Weber, one of the few German authors dealing with the subject matter, noted in 1934:

> It has gone almost unnoticed by the German public that a movement to establish an international criminal jurisdiction has started after the World War. The German reservation is rooted in the fact that this movement has at its origin the allegation of Germany's responsibility for and during the war. Such allegation made it impossible for a German to take a positive attitude towards the said movement.[6]

'Versailles-Nuremberg-The Hague' (2006) 40 The American Lawyer 16 ('Kreß, 'Versailles-Nuremberg-The Hague"') (each study contains detailed further references).
4 'Coalition policy defined, Mr. Lloyd George's pledges', *The Times* (6 December 1918) 9.
5 For a fascinating account of this first attempt with many detailed references, see Kirsten Sellars, *'Crimes Against Peace' and International Law* (CUP 2013) 1–11.
6 Helmut von Weber, *Internationale Strafgerichtsbarkeit* (Ferd Dümmlers Verlag 1934), preface.

2 Nuremberg

Robert Jackson's success at Nuremberg in setting a 'creative precedent' for the international criminalization of waging a war of aggression, bolstered this negative German position towards international criminal law in general and crimes against peace in particular for quite a while.[7] Interestingly, about 80% of the German population had considered the Nuremberg trial against the Major War Criminals to be 'fair' at the time when the trial was being conducted, but already in 1950 public opinion changed dramatically and only 38% of the Germans held that view any longer.[8] While West Germany's political leaders generally tended to avoid addressing the topic in political and patriotic terms, they invested much energy to persuade the Occupying Powers to release the imprisoned German war criminals. This tireless endeavour met with success: by 1958, all those sentenced to imprisonment in the Nuremberg-follow up proceedings had been set free. These so-called 'humanitarian initiatives' to seek the early release of those imprisoned for crimes under international law, were complemented by Germany's non-recognition of the Nuremberg precedent on legal grounds. One main objection, which was most prominently applied to the crime against peace, was the retroactive application of this 'new crime' at Nuremberg. Hermann Jahrreiß, Professor of Law at the University of Cologne, had set the tone on the '*nullum crimen*-objection' as early as in the Nuremberg trial itself when he had stated in eloquent terms in support of the defence:

> The regulations of the Charter negate the basis of international law, they anticipate the law of a world state. They are revolutionary. Perhaps in the hopes and longings of the nations the future is theirs. The lawyer, and only as such may I speak here, has only to establish that they are new, revolutionarily new. The laws regarding war and peace between states had no place for them—*could* not have any place for them. Thus they are criminal laws with retroactive force.[9]

---

7 Norbert Frei, 'Der Nürnberger Prozeß und die Deutschen' in Wolfram Wette & Gerd R Ueberschär (ed), *Kriegsverbrechen im 20. Jahrhundert* (Wissenschaftliche Buchgesellschaft 2001) 477–492; see also Ronen Steinke, *The Politics of International Criminal Justice. German Perspectives from Nuremberg to The Hague* (Hart Publishing 2012) ('Steinke, *The Politics of International Criminal Justice. German Perspectives from Nuremberg to The Hague*') 40–61.

8 Norbert Frei, 'Der Nürnberger Prozeß und die Deutschen' (n 7) 478.

9 The quote is from a typescript of Jahrreiß's closing argument. It is part of his personal Nuremberg file that is now in the Archive of the University of Cologne. On Jahrreiß, see Annette Weinke, 'Hermann Jahrreiß (1894–1992): Vom Exponenten des völkerrechtlichen "Kriegseinsatzes" zum Verteidiger der deutschen Eliten in Nürnberg', in Steffen Augsberg & Andreas Funke (eds), *Kölner Juristen im 20. Jahrhundert* (Mohr Siebeck 2013) 163–195.

This, in essence, captured the official legal position that Germany initially took on Nuremberg. And in conformity with this position, Germany distanced herself from the often so-called 'Nuremberg-clause' in Art. 7 (2) of the European Convention on Human Rights that contains a carefully circumscribed exception from the *nullum crimen*-principle.

3 Prevailing Scepticism until the End of the Cold War

The German legal protest against Nuremberg had thus been placed on record. But what were the future prospects of West German international criminal policy at the time of the Cold War? Considering Germany's foreign policy emphasis on multilateralism and the rule of law in international relations, one could perhaps have expected Germany to take a more favourable stance towards international criminal law for the future. The first opportunity to take such a position at the international level came in 1978 when the Sixth Committee of the General Assembly of the United Nations resumed its work on the codification of international criminal law, a task it had abandoned in 1954. But when Germany took the floor in 1980, it spoke out against international criminal law without great diplomatic clouding. According to the record,[10] the German delegation voiced serious doubts about the usefulness of resuming the discussion about the Nuremberg principles. Whether it would be possible to pronounce rules of international criminal law that could gain support from the international community was deemed questionable. While the persisting German difficulties with the Nuremberg precedent are likely to have influenced this less than enthusiastic position, the perhaps more immediate explanation is that, at this moment in time, leading Western powers such as the United States of America, Canada and the United Kingdom were similarly disinclined to revitalize the Nuremberg and Tokyo *acquis*. It would thus take more time before Germany became ready for a new policy on international criminal law.

By and large, Germany's legal scholarship did not display a greater interest in the subject-matter than the country's political establishment. With the noteworthy exceptions of Hans-Heinrich Jescheck,[11] Otto Triffterer[12] and Herbert Jäger,[13] German criminal lawyers and criminologists did not turn their close

---

10   UNGA Sixth Committee (7 October 1980) UN Doc A/C.6/35/Sr. 12.
11   Hans-Heinrich Jescheck, *Die Verantwortlichkeit der Staatsorgane nach Völkerstrafrecht. Eine Studie zu den Nürnberger Prozessen* (Röhrscheid Verlag 1952) *passim*.
12   Otto Triffterer, *Dogmatische Untersuchungen zur Entwicklung des Materiellen Völkerstrafrechts seit Nürnberg* (Eberhard Albert Verlag 1966) *passim*.
13   Herbert Jäger, *Makrokriminalität. Studien zur Kriminologie Kollektiver Gewalt* (Suhrkamp Verlag 1989) *passim*.

attention to the study of crimes under international law and the establishment of an international criminal jurisdiction. And prominent German public and public international lawyers did not make any attempt to conceal their outright policy objections to building on the Nuremberg precedent on international criminal law in general, and on the crime of initiating a war of aggression in particular. As late as in 1994, Helmut Quaritsch, a tireless critic, called the debates within the International Law Commission 'glass bead games by an international sect of lawyers'.[14] And in 1989, when the Cold War drew to a close, Wilhelm Grewe, the eminent historian on international law and the influential international legal adviser of the Foreign Office in Konrad Adenauer's days, articulated the following plainly negative assessment:

> The criminal prosecution of leading individuals for initiating a war of aggression was, as far as the past is concerned, a miscarriage of justice (a victim of which was Rudolf Heß, who, whatever one cares to think about his role in the Third Reich, was jailed for 40 years). As for the future, this was the wrong path to take. In so far as the other crimes listed in the London Statute are concerned, it seems to make little sense to continue to cling to the failed attempts and abandon oneself to the hope that one day there would indeed be a comprehensive international criminal law regime applied by an international criminal court.[15]

3 The German Position during the Negotiations on the Statute of the ICC

1 *The Background: The Evolution of the German Position on International Criminal Law and International Criminal Justice in the 1990s*

As we know, turbulent global developments since the 1990s caused the realist Grewe to be disproved by reality. It is fascinating to see how the German position towards international criminal law has changed in the course of this development.[16] To begin with, Germany was not among the driving forces

---

14 Helmut Quaritsch, *Carl Schmitt. Das international-rechtliche Verbrechen des Angriffskrieges und der Grundsatz 'nullum crimen, nulla poena sine lege'* (Duncker & Humblot 1994) 219.

15 Wilhem Grewe ,'Rückblick auf Nürnberg' in Kai Hailbronner and others (eds), *Festschrift für Karl Doehring* (Springer Verlag 1989) 248–89.

16 For a more detailed account, see Steinke, *The Politics of International Criminal Justice. German Perspectives from Nuremberg to The Hague* (n 7), 74–119 (with many detailed references); see also Kreß, 'Versailles-Nürnberg-Den Haag: Deutschland und das Völker-

when it came to the establishment of the two international criminal courts for the former Yugoslavia and Rwanda. In both cases, the United States, as in Nuremberg, was the key player. Even so, Germany fulfilled her obligation under the relevant Security Council resolution to co-operate with the Yugoslav tribunal. In fact, Germany made the ground-breaking first trial conducted before this tribunal possible, when it terminated its fairly advanced own proceedings against the Serbian defendant *Dusko Tadic* and surrendered him to The Hague. This important instance of early co-operation with the Yugoslav Tribunal indicated a new German openness towards international criminal justice, but in truth it was action upon request.

Since 1997, Germany has been showing her readiness to play an active role on international criminal justice. This new attitude had become possible because in the 1990s a consensus had emerged among all the leading political parties in the country to support the international criminal justice project. The charismatic Head of the Public International Law Section of Germany's Foreign Office, the late Hans-Peter Kaul, who would later become the first German judge at the ICC, most skilfully took advantage of the new political climate. He soon established Germany as a driving force within the group of like-minded States which supported the establishment of an effective permanent international criminal court.[17] If seen from a broader foreign policy perspective, it is remarkable that Germany not only developed a national policy position on the ICC, but was also prepared to defend that position where it deviated from the preferences of France, the United Kingdom and, most importantly, the United States of America. It is possible that the negotiations on the ICC were the first international negotiations touching upon high politics where Germany acted that way. And, the political consensus within Germany on that course of action has remained robust. In 2002, the Christian Democrat, Norbert Roettgen, stated as a member of an opposition party at the time:

> During this term of parliament we had many controversies on legal policy issues. Germany's commitment for an international order of criminal law and criminal justice was no and is no controversy, though, but constitutes a firm common ground of German legal and foreign policy.[18]

---

strafrecht' (n 3) 38–51; Kreß, 'Versailles-Nuremberg-The Hague' (n 3) 28–36 (with many detailed references in each text).

[17] Hans-Peter Kaul, 'Der Beitrag Deutschlands zum Völkerstrafrecht' in Christoph Safferling & Stefan Kirsch (eds), *Völkerstrafrechtspolitik. Praxis des Völkerstrafrechts* (Springer Verlag 2014) ('Kaul, 'Der Beitrag Deutschlands zum Völkerstrafrecht'') 51–84.

[18] Deutscher Bundestag, Plenarprotokoll 14/233, reprinted in Sascha Rolf Lüder & Thomas Vormbaum (eds), *Materialien zum Völkerstrafgesetzbuch. Dokumentation des Gesetzge-*

Hand in hand with this evolution of a new German attitude to the international criminal justice, Germany's perspective on Nuremberg also underwent a change. While the shortcomings of the Nuremberg proceedings that had figured so prominently in Germany's prior approach were not suddenly ignored, more and decisive emphasis was now placed on the fact that a judicial avenue had been chosen to address Germany's wars of aggression under Hitler despite all the challenges that this involved. And, eventually, Germany fully acknowledged that Nuremberg laid the potential for according more weight to the rule of law in future international relations.[19]

As regards the key elements of the German position, it is worth recalling that the latter was never directed to an uncritical extension of the subject matter of international criminal law *stricto sensu*. Quite to the contrary, Germany has consistently been advocating for the limitation of this body of law to the crime of aggression, genocide, crimes against humanity, and war crimes, including those committed in non-international armed conflict. In each case, Germany favoured definitions of the greatest possible precision, and opposed the lowering of general prerequisites of individual criminal responsibility. For example, the express reference to the principle of culpability in the Rules of Procedure and Evidence[20] is due to a German request. Germany was keen, however, to see that her rather narrow concept of international criminal law be construed with full recognition of the principle of universal equality before the law. In the German case, this important point of principle is supported by the historical experience of the Nuremberg precedent which, under the prevailing circumstances at the time, could not live up to this ideal. But in his opening speech, Jackson had stated emphatically, and with particular emphasis on the crime of aggression:

> The ultimate step in avoiding periodic wars, which are inevitable in a system of international lawlessness, is to make statesmen responsible to law. And let me make clear that while this law is first applied against German aggressors, the law includes, and if it is to serve a useful purpose it must condemn, aggression by any other nations, including those which sit here now in judgment.[21]

---

bungsverfahrens (Lit Verlag 2002) ('Lüder & Vormbaum, *Materialien zum Völkerstrafgesetzbuch. Dokumentation des Gesetzgebungsverfahrens*') 95.

19 In accordance with this fresh look at Nuremberg, Germany withdrew her reservation to Art 7 (2) of the European Convention on Human Rights on 5 October 2001.

20 Rule 145 (1) (a) of the Rules of Procedure and Evidence.

21 Secretariat of the International Military Tribunal (ed), *Trial of German Major War Criminals by the International Military Tribunal Sitting At Nuremberg Germany* (Vol II, Allied Control Authority for Germany 1947) 182.

At this point, Germany's reappraisal of Nuremberg becomes particularly clear. The element of victor's justice, which was inevitably present at the time, is not ignored. However, more constructively than in the past, German recognition is now, in line with Jackson's powerful statement of principle, turned into the postulation of 'equality before the law' as the guiding principle for the future. It would have flown into the face of the latter principle to establish the ICC as a 'permanent ad hoc tribunal' of the Security Council. Therefore Germany, together with the great majority of states, was in favour of empowering the international prosecutor to take up situations *proprio motu*, under the control only of the international judges.[22] Germany also—unsuccessfully, as is well known—advocated that the ICC should be vested with universal jurisdiction to ensure universal equality in the application of the law.[23] All this together constitutes the necessary background to fully appreciate the German position on the crime of aggression in Rome and thereafter.

2 The Rome Conference

Just before the Rome Conference,[24] Germany published a position paper on the forthcoming negotiations.[25] The three key messages regarding the crime of aggression were that Germany supports the inclusion of this crime within the jurisdiction of the Court, that the crime should be narrowly defined in line with the relevant historic precedents, and that the competence of the Security Council to determine acts of aggression should not be ignored as this would enhance the prospects of a successful outcome of the negotiations. While the two first pillars of this German position remained unchanged throughout the negotiations, Germany developed its position regarding the position of the Security Council in the course of the negotiations.

Already in 1997, Germany had explained its approach to the crime of aggression in significant detail.[26] She argued that not to include this crime would be a regression from existing customary international law, and would deprive the international community of a desirable instrument of deterrence and

---

22 Art 13(c) in conjunction with Art 15 of the ICC Statute.
23 Hans-Peter Kaul & Claus Kreß, 'Jurisdiction and Cooperation in the Statute of the International Criminal Court: Principles and Compromises' (1999) 2 YIHL 152.
24 For a detailed account of the Rome negotiations on the crime of aggression, see Gerd Westdickenberg & Oliver Fixson, 'Das Verbrechen der Aggression im Römischen Statut des Internationalen Strafgerichtshofes' in Jochen Abr Frowein and others (eds), *Liber amicorum Tono Eitel* (Springer Verlag 2003) 483–525.
25 Kaul, 'Der Beitrag Deutschlands zum Völkerstrafrecht' (n 17) 67.
26 Stefan Barriga & Claus Kreß (eds), *The Travaux Préparatoires of the Crime of Aggression* (CUP 2012) ('Barriga & Kreß, *The Travaux Préparatoires of the Crime of Aggression*') 233.

prevention. The distinctive character of the crime of aggression was seen, she argued, in the serious violation of another State's territorial integrity through the use of military force, irrespective of the commission of other crimes under international law. With respect to the typical case where the crime of aggression does go hand in hand with war crimes, Germany identified the procedural advantage that it might be easier in certain instances to prove the leaders' responsibility for the war as such, rather than to attribute to them the responsibility for war crimes committed on the ground.

From 1997 onwards, Germany was in favour of limiting the substantive definition of the crime to the individual participation in a completed use of military force by one State against another one. She has also been consistently insisting on the absolute leadership character of the crime. In her first detailed proposal of December 1997,[27] Germany explained the need for a narrow definition of the State conduct element of the crime because of the imperative of avoiding, as far as possible, frivolous accusations of a political nature and avoiding any negative impact on the legitimate use of force in conformity with the Charter of the United Nations. Germany favoured 'a viable self-sustained definition'[28] which, in her view, excluded any constitutive substantive effect of a Security Council determination that an act of aggression had occurred.[29] Furthermore, Germany doubted the usefulness of referring to the acts of aggression, as listed in Art. 3 of the 1974 General Assembly definition of aggression, in order to define the State element.[30] In concrete terms, Germany suggested to define the State conduct element as

> an armed attack directed by a State against the territorial integrity or political independence of another State when this armed attack was undertaken in manifest contravention of the Charter of the United Nations and resulted in the effective occupation by the armed forces of the attacking State or in the annexation by the use of force of the territory of another state or part thereof.[31]

When it came to the procedural role of the Security Council, Germany followed the proposal of the International Law Commission to make the proceedings for a crime of aggression dependent on the prior determination of an act of aggression by the Council. In December 1997, Germany was of the view that

---

27 Ibid 234.
28 Ibid 233.
29 Ibid 234.
30 Ibid 236.
31 Ibid 237.

such a solution was 'a merely declaratory clarification of the existing legal situation under the Charter'.[32]

In a slightly revised form, the German proposal was the last one that remained on the negotiation table in Rome,[33] but, as is well known, this proposal also did not meet with success. When the last hope of securing an agreement on the crime of aggression had faded away in the corridors of the World Health Organization in Rome, Germany was quick to support the proposal of the States forming the Non-Aligned Movement[34] that eventually became Art. 5 (1) (d) and Art. 5 (2) of the original ICC Statute.[35] The inclusion of the crime of aggression in the list of crimes under the Court's jurisdiction and the articulation of a kind of normative expectation that States Parties would strive towards the activation of this jurisdiction in the ultimate Rome compromise package should pave the way to the breakthrough that would materialise 12 years later in Kampala.

3   The Preparatory Commission for the ICC: Germany's Informal Discussion Paper of November 2000

In the Preparatory Commission for the ICC,[36] the German delegation made clear its determination not to treat Art. 5 (1) (d) and Art. 5 (2) as dead letters, but to move the discussion on the crime of aggression forward. For this purpose, Germany presented a new discussion paper on the crime of aggression, which was in fact the most detailed of all its written contributions to the negotiation process.[37]

The paper did not repeat the position voiced before and in Rome, namely that proceedings for the crime of aggression should be dependent on the determination of an act of aggression by the Security Council. Instead, the 2000 Paper placed all emphasis on the definition of the State conduct element of the crime. The paper stressed the need firmly to ground that definition 'on established customary law', and thereby to follow the same approach as had been taken when defining the other crimes within the Court's jurisdiction.[38] It was

32   Ibid 234.
33   Ibid 277.
34   Ibid 315.
35   Kaul, 'Der Beitrag Deutschlands zum Völkerstrafrecht' (n 17) 68.
36   For a detailed account of the negotiations in the Preparatory Commission, see Stefan Barriga, 'Negotiating the Amendments on the crime of aggression' in Barriga & Kreß, *The Travaux Préparatoires of the Crime of Aggression* (n 26) 8–14 ('Barriga, 'Negotiating the Amendments on the crime of aggression"').
37   Barriga & Kreß, *The Travaux Préparatoires of the Crime of Aggression* (n 26) 367.
38   Ibid 368 (para 5), 374 (para 24 (2)).

then stated and explained in considerable detail that customary international law had not developed beyond the point of criminalizing the participation in a *war* of aggression.[39] While no decisive importance was attached to maintain the term 'war', it was argued that the substance of that term should be spelled out in the definition. In that context, and in a shift of emphasis compared with her proposal submitted to the Rome conference, Germany no longer suggested that the State use of force either had to result in military occupation or annexation or that such had to be the object of the use of force. Instead, the 2000 Paper stressed the need for the State's use of force to be an 'aggressive and large-scale armed attack on the territorial integrity of another State, clearly without any justification under international law'.[40] The paper went on to assert that such instances of a State use of force 'share the following characteristics':

> Such attacks are of a particular magnitude and dimension and of a frightening gravity and intensity.
>
> Such attacks regularly lead to the most serious consequences, such as extensive loss of life, extensive destruction, subjugation and exploitation of a population for a prolonged period of time.
>
> Such attacks regularly pursue objectives unacceptable to the international community as a whole, such as annexation, mass destruction, annihilation, deportation of forcible transfer of the population of the attacked State or parts thereof, or plundering of the attacked State, including its natural resources.[41]

The paper summarised 'that armed attacks which combine the above-mentioned characteristics are clearly not justified under international law' and that '(b)y the same token, such armed attacks occur "in manifest violation of the Charter of the United Nations"'.[42] The so-defined use of force must effectively occur, so the paper adds in line with the Germany's consistently held position. 'This means that preparatory acts or attempts without actually resulting in an aggressive, large-scale armed attack on the territorial integrity of another State should not fall within the scope of the crime of aggression.'[43]

The German position on the State conduct element, as articulated in the 2000 Paper, is interesting in several respects. Germany clearly articulated the need to

---

39 *Ibid* 370–73 (paras 16–22).
40 *Ibid* 369 (para 10).
41 *Ibid.*
42 *Ibid* (para 11).
43 *Ibid* 374 (para 24 (4)).

remain within the confines of customary international law, and expressed the view that such customary law required a definition of the State act element of the crime that is narrower than the concepts of 'use of force in contravention of Art. 2 (4) of the United Nations Charter' and 'act of aggression as listed in Art. 3 of the 1974 General Assembly definition of aggression.' Germany did not formulate the conviction that customary law required a military occupation or an annexation as a consequence of the use of force or as the latter's objective. She did, however, suggest that the use of force must be particularly serious in quantitative terms. In addition, Germany referred to certain reprehensible consequences or objectives of the use of force, and stated that the qualification of an armed attack as being in 'manifest violation of the Charter of the United Nations' results from the 'combination of these characteristics'. This displays the attempt to define the concepts of 'clearly without justification under international law' and 'manifest violation of the Charter of the United Nations' by reference to a quantitative ('intensity'/'gravity') and a qualitative ('serious consequences' or 'unacceptable objectives') threshold. In respect to the latter, Germany did not replace the originally preferred alternative between military occupation or annexation by another enumerative set of applications, but chose a potentially more inclusive, but less determinate approach by referring to a number of typical examples.

Despite the 2000 German Discussion Paper, the work done on the crime of aggression from February 1999 until July 2000 within the Preparatory Commission for the ICC did not advance the matter significantly. The July 2002 Coordinator's Paper,[44] which was the final outcome of this part of the negotiations, certainly brought the different aspects of the negotiations together in a useful structure. But the impressive number of options and brackets contained in the 2002 Paper dispelled any possible illusion about the difficult way ahead.

4   The Special Working Group on the Crime of Aggression and the Princeton Process

The necessary momentum to overcome these difficulties was only created within the Special Working Group on the Crime of Aggression between 2003 and 2009, and more particularly during the 'Princeton Process' between 2004 and 2007 that comprised a series of informal inter-sessional meetings under the auspices of the Liechtenstein Institute on Self-Determination at the Woodrow Wilson School at Princeton University.[45] Under the masterful chairmanship of

---

44   *Ibid* 412.
45   For a detailed account of the negotiations within the Special Working Group and during the Princeton Prosess, see Barriga, 'Negotiating the Amendments on the crime of aggression' (n 36) 14–41.

Ambassador Christian Wenaweser from Liechtenstein, the Special Working Group, most importantly, was able to achieve the breakthrough with respect to the substantive definition of the crime.

At this point of the negotiations, Germany did not submit another discussion paper, but chose to contribute somewhat less visibly to the process of compromise-building. One member of the German delegation acted as a sub-coordinator to help reaching agreement on the essentially technical legal question of the definition of the conduct of the individual perpetrator and on the interplay of this conduct requirement with the different forms of participations as listed in Art. 25 (3) of the ICC Statute.[46] With respect to the State conduct element, Germany displayed a spirit of compromise while insisting on the need to adopt a threshold which narrowed the definition in comparison with the State conduct described in Art. 2 (4) of the United Nations Charter.

By 2007, it had become clear that an overwhelming majority of delegations wished to refer to the 1974 General Assembly definition, including the latter's concept of 'act of aggression' as the basis of the State conduct element.[47] Although Germany maintained its sceptical view on such a reference within this specific context, she no longer opposed it taking into consideration the need to move forward to an ultimate compromise. But in view of her firmly held conviction that the crime of aggression should be defined in conformity with customary international law, Germany insisted that the reference to the General Assembly definition be qualified in two respects. First, no reference should be made to Arts. 2 and 4 of the latter definition, to avoid the impression that the Security Council could authoritatively determine the State conduct element. Second, the reference to Arts. 1 and 3 of the General Assembly definition should be qualified by a special threshold clause. The compromise, that emerged from the discussions within the Special Working Group, reflected both Germany's concerns. First, the phrase 'subject to and in accordance with provisions of article 2' in Art. 3 of the General Assembly definition was replaced by the words 'in accordance with United Nations General Assembly resolution 3314 (XXIX) of 14 December 1974'.[48] Second, the reference to the concept of 'act of aggression', as circumscribed in Arts. 1 and 3 of the General Assembly definition, was qualified by the words 'which, by its character, gravity and scale constitutes a manifest violation of the Charter of the United Nations'.[49]

---

46 See the 2005 Discussion Paper 1, as reprinted in Barriga & Kreß, *The Travaux Préparatoires of the Crime of Aggression* (n 26) 471.
47 Barriga, 'Negotiating the Amendments on the crime of aggression' (n 36) 25.
48 *Ibid* 27.
49 *Ibid* 28–30.

The resemblance of this threshold clause with the language contained in Germany's 2002 Paper is obvious. This resemblance can be seen in the use of the word 'manifest' in both texts. It is also to be seen in the use of the word 'character' in addition to the words 'gravity' and 'scale', pointing to a qualitative as well as quantitative dimension of the threshold. While the German delegation had much preferred not to use the concept 'act of aggression' in order to define the State conduct element of the crime of aggression, she joined the compromise on the assumption that the essence of her position, as articulated in the 2000 Paper, that is the narrow definition of the crime of aggression in conformity with customary international law, was captured through the threshold clause.

5   The Kampala Review Conference

With one notable exception to which I shall return, the negotiations on the crime of aggression at the Kampala Review Conference from 31 May to 11 June 2010 centered around the three closely intertwined questions of the conditions of the Court's exercise of jurisdiction over the crime, the procedural role of the Security Council, and the entry into force of the amendments.[50] On all three issues, the work within the Special Working Group and during the Princeton Process had considerably advanced the understanding among delegations of the questions involved and to be decided. At the same time, however, the discussions had also revealed an extraordinary level of complexity, which was due to a combination of quite considerable textual ambiguity in Art. 5 (2) and Art. 121 of the ICC Statute, on the one hand, and sharply diverging policy preferences, on the other hand.[51] Predictably, it had proved impossible to overcome the differences among delegations before Kampala.

The essence of the Kampala compromise package on the three outstanding issues may be summarised as follows[52]: The amendments *enter into force for each State* party individually in accordance with the *first* sentence of Art. 121 (5) of the ICC Statute. However, *the Court may exercise its jurisdiction* only with respect to a crime of aggression committed one year after the ratification or acceptance of the amendments by thirty States Parties and after a decision to be taken by a two thirds majority of the members of the Assembly of States Parties to be taken after 1 January 2017, whichever event is later. In cases where the proceedings before the Court are triggered by a State Party referral or by

---

50   For a detailed account of the negotiations at the Kampala Review Conference, see Barriga, 'Negotiating the Amendments on the crime of aggression' (n 36) 46–57.
51   *Ibid* 30–46.
52   For the details, see arts 15 *bis* and 15 *ter* in conjunction with RC/Res. 6; Barriga & Kreß, *The Travaux Préparatoires of the Crime of Aggression* (n 26) 101.

the Prosecutor *proprio motu*, the Court's exercise of jurisdiction over the crime of aggression does not require the Security Council's 'green light'. In these two cases, the Court's exercise of jurisdiction is, however, limited *ratione personae*. The Court shall, first, not exercise its jurisdiction over crimes of aggression arising from an act of aggression committed by or against a *non*-State party. Second, where the crime of aggression arises from an act of aggression allegedly committed by a State Party against another State Party, and where the amendments have entered into force for the State Party which is the victim of the crime of aggression, the Court is still precluded from exercising its jurisdiction over the crime of aggression where the alleged aggressor State had previously declared not to accept the Court's exercise of jurisdiction. The jurisdictional regime adopted in Kampala is therefore *sui generis* in several important respects, and this includes a finely nuanced deviation from the jurisdictional constraints *ratione personae* as foreseen in the *second* sentence of Art. 121 (5) of the ICC Statute. Art. 5 (2) of the ICC Statute provides States Parties with the legal basis to devise such a jurisdiction regime *sui generis* for the crime of aggression because it empowered States Parties to adopt a provision 'setting out the conditions under which the Court shall exercise jurisdiction with respect to this crime'.

In Kampala, Germany did not submit proposals on the three issues in question. Instead, the German delegation tried to assist the compromise-building process through the expression of a spirit of compromise in formal and informal consultations. Germany's flexibility was the result, first, from the recognition of the extraordinary legal and political complexity of the matter and, second, from the fact that she had developed her position in one important respect. In the course of the discussions within the Special Working Group, Germany had abandoned the belief that the determination of an act of aggression by the Security Council was a legal requirement, flowing from the Charter of the United Nations, for proceedings for a crime of aggression before the ICC.[53] From a legal policy perspective, Germany had come to recognize that the rejection of the idea of a Security Council monopoly with respect to criminal proceedings for a crime of aggression by the overwhelming majority of delegations was more in harmony with the idea of an equal application of international criminal law than the contrary position defended by the five permanent members of the Security Council.

---

53   Federal Foreign Office, *Explanatory Memorandum to the Act regarding the Amendments of 10 and 11 June 2010 to the Rome Statute of the International Criminal Court* (17 July 1998) ('Federal Foreign Office, *Explanatory Memorandum to the Act regarding the Amendments of 10 and 11 June 2010 to the Rome Statute of the International Criminal Court*') 12.

During the dramatic last days of the negotiations, the question of the substantive definition of the crime, which seemed to have been conclusively dealt with by the Special Working Group, somewhat surprisingly came back to the negotiation table for a short, but difficult moment. The United States of America, who had returned to the negotiations only shortly before Kampala,[54] had expressed a number of concerns regarding the draft substantive definition of a crime and had submitted a fairly long list of draft Understandings to have these concerns accommodated.[55] In light of the late hour, the American initiative was not met with enthusiasm by most delegations. On the other hand, there was a feeling that it would be unwise not to make a sincere effort to engage with the United States of America in order to broaden and solidify the consensus on such an important question of universal concern. It was within this spirit, that the German delegation accepted the invitation by the President of the Review Conference to act as the Focal Point for consultations. These consultations resulted in the adoption of the sixth and seventh Understandings regarding the substantive definition of the crime which helped preparing the ground for the successful overall result of the negotiations.[56]

4   The German View on the Kampala Compromise

In the Explanatory Memorandum to the German Bill of Ratification, the German Government called the agreement reached in Kampala 'a historical breakthrough' by which 'a major gap in international criminal law' has been closed.[57] The Government highlighted its satisfaction that the Kampala Review Conference adopted its important decision by consensus.[58] With respect to the substantive definition of the crime, the Memorandum emphasizes that 'not every use of force by States which is contrary to international law' will give rise to a crime of aggression. More specifically, the Government stated that the threshold clause is intended

---

54   Barriga, 'Negotiating the Amendments on the crime of aggression' (n 36) 44–45.
55   Barriga & Kreß, *The Travaux Préparatoires of the Crime of Aggression* (n 26) 751.
56   For a detailed account, see Claus Kreß and others, 'Negotiating the Understandings on the crime of aggression', in Barriga & Kreß, *The Travaux Préparatoires of the Crime of Aggression* (n 26) 94–97.
57   Federal Foreign Office, *Explanatory Memorandum to the Act regarding the Amendments of 10 and 11 June 2010 to the Rome Statute of the International Criminal Court* (n 53) 6.
58   *Ibid* 12.

specifically not to include and hence not to criminalize as a crime of aggression actions whose legality is disputed—such as those committed in the course of humanitarian interventions—and situations in which the aggression is not of sufficient severity.[59]

The Memorandum does not explicitly deal with the view that not only the *first*, but also the *second* sentence of Art. 121 (5) of the ICC Statute applies to the crime of aggression, to the effect that *both* the aggressor *and* the victim State Party must have ratified or accepted the Kampala amendments as a prerequisite for the Court's exercise of jurisdiction over a crime of aggression arising out of the act of aggression committed by the former State against the latter. But, by saying that States Parties 'are able to exclude by declaration the jurisdiction of the ICC over the crime of aggression (also known as "opting out")',[60] the Memorandum seems to implicitly point in the direction of the *sui generis*-regime, as set out above.

The German Parliament approved the draft ratification bill unanimously, and on 3 June 2013 Germany deposited its instrument of ratification.

5 Some Preliminary Thoughts on the Question of Domestic Implementation

Germany has ratified the Kampala amendments without making a decision on the question of domestic implementation. Germany is one of the countries that had already included a provision on aggression in its national criminal code before the Kampala compromise was reached. In fact, Art. 26 of the 1949 German Constitution, as a lesson from the country's aggressive conduct in the Second World War, requires the criminalization of the preparation of a war of aggression. In accordance with this constitutional duty, section 80 of the German Criminal Code penalizes the preparation of a war of aggression with German participation, if such preparation leads to the concrete danger that Germany becomes involved in a war. Section 80 has been referred to in the important decisions of the Federal Prosecutor not to initiate criminal proceedings because of Germany's military action in Kosovo (1999) and Iraq (2003).[61] However, as of

---

59 *Ibid* 14.
60 *Ibid* 16.
61 On the latter decision, see Claus Kreß, 'The German Chief Federal Prosecutor's Decision not to Investigate the Alleged Crime of Preparing Aggression against Iraq' (2004) 2 JICJ 245.

yet, the provision has never been tested judicially. The Kampala compromise sheds new light on section 80 and it gives rise to a number of challenging questions with respect to Germany's legislation on the matter.

In 2002, Germany enacted her new Code of Crimes under International Law that codifies customary international criminal law against genocide, crimes against humanity, and war crimes, as well as a limited number of general principles.[62] The first question to be addressed by the German legislator therefore is whether the crime of aggression should make its way into this special Code. Such a legislative move would probably go hand in hand with the deletion of section 80 from the Criminal Code.

Section 80 of the German Criminal Code uses the traditional concept 'war of aggression'. The legislator could make use of the (possible) inclusion of the crime of aggression into the Code of Crimes under International Law in order to bring Germany's national law in line with the definition adopted in Kampala. This could also be used to clarify the absolute leadership character of the crime, which is not explicit from the text of section 80 of the Criminal Code.

One of the many ambiguities of section 80 of the Criminal Code relates to the question as to whether it is only *German* wars of aggression that are covered, or whether wars of aggression *against* Germany are also covered. Any domestic implementation of the Kampala compromise should clarify this important issue. This question is intertwined with the issue of jurisdiction. In its Code of Crimes under International Law, Germany has vested its courts with universal jurisdiction over crimes under international law, while limiting the exercise of this jurisdiction through a number of procedural criteria. A decision will have to be made whether the same or a special jurisdictional scheme shall apply to the crime of aggression.

Last but not least, thought should be given to the question of whether Germany should avail herself of her priority right under the ICC Statute to exercise jurisdiction over the crime of aggression in all cases. The fifth Understanding regarding the Kampala amendments[63] on the crime of aggression,

---

62 On the conceptual ground work, see Claus Kreß, *Vom Nutzen eines Völkerstrafgesetzbuchs* (Nomos Verlagsgesellschaft 2000) *passim*; for an overview about the content of the Code, see Gerhard Werle & Florian Jeßberger, 'International Criminal Law is Coming Home: The New German Code of Crimes Against International Law' (2002) 13 Crim LF 191; for the travaux préparatoires, see Lüder & Vormbaum, *Materialien zum Völkerstrafgesetzbuch. Dokumentation des Gesetzgebungsverfahrens* (n 18) *passim*; for an appraisal of the first 10 years of application, see Florian Jeßberger & Julia Geneuss (Hrsg), *Zehn Jahre Völkerstrafgesetzbuch. Bilanz und Perspektiven eines "deutschen Völkerstrafrechts"* (Nomos Verlagsgesellschaft 2013) *passim*.
63 Kreß, Barriga, Grover and von Holtzendorff in Barriga & Kreß, *The Travaux Préparatoires of the Crime of Aggression* (n 26) 751.

while not capable of changing the application of the complementarity regime under the ICC Statute, may be read as raising an implicit question-mark behind the wisdom of mechanically applying the principle of complementarity to the crime of aggression irrespective of the relevant jurisdictional basis in the given case. And, subsequent scholarly writing has explicitly addressed that question.[64] Therefore, should the decision be made to extend any new German legislation on the crime of aggression to the case where the country is the *victim* of an illegal use of force out of which a crime of aggression has arisen, thought should be given to the question whether such jurisdiction should be exercised as a matter of priority *vis-à-vis* the ICC.

Wisely, the Ministry of Justice, which is leading the conversation on these and other matters within the German government, has decided that, after the country's timely ratification of the Kampala amendments, there is no need to make any decision concerning these complex questions of legislative policy in a rush. Instead, the Ministry has made it clear that careful thought will be given to all the above-listed and several other issues to arrive at a well-considered and satisfactory national legislative choice.

6 Conclusion

This brings me to the end of my little journey through almost hundred years of German history in its connection with the international criminalization of aggression. The story extended from the failed attempt in 1919 to condemn Germany's Emperor William II for bringing about the First World War, to the country's unanimous parliamentary approval and early ratification of the Kampala compromise in 2013. Germany's active role in the negotiations on the crime of aggression in the years between 1997 and 2010, and her unequivocally positive reaction[65] to the outcome of these negotiations are in line with the country's

---

64 Beth van Schaack, 'Par in Parem Non Habet: Complementarity and the Crime of Aggression' (2012) 10 JICJ 133; Jennifer Trahan, 'Is Complementarity the Right Approach for the International Criminal Court's Crime of Aggression? Considering the Problem of "Overzealous" National Court Prosecutions' (2012) 45 Cornell Intl Law J 569.

65 The Kampala compromise has also attracted significant interest within German scholarship. While the shortcomings of the compromise are not ignored, German writers have by and large recognized that the agreement reached in 2010 constitutes a remarkable achievement; see Kai Ambos, 'The Crime of Aggression After Kampala' (2010) 53 German YB Int'l Law 463; Robert Heinsch, 'The Crime of Aggression After Kampala: Success or Burden for the Future?' (2010) 2 GoJIL 713; Claus Kreß & Leonie von Holtzendorff, 'The Kampala Compromise on the Crime of Aggression' (2010) 8 JICJ 1179; Kirsten Schmalenbach, 'Das

positive approach to international criminal law in general since the 1990s. With respect to the crime of aggression, Germany, whose terrible wars of aggression under the Nazi-regime had given rise to the 'creative precedent' set in Nuremberg, has been negotiating in the spirit of the belief expressed by Robert Jackson on behalf of the United States of America at Nuremberg that the application of the international criminal law against aggression must be universalized if it is to serve a useful purpose.

Verbrechen der Aggression vor dem Internationalen Strafgerichtshof: Ein politischer Erfolg mit rechtlichen Untiefen' (2010) 65 Juristen Zeitung 745; for a negative view, however, see Andreas Zimmermann, 'Amending the Amendment Provisions of the Rome Statute. The Kampala Compromise on the Crime of Aggression and the Law of Treaties' (2012) 10 JICJ 209.

CHAPTER 7

Mobilising Law on the Side of Peace: Security Council Reform and the Crime of Aggression

Brian J. Foley

'We therefore propose to charge that a war of aggression is a crime, and that modern International Law has abolished the defense that those who incite or wage it are engaged in legitimate business. Thus may the forces of the law be mobilized on the side of peace.'[1]

1   Introduction

It is hard for me to separate Roger Clark the scholar from Roger Clark the man, which is a strong testament to his integrity. I met him first as a colleague and discovered his work afterward. I'm honoured that he's a friend of mine. He helped me as I began doing work in international law, and he helped me grow as a scholar, teacher, and person.

Clark has mobilised law on the side of peace. He challenged, head-on, the legality of nuclear weapons.[2] Recently, as part of the States Working Group on

---

1   Robert Jackson, 'Report to the President on the Atrocities and War Crimes: June 7, 1945', United States Department of State Bulletin (Government Printing Office 1945) ('Jackson, 'Report to the President on the Atrocities and War Crimes"), at <http://www.yale.edu/lawweb/avalon/imt/jack01.htm> accessed 30 June 2014. With acknowledgment to Matthew Gillett, who used a broader swathe of this language from Jackson as an epigraph to his article, 'The Anatomy of an International Crime: Aggression at the International Criminal Court' (2013) 13(4) ICLR 829.
2   See *Legality of the Threat or Use of Nuclear Weapons* (Advisory Opinion) [1996] ICJ Rep 226; Roger S Clark, 'Is *The Butter Battle Book's* Bitsy Big-Boy Boomeroo Banned? What Has International Law to Say About Weapons of Mass Destruction?' (2013/2014) 58 NYU Sch L Rev 655 ('Clark, 'Is *The Butter Battle Book's* Bitsy Big-Boy Boomeroo Banned?' ') 666 ('That case was a frontal attack on the legitimacy of the weapons themselves, as opposed to their testing'); Roger S Clark, 'The Laws of Armed Conflict and the Use or Threat of Use of Nuclear Weapons' (1996) 7 Crim LF 265 ('Clark, 'The Laws of Armed Conflict and the Use or Threat of Use of Nuclear Weapons' '), 266 (Clark 'was a member of a multinational team representing a coalition of three Pacific states—Marshall Islands, Samoa, and Solomon Islands—that made a joint presentation of the antinuclear side at the oral proceedings in these cases.')

Aggression ('SWGA') for the Statute of the International Criminal Court ('ICC'),[3] Clark helped draft a definition of the international crime of aggression and the jurisdictional conditions for prosecution in the ICC.[4] Gaining international consensus on putting this crime on the books was an enormous accomplishment[5]: it was one thing for the World War II victors to define aggression as perpetrated by the vanquished and powerless Axis powers, but it was quite another thing to define it to apply generally to all nations, 'good guys' and 'bad guys' alike.[6] Clark's work against nuclear weapons and on aggression may have seemed at first like tilting-at-windmills or doomed to failure, or, perhaps worse, doomed to become a long-term effort ending in lousy compromises (and stealing time from scholarly work). The risk and sacrifice may be hard to see in hindsight. These are among the most important tasks of our generation, and Clark rose to the occasion.

Clark and I share a strong passion for reducing, if not entirely eliminating, nations' resort to 'the brutalities and dreadful suffering of war'.[7] This shared passion caused us to move from colleagues to brothers-in-arms, so to speak. I remember Clark gave me a copy of a short paperback in his office, Keith

---

3 A/CONF.183/9, 17 July 1998, and corrected by *proces-verbaux* of 10 November 1998, 12 July 1999, 30 November 1999, 8 May 2000, 16 January 2001 and 17 January 2001 (entry into force: 1 July 2002) ('ICC Statute').

4 Res RC/Res. 6, adopted at the 13th plenary meeting on 11 June 2010. Clark represented Samoa. See Claus Kreß & Leonie von Holtzendorff, 'The Kampala Compromise on the Crime of Aggression' (2010) 8 JICJ 1199 ('Kreß & von Holtzendorff, "The Kampala Compromise on the Crime of Aggression"') (noting that delegates from Samoa and Australia in 2009, at one point during the long process, 'took the initiative to prepare a new draft' of the aggression elements). As a testament to Clark's hard work and influence, Samoa was the second nation to accept and ratify the Kampala Amendments to the Crime of Aggression. So far, 14 nations have done so (30 are required). See 'Amendments on the crime of aggression to the Rome Statute of the International Criminal Court, Kampala, 11 June 2010' ('Kampala Amendments'), at <https://treaties.un.org/Pages/ViewDetails.aspx?src=TREATY&mtdsg_no=XVIII-10-b&chapter=18&lang=en> accessed 30 June 2014.

5 Jennifer Trahan, 'A Meaningful Definition of the Crime of Aggression: A Response to Michael Glennon' (2012) 33 U Pa J Int'l L 907, 912–913 (conference in Kampala 'created a historic achievement.').

6 Beth Van Schaak, '*Par In Parem Imperium Non Habet*: Complementarity and the Crime of Aggression' (2012) 10(1) JICJ 5 ('Up to this point in time, the crime of aggression has been noticeably absent in the penal codes of the nations of the world. Most domestic courts lack jurisdiction—under any jurisdictional basis—over the crime of aggression *stricto sensu*, and there is little purely domestic jurisprudence involving the crime.').

7 Clark, 'The Laws of Armed Conflict and the Use or Threat of Use of Nuclear Weapons' (n 2) 287.

Suter's *Alternatives to War: The Peaceful Settlement of International Disputes*.[8] The title, and Clark's giving me the book as I embarked on my work, served to encourage me in my own efforts to promote peace.[9]

'Thus may the forces of law be mobilized on the side of peace', wrote Justice Robert Jackson in 1945, while preparing, as the U.S. Chief Prosecutor, to try the Nazis for aggression.[10] Jackson reminds us of a crucial point: international law, much of it then and now ostensibly to 'save succeeding generations from the scourge of war',[11] is not always on the side of peace and is capable of being manipulated to support war. We see an example of this when we recall the efforts by the U.S. and U.K. to gain U.N approval to bomb and invade Iraq in 2003; these efforts were based in large part on tendentious, tortured legal arguments, including that force was authorized based on Security Council resolutions more than a decade old.[12] To foster peace, laws must be written and applied with the proper attitude.[13] Roger Clark has laboured on the side of peace. He is an optimist, a wise one who understands that changing international law is a long term game. He has spent much of his career doing the hard, often tedious, usually incremental, and I am sure sometimes frustrating work of bringing the law to this side.[14]

---

8   Keith Suter, *Alternative to War: The Peaceful Settlement of International Disputes* (Women's International League for Peace & Freedom, Australian Section 1981).
9   I don't know Clark's views on the book.
10 Jackson, 'Report to the President on the Atrocities and War Crimes' (n 1).
11 Charter of the United Nations (signed on 26 June 1945, entered into force 24 October 1945) 1 UNTS 16, Preamble.
12 See Sean D Murphy, 'Assessing the Legality of Invading Iraq' (2004) 92 Geo L J 173, 256 (assessing these arguments and concluding they are unconvincing). Below, I discuss what should be the proper focus of the Security Council when considering the question of whether force should be authorised: force must be used as a last resort to preventing irreparable harm to human life. Given the gravity of the decision, reliance on legalistic arguments seems satirical.
13 I discuss the importance of attitude in 'Avoiding a Death Dance: Adding Steps to the International Law on the Use of Force to Improve the Search for Alternatives to Force and Prevent Likely Harms' (2003) 29 Brook J Int'l L 129 ('Foley, 'Avoiding a Death Dance''), 132, 156, 173.
14 Clark, 'Is *The Butter Battle Book's* Bitsy Big-Boy Boomeroo Banned?' (n 2) 658: ('Throughout my professional life, I have been involved in efforts to use international law to rid the world of the other ultimate weapon—the nuclear one—for which the Boomeroo is no doubt a metaphor. I have never given up the conviction that law has something useful to say in this endeavour. But the older I get, the more impatient I get.'). Later in the article, at 673, Roger returns to this: 'This grandpa is a little impatient that general and complete disarmament is not yet with us!' The *Butter Battle* article contains some wonderful autobiographical material regarding Clark's work against nuclear weapons, 659–70.

For this *Festschrift*, I decided to look at how a proposal I have made to improve the Security Council's decision-making when it considers whether to authorize military force coheres with the ICC crime of aggression. I will describe my proposal, which is aimed at preventing unnecessary wars. I will then discuss how the crime of aggression, even in its current form with significant limits on the ICC's jurisdiction over alleged aggressors, also can help us avoid unnecessary wars, and how it could even spark Security Council reform.

2 Mobilising the Security Council's decision-making, on the Side of Peace

My international law work has focused on the fact that the decision to use military force, the most horrific, destructive, ultimately uncontrollable action a government or the UN can undertake, is governed by very little legal process. As jurists, we're used to the idea that the intensity of the process required to test a government's decision roughly equates with the gravity of the decision. But there's less *required* testing of a nation's evidence and rationale for going to war than there is for a restaurant seeking a liquor license.[15] And for many years, there was little chance that a those in leadership roles who bomb and invade other nations would be hauled into court to defend charges of aggression.[16] My work can be described as an effort to require that good thinking be applied to the decision of whether to authorize the use of military force; and, if force is authorized, to require that good thinking be applied to the task of finding ways to limit the likely harms of using this force.[17]

---

15 See Clark, 'Is *The Butter Battle Book's* Bitsy Big-Boy Boomeroo Banned?' (n 2) 657–58 ('Surely the law, which seems to deal fairly effectively with such mundane issues as defective widgets and the like, can be brought to bear on weapons of mass destruction. The law is a great engine, in some situations, for promoting dialogue, and this one—with such high stakes—must be one of those situations.').

16 Drafting the crime of aggression was completed only in 2010, and the law will not take effect until at least 1 January 2017, when the ICC's jurisdiction over this crime is activated. Kampala Amendments (n 4), Annex I, art 15*ter* (3); Roger S Clark, 'Amendments to the Rome Statute of the International Criminal Court Considered at the first Review Conference on the Court, Kampala, 31 May–11 June 2010' (2010) 2 GoJIL 689 ('Clark, 'Amendments to the Rome Statute of the International Criminal Court Considered at the first Review Conference on the Court, Kampala, 31 May–11 June 2010"'), 702.

17 See Clark, 'Is *The Butter Battle Book's* Bitsy Big-Boy Boomeroo Banned?' (n 2) 658 ('International law has a role in matters of war and peace, and in mitigating the worst effects of war should efforts to prevent it fail.') My focus has been on the *jus ad bellum* as

The Just War standard and UN Charter set out rules for when nations may use military force, but the effectiveness of these rules has been limited by the lack of enforcement mechanisms. Nations and their leaders have been able to violate them with impunity.[18] For example, since World War II, it has been more likely that a person would be tried and punished for torturing a POW than for starting a war of aggression.[19] It seems that the UN Charter has been reduced to something that international leaders, jurists, and public intellectuals generally refer to before, during, and after wars, only in a rigid, *j'accuse* fashion.[20] Now and then, political leaders might deign to argue that their military action did not violate the Charter. And, unfortunately, the Security Council

---

opposed to the *jus in bello* (international humanitarian law) because it is far more important to find alternatives to war than to regulate it or even to punish people afterwards (this is especially the case with the *sui generis* IHL issue of nuclear weapons! I suppose that this puts me firmly on the side of 'peace' in what Noah Weisbord has described as the 'peace vs. justice' debate. See Noah Weisbord, 'Judging Aggression' (2011) 50 Colum J Transnat'l L 82 ('Weisbord, 'Judging Aggression''), 87.) That all said, I like Clark's view of the IHL: 'Perversely perhaps, such rules and principles regulate the ethics (and modalities) of killing people… [But t]hrough the ages many religious and philosophical ideas have been poured into the mould in which modern humanitarian law has been formed. They represented the effort of the human conscience to mitigate in some measure the brutalities and dreadful suffering of war', see Clark, 'The Laws of Armed Conflict and the Use or Threat of Use of Nuclear Weapons' (n 2) 287.

18 UN General Assembly, Rome Statute of the International Criminal Court (adopted 17 July 1998, entered into force 1 July 2002) 2187 UNTS 3 ('Rome Statute'), Preamble ('The States Parties to this Statute [are] [d]etermined to put an end to impunity for the perpetrators of these crimes and thus to contribute to the prevention of such crimes…'). Indeed, '[u]pon activation of the amendments in 2017, the ICC will be the first international court since the International Military Tribunals in Nuremberg and Tokyo to hold individuals responsible for the crime of aggression' (The Global Campaign for the Ratification and Implementation of the Kampala Amendments on the Crime of Aggression, at <http://crimeofaggression.info/?show=gallery> accessed 30 June 2014).

19 The law of war can be illogical when it comes to matters of degree, as Clark has noted colourfully. See Clark, 'Is *The Butter Battle Book's* Bitsy Big-Boy Boomeroo Banned?' (n 2) 669 ('If using one poisoned arrow or one barbed lance to kill one person, or using a poison gas container to kill scores, is a war crime, why is it not a war crime to use a nuclear weapon or a Bitsy Big-Boy Boomeroo [a weapon in Dr Seuss's *The Butter Battle Book*] which can kill hundreds of thousands?'). See also Clark, 'The Laws of Armed Conflict and the Use or Threat of Use of Nuclear Weapons' (n 2) 288.

20 But see Murphy (n 12) 257 ('Even though, ultimately, such laws and institutions cannot prevent a major power from pursuing its fundamental national security interests, the invasion of Iraq demonstrates that, even for a major power, such laws and institutions cannot be ignored.').

rarely makes any pronouncement regarding the legality of a use of force and 'has been leery of actually using the word "aggression"'.[21] The U.S.-led coalition to invade Iraq in 2003 and NATO when it bombed Kosovo in 1999 bypassed the Security Council; the Council gave no authorisation, but neither did it do anything to stop the actions.[22] There were no war crimes trials afterward, either. The Council promoted neither peace nor justice.

The thrust of my work is that the Security Council should reform its practice to be more proactive in avoiding war: it should rigorously test claims and evidence for war *before* any shots are fired, in a process somewhat akin to that governing motion for a preliminary injunction. If leaders were forced to set forth their claims and evidence and subject them to probing and challenge, good cases would lead to popular support. Bad cases would lead to the opposite—which might prevent a war. Also, alternatives to using force might reveal themselves more easily through such a process. The textual basis for such a rigorous inquiry is in the UN Charter's requirement of necessity, a requirement that should be taken seriously.[23] In short, why not require deliberation for such an important undertaking, an undertaking that, even if justified, will result in enormous damage, including the injury and even death of large numbers of innocent people?[24] This really isn't too much to ask![25]

One might counter that we don't have the luxury to deliberate over war, which seems to require immediate action. But outside of defending against an actual or truly imminent attack, that's not the model anymore, at least for U.S.

---

21 Clark, 'Amendments to the Rome Statute of the International Criminal Court Considered at the first Review Conference on the Court, Kampala, 31 May–11 June 2010' (n 16) 689, 700.

22 See 2005 World Summit Outcome, UNGA Res 60/1 ('2005 World Summit Outcome'), paras 139–140, UN GAOR, 60th Sess., UN Doc A/RES/60/1 (2005) para 197 ('One of the reasons why states may want to bypass the Security Council is a lack of confidence in the quality and objectivity of its decision-making.').

23 See Foley, 'Avoiding a Death Dance' (n 13) 140–43.

24 There is actually more required process for a restaurant to obtain a liquor license than there is for the Security Council to follow when dealing with whether to authorise the use of military force. See Clark, 'Is *The Butter Battle Book's* Bitsy Big-Boy Boomeroo Banned?' (n 2) 657–58 ('Surely the law, which seems to deal fairly effectively with such mundane issues as defective widgets and the like, can be brought to bear on weapons of mass destruction. The law is a great engine, in some situations, for promoting dialogue, and this one—with such high stakes—must be one of those situations. International law has a role in matters of war and peace, and in mitigating the worst effects of war should efforts to prevent it fail.').

25 Exclamation points are rare in scholarly writing. One thing I love about reading Clark's work is that he doesn't shy away from using them. When I read them, I often hear him laughing.

wars. Even after the 11 September attacks, the U.S. didn't strike back until almost three weeks later, when it invaded Afghanistan. (And those three weeks were spent planning for war rather than planning to *prevent* a war.) The Bush Administration subsequently announced an aggressive 'national security strategy' of pre-emptive self-defence.[26] (President Obama appears to follow this strategy, given his threats to Iran and his use of drone strikes.[27]) The challenge with such an aggressive strategy is that the evidence of an enemy's plotting and planning might be murky, especially if the enemy seeks to rely on the element of surprise. The perennial U.S. confrontation with Iran is a good example. Is Iran *actually* building an atomic bomb? If so, would it *actually use it* against the United States or Israel or anyone else? If not, then there are unnecessary costs in going to war. On the other hand, if the U.S. were to remain passive in the face of an actual threat, there would be unnecessary costs as well.

The process I have envisioned for preventing war or at least limiting its harms would provide at least five basic steps.[28] *First, when confronted with an apparent threat to international peace and security, determine whether the military force would be required to prevent a serious irreparable harm.* The sorts of serious irreparable harm to be prevented by using force would be harms involving dangers to human life.[29] Such dangers include a rogue nation's acquiring an atomic bomb with the intent to use it; a nation's harbouring

---

26 The National Security Strategy of the United States of America September 2002, at <http://nssarchive.us/?page_id=32> accessed 30 June 2014. This infamously claimed the right to preemptive self-defense: 6, 15, 16.

27 See National Security Strategy May 2010, at <http://nssarchive.us/?page_id=8> accessed 30 June 2014. The 2010 Strategy avoids any use of the term 'preemption' in any form, but there are almost 35 uses of 'prevent' and two of 'prevention', and four of 'preventing', in various contexts, including non-military. The stated guidelines for using military force mention the concepts of necessity and seeking options (2010 Strategy, 22) ('While the use of force is sometimes necessary, we will exhaust other options before war whenever we can, and carefully weigh the costs and risks of action against the costs and risks of inaction. When force is necessary, we will continue to do so in a way that reflects our values and strengthens our legitimacy, and we will seek broad international support, working with such institutions as NATO and the UN Security Council.'). The 2010 Strategy, however, still claims the right to act unilaterally: 'The United States must reserve the right to act unilaterally if necessary to defend our nation and our interests, yet we will also seek to adhere to standards that govern the use of force' (2010 Strategy, 22).

28 See Brian J Foley, 'Reforming the Security Council to Achieve Collective Security', in Russell A Miller & Rebecca M Bratspies (eds), *Progress in International Law* (Koninklijke Brill NV 2008) ('Foley, 'Reforming the Security Council to Achieve Collective Security"') 575–79.

29 Ibid 576.

terrorists bent on launching large scale attacks; genocide; and mass murder. This should be a short list. It would decidedly not include efforts to control another nation's resources or to create or maintain political hegemony.

If there is evidence that using force could prevent irreparable harm, then the *second step in the process for preventing a war or at least limiting its harms would be a search for alternatives to using military force.*[30] Such a search is required by the UN Charter (and, indeed, in the Just War standard)[31] in that Article 42 of the Charter states:

> Should the Security Council consider that measures provided for in Article 41 would be inadequate or have proved to be inadequate, it may take such action by air, sea, or land forces *as may be necessary* to maintain or restore international peace and security. Such action may include demonstrations, blockade, and other operations by air, sea or land forces of Members of the United Nations.[32]

This is a demanding requirement! The 'measures provided for in Article 41' are specifically 'measures not involving the use of armed force.'[33] And the measures suggested in Article 42 (limited by necessity) include measures short of all-out war; Article 42 sets forth an approach moving from non-forceful measures to forceful ones, escalated only if *necessary*.

Creativity would be required. A nation seeking to wage war would have to show that it had tried alternatives to military force and that these alternatives had failed, or it would have to show that untried alternatives most likely would fail. I envision the Security Council brainstorming or using other methods to boost creativity.[34] This 'step' would be on-going. Efforts to come up with solutions, and tenacious diplomacy to broker a *war-avoiding* deal would have to continue, even after war has begun.

The third step in the process for preventing a war or at least limiting its harms would be to set forth clearly the likely harms posed by the use of military force and

---

30 Ibid 577; Foley, 'Avoiding a Death Dance' (n 13) 143–57. I would also suggest a search for alternatives to using other highly destructive measures, such as sanctions that could lead to starving and otherwise harming the civilians.
31 Foley, 'Reforming the Security Council to Achieve Collective Security' (n 28) 577; Foley, 'Avoiding a Death Dance' (n 13) 141–43.
32 UN Charter (n 11), art 42 (emphasis added).
33 UN Charter (n 11), art 41.
34 Perhaps they could do this behind closed doors, if they're afraid of looking undignified. But that seems a small price to pay if such a session could avoid the serious costs of war!

seek ways to limit them.[35] Creativity would be required here, too. Military strategies can be shaped in various ways to avoid particular harms. For example, what would be the relative costs of inserting ground troops into the conflict as opposed to high altitude bombing? High altitude bombing is safer for the attacking nation's military (and therefore politically safer for leaders), but it is brutal for innocents on the ground.[36] Many variables, including the long-term effects of weapons such as depleted uranium, would have to be weighed.

The fourth step would be a cost-benefit analysis to balance the irreparable harm that military force is proposed to prevent against the likely harms of using the force. Would using force cause more harm than good? For example, it would make little sense to try to prevent a genocide by a military campaign that would likely end up killing an equal number of innocent civilians.[37]

The fifth step would be for the Security Council to maintain control over the use of force. It is not enough to authorize the use of force and then give a coalition *carte blanche* to choose targets or determine the level of force. For example, the coalition bombing of Baghdad in 1991, or the NATO bombing of Belgrade in 1999 (where the Security Council was bypassed), were unnecessary, and the costs to civilians outweighed any benefits, as these cities were far from the actual battlefields.

Throughout the process, the burden of persuasion would be on the proponents of using force; the burden should be at least 'clear and convincing evidence'.[38] Or, perhaps, at least with pre-emptive wars and other wars of choice, the highest legal standard, 'beyond a reasonable doubt', should be applied. Anyone proposing to unleash the destruction and havoc of war should be forced to meet the highest standard to show that war is justified and that no reasonable alternatives exist.

---

35 Foley, 'Reforming the Security Council to Achieve Collective Security' (n 28) 577–578; Foley, 'Avoiding a Death Dance' (n 13) 157–62.

36 As seen in Kosovo, an instance where NATO powers bypassed the Security Council altogether (Foley, 'Reforming the Security Council to Achieve Collective Security' (n 28) 584–86). To 'innocents' I should add 'conscripts', whose fate should be considered (Foley, 'Avoiding a Death Dance' (n 13) 61, 171). *Jus in bello* concepts would come into play here.

37 I'm not sure what proportion of innocents killed by the humanitarian intervention to innocents saved by the intervention would be appropriate. In any event, here is a benefit of ICC jurisdiction over genocide: It gives the world an option beyond using military force to punish, to show that 'we' are 'serious' about addressing outrageous crimes.

38 See Jules Lobel, 'The Use of Force to Respond to a Terrorist Attack: The Bombing of Sudan and Afghanistan' (1999) 24 Yale J Int'l L 537, 551 (suggesting that this standard apply to uses of force in self-defence).

The process described above is 'portable'. It could be applied by the UN Security Council or by congresses and parliaments. It could be followed by any of the world's almost 200 nations, especially those under request (or pressure) to join a coalition. One nation could invite the leaders of another nation proposing to use military force to lay out their claims and evidence. And, if governments fail to provide such a forum, NGOs or other civil society organizations could step up and hold hearings or debates and stream them over the Internet.

The benefits: a proposed war that would actually prevent imminent irreparable harm and for which no reasonable alternative exists would garner wide support—and damages from it would be limited. A proposed war that is not justified might not garner sufficient support and could end up being avoided altogether.[39]

3 Even a (So-far) Imperfect 'Crime of Aggression' Helps Mobilise Law on the Side of Peace

The crime of aggression was created ostensibly to bring 'justice' in the form of judicial punishment of individuals. Merely having the crime on the books, can also help deter leaders from committing aggression in the first place, and, as such, promotes peace. However, reaching consensus at Kampala required imposing severe limits on the ICC's exercise of jurisdiction over alleged aggressors,[40] with the result that the prospect of impunity remains for some

---

39 For example, go back to 2003. Had the Security Council exposed U.S. claims for war as supported only by shaky an evidence (such as the forged documents used to allege that Iraq sought uranium from Niger; claims about Iraq's nuclear program that had been gained from coercive interrogation; information from an informant so distrusted that intelligence officials had nicknamed him 'Curveball'), the war might have been avoided. In addition, the idea of toppling a dictator to prevent from using weapons of mass destruction might spark him to use those weapons when he otherwise wouldn't have. I have set forth more fully a 'counterfactual' case study of how this process could have worked had it been applied in 2003, a well as to the 1999 NATO airstrikes in Kosovo and the Federal Republic of Yugoslavia (Foley, 'Reforming the Security Council to Achieve Collective Security' (n 28) 580–86).

40 For explanations see Kreß & von Holtzendorff, 'The Kampala Compromise on the Crime of Aggression' (n 4) 1179, 1194–99; 1201–16; Clark, 'Amendments to the Rome Statute of the International Criminal Court Considered at the first Review Conference on the Court, Kampala, 31 May–11 June 2010' (n 16) 699–706. Clark noted, 'Obtaining such a comprehensive consensus was no mean feat!' (706). Such severe limits are not imposed on ICC jurisdiction over other crimes in the Rome Statute.

leaders who commit aggression. Nevertheless, the imperfect Kampala compromise version of aggression is a significant improvement in international law.[41] In this section, I will discuss how having the crime of aggression on the books can help prevent war, and how the jurisdictional limits reached by compromise at Kampala may create a dynamic that could spark significant reform to the Security Council's process along the lines I have sketched out above.

A   *Benefits from Defining 'Aggression'*

We cannot overlook the importance of the fact that a consensus was reached on defining 'aggression' as an international crime that may be prosecuted in the ICC. As Joanna Harrington wrote shortly after the Kampala conference, '[i]t is easy to forget that defining an act of aggression was not an easy task. For a state to be accused of an act of aggression carries obvious political costs and the international efforts to define aggression in the 1970s illustrate the difficulties'.[42] A prosecution for the crime of aggression is no longer merely victor's justice.

Providing the world with an agreed-upon definition of the elements of 'aggression'—even with severe limits on jurisdiction—is a major step in mobilising law on the side of peace.[43] For example, unlike the General Assembly definition from the 1970s, the ICC definition cannot be undercut by the Security

---

41   As with practically any new law, there are still many open issues that ICC judges will need to interpret in actual cases. Roger Clark has shown these issues in a novel and helpful way by publishing a law school exam he wrote concerning aggression and a sample answer. See Roger S Clark, 'Alleged Aggression in Utopia: An International Criminal Law Examination Question for 2020', in William A Schabas, Yvonne McDermott & Niamh Hayes (eds), *The Ashgate Research Companion to International Criminal Law: Critical Perspectives* (Ashgate 2013) ('Clark, 'Alleged Aggression in Utopia'') 63.

42   Joanna Harrington, 'An End to War Through a Court of Law? Perhaps—and in Time', EJIL: *Talk!*, 14 June 2010, at <http://www.ejiltalk.org/an-end-to-war-through-a-court-of-law-perhaps-and-in-time/> accessed 13 July 2010. For a brief history of the drafting of the elements of aggression, see Clark, 'Amendments to the Rome Statute of the International Criminal Court Considered at the first Review Conference on the Court, Kampala, 31 May–11 June 2010' (n 16) 692–99; Kreß & von Holtzendorff, 'The Kampala Compromise on the Crime of Aggression' (n 4) 1199–1201; 1210–11.

43   Gaining consensus on this definition appears to have been the result of skilful negotiation. As Clark has written, 'The major achievement in this part of the negotiation in the period of the Special Working Group [ie, in the years leading to the Kampala conference] was to de-couple the definition [of the crime] from the conditions [for jurisdiction over individuals accused of committing it]'. Clark, 'Amendments to the Rome Statute of the International Criminal Court Considered at the first Review Conference on the Court, Kampala, 31 May–11 June 2010' (n 16) 700.

Council's deciding that conduct that meets the definition is nevertheless not aggression, or that conduct that is not included in the definition nevertheless is aggression. The conclusion of whether aggression has occurred, in short, is now a question of law, not politics.[44]

The ICC definition can in itself help shape the dialogue in the crucial run-up to a war, and might help prevent an unnecessary war. If a proposed use of military force looks like aggression to a critical mass of people, populations may withhold political support from their governments, which could cause leaders to abandon plans to use military force.

There are also benefits from merely identifying a leader as an aggressor, even if that leader is never prosecuted. Sometimes it may be more important merely to identify someone as a 'criminal' than it is to punish him. A leader identified as having committed aggression but not prosecuted could suffer a loss of credibility and support, rendering him or her unable to aggress again. So some of the purposes of punishment—incapacitation, specific and general deterrence and retribution (here, loss of power)—could be realized. Hitler without state power would have been just another nut in a beer hall.[45]

B   *The 'Crime of Aggression' Will Still Promote Peace, Despite Limits on the ICC's Jurisdiction*

There are several limits on the ICC's jurisdiction over aggression, which means that in some cases of even blatant aggression, prosecutions may be thwarted.

---

[44] The General Assembly resolution in 1974 was seen as insufficient for the ICC. See UNGA Res 3314 (XXIX) (14 December 1974) 29 UN GAOR 29th Session Supp No 31 UN Doc A/9631, 142. As Clark explains, 'The ultimate drafting of 8*bis* is aimed at avoiding the open-ended nature of Resolution 3314 which says, essentially, that the Security Council may decide that something that meets the definition is nonetheless not aggression and, on the other hand, that acts other than those on the list may be regarded by the Security Council as aggression. As a political body, the Security Council may act in a completely unprincipled and arbitrary manner'. Clark, 'Amendments to the Rome Statute of the International Criminal Court Considered at the first Review Conference on the Court, Kampala, 31 May–11 June 2010' (n 16) 696. See also Weisbord, 'Judging Aggression' (n 17) 95 (arguing that the fact that ICC can act outside of Security Council control marks a historic shift from politics to law in regulating use of force).

[45] I've also broached the subject elsewhere of 'buying out' dictators or other leaders bent on aggression and giving them a safe haven. Brian J Foley, 'Dealing With Dictators—Payoffs vs. Punishment—Spare the Rod, Spare the Children', *Lawpaganda*, 8 March 2014, at <http://lawpaganda.com/2014/03/08/dealing-with-dictators-payoffs-vs-punishment-spare-the-rod-spare-the-children/ accessed July 11 2014. Better to avoid war, even if it means denying the collective urge to punish such a dictator formally.

But I will take an optimistic view to show how these limits on post-war punishment will not necessarily thwart efforts to prevent war in the first place.

1   The Limits

There are three ways for the ICC to exercise jurisdiction over alleged aggressors. The first is for the Security Council to refer a case to the ICC.[46] The Council could refer a case concerning any nation (even non-parties to the ICC statute), as the Council would make the referral under Chapter VII of the UN Charter.[47] This is the broadest and most straightforward basis for ICC jurisdiction. Notably, the Security Council can essentially block any ICC prosecution, including of aggression: the Security Council can pass a resolution deferring any ICC investigation or prosecution of *any* crime for a year (and the Security Council cam renew that resolution).[48]

The second and third ways for the ICC to exercise jurisdiction over aggression is where a nation that is a party to the ICC statute ('State Party'), or the Prosecutor on his or her own motion (*proprio motu*), refers a case.[49] These referrals are more limited than Security Council referrals, in several ways.[50] One is that these referrals must concern aggression by a State Party. Aggression by a non-State Party against a State Party, for example, will not suffice.[51] Nations

---

46   Rome Statute (n 18); Kampala Amendment (n 4), art 15*ter;* art 13(b).
47   Rome Statute (n 18); Kampala Amendment (n 4), Annex III, Understandings, para 2; art 13(b).
48   See Rome Statute (n 18) art 16 (allowing such delay for all ICC crimes); Kampala Amendment (n 4), Annex I, art 15*bis* (8). Permanent Parties could prevent such a resolution through the veto power, of course.
49   Rome Statute (n 18); Kampala Amendment (n 4), art 15b*is;* art 14.
50   Kreß and Hotzendorff explain:
>   This is by far the most complex part of the negotiations related to the question of whether there should be a Security Council monopoly with respect to aggression proceedings. Draft Article 15 bis of the ICC Statute, which deals with State Party referrals and proprio motu investigations, answers this question in the negative and only provides for the special judicial filter that the Pre-Trial Division must, in all cases, authorize the commencement of an investigation. This in itself constitutes a major achievement in light of the fundamental aspiration of the ICC Statute towards the equal application of international criminal law. Yet the insistence on a Security Council monopoly was a most powerful one, and it thus comes as no surprise that a high price had to be paid for overcoming it. Partly for this reason, draft Article 15 bis ICC Statute is of quite considerable complexity.

Kreß & von Holtzendorff, 'The Kampala Compromise on the Crime of Aggression' (n 4) 1212.
51   Kampala Amendment (n 4), Annex I, art 15*bis* (5). There is therefore no 'territoriality' component of jurisdiction, unlike for other ICC crimes (Clark, 'Amendments to the Rome Statute of the International Criminal Court Considered at the first Review Conference on

may protect their nationals from this sort of referral by not signing on to the ICC statute.

Another limit on State and Prosecutor *proprio motu* referrals is that, after the Prosecutor decides there is a reasonable basis to investigate the alleged aggression, the Prosecutor must 'first ascertain whether the Security Council has made a determination of an act of aggression committed by the State concerned'.[52] If there is a Security Council determination that there was aggression, the Prosecutor may proceed.[53] If the Security Council is silent about the issue after six months from being notified by the Prosecutor,[54] the prosecution may proceed, but with a further limit: the Prosecutor must gain approval from the ICC's Pre-Trial Division.[55] The Pre-Trial Division consists of at least six judges. This appears to create a more rigorous review than the review of referrals for the other ICC crimes, for which the Prosecutor must win approval of the Pre-Trial *Chamber*, which usually consists of three judges.[56]

The conditions for ICC jurisdiction over aggression seem to give, as a practical matter, the Security Council the ability to impose serious limits on prosecutions or even to block them (without using its power to defer an investigation or prosecution under Article 13 of the ICC Statute), even though the Security Council's determination is not binding on the ICC.[57] That is because the lack of Security Council support could have a strong persuasive effect. For example, if after notification by the Prosecutor the Security Council were silent for six months, or if the Security Council were to determine that no aggression occurred, the implication may be that the case against the alleged aggressors is

---

the Court, Kampala, 31 May–11 June 2010' (n 16) 705, noting 'It is probably another example of a small but powerful minority protecting its own position in a consensus negotiation.').

52 Kampala Amendment (n 4), Annex I, art 15*bis* (6).
53 Kampala Amendment (n 4), Annex III, Understandings, para 7.
54 Kampala Amendment (n 4), art 15*bis* (6–8).
55 Kampala Amendment (n 4), art 15*bis*(8); Kampala Amendment (n 4), Annex III, Understandings, para 8.
56 See Rome Statute (n 18) arts 39(1) (Pre-Trial Division must have at least six judges) and 39(2)(b)(iii) (Pre-Trial Chamber functions can be carried out by three, or even one, judge from the Pre-Trial Division). Weisbord explains:

> The decision to buttress the pre-trial chamber in aggression cases, unnecessary in any other type of ICC case, was intended to assuage those states concerned that the pre-trial judges might be biased or vulnerable to political pressure. The reasoning was that adding more judges whose personal and political proclivities would counterbalance each other offset those risks.

See Weisbord, 'Judging Aggression' (n 17) 96.
57 Kampala Amendment (n 4), Annex I, art 15*bis* (9).

weak. The Prosecutor might drop the matter rather than taking it to the Pre-Trial Division; or, if the Prosecutor decided to take it to the Pre-Trial Division, those judges might not let the case go forward. This outcome could obtain especially in some of the first ICC aggression cases, as the Prosecutor or Pre-Trial Division might believe that defeat of the prosecution at the ICC could be devastating for the ICC's credibility. Or, the implication may be that that an aggression prosecution would open a political can of worms. So it seems likely that in some instances, a case would not proceed without the support of the Security Council, except in an egregious case where it appears that there has been an abuse of power by the Security Council or a Permanent Member.

Finally, there is what Clark called a 'strange' jurisdictional limit on a State or prosecutor's referral: any State that has signed onto the ICC Statute is free to 'opt out' of jurisdiction over its nationals for the crime of aggression.[58] This provision is unique among the four ICC crimes and has been highly criticised,[59] as it smacks of letting a person charged with murder prohibit a court from prosecuting him.

2   Optimism about Opting Out

Will the opt-out loophole render, as a practical matter, ICC prosecutions for aggression illusory? Perhaps, but I am cautiously optimistic that it will not, perhaps even more optimistic than Clark, who noted that even a nation that becomes one of the 30 nations required to pass the aggression, amendments might nevertheless opt-out of ICC jurisdiction over its nationals for aggression: 'It would take some nerve to help make up the thirty and then opt out, but one should never underestimate the acrobatic ability of the diplomatic mind in construing the national interest!'[60] I want to follow Clark's overall spirit of optimism, reflected in his life and work, and show how there may be instances where the 'national interest' of any nation might be construed against opting-out.

First, the leaders of a nation that has opted out could not be sure before beginning a military action that the Security Council would not refer the

---

58   Clark, 'Amendments to the Rome Statute of the International Criminal Court Considered at the first Review Conference on the Court, Kampala, 31 May–11 June 2010' (n 16) 703.

59   See, eg Weisbord, 'Judging Aggression' (n 17) 133 (nations opting out can become 'above the law'); Kevin Jon Heller, 'The Sadly Neutered Crime of Aggression' *Opinio Juris*, at <http://opiniojuris.org/2010/06/13/the-sadly-neutered-crime-of-aggression/> accessed 3 July 2014.

60   Clark, 'Amendments to the Rome Statute of the International Criminal Court Considered at the first Review Conference on the Court, Kampala, 31 May–11 June 2010' (n 16) 704–05. Clark was not saying that there was no jurisdiction over nationals from States Parties that did not additionally expressly pass the aggression amendments.

matter to the ICC under Article 15*ter*, which allows for jurisdiction over non-State Parties, so the opt-out would not help leaders here. Even a remote possibility of prosecution could have a deterrent effect.[61]

Second, the leaders protected by the opt-out might nevertheless face (or trigger) vigorous prosecution for other ICC crimes related to their aggression, which, unlike prosecutions for aggression, they cannot opt out of.[62]

Third, individual leaders contemplating aggression (or a war that could be seen as a close case) could not be sure that their nation would opt-out to prevent a prosecution, or would maintain that nation's opt-out declaration, which can be withdrawn at any time.[63] (Notably, winning the war is no longer the way for leaders to avoid prosecution for war crimes.[64]) Politicians are likely well aware that even popular wartime leaders may later fall out of political favour, and their successors might decide that the costs of opting out of jurisdiction

---

61 The deterrent effect can also help stop a war that has already started: leaders could be offered immunity for aggression as part of a ceasefire deal. See Weisbord, 'Judging Aggression' (n 17) 110.

62 See Manuel J Ventura & Matthew Gillett, 'The Fog of War: Prosecuting Illegal Uses of Force as Crimes Against Humanity' (2013) 12 Wash U Global Stud L Rev 523.

63 Kampala Amendment (n 4), art 15bis(4). The language of the statute is ambiguous regarding whether an opt-out must occur before the aggression is committed, or before any investigation or prosecution for aggression is committed. See Crime of Aggression (n 4), Annex I, art 15bis (4). Astrid Reisinger Coracini argues that it is the former:

> Article 15bis (4) refers to a previous declaration. The formulation appears to intend excluding the lodging of an ad hoc declaration upon the commission of an act of aggression. This does not only include declarations lodged in the immediate context of an act of aggression. A declaration lodged 'previously' with the intent to avert the exercise of the Court's jurisdiction, may be conduct that depending on the circumstances falls under the definition of the crime of aggression as part of the planning and preparation of an act of aggression. As a criminal act falling under the jurisdiction of the Court, it may eventually be considered invalid.

Astrid Reisinger Coracini, 'The International Criminal Court's Exercise of Jurisdiction Over the Crime of Aggression—at Last…in Reach… Over Some', 2 GoJIL 745 ('Coracini, 'The International Criminal Court's Exercise of Jurisdiction Over the Crime of Aggression—at Last…in Reach… Over Some"), 777 (2010) (citation omitted).

64 James Carroll, *House of War: The Pentagon and the Disastrous Rise of American Power* (Houghton Mifflin Harcourt 2006) 533 fn 233 (discussing the film *The Fog of War* in which former U.S. Secretary of Defence Robert MacNamara recalls U.S. Air Force General Curtis LeMay saying, regarding U.S. bombing of Japanese civilians in World War II, "'If we'd lost the war, we'd all have been prosecuted as war criminals." And I think he's right. He, and I'd say I, were behaving as war criminals. LeMay recognized that what he was doing would be thought immoral if his side had lost. But what makes it immoral if you lose and not immoral if you win?').

would outweigh letting the unpopular former leaders be tried for aggression in the ICC. Subsequent leaders could end up scapegoating now-unpopular wartime leaders for a costly war and permit an ICC prosecution to proceed, and thereby boost their own (and their tarnished nation's) power and credibility nationally and internationally.[65]

Fourth, any nation exercising the opt-out could be subjected to shame or illegitimacy, which could affect that nation in a multitude of international arenas.[66] A nation contemplating opting out, might, of course, see such shame and resulting parade of horribles as merely speculative when compared to the very real possibility of its own leaders being convicted of aggression (with all sorts of diplomatic dirty laundry coming out in the process). Nevertheless, a nation that opts out of such a prosecution rather than trying to vindicate itself (through its nationals) in the ICC might find it difficult, the next time around, to assemble a 'coalition of the willing' or to gain Security Council authorization to use force.[67] Leaders of nations that have not opted out might be nervous about joining forces with opt-out nation leaders, because those leaders may see themselves as immune from prosecution for aggression and act accordingly, putting the non-opt-out leaders at risk of prosecution.

Fifth, leaders contemplating using military force would also know that there is a less 'shameful' way for their nation to 'avoid' ICC jurisdiction but still scapegoat them: the nation could, on its own, prosecute its wartime leaders

---

65 There may be political pressure on the government from civil society organisations against opting-out (Weisbord, 'Judging Aggression' (n 17) 95–6).

66 See Robert F Drinan, *The Mobilization Of Shame: A World View Of Human Rights* (Yale University Press 2001). See also Weisbord, 'Judging Aggression' (n 17) ('The hope of proponents of the Kampala outcome is that, over time, the rule will become widely accepted and even powerful states will face domestic constituencies, political processes and multilateral pressures that militate against its violation.'). A nation may have a right to opt out but may have no justification to do so. Philosophy professor Daniel Haybron wonderfully explains:
    You may have the right to let your neighbour starve, though you have food enough to share. You have, in short, the right to be a deplorable, despicable, contemptible jerk. [...] But of course you wouldn't be justified in doing any of these things. What makes living with each other bearable, and civilization possible, is the willingness of all parties to limit the exercise of their rights. [...] Perhaps because this sort of thing has become somewhat of a problem, contemporary English vernacular has a special name for people who act as badly as they have a right to, and it has become quite popular. [...] We call such people assholes.
    Daniel M Haybron, *Happiness: A Very Short Introduction* (Very Short Introductions Series, OUP 2013) 96–7.

67 Rather than opting out, a State might try to help its nationals defend themselves in court, or, more cynically, try to get the Security Council to pass a resolution delaying or deferring the matter. See Rome Statute (n 17) art 16.

under that nation's own version of aggression (or for similar or related crimes), which could obviate any ICC prosecution under the ICC's complementarity principle.[68]

Last, even if a State opts out of ICC jurisdiction over aggression as a way of protecting its own leaders from prosecution, the opt-out might not be the end of the international legal affair. One can imagine that a victim state might claim national jurisdiction over aggressors and try them under its own laws in its own national courts, even *in absentia*.[69] Indeed, *any* state might attempt to try aggressors under a claim of universal jurisdiction.[70] One can also imagine an informal tribunal created by an NGO or a civil society organisation staging some sort of 'trial'.[71] These 'trials' could be streamed over the Internet. That process would not land the leader in prison but could ultimately cause the leader to fall out of favour at home and abroad.

We must keep in mind that the crime of aggression is new on the books. It might take some failed attempts to prosecute to spark a critical mass of nations to increase the ability of the ICC to gain jurisdiction over alleged aggressors. Indeed, the opt-out provisions might even be eliminated if they end up being used as a cynical way of blocking a strong case. The very desire for impunity that animates the ICC Statute[72] could grow and lead to a rethink of the opt-out provisions.[73]

---

68   Kreß & von Holtzendorff, 'The Kampala Compromise on the Crime of Aggression' (n 4) 1216–17.

69   See Appendix, Benjamin B Ferencz (2013) 'A New Approach to Deterring Illegal Wars', in Donald M Ferencz, 'Aggression in Legal Limbo: A Gap in the Law that Needs Closing' (2013) 12 Wash U Glob Stud L Rev 507, 521.

70   See Kreß & von Holtzendorff, 'The Kampala Compromise on the Crime of Aggression' (n 4) 1216–1217 (noting that Kampala Amendments (n 4), Annex III, Understandings, para 5 suggests that states may try only their own nationals); Clark, 'Alleged Aggression in Utopia' (n 41) 70–71 (noting lack of clarity on this issue and that the Understanding did not cure it); Clark, 'Amendments to the Rome Statute of the International Criminal Court Considered at the first Review Conference on the Court, Kampala, 31 May–11 June 2010' (n 16) 705 n 57 (same). But see Michael P Scharf, 'Universal Jurisdiction and the Crime of Aggression' (2012), 53 Harv Int'l L J 357, 388 ('the Nuremberg trial and its progeny crystallized the right under customary international law of states to exercise universal jurisdiction over the crimes within the Nuremberg Charter, including aggression, and therefore an interpretative statement that the Kampala amendments should not be considered as creating such a right is without import.')

71   See generally Arthur J Klinghoffer & Judith Apter Klinghoffer, *International Citizens' Tribunals: Mobilizing Public Opinion to Advance Human Rights* (Palgrave 2002).

72   Rome Statute (n 17) Preamble.

73   See Coracini, 'The International Criminal Court's Exercise of Jurisdiction Over the Crime of Aggression—at Last…in Reach… Over Some' (n 63) ('The responsibility to counter

4 The 'Crime of Aggression' Could Spark Security Council Reform

Including aggression among the crimes in the ICC Statute could create dynamics that spark the sort of Security Council reform I have proposed. That is because the Security Council will be the subject of more intense focus as a result of its role in the ICC jurisdictional limits on aggression.

For example, given even a remote possibility of an ICC prosecution, leaders contemplating using military force might take their case to the Security Council for authorisation—despite that such approval isn't binding on the ICC later.[74] That is because a fairly rigorous inquiry leading to authorisation could help persuade, later, a State considering making a referral or an ICC prosecutor or Pre-Trial Division or the ICC judges that the military campaign was not aggression, or that, if it is a close case, there was no '*manifest* violation of the UN Charter'.[75] Indeed, national leaders may *want* such an inquiry when they seek authorisation, to provide them with an informal, practical sort of (albeit not-legally-binding[76]) 'advice of Security Council' defence to any subsequent ICC prosecution along with the later persuasive effect the authorisation may have. Of course, such leaders risk that the Security Council might not authorise their use of force, but some leaders would take that risk into account and seek authorisation anyway. This increased use of the Security Council could become a more standard practice and could expose weak cases for war—resulting in nations declining to wage those wars, as I have described above.

Another dynamic created by ICC jurisdiction over aggression is that the Security Council's work in approving a particular use of force will be subject to subsequent scrutiny by States and by the ICC prosecutor, and perhaps ultimately by the ICC judges. This is progress: *Until now there has been no formal institutionalized review of the Security Council's decision-making regarding use of force.* There has been a serious lack of accountability, and the Security Council has failed to make any determination regarding the legality of several

---

shortcomings in the context of State Party referrals and *proprio motu* investigations now rests with the States Parties. The Court's jurisdictional reach grows with each unconditional ratification of the amendments. Once the regime is well accepted, a review of Article 15*bis* in light of a uniform jurisdictional regime for all core crimes is not excluded.').

74 Kampala Amendment (n 4), Annex III, Understandings, para 9.
75 Kampala Amendment (n 4), Annex I, art 8*bis* (1) (emphasis added). It remains to be seen how this phrase will be interpreted. For example, the fact that the leaders followed the Charter's required process by seeking and receiving Security Council authorisation to use military force could lead or tend to lead ICC actors to conclude that there was no 'manifest' violation of the Charter.
76 See Kampala Amendment (n 4), Annex II, Introduction, paras 2 & 4.

uses of force.[77] The good news is that in future ICC proceedings, any Security Council failure to delve deeply into the arguments for waging war will become obvious. That is because determining aggression requires inquiry into the conditions surrounding the decision to use military force in the first place. So the Security Council, to maintain its relevance and its authority,[78] and to avoid looking in hindsight like a rubberstamp, or even to avoid the appearance of *complicity* in a war of aggression, may probe much more deeply than we have seen it do up to now into politicians' arguments and evidence that military force is necessary in a given situation.[79] Scrutiny *of* the Security Council should lead to deeper scrutiny *by* the Security Council. Deep scrutiny by the Security Council could expose weak or even fraudulent cases for war, which could prevent those wars.

Last, all of this scrutiny may result in wider exposure of the shortcomings of the Security Council's overall process for deciding whether to approve military force. As a result, the Security Council could end up adopting, formally or informally, a rigorous process such as the one I describe above, which could prevent unnecessary wars.

5 Conclusion

I had not taken the opportunity until this *Festschrift* to contemplate how the criminalisation of aggression cohered with my proposal for Security Council reform. Nor, until this *Festschrift*, was I inclined to look at the limitations on the ICC's jurisdiction over aggression with much optimism. But reflecting on the legacy of Roger Clark made me think more broadly and productively than I would have otherwise, leading me to see new possibilities for mobilising the Security Council's process for authorising the use of military force on the side of peace.

---

77   Clark, 'Amendments to the Rome Statute of the International Criminal Court Considered at the first Review Conference on the Court, Kampala, 31 May–11 June 2010' (n 16) 696 ('As a political body, the Security Council may act in a completely unprincipled and arbitrary manner').

78   See 2005 World Summit Outcome (n 22).

79   See Weisbord, 'Judging Aggression' (n 17) 97 ('The hope of a number of the drafters is that the involvement of the ICC will spur the Council to respond to breaches of the peace in a more principled manner than it has in the past. Going forward, if the Council does not do its job, the court can step up to the plate.').

CHAPTER 8

From the Shoulders of Giants: Harold Nicolson's Peacemaking 1919 and the Congress of Vienna

Pam Jenoff[1]

> 'If I have seen further, it is by standing on the shoulders of giants.'
> SIR ISAAC NEWTON[2]

1   Introduction

I was elated to be asked to contribute an essay to this volume honoring my epic colleague and mentor, Roger Clark, with whom I've had the pleasure of working these past five years at Rutgers School of Law–Camden. I was further delighted to be asked to write on two works by Harold Nicolson: *Peacemaking 1919*[3] and *The Congress of Vienna: A Study in Allied Unity*,[4] which *Festschrift* coordinator Suzannah Linton has described as 'two of Roger's favourite works on diplomacy and the formation of international organizations.'[5] Nicolson has long been a subject of interest for me[6] because he (like myself on a much smaller scale) was a diplomat[7] turned writer[8] and brought the two together so well.

In titling this piece, I was struck by the apropos of Newton's 'From the Shoulders of Giants' quote.[9] It reflects how, learning from our mentors and

---

1 I would like to thank Librarian Genevieve Tung for her extensive research assistance with this project.
2 Letter from Isaac Newton to Robert Hooke (5 February 1675), in H W Turnbull (ed), *The Correspondence of Isaac Newton, vol 1* (CUP 1959) ('*Letter from Isaac Newton to Robert Hooke*') 416.
3 Harold Nicolson, *Peacemaking 1919* (Grosset & Dunlap 1965) ('*Nicolson, Peacemaking 1919*').
4 Harold Nicolson, *The Congress of Vienna: A Study in Allied Unity 1812:1822* (Viking 1961) ('*Nicolson, The Congress of Vienna*').
5 Email from Suzannah Linton (2 October 2013).
6 I first read *Peacemaking 1919* during my post-graduate studies at Cambridge, where I wrote my thesis 'Race Relations Between Japan and the West 1895–1925' focusing on the rejection of the racial equality clause from the League of Nations covenant at the Paris Peace Conference.
7 Prior to studying law, I was a Foreign Service Officer with the United States Department of State.
8 I am the author of seven novels and one short story in an anthology, set primarily in Europe during the first half of the 20th century.
9 Letter from Isaac Newton to Robert Hooke (n 2) 416.

benefitting from their years of experience, we can see further and understand more.[10] It reflects how more junior scholars such as myself can benefit from the perspective of 'giants' like Roger Clark. And, it reflects how Harold Nicolson, as a junior diplomat serving the world's leaders, was able to gain a bird's eye view and unique perspective on the Paris Peace Conference, in a way that would influence not just his writing of *Peacemaking 1919*[11] but all of his future writing, government service and other endeavors.

Interestingly, despite his affinity for Nicolson's work, Roger himself has not actually cited to Nicolson in his work. However, Roger describes Nicolson as influential on his own vast body of scholarship, teaching, and work with governments and international organizations. Roger has taught a course on international organizations for many years.[12] He has written extensively on international organizations.[13] He had a role in creating the International Criminal Court.[14] He has appeared before the International Court of Justice in the *Nuclear Weapons* case.[15] As a Non-Governmental Organization representative in the 70s and 80s, he worked to make the United Nations organizations on human rights and decolonization more effective.[16]

Nicolson's works are instructive to a scholar and leader in international law and diplomacy such as Roger, not only for their historical content, but for the insight they provide into many of our present global challenges. Indeed, Roger, like Nicolson, has undoubtedly been influenced in his writing by the many international endeavors to which he has been a contributor. Honoring Roger with this essay, I will endeavor to give a brief overview of *Peacemaking 1919* and *The Congress of Vienna* and the way in which Nicolson's view in them was shaped and changed by his experiences.

---

10   Indeed, I have often borrowed the 'shoulder of giants' quote to describe my own experiences as Special Assistant to the Secretary of the Army at the Pentagon, where I had the opportunity to travel the world and witness operations at the most senior levels of government— experiences which have subsequently influenced my own writing.
11   Nicolson, *Peacemaking 1919* (n 3).
12   Roger teaches a wide array of international courses at Rutgers Law. Rutgers School of Law, Camden, Faculty Biography for Roger S. Clark, <https://camlaw.rutgers.edu/directory/rsclark/> accessed 16 June 2014.
13   Roger S Clark, *A United Nations High Commissioner for Human Rights* (Martinus Nijhoff 1972); Roger S Clark, *The United Nations Crime Prevention and Criminal Justice Program*: Formulation of Standards and Efforts at their Implementation (University of Pennsylvania Press for Procedural Aspects of International Law Institute 1994).
14   Faculty Biography for Roger S Clark (n 12).
15   *Ibid.*
16   *Ibid.*

2 Biographical Background

Harold Nicolson was born in Persia in 1886.[17] The son of a diplomat, he lived in Turkey, Morocco, Russia and Spain before attending college at Oxford.[18] Nicolson himself entered diplomatic service in 1909.[19] In 1914, he had the distinction of handing Britain's declaration of war to the German ambassador in London.[20] He was a relatively minor diplomat at the Paris Peace Conference.[21] He served as the personal assistant to the first Secretary General of the League of Nations.[22]

Nicolson resigned from diplomatic service in 1929.[23] He stood successfully for a seat in Parliament in 1935 and was one of the first officials to warn of the dangers of fascism.[24] Nicolson left Parliament in 1945 and ran unsuccessfully once more, but never returned to public office.[25] He was appointed Knight Commander of the Royal Victorian Order (KCVO) in 1953.[26]

3 Bibliographic Background

Nicolson is the author of numerous books and articles, among which *Peacemaking 1919*[27] and *The Congress of Vienna: A Study in Allied Unity*[28] are the best known.[29]

---

17 James Lees-Milne, *Harold Nicolson: A Biography* (Shoe String Press 1982) ('*Lees-Milne, Harold Nicolson: A Biography*'); Derek Drinkwater, *Sir Harold Nicolson and International Relations: The Practitioner as Theorist* (OUP 2005) ('*Drinkwater, Sir Harold Nicolson and International Relations: The Practitioner as Theorist*') 17.
18 Drinkwater, *Sir Harold Nicolson and International Relations: The Practitioner as Theorist* (n 17) 19.
19 *Ibid.*
20 *Ibid.*
21 *Ibid.*
22 *Ibid.*
23 *Ibid.*
24 *Ibid.*
25 *Ibid.*
26 *Ibid.*
27 Nicolson, *Peacemaking 1919* (n 3).
28 Nicolson, *The Congress of Vienna* (n 4).
29 Nicolson is the author of roughly two dozen other books, including *Portrait of a Diplomatist* (1930), *Curzon: The Last Phase, 1919–1925: A Study in Post-War Diplomacy* (1934), *Diplomacy: a Basic Guide to the Conduct of Contemporary Foreign Affairs* (1939), *Why Britain is at War* (1939), *The Evolution of Diplomacy* (1954), *The Age of Reason* (1700–1789) (1960), works on Tennyson and Byron, and some novels.

A Peacemaking 1919[30]

Peacemaking 1919 is widely regarded as one of the seminal accounts of the Paris Peace Conference.[31] The book chronicles the negotiations at the Paris Peace Conference, which had taken place after the end of the First World War.[32]

Myriad works have been written about the Paris Peace Conference, which had an unparalleled influence over subsequent events in the 20th century. Among these, however, scholars regard Nicolson's work as uniquely insightful in that he was an author who was also a participant, serving as a junior staffer to the British delegation.[33] His writing therefore provides unique insight into the workings of the conference.[34] One contemporary noted, 'Nothing else known to me conveys so accurately and so effectively the feelings of a subordinate engaged in the peace negotiations—his hopes and doubts, his moods and distractions.'[35]

Thus, Nicolson's role at the conference gives him perspective not available to other authors.[36] However, critics have noted the inherent bias in Nicolson's work given his personal involvement, most notably, his proclivity toward treating his superiors in the British delegation with kid gloves in his analysis.[37]

Peacemaking 1919 was written in two parts.[38] The first is a historic analysis of the world powers attempt to formulate peace, redistribute colonial holdings and create the League of Nations as a way to avoid further conflict.[39] The second half is a diary of Nicolson's experiences as a delegate at the Paris Peace Conference, detailing the day-to-day deliberations of the parties.[40]

Nicolson, by his own description, had come to the Paris Peace Conference holding out high hopes for the ability of the allied powers to make lasting peace, as articulated most notably in President Wilson's Fourteen Points.[41] However,

---

30 Nicolson, *The Congress of Vienna* (n 4).
31 Charles Seymour, 'Peacemaking 1919' (1934) 49 Polit Sci Q. 119 ('Seymour, Peacemaking 1919'); Denis Stairs, 'The Book That Influenced Me Most' (2002) Policy Options 7 ('Stairs, 'The Book That Influenced Me Most'') 7–8.
32 Nicolson, *Peacemaking 1919* (n 3) v–vii.
33 Ibid.
34 Seymour, 'Peacemaking 1919' (n 31) 119.
35 Clive Day, 'Peacemaking 1919: Being Reminiscences of the Paris Peace Conference' (1934) 39 Am Hist Rev 529.
36 Seymour, 'Peacemaking 1919' (n 31) 119
37 Ibid.
38 Nicolson, *Peacemaking 1919* (n 3) v–vii.
39 Ibid.
40 He also wrote a new introduction ten years after the initial publication, see Stairs, 'The Book That Influenced Me Most' (n 31) 7.
41 President Wilson outlined his Fourteen Points in a speech in January 1918 in which he described his principles for the new world order after the war, including free trade,

his writing makes clear that he became disillusioned with Wilson and his inability to implement his goals against the political realities of the conference and divergent interests of the allies post-conflict.[42] Indeed, the chapters of his book bear titles such as 'Delay', 'Misfortunes', 'Mistakes', 'Disorganization', 'Quarrel' and 'Failure' leaving little doubt as to his overall negative view of the proceedings.[43]

Through his experiences at the conference, Nicolson became disillusioned with the shady deals and self-serving commitments of the powers. 'What may remain unrecorded, is the atmosphere of those unhappy months, the mists by which we were enshrouded.'[44] He focuses on the compromises that had to be made in the treaty.[45] In essence, Nicolson goes from high ideals to profound disillusionment:[46] In the words of one critic, 'it is the contrast between youthful aspirations, accompanied by the high-spirited belief in "we can because we ought" and the mature knowledge that we must restrict ourselves to the compossibles.'[47] His personal transformation seems to mirror that of the conference—from unbridled, youthful optimism to disillusionment at the end result, which manifested compromises to the point of being no longer recognizable.

In his writing, Nicolson places most of the blame for the failure on Wilson.[48] He had high hopes for Wilson, which were frustrated by Wilson's failure to have the League of Nations ratified by Congress and to achieve many of the key aims of the Fourteen Points.[49] Critics have pointed out several assumptions implicit in Nicolson's work: first, he assumed that Wilson had the power to make those realities happen.[50] He also assumed that Wilson's failure was at the Paris negotiations, rather than afterwards when he returned to America and was unable to persuade Congress to ratify the treaty.[51] As a result, America never joined the League of Nations, severely undercutting any effectiveness the organization might have had.[52]

---

open agreements, democracy and self-determination, see Nicolson, *Peacemaking 1919* (n 3) 39–40.
42   Seymour, *Peacemaking 1919* (n 31) 120.
43   Nicolson, *Peacemaking 1919* (n 3) v–vii.
44   *Ibid* 6.
45   Seymour, *Peacemaking 1919* (n 31) 121.
46   *Ibid*.
47   Andrew McFadyean, 'Peacemaking 1919 by Harold Nicolson'(1933) 12 Int Aff 661–62.
48   Seymour, *Peacemaking 1919* (n 31) 120.
49   *Ibid*.
50   *Ibid*.
51   *Ibid*.
52   *Ibid*.

The time frame in which *Peacemaking 1919* was penned is significant. Nicolson wrote the book more than a decade after the conference had ended and the work reflects the perspective of the years and distance from the actual events. His disillusionment was undoubtedly exacerbated by the fact that he wrote *Peacemaking 1919* in the late 1920s and early 1930s as fascism in Europe was on the rise and the failure of 1919 was becoming undeniable.

Yet even a decade later, Nicolson recognizes in his work the temporal limits of his perspective, noting: 'The history of the Conference of Paris has yet to be written. It will be many years before the complete material can either be rendered available or digested.'[53]

B   *The Congress of Vienna: A Study in Allied Unity*

The Congress of Vienna: A Study in Allied Unity[54] is a historical analysis of the Congress of Vienna which, two centuries before the Paris Peace Conference, sought to restore the world order in the wake of the Napoleonic Wars.[55] Interestingly, while the Paris Peace Conference was deemed an almost immediate failure, the Congress of Vienna is widely regarded as more successful, having resulted in peace for almost 100 years.[56]

The Congress of Vienna occurred decades before Nicolson was born, and the book does not benefit from the same firsthand account as he was able to give in *Peacemaking 1919*. He nevertheless infuses *The Congress of Vienna: A Study in Allied Unity* with human sketches of those who participated. As one reviewer noted, 'His swift moving sketches of the leading participants are skillfully spotted and underscore the highly important essential for us once more—that diplomatists in any environment are still human beings.'[57]

Nicolson offers a number of criticisms of the Congress of Vienna that may provide instructive in the present day. First, Nicolson faults the delegates for failing to articulate clear objectives at the outset of the conference.[58] He also notes that the conference was flawed because the common causes of war were divided by self-interest in peacetime: '…factors which create dissension between

---

53   Nicolson, *Peacemaking 1919* (n 3) 30.
54   *Ibid.*
55   Genevieve Peterson, 'The Congress of Vienna: A Study in Allied Unity 1812–1822' (1947) 62 Polit Sic Q 155 ('Peterson, 'The Congress of Vienna: A Study in Allied Unity 1812–1822").
56   *Ibid.*
57   Malcom Moos, 'The Congress of Vienna' (1947) 9 The J Polit Sci 458 ('Moos, 'The Congress of Vienna").
58   John K Zeedner, 'The Congress of Vienna: A Study in Allied Unity 1812–1822' (1947) 33 The Cathol Hist Rev 229–30.

independent states temporarily bound.'[59] He cautions against the dangers of allowing separate postwar interests to overshadow the common purpose forged in war.[60]

Finally, he notes that those crafting peace should take care to safeguard against new aggression that results from changes in world equilibrium.[61] Thus, Nicolson notes,

> Then, as now Great Britain (at first alone and thereafter assisted by powerful allies) had destroyed a totalitarian system which sought to engulf the world. Then as now the common purpose which had united the Nations in the hour of danger ceased, once victory had been achieved, to compel solidarity [...] Then as now there were those who felt that destroying one menace to peace and independence of nations they had succeeded only in creating another and graver menace in its place.[62]

Interestingly, although it covers an earlier period in history, Nicolson wrote *The Congress of Vienna: A Study in Allied Unity* in 1946, some fifteen years after *Peacemaking 1919*.[63] The timing of this book is also significant—he wrote *The Congress of Vienna: A Study in Allied Unity* in 1946 as the full scope of destruction from the Second World War was coming to light and the United Nations was being formed on the eve of the Cold War.[64] It is therefore apropos and pointed that he notes that the 'balance of power is one of the most stable guarantees of peace.'[65]

4   Taken Together

Taken in tandem, *Peacemaking 1919* and *The Congress in Vienna: A Study in Allied Unity* represent two points in time along the trajectory of Nicolson's career. They show the transformation from idealistic junior diplomat to seasoned diplomat, and later to sanguine politician.

---

59   Ibid.
60   Vernon J Puryear, 'The Congress of Vienna: A Study in Allied Unity 1812–1822' (1947) 252 Ann Am Acad Polit Soc Sci 134 ('Puryear, 'The Congress of Vienna: A *Study* in Allied Unity 1812–1822"').
61   Moos, 'The Congress of Vienna' (n 57).
62   Nicolson, *The Congress of Vienna* (n 4).
63   Peterson, 'The Congress of Vienna: A Study in Allied Unity 1812–1822' (n 55) 155.
64   *Ibid* 155.
65   Nicolson, *The Congress of Vienna* (n 4).

There are a number of similarities between the two works that belie a certain consistency to Nicolson's approach as historian. First, both books are in a sense case studies on the rise and fall of coalitions, analyzing each diplomatic move.[66]

In both works, Nicolson cautions throughout that history must be used in its appropriate context and that parallels not be overdrawn.[67] Thus, to Nicolson history is not a crystal ball that will predict the future, but rather an opportunity to see from the shoulders of giants the paths that might lie ahead. To that end, Nicolson employs analogies which can deepen understanding of present day conflicts and issues in diplomacy. However, he does not necessarily believe that the future will inevitably follow the same path.[68] He notes,

> We can learn little from history unless we first realize that she does not, in fact, repeat herself. Events are not affected by analogies; they are determined by combinations of circumstances. And since circumstances vary from generation to generation it is illusive to suppose that any pattern of history, however similar it may at first appear, is likely repeat itself exactly in the kaleidoscope of time.[69]

Finally, Nicolson is consistent in his attributing the failure of the two international conferences to the post-conflict private interests that trump the common cause of defense during wartime. Thus, once the danger to national existence was gone, the coalition deteriorated.[70]

Notwithstanding these commonalities, the two books reflect marked differences. *Peacemaking 1919* is a hybrid of Nicolson's own diary, and a backward reflection two decades later when the failures of that endeavor were wreaking their full havoc.[71] Conversely, *The Congress of Vienna: A Study in Allied Unity* is a purely historical study. The difference in Nicolson's view as participant and that as historian are readily apparent, one having been written with a bird's eye view on the past and the other witnessing history from the shoulder of giants with all of the biases and filters that involves.[72]

---

66 H M Spitzer, 'The Congress of Vienna: A Study in Allied United 1812–1822' (1946) 109 World Aff 301.
67 *Ibid.*
68 *Ibid.*
69 Nicolson, *The Congress of Vienna* (n 4).
70 Zeedner, 'The Congress of Vienna: A Study in Allied Unity 1812–1822' (n 58) 229.
71 Seymour, 'Peacemaking 1919' (n 31) 119.
72 *Ibid.*

Second, they were written at different points in Nicolson's career. Nicolson wrote *Peacemaking 1919* in 1931, just after coming out of diplomatic service and as he was about to embark on a political career. His diary demonstrates an earlier view of unbridled optimism at Wilson, and his ability to shape destiny.[73] He, at that time, possessed an idealistic view of what the world powers should have been able to achieve and he offers recrimination and disillusionment at Wilsons' failure to do so.[74]

Conversely, Nicolson writes about the Congress of Vienna two centuries earlier at a later date—1946.[75] A number of factors color his worldview at this point. First, Nicolson has served a number of years in Parliament and has recently lost election.[76] Though he would again try to run for office he would be unsuccessful and not return to government.[77] Second, at this point he can see the full spectrum of destruction the failure of 1919 has wrought.[78] Thus, his view at the writing of *The Congress of Vienna* is a more sanguine, if not cynical one. Here, he seems to have shifted, and instead of faulting the powers for failing to adhere to principles, he criticizes them for not predicting and adjusting to realities of the new world order post conflict.

Thus, *Peacemaking 1919* is predominantly from the view of a diplomat, whereas *The Congress of Vienna: A Study in Allied Unity* represents the more seasoned view of a politician. For example, in *Peacemaking: 1919* he is disillusioned with the way Wilson bent his ideals to the realities of the world order. However, in *Congress of Vienna*, he faults the negotiators for failing to adjust course to respond to the dangers that had emerged post-conflict. As one historian noted,

> The young idealist of 1919 began to fuse realist and idealist approaches to international affairs during the 1920s, and by the late 1930s had formulated a liberal realized conception of international relations, which he applied to international order, diplomacy, the foreign affairs maelstrom of interwar Europe, European integration, world government and peace.[79]

73　Ibid.
74　Ibid.
75　Nicolson, *The Congress of Vienna* (n 4).
76　Ibid.
77　Ibid.
78　Ibid.
79　Drinkwater, *Sir Harold Nicolson and International Relations: The Practitioner as Theorist* (n 17) 205.

5 Conclusion

Nicolson's perspective and analysis in both *Peacemaking 1919* and *The Congress of Vienna: A Study in Allied Unity* were clearly both influenced by his experiences as a junior delegate at the Paris Peace Conference. By witnessing history 'from the shoulders of giants', he saw the failure of the peace conference as it took place, and the devastating consequences in the decades to follow. This affected his political views and his writing. As one observer has noted, Nicolson sought to:

> resolve the tension between realities and hopes, between the disheartening evidence of history and over-sanguine future expectations […] Even for an optimist like Nicolson it was a daunting exercise. Establishing positive coexistence for realism and practical idealism in the twentieth century international relations environment was difficult enough. Harnessing their respective strengths and ameliorating their particular weaknesses in an attempt to improve the international society of tomorrow was a significant undertaking.[80]

Our colleague and mentor, Roger Clark, has found Nicolson's work instructive in his own groundbreaking work in human rights. He has also incorporated his own tremendous contributions to international organizations and initiatives in his own scholarship. By learning from his own experiences, and Nicolson's writing, and employing both in his own teaching and scholarship, Roger has provided an opportunity for the rest of us to stand on the shoulders of giants—notably, his own.

---

[80] *Ibid.*

CHAPTER 9

The Rule of Law, the International Justice System and Africa

Daniel David Ntanda Nsereko [*]

1   Introduction

Africa severely lags behind other continents in terms of human and economic development. Of the 49 states that the UN has designated as the 'Least Developed Countries' ('LDC'), 34 (or 69%) are African.[1] This means that of all the members of the African Union, 63% fall within the LDC category. The disparities between the developed world and Africa as indicated by the data are indeed enormous.[2] Yet all human beings are created equal in dignity and rights.[3]

---

[*]   An essay in honour of Professor Roger Clark. It is based on the 2013 Annual Benedicto Kiwanuka Lecture, which the author delivered at Makerere University, Kampala, Uganda, on 14 November 2013. The views he expresses herein are solely his and do not represent the Special Tribunal for Lebanon or the International Criminal Court. The author also acknowledges the assistance of Mr Brian Rifkin in the preparation of this essay. He however remains solely responsible for the views expressed therein.

[1]   UN Conference on Trade and Development, 'The Least Developed Countries Report 2012—Harnessing Remittances and Diaspora Knowledge to Build Productive Capacities' (26 November 2012) UN Doc UNCTAD/LDC/2012.

[2]   The human development indicators in these countries reveal an abysmal picture. As of 2013, in a majority of these countries the people lived in abject poverty, earning less than USD $1.25 a day. *See* 'Poverty Overview' (World Bank) http://www.worldbank.org/en/topic/poverty/overview accessed 17 April 2014). While average global life expectancy in 2013 was 70 years, with Japan at the top with 86.4, in Africa it was 60 years, with Sierre Leone at the bottom of the rung with 47.5 years. (*See* 'Life expectancy: Life expectancy: Data by country' (World Health Organisation) at <http://apps.who.int/gho/data/node.main.688?lang=en%3E?%3E> accessed 17 April 2014; Lucy Kinder, 'Countries with highest and lowest life expectancies for people born in 2013 charted' *The Telegraph* (9 January 2014). When it comes to literacy, we find that the majority of developed countries have rates of 99% or above. In Sub-Saharan Africa, on the other hand, the literacy rates hover in the sixties and in some cases are as low as 29%. (*See*, UNESCO Institute for Statistics, 'Adult And Youth Literacy, 1990–2015 Analysis of data for 41 selected countries' at <http://www.uis.unesco.org/Education/Documents/UIS-literacy-statistics-1990-2015-en.pdf> accessed 17 April 2014). As for democracy and good governance, howsoever defined, there is still a huge deficit in Africa. For instance, free and fair elections are an exception for most of the African countries (*see* Edwin Odhiambo Abuya, 'Can African States Conduct Free and Fair Presidential Elections?' (2010) 8 Northwestern JIHR) 2.

[3]   Universal Declaration of Human Rights (adopted 10 December 1948) UNGA Res 217 A(III) (UDHR) art 1.

It is imperative that Africa pull itself out of this sorry situation. In my view, Africa can only develop in conditions of peace and freedom; not amidst incessant wars and armed conflicts, in the course of which 'unimaginable atrocities that deeply shock the conscience of humanity' are often committed.[4] Yet, there can be no peace without justice. And there can be no justice when the perpetrators of injustices are apparently not accountable and, consequently, continue their conduct with impunity. This is so because the perpetrators of these atrocities are often the enforcers of the law or have influence on the national law enforcement machinery. Impunity is thus rife and the rule of law inert.

Thankfully, at the demise of the Cold War, the international community established an international criminal justice system to complement national justice systems and to ensure that nations and peoples can access justice through the rule of law and ultimately pursue development. This system was made possible and remains essential because the nature and magnitude of so many atrocities qualify them as international crimes; they violate internationally cherished values, have international reverberations, and often constitute a threat to peace and the security of mankind.

Today, the central and most visible mechanism created to attain these goals is the International Criminal Court ('ICC'). Former UN Secretary-General Kofi Annan welcomed the establishment of the ICC as 'a gift of hope to future generations, and a giant step forward in the march towards universal human rights and the rule of law.'[5] Nevertheless, this Court has lately come under acerbic criticism by some African states.

Roger Clark, to whom this essay is dedicated, devoted most of his academic and professional life advancing the cause of the rule of law in lecture halls, diplomatic conferences and scholarly publications. He played a key role in the establishment of the ICC as a member of the delegation of Samoa at the Rome Diplomatic Conference, during the Prepcoms and at the sessions of the Assembly of States Parties. This essay attempts to further advocate the critical importance of the rule of the law and, specifically, the ICC in Africa.

The essay first discusses certain basic aspects of the rule of law particularly relevant to ending impunity and achieving justice in Africa. It then examines them as they are reflected in the Principles of International Law Recognized in the Charter of the Nuremberg Tribunal and in the Judgment of the Tribunal in 1950, and later refined by the International Law Commission. Commonly known as the Nuremberg Principles, they constitute the basic principles of

---

[4] UNGA Rome Statute of the International Criminal Court (adopted 17 July 1998, entered into force 1 July 2002) 2187 UNTS 3 ('Rome Statute') Preamble.

[5] 'Secretary-General says establishment of International Criminal Court is major step in march towards universal human rights, Rule of Law' (UN Press Release L/2890 20 July 1998).

international criminal law, which, in turn, inform the provisions of the Rome Statute of the ICC. In doing so, the essay considers how these principles, as applied by the ICC, help advance the rule of law in Africa and, ultimately, justice, peace and development. In this respect, the essay attempts to counter some of the African criticisms of the Court as it endeavours to live up to these principles.

2   The Rule of Law in the Fight against Impunity

Aristotle said over two thousand years ago that the rule of law was better than the rule of any individual.[6] John Adams, one of the drafters of the American Declaration of Independence and the second President of the United States, advocated a type of constitution that would ensure for the American people 'a government of laws and not of men.'[7] But what is the rule of law? As the phrase suggests, the rule of law is about legality. It is not, however, conformity with just any law, but rather a particular conceptualisation of a legal system that ensures and promotes justice. Certain aspects of the rule of the law are essential to fighting impunity.

The rule of law requires that in any human society there must exist a set of rules that governs the conduct of the members of that community. Most importantly, it requires that those who exercise power do so under the authority of and consistent with the pre-existing rules. The law in this sense serves as an antidote to chaos, arbitrariness and abuse of power.

Equally important is that everyone must be under the law. As Lord Denning said, 'Be you ever so high, the law is above you.'[8] Every citizen must be accountable for his or her actions and amenable to the jurisdiction of ordinary courts. The culture of impunity, or *banankola ki*, so rife and rampant in much of Africa, is repugnant to the rule of law. It encourages aggrieved citizens to take the law in their own hands and thereby breeds lawlessness and violence in society. For a developing country, impunity and lawlessness further discourage economic development. In a constitutional government, this aspect of the rule of law denies unlimited powers to any of the three branches of government. The powers granted to one branch must be limited by the powers granted to the others.

---

6   Aristotle, *Politics* (Penguin Classics 1981) Book 3, ch 16.
7   Constitution of the Commonwealth of Massachusetts (1780) Part The First, art XXX, at <https://malegislature.gov/Laws/Constitution> accessed 19 September 2014.
8   *Gouriet v Union of Post Office Workers and Others* [1977] QB 729, 762. The statement is actually attributable to one Dr Thomas Fuller who is reputed to have written it in 1737.

None of the three branches is above the law, or free to do or decide as it wishes. This idea was known in Uganda to our ancestors. They expressed it in the Luganda adage as *'mpaawo kyetwala: Kabaka afugibwa Kibaale.'* It means that no one is above the law; even the *Kabaka* (the King) is subject to the jurisdiction of *Omutaka Kibaale*, an important clan leader.

To ensure that everyone in the country is within the reach of the law, a country must have an independent and impartial judiciary, with judges who must apply the law without fear or favour, malice or ill will. Stressing the value of judicial independence, Lord Chief Justice Phillips of Great Britain said in 2007, 'A judge should value independence above gold, not for his or her own benefit, but because it is of the essence of the rule of law.'[9] I add that when citizens know that their courts are independent and impartial, they will readily and confidently refer their disputes to them for adjudication and accept and carry out their judgments and orders; they will be less inclined to resort to self-help measures, including violence, which often have catastrophic consequences. Also important for a developing country, when potential investors know that legal disputes between them and others in such country will be adjudicated by impartial and independent judges, this knowledge will be an important factor in the decision to invest or not to invest.

3   The International Justice System

(a)   *Rule of Law among Nations*

How does the idea of the rule of law connect with the international justice system? In one of his famous poems, the English poet, John Donne, wrote:

> No man is an island entire by itself.
>   Every man is a piece of the continent[10]

Donne was suggesting that the human person, as a social being, cannot exist without his or her fellows. We are all interconnected and interdependent. Similarly, no state can be on its own. As Donne observed, a state is 'a piece of the continent, a part of the main.'[11] Individual states belong to a larger community

---

9   Lord Phillips, 'Judicial Independence', Speech at the Commonwealth Law Conference 2007 in Nairobi, Kenya, 12 September 2007, at <https://www.judiciary.gov.uk/wp-content/uploads/JCO/Documents/Speeches/lcj_kenya_clc_120907.pdf> accessed 17 April 2014.
10   John Donne, *Devotions upon Emergent Occasions* (1624) Mediation XVII.
11   *Ibid.*

of sovereign nations, the international community. Members of this community have inextricably shared interests, values, and resources and, above all, a shared humanity. As is true for individual states, for the international community to continue to exist as such, it must have rules that regulate the relations between its members *inter se*. According to a Latin maxim, *ubi societas ibi jus*, where there is society there is law. It is inconceivable how it could be otherwise. Explaining the rationale for law in the international community, Elihu Root wrote almost a century ago:

> Men cannot live in neighbourhood with each other without having reciprocal rights and obligations toward each other arising from their being neighbours. [...] It is not a matter of contract. It is a matter of usage arising from the necessities of self-protection. It is not a voluntary matter. It is compelled by the situation. The neighbours generally must govern their conduct by accepted standards or the community will break-up. It is the same with nations.[12]

The rule of law is essential for peaceful and harmonious relations among the members of the international community. The rule of law serves to elevate law over power and to protect weak and fledgling states from the mighty and overbearing. The UN Charter, which may be referred to as the constitution of the international community, confirms this assertion. In its preamble the founding fathers indicated their determination 'to establish conditions under which justice and respect for the obligations arising from treaties and other sources of international law can be maintained.'[13] The Charter is supplemented by the General Assembly's Declaration of Principles of International Law concerning Friendly Relations and Co-operation among States in Accordance with the Charter of the United Nations. In its preamble this Declaration underscores 'the paramount importance of the Charter of the United Nations in the promotion of *the rule of law among nations*.'[14] It also lists the core principles that underpin concord, harmony and peaceful life in the community. The principles include non-use or threat of use of force and condemnation of aggression as a crime against the peace; resolving international disputes by peaceful means; respect for the sovereign equality of states; equal rights and self-determination of peoples; fulfilment in good faith of

---

12   Elihu Root, 'A Requisite for the Success of Popular Diplomacy' (1922) 1 Foreign Affairs 3, 8.
13   Charter of the United Nations (signed on 26 June 1945, entered into force 24 October 1945) 1 UNTS 16 (UN Charter) Preamble.
14   UN General Assembly Res 2625 (24 October 1970) UN Doc A/RES/2625(XXV) Preamble.

international obligations; and universal respect for and observance of human rights and fundamental freedoms.[15]

(b) Nuremberg Principles

That conflicts or misunderstandings and deviant behaviour in any community occur is undeniable and inevitable. What is important, however, is that such conflicts are resolved and deviant behaviour neutralized in an orderly and fair manner. This is the hallmark of a civil or well-ordered society. For that reason, the international community has for long developed means of peacefully settling inter-state disputes and of dealing with deviant members. These means include: negotiation, enquiry, mediation, conciliation, arbitration and adjudication. The international community has also built institutions to resolve the disputes or deal with deviance. This is what we may refer to as the international justice system. Prominent in this system is the International Court of Justice ('ICJ'), the successor to the Permanent Court of International Justice. This Court resolves disputes between states as such.

However, the behaviour of rogue states, such as Nazi Germany and its Axis partners, prior to and during World War II, spurred the international community to develop new legal principles and to establish new institutions with the view to making the international justice system more effective. These principles of international criminal justice are based on, and reflect, the elements of the rule of law discussed above. They acknowledge that a system of international justice that does not hold individuals accountable for the atrocities they commit in violation of international law is not compatible with the rule of law, and thus does not ensure justice for the international community. First recognized in the Charter and Judgment of the International Military Tribunal ('IMT') that tried certain major war criminals for 'crimes against peace,'[16] they were later formulated and refined by the International Law Commission.[17]

The principles, known as the Nuremberg Principles ('Principles'), include a list of crimes that are punishable under international law: crimes against peace, war crimes and crimes against humanity; the crime of genocide was later added to the list by treaty.[18] They also include the notion of individual

---

15 UN General Assembly Res 2625 (n 14).
16 Charter of the International Military Tribunal—Annex to the Agreement for the prosecution and punishment of the major war criminals of the European Axis ('London Agreement') (signed 8 August 1945) 82 UNTC 280.
17 'Principles of International Law Recognized in the Charter of the Nuremberg Tribunal and in the Judgment of the Tribunal' (1950) II Ybk of the Intl L Commission 97.
18 UNGA Convention on the Prevention and Punishment of the Crime of Genocide (signed 9 December 1948) 78 UNTS 277.

criminal responsibility for international crimes; the irrelevance of domestic law; the irrelevance of official capacity; the non-applicability of the defence of superior order and command responsibility; and the right to a fair trial.[19] The Principles have been incorporated into the statutes of the various international criminal tribunals, most notably the ICC.[20] The Principles have further been augmented in the ICC Statute by the principle of complementarity. They constitute the basic principles of international criminal law today and play an indispensable role in the fight against impunity. Yet despite their virtuous goals, their application by the ICC in cases involving certain African defendants has led to a cacophony of complaints against the international justice system. In my view, the complaints are groundless. For limitation of space, this essay discusses only certain of these Principles which to date have been contentious.

Individual Criminal Responsibility

The first Principle declares that '[a]ny person who commits a crime under international law is responsible therefor and liable to punishment.'[21] International crimes, by their nature and magnitude, are most often committed by state officials or agents on orders of the government, or in furtherance of government policy. Save for the cases of rebel movements, these crimes have in the past been called crimes of state which, indubitably, involve state responsibility. What then is the rationale for punishing the individual, and not the state on whose behalf the individual acts?

The answer is that, under the current state of international law, a state as such cannot be punished. If it were to be punished, such punishment would most likely take the form of economic or other sanctions. Yet, when sanctions are imposed on a state, it is ultimately the ordinary and innocent citizens who

---

19   Principles of International Law Recognized in the Charter of the Nuremberg Tribunal and in the Judgment of the Tribunal (n 17).

20   *See* Rome Statute (n 4) art 22–33.

21   Principles of International Law (n 17). In line with this Principle, the Rome Statute provides: 'A person who commits a crime within the jurisdiction of the Court shall be individually responsible and liable for punishment in accordance with this Statute.' Rome Statute (n 4) art 25(2). Statutes of other international tribunals provide similarly, see UN Security Council, Statute of the International Criminal Tribunal for the Former Yugoslavia (25 May 1993) UN Doc S/Res/827, art 7 (1); UNSC, Statute of the International Criminal Tribunal for Rwanda (8 November 1994) UN Doc S/Res/955, art 6(1). See also the following cases: *Prosecutor v Akayesu* (Trial Judgement) ICTR-96-4-T (2 September 1998); *Prosecutor v Jelisić* (Trial Judgement) IT-95-10-T (14 December 1999); *Prosecutor v Krstić* (Trial Judgement) IT-98-333-T (2 August 2001); *Prosecutor v Tadić* (Appeal Judgement) IT-94-1-A (15 July 1999).

suffer their brunt. Here one recalls the terrible effects on the civilian population of the sanctions imposed on Iraq following its invasion of Kuwait in 1990. Thousands of innocent children and members of other vulnerable groups died for lack of food and medicine.[22] And yet there was no immediate change of behaviour by the government of Iraq. Again, in South Africa, it was the innocent citizens who suffered from the social and professional isolation under the sanctions imposed on the apartheid government.[23] It was, in part, to address the inadequacy of state punishment as a means of ensuring law abidingness and combatting impunity that Nuremberg established the principle of individual criminal responsibility for international crimes. In its often quoted words, the IMT declared that:

> Crimes against international law are committed by men, not by abstract entities, and only by punishing individuals who commit such crimes can the provision of international law be enforced.[24]

As thus articulated, the aim of international criminal law is to punish the individuals who conceive, plan, initiate, order, or execute international crimes, albeit in the name of and on behalf of the state; and the aim of punishment is deterrence. To borrow a leaf from the law of corporate criminal responsibility, a state, as a mere fiction, 'is incapable of acting or speaking or even thinking except so far as its officers have acted, spoken or thought.'[25] Therefore, individuals must not be allowed to commit heinous crimes and hope to escape responsibility by hiding behind the mask of the state. They must individually and in their personal capacity account for what they did or omitted to do. The veil must be lifted or pierced. This view is particularly apt with respect to the crime of aggression, which is a leadership crime.

For completeness, I must also add that the fact that an individual has been convicted of and punished for crimes committed on a state's territory does not relieve that state of its responsibility under international law to pay

---

22   Barbara Crossette, 'Iraq Sanctions Kill Children, U.N. Reports' (*The New York Times*, 1 December 1995); David Cortright, 'A Hard Look at Iraq Sanctions: Death rates are alarming but lower than claimed. Saddam shares responsibility' (*The Nation*, 15 November 2001).
23   Alexander Laverty, 'Impact of Economic and Political Sanctions on Apartheid' (The African File, Final Paper: MMW 6 Spring 2007), at <http://theafricanfile.com/politicshistory/impact-of-economic-and-political-sanctions-on-apartheid/> accessed 17 April 2014.
24   International Military Tribunal (1947) Vol. I, Trial of the Major War Criminals before the International Tribunal: Nuremberg, 14 November 1945–1 October 1946, 223.
25   *Director of Public Prosecutions v Kent and Sussex Contractors Ltd.* [1944] KB 146, 155.

reparations, where those crimes are attributable to it.[26] Similarly, the fact that a state incurs state responsibility for what its officials did does not absolve the officials from individual criminal responsibility and punishment.[27]

Irrelevance of Domestic Law

The second Principle enunciates that '[t]he fact that internal law does not impose a penalty for an act which constitutes a crime under international law does not relieve the person who committed the act from responsibility under international law.'[28] For instance, aggression, an international crime, is currently not a crime under the laws of Uganda. Nevertheless, provided that other conditions under the Statute are met, an individual charged with the crime of aggression before the ICC would not be allowed to invoke this lacuna in Uganda's law as an excuse for engaging in acts of aggression against another state and to escape criminal responsibility. If this were permitted, international law generally, and international criminal law in particular, would be flouted with impunity.[29]

Irrelevance of Official Capacity

Under this Principle, 'The fact that a person who committed an act which constitutes a crime under international law acted as Head of State or responsible Government official does not relieve him or her of responsibility under international law.'[30] In line with this Principle, the Statute of the ICC explicitly rejects any form of immunity that serving Heads of State and other high-ranking government officials may enjoy under national or customary international law. Article 27 pointedly provides:

> The Statute shall apply to all persons without distinction based on official capacity. In particular, official capacity as Head of State or Government, a member of a Government or parliament, an elected representative or a government official shall in no case exempt a person from criminal responsibility under this Statute nor shall it, in and of itself, constitute a ground for reduction of sentence.

---

26   Thomas Franck, 'Symposium—Judgment at Nuremberg, Individual Criminal Liability and Collective Civil Responsibility: Do They Reinforce or Contradict One Another?' (2007) 6(3) Washington University Global Studies Law Review 567.
27   Thomas Franck (n 26).
28   Principles of International Law Recognized in the Charter of the Nuremberg Tribunal and in the Judgment of the Tribunal (n 17).
29   See *Alabama Claims Arbitration* (*United States v Great Britain*) (1872) 1 Intl Arb 495.
30   Principles of International Law Recognized in the Charter of the Nuremberg Tribunal and in the Judgment of the Tribunal (n 17).

> Immunities or special procedural rules which may attach to the official capacity of a person, whether under national or international law, shall not bar the Court from exercising its jurisdiction over such person.[31]

It is particularly the application of these provisions in cases involving serving African heads of state[32] which has evoked bitter criticism from Africa. It has led some to label the ICC as a western institution imposed on Africa to humiliate it and to subvert the national sovereignty of African states.[33] Others have called it a tool of the American administration.[34] At its summit in October 2013, the African Union ('AU') even purported to assert an exception to its provisions. The AU 'decided' that 'no charges shall be commenced or continued before any international Court or Tribunal against any serving AU Head of State or Government or anybody acting or entitled to act in such capacity during their term of office.'[35] In so deciding, the AU purportedly acted under 'principles deriving from national laws and international customary law by which sitting heads of State and other senior state officials are granted immunities during their tenure of office.'[36] Additionally, the AU in effect ordered African States Parties to 'propose relevant amendments to the Rome Statute, in accordance with Article 121 of the Statute,' presumably to grant immunity to sitting Heads of State.[37]

With great respect, claims to immunity for anyone charged with crimes before the ICC, or any other international criminal tribunals, have no basis in law. The immunity recognized under international customary law, which the AU

---

31 Rome Statute (n 4) art 27. The Statutes of all other international criminal tribunals carry similar provisions. See for example, ICTY Statute (n 21) art 7 (2); ICTR Statute (n 21) art 6 (2); UNSC Statute of the Special Court for Sierra Leone (16 January 2002) UN Doc S/Res/1315, art 6 (2); Charter of the International Military Tribunal (n 16) art 7.

32 *See Prosecutor v Al Bashir* (Decision on the Prosecutor's Application for a Warrant of Arrest against Omar Hassan Ahmad Al Bashir) ICC-02/05-01/09 (4 March 2009); *Situation in the Libyan Arab Jamahiriya* (Decision on the 'Prosecutor's Application Pursuant to article 58 as to Muammar Mohammed Abu Minyar Gaddafi, Saif Al-Islam Gaddafi and Abdullah Al-Senussi') ICC-01/11, (27 June 2011).

33 The Editorial Board, 'Kenya and the International Criminal Court' (*The New York Times*, 9 November 2013); Reason Wafawarova, 'ICC: Racial stereotyping, politicisation of justice' (*The Herald*, 5 June 2013); 'ICC, A Tool To Recolonise Africa' (*African Business Magazine*, 1 September 2011).

34 Mahmood Mamdani, 'Darfur, ICC and the New Humanitarian Order' (*Pambazuka News*, 17 September 2008).

35 African Union, Decision on Africa's Relationship with the International Criminal Court (12 October 2013) Decision No. Ext/Assembly/AU/Doc.1, para 10(i).

36 *Ibid* para 9.

37 *Ibid* para 10(vi).

invokes, is immunity from the jurisdiction of *domestic courts*.[38] That immunity is predicated on the notion of the sovereign equality of all states. It is articulated in the Latin maxim as *par in parem non habet imperium*, or 'an equal has no power over an equal.' Under this notion, in the absence of a law or treaty stipulating the contrary, one state cannot subject another state, as embodied by its Head of State or his emissaries, to its courts' jurisdiction and processes.[39] To do so, as the ICJ found in the *Yerodia* case between the Democratic Republic of Congo and Belgium,[40] would be to infringe on that state's sovereign independence. Quite clearly, issues of sovereign equality are not relevant in cases before international tribunals. For that reason, the Special Court for Sierra Leone ('Special Court') rejected Mr. Charles Taylor's claim for immunity, as a sitting Head of State, founded on arguments of state sovereignty or equality. In doing so the Appeals Chamber of the Special Court declared that:

> The principle of state immunity derives from the equality of sovereign states and therefore has no relevance to international criminal tribunals which are not organs of state but derive their mandate from the international community.[41]

The Trial Chamber of the Special Court, after convicting Mr. Taylor of what it described as 'some of the most heinous and brutal crimes recorded in human history',[42] observed:

> The lives of many more innocent civilians in Sierra Leone were lost or destroyed as a direct result of his actions. As President and as Commander-in-Chief of the Armed Forces of Liberia, Mr. Taylor used his unique position, including his access to state machinery and public resources, to aid and abet the commission of crimes in Sierra Leone, rather than using his power to promote peace in the region. The Trial Chamber finds that Mr. Taylor's special status, and his responsibility at the highest level, is an aggravating factor of great weight.[43]

---

38   William Davison, 'African Leaders Want Prosecution Immunity for Heads of State', (*Bloomberg*, 12 October 2013).

39   Yoram Dinstein, 'Par in Parem Non Habet Imperium' (1966)1 Isr L Rev 407, 410–12.

40   *Arrest Warrant of 11 April 2000 (Democratic Republic of the Congo v. Belgium)* [*The Yerodia case*] (14 February 2022) ICJ Rep 2002, 3, paras 62–63.

41   *Prosecutor v Taylor* (Decision on Immunity from Jurisdiction) SCSL-2003-01-1, (31 May 2004) para 51.

42   *Prosecutor v Taylor* (Sentencing Judgment) SCSL-03-01-T (30 May 2012) para 70.

43   *Ibid* para 97.

Sentencing Mr. Taylor to 50 years imprisonment, the Special Court also declared that 'leadership must be carried out by example, by the prosecution of crimes not the commission of crimes.'[44] In my view, the Special Court's pronouncements give full force and effect to the requirements of the rule of law. They echo the Rome Statute's goal of ending impunity for the perpetrators of the most serious crimes of concern to the international community, which 'must not go unpunished.'[45] They need to be echoed elsewhere in Africa and beyond with an ever increasing crescendo.

The AU Resolution also invoked national laws. It is true that many African countries confer immunity to serving heads of state, for crimes that they might commit *whilst* they are in office.[46] Many seem to extend such immunity to *any* crime.[47] However, a few of them, such as Kenya, limit the immunity to ordinary crimes. Section 143(4) of the Kenyan Constitution categorically provides that Head-of-State immunity 'shall not extend to a crime for which the President may be prosecuted under any treaty to which Kenya is a party and which prohibits such immunity.'[48] Kenya is a party to the ICC Statute. According to these provisions, were its President to be indicted before its national courts for crimes such as those with which Mr Uhuru Kenyatta is indicted before the ICC, he would not be entitled to immunity. This renders all the more surprising Kenya's hardihood in claiming immunity for Kenyatta before the ICC.

Be that as it may, for those states that confer absolute immunity on their Heads of State, one has to wait until an incumbent vacates office before instituting or continuing any court proceedings against him or her for any crime before the national courts. In contrast, the ICC need not wait. If it did, it would be failing in its mandate of ensuring that 'the most serious crimes of concern to the international community as a whole [do] not go unpunished.'[49] The Court would also be failing in its mission of protecting hapless victims. This would be particularly true in those countries, particularly in Africa, where Heads of State hold office virtually for life. As long as they stay in office they cannot be prosecuted. Admittedly, statutes of limitation are not applicable to

---

44 *Ibid* para 102.
45 Rome Statute (n 4), Preamble; *Prosecutor v. Al Bashir* (n 32) para 42.
46 Constitution of the Republic of Uganda (22 September 1995) art 98(4). 'While holding office, the President shall not be liable to proceedings in any court.' For a similar provision see Constitution of Botswana (30 September 1966) art 41(1).
47 Constitution of the Republic of Uganda (n 46).
48 The Constitution of Kenya (27 August 2010) 143(4).
49 Rome Statute (n 4) Preamble.

the kind of crimes within the jurisdiction of the ICC,[50] and indictments can be instituted at any time.[51] Nevertheless, one should not be oblivious to the adage that justice delayed is justice denied. Moreover, as one commentator observed, 'a policy of refusing to prosecute sitting heads of state could easily become an incentive for leaders facing criminal charges to do whatever it takes to remain in office, including committing more of the mass atrocities that the ICC is supposed to be helping to prevent.'[52]

African states that are today critical of the ICC on the issue of Head-of-State immunity took part in the negotiations for the Court's Statute, and subsequently ratified it. These states knew, or ought to have known, that the Statute which they ratified forbids Head-of-State immunity. They knew, or ought to have known, that the ICC was not created to try only rebel leaders and the opponents of incumbent leaders. It was created to try *anyone*, irrespective of official status, who commits any crime within the jurisdiction of the Court. It surely does not lie in the mouths of these states to make such criticisms, which only make them look confused about their international commitments.

Related to the issue of immunity is the obligation of States Parties, and in the case of Security Council referrals, all UN member states, to co-operate with the Court in matters of arrest and surrender of indicted persons. Some African States Parties to the Rome Statute declined to arrest and hand over to the Court Hassan Ahmad Al Bashir of the Sudan,[53] for whose arrest the Pre-Trial Chamber issued a warrant to be executed when he visited them.[54] In declining, they claimed to be abiding by the AU stance of non-cooperation with the ICC,[55] and

---

50 Convention on the Non-Applicability of Statutory Limitations to War Crimes and Crimes against Humanity, UNGA Res 2391 (XXIII) (26 November 1968). *See also* Rome Statute (n 4) art 29: 'The crimes within the jurisdiction of the Court shall not be subject to any statute of limitations.'

51 The seriousness and heinousness of these crimes are no less compelling with the passage of time. Moreover, most of these crimes have long-lasting consequences for the affected communities and, indeed, the entire international community. This explains why seventy years after World War II, countries are still hunting down and prosecuting Nazi war criminals.

52 Kenneth Roth, 'Africa Attacks the International Criminal Court' (*The New York Review of Books*, 6 February 2014).

53 The states include Djibouti, Kenya, Chad, Malawi and the Democratic Republic of the Congo. However, with the change of government in Malawi, the new President, Mrs. Banda, declared that Malawi would arrest Mr. Al Bashir if he went there again.

54 See *Prosecutor v. Al Bashir* (n 32).

55 African Union, Decision on International Jurisdiction, Justice and the International Criminal Court (ICC) (26–27 May 2013) Doc. Assembly/AU/13 (XXI) para 4. The Assembly

the constraints of international law, which they thought granted him immunity from arrest and prosecution.[56] It is submitted that in doing so such states were in violation of their legal obligation. First, as was noted above, the principle of head-of-state immunity does not extend to persons being prosecuted before international criminal tribunals. Second, under the Rome Statute,[57] States Parties have an obligation to cooperate with the Court, when requested, to arrest and surrender to it all indicted individuals who come to their territory. In the case of Security Council referrals, all states, whether or not parties to the Rome Statute, assume a similar obligation under the UN Charter.[58] This is so because the referrals are made under the Council's Chapter VII peace and security powers, which override all other pre-existing legal obligations. According to both a general principle of law and the law of treaties, an undertaking freely and voluntarily assumed must be carried out in good faith.[59] This principle, expressed in Latin as *pactum sunt servanda*,[60] is known to Ugandans. It is expressed in the Luganda language as *akalagaane tekajja buliika*: to be required to honour one's contractual obligations is not an exaction, extortion or undue pressure. Therefore, when individuals for whose arrest warrants may have been issued come to its territory, a State Party must arrest and surrender them to the ICC in accord with its treaty obligations.[61] Lastly, it is wrong for an

---

of the Union 'REAFFIRMS the Member States such as Chad that had welcomed President Omar Al Bashir of The Sudan did so in conformity with the decisions of the Assembly and, therefore, should not be penalized.' The Republic of Botswana entered a reservation on the entire decision.

56 Gwen P Barnes, 'The International Criminal Court's Ineffective Enforcement Mechanisms: The Indictment of President Omar Al Bashir' (2011) 34 (6) Fordham Int'l LJ 1584, 1605–6; Alex Bell, 'African leaders under fire for seeking ICC immunity' (SW *Radio Africa*, 14 October 2013).

57 *See* Rome Statute (n 4) art 86, 89.

58 *See* UN Charter (n 13) art 24(1), 25, 103.

59 Vienna Convention on the Law of Treaties (adopted 22 May 1969, entered into force 27 January 1980) 1155 UNTS 331, art 26.

60 Vienna Convention on the Law of Treaties (n 59).

61 *See Prosecutor v Al Bashir* (Corrigendum to the Decision Pursuant to Article 87 (7) of the Rome Statute on the Failure by the Republic of Malawi to Comply with Cooperation Requests Issued by the Court with Respect to the Arrest and Surrender of Omar Hassan Ahmad Al Bashir) ICC-02/05-01/09-139-Corr (13 December 2011) para 41. The Pre-Trial Chamber I stated as follows: '[A]ll the States referenced above have ratified this Statute and/or entrusted this Court with exercising 'its jurisdiction over persons for the most serious crimes of international concern.' It is facially inconsistent for Malawi to entrust the Court with this mandate and then refuse to surrender a Head of State prosecuted for orchestrating genocide, war crimes and crimes against humanity. To interpret article 98(1)

African State Party to refuse to co-operate with the court in deference to AU decisions or obligations. This is particularly so in the case of Security Council referrals such as that implicating Mr. Al Bashir. As we have noted earlier, their obligation to co-operate, which they assumed under the UN Charter, prevails over any other obligations that they may have under any other treaty, including the Constitutive Act of the African Union.[62]

Complementarity

The principle of complementarity articulated in the ICC Statute derives from the failure in many cases of territorial states, as well as other states competent under the universality principle, to arrest and to prosecute perpetrators of international crimes.[63] The ICC Statute provides that the Court 'shall be complementary to national criminal jurisdictions.'[64] This means that the ICC is a court of last resort. Its powers to act are subordinate or secondary to those of the territorial state, which has the right to act first. This right is based on respect for the territorial state's sovereignty and also on other practical and logistical considerations, such as cost-effectiveness.[65] However, if that state does not exercise its powers at all, or if where it purports to do so, it does not do so genuinely, the ICC may step in and act on behalf of the international community.

This explains why, in the sequel of the post-elections violence in Kenya, Kenyan leaders, with the mediation of Mr. Kofi Annan, undertook to set up national judicial mechanisms to try and punish persons that were the most responsible for orchestrating the violence. The seriousness and magnitude

---

in such a way so as to justify not surrendering Omar Al Bashir on immunity grounds would disable the Court and international criminal justice in ways completely contrary to the purpose of the Statute Malawi has ratified.'

[62] UN Charter (n 13) art 103. See also *Prosecutor v Al Bashir* ('Decision on the Cooperation of the Democratic Republic of the Congo Regarding Omar Al Bashir's Arrest and Surrender to the Court'), Case No. ICC-02/05-01/09, 9 April 2014, in which Pre-Trial Chamber II cited the Democratic Republic of the Congo for non-cooperation, echoing the above arguments. The Chamber also pointed out that Security Council 1509 (2005), referring the Darfur situation to the ICC, specifically decided that 'the Government of the Sudan...shall cooperate fully with the Court and the Prosecutor pursuant to this resolution', and interpreted the resolution as having indirectly taken away any immunity that Al Bashir might have enjoyed under customary international law and envisaged under article 98 (1) of the Rome Statute.

[63] Principles of International Law Recognized in the Charter of the Nuremberg Tribunal and in the Judgment of the Tribunal (n 17).

[64] Rome Statute (n 4) art 1.

[65] Yuval Shany, *Assessing the Effectiveness of International Courts* (OUP 2014) 243.

apparently qualified the violence as crimes against humanity and of concern to the international community. It was only after the Kenyan government failed to set up those mechanisms that Kofi Annan handed the matter over to the ICC Prosecutor, as had been agreed.[66] With the approval of the Court's Pre-trial Chamber, the Prosecutor initiated the investigation and the subsequent indictment of six prominent Kenyans, including Mr. Kenyatta and Mr. Ruto.[67] ICC action was meant to ensure that those most responsible for the violence would not go unpunished and that the thousands of victims and their survivors would not be denied justice. As Kofi Annan points out,

> There have been active efforts to paint the I.C.C. cases as an assault on Kenya's sovereignty. The supporters of Mr. Kenyatta and his running mate, Mr. Ruto, who won the presidential election earlier this year despite the charges against them, have spoken often of the meddling of 'foreign powers.' But the record is clear and there should be no doubt: it was the Kenyan government's own failure to provide justice to the victims and their survivors that paved the way to the I.C.C., a court of last resort. Nor do these trials reflect the court's unfair targeting of Africa, as has also been alleged. They are the first steps toward a sustainable peace that Kenyans want, deeply, and can only be assured of if Kenya's leaders are not above the law.[68]

Under the Court's Statute,[69] both the accused and a state having jurisdiction can challenge the admissibility of a case before the Court. Accordingly, Kenya could have stopped ICC action if it were able to present 'evidence of a sufficient degree of specificity and probative value that demonstrates that it is indeed investigating the case.'[70] But, alas, as the ICC Appeals Chamber confirmed, Kenya failed to do so; and the trials had to continue. In contrast, in the case of *Prosecutor v. Abdullah Al-Senussi*, Libya, with concrete evidence, was

---

66   Xan Rice, 'Annan hands ICC list of perpetrators of post-election violence in Kenya' (*The Guardian*, 9 July 2009).
67   *Situation in the Republic of Kenya* (Decision Pursuant to Article 15 of the Rome Statute on the Authorization of an Investigation into the Situation in the Republic of Kenya) ICC-01/09 (31 March 2010); Human Rights Watch, 'ICC: Judges Approve Kenyan Investigation' (31 March 2010).
68   Kofi Annan, 'Justice for Kenya' (*The New York Times*, 9 September 2013).
69   Rome Statute (n 4) art 19.
70   *Prosecutor v. Ruto and others*, and *Prosecutor v. Muthaura and others* (Appeals Chamber Judgment) ICC-01/09-02/11 OA (30 August 2011) para 2. See also *Prosecutor v. Katanga and others* (Appeals Chamber Judgment) ICC-01/04-01/07 OA 8 (25 September 2009).

successful in convincing the Pre-Trial Chamber that it was able and willing to exercise jurisdiction over Mr. Al-Senussi and that it was genuinely doing so.[71] In all these cases, as the Appeals Chamber stressed, the Court bases its decisions on facts established by evidence, and not on 'impulse, intuition and conjecture or on mere sympathy or emotion.'[72]

4   Concluding Remarks

This essay has dwelt at length on the ICC. The ICC is a central and prominent component of the international justice system. It is a conspicuous symbol of the rule of law. Like the biblical serpent that Moses hoisted in the desert, the Court serves to give a ray of hope to the millions of victims of heinous crimes world-wide. It also serves to put on notice individuals, particularly those in positions of power, that no one is above the law; and that in The Hague there is a Prosecutor who is monitoring their activities and is vested with power to indict them before that Court should they commit those crimes. This is real deterrence. In my view, the very issuance of a warrant of arrest is a deterrent in itself. The person for whose arrest the warrant is issued becomes selective as to which countries to visit, for fear of arrest. On this point, I should stress how monumentally important it is that the Court's Statute is ratified by a large number, if not all, of the countries of the world. Such universal ratification would blanket the globe with law, and would ensure that no country is a safe haven for perpetrators of heinous crimes.

A view that the ICC is a western imposition, established to hound African states, must be refuted. On the contrary, the Court is a consent-based institution, whose Statute states freely and voluntarily sign.[73] To date, 122 states have done so, 34 of which are African. In fact, African states constitute the single largest bloc in the Assembly of States Parties. By signing the Statute, states

---

71   *Prosecutor v Gaddafi and others* (Decision on the admissibility of the case against Abdullah Al-Senussi) ICC-01/11-01/11 (11 October 2013) para 167. The Pre-Trial Chamber held that it was satisfied that the evidence placed before it 'demonstrates that the Libyan competent authorities are taking concrete and progressive steps directed at ascertaining the criminal responsibility of Mr Al-Senussi for substantially the same conduct as alleged in the proceedings before the Court.'

72   See *Ruto and others* (n 70) para 61, citing *Situation of Uganda* (Appeals Chamber Judgement) ICC-02/04-179 (OA) and ICC-02/04-01/05-371 (OA 2) (23 February 2009) para 36.

73   Dapo Akande, 'The Jurisdiction of the International Criminal Court over Nationals of Non-Parties: Legal Basis and Limits' (2003) JICJ 1, 620–21.

accept the jurisdiction of the Court to try their nationals or any other persons who might commit international crimes on their territory.[74] The only exception here is when the UN Security Council, in exercise of its peace and security powers, refers a situation to the Court; it did so in the cases of Libya and the Sudan.[75] Therefore, given the large number of African States Parties and the fact that most of the situations before the Court to date were referred to it by African states, the Court is clearly not anti-Africa.

Furthermore, the fact that all the situations before the Court to date originate from Africa does not, *per se*, mean that the Court is targeting Africa, as some have persistently charged. No, the Court is targeting impunity, or *banankola ki*, in Africa. It is merely targeting individuals in Africa in their personal capacity. It is acting to ensure that justice is done for the millions of victims in Africa. It would be good were the court able to prosecute perpetrators of heinous crimes in other countries. However, this court's current inability to do so should not mean that it should not prosecute African perpetrators, particularly those referred to it. As the saying goes, the fact that you cannot catch every burglar does not mean that you should not catch the one you can.

In this respect, one finds it paradoxical that some of the most vociferous critics of the Court today are, at the same time, the ones that were most zealous in referring situations or handing their opponents over to the Court for investigation or trial. These critics must be reminded that the Court was not established only for government opponents.[76] The Court was established to try all persons, irrespective of official status, who commit crimes within its mandate. This is what its Statute calls for and what the rule of law demands.

Here, one must note Kofi Annan's most apt observation that '[t]oo often, the individual interests of leaders have been misconstrued as interests of their country.'[77] This observation should serve to warn Africans and others about the veiled motives behind some of the criticisms against the Court; it should also

---

74 'Jurisdiction and Admissibility' (ICC Website) at <http://www.icc-cpi.int/en_menus/icc/about%20the%20court/icc%20at%20a%20glance/Pages/jurisdiction%20and%20admissibility.aspx> accessed 17 April 2014.

75 International Peace Institute, Meeting Note: 'The Relationship between the ICC and the Security Council: Challenges and Opportunities' (March 2013) at <http://www.regierung.li/files/medienarchiv/icc/IPI_E-Pub-Relationship_Bet__ICC_and_SC__2__01.pdf?t=635627301599415400> accessed 17 April 2014.

76 For example: Joseph Kony (Uganda), Bosco Ntaganda (Rwanda), Lubanga Dyilo (DRC), Katanga (DRC), Pierre Bemba and Laurent, (Central African Republic), and Gbagbo and Blé Goudé (Ivory Coast).

77 Kofi Annan, 'Strong and Cohesive societies: the foundations for sustainable peace', Third Annual Desmond Tutu International Peace Lecture, University of the Western Cape

particularly embolden Africans in our support for the Court. Africans have suffered too much and for too long under the rule of strongmen. Africans need to support institutions, such as the ICC, that assure them of the rule of law instead. It is true that proceedings before the Court tend to be costly and protracted. These shortcomings are inherent and inevitable in any international trial of complex mass crimes, involving millions of victims and hundreds of witnesses.[78] Yet even with these shortcomings, the court is indeed 'a beacon of hope for those who seek justice.'[79]

(7 October 2013) para 37, at <http://kofiannanfoundation.org/newsroom/speeches/2013/11/third-annual-desmond-tutu-international-peace-lecture> accessed 17 April 2014.

[78] On this point, Willy Mutunga, the Chief Justice of Kenya opined thus: '[T]]he international justice system [...] has, over the years, focused on power, wealth, impunity and justice for the wretched of the earth, the poor, the victims of violence and injustice. Global citizens have fought long and hard for the ICC to become a reality. That struggle continues. Though the international justice [system] has its limitations, deficits and gaps we cannot throw out the baby with the bath water. We must improve on our international justice system.' *See* Willy Mutunga, 'Wayamo/IPR Meeting on Media and International Justice System' (Strathmore University, Nairobi, 26 November 2012) 1, at http://www.wayamo.com/sites/default/files/pdfs/Willy%20Mutunga.pdf accessed 25 September 2014.

[79] James A Goldston, 'International Justice Must Start at Home' (*The New York Times*, 17 July 2013).

CHAPTER 10

Global Citizenship

Kennedy Graham

> This essay is compiled in honour of Roger Clark: law teacher without peer, raconteur par excellence, mentor, colleague and friend—leading member of the emerging cadre of global citizens.

The idea of global citizenship is as old as political thought. It rests on five millennia of unrealised universalism, qualified by four centuries of dominant nationalism. The contemporary age is witness to the articulation of universalism in human rights within the context of national political thought. How the tension between universalism and individualism will play out through this century is the focus of enquiry here.

A study of 'global citizenship' requires, first, definitional and conceptual clarification. This facilitates an exploration of the philosophical foundations of the concept, including the values underpinning it. As the world changes, so does the socio-psychological dimension of an individual's modern sense of identity and loyalty. Those evolving values and the social psychology of modern life lay the foundation for strengthened juridical concepts relevant to global citizenship which in turn, ultimately, will bestow it a constitutional status with institutional expression.

The structure of this essay reflects the above reasoning, with conclusions derived at the end.

1   Definitional and Conceptual Meaning

The distinction between 'global' and 'international' is at the core of contemporary political thought. Whereas 'international' involves the relations between nation-states on issues of common concern, 'global' involves recognition of a unified human interest in, and responsibility for, issues of universal concern. With international issues there is always a 'we / them' dimension in analytical discourse; with global issues there is always, and only, 'we'. There is also a difference in scale: an international issue may be sub-global; a global issue, by definition, cannot.

'Citizenship' has two meanings:

- the state of being vested with the rights, privileges and duties of a citizen;

- the character of an individual viewed as a member of society, behaviour in terms of the duties, obligations and functions of a citizen.[1]

The distinction is important; a person may exhibit behavioural characteristics independent of whether s/he is of that particular state of being. This is critical because it raises the question whether a person can acquire and exhibit behavioural characteristics pertaining to a state of being which does not actually exist, or at least which is not fully developed.

If, in the second definition, there are two components that are mutually independent, namely, character viewed as a member of society on the one hand and citizen-like behaviour on the other, then a person could indeed exhibit characteristics that are evocative of, but not formally tied to, a state of being.

The issue therefore becomes empirical, rather than theoretical, whether citizenship is confined to the national level or can be seen as applying to the regional or global level—and whether it rests on a community or a society, with or without a polity.

Citizenship at the Regional Level

In the contemporary age, is there such a thing as 'regional citizenship'? Clearly the Africans, Americans and Europeans reside in a specific (regional) locality. All three regional peoples have a common cultural or historical heritage. Asia is so large and heterogeneous that it may not meet any of the necessary characteristics.[2]

Over the past half-century, Europeans have broken from the definitional constraint of a 'citizen' being confined to the nation-state. Through socio-political engineering, they have lifted citizenship to the supra-national level. Serving the European Union ('EU') today is a European Council (the executive branch of ministers from the member states); a European Commission (the bureaucratic body serving the Council); and a European Parliament (the representatives of the peoples of each member nation-state elected on the basis of political philosophy and party affiliation rather than national identity).

Other regional organizations are less developed. The African Union ('AU'), however, is strong and visionary. It has the concept of an 'AU Government' for a 'United States of Africa' actively under consideration.[3] And it leads the world

---

[1] See <http://dictionary.reference.com/browse/citizenship> accessed 4 August 2014.
[2] See Kennedy Graham & Tania Felicio, *Regional Security and Global Governance* (VUB Press 2006) 85–88, 178–89.
[3] Since its 2007 Summit, the African Union ('AU') has had an audit of the idea at head-of-government level, with annual reports.

in one critical dimension: it can decide by majority without veto, at head-of-government level, to intervene militarily in a member state if 'grave circumstances' have occurred (genocide, war crimes, or crimes against humanity).[4] This is not to be found in any other organization—including the United Nations ('UN') at the global level.

It seems clear that peoples within the EU can credibly be seen as European citizens—verified by possession of a passport, payment of taxes, and direct electoral representation. It could be said that the Europeans 'share in government', and that the Africans aspire to do that, while the peoples of the Americas and of Asia do not.

Citizenship at the Global Level

Does the emergence of 'regional citizenship' have implications for 'global citizenship'? In a theoretical sense it does, but the difference in scale is enormous. Is there a global community or a global society; if so does it have political reflection in a global polity?

A 'community' is a social group 'of any size' with three characteristics: its inhabitants reside in a specific locality, they share in government, and they have a common cultural and historical heritage.[5] A 'society' is a community that has evolved certain stronger governmental characteristics.[6]

Humanity has not developed a global polity, notwithstanding the international organizational network that has been built during the 20th century. But it may be said that a 'global community of peoples' exists, though not yet a 'global society'. In this schema, a community is a precondition of a society which is a precondition of a polity.

---

4 Constitutive Act of the African Union, OAU Doc. CAB/LEG/23.15 (adopted 11 July 2000, entered into force 26 May 2001) art 4 h.

5 Community: 1. A social group of any size whose members reside in a specific locality, share government, and often have a common cultural and historical heritage; 2. A locality inhabited by such a group; 3. A social, religious, occupational, or other group sharing common characteristics or interests and perceived or perceiving itself as distinct in some respect from the larger society within which it exists (usually preceded by the): the business community; the community of scholars; 4. A group of associated nations sharing common interests or a common heritage; 5. Ecclesiastical: a group of men or women leading a common life according to a rule.

6 Society: 1. An organized group of persons associated together for religious, benevolent, cultural, scientific, political, patriotic, or other purposes; 2. A body of individuals living as members of a community; 3. The body of human beings generally, associated or viewed as members of a community: the evolution of human society; 4. A highly structured system of human organization for large-scale community living that normally furnishes protection, continuity, security, and a national identity for its members: American society; 5. Such a system characterized by its dominant economic class or form: middle-class society; industrial society.

If a 'citizen' is defined as a member of a polity who owes allegiance to its government and is entitled to its protection, then no global citizen exists because no global polity exists. Indeed, by the standard definition no global polity can exist since the definition is constrained to a state or nation that, by its nature is sub-global (sub-universal).

A person could, however, be a member of a society without being a citizen of that society's non-existent polity. Thus, a person could be a member of an existing 'global society' without necessarily being a citizen of a 'global polity'. So the contemporary definition of a citizen needs to be relaxed if the concept 'global citizenship' is to have meaning.

2 Philosophical Foundations

The philosophical idea of universalism derives from classical notions of natural law—Plato's original conception of the ideal community that was a 'city established on principles of nature'.[7] Greek philosophy drew the distinction between nature, which was immutable and immanent, and law which was changeable and anthropocentric. Socratic and Aristotelian thought viewed natural justice as in accordance with 'right', which laid the basis for natural law that was in accordance with 'nature'.

Stoicism developed an alternative concept of natural law—one that derived from an eternal rational and purposeful order to the universe. The means by which rational beings lived in accordance with this order, through 'virtue', was natural law—reflecting the 'divine spark' within each human.

Roman thought took this a stage further; Cicero taught that law was based on what Nature has given to humanity and which serves to unite it. Whereas positive law was established by government for the stability and safety of society, natural law determined whether such positive law was true and just.[8]

Classical Christianity, culminating in Thomist thought, adopted natural law,[9] thus influencing both English common law and American constitutional jurisprudence, and also Islamic theory.

---

7   Plato, *The Republic* I, Bk. IV 428E, in P Shorey trans. (William Heinemann 1953) 351.
8   '...Nature has implanted in the human race so great a need of virtue and so great a desire to defend the common safety, that the strength thereof has conquered all the allurements of pleasure and ease' in Cicero, *De Republica* Bk 1, sec 1; and De Legibus Bk 1, sec. 16–17, in CW Keyes trans (William Heinemann 1928) 7, 315–33.
9   See Thomas Aquinas, *Summa Theologica*, Bks I-II, questions 90–106 (Benziger Bros 1947).

In the European Enlightenment, liberal natural law derived from a merger of medieval theory and its Hobbesian revision. Grotius based international law on natural law precepts, while Jefferson's inalienable rights underpinned Euro-American thought and, two centuries later, the universal declaration of human rights. Kant's 'perpetual peace' is based on two conditions: a world-wide set of constitutional republics and international organization.

More recently, Habermas explored the notion of a political constitution for a pluralist world society.[10] In contemporary thought, 'new natural law' theory as developed by Finnis focuses on 'basic human goods' such as human life, knowledge and aesthetic experience, all of which are self-evidently and intrinsically worthwhile.[11]

These tensions between natural law and positive law continue to play a key role in the development of international law.

Global Values

Natural law rests on the notion of what is eternally good for humanity, comprising intrinsic truths discoverable through divine revelation or secular reasoning. This presupposes a set of eternal values which philosophy and political theory seek to identify.

In classical theory, from Greco-Roman to Islamic and Christian doctrine, these have reflected an appreciation of the civic 'virtues'—honesty, humility, piety, charity, courage. Eastern theory, from Taoism, Confucianism and Hinduism to Buddhism, has developed complementary values of sincerity, courtesy, and harmony.

These traditional values have never been repudiated. They have, however, become supplemented in the modern age by an aspirational set of secular values designed to unite societies and underwrite the obligations and rights of their citizens. The bifurcation of universal rights through Cold War ideology into separate political and economic contexts slowed progress in modernising the concept of global citizenship.

With the end of the Cold War, the 'end of history' was announced through the proclaimed triumph of Western liberalism.[12] An alternative prognosis was advanced in the 'clash of civilizations' thesis.[13] The UN itself explored these

---

10 Jürgen Habermas, 'A Political Constitution for a Pluralist World Society' (2007) 34(3) J Chinese Philos 331.
11 John Finnis, *Natural Law and Natural Rights* (Clarendon Law Series 2nd ed. 2011).
12 Francis Fukuyama, 'The End of History?' (1989) National Interest 3; Francis Fukuyama, *The End of History and the Last Man* (Free Press 1992).
13 Samuel Huntingdon, *The Clash of Civilizations* (Simon Schuster 1996).

issues in the post-Cold War period with an Iranian-inspired project on a 'dialogue among civilizations' followed by a regional project led by Spain and Turkey on an 'alliance of civilizations'.

The first formal statement of a set of global values was made by the UN General Assembly in the Millennium Declaration.[14] The updated version of 2005 remains the current version, with seven values identified: freedom, equality, solidarity, tolerance, respect for all human rights, respect for nature, and shared responsibility.[15]

These values are rudimentary, scarcely sufficient to inspire any real global patriotism. But they are the first formal articulation of global human values. And they thus provide the prototype set of values that can underpin the development of global citizenship.

3   The Socio-Psychological Dimension

The individual commitment to global citizenship is sourced not in philosophical thought but rather the practical aspects of daily life. Indeed, it is only the socio-psychological dimension of human life that can sustain the more abstract levels of thought. These consist of a sense of belonging and affection, a rallying cry for action. This requires a number of things: a founding narrative; a set of symbols; an oath of loyalty; an educational curriculum; and political leadership as an embodiment of the concept.

Narratives

There is no global narrative as yet; at least one that is depicted as such.

Notions of identity and thus loyalty are intimately related to narratives with deep historical roots. The ancient epics or spiritual sources—the Vedas, the Tao and I-Ching, Gilgamesh and Shahnameh, Ramayana and Mahabharata, the Iliad and Odyssey, the Torah and the Edda—all give rise to a binding cultural affiliation, with active political loyalty as the derivative.

Is there anything comparable for humanity as a whole? It is possible that a global narrative is emerging. It takes the form of space-borne imagery of planet Earth, together with modern insights into the place of human life in the Cosmos. The Apollo 8 photographs of the 1960s instantaneously became iconic images for the first generation of fledging global citizens. The newly-acquired self-image of our planet and the developing saga of human stewardship in the

---

14   'Millennium Declaration', UNGA Res 55/2, 8 September 2000.
15   '2005 World Summit Outcome' (24 October 2005) UNGA Res A/RES/60/1, para 4.

Anthropocene, are fertilising something new. The weaving of a single fabric of human thought—with a coherent relationship between early mythology, traditional religion and modern science—is perhaps the key to forming such a narrative.

The global narrative may take a different twist as well. The interaction between science, modern technology and the ecological crisis may see humans undertaking action in ways difficult to perceive even today. Issues of cloning, species self-determination through the genome project, and the unpredictability of artificial intelligence may prompt humans to act in a transnational manner that challenges traditional precepts of international law. Such actions may be accompanied, for self-justification, by claims of global citizenship—not necessarily reflective of the global public good.

Symbols

If the notion of 'global citizenship' cannot yet be expressed in legal manner, it nonetheless can be used as a symbol of identity and of loyalty, such as flags, passports and anthems.

The concept of 'global citizenship' evokes sentiments of identity and loyalty. Identity is critical. The central square of Bruges in Belgium, lined with exquisite 17th-century architecture, exhibits a 21st-century notion of identity. Above the municipal building fly five flags together: the Bruges flag for the town; the West Flanders flag for the province; the Flanders flag for the Belgian region, the Belgium flag for the nation-state; and the EU flag for Europe. It is significant, and evocative of our stage of progression, that a sixth, the UN flag, is missing.

Passport ownership is of similar significance. The passport is a symbol of citizen identity. The Europeans now carry a European passport, with the name of the member state below the governing title.

Most people recognise the national anthems of most major countries as well as one's own. Anthems have a powerful effect on the human psyche—reinforcing the tug of nationalism. On its 25th anniversary, a 'Hymn to the UN' was produced on the request of the Secretary-General. Unofficial and uninspiring, it remains virtually unknown. In 2013, India proposed to UNESCO that it undertake a project to develop an Earth Anthem, but the agency declined on grounds of cost constraint. An Indian poet-diplomat wrote one but it too remains unknown.

Oaths

Buttressed with flags and passports, we take oaths of loyalty as citizens. New citizens swear an oath to the head of state in a ceremony rich with symbolism, recognising the national 'sovereign' and being prepared, at least theoretically, to die for their new country. Native-born citizens are assumed to carry that commitment from birth; unlike some religious institutions which thoughtfully require an elective confirmation upon a certain age.

If the same individual becomes an international civil servant at the United Nations, s/he effectively repudiates a certain level of that loyalty. A UN official swears not to take instructions from any country, including one's own. The UN official has effectively withheld national loyalty from one's own country.[16]

The notion of loyalty can be taken a step further. Under the notion of global citizenship, an individual whose self-perception is that of a 'global citizen' may adopt the same position as a UN official—as if s/he had sworn the same UN oath of loyalty. If s/he believes the government's policy and actions threaten broader interests, s/he may take a stance of civil disobedience. The individual may end up charged under domestic law, but the prescriptive stance is politically authentic.

These considerations are not new. Conscientious objection against military conscription caused particular angst in World War I. Today many activists risk legal action in protest against a number of 'global issues'—nuclear weapons, environmental destruction, intrusive espionage. But the legal defence is changing—no longer moral-religious exemption from secular military authority, but secular legal argumentation in the name of a higher political authority.

The associated test of loyalty is a readiness to sacrifice one's life for a cause or an entity. In the 20th-century, the dominant question in this respect for the national citizen was: 'Will I die for my country?' In the course of the 21st century, the question may well become: 'Will I die for humanity?'

UN peacekeepers already risk their lives for humanity. But the fact that they are soldiers from the armed forces of a UN member state raises ambiguities. They are prepared, by virtue of their role, to risk their lives, but for whom? They accept the orders of their immediate commanding officer who will usually be from the same country.

Their national contingents, however, operate under the overall command of a senior military officer from another country. They have sworn an oath of loyalty—to the UN. But who decided when Belgian troops would withdraw to barracks in Rwanda in the face of genocide? Was it the UN commander? That is unlikely—he was striving to protect the vulnerable people. Essentially the Belgian troop leader took orders direct from Brussels, not from the UN Secretariat or UN commander. If and when the day comes that UN soldiers are

---

16   Kennedy Graham, 'National Loyalty and the Global Interest' (blogpost, 21 December 2011) <https://home.greens.org.nz/node/27675> accessed 8 August 2014.

recruited as UN soldiers, with no attachment to their nation-state (just as with UN officials), problems of divided loyalty will diminish.

Curricula

Global citizenship education is a vibrant part of the curriculum today. Some see it as difficult to operationalize; unclear whether the very notion of 'global citizenship' is a metaphor or an oxymoron.[17]

The notion of 'global citizenship' has recently gained prominence in development discourse with the UN's Global Education First Initiative (2012).[18] Among the three priority areas outlined in the Initiative, the third aims to foster 'global citizenship'.

The civil society is the more advanced in terms of global citizenship than perhaps any other dimension of societal life. It includes the following:

- Cosmopolitan identity: Individuals identify with one another in a manner that transcends their national loyalties.
- Political movement: The World Federalist Movement proposed the idea of world government since the time of the League of Nations in the early 20th century. Its international counterpart is the World Federation of UN Associations, whose national branches are devoted to strengthening rather than replacing the UN.
- Religious movements: The spiritual and religious underpinning of global citizenship remains strong. Indeed the first global gathering—the 'Parliament of the World's Religions'—was convened in 1893. Baha'ai is a faith-based religious movement that puts global unity as its first defining tenet. Humanity's Team is an international spiritual movement whose purpose is to communicate the 'timeless truth that we are all One, with God and life'.
- Research institutes: Many of the modern research institutes are based on the idea of a unified world.[19] At the national level, think-tanks are

---

17   Lynn Davies, 'Global Citizenship: Abstraction or Framework for Action?' (2006) 58(1) Educational Review 5.
18   Sobhi Tawil, Education for 'Global Citizenship' (August 2013) UNESCO Working Paper 07.
19   The Earth Policy Institute produces regular analyses of global challenges and offers prescriptive solutions. The Ecological Footprint Network produces penetrating analyses of the global economy's ecological overshoot. The Stockholm Resilience Centre has developed the concept of the planetary boundaries and a 'safe operating space for humanity'. The Global Institute for the Prevention of Aggression works to ensure that aggression becomes a leadership crime in international law.

designed to encourage national establishments to have regard for the higher global interest.[20]

Leadership

National political leaders are not global citizens in a formal sense. The charismatic figures of recent times always remained national leaders. They may have attained world-wide stature and influence but that is not to be mistaken for global leadership, for they are not formally speaking on behalf of all the world's peoples.

The UN Secretary-General is the closest official embodiment of a global leader.[21] Yet, with the exceptions of Dag Hammarskjöld and Kofi Annan, no UN leader has exhibited the charisma and courage to be effective in that capacity. The selection process is fashioned by the major powers to prevent this.[22] The Secretary-General is seen as an international civil 'servant'—the 'world's top diplomat', but without political rank. This is far removed from Roosevelt's notion of a 'World Moderator' with political powers heading the UN.

4   Juridical Concepts

Juridical thought of the 20th century has laid down a basis for global citizenship. This takes three forms: declaratory treaty pronouncements pertaining to human proprietorship and custodianship; individual human rights and responsibilities; and individual criminal liability.

Human Proprietorship

Universalism was embraced in juridical thought through the 20th century in assertive ways.[23] Even more progressive are the concepts spawned by the inde-

---

20   An example is the New Zealand Centre for Global Studies, see <www.nzcgs.org> accessed 9 October 2014.
21   See *To Speak for the World: Speeches & Statements by Dag Hammarskjöld* (Atlantis 2005).
22   Brian Urquhart, *A World in Need of Leadership: Tomorrow's United Nations* (Ford Foundation 1990).
23   The Antarctic Treaty (1959) recognised that 'it is in the interest of all mankind that Antarctica shall continue for ever to be used exclusively for peaceful purposes and shall not become the scene or object of international discord; the continent a demilitarized zone in the interests of mankind'. The NPT (1968) considered 'the devastation that would be visited upon all mankind by a nuclear war and the consequent need to make every effort to avert the danger of such a war and to take measures to safeguard the security of

pendent commissions that are often called for by, and which report to, the UN Secretary-General.[24] These provide the fertile field of conceptual change from which UN member states may develop declaratory pronouncements that, in turn, become binding obligations in due course. 'Global citizens' tend to be the first to embrace such conceptual change and give it political oxygen, through academic scrutiny and civil activism.

Individual Human Rights

Probably the most potent expression of 'global citizenship' is found in the development of universal human rights over the past century.

- The self-determination of peoples, first captured in the League's Covenant of 1919 and fleshed out in the UN Charter;
- The possession of universal human rights by the individual in the Universal Declaration (with binding force in the two covenants), given an unexpected sharp edge through the empowerment to lodge a complaint against one's own national government for breaches;
- The right of the citizen of a nation-state to protection by the international community (through the UN Security Council) if one's own government has proved unable or unwilling to meet its primary responsibility in that regard. The 'Responsibility to Protect' doctrine, adopted by the UN General Assembly in resolution 60/1 of 2005.[25]

---

peoples'. The UN Outer Space Treaty (1967), recognizing the common interest of all mankind in the progress of the exploration and use of outer space for peaceful purposes, declared that the exploration and use of outer space, including the moon and other celestial bodies, shall be carried out for the benefit and in the interests of all countries, irrespective of their degree of economic or scientific development, and shall be the province of all mankind. The UN Framework Convention on Climate Change (1992) acknowledged that 'change in the Earth's climate and its adverse effects are a common concern of humankind.'

24 The principal examples are the reports on 'common security' (Palme, 1982); sustainable development (Brundtland, 1987); 'responsibility to protect' civilians (Evans-Sahnoun, 2001); and 'global governance' (Carlsson-Ramphal, 2005).

25 The R2P concept has been described by a leading international lawyer as '...the most important shift in our conception of sovereignty since the Treaty of Westphalia in 1648. It is the foundation of an international order that recognizes the rights and responsibilities of individuals as well as states', Anne-Marie Slaughter, Comments on Richard H Cooper & Juliette Voinov Kohler (eds), *Responsibility To Protect: The Global Moral Compact for the 21st Century* (Macmillan-Palgrave 2009) at <http://www.palgrave.com/page/detail/Responsibility-to-Protect/?K=9780230618404> accessed 4 August 2014.

These rights give unprecedented strength to self-identity and civic action by a 'global citizen'. Many individuals avail themselves of it.

Individual Criminal Liability

The progression towards global citizenship took a giant step in the form of the International Criminal Court ('ICC') whose jurisdiction commenced in July 2002.

The ICC is the culmination of a century of effort since World War I and the charges against Kaiser Wilhelm as an individual of crimes against peace (in fact never pursued), the Nuremburg/Tokyo war crimes trials of the 1940s, and specific war crimes tribunals for Rwanda and former Yugoslavia of the 1990s.

The Rome Statute of the ICC deals with individuals under criminal charges. Three crimes are justiciable—genocide, war crimes and crimes against humanity. Proceedings against nine individuals have been completed; one has been convicted, four charges have been dismissed and one withdrawn, while three have died before trial. A fourth crime, also in the Rome Statute, is of a different order. The crime of aggression applies to political and military leaders, and is likely to become justiciable within the decade.

The critical difference between the International Court of Justice ('ICJ'), which adjudicates between disputant states, and the ICC which judges individuals under international criminal law, will lend strength to 'global citizens' to hold their compatriots to account. Indeed, the assertion of universal jurisdiction over certain crimes towards all independent of state ratification of treaties takes that empowerment beyond a national to a global reach. As the Rome Statute puts it: 'Individual criminal responsibility: 1. The Court shall have jurisdiction over natural persons pursuant to this Statute; 2. A person who commits a crime within the jurisdiction of the Court shall be individually responsible and liable for punishment in accordance with this Statute.'[26]

With a touch of irony, individuals charged under the ICC are the first real global citizens.

5 Global Constitutionalism

These juridical concepts have laid the basis for the idea of global constitutionalism—the most profound expression of global citizenship. The distinction between a world of citizens belonging to nations that cooperate under a

---

26 Rome Statute of the International Criminal Court (adopted 17 July 1998, entered into force 1 July 2002) 2187 UNTS 90, art 25.

charter and a world of global citizens who have united under a global constitution is profound. The progression, if there is to be one, can be evolutionary or revolutionary. The evolutionary approach has been described in similar terms by two of the 20th century's two most insightful thinkers on the subject—Dag Hammarskjöld and Phillip Allott.

Hammarskjöld identified stages of human thought in what he saw as a natural progression from the national to the global. He identified three aspects of that progression.

First, the UN Organization is to be seen as a dynamic organization, with the inherent capacity to adapt and transform in response to the continuous process of global societal transition.

> [I]nternational constitutional law is still in an embryonic stage; we are still in the transition between institutional systems of international coexistence and constitutional systems of international co-operation. It is natural that, at such a stage of transition, theory is still vague.... Those who advocate world government, and this or that special form of world federalism, often present challenging theories and ideas, but we, like our ancestors, can only press against the receding wall which hides the future.[27]

Secondly, the Charter should be treated as a teleological instrument, containing implied powers to facilitate and legitimise a constitutional framework.

> ...the United Nations is an experimental operation on one of the lines along which men at present push forward in the direction of higher forms of an international society. It is obvious that we cannot regard the line of approach represented by the United Nations as intrinsically more valuable than other lines, in spite of the fact that, through its universality, it lies closer to, or points more directly towards, the ideal of a true constitutional framework for world-wide international co-operation [...] the United Nations is an effort just as necessary as other experiments, and nothing short of the pursuit of this specific experiment with all our ability, all our energy and all our dedication, can be defended. In fact, the

---

27   Dag Hammarskjöld, 'The development of a Constitutional Framework for International Cooperation': address at University of Chicago, 1 May 1960, in 'To Speak for the World: Speeches and Statements of Dag Hammarskjöld', Ed. Kai Falkman (Atlantis; Stockholm, 2005) 160, 164. See also Manuel Fröhlich, 'The Quest for a Political Philosophy of World Organization', in Sten Ask & Anna Mark-Jungkvist, *The Adventure of Peace: Dag Hammarskjöld and the Future of the United Nations* (Palgrave Macmillan 2006) 130–45.

> effort seems already to have been carried so far that we have conquered essential new ground for our work for the future. This would remain true in all circumstances and even if political complications were one day to force us to a wholly new start.[28]

Thirdly, there was a need to place this in the context of humanity's 'evolving self-consciousness' as a species, in which the UN was the lead agent.

> The United Nations is an organic creation of the political situation facing our generation. At the same time, however, the international community has, so to say, come to political self-consciousness in the Organization and, therefore, can use it in a meaningful way in order to influence those very circumstances of which the Organization is a creation.[29]
>
> And:
>
> The United Nations is a positive response by the world community to the fundamental needs of our time.... Its efforts are significant insofar as they show the growing maturity of the Organization as an instrument by means of which the nations can solve conflicts threatening the natural evolution of the world community.[30]

Taking this thought further three decades after Hammarskjöld, Allott speaks of the 'self-constituting of international society'—an international community into a global community.

> It may be that the hallowed diplomatic concept of 'international security' is changing into something much more like the ancient and hallowed constitutional concept of the 'public order', so that a collapse of internal constitutional order or a massive abuse of constitutional power within a state may come to be seen as a threat to international public order, which international society, and hence international law, cannot ignore.... Central to this challenge is the question whether we can see signs of an

---

28 See <http://www.un.org/depts/dhl/dag/docs/chicagospeech.pdf> accessed 9 October 2014.

29 Secretary-General's Introduction to the Annual Report of the United Nations, 1960, in Manuel Fröhlich, *Political Ethics and the United Nations: Dag Hammarskjöld as Secretary-General* (Routledge 2008) 37.

30 Secretary-General's Introduction to the Annual Report of the United Nations, 1953, in Manuel Fröhlich, *Political Ethics and the United Nations: Dag Hammarskjöld as Secretary-General* (Routledge 2008) 27.

emerging public mind of international society, since it is in the public mind of society that a society stores its ideas about itself and its high values, and in which a permanent struggle about its ideas and values is enacted. The hypothesis proposed in Eunomia suggests that a society constitutes itself, not only on the form of law and legal institutions and not only in the real world struggles, political and economic and personal in everyday life, but also in society's struggle about ideas. The self-constituting of the international society of the 21st century will be no different.[31]

The constitutional dimension of global thinking is even more recently reflected in the 2005 work of Macdonald and Johnston:

> [I]t now appears that the purposes and principles of the UN Charter are no longer being served sufficiently in light of new concerns… [I]t seems timely to reconsider the case for strengthening the constitutional framework of norms and institutions that seemed to offer the promise of fulfilment in the second half of the 20th century […] The depiction of the organized world community as a 'constitutional order' goes far beyond the present reality of the UN and its Charter. Yet certain specialized areas of international law have been developed systematically to the point of having permanent global mechanisms with rule-making, executive, administrative and judicial roles.[32]

This school of thought, derived from Wilsonian doctrine of the early-20th century, lays the constitutional basis for 'global citizenship', not only enjoying full rights and responsibilities but their juridical and institutional expression.

6 Institutional Structures

With the constitutional basis thus contested between national legal sovereignty and global normative aspiration, contemporary international institutions struggle for identity and efficacy.

The UN Charter is seen as a 'quasi-constitution' for governing relations among sovereign and equal nation-states towards 'common ends'. The Organization, as the institutional dimension, has 193 member states.

---

31 Philip Allot, *Eunomia: New Order for a New World* (OUP 2001) xvi, xx.
32 Ronald St John Macdonald & Douglas Johnston, *Towards World Constitutionalism: Issues in the Legal Ordering of the World Community* (Martinus Nijhof 2005) xiii–xviii.

Whereas the League of Nations Covenant opened with 'we the High Representatives' of each government, the UN Charter opens with the phrase 'We the peoples of the United Nations'. The difference is critical. In the Charter, the peoples of each nation-state delegate the powers and responsibilities in the Charter to their respective governments. So in a philosophical sense, the peoples of the world control the United Nations.

It follows that, were they disposed to do so, they could amend it. Does this make them 'global citizens'? In seeking to amend the United Nations, they would need to act through the governments to which they gave delegated authority to act in their names. Governments will not act unless they have a clear and compelling mandate.

It is in this cauldron of contested opinion that governments search for insightful policy at the international organizations—both the UN and Bretton Woods systems.

One largely unnoticed opportunity exists for progress in 'individualising' formal international relations. The UN Charter, at article 28(b), provides that member states can be represented at the Security Council by official representatives 'or by other individuals'.

Electoral Representation

The European Parliament is the second largest parliament in the world, with almost 800 members representing about 400 million voters. Based on direct universal suffrage since 1979, it shares equal legislative and budgetary powers with the Council which is composed of the ministers of the member states.

The distinctive feature of the European Parliament is that MEPs sit according to political party and not according to nation-state. This contrasts with the Inter-Parliamentary Union at the global level. There, members of national parliaments sit behind national name-plates, irrespective of political party persuasion. The difference depicts the vast distinction between 'citizenship' at the regional and the global levels.

Political Expression

So long as the nation-state remains the central institutional expression of citizenship, global citizens search for ways of facilitating the progression to the global level. One new concept serves usefully for the purpose. The 'planetary interest' has been defined as 'The interests of the planet, comprising: (1) the survival and viability of humanity, contingent on maintenance of the physical integrity of Earth and the protection of its ecological systems and biosphere from major anthropogenic change; and (2) the universal improvement in the human condition in terms of basic human needs and fundamental human rights'.[33]

From this definition, three propositions are advanced:

1. That the 'planetary interest' is the valid criterion for official policy on any issue that is genuinely a global problem.
2. That, once the planetary interest is identified, the 'legitimate national interest' of all countries fit harmoniously within the global solution to the problem.
3. That 'legitimate global power' can be developed and applied on behalf of all peoples of the world, in cases where a global problem requires a global solution.

The concepts of 'legitimate global power' and the 'legitimate national interest', developed for the 21st century, compare with the traditional notion of a competitive national interest that marked 20th-century diplomacy in trade and military relations. Through the use of these concepts the way is free for a 'global citizen' to judge whether a government is pursuing a 'legitimate national interest' on a particular issue.

7 Conclusions

Global citizenship is, in essence, the philosophical-political foundation of future global governance of an indeterminate kind. It will not fashion the nature of that governance system, nor will it manage it. It will be, in the first instance, a precondition of the emergence of the system. It will then act as the continuing legitimation of that system.

Global citizenship in the early-21st century is a state of being. It can exist prior to the system of global governance that reflects it; indeed it must precede it to act as a precondition. It is the individual expression of the evolution of human thought, sourced in the notion of universalism embraced by the ancients, strengthened over the centuries through religious and secular enquiry, gathering pace in the globalising world of modern technology and telecommunication. What is unknown is whether the process of globalisation succumbs to ideological tension—between a corporate-dominated or a political-dominated world.

---

[33] Kennedy Graham (ed), *The Planetary Interest* (UCL Press 1999) 7.

An individual today, in the early 21st century, can genuinely claim to be a global citizen, in the sense that s/he perceives oneself to carry values and convictions—principles of conduct—that have primary claim to the planet and humanity. This is an informal psychological state of being. It can coexist with the formal, political, national citizenship. In the abstract they are not incompatible.

The dilemma for today's prototype 'global citizen' arises when the actions of one's government on the world stage conflicts with one's individual convictions as a global citizen. In such instances, the dilemma concerns one's loyalty in terms of publicly-articulated political prescription. Does a 'global citizen' condemn, and dissociate oneself from, the government's actions and refuse to obey them, if the issue is sufficiently critical? If so, then one's loyalty to informal global citizenship overrides one's formal loyalty to national citizenship.

The following propositions are advanced, by way of conclusion:

1. Global citizenship is politically necessary; otherwise, nation-states will forever remain divided, competitive and antagonistic in an age of globally-destructive technology.
2. A global community exists, comprised of a mosaic of nation-states, ethnic peoples, private sector and civil society.
3. A global society is emerging from that community, associated with a strengthening of the notion of 'global citizenship'.
4. A 'global polity' does not yet exist, in the form of global government; but today's 'global citizenship' provides the foundation for global governance to strengthen towards that, as yet indefinable, end-state.

CHAPTER 11

From Dr Strangelove to Dr Suess: Contributions of Professor Roger Clark on the Legal Norm against Nuclear Weapons

Alyn Ware

> 'The destructive power of nuclear weapons cannot be contained in either space or time. They have the potential to destroy all civilization and the entire ecosystem of the planet.'
> International Court of Justice, 1996[1]

On 1 March 2013, New York Law School held a conference on *Exploring Civil Society through the Writings of Dr Seuss.* The conference examined aspects of civil society reflected in a selection of books by Theodor Seuss Geisel,[2] including tolerance, punishment, equality, war, civil and human rights, land use and property rights, and corporate responsibility. One of the sessions discussed *The Butter Battle Book,* a picture book published by Geisel in 1984 in response to U.S. President Ronald Reagan's escalation of the nuclear arms race with the Soviet Union, a policy that he characterized as evincing 'deadly stupidity.'[3]

The story revolves around two peoples—the Yooks and the Zooks—who have fundamentally different ways of spreading butter on bread and eating it (an analogy about different economic and political systems). They perceive their neighbours' system as unacceptable and threatening their moral and political order. In response they build a wall between their societies which they guard with increasingly destructive weapons until they both have a 'Big Boy Boomeroo' which could destroy everyone.[4]

Professor Roger Clark, a New Zealand-born Professor of International Law at Rutgers School of Law, gave a presentation on *The Butter Battle Book* and

---

[1] *Legality of the Threat or Use of Nuclear Weapons* (Advisory Opinion) 1996, at <http://www.icjcij.org/docket/files/95/7495.pdf> accessed 14 January 2015, para 35.
[2] Dr Seuss is the pen-name for Theodor Seuss Geisel, a popular children's picture book author.
[3] John Hursh, 'International Law, Armed Conflict, and the Construction of Otherness: A Critical Reading of Dr Seuss's *The Butter Battle Book* and a Renewed Call for Global Citizenship' (2013–2014) 58 NY L Sch LR 618.
[4] Dr Seuss, *The Butter Battle Book* (Random House 1984).

international law with respect to nuclear weapons.[5] Clark recognises that *The Butter Battle Book* does not mention international law in the storyline. However, the issues it raises give clarity to the application of international law to nuclear weapons—a key political issue which impacts on the survival of humanity. As Clark says,

> Surely the law, which seems to deal fairly effectively with such mundane issues as defective widgets and the like, can be brought to bear on weapons of mass destruction...it [the book] is surely an invitation to imagine how law might be used to get out of such situations....[6]

Clark then evokes aspects of *The Butter Battle Book* to analyse political and legal dimensions of nuclear deterrence. Clark argues that the moral and philosophical opposition to nuclear weapons depicted in *The Butter Battle Book* finds support in international law, particularly international humanitarian law, as affirmed by the International Court of Justice in its 1996 Advisory Opinion.[7] Accordingly, nuclear weapons should be banned and eliminated.

However, like in *The Butter Battle Book*, the power of politics and the promotion of 'fear of the other' have so far prevented this. Indeed, *The Butter Battle Book* bears some similarities to the Dr Strangelove complex depicted by Peter Sellers in the movie '*Dr Strangelove or: How I Learned to Stop Worrying and Love the Bomb*,'[8] which depicts a combination of nuclear deterrence postures, political suspicions and misplaced faith in the bomb, leading to the inadvertent but inevitable destruction of the world.

---

5 Roger S. Clark, 'Is the Butter Battle Book's Bitsy Big-Boy Boomeroo Banned? What Has International Law to Say About Weapons of Mass Destruction?' (2013–2014) 58 NY L Sh LR 655. By coincidence, one year after *The Butter Battle Book* was published, a real Butter Battle over nuclear weapons policies occurred between the US and New Zealand instigated by Ronald Reagan. In an effort to pressure New Zealand to reverse its decision in 1984 to ban all nuclear-armed ships from port visits, 'President Reagan placed a moratorium on trade deals with New Zealand just as representatives of the New Zealand Dairy Board (which markets butter and cheese) were in Washington': at 665 note 43. The Dairy Board representatives returned to New Zealand empty-handed (no trade deals) and somewhat red-faced. However, the moratorium was short-lived: 'Sympathetic women's organizations in the United States participated in a 'girlcott' campaign,' which prevented US Congress ratification of the US administration's boycott and resulted in doubling of New Zealand dairy sales to the US over the following five years: at 665–6 note 43.
6 Clark, 'Is the Butter Battle Book's Bitsy Big-Boy Boomeroo Banned? What Has International Law to Say About Weapons of Mass Destruction?' (n 5) 657.
7 See n 1.
8 Stanley Kubrick (dir) (Columbia Pictures 1964).

Legal scholars might wince at the notion that complex legal questions can be considered in terms of simple morals or principles able to be depicted in children's picture books or Hollywood movies. However, Christopher Weeramantry, former Vice-President of the International Court of Justice, and John Burroughs note that

> The principles underlying international law are based upon universally accepted values and moral standards. They can be understood by every schoolchild. When children are informed about them their eyes light up with appreciation that the international world is governed by principles which are so acceptable to them. International law represents the essence of the progress of civilization towards a world ruled by law rather than a world ruled by force.[9]

Weeramantry and Burroughs also note that the illegality of nuclear weapons under international law is obvious and easily understandable by lawyer and non-lawyer alike. The threat or use of nuclear weapons would violate general principles of humanity enshrined in international humanitarian law, including the prohibitions in wartime against causing unnecessary suffering, indiscriminate harm (impact on non-combatants), disproportionate harm, damage to neutral states and long-term damage to the environment. 'The jus in bello covers all uses of force. There can be no exceptions without violating the essence of its principles.'[10]

Weeramantry notes that nuclear weapons are also in violation of religious and ethical principles which provide a strong underpinning for international law:

> Support of the nuclear bomb with its potential to destroy all civilizations and all the values we cherish, is a gross betrayal of the basic teachings of every religion. Every one of them is categorically opposed to the use of weapons that cause cruel and unnecessary suffering. No government in the world can afford to be guilty of this fundamental breach of the teachings to which the bulk of its people are committed.[11]

---

9   Christopher G Weeramantry & John Burroughs, *International Law and Peace* (Hague Appeal for Peace 1999), at <http://www.haguepeace.org/files/morePeaceLessons/International%20Law%20and%20Peace%20%28Weeramantry%20Sri%20Lanka%20and%20Buroughts%20USA%29.pdf > accessed 20 January 2015.

10 *Legality of the Threat or Use of Nuclear Weapons* (Dissenting Opinion of Judge Weeramantry) 1996, at <http://www.icj-cij.org/docket/files/95/7521.pdf> accessed 14 January 2015, 513.

11 Christopher Weeramantry, 'The Time to Act is Now' *Securing a Nuclear Weapon-Free World Today: Our Responsibility to Future Generations*, Booklet for the 2010 Review Conference of the Parties to the Treaty on the Non-Proliferation of Nuclear Weapons 3–28 May 2010 (World Future Council 2010) 13, 13.

However, the implementation of this norm clashes with the politics of power and money. The most powerful countries in the United Nations system are the five permanent members of the Security Council, each of which has the power of veto over any Security Council decision—a power held only by these five. These are the same five countries recognised under the Nuclear Non-Proliferation Treaty ('NPT') to be 'Nuclear Weapon States.' They are also the only ones always to have a judge from their country sitting on the International Court of Justice. Their arguments for the nuclear status quo are supported by strong corporate interests.[12]

Upholding and advancing the law against nuclear weapons in this context requires a mix of sound legal argument, political nuance and clarity of communication to cut through the legal obfuscation used to defend the bomb.

Commander Robert Green notes that in the fable *The Emperor's New Clothes*, it was a boy, unburdened by authoritarian dictates on what he should think, who thus saw clearly the simple reality and challenged the power of the ruler who had been hoodwinked by the greedy weavers. Green notes that such clarity of perception and thinking is required to cut through the doctrine of nuclear deterrence which has been advanced by the powerful nuclear States as a doctrine that should be accepted without question.[13]

Professor Roger Clark has made considerable contributions to the debate on nuclear weapons and the law, which indeed cut through the nuclear deterrence priesthood with a clarity of thinking supported by considerable legal expertise. His writings and classes have done much to educate law students and other law scholars. Moreover, Clark has been incredibly effective in bringing this clear legal thinking into key legal, diplomatic and political processes which have had considerable impact on the development and implementation of international law and the norm against nuclear weapons.

This includes, *inter alia*, participation in the *Nuclear Tests* Cases before the International Court of Justice, the International Court of Justice *Advisory Opinion on the Legality of the Threat or Use of Nuclear Weapons*, advancing the criminality of nuclear weapons in the negotiations of the Statute for the International Criminal Court ('ICC'), participation in the drafting of a Model

---

12   Nuclear weapons production is a multi-billion dollar industry with over US$100 billion spent annually by the nine nuclear-armed States, most of this going to a small number of corporations. See 'Dirty Dozen: corporate partners in mass destruction' (*Reaching Critical Will*), at <http://www.reachingcriticalwill.org/resources/publications-and-research/research-projects/6202-dirty-dozen-corporate-partners-in-mass-destruction> accessed 15 January 2015.

13   Robert Green, *The Naked Nuclear Emperor: Debunking Nuclear Deterrence* (Disarmament & Security Centre 2000); see also Robert Green, *Security Without Nuclear Deterrence* (Disarmament & Security Centre 2010).

Nuclear Weapons Convention circulated by the UN Secretary-General as a guide to nuclear disarmament negotiations, and serving on the legal team for the case lodged by the Marshall Islands in the International Court of Justice against the nuclear-armed States.

1   Nuclear Tests Cases

In 1962, France announced that it would commence nuclear tests, i.e. nuclear weapons detonations, in French Polynesia, a group of islands in the Pacific under French control. By this time, the devastating health and environmental impact of French tests in Algeria and the US nuclear tests in the Marshall Islands was coming to light. As such, the announcement was greeted with considerable concern in the Pacific.

In 1964 and 1965, a group of young university students and lawyers, including Roger Clark, petitioned the New Zealand government to contest the legality of impending French nuclear tests in the International Court of Justice ('ICJ'). They argued that New Zealand would have a case against France on a number of grounds: (a) that the transborder impact of the radiation released by the tests infringes on the sovereignty of other countries in the Pacific including New Zealand, (b) that the closure by France of sections of the high seas during the tests was in violation of the right of freedom of the high seas; and (c) the Partial Test Ban Treaty prohibiting atmospheric tests had achieved customary status even though France had not yet signed or ratified it.

Keith Holyoake, the Foreign Minister of the Conservative New Zealand government of the time, replied that this was 'one of the dumbest, stupidest ideas he had ever heard.'[14] However, as the French nuclear tests continued and opposition to them grew, the incoming Labour government of 1972 took a different view and initiated proceedings in the ICJ against France, in conjunction with a similar case lodged by Australia. During the proceedings France announced that it would end its atmospheric nuclear tests (shifting them underground) thus resulting the in the case being dropped.[15]

In 1995, New Zealand petitioned the ICJ to re-examine the case on the basis of the French underground testing program. The Court declined to take up the case. However, as in 1974, the political goal of New Zealand—to end the testing program being challenged—was achieved.

---

14   Cited in Clark, 'Is the Butter Battle Book's Bitsy Big-Boy Boomeroo Banned? What Has International Law to Say About Weapons of Mass Destruction?' (n 5) 664.
15   Nuclear Tests Case (*New Zealand v. France*) (Merits) [1974] ICJ Rep 457, at <http://www.icj-cij.org/docket/files/59/6159.pdf> accessed 15 January 2015.

2 The ICJ Case on the Threat and Use of Nuclear Weapons

In 1992, a global civil society campaign was launched in Geneva which aimed to obtain an advisory opinion from the ICJ on the legality of nuclear weapons. The World Court Project had been proposed by New Zealand anti-nuclear activists during the dispute between New Zealand and the United States over New Zealand's decision to ban the port visits of nuclear-armed vessels.[16] In 1994 the campaign succeeded in moving the United Nations General Assembly to formally request the ICJ to render its opinion on whether the threat or use of nuclear weapons is in any circumstance permitted under international law.[17]

Weeramantry argues that this is the most important case ever to have come before the ICJ.

> In the historical context of the court, this is the most important case that ever came before the international court. So many countries making submissions, we had witnesses, we had weeks of hearings and deliberations, and it was an issue of importance to the entire history of the world, because my personal view is that the future of humanity depends, to a large extent, on our being able to get rid of nuclear weapons…So certainly in all the—so many decades—of the court's existence, there was never a more important case.[18]

Indeed, 44 countries participated in the ICJ process through written and/or oral submissions,[19] more than twice the number of countries for any previous case in the history of the court.[20]

---

16   Kate Dewes and Robert Green, *Aotearoa/New Zealand at the World Court* (Disarmament & Security Centre 1999), at <http://www.disarmsecure.org/Aotearoa_New_Zealand_At_The_World_Court.pdf> accessed 15 January 2015.

17   *Legality of the Threat or Use of Nuclear Weapons* (Request for an Advisory Opinion) (1994), at <http://www.icj-cij.org/docket/files/95/7646.pdf> accessed 15 January 2015.

18   Masato Tainaka, 'Nuke Judgment: Weeramantry: Small proviso ruins chance to declare nuclear weapons illegal', The Asahi Shimbun (1 August 2014), at <http://ajw.asahi.com/article/behind_news/politics/AJ201408010085> accessed 15 January 2015.

19   Participating countries included Australia, Azerbaijan, Bosnia and Herzegovina, Burundi, Colombia, Costa Rica, DPRK, Ecuador, Egypt, Finland, France, Germany, India, Indonesia, Iran, Ireland, Italy, Japan, Kazakhstan, Lesotho, Lithuania, Marshall, Islands, Mexico, Moldova, Nauru, Netherlands, New Zealand, Norway, Papua New Guinea, Philippines, Russia, Rwanda, Qatar, Samoa, San Marino, Saudi Arabia, Solomon Islands, Sri Lanka, Sweden, Uganda, Ukraine, United Kingdom, USA and Zimbabwe.

20   The ICJ matters which had the next highest number of participating states prior to this case were the 'Apartheid' case (*Legal Consequences for States of the Continued Presence of South Africa in Namibia (South West Africa) notwithstanding Security Council Resolution*

Roger Clark served as Agent in the case for Samoa, a Pacific Island close to French Polynesia, where France was still conducting nuclear tests at the time. Samoa joined with the Solomon Islands and the Marshall Islands to present compelling factual information on the impact of nuclear tests, and legal arguments against the threat or use of nuclear weapons to the Court.[21] Indeed the conclusion by the Court that '[t]he destructive power of nuclear weapons cannot be contained in either space or time' came directly from the testimony of the Marshall Islands, which has suffered considerably from the 67 nuclear tests carried out in their territory by the United States. The testimony to the Court from Marshall Islander Lijong Eknilang indicates why the small Pacific Island countries were so active in this case.

> On the morning of 1 March 1954, the day of the 'Bravo' shot, there was a huge, brilliant light that consumed the sky. We all ran outside our homes to see it. The elders said another world war had begun...Not long after the light from Bravo, it began to snow in Rongelap. We had heard about snow from the missionaries and other westerners who had come to our islands, but this was the first time we saw white particles fall from the sky and cover our village...
>
> My own health has suffered very much, as a result of radiation poisoning. I cannot have children. I have had miscarriages on seven occasions. On one of those occasions, I miscarried after four months. The child I miscarried was severely deformed; it had only one eye...
>
> Women have experienced many reproductive cancers and abnormal births...they give birth, not to children as we like to think of them, but to things we could only describe as 'octopuses', 'apples', 'turtles', and other things in our experience. We do not have Marshallese words for these kinds of babies because they were never born before the radiation came...

---

276 (Advisory Opinion) 1970) with 12 participating States, the 'Genocide' case (*Reservations to the Convention on the Prevention and Punishment of the Crime of Genocide* (Advisory Opinion) 1950) with 13 participating States. Since the nuclear weapons case, there have been two advisory opinions which have also had high numbers of participating States— the Kosovo case (*Accordance with International Law of the Unilateral Declaration of Independence in Respect of Kosovo* (Advisory Opinion) 2010) with 35 participating States, and the Palestine-Israel Wall case (*Legal Consequences of the Construction of a Wall in the Occupied Palestinian Territory* (Advisory Opinion) 2003) with 46 participating States.

21   See Roger S Clark and Madeleine Sann (eds), *The case against the bomb: Marshall Islands, Samoa, and Solomon Islands before the International Court of Justice in Advisory Proceedings on the Legality of the Threat or Use of Nuclear Weapons: Questions Posed by the General Assembly and the World Health Organization* (Rutgers-Camden School of Law 1996).

> The most common birth defects on Rongelap and nearby islands have been 'jellyfish' babies. These babies are born with no bones in their bodies and with transparent skin. We can see their brains and hearts beating. The babies usually live for a day or two before they stop breathing. Many women die from abnormal pregnancies and those who survive give birth to what looks like purple grapes which we quickly hide away and bury.
>
> My purpose for travelling such a great distance to appear before the Court today, is to plead with you to do what you can not to allow the suffering that we Marshallese have experienced to be repeated in any other community in the world.[22]

The ICJ concluded that 'the threat or use of nuclear weapons would generally be contrary to the rules of international law applicable in armed conflict,'[23] that it could not reach a conclusion one way or the other regarding legality of threat or use in the 'extreme circumstance of self-defence when the very survival of a State is at stake',[24] and that 'there exists an obligation to pursue in good faith and bring to a conclusion negotiations leading to nuclear disarmament in all its aspects under strict and effective international control.'[25]

Although this did not rule nuclear weapons as illegal outright, it advanced the legal norm against nuclear weapons in three key ways.

Firstly, it affirmed that the 'threat or use of nuclear weapons should also be compatible with the requirements of the international law applicable in armed conflict, particularly those of the principles and rules of international humanitarian law'.[26] Thus, even in cases where nuclear weapon States argue military necessity for the threat or use of nuclear weapons in the extreme circumstance of the very survival of a State, they cannot exempt such threat or use from the restrictions imposed by international humanitarian law. This includes the prohibitions against causing unnecessary suffering, indiscriminate harm, disproportionate harm, damage to neutral states and long-term damage to the environment. Some analysts have argued that this precludes any possible use of nuclear weapons.

---

22   *Legality of Threat or Use of Nuclear Weapons in Armed Conflict* (*Request for an Advisory Opinion*) (Public Sitting) 14 November 1995 CR 1995/33, at <http://www.icj-cij.org/docket/files/95/5943.pdf#view=FitH&pagemode=none&search=%22Eknilang%22> 25–28.
23   *Legality of Threat or Use of Nuclear Weapons in Armed Conflict* (Advisory Opinion) [1996] ICJ Rep 226, 266.
24   Ibid.
25   Ibid 267.
26   Ibid 266.

Secondly, the decision turns the Lotus principle on its head with respect to nuclear weapons. Prior to the decision, the illegality of specific uses of nuclear weapons had to be proved, something virtually impossible as the targeting plans of the nuclear weapon States are classified. Following the decision, any specific threat or use is presumed illegal unless it can be proven to be an exception to the provisions affirmed by the Court. Indeed, a Scottish Court, in hearing a case concerning 'Ploughshares activists' who damaged nuclear weapons equipment at the UK nuclear naval base in Faslane, upheld the activists' defence that the nuclear weapons system was illegal as it included nuclear weapons that could not be used without violating international humanitarian law, and it was deployed with the weapons ready to be used despite there being no immediate threat to the very survival of the United Kingdom.[27]

Thirdly, the ICJ decision demolishes the conditionality placed on nuclear disarmament by the nuclear weapon States. These States have accepted that they have an obligation under Article VI of the NPT to pursue negotiations on nuclear disarmament. However, prior to the ICJ decision they argued that Article VI also calls for negotiations on a treaty on general and complete disarmament and that progress on nuclear disarmament is thus conditional on progress on conventional disarmament. With the Court demolishing this argument of conditionality, the nuclear weapon States were forced, at the subsequent Nonproliferation Treaty ('NPT') Review Conference in 2000, to agree to an 'unequivocal undertaking to achieve the total elimination of nuclear weapons.'[28]

3   International Criminal Court

International law took a big leap forward in 1998 with the adoption of the Rome Statute establishing an International Criminal Court. Despite some flaws in the statute, and the fact that some key countries are not yet parties to it, the establishment of the court has nonetheless enhanced the norm of individual responsibility for crimes against humanity, war crimes and genocide. It provides an international mechanism, complementary to national criminal systems, by which the norm can be implemented.

---

[27]   See 'Trident disarmers acquitted in Scotland based on the International Court of Justice opinion' (*Lawyers' Committee on Nuclear Policy*), at <http://lcnp.org/wcourt/Gimblett.htm> accessed 19 January 2015.

[28]   See Daryl Kimball, 'U.S. Implementation of the "13 Practical Steps on Nonproliferation and Disarmament" Agreed to at the 2000 NPT Review Conference' (*Arms Control Association*, 4 April 2002), at <http://www.armscontrol.org/aca/npt13steps> accessed 19 January 2015.

A positive feature of the negotiations for the ICC was that small countries and NGOs played just as important a role as the larger, more powerful countries when negotiating the crimes and procedures to be incorporated into the Statute. One exception to this was in the case of nuclear weapons. The initial negotiating draft for the Statute included as war crimes the employment of expanding bullets and chemical weapons (poison weapons, asphyxiating, poisonous or other gases, and all analogous liquids, materials or devices). A number of countries—including Samoa, New Zealand, Mexico and the Philippines—proposed that the employment of nuclear weapons should be included as a war crime. Roger Clark, who represented Samoa in the ICC negotiations, repeated the reference made by the Solomon Islands to French writer Balzac in the ICJ hearings, who said: 'that laws are like spider webs through which the big flies pass and the little ones get caught.'[29]

> Did we mean what we said in Nuremberg and Tokyo when we tried (and hanged) the defeated for war crimes. Does the law apply to us? Just down the road at The Hague the Tribunal for the Former Yugoslavia is gearing up for the first international trials since Tokyo. What is required to be consistent? Is it possible to think that it is illegal to kill one person with a dum-dum bullet or by torture but not hundreds of thousands with a weapon of mass destruction? If so, the law is an ass.[30]

The proposal to include specific prohibition of nuclear weapons in the draft Statute was of course unacceptable to the nuclear-armed States (except for India) and those States under extended nuclear deterrence relationships (NATO countries, Japan, South Korea and Australia). In order to enable at least some of these countries to sign and ratify the Statute, the proposal had to be dropped.

---

29 Cited in *Legality of Threat or Use of Nuclear Weapons in Armed Conflict (Request for an Advisory Opinion)* (Public Sitting) 14 November 1995 CR 1995/32, at <http://www.icj-cij.org/docket/files/93/5968.pdf> accessed 19 January 2015, 54; see also Roger S Clark, 'Letters Regarding his Representation of the Government of Samoa in the International Court of Justice (1995–1996)' (Exploring Civil Society Through the Writings of Dr Seuss symposium, New York, 1 March 2013), at <http://www.nylslawreview.com/wp-content/uploads/sites/16/2013/02/Seuss-and-Society.CLE-Materials.full_.pdf> accessed 19 January 2015.

30 Roger S Clark, 'Letters Regarding his Representation of the Government of Samoa in the International Court of Justice (1995–1996)' (Exploring Civil Society Through the Writings of Dr Seuss symposium, New York, 1 March 2013) <http://www.nylslawreview.com/wp-content/uploads/sites/16/2013/02/Seuss-and-Society.CLE-Materials.full_.pdf> accessed 19 January 2015.

However, the criminality of nuclear weapons use is covered by other more general provisions in the Statute. This includes article 8(b)(iv) of the Statute ('War Crimes') which makes it a crime intentionally to launch 'an attack in the knowledge that such attack will cause incidental loss of life or injury to civilians or damage to civilian objects or widespread, long-term and severe damage to the natural environment which would be clearly excessive in relation to the concrete and direct overall military advantage anticipated.'[31]

Following the adoption of the ICC Statute, France attempted to rule out the possibility of nuclear weapons use coming under ICC jurisdiction by adding an interpretative declaration to its instrument of ratification. France stated that the war crimes provisions of the Statute 'relate solely to conventional weapons and can neither regulate nor prohibit the possible use of nuclear weapons nor impair the other rules of international law applicable to other weapons necessary to the exercise by France of its inherent right of self-defence'.[32]

New Zealand responded by adding its own interpretive declaration upon ratifying the Statute, squarely rejecting any nuclear exemption. New Zealand stated that it would be inconsistent with principles of international humanitarian law to purport to limit the scope of article 8, in particular article 8(2)(b), to events that involve conventional weapons only[33]:

> New Zealand finds support for its view in the Advisory Opinion of the International Court of Justice on the *Legality of the Threat or Use of Nuclear Weapons*...where the Court stated that the conclusion that humanitarian law did not apply to such weapons 'would be incompatible with the intrinsically humanitarian character of the legal principles in question which permeates the entire law of armed conflict and applies to all forms of warfare and to all kinds of weapons, those of the past, those of the present and those of the future.'[34]

Clark notes that the use of nuclear weapons might also be covered by article 6 of the Statute which makes it possible to prosecute those responsible for

---

31 Rome Statute of the International Criminal Court (adopted 17 July 1998) art 8(b)(iv).
32 Rome Statute of the International Criminal Court (adopted 17 July 1998) Interpretative Declaration of France, at < https://treaties.un.org/Pages/ViewDetails.aspx?mtdsg_no=XVIII-10&chapter=18&lang=en#13> accessed 19 January 2015.
33 Rome Statute of the International Criminal Court (adopted 17 July 1998) Interpretative Declaration of New Zealand, at <https://treaties.un.org/Pages/ViewDetails.aspx?mtdsg_no=XVIII-10&chapter=18&lang=en#13> accessed 19 January 2015.
34 *Ibid*; see also *Legality of the Threat or Use of Nuclear Weapons* (Advisory Opinion) 1996 http://www.icj-cij.org/docket/files/95/7495.pdf, accessed 14 January 2015, para 86.

genocide and various provisions under the Statute's crimes against humanity provision (article 7) which provides for ICC jurisdiction over acts committed as part of a widespread or systematic attack directed against any civilian population, with knowledge of the attack.[35] As he points out,

> [in] the Nuclear Weapons advisory proceedings, some of the anti-nuclear states argued 'that the number of deaths occasioned by the use of nuclear weapons would be enormous; [and] that the victims could, in certain cases, include persons of a particular national, ethnic, racial or religious group.' They argued, moreover, 'that the intention to destroy such groups could be inferred from the fact that the user of the nuclear weapon would have omitted to take into account the well-known effects of the use of such weapons.[36]

4   Model Nuclear Weapons Convention

In 1997 the United Nations Secretary General circulated a Model Nuclear Weapons Convention ('Model NWC') to UN members as a guide to support the implementation of UN General Assembly Resolution 51/45M calling on implementation of the 1996 ICJ Advisory Opinion through negotiations leading to the early conclusion of a nuclear weapons convention prohibiting the development, production, testing, stockpiling, deployment, transfer, threat or use of nuclear weapons and providing for their complete elimination.[37]

The Model NWC was prepared over nine months by a small group of disarmament experts and international lawyers including Roger Clark. It was modelled to some degree on the Chemical Weapons Convention which prohibits chemical weapons and provides a phased process for the elimination of stockpiles under international verification, implementation and compliance procedures. However, the Model NWC also includes additional innovative measures, some proposed by Clark, such as strong individual responsibility measures, criminal law and protection for whistle-blowers.

---

35   Roger S Clark, 'The International Criminal Court and Nuclear Weapons' (presentation at a New Zealand/Switzerland sponsored discussion on Nuclear Weapons and International Law, New York, 18 October 2013).
36   Clark, 'Is the Butter Battle Book's Bitsy Big-Boy Boomeroo Banned? What Has International Law to Say About Weapons of Mass Destruction?' (n 5) 671.
37   UNGA 'Model Nuclear Weapons Convention' (1997) UN Doc A/C.1/52/7.

The Model NWC was revised in 2007,[38] taking into consideration relevant developments over the previous decade, and circulated by the new UN Secretary General Ban Ki-moon as part of his Five Point Plan for Nuclear Disarmament.

Clark notes that although the revised Model NWC has not yet triggered actual negotiations, the exercise has been useful in outlining the legal, technical and institutional elements required to achieve a nuclear-weapon-free world, and thus shifting from a purely idealistic goal to a practical task-oriented endeavour. It thus 'demonstrates the feasibility and practicality of nuclear disarmament.'[39]

5   Marshall Islands Cases on the Nuclear Disarmament Obligation

On 24 April 2014, the Republic of the Marshall Islands filed applications in the ICJ to hold the nine nuclear-armed states accountable for violations of international law with respect to their nuclear disarmament obligations under the 1968 NPT and customary international law. The respondent nuclear-armed states are the United States, United Kingdom, France, Russia, China, India, Pakistan, North Korea, and Israel.

The relief requested is a declaratory judgment of breach of obligations relating to nuclear disarmament and an order to take, within one year of the judgment, all steps necessary to comply with those obligations, including the pursuit, by initiation if necessary, of negotiations in good faith aimed at the conclusion of a convention on nuclear disarmament in all its aspects under strict and effective international control.

Clark, who is a member of the legal team representing the Marshall Islands, is confident that the merits of the case are strong. In the 18 years since the Court concluded unanimously that '[t]here exists an obligation to pursue in good faith and bring to a conclusion negotiations leadings to nuclear disarmament in all its aspects under strict and effective international control',[40] the nuclear-armed States have not even commenced such negotiations, let alone brought them to a conclusion.

---

[38]   UNGA 'Revised Model Nuclear Weapons Convention' (1998) UN Doc A/62/650.
[39]   Roger S Clark, 'Roger Clark: Peter Weiss Tribute 2 April 2014 (Law's Imperative: A World Free of Nuclear Weapons)' (The Lawyers' Committee on Nuclear Policy Inc), at <http://lcnp.org/events/04_02_14/Roger%20Clark.pdf> accessed 20 January 2015.
[40]   *Legality of the Threat or Use of Nuclear Weapons* (Advisory Opinion) 1996, at <http://www.icj-cij.org/docket/files/95/7495.pdf> accessed 14 January 2015, 267.

On the other hand, if the 1996 advisory Opinion did not have much impact on the nuclear-armed States, can one expect a contentious case to do much more? Perhaps Clark summed this up in his reference to the end of the *Butter Battle Book* where the boy asks his grandfather how the conflict between the Yooks and the Zooks ended. The grandfather's reply was: 'be patient…we'll see, we'll see.'[41]

---

41   Cited in Clark, 'Is the Butter Battle Book's Bitsy Big-Boy Boomeroo Banned? What Has International Law to Say About Weapons of Mass Destruction?' (n 5) 672.

PART 3

Essays on Human Rights

∴

CHAPTER 12

Updating the Standard Minimum Rules for the Treatment of Prisoners

Nigel S. Rodley, Andrea Huber and Lorna McGregor

1   Introduction

It is a privilege to have the opportunity to contribute to this *liber amicorum* in honour of Roger Clark, one of a rare group whose interests and professional career have straddled the human rights and criminal justice sectors of United Nations activity. Indeed, he has played a key role ensuring that the criminal justice sector maintained a human rights orientation. He was able to do this, both as a Member of the former UN Committee on Crime Prevention and Control and as a member of New Zealand delegations to UN Congresses on the Prevention of Crime and the Treatment of Offenders. Co-author Nigel Rodley had the privilege and pleasure of working with him, first as a representative of Amnesty International and later as UN Special Rapporteur on the question of Torture. A key source in the field is his book *The United Nations Crime Prevention and Criminal Justice Programme: Formulation of Standards and Efforts at Their Implementation*.[1] Four chapters of the book deal with UN 'norms and standards' in criminal justice and their implementation. The essay that follows is about the oldest, but still best known, of those norms and standards: the 1955 Standard Minimum Rules for the Treatment of Prisoners (SMR).[2] The SMR are undergoing a process of 'updating'. This essay is about that process.

a   History of the Standard Minimum Rules for the Treatment of Prisoners

The United Nations Standard Minimum Rules for the Treatment of Prisoners ('SMR') were adopted by the First UN Congress on the Prevention of Crime and the Treatment of Offenders in 1955. They were then approved by the Economic and Social Council in 1957.

The SMR were not, however, the first intergovernmental foray into the field of criminal justice policy and penal reform. A fifty-five rule draft had been

---

1   It was published by University of Pennsylvania Press in 1994.
2   *Ibid* 98–100.

adopted by the International Penal and Penitentiary Commission, an affiliate of the League of Nations, as early as 1935. In 1950, the Commission was dissolved by the UN, which assumed its functions.[3] The 1955 Congress then had the task of considering a substantially updated and extended ninety-four-rule text that, subject to one amendment in 1977, became the text of the present SMR.[4] In 1977, a new Rule 95 was adopted to ensure that relevant parts of the SMR would apply to persons arrested or imprisoned without charge, in addition to those so held on the basis of criminal charges.[5]

The SMR have served for some six decades as a 'blueprint'[6] for humane prison rules. They have inspired the rules and inspection practices of numerous jurisdictions.[7] Of particular importance has been their role in giving those charged with applying international human rights law, guidance as to the content of key norms. These norms are the prohibition of torture or cruel, inhuman or degrading treatment or punishment[8] and the obligation to treat persons deprived of liberty with humanity and respect for the inherent dignity of the human person.[9]

Thus, the Human Rights Committee, established under the International Covenant on Civil and Political Rights (ICCPR) invited states to indicate to what extent they were applying the SMR,[10] when addressing the Article 10(1)

---

3   William Clifford, 'The Standard Minimum Rules for the Treatment of Prisoners' (1972) 66 AJIL 232, 233.
4   UNGA Res 415 (V) (1 December 1950).
5   ECOSOC Res 2076 (LXII), amending Section E (Rule 95), 13 May 1977, following a recommendation by the Committee on Crime Prevention and Control at its Fourth Session.
6   Clifford, 'The Standard Minimum Rules for the Treatment of Prisoners' (n 3) 234.
7   See, for recent examples, the South African Department of Corrections White Paper on Corrections in South Africa (2005) Sect 2.4 and Chs 8 and 9, at <http://www.google.co.uk/url?sa=t&rct=j&q=&esrc=s&source=web&cd=3&ved=0CC4QFjAC&url=http%3A%2F%2Fwww.dcs.gov.za%2FAboutUs%2FCOE%2FDocuments%2FWhitePaper%2FWHITE%2520PAPER%2520-%2520Interactive.doc&ei=mxTuU6qkEsPF7AbhnYCQDg&usg=AFQjCNHljtiKhlZyaMpteJdE3rfvtRONBg&bvm=bv.73231344,d.ZGU> accessed 15 August 2014; the Irish Inspector of Prisons, Standards for the Inspection of Prisons in Ireland (2009) sect 2.4, at <http://www.inspectorofprisons.gov.ie/en/IOP/Standards%20for%20the%20Inspection%20of%20Prisons%20in%20Ireland.pdf/Files/Standards%20for%20the%20Inspection%20of%20Prisons%20in%20Ireland.pdf> accessed 15 August 2014.
8   See International Covenant on Civil and Political Rights ('ICCPR') Article 7; African Charter on Human and Peoples Rights Article 5; American Convention on Human Rights Article 5; European Convention on Human Rights Article 3; see, generally, Nigel Rodley & Matt Pollard, *The Treatment of Prisoners under International Law* (3rd edn, OUP 2009) ('Rodley & Pollard, *Treatment of Prisoners*').
9   ICCPR art 10(1).
10 Human Rights Committee, General Comment No 21(1992) (Rights of detainees), para 5.

obligation to treat prisoners with humanity. It has also invoked the SMR in finding violations of the Article 7 prohibition of torture or ill-treatment.[11]

The former European Commission of Human Rights was inspired by the SMR in framing its analysis of conditions of detention of Greek political prisoners under the military regime that took power in 1967. It found some of the conditions amounted to inhumane or degrading treatment. The European Court of Human Rights has frequently invoked the later regional version of the SMR, the European Prison Rules,[12] as well as occasionally the SMR.[13] The Inter-American Court of Human Rights has used the SMR as a basis for finding a violation of Article 5(1) (physical, mental and moral integrity) and 5(2) (inhuman and degrading treatment)[14] under the American Convention on Human Rights. Meanwhile, as early as 1995, the African Commission on Human and Peoples' Rights referred to the obligations of states party to the African Charter on Human and Peoples' Rights, under both that Charter and the SMR.[15]

The continuing authority of the SMR as a universal instrument for the interpretation of universal legal norms is self-evident.

b   *The Revision Process*

Substantially unchanged since 1955, the SMR have unsurprisingly been outpaced by the multitude of standards that have subsequently been developed in human rights and criminal justice.

When in December 2010, the UN General Assembly adopted resolution 65/230, it requested the Commission on Crime Prevention and Criminal Justice (Crime Commission) to establish 'an open-ended intergovernmental expert group (...) to exchange information on best practices (...) and on the revision of existing United Nations standard minimum rules for the treatment of prisoners so that they reflect recent advances in correctional science and best practices'.[16] So far, there have been three meetings of the intergovernmental expert group ('IEGM').[17]

---

11   *Mukong v Cameroon,* CCPR/C/51/D/458/1991 (1994), para 9.3.
12   For example, *Ramirez Sanchez v France* [GC] (no 59450/00) ECHR 4 July 2006, paras 85, 130; for other cases see Rodley & Pollard, *Treatment of Prisoners* (n 8), 395, note 88.
13   For example, see *Dickson v United Kingdom* [GC] (no 44362/04) ECHR 8 November 2005, para 30; for other cases see Rodley and Pollard, *Treatment of Prisoners* (n 8).
14   *Raxcacó-Reyes v Guatemala* (2005) Series C No 133, paras 99–102.
15   Resolution on Prisons in Africa, ACHPR/Res.19(XVII) 95.
16   UN General Assembly resolution 65/230, Twelfth United Nations Congress on Crime Prevention and Criminal Justice, 1 April 2011, UN Doc. A/RES/65/230 (2011), para 10, at <http://daccess-dds-ny.un.org/doc/UNDOC/GEN/N10/526/34/PDF/N1052634.pdf?OpenElement> accessed 18 May 2012.
17   The reports to the Crime Prevention and Criminal Justice are found in UN docs UNODC/CCPCJ/EG.6/2012/1 (Vienna, 31 January – 2 February 2012) ('First IEGM Report'); UNODC/

The somewhat cryptic formulation of the 2010 resolution may have been a reflection of the reluctance, at the time, to engage in redrafting the SMR. This reluctance can partly be explained by concern about the prospect of entrenched negotiations and partly by anxiety about the risk of retrogression rather than improvement.

However, the development of an alternative approach,[18] which has become known as 'targeted revision', offered a compromise. This approach leaves the structure and most of the rules unchanged while reviewing text considered the most outdated in nine areas identified. These were:

a. Respect for prisoners' inherent dignity and value as human beings;
b. Medical and health services;
c. Disciplinary action and punishment, including the role of medical staff, solitary confinement and reduction of diet;
d. Investigation of all deaths in custody, as well as any signs or allegations of torture or inhuman or degrading treatment of prisoners;
e. Protection and special needs of vulnerable groups deprived of their liberty, taking into consideration countries in difficult circumstances;
f. The right of access to legal representation;
g. Complaints and independent inspection;
h. The replacement of outdated terminology;
i. Training of relevant staff to implement the Standard Minimum Rules.[19]

At the same time, the IEGMs and the Crime Commission repeatedly pledged that 'any changes to the SMR should not lower any of the existing standards'.[20]

Progress has since been made in two subsequent Expert Group meetings, made possible by an extension of its mandate by the Crime Commission. The second IEGM in December 2012 identified the Rules to be revised and the

---

CCPCJ/EG.6/2012/4 (Buenos Aires, 11–13 December 2012) ('Second IEGM Report'); and E/CN.15/2014/19 (Vienna, 25–28 March 2014) ('Third IEGM Report').

18 Included as one of four options suggested by the Secretariat to the first intergovernmental Expert Group meeting (IEGM): First IEGM Report (n 17) para 35.
19 *Ibid*, para 5.
20 The clause committing to not lower any of the existing standards has been affirmed and reiterated in the reports and recommendations of all Expert Group meetings (First IEGM report, para 4; Second IEGM Report (n 17) para 4; Third IEGM Report (n 17) para 8(f)) and all resolutions of the Crime Commission relating to the review, most recently in Commission on Crime Prevention and Criminal Justice, 23rd Session, Report E/2014/30; E/CN.15/2014/20, Draft General Assembly Resolution 11. It has also been reflected in Human Rights Council resolution A/HRC/24/12 of 23 September 2013, OP16 and in the resolution of the UN General Assembly on 'Torture and other cruel, inhuman or degrading treatment or punishment' A/RES/68/156, OP 38.

issues to be considered for incorporation, change or deletion from the current text.[21] A first set of provisions was negotiated at the third IEGM in March 2014.[22] Relevant documentation of the process includes two UNODC Working Papers,[23] submissions by Member States[24] and by various UN and regional bodies.[25] A group of non-governmental experts provided a concrete proposal for a revised text of the Rules identified.[26]

2 The Issues

a *Respect for Prisoners' Inherent Dignity and Value as Human Beings*

The SMR were adopted before the spate of human rights standard-setting in the decades following the 1960s in bodies dealing with crime policy and penal

---

21 Second IEGM Report (n 17) para 11.
22 Third IEGM Report (n 17) para 24.
23 'Working Paper prepared by the Secretariat', 6 November 2012, UNODC/CCPCJ/EG.6/2012/2, at <http://www.unodc.org/documents/justice-and-prison-reform/EGM-Uploads/E-V1257278.pdf> accessed 18 May 2014 and 'Working paper prepared by the Secretariat', 29 November 2013, UNODC/CCPCJ/EG.6/2014/CRP.1, at <http://www.unodc.org/documents/justice-and-prison-reform/EGM-Uploads/IEGM_Brazil_Jan_2014/IEGM_Vienna_25-28-March-2014/English.pdf> accessed 18 May 2014.
24 All state submissions are available at <http://www.unodc.org/unodc/en/justice-and-prison-reform/expert-group-meetings6.html> accessed 18 May 2014; see also UNODC, Summaries of replies from Member States to the Notes Verbales of 8 March 2011 and 11 September 2012, 30 November 2012, UNODC/CCPCJ/EG.6/2012/CRP.1, at <http://www.unodc.org/documents/justice-and-prison-reform/EGM-Uploads/IEGM-SMR_II_CRP_prepared_by_the_Secretariat.pdf> accessed 18 May 2014.
25 See in particular 'Report of the Special Rapporteur on Torture submitted to the UN General Assembly 2013', 9 August 2013, UN Doc. A/68/295, submission of the Committee Against Torture, the Subcommittee on Prevention of Torture and Other Cruel, Inhuman or Degrading Treatment of Punishment, the Inter-American Commission on Human Rights and the World Health Organization, all available at <http://www.unodc.org/unodc/en/justice-and-prison-reform/expert-group-meetings6.html> accessed 18 May 2014.
26 'Summary of an Expert Meeting at the University of Essex on the Standard Minimum Rules for the Treatment of Prisoners Review', 21 November 2012, UNODC/CCPCJ/EG.6/2012/NGO/1, available in Arabic, English, French, Spanish and Russian, at <http://www.unodc.org/unodc/en/justice-and-prison-reform/expert-group-meetings5.html#_ftn3> ('Essex I') accessed 18 May 2014; and 'Second Report of the Essex Expert Group on the Review of the Standard Minimum Rules for the Treatment of Prisoners', 20 March 2014, available at <http://www.unodc.org/documents/justice-and-prison-reform/EGM-Uploads/PRI_ESSEX-2nd-paper.pdf> ('Essex II'). Co-author Nigel Rodley chaired the meetings organized by the University of Essex Human Rights Centre, led by its Director, co-author Lorna McGregor; and by Penal Reform International, led by its Policy Director, co-author Andrea Huber.

reform. So, there was no explicit reference to human rights or human rights instruments in the original SMR.[27] In the intervening period, many UN instruments relevant to both sectors—crime prevention/criminal justice and human rights—have been adopted. It was, therefore, natural that, as part of the revision process, thought be given to providing or extrapolating underlying human rights dimensions of the matter.

This must be taken as explaining the choice of the first issue to be addressed by the IEGM: the notion of 'respect for prisoners' inherent dignity and value as human beings. This language is evidently inspired by the key human rights law text on the subject, Article 10 of the International Covenant on Civil and Political Rights ('ICCPR'), the first paragraph of which reads: 'All persons deprived of their liberty shall be treated with humanity and with respect for the inherent dignity of the human person'.

Non-governmental experts have made a number of recommendations, including incorporation of this ICCPR Article 10(1) language into the SMR. This has not yet been determined. The only changes so far agreed in the IEGM have been minor ones to rules thought to be specifically relevant to the broad norm, notably, Rule 6 (non-discrimination), Rule 58 (desired outcome of imprisonment being reintegration into society) and Rule 59 (provision of services that would promote the same outcome).[28] Given the scepticism that the rehabilitation goal has generated in recent years (ranging from challenges to the legitimacy of the goal of what is intended as punishment, through questions about its viability in the light of decidedly unsuccessful experience), there is some slight comfort, especially to those who believe it has not been effectively put into practice, in its reaffirmation in the proposed revised Rule 58.

Principles of general application, such as the ICCPR Article 10(1) norm, as well as the fundamental principle of international human rights law prohibiting torture or cruel, inhuman or degrading treatment or punishment, remain to be considered for incorporation into the text. While those principles are fully established under existing international law, it would be helpful, if only for awareness-raising of detention personnel, that the core international instrument of their profession highlight them. The same goes for such other fundamental principles as that according to which prisoners retain all those rights whose restriction is not 'demonstrably necessitated by the fact of incarceration'.[29]

---

27 It is no accident that 'new' Rule 95, by contrast, refers to ICCPR Article 9 (liberty and security of person).
28 Third IEGM Report (n 17) para 24.
29 Basic Principles on the Treatment of Prisoners, General Assembly resolution 45/111 (1990), Annex, para 5.

The Second IEGM considered the importance of prisoner safety under the present topic.[30] Many of the areas identified for review although not yet agreed upon within the targeted revision of the SMR relate to the safety and personal security of prisoners. However, the current text of the SMR and the revision process do not contain a general provision on the obligation to ensure the safety and personal security of prisoners. This omission contrasts to later international standards on the treatment of prisoners such as the European Prison Rules, which in Rule 52(2) requires procedures to be put in place 'to ensure the safety of prisoners, prison staff and all visitors and to reduce to a minimum the risk of violence and other events that might threaten safety'. A provision of this nature within the SMR would provide an overarching framework within which to locate specific obligations such as the use of force or the proposed inclusion of the prohibition of torture and other cruel, inhuman or degrading treatment.

Beyond a general provision on safety, neither the current version of the SMR, nor as yet the targeted revision process includes a range of other obligations recognised within international human rights law as directly related to the safety and personal security of prisoners. For example, it is well-recognised, including within a recent report of the UN Secretary General, that overcrowding can pose a grave risk to the safety and personal security of prisoners.[31] The obligation to exercise meaningful and effective control over prisons and not control them from the perimeters is based on safety.[32] Regional and UN human rights bodies and UN Special Procedures have also underscored the obligation upon states to prevent and protect prisoners from inter-prisoner violence, self-harm and suicide.[33] Moreover, the current process does not provide for the obligation to identify and respond effectively to common risks to the safety and personal security of prisoners that arise from the prison estate, its management and maintenance, such as fires and floods.[34] Finally, substantial best practice on prison management has developed in areas such as conflict

---

30 Second IEGM Report (n 17) para 11(a)(iii).
31 Report of the UN Secretary-General, 'Human Rights in the Administration of Justice: Analysis of the International Legal and Institutional Framework for the Protection of all Persons Deprived of their Liberty' (5 August 2013), para 49.
32 Inter-American Commission on Human Rights, 'Report on the Human Rights of Persons Deprived of Liberty in the Americas' (31 December 2011) OEA/Ser.L/V/II Doc. 64 ('Inter-American Commission on Human Rights', 'Report on the Human Rights of Persons Deprived of Liberty in the Americas'), para 53.
33 See for example, UN Special Rapporteur on Torture, UN Doc. A/68/295 (9 August 2013), para 48.
34 Inter-American Commission on Human Rights, 'Report on the Human Rights of Persons Deprived of Liberty in the Americas' (n 32).

resolution which offer alternatives to the use of force and restraints, which, if incorporated into the SMR would provide further effective ways in which to secure prisoner safety and personal security.

While non-governmental experts have argued for the inclusion of a general principle of prisoner safety and personal security in addition to more detailed rules in key areas that are known to pose grave risks to prisoner safety and personal security, it is not clear at the time of writing whether these recommendations will be included within the revision agenda at future IEGM meetings.

b   Medical and Health Services

Given the typically poor health profile of the majority of people in prison, the inadequacy of SMR provisions on 'Medical services' (Rules 22 et seq.) compared to modern standards is particularly significant, failing to mirror the right to the enjoyment of the highest attainable standard of physical and mental health[35] or to meet current standards of medical ethics.[36]

In its third meeting, the IEGM negotiated text recognising the provision of healthcare for prisoners as a State responsibility, to be provided free of charge, without discrimination on the grounds of legal status and equivalent to that in the community. Organisation of health services in close relationship to the general public health administration and continuity of treatment and care were also envisaged in a new rule.

Negotiations stalled over the inclusion of specific health needs of vulnerable groups, and have not yet started on other elements the IEGM committed to consider. These include the incorporation of provisions on specific, evidence-based healthcare with regard to HIV/AIDS, hepatitis and tuberculosis, mental illnesses as well as to alcohol and drug dependence treatment, neither of which is captured in the SMR to date. Incorporation of a requirement to maintain accurate and up-to-date medical files and the principle of respect for the confidentiality of medical information are also still to

---

35   As enshrined in Article 12 of the International Covenant on Economic, Social and Cultural Right ('ICESCR'); *see also* UN Committee on Economic, Social and Cultural Rights, 'General Comment No. 14: The Right to the Highest Attainable Standard of Health', 11 August 2000, UN Doc. E/C.12/2000/4, paras 12(a)-(d), and Principle 9 of the Basic Principles for the Treatment of Prisoners.

36   For example, the Principles of Medical Ethics relevant to the Role of Health Personnel, particularly Physicians, in the Protection of Prisoners and Detainees against Torture and Other Cruel, Inhuman or Degrading Treatment or Punishment, UN General Assembly Resolution 37/194 (1982).

be negotiated, alongside text recommending a comprehensive approach, including curative as well as preventive elements and hygiene.

Medical staff's primary duty of care, their independence and the requirement of informed consent also remain on the agenda of future negotiations. The same applies to the incorporation of an obligation of healthcare personnel to record and report signs of torture and other ill-treatment.

c   *Disciplinary Action and Punishment*

Current SMR provisions on disciplinary measures fail to reflect the obligation to abstain from and prevent torture and other forms of ill-treatment, both in terms of impermissible measures as well as providing sufficient guidance on the boundaries of justified security measures.

In its first deliberations on the subject, the IEGM negotiated a recommended new Rule 27, which explicitly introduces the requirement of proportionality of disciplinary punishment and encourages the use of conflict prevention, mediation and other alternative dispute prevention and resolution mechanisms.[37] Remarkably, the IEGM also formulated a recommended new Rule 34*bis* on body searches, an area particularly prone to abuse, yet lacking explicit guidance in international standards to date. The suggested rule would introduce the principles of legality, proportionality and necessity, respect for the dignity and privacy of the individual as well as the requirement, for the purpose of accountability, to keep appropriate records of body searches. Furthermore, the draft rule requires intrusive searches (including strip searches and body-cavity searches) to be conducted 'only if absolutely necessary', in private and by trained staff of the same sex as the prisoner.[38]

Negotiations on other elements previously identified for consideration have not yet started. These include in particular the deletion of a reduction of diet[39] as a punishment (Rule 31) and the role of medical personnel in certifying prisoners fit for punishment (Rule 32), both of which are questionable under international human rights standards or medical ethics. The incorporation of a prohibition or restrictions on other (disciplinary) measures such as solitary confinement, collective punishment and the suspension of (family) visits, recommended in various submissions to the IEGM, also remain to be discussed.

---

37   A new Rule 30(1) was suggested to incorporate the obligation to promptly report any disciplinary offence to the competent authority and investigate it without undue delay.
38   Negotiations on a separate Rule, guiding searches of visitors (Rule 37*bis*), started, but were not yet concluded.
39   Recommendations to the expert group have stressed the need to explicitly anchor a prohibition of the suspension or restriction of not only food but also of water.

In light of the abusive use of solitary confinement across the globe, as documented by the UN Special Rapporteur on Torture, deliberations on restrictions to this measure, whether as disciplinary punishment or for other purposes, will constitute an important, but complex element of the review.

Unfortunately, to date deliberations of the IEGM have not so far taken into consideration the recommendation to also update Rule 33 which covers the use of force and restraints.[40] In practice, the use of force including lethal force, is deployed to quell prison unrest (itself often induced by inhumane and abusive conditions of detention) and prone to abuse.[41] Existing Rule 54 already indicates that when force is used it should be the minimum necessary (principle of necessity). However, while the BPUFF make clear that any force used should not exceed the harm threatened (principle of proportionality)[42] the SMR lack an explicit provision and would therefore benefit from an amendment reflecting this principle.

Similar concerns motivate proposals to amend Rule 33 to ensure respect for the principle of proportionality and to exclude altogether contemporary forms of restraint that, like the already prohibited use of chains and irons, are inherently degrading. It has been proposed that body-worn electro-shock devices should expressly fall into the same category of absolute prohibition.[43]

d   Investigations of Deaths in Custody and of Indications of Torture

Since the adoption of the SMR, the world has become used to euphemisms such as 'killed while trying to escape' (meaning murdered by the detaining authorities) and to testimonies of torture that often leads to death. As a result, a wide variety of standard-setting instruments, aimed at preventing extra-legal killings and torture and promoting accountability for their commission, have been adopted.

Some, like the SMR before them, were adopted in the crime prevention sector of the UN, including the UN Basic Principles on the Use of Force and Firearms by Law Enforcement Officials and the Principles on the Effective Prevention and Investigation of Extra-legal, Summary and Arbitrary Executions.

---

40   See Essex I (n 26) ch F, Rule 33 and Essex II (n 26) ch C, paras 40 et seq.
41   For example, *Montero-Aranguren* et al. (*Detention Centre of Catia*) *v Venezuela* (2006) I-ACtHR, Ser C, No 150.
42   See especially Principle 16.
43   Essex I (n 26) 24–26. 'Body-worn electro-shock devices' include electro-shock cuffs, sleeves and belts designed for restraining human beings by administration of electric currents. See Amnesty International, *No more delays: Putting an end to the EU trade in "tools of torture"*, AI Index No ACT 30/062/2012, 13–17.

Others, such as the Body of Principles for the Protection of all Persons under any Form of Detention or Imprisonment were drafted in the human rights bodies. One, the Principles on the Effective Investigation and Documentation of Torture and other Cruel, Inhuman or Degrading Treatment or Punishment, was drafted by civil society and introduced to the UN General Assembly by the Special Rapporteur on the question of torture.[44]

What they all have in common is a focus on the requirement for a prompt, independent, impartial and effective investigation of suspicious deaths or of allegations of indications of torture. Moreover, like the SMR, they have all been cited with approval by UN treaty bodies and regional human rights courts.[45]

Yet, apart from the (preliminary) obligation to notify the family of a prisoner, in the case of death or serious injury (Rule 44), the SMR are silent on the question of the duty to investigate suspicious deaths or injuries. This no doubt explains the decision to include in the current review: 'Investigation of all deaths in custody, as well as any signs or allegations of torture or inhuman or degrading treatment or punishment'.

As of the time of writing, the IEGM has not discussed this area. When it does, it may be expected to consider proposals from non-governmental experts. These focus not so much on the investigatory process of the detaining institution (all should be presumed to have these), but on independent investigations, that is investigations from outside the institution. So, while proposing an obligation to report incidents to a superior level and to medical staff, recommendations stress the obligation to facilitate and cooperate with investigations outside the institution.[46] In particular, a key obligation would be on the institution's director him or herself to report the fact of incident to the relevant independent investigative body. In fact, this would barely be doing more than putting into the active voice the obligation found in the BPUFF that provides: 'In cases of death and serious injury or other grave consequences, a detailed report shall be sent promptly to the competent authorities responsible for administrative review and judicial control.'[47]

---

44 UNGA Res 55/89 (2000); *see* Rodley and Pollard, *Treatment of Prisoners* (n 8) 149–50.
45 Rodley and Pollard, *Treatment of Prisoners* (n 8) 257–260, 268–271.
46 University of Essex Human Rights Centre, 'Second Report of Essex Expert Group on the Review of the Standard Minimum Rules for the Treatment of Prisoners' (March 2014), 17–19.
47 Principle 22.

e   *Protection and Special Needs of Vulnerable Groups Deprived of Their Liberty*

From the outset, the IEGM proposed that the targeted revision of the SMR include consideration of the 'protection and special needs of vulnerable groups deprived of their liberty' and 'consideration of the requirements and needs of prisoners with disabilities' specifically. The second IEGM report recommended the addition of a paragraph to Rule 6 'addressing prisoners with special needs, including women; children; older prisoners; prisoners with disabilities; prisoners with mental health needs; sick prisoners, in particular AIDS patients, tuberculosis patients, or prisoners with terminal illness; sick drug dependent prisoners; ethnic and racial minorities and indigenous peoples; foreign national prisoners; lesbian, gay, bisexual and transgender (LGBT) prisoners; prisoners under sentence of death and people in other situations of vulnerability.'[48] The third IEGM report does not refer to this recommendation but rather reiterates the existing discrimination clause within Rule 6.

Beyond discussions on the categories of vulnerable groups in the discrimination sub-clause of Rule 6, discussions have yet to take place into how the SMR might be revised to provide concrete protection to prisoners in a position of vulnerability. As noted above, the absence of safety and personal security from the SMR, not yet discussed in the review process, has an impact on the articulation of specific rules designed to protect such prisoners. In the future, specific rules on the rights and particular needs of prisoners in a position of vulnerability might be articulated to address problems of violence and discrimination, incorporating measures such as risk and needs assessment and training of prison staff.

In relation to prisoners with disabilities, the SMR currently contain language such as in Rules 82 and 83 that is unacceptable today, for instance the very heading of the section: 'Insane and mentally abnormal prisoners'! The SMR also fail to reflect current international standards and norms on states' obligations towards persons with disabilities as reflected in the UN Convention on Persons with Disabilities, in particular the key principles of accessibility and reasonable accommodation. Despite the inclusion of prisoners with disabilities as a specific agenda item from the outset of the review process, none of the IEGM meetings have examined how to bring the SMR into line with the principles advanced in the UN Convention and how to apply them to the specific context of prison. The second IEGM meeting and report were of significant concern in that the report makes no reference to considering the specific requirements and needs of prisoners with disabilities, but rather refers to the need to update the outdated terminology in Rules 82 and 83.[49] This omission is

---

48   At para 11(e)(i).
49   At para 11(h)(iv)–(vii).

carried through to the third IEGM report. It is hoped that the issue is returned to the agenda substantively in order to bring the SMR into line with the UN Convention and not treated merely as a matter of updating terminology.

f   The Right of Access to Legal Representation

Within the current text of the SMR, a right of access to legal representation is only recognised within Rule 93, which only applies to pre-trial detention, and for the purposes of defence. Rule 37 on contact with the outside world contains no reference to legal representation.

Rule 37 therefore requires revision to recognise that legal representation may be necessary after conviction, for example in order to appeal and to apply for early release and probation arrangements. It also may be necessary in relation to complaints of ill-treatment for which access to a lawyer reflects a fundamental safeguard in international law. Moreover, a prisoner may need to have access to a lawyer with regard to personal matters such as divorce, property or custody arrangements. Both Rules 37 and 93 would also benefit from updating in line with other international norms and standards adopted after the SMR such as the UN Basic Principles on the Role of Lawyers, the UN Principles and Guidelines on Access to Legal Aid in Criminal Justice Systems and the Kampala Declaration on points such as the ability to communicate and consult with a lawyer or paralegal without delay, interception or censorship and effective access to legal aid at all stages in the criminal process.

The second IEGM report recommended for consideration the inclusion of a right to 'access legal advice [and] to the information with which every prisoner should be provided upon admission' (Rule 35(1)); the addition of a 'qualified right to legal advice in disciplinary proceedings' (Rule 30); and in Rule 37, 'the right to meet and consult with a legal advisor of own choice to all prisoners, at their own expense, on any legal matter, and under similar conditions as established in Rule 93, to be complemented by access of imprisoned persons to legal aid mechanisms to the maximum extent possible, including at the pre and post-trial stages, in line with international, standards and norms.'[50] Due to time constraints, the third IEGM did not discuss the right of access to legal representation which should be taken up again at a future meeting.

g   Complaints and Independent Inspection

In the second IEGM report, the inclusion of the right of access to external means of complaint in rule 36 [and the] reinforcement of the importance of monitoring and independent inspection (rules 36 and 55) were recommended. Rule 36 currently provides that prisoners can make complaints to the prison director

---

50   At para 11(f)(i)–(iii).

each week and to the inspector of prisons. The Rule does not contain any entitlement to complain to the central prison administration or to external bodies as provided in other international standards such as the UN Body of Principles. It also does not provide for the confidentiality of the complaint which is a key provision in relation to protecting against reprisals or to the right to appeal or challenge rejected complaints or complaints that are delayed significantly.

Rule 55 within the current SMR deals with inspections to ensure lawfulness and for the laconic purpose of 'bringing about the objectives of penal and correctional services', but does not require that they are independent or that they focus on the rights of prisoners, and in particular the identification of any risks of torture or other cruel, inhuman or degrading treatment or punishment as incorporated within a wide array of international norms and standards adopted since the SMR such as the Istanbul Principles. The Rule also does not make specific provision for the need for independent inspectors to have access to all facilities within a prison as reflected in OPCAT.

While the second IEGM report makes an extensive range of recommendations for the revision of the SMR in the areas of complaints and independent inspections,[51] as with the right to legal representation, the third IEGM did not have time to discuss this area of revision.

h Other Areas

Other areas identified for revision envisage the replacement of outdated terminology and training.

While initially Rules 82 and 83, titled 'Insane and mentally abnormal prisoners', were perceived as an area strikingly outdated, in the second IEGM report only a change in terminology is envisaged.[52] Gender-neutral formulations were also listed under 'replacement of outdated terminology'.[53]

With regard to training, preliminary discussion envisaged the inclusion of the requirement of training in 'international and regional human rights instruments (...) and (...) national legislation and codes of conduct', 'prohibitions of prison staff in the exercise of their functions' and 'security matters, including the use of force and management of violent offenders, with a focus on preventive and defusing techniques.' Future IEGMs may also consider

---

51 At para 11(g)(i)–(x).
52 Other terms potentially replaced, pending further discussions, include 'Borstal institutions' by 'juvenile detention centres', 'register' to 'record-keeping' and/ or 'prisoner file management system', 'medical services' by 'health-care services' and 'dental officer' (with no term identified yet).
53 Given not all Rules of the SMR are under revision, the selective listing of Rules and paragraphs in the report of the Buenos Aires IEGM, suggesting to replace 'he' by 'he or she' and 'his' by 'his or her' appears oversimplified.

capturing the need for specialised training for staff with special functions and with regard to prisoners in situations of vulnerability.

Non-governmental experts have highlighted additional training elements for explicit incorporation, such as training on risk assessment, conflict resolution, suicide and self-harm prevention and the use of restraints. The necessity of regular retraining and of not only theoretical but practical instruction has also been emphasised.[54]

While record-keeping has not been discussed as a stand-alone topic, Rule 7[55] has been listed for revision within the area on investigations of deaths in custody.[56]

In this context, the second IEGM committed to look into a requirement to include in prison files 'information on the circumstances and causes of death and of serious injuries of a prisoner', as well as 'cases of torture, confinement and punishments'. Incorporation of an 'information system on prison capacity and occupancy rate' was identified as another issue for consideration.

Beyond this remit, non-governmental experts have stressed the need and benefit of bringing case management up to date with modern standards to deliver good prison management and to implement the obligation to prevent torture and ill-treatment, unofficial detention and enforced disappearance. It is also necessary to avoid the all-too-frequent problem of people being detained beyond the authorized period. Recommendations relate to the keeping of a central file register as well as separate individual files and medical files, to the transfer and storage of data and to regular analysis of information to enable the central administration to identify systemic concerns.[57]

3   Conclusion

While at the outset of the process the appetite for revising the SMR was limited, the 'targeted revision' approach has since been endorsed by an increasing

---

54   Essex II (n 26) ch G, paras 105 et seq; *see* also Expert Meeting at the University of Essex on the Standard Minimum Rules for the Treatment of Prisoners Review, 20 November 2012, ch K.

55   Rule 7 is titled 'Register' and states that a bound registration book shall be kept in every place where persons are imprisoned with numbered pages in which shall be entered in respect of each prisoner received, with information concerning identity, reasons for commitment and authority therefor, day and hour of admission and release. It further emphasises that no one shall be received in an institution without a valid commitment order.

56   Note that within the area of replacing outdated terminology (area h), replacement of 'register' to 'record-keeping' and/ or 'prison file management system' has been suggested to reflect technological advance in information management systems.

57   Essex II (n 26) ch F, paras 84 et seq, available at <http://www.unodc.org/documents/justice-and-prison-reform/EGM-Uploads/PRI_ESSEX-2nd-paper.pdf> accessed 18 May 2014.

number of states, illustrated by the growing co-sponsorship of the respective Crime Commission resolution.[58] The process of revision has prompted a 'renaissance of the SMR', a positive development in itself.

Based on the agreement of the overall approach, areas and Rules to be reviewed, concrete negotiations on revised text started at the third IEGM in April 2014. A fourth and possibly fifth IEGM will be necessary to continue deliberations and finalise a proposed revised text to be put forward to the Crime Commission for consideration and adoption.

The process provides a historic opportunity, but it comes with limitations too. Identification of the 'most outdated' provisions does not of course mean that all other Rules are entirely fit for purpose. States agreed to bring the SMR into line with existing standards, yet it is apparent that their aspirations are not as visionary as that of the drafters of the initial set of SMR who provided us with a text that still holds value six decades later.

It is however likely that a number of SMR provisions are going to be substantially improved, prompting subsequent revision of national prison rules, policies and practices of key importance to the lives of detainees across the globe and/or providing a tool to advocate to this end. Revisions to other Rules may fall short of expectations, sacrificed to the limited scope of the process and pushback by states in certain areas, and due to the tradition of consensus at the Crime Commission.

The review is significant in addressing the anomaly that these standards have remained the benchmark for detention conditions even though some of them have become incompatible with recognised standards of human rights. The SMR Review may not deliver a 'refurbishment' of the SMR, but if nothing else an overdue repair.

In any event, other instruments from both the human rights sectors of UN activity have already provided much of the needed modernization of the principles and, yes, rules reflected in the SMR. The most important task is to make that *acquis* easily accessible to policy makers, prison administrators and personnel and those charged with monitoring compliance. We must at least hope and work to ensure that the promise of no backtracking on the *acquis* is kept.

Postscript

Since this chapter went to press, a fourth IEGM took place in Cape Town, South Africa from 2–5 March 2015. The Expert Group proposed a set of revised SMR

---

58   Ten member states have co-sponsored the respective resolution in 2012, 20 in 2013 and 28 member states in 2014.

to the Crime Commission,[59] recommending endorsement and submission of the entire set of revised SMR for approval by the General Assembly (via ECOSOC).[60]

Most of the issues identified above were addressed, and the proposed revised text largely reflects the authors' proposals. A draft resolution has been tabled at the 24th session of the Crime Commission (18–22 May 2015) endorsing the proposals of the IEGM.[61] Tracking the headings under section 2 above, the following appear to be the most significant results of the meeting:

a. Rule 6 (1) (basic principles) affirms the obligation to treat prisoners with respect for their inherent dignity and to refrain from torture or similar prohibited ill-treatment or punishment. It includes a general requirement that the safety of prisoners and others within the institution be ensured at all times, though there is little specificity about the operative implications.

b. Rules 22–26 (medical services) respond positively to all the issues mentioned above, in particular, requiring respect for medical ethics that, *inter alia*, expect health personnel to provide independent medical care, applying the standards prevailing in the outside world.

c. Rule 27 (disciplinary issues) requires disciplinary penalties to be proportionate. Rule 31 eliminates reference to the possibility of reduction of diet, while insisting that general living conditions be enjoyed by all prisoners. All separation from the general prison population must be subject to law or general regulation (Rule 27), while solitary confinement (separation for more than 22 hours) must never be indefinite or prolonged for more than fifteen days (Rule 31). Rule 54 on the use of force has not been updated.

d. Rule 7 (investigation of deaths or torture) provides detailed rules for file management. Rule 44 bis provides guidance on independent investigations of custodial deaths, disappearances, injury or torture or other prohibited ill-treatment.

---

59 UN Doc E/CN.15/2015/17, Note by the Secretariat on the report of the open-ended intergovernmental Expert Group on the Standard Minimum Rules for the Treatment of Prisoners.

60 The IEGM further recommended the revised Rules be known as the 'Mandela Rules' to honour the legacy of Nelson Mandela.

61 The Thirteenth UN Congress on the Prevention of Crime and the Treatment of Offenders welcomed (Doha, 12–19 April 2015; Doha Declaration, A/CONF.222/L.6, para 6); Draft resolution E/CN.15/2015/L.6, "United Nations Standard Minimum Rules for the Treatment of Prisoners (the Mandela Rules)".

e. There are few amendments on the protection of vulnerable groups, but Rule 23 deals with children staying in prison with a parent. Rule 6 adds the principle of reasonable accommodation and full and effective access to prison life for prisoners with disabilities as a general principle.
f. Rules 30 and 37 ter provide for comprehensive access to legal representation, not just before trial, and defence in disciplinary hearings.
g. Rule 55 provides for independent inspection of prisons.

CHAPTER 13

The High Commissioner for Human Rights on the Legal Obligation of Corporations to Respect International Human Rights Norms

Chile Eboe-Osuji*

> Justice is the foundation of all social life and the secure bond of all civil intercourse. Human society, instead of being an interchange of friendly assistance, would be no more than a vast system of robbery if no respect were shown for the virtue which gives each his own.[1]

1 Roger

For some time now, I have had a modest, applied association with international criminal law. It is not surprising, then, that the editors of this volume had initially pre-assigned my contribution to the segment of essays on international criminal law—a branch of international law in which Roger S Clark is very well known. Indeed, it was things concerning the International Criminal Court (where I now work) that introduced Roger and me to one another (though I would not suppose that the editors would have known that). And, here is that aspect of the story. Nigeria had nominated me for election as an ICC judge, in 2008. During the Assembly of States Parties meeting at the end of that year, the Coalition for the International Criminal Court organised (as a side event) a public forum for all the candidates. The idea was to have all the candidates make short speeches from a platform and then answer questions from the floor that was comprised mostly of ASP delegates (who found time to attend) and NGO representatives. Some of the wiser candidates stayed away—and were

---

* Acknowledgements are due to Jan Hessbruegge for his assistance to me during my tenure as the High Commissioner's legal advisor and especially for his assistance with what formed the germ of the second part of this paper. Gratitude is also due to Mary-Anne Power, Clare Lawson, Avani Singh, Aman Aman, Jayoung Jeon and Anna Read for their assistance in finalising this paper in its current shape.

1 Emmerich de Vattel, *The Law of Nations or the Principles of Natural Law* (first published 1758, Charles G Fenwick tr, Carnegie Inst of Wash 1916) (Vattel, *The Law of Nations or the Principles of Natural Law*) Book II, Chap V, 135.

later elected. Others—including me—stepped up and made speeches and took questions from the floor. And I was not elected. But, one of the consolations that I took away from that experience was Roger's strong support for my candidacy—and (to my surprise) my speech. Although he alone would know why he complimented a speech that never swayed the voters, I must confess that his compliments made more tolerable the disappointment of my failure at the polls. And, in the nature of things, it made me like the man. In light of what *Keane* (the British rock band) would call 'an invisible wall' between those who become judges and the rest of humanity (beyond immediate family members), I do consider the subsequent interaction between Roger and me as an extended and most rewarding consolation prize for my non-election to the ICC bench in 2009.

I must, however, defy predictability. I shall not write about international criminal law or the ICC. I shall, rather, write on international human rights law—another branch of international law in which Roger is very well-known.

But, I must first register another aside on Roger and me in the context of international criminal law. It relates to the imperfections of treaty negotiations and the resulting dangers of placing too much faith in the facility of *travaux préparatoires* as the Rosetta Stone that deciphers legislative intent in the construction of treaties. I had served as an expert to the delegation of Nigeria in the Special Working Group on the Definition of the Crime of Aggression in the Rome Statute. My place to sit was behind Angela Nworgu who, at the time, was the legal adviser to the Permanent Mission of Nigeria to the UN in New York. Roger was a leading voice during the Group's working sessions. I recall an episode during a drafting session at the Princeton Club in New York. A certain wording had been proposed in the draft provision then under consideration. It generated much debate among the Group. As often happens, some in the Group did not care for the wording and others argued to retain it. I held my peace. For, I had every confidence in the ability of the CD lawyers[2] negotiating the text to work it out satisfactorily. [I continue to marvel at their patience, persistence and ability to bring together diverse views, perspectives and understandings in the successful negotiation of the text of multilateral treaties. Notably, the maxim *quot homines tot sententiae* has no higher value than in multi-lateral treaty negotiations.] Eventually, the argument in the matter at hand was made by someone that the wording should remain, as a *convenient* formulation. At that point in the debate, a palpably weary mood had primed the group to accept the formulation on that basis and move on to something

---

2 The legal professionals of the *corps diplomatique* constitute a very crucial pedigree of international lawyers.

else. It was then that I bleated in respectfully, with the view that a compromise settlement driven merely by the *convenience* of the formulation was an ill-advised reason to adopt the wording. From my experience in the courtrooms, I felt called upon to testify, the wording in question may end up generating just as much debate later in the courtroom in an eventual case; and the lawyers and judges left to construe the provision may suppose that the drafters had deliberately and carefully chosen the formulation for a specific purpose (informed, perhaps, by a certain policy choice that the interpreters would suggest), rather than merely a convenient formulation settled upon after an extended back-and-forth in a debate-weary drafting committee. There is a legal maxim to the effect that the legislature uses no word in vain. Roger immediately saw the point and spoke up. He suggested that the formulation should be abandoned. Everyone immediately agreed with him.

That episode in my own participation in the drafting history of the definition of the crime of aggression in the Rome Statute gives empiric meaning to Roger's observation made elsewhere: 'Drafting by consensus, the norm in both exercises, the Statute and the Elements, leads sometimes to awkward compromises. An adamant minority can carry the day.'[3] These observations, informed no doubt by Roger's own experience, are wholly consistent with the views expressed years before by Sir Ian Sinclair QC who, too, was a very experienced hand in treaty negotiations and a former Legal Adviser to the UK Foreign and Commonwealth Office. In an early note of caution (in 1968) concerning easy resort to *travaux*, Sir Ian had argued (before the UN Conference on the Law of Treaties) that *travaux* are 'unequal, because not all delegations spoke on any particular issue...'.[4] This is very much similar to Roger's later observation that 'an adamant minority can carry the day.' In his subsequent writings, Sir Ian continued his *travaux* caution in other respects. As he wrote later:

> Recourse to *travaux préparatoires* of a treaty must always be undertaken with caution and prudence...[T]he obscurity of a particular text will often find its origins in the *travaux préparatoires* themselves. *The natural desire of negotiators to bring negotiations to a successful conclusion will often result in the adoption of vague or ambiguous formulations.* Sometimes the parties will have deliberately wished to avoid too much precision in

---

3   Roger S. Clark, 'The Mental Element in International Criminal Law: the Rome Statute of the International Criminal Court and the Elements of Offences' (2001) 12 Crim LF 291, 295.
4   United Nations, 'United Nations Conference on the Law of Treaties, Official Records, Summary of records of plenary meetings and of the meetings of the Committee of the Whole' (22 April 1968) UN Doc. A/CONF.39/11, 178, para 8.

order to allow themselves in future to argue that the provision as formulated does not commit them to an inconvenient or too onerous obligation. Finally, the *travaux préparatoires* are unlikely to reveal accurately and in detail what happened during the negotiations, since, more often than not, they will not disclose what may have been agreed between the heads of delegations during private corridor discussions.[5] [Emphasis added.]

Those observations implicate the phenomenon described in the narrative appearing above. At the ICC, a note of caution has also been sounded as regards undue resort to *travaux*.[6]

• • •

For my next observation, I must assume that New Zealand is a country that provokes much warmth in Roger's heart. But, it is an assumption that I never make with confidence. For, I have many friends from France, Nigeria and the US who are reluctant to project much warmth in their hearts, when they speak of their countries. But I have never met a New Zealander guilty of a similar attitude. I assume Roger is no exception to the rule. The emphasis is on *much* warmth, of course. I have known some Kiwi women go so far down the road of sacrilege as rolling their eyes at the mention of the sport of rugby in general. But the behaviour is never extended to the All Blacks on an international assignment—let alone to the country itself.

But, regardless of Roger's feelings about his country, New Zealand is a country that provokes much warmth in my own heart. Thanks largely to New Zealand, even I have acquired a taste for rugby—a very strange taste indeed for a Nigerian.[7] A leading reason is this. I was finally elected as a judge of the ICC, after 15 rounds

---

5   Ian Sinclair, *The Vienna Convention on the Law of Treaties* (2nd edn, Manchester University Press 1984) 142.
6   See *Prosecutor v Uhuru Muigai Kenyatta* (Decision on Defence Request for Conditional Excusal from Continuous Presence at Trial) 18 October 2013, majority Decision of Judge Fremr and Judge Eboe-Osuji, paras 76–80. See also *Prosecutor v Ruto and Sang* (Decision on Prosecutor's Application for Witness Summonses and resulting Request for State Party Cooperation) 17 April 2014, majority Decision of Judge Eboe-Osuji and Judge Fremr, paras 141–45.
7   In Nigeria, national life revolves around football. And, please, do not call the beautiful game 'soccer'. It is not easy to explain to a Nigerian how any sport should be taken seriously if all that the player does is run around the field mostly carrying the ball in the hands. True sporting finesse and prowess are achieved by the sheer ability to run, jump, and dribble, feint and twist and turn, and kick and more—and score: all with the feet, not the hands! [So you know, I write this one week to the start of Brazil 2014. And the Super Eagles will be there.]

of voting, at the 2011 ASP. The very last of the six judges to be elected during that election! Roger's country, New Zealand, threw unflinching support behind me all the way—just as Roger himself had always done. I knew that, because New Zealand is Nigeria's neighbour—in multilateral diplomatic gatherings like the UN General Assembly, the UN Human Rights Council and the ICC Assembly of States Parties. I sat with the Nigerian delegation during the voting at the 2011 ASP. How did I know that New Zealand was supporting me all along? During these elections, you see, sponsoring States would often distribute assorted campaign memorabilia, with varying worth in utility and money. The mementoes would include bookmarks with candidates' photos, scarves, and USB sticks of various memory sizes. There were also manila folders or wallets in *vero cuoio* or faux leather, engraved with candidates' names, and so on. The Nigerian delegation very modestly ('modestly' is emphasised) handed out small 'beau-coup.com' mint boxes worth $2.50 a piece (before bulk-purchase discount was applied), with the name and photo of yours truly (embarrassment fully admitted). The idea was that each voting delegate could slip the mint box unobtrusively into any clothes pocket or wallet however small, and bring out the box over and over again and nibble mints—after coffee, lunch and the endless stream of campaign receptions that were on offer by the various Diplomatic Missions at the UN in New York during that period. The Nigerian mint boxes became a hit. Everyone, it appeared, loved them. Even the delegates whom I presumed were not voting for me during rounds were seen enjoying my mints! And, how, you may ask, did I figure out the delegates who were not voting for me? Well, they would be popping my mints into their mouths right in front of me, while doing their very best to avoid eye contact. Not so, New Zealand. Roger's country was voting for me, round after round, and generally giving moral support in between rounds of voting, all through the 15 rounds. And they were genuinely happy (as were their Antipodean neighbours) when I was voted in at last—in the very last round.

I have other reasons for fond feelings for New Zealand. My wife's parents are regular snowbirds that migrate every year from the northern hemisphere to roost in the magnificent south island of New Zealand. Their neighbours down under love our children.

• • •

My last full-time position before my 'upgradement'[8] to the ICC Bench was in the post of the Legal Adviser to the UN High Commissioner for Human Rights,

---

8   In fairness to friends and assistants who reviewed this paper in draft, I should inform that some had politely queried the use of this vocable, possibly on grounds that it is not a 'word'.

beginning in the summer of 2010. In that position, I got used to the High Commissioner and her personal secretaries passing crumbs of literature down to me, in the form of books on law and human rights that could find no space on the bookshelves in the High Commissioner's personal office or the OHCHR library. Occasionally, the authors would graciously send their books directly to me, in my very own right as 'Queen Navi's' humble chamber lawyer-in-chief. One of those gracious souls was my good friend, Roger. And his was one of the very first that I received, as soon as I arrived in Geneva to take up my new post. It was not a new book. The book's vintage is accurately portrayed in Roger's own scribble that said: 'Chile: An historical artefact for your Collection! Roger.' The publisher is Martinus Nijhoff of The Hague. (They are my publishers, too). The publication year was 1972. I had been born by then, aged all of ten. That bears true testament to *the book's* senescence. It is evident that I have emphasised *'the book's'* senescence and not my own; nor that of *anyone else* already born let alone *writing seminal books* by that time. [I must trust that the difference is possible to see in a kind world full of good faith☺.] The book bears the title: *A United Nations High Commissioner for Human Rights*. The book is truly informative (as will be seen presently). Among other things, we learn what the 'S' stands for in the Americanism that Roger employs consistently in writing his own name: 'Roger S. Clark'. The book teaches that 'S' is for 'Stenson'. The author's brief biography, appearing at the back of the book, indicates that Roger's career as a law teacher started in 1964, when he taught law at Victoria University of Wellington (his alma mater). I was two. And, here, I must revisit my earlier disclaimer about not implicating anyone's antiquary (including my own). That is not at all the point. The point, rather, is this. Most of those who will be contributing to (or reading) this Festschrift would comfortably belong to the 'age-grade' (as we say in Africa) of international lawyers who would have been Roger's law students. For that reason alone, the honour we do him here he so richly deserves. As an African, after all, I am both bound and hardwired to venerate age—perhaps, an adaptation trait possibly explained by the Igbo proverb: 'Those who honour their elders will live as long.' But, there are many reasons beyond that to honour Roger. They specifically include his substantive,

---

I do wholly accept the concern as entirely correct, if the point is that 'upgradement' is not listed in any dictionary. But beyond that point, reasonable people may disagree. For, if a 'word' is accepted as meaning any sound or combination of words or letters intuitively recognised by native speakers as a basic unit of meaningful speech, 'upgradement' is readily understood as a 'word'. It is not necessary, then, to follow Ambrose Bierce in his devilish definition of 'dictionary' as a 'malevolent literary device for cramping the growth of a language and making it hard and inelastic.' Bierce insists, however, that his own Devil's Dictionary 'is a most useful work'.

extensive, consistent and stalwart service in the scholarship of international human rights law, going back half a century—one example of which is his book *A United Nations High Commissioner for Human Rights*.

• • •

In the book, Roger, among other things, traced the background of the various past and then present (as of 1972) proposals for the post of the High Commissioner for Human Rights, reviewing who gave the proposals momentum and what brought inertia. He reviewed the proposed functions of the post, as set out in the ECOSOC resolution 1237(XLII) of 6 June 1967 which recommended that the General Assembly adopt a draft resolution establishing the post. He considered matters of administration of the Office of the High Commissioner and its relationship with the Secretary-General and other UN agencies. He considered the question of the legality of using a resolution, rather than a convention, to create the post. And—quite significantly for the larger purpose of this essay—Roger stressed the role of the High Commissioner for Human Rights '*as a catalyst for the creation of international customary law by the collective process.*'[9] [The emphasis is Roger's.] Richard N Gardner captured the essence of the book in the foreword he wrote. In 1972, Gardner held the chair of Henry L Moses Professor of Law and International Organization at Columbia University. It was in that capacity that he had supervised the doctoral thesis at Columbia that Roger ultimately converted into the book. And, in the foreword to the book, Professor Gardner wrote as follows: 'This book by Roger Stenson Clark explores the history and the future prospects of the High Commissioner *proposal* with careful scholarship and shrewd judgment.'[10] [Emphasis added.] And Professor Gardner concluded the foreword with the following prediction:

> Mr Clark quite rightly sees the High Commissioner as part of the international political process, as a catalyst for the creation of international customary law, as a promoter of human rights standards—not as a judge or enforcer. Like most proposals for practical next steps toward world order, the idea of the High Commissioner for Human Rights may be attacked as too modest by some and too ambitious by others. Strong opposition from a minority of members has so far prevented affirmative action by the General Assembly. These members may well succeed in blocking action for another few years. But I think they will lose in the end. The High

---

9   Roger S Clark, *A United Nations High Commissioner for Human Rights* (Martinus Nijhoff 1972) 148.
10   Richard N Gardner, 'Foreword', *ibid* xi–xii.

Commissioner for Human Rights is an idea whose time has come. I commend this excellent book to all who would understand its history and, even more important, assess its future potential for international organization and human dignity.[11]

That was 1972. At the time, the position of 'the High Commissioner for Human Rights' was still an 'idea' or, at best, a 'proposal'. It was not Roger's idea or proposal, of course. But, his book was a remarkable contribution to international legal scholarship in the manner of one of the most stalwart and most coherent urgings for the idea at the time. He took on each of the major arguments of the day that had fostered hesitation, foot-dragging or outright hostility ever since the idea of the position had worried the consciousness of the United Nations 'in various forms since 1947.'[12]

The idea finally became the office in 1993. The Vienna Declaration and Programme of Action adopted on 25 June 1993, at the conclusion of the World Conference on Human Rights, had made concrete recommendations for strengthening and harmonising the efforts of the UN in the field of human rights. As may be recalled, one of those concrete recommendations was a call for the establishment of the post of High Commissioner for Human Rights. The call was made in the following words:

> The World Conference on Human Rights recommends to the General Assembly that when examining the report of the Conference at its forty-eighth session, it begin, as a matter of priority, consideration of the question of the establishment of a High Commissioner for Human Rights for the promotion and protection of all human rights.[13]

On 20 December 1993, the General Assembly heeded the call and adopted resolution 48/141, creating the post.[14] Secretary General Boutros Boutros-Ghali appointed Mr José Ayala Lasso as the first High Commissioner. Mr Ayala Lasso assumed office on 5 April 1994.[15] The Rwandan genocide broke out the very

---

11   *Ibid* xv.
12   *Ibid* 2.
13   Vienna Declaration and Programme of Action (adopted by the World Conference on Human Rights in Vienna on 25 June 1993) Pt II, para 18.
14   See 'High Commissioner for the promotion and protection of all human rights' (20 December 1993) UNGA Res A/RES/48/141.
15   See UNCHR, 'Report of the UN High Commissioner for Human Rights, Mr J.A. Lasso, on his mission to Rwanda of 11–12 May 1994' (19 May 1994) UN Doc No E/CN.4/S-3/3, para 12.

next day. There is no connection, of course, between the appointment of Mr Ayala Lasso and the Rwandan genocide. I mention the two events merely because both Ms Pillay (the High Commissioner whom I served in the capacity of legal advisor from 2010 to 2012) and I had earlier worked at the ICTR that inquired into the Rwandan genocide. She was a judge (and also served as the President of the Tribunal) there and I had served in various capacities including as a prosecution counsel.[16]

2 Kiobel

As the High Commissioner's legal advisor, one of my tasks was to coordinate and represent the High Commissioner in her *amicus curiae* interventions in court cases around the world that concerned human rights. This was as part of her mandate 'to promote the universal respect for and observance of all human rights'.[17] There was a rigorous consultation process (laid out in the 'OHCHR Standard Operating Procedures for Interventions before International, Regional and National Courts') that I was required to undertake across the various divisions and sections in the OHCHR, before making a recommendation to the High Commissioner to intervene in a case. It was in that capacity and through that process that I had carriage of the High Commissioner's intervention in the *El-Masri* case[18] and the *Hirsi* case[19] before the European Court of Human Rights, involving questions of human rights violations respectively in the contexts of rendition and interception of migrant boats on the high seas.

And, then, there was *Kiobel*.[20] The case had held out the potential that the US Supreme Court would pronounce itself on the question whether international law requires corporations to respect international human rights norms—as a matter of legal obligation (and not merely as a matter of the moral expectation to do the right thing or 'corporate social responsibility' as

---

16 An aside: when I was prosecuting Colonel Théoneste Bagosora in Arusha, I had to review, as part of the potential *res gestae* evidence in the case, videos of Mr Ayala Lasso meeting with Colonel Bagosora during Mr Ayala Lasso's visit to Rwanda in May 1994, while the genocide was in its full pyroclastic flow. It is not easy to image how trying the occasion must have been for the newly-minted High Commissioner—as he tried to do his best in the midst of the genocidal inferno that was so rapidly engulfing the country, sitting face-to-face with the reputed linchpin of the genocide.
17 See A/RES/48/141 (n 14) para 3(a).
18 *El-Masri v The Former Yugoslav Republic of Macedonia*, Application no. 39630/09.
19 *Hirsi Jamaa and Others v Italy*, Application no. 27765/09.
20 *Kiobel et al. v Royal Dutch Petroleum Co et al.*, 621 F 3d 111 ('Kiobel Second Circuit').

was the vogue terminology at one point). The prospect that such an important national apex court would pronounce itself on a question so important propelled one of Roger's younger compatriots in the New York Office of the OHCHR to bring the case to my attention, with an ardent urge for me to recommend the High Commissioner's *amicus curiae* intervention. Paul Oertley is a very bright lawyer with a big heart for human rights. It would not surprise me to see him also receiving high accolades in future for having done great things in the area of human rights and international law, just like Roger. Sensing that my Nigerian nationality might cause hesitation in my inclination to recommend the case to the High Commissioner for intervention (as I might not want to be seen as promoting or seeking attention for a legal cause specifically relating to my own country), Paul intensified his urge for the recommendation. He was right in pre-sensing my shyness for the indicated reason. But, the shyness did not endure; thanks also to similar urgings that came from Paul's friend and former office mate, Jan Hessbruegge (of Germany), who was my trusty, able and competent assistant at the OHCHR. The recommendation for intervention was made in the end. After reviewing the matter, Navi did not hesitate at all in giving approval and guidance for the intervention. So, we engaged the process.

•••

As must be familiar to most who have followed the case, *Kiobel v Royal Dutch Petroleum Co* concerned a compensation claim for alleged complicity in crimes against humanity (amongst other wrongful conducts) brought in the US Federal Court. The plaintiffs were the relatives of the late Ken Saro-Wiwa and other Nigerians who were, at all material times, residents of the Ogoni part of the Niger Delta region.

The defendants Royal Dutch Petroleum Company and Shell Transport & Trading Company, plc, were holding companies respectively incorporated in the Netherlands and the UK. At all material times, they were engaged in oil exploration and production in Ogoniland, through their joint subsidiary company Shell Petroleum Development Company (Nigeria) Ltd—also a defendant in the case. In the statement of claim, it was alleged that SPDC had enlisted the assistance of the Nigerian military government of the day to suppress violently the protests of the Ogoni people against environmental degradation that allegedly resulted from the operations of SPDC.

In a tale of horror that brings James Cameron's *Avatar* to mind, it was alleged that throughout the early 1990s, the Nigerian soldiers and police attacked Ogoni villages. They killed and raped and beat and arrested the residents, and destroyed and looted property belonging to the villagers. It was alleged that

SPDC aided and abetted these atrocities in a manner that went beyond instigating and procuring them. It was alleged in particular that SPDC had, among other things, provided logistical support for the attacks, such as by providing food, transport, and emolument to the attackers and allowed them the use of SPDC premises as staging posts for the attacks.

The plaintiffs eventually emigrated to the US. They were granted asylum and, eventually, permanent residency. They brought their claim under the *Alien Tort Statue* (ATS), a piece of legislation passed by the First Congress of the United States in 1789, as part of the *Judiciary Act*.

The ATS allows non-US citizens to bring civil claims in the US Federal Court, for wrongful conduct that amounts to violation of international law. In the words of the statute, '[t]he district courts shall have original jurisdiction of any civil action by an alien for a tort only, committed in violation of the law of nations or a treaty of the United States.'[21]

What attracted the High Commissioner's interest in the case was the broader legal question whether corporations (as juristic persons)—as opposed to human beings—are contemplated as defendants that could be sued for breach of international law, in particular human rights law. In other words, does international law require corporations to respect international human rights norms? A positive answer had been assumed all along in the jurisprudence of the US federal court.[22] But, along came *Kiobel* to challenge that assumption, by engaging that question in a deliberate way. In September 2010, the Second Circuit of the US Court of Appeals (by majority) answered that question in the negative, when it dismissed the *Kiobel* plaintiffs' claim.[23] It had reasoned, among other things, that 'corporate liability is not a discernable—much less universally recognized—norm of customary law.' The majority of the Second Circuit was emboldened in that ruling by an open *quaere* that the US Supreme Court had posed in a footnote in *Sosa v Alvarez-Machain*: 'whether international law extends the scope of liability for a violation of a given norm to the perpetrator being sued, if the defendant is a private actor such as a corporation or individual.'[24] In answering that question in *Kiobel*, the Second Circuit majority found that international law does not recognise corporations as legal culprits that violate international law. Therefore, corporations enjoy immunity from lawsuits under the ATS.

---

21   28 USC para 1350.
22   See, for instance, *Filártiga v Peña-Irala*, 630 F 2d 876.
23   Kiobel Second Circuit (n 20).
24   *Sosa v Alvarez-Machain*, 542 US 692 (2004) 732, fn 20.

But, the appellate jurisprudence of the US Federal Court, in the wake of the Second Circuit judgment in *Kiobel*, conveyed no uniform answer to the question. The Seventh, District of Columbia and Ninth Circuits Courts of Appeal came to the opposite conclusion, respectively in *Flomo v Firestone Natural Rubber Co LLC*,[25] *John Doe VIII et al. v Exxon Mobil Corporation* et al.,[26] and *Sarei v Rio Tinto (V)*.[27]

Because of this split of opinions among the US federal appellate Circuits, the US Supreme Court accepted *Kiobel* for hearing, in an initial hope, perhaps, of finally settling that legal question.

The hope was initial—considering, as it turned out, that the Supreme Court did not in the end settle the question whether international law requires corporations to respect international human rights norms. The Supreme Court had granted leave on 17 October 2011 to litigate that question. Briefs were filed by parties and interveners including the High Commissioner. The case was argued orally on 28 February 2012. But, by an unexpected announcement made on 5 March 2012, the Supreme Court reopened the case for further written and oral submissions. The parties were directed to file supplemental briefs addressing the question: 'Whether and under what circumstances the Alien Tort Statute...allows courts to recognize a cause of action for violations of the law of nations occurring within the territory of a sovereign other than the United States.'[28] The objective of the extended litigation was to promote the jurisdictional question as the central question in the case, rather than the earlier dominant focus on whether international law recognises corporate obligation to respect international human rights law. Following the submission of the further briefs, the further oral arguments were conducted on 1 October 2012.

In the Supreme Court's judgment delivered on 17 April 2013, the outcome rested upon the extended question—of jurisdiction.[29] In his concurring opinion, Justice Kennedy correctly informed that '[t]he opinion for the Court is careful to leave open a number of significant questions regarding the reach and interpretation of the Alien Tort Statute.' One of those significant questions left open in the judgment is the original question that the Supreme Court had posed in the initial round of the litigation before it—i.e. whether international law recognises corporate obligation to respect international human rights law.

From the various opinions of the Justices, observers are left to speculate that the Justices were equally split on the initial question, possibly with Justice

---

25   *Flomo v Firestone Natural Rubber Co LLC*, 643 F 3d 1013 (2011).
26   *John Doe VIII et al. v Exxon Mobil Corporation et al.*, 654 F 3d 11 (2011).
27   *Sarei et al. v Rio Tinto et al.*, 671 F 3d 736 (2011).
28   *Kiobel v. Royal Dutch Petroleum*, no 10–1491 (order dated 03/05/12).
29   *Kiobel v Royal Dutch Petroleum Co*, 133 S Ct 1659 (2013) ('Kiobel Supreme Court').

Kennedy holding the wild card. The only question, the speculation would continue, on which unanimity could be achieved, as was indeed evident from the outcome of the appeal, was on the extended question. These are speculations and they are neither here nor there. It is more useful to concentrate on the published opinions themselves. It is perhaps helpful, then, to review briefly the various opinions expressed differently, even as the Justices all agreed on the outcome of the case.

•••

Chief Justice Roberts delivered the Court's majority opinion. He was joined by Justices Scalia, Kennedy, Thomas, and Alito. It was on the presumption against extra-territoriality that they hung their answer to the extended question. They found that in American law, there exists a presumption against extraterritorial application of legislation, in the absence of clear statutory language.[30] The presumption is rooted in the need to minimise 'the danger of unwarranted judicial interference in the conduct of foreign policy'—foreign policy being a delicate field fraught with the risk of possibilities of international discord. It is better, reasoned the majority, that judges do not boldly strike out into the uncertain world of foreign relations unless the legislature has clearly given judges the green light so to proceed. In the outcome, the majority reasoned that neither the text of the ATS nor its history (rooted in the improbability that the First Congress of a fledgling American republic, seeking acceptance from the international community, would have had the confidence to legislate beyond its shores) suggested that the legislature had given that green light in the ATS. Hence, the rule against extraterritoriality of US legislation applied in a terminal way to the suit of the *Kiobel* plaintiffs.

Justices Alito and Thomas added a separate concurring opinion, to amplify the reasoning of the majority and broaden the test against extraterritorial application. In so doing, they reasoned that even when ATS 'claims touch and concern the territory of the United States, they must do so with sufficient force to displace the presumption against extraterritorial application.'[31] According to the broader test, only conduct that satisfies the requirements of 'definiteness and acceptance among civilized nations' can be said to have been the 'focus' of congressional concern when Congress enacted the ATS.[32] As a result, they concluded

---

30   Ibid 4.
31   Kiobel Supreme Court (n 29) Opinion of Alito J, 1 (quoting the majority Opinion of Chief Justice Roberts).
32   Ibid 2.

that a putative ATS cause of action would fall within the scope of the presumption against extraterritoriality, and would therefore be barred, unless the 'domestic conduct is sufficient to violate an international norm that satisfies *Sosa*'s requirements of definiteness and acceptance among civilised nations.'[33] On this theory, it is arguable that federal courts may not recognise private claims under federal common law for violations of every international law norm.

The concurring minority opinion of Justice Breyer (joined by Justices Ginsburg, Sotomayor and Kagan) agreed with the majority's dispositif that the *Kiobel* claim should be dismissed, but for different reasons.[34] Interestingly, they particularly rejected the majority's reliance on the presumption against extraterritoriality.[35] According to the minority, the presumption rests on the fact that Congress ordinarily legislates with respect to domestic and not foreign matters.[36] The presumption is thus inapplicable to the ATS, which was enacted with 'foreign matters' specifically in mind: notably, the text of the statute also refers explicitly to 'alien[s],' 'treat[ies],' and 'the law of nations'.[37] In fact, as the majority notes, anti-piracy actions that are generally accepted as covered by the ATS have extraterritorial orientation. As with harbouring pirates (which provoked the concern of other nations in past centuries), harbouring 'common enemies of all mankind (which include torturers and perpetrators of genocide)' provokes similar concerns today. This, according to the minority, defines the 'substantive grasp' of the ATS in today's context.[38] Thus, the minority concluded that the reasoning of their colleagues in the majority fails fairly to support the use of any presumption against extraterritoriality in relation to the ATS. Rather, it suggests the contrary: that the majority failed to ask, 'who are today's pirates'[39] that permitted the ATS its valid extraterritorial reach in the past.

---

33   Ibid.
34   *Ibid* Opinion of Breyer J, 1.
35   *Ibid* 3–6.
36   *Ibid* 3.
37   Ibid.
38   *Ibid* 5–8; See 'As I have indicated, we should treat this Nation's interest in not becoming a safe harbour for violators of the most fundamental international norms as an important jurisdiction related interest justifying application of the ATS in light of the statute's basic purposes—in particular that of compensating those who have suffered harm at the hands of, eg torturers or other modern pirates.—Nothing in the statute or its history suggests that our courts should turn a blind eye to the plight of victims in that "handful of heinous actions." To the contrary, the statute's language, history, and purposes suggest that the statute was to be a weapon in the "war" against those modern pirates who, by their conduct, have "declar[ed] war against all mankind."'
39   *Ibid* 5.

According to Breyer J., it is logical to assume that Congress intended the jurisdictional reach of the statute to match this underlying 'substantive grasp', in the present day context.[40] In that connection, Breyer J enunciated three jurisdictional principles that derive from this 'substantive grasp' and the practices of foreign relations law.[41] According to this hypothesis, jurisdiction is afforded in the ATS where: (1) the alleged tort occurs on American soil; (2) the defendant is an American national; or, (3) the defendant's conduct substantially and adversely affects an important American national interest—including a distinct interest in barring the United States to torturers or other common enemies of mankind as a safe haven (free of civil as well as criminal liability).[42] In other words, extraterritorial application is possible. This hypothesis, in the view of the minority, is consistent with not just the substantive view of the ATS that the Supreme Court took in *Sosa*,[43] but also with the Restatement of Foreign Relations Law, treaties the United States has ratified, the practice of American Courts and the practice of other states as well as international norms.[44]

The Breyer minority also reasoned that limiting the actions to cases where 'distinct American interests are at issue' would prevent the United States from being the custodian of morality for the whole world.[45] Besides that, further limiting principles such as exhaustion, *forum non conveniens*, and comity would do the same.[46] So would a practice of courts giving weight to the views of the Executive Branch of the government.[47]

---

40 *Ibid* 6.
41 *Ibid* 7: The Restatement (Third) of Foreign Relations Law (in § 402) recognises, subject to §403's 'reasonableness' requirement, that a nation may apply its law [for example, federal common law, see 542 US, at 729–730] not only (1) to 'conduct' that 'takes place [or to persons or things] within its territory' but also (2) to the 'activities, interests, status, or relations of its nationals outside as well as within its territory,' (3) to 'conduct outside its territory that has or is intended to have substantial effect within its territory,' and (4) to certain foreign 'conduct outside its territory…that is directed against the security of the state or against a limited class of other state interests.' In addition, §404 of the Restatement explains that a 'state has jurisdiction to define and prescribe punishment for certain offenses recognized by the community of nations as of universal concern, such as piracy, slave trade,' and analogous behaviour.
42 *Ibid* 1–2.
43 *Ibid* 14.
44 *Ibid* 8–13.
45 *Ibid* 7.
46 *Ibid* 7, 3.
47 *Ibid* 7, 13–14.

All that said, the minority ultimately concurred with the majority in the failed outcome of the case for the *Kiobel* plaintiffs. For, in applying even its own jurisdictional principles to the *Kiobel* case, the minority concluded that the ATS did not anchor jurisdiction for the Federal Court, because of the lack of a direct nexus connecting the cause of action, the plaintiffs and the defendant companies to the United States.[48] Even if the defendants' New York offices were to be considered a sufficient basis generally to claim jurisdiction,[49] it would be farfetched for the minority to accept, based solely on this minimal and indirect presence, that this legal action would vindicate a distinct American interest 'such as in not providing a safe harbour for an "enemy of all mankind." '[50]

∙ ∙ ∙

My own current position on the Bench of the ICC recommends against—and affords the happy privilege of not doing the work of—engaging in extensive normative commentary on the various opinions of the Justices. The restraint is even more pressing as I am now not engaged in any task that makes such an exercise necessary. But, in honour of Roger, I may hazard three quick observations on the judgment.

∙ ∙ ∙

It may first be observed that to anyone unfamiliar with the rules of litigation procedure, the approach adopted by the Supreme Court in disposing of *Kiobel* may seem awkward, because of the manner in which the adopted approach came about. The awkwardness is certainly traceable to the origins of the appeal, in the question answered by the Second Circuit in its own judgment. That awkwardness was made apparent when the Supreme Court reopened the written and oral submissions for purposes of the extended question of jurisdiction on which the judgment was finally resolved by both the majority and the minority. In the end, however, the approach ultimately comprised in the judgment of the Supreme Court is entirely consistent with the standard method of threshold adjudication in tort litigation. According to that method, the first hurdle is usually jurisdictional. Does the court have jurisdiction in the case? And, if it

---

48   *Ibid* 14.
49   *Ibid*. Their only presence in the United States consists of an office in New York City (actually owned by a separate but affiliated company) that helps to explain their business to potential investors.
50   *Ibid* 14–15.

does, is there any serious reason to decline the jurisdiction that it has? Upon scaling that jurisdictional hurdle, the second hurdle is confronted: in the question whether the suit is bereft of a cause of action known to law.

In *Kiobel*, the Supreme Court had started out with the second hurdle[51]—or, depending on one's perspective, a version of it that might have been bound up with the first hurdle—as that is the question engaged in the issue whether international law imposes on corporations an obligation to respect human rights norms. But, in reopening the appeal, to focus clearly on the issue of jurisdiction, the Court returned to the traditional, streamlined approach: which was to resolve the issue of jurisdiction as the starting threshold matter. In the outcome, the claim of the *Kiobel* plaintiffs met its demise at that first hurdle. With the case thus resolved, the Court did not engage the second hurdle as a matter of *ratio decidendi* of the judgment.

It is important to keep the streamlined approach keenly in mind, in order to avoid (a) a temptation (for the judgment's enthusiasts) of stretching the *ratio decidendi* of the judgment in a manner that troubles the second threshold hurdle that the Court left undecided in the end; or, (b) a worry (for the judgment's critics) that its *ratio decidendi* may be so elastic as to be readily stretched genuinely to cover the second hurdle, thus rendering that second hurdle virtually academic in future cases.

⋯

My second observation is that from the perspective of international law, both the majority and the minority are right in their reasoning. Both views are consistent with international law as regards assumption of jurisdiction over extraterritorial conduct. This is in the sense that international law does not, as a general proposition, forbid the exercise of extraterritorial jurisdiction

---

51   The initial question was posed as follows:

'1. Whether the issue of corporate civil tort liability under the Alien Tort Statute ("ATS"), 28 U.S.C. § 1350, is a merits question, as it has been treated by all courts prior to the decision below, or an issue of subject matter jurisdiction, as the court of appeals held for the first time.

2. Whether corporations are immune from tort liability for violations of the law of nations such as torture, extrajudicial executions or genocide, as the court of appeals decisions provides, or if corporations may be sued in the same manner as any other private party defendant under the ATS for such egregious violations, as the Eleventh Circuit has explicitly held.'

See <http://www.law.cornell.edu/supct/cert/10-1491_feb2012> accessed 4 August 2014.

(*Lotus* case).[52] Nor does it strictly require its exercise. As confirmed in the *Hissene-Habre Case*, the most that international law does (in some treaties) is require a State to choose either to exercise jurisdiction or surrender the culprit.[53] [It is a different matter, of course, if there is an international forum that could exercise the type of jurisdiction contemplated by the complaint.] In cases in which the *aut dedere aut judicare* norm does not apply, States are free to decline jurisdiction. Jurisdiction is then a matter of choice—always keeping in mind the difference between the existence of jurisdiction as a question of law, on the one hand, and, on the other hand, its actual exercise as a practical question of policy or convenience or both. The *Kiobel* majority, as a competent agent of US state practice, has expressed for the American judiciary the newfound choice to decline jurisdiction on the basis of their formulated view of a presumption against extraterritorial application of US legislation. Nothing in international law prevents their expression of that choice. On the other hand, the minority view is also valid in recognising that the choice could very well have been properly made in the opposite direction. They, too, are correct in that view.

•••

My third observation is that the drift seen in *Kiobel* is traceable to the wind of *Sosa v Alvarez-Machain*.[54] Some may say that the facts of the two cases present different moral arguments for the intervention of justice as represented by the bench of the US Supreme Court. *Sosa* concerned a lawsuit brought by Humberto Alvarez-Machaín, a Mexican man indicted in the United States for complicity in a Mexican drug cartel's torture and murder of Enrique Camarena-Salazar, a special agent of the US Department of Justice's Drug Enforcement and Administration. It was alleged that Alvarez, a medical doctor, had prolonged the life of the special agent for purposes of extended interrogation and torture over a period of two days. When the US Government could not persuade the Government of Mexico to extradite Alvarez to the US for trial, the DEA hired Mexican bounty hunters, including José Francisco Sosa, to abduct Alvarez and bring him to the US—for the purpose of prosecution. As planned, the bounty hunters successfully abducted Alvarez from his house and held him overnight in a motel. They brought him the next day to El Paso, Texas, by

---

52   See *The Lotus Case (France v Turkey)* [1927] PCIJ Rep Series A No 10, 4.
53   See *Questions relating to the Obligation to Prosecute or Extradite (Belgium v Senegal)*, Judgment [2012] ICJ Rep 422.
54   *Sosa v Alvarez-Machain* (n 24).

private plane and handed him over to US federal agents who duly placed him under arrest. At the ensuing criminal trial, the charges against Alvarez were dismissed at the end of the case for the prosecution, on a defence motion of 'no case to answer'. Upon his acquittal, he commenced proceedings against the US Government and Sosa for the tort of false arrest and imprisonment, invoking both the ATS and the Federal Tort Claims Act. As the US Supreme Court observed, 'Alvarez's arrest...was said to be "false", thus tortious, only because, and only to the extent that, it took place and endured in Mexico.'[55] Notably, the DEA had no legal authority to make the arrest in Mexico; thus forcing them to employ Mexican bounty hunters, private operatives, in effecting the arrest and the overnight detention in Mexico.

Thus, the ATS claim in the case was on the theory that Sosa's abduction and detention of Alvarez in Mexico were torts in violation of the law of nations. The US Supreme Court ultimately rejected the claim on the formula that, for purposes of the ATS, '[a]ctionable violations of international law must be of a norm that is specific, universal and obligatory'.[56] Applying that formula to Alvarez's ATS claim, the Supreme Court concluded that 'a single illegal detention of less than a day, followed by the transfer of custody to lawful authorities and a prompt arraignment, violates no norm of customary international law so well defined as to support the creation of a federal remedy.'[57] It is, perhaps, to be noted in this connection that Alvarez had invoked a 'general prohibition of "arbitrary" detention defined as officially sanctioned action exceeding positive authorization to detain under the domestic law of some government, regardless of the circumstances.'[58] The Supreme Court was not persuaded; observing among other things that Alvarez 'cites little authority that a rule so broad has the status of a binding customary norm today. He certainly cites nothing to justify the federal courts in taking his broad rule as the predicate for a federal lawsuit, for its implications would be breathtaking.'[59] According to the Court, 'Any credible invocation of a principle against arbitrary detention that the civilized world accepts as binding customary international law requires a factual basis beyond relatively brief detention in excess of positive authority.'[60] Ultimately, the Court concluded as follows: 'Whatever may be said for the broad principle Alvarez advances, in the present, imperfect world, it expresses

---

55   *Ibid* 700.
56   *Ibid* 732.
57   *Ibid* 738.
58   *Ibid* 735.
59   *Ibid.*
60   *Ibid* 737.

an aspiration that exceeds any binding customary rule having the specificity we require.'[61]

Beyond the actual substance of *Sosa's ratio decidendi*, there may be some temptation to view the territorial sovereignty of Mexico (who had not authorised the operation) as giving the factual matter an added dimension as a tort committed 'in violation of international law'; on the basis of the principle of international law that insists that States must respect the territorial integrity of one another.[62] Even so, the violation is arguably offset by the interest or jurisdiction that States have in the protection of their citizens abroad, coupled with the very limited infringement of sovereignty involved in the counter-measure operation; although the better course of action must always remain the pacific settlement of international disputes. As the factual anchor of *stare decisis* in *Sosa*, it is possible to consider, therefore, that the intensity of moral stench is markedly different—and necessarily lighter—in a case where a man accused of complicity in torture and murder is briefly abducted and detained and immediately transferred to *lawful* authorities for purposes of bringing him to trial, thus precluding his possible impunity. The factual circumstances of *Sosa* are, thus, highly distinguishable from those of *Kiobel*, where the allegation was of complicity in gross human rights violations in the manner of killing, raping, beating and arresting of residents of a community; and the looting and destruction of their property, in addition to the degradation of their environment—none of it done with any pretence of a claim to a higher legal purpose.

Should these differences in the moral odour of the respective facts of the two cases make a difference in the judicial choice of recognition of causes of action under the ATS? It may be noted in that connection that the Supreme Court had acknowledged in *Sosa* that the common law drain that is hitched to the ATS for purposes of distilling what, in any given case, is 'a tort in violation of the laws of nations' is no longer to be understood in American federal jurisprudence as 'a discoverable reflection of universal reason but, in a positivistic way, as a product of human choice.'[63] By 'human choice' is meant judicial

---

61   *Ibid* 738.
62   It should be said, however, that Alvarez's case at the Supreme Court did not rest on violation of the territorial sovereignty of Mexico. Indeed, at the court below, a three-judge panel of the Ninth Circuit had rejected the argument as beyond Alvarez's *locus standi*. As the Court of Appeals had put it: 'Alvarez's claim that Sosa should be liable under the ATCA because his kidnaping violated Mexican territorial sovereignty fails. Alvarez lacks standing to sue for the violation. [...] Alvarez does not have a legally protected interest in Mexican sovereignty. [...] Only Mexico has standing to object to encroachments on its territorial sovereignty.' See 266 F 3d 1045, para 22.
63   See *Sosa v Alvarez-Machain* (n 24) 729.

choice.[64] Such judicial choice making was premised on the understanding that the 'law of nations' comprised two principal elements. The first and more prominent of the elements covers 'the general norms governing the behaviour of national states with each other'.[65] But, the second and 'more pedestrian element' regulates 'the conduct of individuals situated outside the domestic boundaries and consequently carrying an international savor.'[66] As the Supreme Court observed in *Sosa*, this second and 'more pedestrian element' of international law is the part that 'fall[s] within the judicial sphere, as a body of judge-made law' in US federal law.[67] And, the majority of the Supreme Court, in *Sosa*, rejected Justice Scalia's insistence, obviously consistent with his characteristic originalist approach to the interpretation and application of constitutional and statutory texts, that beyond the conduct specifically, universally and obligatorily forbidden by the law of nations in 1789 (when the ATS was enacted), US federal courts should be understood as precluded 'from recognising any further international norms as judicially enforceable today, absent further congressional action.'[68] The majority reviewed the considerations that persuaded them 'that the judicial power should be exercised on the understanding that the door is still ajar subject to vigilant door-keeping, and thus open to a narrow class of international norms today.'[69] It remains, of course, something in the order of judicial choice making, that the Court insisted that while the door should be kept ajar, only 'a narrow class of international norms [of] today' may come in. While the Court did not nominate the eligible candidates in terms, it is still worthy of note that the Court had indicated that earlier judicial precedent 'did not…bar any judicial recognition of new substantive rules, no matter what the circumstances'.[70] Thus, in the drift of *Sosa*, the Court in *Kiobel* revisited the question of whether the ATS allows courts to recognise a cause of action for violations of the law of nations occurring outside the United States.

∙ ∙ ∙

It is against that background that the intervention of the High Commissioner in the *Kiobel* litigation at the US Supreme Court is to be appreciated. Again, it

---

64 *Ibid* 725–26.
65 *Ibid* 714.
66 *Ibid* 715.
67 *Ibid*.
68 *Ibid* 729.
69 *Ibid*.
70 *Ibid*. See also *Erie Railroad Co v Tompkins*, 304 US 64 (1938).

is recalled that the Supreme Court decided *Kiobel* on the basis of the additional question (regarding extraterritorial application of US legislation) posed by the Court, and not on the basis of the original question whether corporations are bound to respect international human rights law. At least, *Kiobel* did not result in a judgment of one of the most important national supreme courts in the world saying that corporations are not bound to respect international human rights law or international humanitarian law.

But, the effect of side-stepping the initial question was that its answer is now left—once more—to the discordant jurisprudence of the US federal appellate bench, which in the preponderance appeared to be in the affirmative on that particular question, leaving in the minority (among the US federal courts of appeal) the position expressed by the Second Circuit majority in *Kiobel*.

It helps to recall here that the position before the *Kiobel* litigation was that the US Supreme Court had only posed the following *quaere* in footnote 20 in *Sosa*: 'A related consideration is whether international law extends the scope of liability for a violation of a given norm to the perpetrator being sued, if the defendant is a private actor such as a corporation or individual'.[71] That 'related question' (as to international law's clear recognition of the parties that it encumbers with legal obligation) was not addressed by the Supreme Court on the occasion of their judgment in *Sosa*. The Court's concern on that occasion, as we have seen, was limited to settling the proposition that, for purposes of conduct sought for redress under the ATS, '[a]ctionable violations of international law must be of a norm that is specific, universal and obligatory'.[72]

In *Kiobel*, the US Court of Appeals for the Second Circuit threw down the gauntlet of the related question that the Supreme Court had posed in footnote 20 of *Sosa*. And, by a majority, the Second Circuit answered that question in the negative—i.e. that international law did not recognise corporations as bearing a legal obligation to respect human rights. But, as indicated earlier, other US federal appellate courts—particularly the Seventh, Eighth and Ninth circuits—equally picked up that gauntlet from the opposite direction and disagreed with the Second Circuit majority.[73]

It is here that the position of the High Commissioner adds value, from the perspective of the role that Roger had (in *A United Nations High Commissioner for Human Rights*) envisioned for the High Commissioner as a catalyst in the

---

71   *Sosa v Alvarez-Machain* (n 24) 732.
72   *Ibid* 732 (quoting *In re Estate of Marcos Human Rights Litigation*, 25 F 3d 1467, 1475).
73   See *Flomo v Firestone Natural Rubber Co LLC* (n 25); *John Doe VIII et al. v Exxon Mobil Corporation et al* (n 26); *Sarei et al. v Rio Tinto et al* (n 27).

formulation of customary international law. In her intervention, the High Commissioner identified herself with the US federal appellate judges that had decided that international law recognised a corporate legal obligation to respect international human rights norms.

In the following section, I shall recall the essential legal considerations that motivated the High Commissioner's position in that regard, much of which were articulated in the High Commissioner's intervener brief before the US Supreme Court. It is important to stress, however, that the discussion that I embark upon below is not made in the precise text of the brief submitted on behalf of the High Commissioner. The brief itself may be found at the website footnoted here.[74] [Counsel of Record before the Supreme Court was Professor David Sloss of Santa Clara University School of Law in California. I had first approached Roger to do the honours of conveying the position of the High Commissioner to the Supreme Court, since I lacked right of audience as the High Commissioner's legal counsel with no professional affinity to the US legal profession let alone of the Bar of the US Supreme Court. It turned out also that Roger was similarly without a right of audience before the Supreme Court—despite his long years in the US! With Roger unable to assist, Jenny Martinez of Stanford Law School put me in touch with David Sloss of Santa Clara Law School, who very graciously agreed to finalise the brief largely in his own style, and filed it as our counsel of record. I merely received mention on the brief, assisted by Jan Hessbruegge.]

Before recalling the position expressed by the High Commissioner, it must be noted that the US Government—presumably influenced by Harold Koh, the Legal Adviser to the State Department and his principal at the time (Mrs Hilary Rodham Clinton)—had also intervened and similarly argued that corporations are under a legal obligation to respect human rights. For their own part, the Governments of the Netherlands and the UK (the principal host states of the multinational defendants Royal Dutch Petroleum Company and Shell Transport & Trading Company, plc) and Germany took the opposite view in their own interventions. It is not my aim here to review the positions of the various governments who had intervened. I merely point out that they, too, had intervened in the case and expressed positions that were not all consonant with those of the High Commissioner.

---

74   Brief of Amicus Curiae Navi Pillay, the United Nations High Commissioner for Human Rights, in Support of Petitioners: <www.americanbar.org/content/dam/aba/publications/supreme_court_preview/briefs/10-1491_petitioner_amcu_navipillay.authcheckdam.pdf> accessed 27 December 2013.

3 An Overview of the High Commissioner's Position on the Civil Legal Responsibility of Corporations in International Law

In summary, the High Commissioner's position was that to hold corporations liable for human rights violations is fully consistent with international law. At the heart of the debate is the value that must be attached to the idea of the rule of law. A value that lends itself to the following simple statement: 'Be you never so high, the law is above you.'[75]

The battle for the rule of international law over perpetrators of human rights violations has been fought and won against individuals (however high and mighty), against groups and organisations, and against States. On a proper understanding of contemporary international law, corporations are also subject to the rule of law on the international plane, in which they operate so ubiquitously. Under that law, they are accountable for human rights violations.

The proposition that corporations may be held accountable for human rights violations, pursuant to the US *Aliens Tort Statute*, now finds the clear support of *stare decisis*[76] in *Flomo v Firestone Natural Rubber Co LLC*,[77] *John Doe VIII et al. v Exxon Mobil Corporation et al.*,[78] and *Sarei v Rio Tinto (V)*.[79] In particular, corporations are not immune from responsibility under international law if they engage—or become complicit—in conducts amounting to international crimes such as genocide, crimes against humanity and/or war crimes.

That proposition is eminently correct in—and wholly consistent with—international law; and salutary in its development in particular and the rule of law in general. It is a legal proposition that is solidly validated by the following considerations among others: it is consistent with the international legal principle of effective remedy for human rights violations; it is consistent with the international legal policy of disavowal of impunity for human rights violations; it is consistent with the international practice of complementarity between international and domestic legal regimes for the protection of human rights; it

---

[75] Tom Bingham, *The Rule of Law* (Penguin 2010) ('Bingham, *The Rule of Law*') 4, quoting Dr Thomas Fuller (1654–1734).

[76] Until recently, the proposition was only a legal assumption in the US federal appellate jurisprudence.

[77] *Flomo v Firestone Natural Rubber Co LLC* (n 25).

[78] *John Doe VIII et al. v Exxon Mobil Corporation et al* (n 26).

[79] *Sarei et al. v Rio Tinto et al* (n 27).

is consistent with general principles of law recognised by civilised nations—in and of itself and as a source of international law; and, in the nature of things, it serves as an avenue of orderly redress, according to the rule of law, the absence of which might drive boiling frustration to recourse of extra-legal means of redress for perceived wrongs.

Conversely, for all those reasons, the opposite proposition lacks support as a matter of law or policy or both. It is wholly undesirable. The paradigm of that opposite proposition is the exceptional decision of the majority of the appeals judges, in *Kiobel*, that corporations may not be held accountable for human rights violations, because such attribution of liability is unknown to international law.[80]

Corporate Civil Liability is Consistent with the International Legal Principle of Effective Remedy for Human Rights Violations

Much like a very familiar principle in common law jurisdictions, international law requires effective remedy for breach of a right guaranteed by international law. In the *Case Concerning the Factory at Chorzów,* the Permanent Court of International Justice classically stated that principle as follows: 'it is a principle of international law, and even a general conception of law, that the breach of an engagement involves an obligation to make reparation in an adequate form.'[81] In international law, the term 'breach of an engagement' (as employed in the passage quoted above), such as 'involves an obligation to make reparation in an adequate form', is generally accepted to mean commission of 'an act [or omission] contrary to international law'. That much is evident in another passage in the same *Chorzów Factory* case where the Court explained how reparation may be made: 'Restitution in kind, or, if this is not possible, payment of a sum corresponding to the value which a restitution in kind would bear; the award, if need be, of damages for loss sustained which would not be covered by restitution in kind or payment in place of it—such are the principles which should serve to determine

---

80   Kiobel Second Circuit (n 20) 112. Specifically, the Second Circuit Court of Appeals wrote: 'Because customary international law consists of only those norms that are specific, universal, and obligatory in the relations of States *inter se*, and because no corporation has ever been subject to *any* form of liability (whether civil or criminal) under the customary international law of human rights, we hold that corporate liability is not a discernible—much less universally recognized—norm of customary international law that we may apply pursuant to the ATS'.

81   *Case Concerning the Factory at Chorzów (Germany v Poland)* (Merits) (Claim for Indemnity) [1928] PCIJ Rep Series A No 17, 29.

the amount of compensation due for *an act contrary to international law*.'[82] [Emphasis added.]

In contemporary international law, since 1948, this principle has come to be known as the principle of effective remedy or effective reparation. It is a golden thread that customarily runs through all modern international human rights instruments. Professor Theo van Boven, an expert in the field of reparation for human rights violations, observed the legal phenomenon in the following way: 'As the result of an international normative process the legal basis for a right to a remedy and reparation became firmly anchored in the elaborate corpus of international human rights instruments, now widely ratified by States.'[83]

A sample of the statement of this principle may be found in the *Universal Declaration for Human Rights* (article 8), which provides as follows: 'Everyone has the right to an effective remedy by the competent national tribunals for acts violating the fundamental rights granted him by the constitution or by law.' Similarly, in the *International Covenant on Civil and Political Rights* (article 2(3)), the principle is stated in the manner of requiring 'each State Party... to take the necessary steps, in accordance with its constitutional processes and with the provisions of the present Covenant, to adopt such other measures as may be necessary *to give effect* to the rights recognized in the present Covenant' (article 2(2)) (emphasis added). The principle is reiterated in the ICCPR in the manner of requiring each State Party to ensure: (a) 'that any person whose rights or freedoms as herein recognized are violated shall have an effective remedy'; (b) 'that any person claiming such a remedy shall have his right thereto determined by competent judicial, administrative or legislative authorities, or by any other competent authority provided for by the legal system of the State, and to develop the possibilities of judicial remedy'; and, (c) 'that the competent authorities shall enforce such remedies when granted' (article 2(3)).

---

82 *Ibid* 47. See also United Nations, 'Report of the International Law Commission on the work of its fifty-third session' (23 April–1 June and 2 July–10 August 2001) 35, para 7, UN Doc A/56/10 in the Yearbook of the International Law Commission (2001) vol II (2).

83 Theo van Boven, 'Victims' Rights to a Remedy and Reparation: The New United Nations Principles and Guidelines' in Carla Ferstman and others (ed), *Reparations for Victims of Genocide, War Crimes and Crimes Against Humanity: Systems in Place and Systems in the Making* (Brill 2009) 21.

THE OBLIGATION OF CORPORATIONS TO RESPECT HUMAN RIGHTS NORMS   179

This principle of effective remedy is a regular feature of international human rights instruments at both the multi-lateral[84] and regional[85] levels.

---

84   In the International Convention on the Elimination of All Forms of Racial Discrimination (art 6), the principle is stated as follows: 'States Parties shall assure to everyone within their jurisdiction effective protection and remedies, through the competent national tribunals and other State institutions, against any acts of racial discrimination which violate his human rights and fundamental freedoms contrary to this Convention as well as the right to seek from such tribunals just and adequate reparation or satisfaction for any damage suffered as a result of such discrimination.' In the Convention against Torture and other Cruel, Inhuman or Degrading Treatment or Punishment (art 14), one also finds the principle states as follows: '(1) Each State Party shall ensure in its legal system that the victim of an act of torture obtains redress and has an enforceable right to fair and adequate compensation including the means for as full rehabilitation as possible. In the event of the death of the victim as a result of an act of torture, his dependents shall be entitled to compensation. (2) Nothing in this Article shall affect any right of the victim or other person to compensation which may exist under national law.' In the International Convention on the Protection of the Rights of All Migrant Workers and Members of Their Families (article 83), the same principle appears as follows: 'Each State Party to the present Convention undertakes: (a) To ensure that any person whose rights or freedoms as herein recognized are violated shall have an effective remedy, notwithstanding that the violation has been committed by persons acting in an official capacity; (b) To ensure that any persons seeking such a remedy shall have his or her claim reviewed and decided by competent judicial, administrative or legislative authorities, or by any other competent authority provided for by the legal system of the State, and to develop the possibilities of judicial remedy; (c) To ensure that the competent authorities shall enforce such remedies when granted.'

85   According to the European Convention on Human Rights (art 13) 'Everyone whose rights and freedoms as set forth in this Convention are violated shall have an effective remedy before a national authority notwithstanding that the violation has been committed by persons acting in an official capacity.' The American Convention on Human Rights (art 25) provides as follows: '(1) Everyone has the right to simple and prompt recourse, or any other effective recourse, to a competent court or tribunal for protection against acts that violate his fundamental rights recognized by the constitution or laws of the state concerned or by this Convention, even though such violation may have been committed by persons acting in the course of their official duties. (2) The States Parties undertake: (a) to ensure that any person claiming such remedy shall have his rights determined by the competent authority provided for by the legal system of the state; (b) to develop the possibilities of judicial remedy; and (c) to ensure that the competent authorities shall enforce such remedies when granted.' Also in article 63(1) of the same Convention, it is provided: 'If the Court finds that there has been a violation of a right or freedom protected by this Convention, the Court shall rule that the injured party be ensured the enjoyment of his right or freedom that was violated. It shall also rule, if appropriate, that the consequences

It is indeed a traditional view in international law that the duty to make reparation for an injury is inseparable from the concept of responsibility itself for an internationally wrongful act.[86]

In recent times, greater emphasis has been placed on reparation for victims of human rights violations—especially as concerns the manner of such violations that also amount to violations of international criminal norms.[87] This new emphasis is consistent with developments in national jurisdictions, which have been focusing on civil reparation for victims of crimes as efforts that complement criminal punishment for criminal conducts.[88]

Evidence of this new found emphasis is seen in article 75(1) of the Rome Statute, which requires the ICC to establish principles relating to reparation for victims, including restitution, compensation and rehabilitation. The statutes of the older international criminal tribunals were, in contrast, silent on

---

of the measure or situation that constituted the breach of such right or freedom be remedied and that fair compensation be paid to the injured party.' And in the Protocol to the African Charter on Human and Peoples' Rights on the Rights of Women in Africa (art 25) it is provided: 'States Parties shall undertake to: (a) provide for appropriate remedies to any woman whose rights or freedoms, as herein recognised, have been violated; (b) ensure that such remedies are determined by competent judicial, administrative or legislative authorities, or by any other competent authority provided for by law.'

86 See FV García Amador y Rodríguez, Louis B Sohn & Richard R Baxter, Recent Codifications of the Law of State Responsibility for Injuries to Aliens (Brill 1974) 8–9.

87 See, for instance, International Commission of Jurists, Corporate Complicity & Legal Accountability, vol 2 (Criminal Law and International Crimes) (Report of the International Commission of Jurists Expert Legal Panel on Corporate Complicity in International Crimes) (International Commission of Jurists 2008) 6–7; Carla Ferstman and others (ed), *Reparations for Victims of Genocide, War Crimes and Crimes Against Humanity: Systems in Place and Systems in the Making* (Brill 2009); Conor McCarthy, 'Reparations under the Rome Statute of the International Criminal Court and Reparative Justice Theory' [2009] 3 IJTJ 250; Frederic Megret, 'Justifying Compensation by the International Criminal Court's Trust Fund for Victims: Lessons from Domestic Compensation Schemes' [2010–2011] 36 Brooklyn JIL 123.

88 See the Explanatory Report to the European Convention on the Compensation of Victims of Violent Crimes, para 1, available at <http://conventions.coe.int/treaty/en/Reports/Html/116.htm> accessed 4 August 2014. See also JUSTICE, 'A Report by JUSTICE: Compensation for Victims of Crimes of Violence' (1962) paras 2, 76; Robert E Scott, 'Compensation for Victims of Violent Crimes: An Analysis,' [1967] 8 William & Mary Law Review 277, 278; Jo Goodey, 'Compensating Victims of Violent Crime in the European Union With a Special Focus on Victims of Terrorism' [a discussion paper for National Center for Victims of Crime, May 2003] at <www.ncvc.org/ncvc/AGP.Net/Components/documentViewer/Download.aspxnz?DocumentID=32594> accessed 4 August 2014.

reparation, beyond empowering judges to make orders of restitution of property as an incident of findings of guilt;[89] although the Judges of those tribunals did manage to adopt rules that minimally authorised the Registrars to transmit judgments to national authorities with the aim of facilitating compensation proceedings in the domestic arena.[90]

Efforts on the part of the UN High Commissioner for Human Rights in this regard include setting up a high level panel to inquire, report and recommend on reparation for victims of sexual violence in armed conflicts in the Democratic Republic of the Congo.[91]

Although the general rule of effective remedy, as a principle of international law, originated, as with much else in inter*nation*al law, in the traditional consciousness of responsibility of States, there is no principle of international law that is known to except corporations from the rule. Such an exception from a general rule must be founded upon a rational theory that validates the exception. It cannot depend upon a casuistic determination to preserve, defend or exploit an ill-*perceived* loophole in the law. Indeed, such an exception in this case would be highly incongruous to both common sense and the general grain of international law.

'Reparation', notably, is a compound term in international law. This is conveniently illustrated by the usage appearing in the International Law Association's Declaration of International Law Principles on Reparation for Victims of Armed Conflict (Substantive Issues) (2010).[92] In the first paragraph of article 1 of the ILA Declaration, the root definition of 'reparation' is stated as covering 'measures that seek to eliminate all the harmful consequences of a violation of rules of international law applicable in armed conflict and to re-establish the situation that would have existed if the violation had not occurred.'[93] And, in

---

89 See art 24(3) common to the Statutes of the International Criminal Tribunal for Rwanda and of the International Criminal Tribunal for the former Yugoslavia. See also rule 105 common to the Rules of Procedure and Evidence of both of tribunals. See Antonio Cassese, *International Criminal Law* (2nd edn, OUP 2008) 422–23.

90 Rule 106 common to the Rules of Procedure and Evidence of both of ICTR and ICTY authorises the Registrar to transmit judgments to national authorities, in order to enable victims of the convict to 'bring an action in a national court or other competent body to obtain compensation,' pursuant to 'relevant national legislation': see rule 106.

91 UNHCHR, 'Report of the Panel on Remedies and Reparations for Victims of Sexual Violence in the Democratic Republic of Congo to the High Commissioner for Human Rights' (March 2011) available at <http://www.refworld.org/docid/4d708ae32.html> accessed 6 June 2014.

92 International Law Association, Resolution 2/2010 adopted at the 74th Conference of the International Law Association, held at The Hague, The Netherlands, 15–20 August 2010.

93 *Ibid* art 1(1).

the second paragraph of article 1, the particular measures comprising the term 'reparation' are specified as 'restitution, compensation, satisfaction and guarantees and assurances of non-repetition, either singly or in combination.'[94]

The ILA definition is a synthesis of meanings of reparation appearing in earlier international documents from UN sources, such as the General Assembly, the Economic and Social Council, the Commission on Human Rights, and the International Law Commission. The earliest of these instruments, the International Law Commission's *Articles on the Responsibility of States for Internationally Wrongful Acts* (2001), provides as follows: 'Full reparation for the injury caused by the internationally wrongful act shall take the form of restitution, compensation and satisfaction, either singly or in combination...'[95] Similarly, in the *Basic Principles and Guidelines on the Right to a Remedy and Reparation for Victims of Gross Violations of International Human Rights Law and Serious Violations of International Humanitarian Law* (2005)—as adopted in identical terms by the UN General Assembly, the UN Economic and Social Council,[96] and the Commission on Human Rights[97]—included within the notion of 'full and effective reparation' are 'restitution, compensation, rehabilitation, satisfaction and guarantees of non-repetition.' [See common paragraph 18 of both documents.]

Thus, the proposition that corporations are not accountable in international law for violations of international human rights law is a proposition that pointedly misses or ignores the principle of effective remedy for human rights violations, as a fundamental principle of international law. Without limiting the value of the other types of reparation, guarantees of non-repetition as a manner of reparation truly underscore the elementary flaw in the proposition that corporations are not accountable in international law for human rights violations. It simply means that corporations may continue to violate human rights in particular instances and may never feel a compelling need to cease and desist. But it would be more than an act of 'passive injustice'[98] to accept such a grotesque interpretation of international law.

---

94 *Ibid* art 1(2).
95 See art 34 of the ILC Draft Articles on the Responsibility of States for Internationally Wrongful Acts. See also annex to UNGA Res 56/83 of 12 December 2001, UN Doc A/RES/56/83 (2001) and corrected by document A/56/49(Vol. 1)/Corr. 4.
96 See ECOSOC Res 2005/30 (25 July 2005) UN Doc E/RES/2005/30.
97 See UNCHR Res 2005/35 (19 April 2005) UN Doc E/CN.4/RES/2005/35.
98 As Judith Shklar usefully reminds us, 'passive injustice' includes the silent acceptance of 'laws that we regard as unjust, unwise or cruel', Judith N Shklar, *Faces of Injustice Storrs Lectures on Jurisprudence, Yale Law School 1988* (Yale University Press 1990) 6.

In the circumstances, a rule of law that recognises an exemption of corporations from the same liability for human rights violations that encumbers everyone else in international law—States at one end, individuals at the other and other groups and organisations in between[99]—is nothing less than a brazen perpetuation of the axiom that 'corporate status has long implied economic and political power without accountability.'[100] Such a state of affairs is more than really awkward in an international legal order that has continually denounced the absence of accountability for human rights violations. In short, corporations are not above the law that binds every other participant as regards the events of concern to international law. In particular, a corporation cannot be allowed to commit genocide, crimes against humanity or war crimes while every other participant on the plane of international law is prohibited from doing so.

In addition to the foregoing considerations, one must at all times keep in view the clear pronouncement of the ICJ as follows: 'Responsibility is the necessary corollary of a right.'[101] This is a clear redux of the Hohfeldian jural correlativity, in which a right in someone entails an obligation on someone else implicated in its violation. As a principle of international law, this simply means that the person implicated in the violation of the right bears an *obligation* to make reparation for the violation.

Corporate Civil Liability is Consistent with the International Legal Policy of Disavowal of Impunity for Human Rights Violations

As a matter separate from international law's requirement that perpetrators of human rights violations must offer guarantees of non-repetition, there is a clear international legal policy of disavowal of impunity for human rights violations already committed.

This disavowal is seen in a strong current of legal policy that is steadily washing away the stilts of impunity for human rights violations. The clear direction of this policy is to require accountability on the part of every person or entity that enjoys recognition in international law. Elements of that policy include notions such as: state responsibility for human rights violations;

---

99   See Phillipe Sands & Pierre Klein, *Bowett's Law of International Institutions* (6th ed, Sweet and Maxwell 2009), Ch 15. See also Andrew Clapham, *Human Rights of Non-State Actors* (OUP 2006) 30, Sect 2.2.

100 See David Millon, 'The Ambiguous Significance of Corporate Personhood' (2001) 2 Stanford Agora 1. Also see generally Stephen Tully, *Corporations and International Lawmaking* (Martinus Nijhoff 2007), especially chs 1 and 2.

101 *Barcelona Traction, Light and Power Company, Limited* (*Belgium v Spain*) (Judgement) [1970] ICJ Rep 3, para 36.

individual criminal responsibility for gross human rights violations; denial of immunity for even heads of state and government for gross human rights violations; complementarity of jurisdiction between national judiciaries and the international criminal courts and tribunals in respect of gross violations of human rights; and, responsibility of States and the international community to protect persons from gross human rights violations.

This current of international legal policy has stripped the cloak of impunity from the oldest subject of international law: the State. The spirit of accountability has moved international law to the place where it is taken for granted nowadays that a State may be held accountable by way of civil remedies for the violation of human rights attributable to it. It is, however, important to recall that this was not always the case. It used to be the case that States were not accountable in international law for human rights violations, because the humans that now enjoy the rights were not then recognised as subjects of international law. Gradually, developments in international law overruled that objection. Humans were eventually recognised as subjects whose rights were protected in international law. Then the next objection was raised that States could not be held accountable for the violation of their citizens' rights in the hands of their own Governments, because of notions of sovereignty that prevented States from concerning themselves with what was considered the internal affairs of one another. How State officials treated their own citizens was then considered an internal affair of that State. Eventually, that objection, too, was overridden by international law. It was found that the obligation to respect human rights entailed an incidental obligation of accountability owed to the whole world—or obligation *erga omnes*, as the ICJ termed it in the *Barcelona Traction* case.[102] The doctrinal products of this obligation *erga omnes* include the idea of universal jurisdiction for the criminal prosecution of suspects of gross human rights violations that engaged criminal responsibility; the establishment of international criminal courts and tribunals; and, most recently, the acceptance of the doctrine of responsibility (on own national authorities and the international community) to protect citizens from the most serious forms of violations of rights (specifically in the manner of genocide, crimes against humanity and war crimes).[103]

---

[102] *Ibid*, paras 33–34.

[103] See '2005 World Summit Outcome', UNGA Res 60/1 (24 October 2005) UN Doc A/60/L.1, paras 138–139. See also UNCA, 'A more secure world: our shared responsibility—Report of the High-level Panel on Threats, Challenges and Change' (2 December 2004) UN Doc A/59/565.

Human beings, for their part, are no longer permitted by international law to enjoy impunity for gross human rights violations. Individual responsibility for human rights violations was once considered outside the purview of international law. In this regard, it was notably argued in Nuremberg that 'international law [was] concerned with the actions of sovereign States and provide[d] no punishment for individuals; and further, that where the act in question [was] an act of state, those who [carried] it out [were] not personally responsible, but [were] protected by the doctrine of the sovereignty of the State.'[104] But the judges of the International Military Tribunal (IMT) in Nuremberg rejected that argument—quite significantly relying on the jurisprudence of the US Supreme Court.[105] As part of their reasoning, the IMT delivered the following classic international legal dictum: 'Crimes against international law are committed by men, not by abstract entities and only by punishing individuals who commit such crimes can the provisions of international law be enforced.'[106] This judgment resulted in the crystallisation of the international law principle of individual criminal responsibility for international crimes, most of which constitute gross violation of human rights.

Unfortunately, the point of that classic Nuremberg dictum might have been misinterpreted in the *Kiobel* case, by the majority of the US Court of Appeals for the Second Circuit. The point of the dictum was not to limit responsibility to individuals alone, as the Second Circuit majority suggested.[107] The point rather was to reject an argument of impunity, by extending accountability to the human defendants, which was then unheard of in international law, according to the lawyers representing the human defendants in question.

It is important to understand that the IMT did not override the suggestion of Germany's state responsibility—as a matter of civil remedies—for the Nazi violations. What the IMT did was to pierce the veil of state, in order to extend criminal responsibility to the individual culprits of the actions attributable to the State. The sounder interpretation of what the IMT said would lie more in the following analogy: the fact that domestic law would allow a lifting of the corporate veil in order to visit liability (criminal or civil) on *individuals* says little about the idea of the liability of the corporation itself. That analogy is aptly engaged in this current discussion.

---

104 *Judgment of the Nuremberg International Military Tribunal,* The Trial of German Major War Criminals: Proceedings of the International Military Tribunal sitting at Nuremberg, Germany, Part 22 (22 August 1946–1 October 1946) 446.
105 *Ibid* 446, referring to *Ex Parte Quirin* 317 US 1 (1942).
106 *Ibid* 447.
107 Kiobel Second Circuit (n 20) 119.

It must be said that what the IMT considered and rejected in the Nuremberg judgment was in essence the same argument of impunity that was accepted by the Second Circuit majority in *Kiobel*. For, notably, at the time of the judgment of the Nuremberg Tribunal, individual criminal responsibility was not a *universally recognised norm of customary international law*. It is hard, therefore, to resist the speculation that had the *Kiobel* Second Circuit majority dominated the bench of the IMT in 1946, they might have likely held that the individual defendants were not accountable because '[individual responsibility] has not attained a discernable, much less universally recognized, norm of customary law', as they held in 2010 in respect of 'corporate liability' for the same reason of want of 'universal' recognition.[108] It is thus difficult to ignore the dissenting opinion of Leval J (to the decision of the Court of Appeals for the Second Circuit in *Kiobel*) as he observed as follows: 'If past judges had followed the majority's reasoning, we would have had no Nuremberg trials, which for the first time imposed criminal liability on natural persons complicit in war crimes; no subsequent international tribunals to impose criminal liability for violation of international law norms; and no judgments in U.S. courts under the ATS, compensating victims for the violation of fundamental human rights.'[109]

As with States and individuals, aggregate entities have not escaped punitive legal censure for violation of international legal norms including human rights. Such aggregate entities included the political/administrative groups and organisations that were held accountable in Nuremberg for criminal violations, including persecution of Jews, slave labour and mistreatment of POWs. Pursuant to the Charter of the Nuremberg Tribunal, the Tribunal declared the following entities as criminal groups or organisations, as a measure of accountability for their violations: the Leadership Corps of the Nazi Party, *Die Geheime Staatspolizei* (Gestapo), *Der Sicherheitsdienst des Reichsführer SS* (SD), and *Die Schutzstaffeln der Nationalsozialistischen Deutschen Arbeiterpartei* (commonly known as the SS).[110] Indeed, contrary to the assertions of the *Kiobel* majority of the Second Circuit,[111] these entities were among the groups and organisations

---

108   Kiobel Second Circuit (n 20) 149.
109   *Ibid* 153.
110   *Nuremberg Judgment* (n 104) 473–481.
111   As the *Kiobel* majority incorrectly observed in relation of the power granted by the Nuremberg Charter to declare groups and organisations as criminal: 'Such a declaration following indictment, however, did not result in the organization being *punished* or having liability assessed against it': Kiobel Second Circuit (n 20) 137 [emphasis added].

dissolved by the Allied Control Authority in Germany, as *punishment* for their complicity in Nazi atrocities.[112] That was collective state practice in action.

There is no convincing reason to accept that entities such as those would be held accountable for gross violations of human rights, while denying similar accountability to entities organised as business corporations.[113] And, indeed, business corporations never truly escaped such censure. For, other tribunals at Nuremberg were on record as explicitly recognising the liability of corporations for violations of international law, in the judgments against executives of I G Farbenindustrie and Krupp, two corporations implicated in international crimes of the Nazi Regime. In the *Krupp* case—a case conducted within the US military justice system in the American occupation zone of Nuremberg pursuant to Control Council Law No 10[114]—the US Military Tribunal held as follows:

> We conclude from the credible evidence before us that the confiscation of the Austin plant based upon German-inspired anti-Jewish laws and its subsequent detention by the Krupp firm constitute a violation of Article 48 of the Hague Regulations which requires that the laws in force in an occupied country be respected; that it was also a violation of Article 46 of the Hague Regulations which provides that private property must be respected; that the Krupp firm, through defendants…, voluntarily and without duress participated in these violations…and that there was no justification for such action.[115]

In the *I.G. Farben* case, the Nuremberg Military Tribunal held that the Farben conglomerate had violated the prohibition of pillage under Article 47 of the Hague Regulations on the Laws and Customs of War:

---

112 Control Council Law No 2 (Providing for the Termination and Liquidation of the Nazi Organizations) of 10 October 1945 abolished 62 Nazi Organisations; and, a 63rd group was abolished by Control Council Law No 58 (Supplement to Appendix to Control Council Law No 2 Providing for the Termination and Liquidation of Nazi Organizations) of 30 August 1947.

113 As Posner J, writing for the Second Circuit in *Flomo*, correctly observed: 'At the end of the Second World War the allied powers dissolved German corporations that had assisted the Nazi war effort, along with Nazi government and party organizations—and did so on the authority of customary international law': Flomo (n 25) 1017. Notably, Control Council Law No. 9 (Providing for the Seizure of Property owned by I.G. Farbenindstrie and Control thereof) of 30 November 1945.

114 The case was not heard by the International Military Tribunal.

115 *United States v Krupp*, IX Trials of War Criminals before the Nuremberg Military Tribunals (1952) 1351–52.

> Similarly, where a private individual or a juristic person becomes a party to unlawful confiscation of public or private property by planning and executing a well-defined design to acquire such property permanently, acquisition under such circumstances subsequent to the confiscation constitutes conduct in violation of the Hague Regulations.
>
> ...The result was the enrichment of Farben and the building of its greater chemical empire through the medium of occupancy at the expense of the former owners. Such action on the part of Farben constituted a violation of rights of private property, protected by the Laws and Customs of War. And in the instance involving private property, the permanent acquisition was in violation of the Hague Regulations which limits the occupying power to a mere usufruct of real estate. The forms of the transactions were varied and intricate, and were reflected in corporate agreements well calculated to create the illusion of legality. But the objective of pillage, plunder and spoliation stands out, and there can be no uncertainty as to the actual result...
>
> With reference to the charges in the present indictment concerning Farben's activities in Poland, Norway, Alsace Lorraine and France, we find that the proof established beyond a reasonable doubt that offences against property as defined in Control Council Law No. 10 were committed by Farben, and that these offences were connected with, and an inextricable part of the German policy for occupied countries as above described.[116]

The Nuremberg judgments thereby made the point that responsibility under international law for gross violations of international law also extends to corporations, although they did not have the jurisdiction to hold corporations responsible. However, the absence of a mode of judicial enforcement for a norm of international law does not call into question its existence, but is a typical characteristic of international law.

Even the acceptance (purely for purposes of argument) of an absence of a clearly recognised principle of corporate liability in international law, could never amount to a hindrance of the development of international legal jurisprudence in that direction, as Leval J in *Kiobel* (as seen above) and Posner J in *Flomo* correctly recognised.[117] That is precisely how customary international law develops. States seldom assemble in one place to agree to initiate a rule of

---

116 See *US v Krauch, et al.* [I.G. Farben Case] VIII Trials of War Criminals Before the Nuremberg Military Tribunals, iii–iv (1952) 1131–32, 1140–41.

117 In the words of Posner J: '[S]uppose no corporation *had* ever been punished for violating customary international law. There is always a first time for litigation to enforce a norm;

customary international law. Evolution of a customary norm generally begins with one or more States (in their laws or state practice) developing or identifying an initial good idea intended as a legal rule concerning international relations. The absence of overpowering objection, coupled with widespread subsequent practice, by other States produces the custom in the given respect. This process of formation of customary international law was recognized many years ago by the Supreme Court of the United States.[118]

As will become clear presently, it is not necessary to wait for the development of customary international law of corporate liability, in order that it may be recognised in international law. Customary international law is not the only source of international law. General principles of law recognised by civilised nations are an equally strong source of international law, when international treaties and customary international law are silent on a given matter. As is demonstrated next, corporate liability is indeed a general principle of law recognised by civilised nations.

Corporate Civil Liability Exists under International Law by Virtue of General Principles of Law Recognised by Civilised Nations

In the reasoning of the majority of the Second Circuit in *Kiobel*, there appeared to have been a near elision of 'general principles of law recognised by civilised nations' as one of the principal sources of international law—to which reference may be made for purposes of ascertaining the correct answer to a question of international law. The focus of the *Kiobel* majority's attention appeared exclusively trained on customary international law. But treaties and customs (in the nature of consistent and universal practice of States in their relations with each other) are not the only places to look for such answers. According to article 38(1)(c) of the ICJ Statute, general principles of law recognised by civilised nations are an important third source of international law, in the absence of readily available answers in treaties and customary international law. Indeed, this was the recognised source of the rule (discussed earlier) that every breach of international law involves an obligation to make reparation.[119]

---

there has to be. There were no multinational prosecutions for aggression and crimes against humanity before the Nuremberg Tribunal was created': *Flomo* (n 25) 1017.

118 As was accepted in the *Paquete Habana:* 'Many of the usages which prevail, and which have the force of law, doubtless originated in the positive prescriptions of some single State, which were at first of limited effect, but which, when generally accepted, became of universal obligation': 175 US 677, 711 (1900).

119 According to the *Encyclopædia Britannica* (Academic Edition): 'A third source of international law identified by the ICJ's statute is "the general principles of law recognized by civilized nations." These principles essentially provide a mechanism to address international

Therefore, it was not correct procedure for the *Kiobel* Second Circuit majority to have failed to look at this important source of international law, having failed to find the answer they were looking for in treaties and customary international law.

According to Professor Manley Hudson, a pre-eminent American international lawyer of his age (a former Judge of the Permanent Court of International Justice and former Harvard Professor), 'general principles of law recognized by civilized nations', as a source of international law, 'empowers the Court to go outside the field in which States have expressed their will to accept certain principles of law as governing their relations *inter se*, and to draw upon principles common to various systems of municipal law or generally agreed upon among interpreters of municipal law. It authorizes use to be made of analogies found in the national law of the various States. It makes possible the expansion of international law along lines forged by legal thought and legal philosophy in different parts of the world.'[120] Similarly, in the ICJ's *International Status of South West Africa* Advisory Opinion, Sir Arnold McNair (in his Separate Opinion) observed as follows: 'International law has recruited and continues to recruit many of its rules and institutions from private systems of law. Article 38(1)(c) of the Statute of the Court bears witness that this process is still active, and it will be noted that this article authorizes the Court to "apply... (c) the general principles of law recognized by civilized nations"'.[121] More succinctly, Lord Phillimore who proposed the formulation now embodied in article 38(1)(c) of the ICJ Statute had explained general principles as those 'accepted by all nations in *foro domestico*.'[122]

As a source of international law, general principles of international law are directly derived from shared features of municipal legal systems. They do not require an intermediate process of uniform practice of states in their relations with each other. Hence, general principles of law must not be confused with

---

issues not already subject either to treaty provisions or to binding customary rules. Such general principles may arise either through municipal law or through international law, and many are in fact procedural or evidential principles or those that deal with the machinery of the judicial process, eg the principle, established in *Chorzow Factory* (1927–28), that the breach of an engagement involves an obligation to make reparation': www.britannica.com/EBaccessed/topic/291011/international-law/233501/General-principles-of-law accessed 4 August 2014.

120 Manley O Hudson, *The Permanent Court of International Justice, 1920–1942* (The Macmillan Company 1943) 611.
121 *International Status of South West Africa,* Advisory Opinion [1950] ICJ Rep 128, 148.
122 See Bin Cheng, *General Principles of Law as applied by International Courts and Tribunals* (CUP 1993) 25.

customary international law, which depends on universality of the practice of states oriented towards *the international plane*.[123]

The usual concern in relying on general principles of law derived from municipal law, as a source of international law, has always been whether their application could lead to distortion and injustice in international law in particular regards.[124] Hence, in the absence of treaty or custom, municipal law offers a rich source of principles of law and justice in the international sphere. The main limiting concern, apart from universal following, is the need to avoid distortion or injustice in the international sphere.

Naturally, any concern about distortion or injustice would then require specific and rational considerations that engage reasonable apprehension of it. Corporate civil liability for human rights violations engages no such concern. For, the idea of corporate personality and the appurtenances of it—specifically in terms of corporate rights and responsibilities—have already been recognised in international law. In the recent case of *Ahmadou Dadio Diallo* (*Guinea v Democratic Republic of the Congo*) (*Preliminary Objections*), the ICJ dealt with the question of corporate personality and its consequences in the following way:

> 60. The Court notes that the Parties have referred frequently to the case concerning the *Barcelona Traction, Light and Power Company, Limited* (*Belgium* v *Spain*). This involved a public limited company whose capital was represented by shares. The present case concerns SPRLs whose capital is composed of *parts sociales* (see paragraph 25 above).

---

[123] According to Professor Bin Cheng, a renowned authority on general principles of law as a source of international law: 'In Article 38[(1)(a)]…custom is used in a strict sense, being confined to what is a general practice among States accepted by them as law. General practice among nations, as well as the recognition of its legal character, is therefore required. …In the definition of the third source of international law [general principles of law recognized by civilized nations], there is also the element of recognition on the part of civilised peoples, but the requirement of general practice is absent. […] The recognition of these principles in the municipal law of civilised peoples, where the conception of law is already highly developed, gives the necessary confirmation and evidence of the juridical character of the principle concerned.' Bin Cheng, *ibid* 23–24.

[124] See, for instance, Robert Jennings and Arthur Watts, *Oppenheim's International Law*, vol 1 (Peace) (9th ed, Longman 1996) 37: 'In thus opening the way for the operation as international law of general principles of municipal jurisprudence, it must be noted that such principles are in the municipal sphere applied against a background of national laws and procedures. Unless there is some sufficient counterpart to them in abstracting the principles from the various municipal rules, the operation of the principles as a source of particular rules of international law will be distorted.'

61. As the Court recalled in the *Barcelona Traction* case, "[t]here is... no need to investigate the many different forms of legal entity provided for by the municipal laws of States" (I.C.J. *Reports 1970*, p. 34, para. 40). *What matters, from the point of view of international law, is to determine whether or not these have a legal personality independent of their members. Conferring independent corporate personality on a company implies granting it rights over its own property, rights which it alone is capable of protecting.* As a result, only the State of nationality may exercise diplomatic protection on behalf of the company when its rights are injured by a wrongful act of another State. In determining whether a company possesses independent and distinct legal personality, international law looks to the rules of the relevant domestic law.[125] [Emphasis added.]

Indeed, in the *Barcelona Traction* case itself, the first case in which the ICJ pronounced upon the concept of corporate personality, the Court clearly recognised that '[t]*hese entities have rights and obligations peculiar to themselves*.'[126] [Emphasis added.] There is therefore no question that corporations have obligations for their own errors in international law.

Particularly to be noted, in the *Barcelona Traction* case, was the Court's recognition of the profound influence of corporations in international affairs. Speaking about diplomatic protection as it relates to corporations, the Court made that observation in the following way:

From its origins closely linked with international commerce, diplomatic protection has sustained a particular impact from the growth of international economic relations, and at the same time from *the profound transformations which have taken place in the economic life of nations. These latter changes have given birth to municipal institutions, which have transcended*

---

125 *Ahmadou Dadio Diallo (Republic of Guinea v Democratic Republic of the Congo)* (Preliminary Objections) [2007] ICJ Rep 582 paras 60–61.
126 Barcelona Traction, Light and Power Company, Limited (*Belgium v Spain*) (n 101) para 39. Similarly, in his commentary on corporations in international law, Professor Peter Muchlinski of the London School of Economics, observed as follows: 'The act of incorporation creates a legal person separate from the owners and managers of the underlying enterprise. This allows for the creation of a separate capital fund to be applied for the purposes of the corporation, in that *the corporation acquires the right* to own its own assets, to enter into contracts in its own name, to pledge its assets to creditors, and to *be held liable for its actions*.' [Emphasis added.] Peter Muchlinski, 'Corporations in International Law' in Rudiger Wolfrum (ed), *Max Planck Encyclopaedia of International Law* (OUP 2010) ('Muchlinski, 'Corporations in International Law'') para 2.

frontiers and have begun to exercise considerable influence on international relations. One of these phenomena which has a particular bearing on the present case is the corporate entity.[127] [Emphasis added.]

And speaking about the need to accord corporations recognition in international law, the ICJ continued as follows:

In this field international law is called upon to recognise institutions of municipal law that have an important and extensive role in the international field. This does not necessarily imply drawing any analogy between its own institutions and those of municipal law, nor does it amount to making rules of international law depend upon categories of municipal law. All it means is that *international law has had to recognise the corporate entity* as an institution created by States in a domain essentially within their domestic jurisdiction.[128] [Emphasis added.]

Naturally, for purposes of protection of the rights of these municipal institutions that have so transcended frontiers and exerted such considerable influence in international relations, 'calls for a transparent, stable, and predictable investment environment have given rise to specialized rules of international law that offer protection to the assets of corporate investors among others.'[129] That is to say, a robust subset of international law has been developed regarding international commercial arbitration, investment disputes and mixed claim courts, dealing with the protection of rights of corporations.

It is appropriate, at this juncture, to observe that the concern noted earlier about distortion associated with general principles of international law is not a one-way street leading away from application of general principles of law that result in distortion and injustice on the international plane. The concern also vexes the reception of a municipal law idea on the international plane and the distortion of it without reasonable justification. That concern was made so clear by the ICJ in the *Barcelona Traction* Case in relation to operation of the idea of corporate personality in international law. As the Court expressed itself:

In turning now to the international legal aspects of the case, the Court must…start from the fact that the present case essentially involves factors derived from municipal law…*If the Court were to decide the case in*

---

127   Barcelona Traction (n 101) para 37.
128   *Ibid* para 38.
129   Muchlinski, *Corporations in International Law* (n 126) para 5.

> *disregard of the relevant institutions of municipal law it would, without justification, invite serious legal difficulties.* It would lose touch with reality, for there are no corresponding institutions of international law to which the Court could resort. Thus the Court has, as indicated, not only to take cognizance of municipal law but also to refer to it. It is to *rules generally accepted by municipal legal* systems which recognize the limited company whose capital is represented by shares, and not to the municipal law of a particular State, that international law refers. *In referring to such rules, the Court cannot modify, still less deform them.*' [Emphasis added][130]

It would then be highly imprudent to suggest or maintain that the corporate right—as opposed to corporate liability—is the only jural correlative that flows in international law from its recognition of corporate personality as an incident of general principles of law recognised by civilised nations. There is no rational warrant for such a suggestion. The jurisprudence of the ICJ flatly negates such a position. So, too, do many international instruments that have imposed legal obligations on corporations.[131] And, it amounts to a distortion of the idea of corporate personality.

In the *Kiobel* judgment, the Second Circuit majority referred to the absence of criminal responsibility on 'juridical persons' in the Statute of the ICC, as having resulted from a sound rejection of the idea during the negotiation of the Statute; thus suggestive of the inclination of international law to allow immunity to corporations for human rights violations.[132] This suggestion rests on uncertain evidential footing. There is contrary information to the effect that the reason that criminal responsibility for juridical persons (which had been in earlier drafts of the Statute) disappeared from the final document was because '[t]ime was running out', not because of a deliberate choice to exclude it.[133]

What seems clear, though, is that a number of States Parties to the ICC Statute have included corporate criminal responsibility in the municipal legislation they have adopted to implement the ICC Statute locally. Hence, a trend towards 'general principles of law recognised by civilised nations' is implicated in that regard.

---

130   *Barcelona Traction* (n 101) para 50.
131   For a summary of these instruments, see the very useful discussion of Professor Harold Hongju Koh in 'Separating Myth from Reality about Corporate Responsibility Litigation' (2004) 7 JIEL 263.
132   Kiobel Second Circuit (n 20) 119.
133   See Per Saland, 'International Criminal Law Principles' in Roy S. Lee (ed), *The International Criminal Court: The Making of the Rome Statute—Issues, Negotiations, Results* (Kluwer 1999) 189–215, 199.

For instance, under article 213-3 of the French Penal Code, corporations and other private legal persons can be prosecuted for genocide and crimes against humanity. If held liable, they can be dissolved, barred from exercising their functions for a certain period, fined, and, in addition, ordered to make reparation and have part or all of their assets confiscated in accordance with articles 131-38, 131-39 and article 213-3 of French Penal Code. Article 689-11 of the French Code of Penal Procedure, as amended in 2010 to implement the ICC Statute, also gives French courts jurisdiction over crimes against humanity and genocide committed abroad by French nationals (corporations and human beings).

In Canada, Section 2 of the *Criminal Code* and Section 1 of *Criminal Code (criminal liability of organizations) Amendment Act* (2003) equate human beings and corporate bodies in the meaning of 'persons'. These definitions are incorporated into the *Crimes against Humanity and War Crimes Act* (enabling the operation in Canada of the norms contained in the ICC Statute) by virtue of Section 2(2) which provides: 'Unless otherwise provided, words and expressions used in this Act have the same meaning as in the *Criminal Code*.' And in the proscriptive part the *Crimes against Humanity and War Crimes Act* chiefly provides: 'Every *person* is guilty of an indictable offence who commits: (*a*) genocide; (*b*) a crime against humanity; or (*c*) a war crime.'

In Australia, the *Criminal Code* 'applies to bodies corporate in the same way as it applies to individuals' with 'modifications…made necessary by the fact that criminal liability is being imposed on bodies corporate'.[134] And a corporation may be found guilty of any offence including an offence punishable by imprisonment.[135] Division 268 of the Australian *Criminal Code* proscribes 'genocide, crimes against humanity, war crimes and crimes against administration of the justice of the International Criminal Court.'

Ultimately, however, an objection founded on a perceived absence of a strong norm of corporate *criminal* responsibility in international law amounts to a mere smoke screen. For the great caution seen in the domestic realm in the area of corporate criminal responsibility is never known to have obscured *civil* liability for wrongs of agents attributable to corporations. In other words, the initial hesitation (though eventually overcome) in domestic legal systems in the direction of corporate criminal liability,[136] inspired by the notion of

---

134   See Section 12.1(1) of the Criminal Code Act 1995 of the Commonwealth of Australia (revised to 2005).
135   *Ibid* Section 12.1(2).
136   See Department of Justice, 'Corporate Criminal Liability' (Discussion Paper, March 2002) available at http://www.justice.gc.ca/eng/dept-min/pub/jhr-jdp/dp-dt/intro.html

individual autonomy in respect of criminal actions,[137] was never felt as regards civil liability of companies for the wrongful acts of its agents acting within their powers.[138]

Corporate Civil Liability is Consistent with the International Practice of Complementarity between International and Domestic Legal Regimes for the Wholesome Protection of Human Rights

The ATS regime as a route to corporate liability for violation of international human rights law is wholly consistent with the practice of complementarity between municipal regimes and international regimes for purposes of comprehensive implementation of international human rights law. The usual practice is to require States to take the necessary steps, in accordance with their constitutional processes and with the provisions of the given international human rights instrument, to adopt such other measures as may be necessary to give effect to the rights recognized in the instrument in question. Article 2(2) of the *International Covenant on Civil and Political Rights* illustrates this practice.[139]

---

accessed 4 August 2014; Markus Wagner, 'Corporate Criminal Responsibility: National and International Responses' (Background Paper for the International Society for the Reform of Criminal Law, 13th International Conference, Commercial and Financial Fraud: a Comparative Perspective, Malta, 8–12 July 1999) available at <www.icclr.law.ubc.ca/Publications/CorporateCriminal.pdf> accessed 4 August 2014; Sara Sun Beale, 'A Response to the Critics of Corporate Criminal Liability' (2009) 46 Am CLR 1481, 1493–95; Andrew Weissmann, Richard Ziegler, Luke McLoughlin & Joseph McFadden, 'Reforming Corporate Criminal Liability to Promote Responsible Corporate Behavior' (U.S. Chamber Institute for Legal Reform 2008); Celia Wells, *Corporations and Criminal Responsibility* (2nd edn, OUP 2001); Wayne R LaFave, *Criminal Law* (5th edn, Thomson-West 2010) §13.5; and David Ormerod, *Smith and Hogan's Criminal Law* (12th edn, OUP 2008) 245–68.

137 Andrew Ashworth, *Principles of Criminal Law* (6th edn, OUP 2009) 146–54.
138 See Beale, 'A Response to the Critics of Corporate Criminal Liability' (n 134) 1481. See also, for instance, International Commission of Jurists, Corporate Complicity & Legal Accountability, vol 3 (Civil Remedies) (Report of the International Commission of Jurists Expert Legal Panel on Corporate Complicity in International Crimes) (International Commission of Jurists 2008).
139 In the terms of art 2(2) of the International Covenant on Civil and Political Rights: 'Where not already provided for by existing legislative or other measures, each State Party to the present Covenant undertakes to take the necessary steps, in accordance with its constitutional processes and with the provisions of the present Covenant, to adopt such other measures as may be necessary to give effect to the rights recognized in the present Covenant.' Similar provisions, in accordance with this practice, may be found in the International Covenant on Economic, Social and Cultural Rights (art 2); the International

THE OBLIGATION OF CORPORATIONS TO RESPECT HUMAN RIGHTS NORMS   197

None of these instruments excludes corporations from the persons whom the State is required to lean upon for purposes of achieving a wholesome protection of international human rights norms.

This rule of complementarity, which relies on national mechanisms as important instruments of enforcement of international law, is a rule of both necessity and good faith (among nations); given the general absence of international mechanisms for a consistent enforcement of international law.[140]

This rule of complementarity that is consistently found in contemporary instruments of international human rights law fully comports with what Vattel described as a mutual duty of nations to support and promote the international order as the 'society of the human race'[141]—by virtue of which nations 'owe one another all the duties which the safety and welfare of that society require.'[142]

An interpretation of the ATS that encompasses corporate liability for violations of international human rights law in accordance with the ordinary US domestic principles of corporate liability is indeed part of that complementarity between international law and its enforcement through municipal enforcement mechanisms.

Corporate Civil Liability in International Law is Consistent with the Idea of Orderly Redress of Grievances According to the Rule of Law

Finally, it may be noted that current events, involving extra-legal solutions embarked upon by people who have felt foreclosed from the processes of the rule of law, recommend a careful consideration of the position that seeks to place corporations beyond the rule of law when they are implicated in violations of international human rights law. These events re-innervate a crucial

---

Convention on the Elimination of All Forms of Racial Discrimination (art 6); the Convention against Torture and other Cruel, Inhuman or Degrading Treatment or Punishment (art 14(1)); the International Convention on the Protection of the Rights of All Migrant Workers and Members of Their Families (art 83); the Convention on the Elimination of All Forms of Discrimination against Women (art 2–8); the Convention on the Rights of the Child (arts 2 and 4); the Optional Protocol to the Convention on the Rights of the Child on the sale of children, child prostitution and child pornography (arts 1, 3, 4); the Optional Protocol to the Convention on the Rights of the Child on the involvement of children in armed conflict (arts 4(2) 6(1) and 6(3)); the Convention on the Rights of Persons with Disabilities (arts 4, 7, 8 etc.); and, the International Convention for the Protection of all Persons from Enforced Disappearance (arts 3, 4, 6 etc).

140   See Mary Ellen O'Connell, *The Power and Purpose of International Law: Insights from the Theory and Practice of Enforcement* (OUP 2008) ch 9 generally, esp 328.
141   Vattel, *The Law of Nations or the Principles of Natural Law* (n 1) Book II, Ch I, 113–114.
142   *Ibid* 113.

forewarning that motivated the adoption of the Universal Declaration of Human Rights 1948—an instrument correctly described by the late Lord Bingham of Cornhill as 'the great post-war statement of principle associated with the name of Mrs Eleanor Roosevelt.'[143] That forewarning was stated in the following way: '*Whereas* it is essential, if man is not to be compelled to have recourse, as a last resort, to rebellion against tyranny and oppression, that human rights should be protected by the rule of law.' It would be mistaken to consider that oppression in the manner of gross human rights violations is the preserve of wicked governments—never effected or connived in by corporations however powerful.

Here, one recognises the accuracy of the observation that 'legal theory will never be as precise as physics'.[144] And international law shares this shortcoming—perhaps more so than any other branch of applied law. Yet, international law, in all its imperfections must be allowed a continued role as an avenue for orderly expression and resolution of grievances: in order to deny the powerless (with no real access to justice) one excuse to resort to less than legitimate means of settling scores with the powerful (including multinational corporations). In answering the question about the *raison d'être* of international law, Martti Koskenniemi reminds us that international law 'provides the shared surface—the *only* such surface—on which political adversaries recognize each other as such and pursue their adversity in terms of something shared, instead of seeking to attain full exclusion—"outlawry"—of the other. Its value and its misery lie in its being the fragile surface of political community among social agents—States, other communities, individuals—who disagree about social purposes but do this within a structure that invites them to argue in terms of an assumed universality.'[145]

These considerations surely accentuate the short-sightedness and general error of the strategy of putting corporations beyond the rule of international law. It is simply not in anyone's best interest—including the corporations'.

4 Concluding Remarks

Before concluding, it is important to note some related developments from Geneva concerning the recognition of the legal obligation of corporations to

---

143 Bingham, *The Rule of Law* (n 75) 6.
144 Thomas A. Smith, 'The Uses and Abuses of Corporate Personality' (2001) 2 Stanford Agora 69, 70.
145 Martti Koskenniemi, 'What is International Law For?' in Malcolm D Evans (ed), *International Law* (OUP 2003) 89, 110–11.

respect human rights. Besides the High Commissioner's position on the matter expressed through her *amicus curiae* intervention in the *Kiobel* case, the matter had also arisen in the context of two efforts associated respectively with the Human Rights Council and its predecessor body, the Human Rights Commission. The later of these efforts was the work of John Ruggie, the Special Representative of the Secretary-General on the issue of human rights and transnational corporations and other business enterprises, culminating in his Report and 'Guiding Principles on Business and Human Rights: Implementing the United Nations "Protect, Respect and Remedy" Framework', issued on 21 March 2011 ('Ruggie Report').[146]

The Ruggie Report had been preceded by an earlier effort by the Sub-Commission on Human Rights. In August 2003, the Sub-Commission had approved the report of its sessional working group,[147] composed of five of its members, including Professor David S. Weissbrodt, a professor of international human rights law at the University of Minnesota. The mandate of the working group was to examine the working methods and activities of transnational corporations. The report of the working group, entitled 'Norms on the Responsibilities of Transnational Corporations and Other Business Enterprises with Regard to Human Rights,'[148] made clear that corporations had a clear legal obligation to promote and respect human rights. The working group had apparently been motivated by 'the principles and obligations under the Charter of the United Nations, in particular the preamble and Articles 1, 2, 55 and 56, inter alia to promote universal respect for, and observance of, human rights and fundamental freedoms'.[149]

It was an important report. But, it attracted some criticism for being much too ambitious in the ranging scheme of rights[150] and monitoring mechanisms (including the UN and other international organisations, as well as national

---

[146] United Nations Human Rights Council 'Report of the Special Representative of the Secretary-General on the issue of human rights and transnational corporations and other business enterprises, John Ruggie—Guiding Principles on Business and Human Rights: Implementing the United Nations "Protect, Respect and Remedy" Framework' (21 March 2011) UN Doc A/HRC/17/31 ('Ruggie Report').

[147] 'Responsibilities of transnational corporations and other business enterprises with regard to human rights', UNCHR Sub-Commission Res 2003/16 UN Doc E/CN.4/Sub.2/2003/L.11, 52 (2003).

[148] UN Doc E/CN.4/Sub.2/2003/12/Rev.2 (2003).

[149] See the first statement in the preamble.

[150] The norms were laid out in the following heads of provisions including the following: general obligations, right to equal opportunity and non-discriminatory treatment, right to security of persons, rights of workers, respect for national sovereignty and human

bodies, 'already in existence or yet to be created') that it contemplated.[151] Also much of this was prescribed in a language of indeterminate newness.[152] *New* regimes of legal liability are never welcomed with the red carpet by powerful interests sought to be encumbered. The business community are powerful indeed. They make things and create wealth that propels economies. Hence, governments do tend to listen when they worry.

A notable feature of the report was the criticism that the working group had aimed to foist upon firms a norm of legal duties approaching those of States. It may indeed be observed that the working group was not always careful to avoid that criticism. A notable anchor for it appears in the recognition indicated in the third statement of the preamble as follows: '*Recognizing* that even though States have the primary responsibility to promote, secure the fulfilment of, respect, ensure respect of and protect human rights, transnational corporations and other business enterprises, as organs of society, are also responsible for promoting and securing the human rights set forth in the Universal Declaration of Human Rights'. The result of the criticisms and protests was the relegation of the report to the archival graveyard of countless stillborn reports and studies of the UN and its many agencies. The ultimate fate of that effort is, perhaps, best summarised in the following words of John Ruggie:

> 2. One early United Nations-based initiative was called the Norms on Transnational Corporations and Other Business Enterprises; it was drafted by an expert subsidiary body of what was then the Commission on Human Rights. Essentially, this sought to impose on companies, directly under international law, the same range of human rights duties that States have accepted for themselves under treaties they have ratified: "to promote, secure the fulfilment of, respect, ensure respect of and protect human rights".

---

rights, obligations with regard to consumer protection, obligations with regard to environmental protection, etc.

151 It is notably provided in paragraph 16 that 'transnational corporations and other businesses enterprises shall be subject to periodic monitoring and verification by United Nations, other international and national mechanisms already in existence or yet to be created...'.

152 To be noted in that regard is the following statement appearing in para 12 of the preamble: '*Noting also* that new international human rights issues and concerns are continually emerging and that transnational corporations and other business enterprises often are involved in these issues and concerns, such that further standard-setting and implementation are required at this time and in the future...'.

3. This proposal triggered a deeply divisive debate between the business community and human rights advocacy groups while evoking little support from Governments. The Commission declined to act on the proposal. Instead, in 2005 it established a mandate for a Special Representative of the Secretary-General "on the issue of human rights and transnational corporations and other business enterprises" to undertake a new process, and requested the Secretary-General to appoint the mandate holder. This is the final report of the Special Representative.[153]

Indeed, on a careful review of the report of the Sub-Commission's working group, there may be something in the view that they had overloaded the circuit of political receptivity of their work. This comes from not only the numerous novel norms they prescribed in detail, but also their effort in seeking to push for recognition the idea that 'even though States have the primary responsibility to promote, secure the fulfilment of, respect, ensure respect of and protect human rights, transnational corporations and other business enterprises, as organs of society, are also responsible for promoting and securing the human rights set forth in the Universal Declaration of Human Rights'.

But, in fairness, the criticism indicated above implicates a fallacy of the red herring. For, it cannot be correct to assert any proposition which suggests ultimately that the *minimum* of obligation that international law recognises for corporations in the matter of respect for human rights necessarily 'impose[s] on companies, *directly…the same range* of human rights duties that States have accepted for themselves *under treaties they have ratified*: "*to promote, secure the fulfilment of,* respect, *ensure respect of* and *protect* human rights".' [Emphasis added.][154] To pitch the argument at such a grossly inflated level of expectation is to reduce the attendant proposition to an obvious level of absurdity, perhaps demonstrated at the most basic element by the realism of the smaller companies that could seldom be in a position to meet such an obligation. It is not even necessary to enquire whether the larger multi-national corporations will be in a position to discharge such levels of obligation. It is only necessary to view the *minimum* legal obligations of corporations at the elementary level of the requirement that they *do* no harm themselves—by respecting human rights and by refraining from complicity in their violation.

In the end, however, it may well be that the Ruggie Report, mindful of the experience of the Sub-Commission's Working Group, implicated a more careful effort that avoided speaking in terms of the 'legal obligation' of corporations

---

153 Ruggie Report (n 146) paras 2, 3.
154 *Ibid* para 2.

to respect human rights or of 'new' norms in that regard. Yet, the Ruggie Report and its annexure[155] still persistently spoke in terms of 'responsibility' of corporations or business enterprises to respect human rights.[156] Some may argue that there is indeed a distinction in the difference of terminology between 'legal obligation' and 'responsibility': the latter being, perhaps, a matter of virtue ethics (especially in the light of the currency that the idea of 'corporate social responsibility' had attained), in a domain removed from juristic deontology. It may, of course, be noted that Ruggie does indeed contemplate the possibility of civil legal or criminal liability as the last bastion of responsibility at the transnational or international plane.[157]

Others may rightly or wrongly argue that not being a jurist by education or expertise or experience subtracted from Dr Ruggie's standing[158] either to make authoritative pronouncements on what is or not a *'legal* obligation' on corporations—a very important question of law—or to have been in a scholarly position properly to expose or discover the applicable law on the matter.

Nevertheless, Ruggie's report, upon close examination, does not truly detract from the proposition that corporations are bound by international law to respect international human rights norms, notwithstanding Ruggie's care in avoiding to state the proposition in those terms.

At any rate, there is no question that the pecking order of the UN High Commissioner for Human Rights in international affairs, together with the personal juristic pedigree of Dr Navi Pillay[159]—as the particular High Commissioner that made the *Kiobel* intervention—does eminently place that intervention among what Roger had in mind and others would agree as the

---

155 'Guiding Principles on Business and Human Rights: Implementing the United Nations "Protect, Respect and Remedy" Framework' (Annexed to Ruggie Report, n 146).

156 See Ruggie Report (n 146) para 6. See also the Guiding Principles on Business and Human Rights (Annexed to Ruggie Report), commentary to Principle 4, Section II, commentary to Principle 11, Principle 12, commentary to Principle 12, Principle 13, Principle 14, commentary to Principle 14, Principle 15, Principle 16, commentary to Principle 16, Principle 19, commentary to Principle 21, commentary to Principle 22, commentary to Principle 23, and, commentary to Principle 29.

157 See the Guiding Principles on Business and Human Rights (Annexed to Ruggie Report) (n 146) commentary to Principle 23.

158 At the time of his report, Dr Ruggie's *curriculum vitae* indicated that his education and expertise were only in the fields of political science and history (in which he holds a doctorate degree).

159 Dr Pillay is a South African lawyer, with both masters and doctorate degrees from the Harvard Law School. She served as a judge in the Appeals Chamber of the ICC. Before that, she served as a judge and the president of the ICTR.

proper role of the High Commissioner as 'a catalyst for the creation of international customary law' or the exposure or discovery of its latent elements in the area of human rights.

∙ ∙ ∙

I finally conclude this commentary by invoking an Igbo proverb which holds that in the bonhomie of irreverent jests, serious truths are often told. But, that is the very description of 'satire' in the English language. The stance against the obligations on corporations to respect international human rights law raises the question whether a jest has become too solemn for laughter, given Bierce's waggish definition of corporation as 'an ingenious device for obtaining individual profit without individual responsibility.'[160] Is it the case that corporations are entitled to any protection that international law may offer, yet remain immune to the obligations that encumber every other subject of international law, requiring respect for human rights norms as a matter of legal norms? The High Commissioner's intervention in *Kiobel* has the value of making that a catalytic open question—in international law at least. Roger, I doubt not, would hope so.

---

160   Ambrose Bierce, *The Devil's Dictionary* (Doubleday Page & Company 1911).

CHAPTER 14

Human Rights as International Constitutional Law

Bertrand G. Ramcharan

1   Introduction

If there is anyone who, for more than half a century, has sought to advance the rule of law internationally, it is my dear and good friend Prof. Dr. Roger Clark. In penning these lines in his honour, therefore, it is appropriate that we spotlight the heart of the international rule of law: international constitutionalism and, more specifically, international constitutional law. We must do so in light of the conditions of a rapidly changing world.

In its edition of 15/16 February, 2014, the Financial Times, under the title 'The World in 2114', serialised three extracts from a recent book, *In 100 years: Leading Economists Predict the Future*, edited by Ignacio Palacios-Huerta.[1] The Financial Times gave its article the banner highlight 'In 100 Years, economists predict that geo-engineering, performance drugs and artificial intelligence will shape our future.' In his article, Professor Martin Weitzman, Professor of Economics at Harvard University, noted that there are several possible forms of purposeful geo-engineering including one that would offer a quick-fix to the problem of increasing temperatures. This is to create a **'space sunshade'** by shooting reflective particles into the stratosphere that block out a small but significant fraction of incoming solar radiation. He encourages further study of this option, remarking that 'The temptation may become very great for a nation to unilaterally engineer the planet out of high temperatures.'[2]

Nobel Laureate in economics, Alvin Roth, Professor of Economics at Stanford University, wrote that the biggest trend of the future is that the world economy will keep growing and becoming more connected. Material prosperity will increase and healthy longevity will rise. Some people will opt for slower-track living while, for others who wish to compete, there will be technological developments to help them. Families will remain one of the main unit of production—certainly of children—and of consumption of all sorts of household goods and comforts. Some of the big changes to medicine will be technological. 'Selecting

---

[1]   Ignacio Palacios-Huerta (ed), *In 100 years: Leading Economists Predict the Future* (MIT Press 2014).
[2]   Financial Times, 15/16 February 2014, 7.

the genetic characteristics of our children will become widely available and tempting.'[3]

Another Nobel Laureate in economics, Robert Shiller, Professor of Economics at Yale University, wrote that the next century carries with it any number of risks as an unprecedented number of people attempt to live well on a planet with limited resources, with more dangerous strategic weapons of mass destruction, and with the flourishing of new information technologies that stir up labour markets and create career risks. Whether it comes sooner or later, an important consequence of artificial intelligence will be a long trend towards unification of global culture. 'Artificial intelligence will take us on a long trend towards unification of global culture.' There is likely to develop a cosmopolitan culture of the people most connected with artificial intelligence, a sort of world elite who, by their constant communications, will tend to develop some loyalties to each other rather than to their neighbours, while billions of others will form a worldwide string of ghettoes!

Even among the elite, the globalisation of culture will not be complete, and there will still be ancient national and traditional, ethnic and religious rivalries, and the potential for war. But, there will be no central authority to be in control of all of these processes that create risks for individuals and for larger society. 'We must approach all these risks with all of the new kinds of risk management functions that we can invent.'[4]

In what can we anchor the world that is coming? It must be, in our submission, the anchor of international human rights. Hence, the importance of human rights as the core of international constitutional law. The case for human rights norms as the core of international constitutional law is buttressed by the evolving threats and challenges facing human kind and the need for new political and legal thinking. We address these two issues before entering into a discussion of human rights as international constitutional law.

2   Threats and Challenges

We are living in a time when the Earth and humanity are under threats never before experienced in human history. The historian Ian Morris, in his widely acclaimed book, *Why the West Rules—for Now: The Patterns of History and What They Reveal About the Future*, argues that 'The great question for our times is…whether humanity as a whole will break through to an entirely new

---

3   *Ibid.*
4   *Ibid.*

kind of existence before disaster strikes us down permanently.'[5] In the twenty-first century social development promises—or threatens—to rise so high that it will change what biology and sociology can do. We are approaching the greatest discontinuity in history. He recalled that the inventor and futurist Ray Kurzwell had presented the concept of the Singularity: 'a future period during which the pace of technological change will be so rapid, its impact so deep… that technology appears to be expanding at infinite speed.' By about 2045, Kurzwell estimated, computers would be able to host all the minds in the world, effectively merging carbon-and-silicon-based intelligence into a single global consciousness. This will be the Singularity. We will transcend biology, evolving into a new, merged being as far ahead of Homo Sapiens as a contemporary human is of the individual cells that merged to create her/his body. While all of this is taking place, the five horsemen of the Apocalypse all seem to be back: climate change, famine, state failure, migration, and disease.

Morris thinks that there are many possible paths that our future might follow, but however much they wind around, most seem to lead ultimately to the same place, Nightfall: Nuclear Armageddon. The twenty-first century is going to be a race. In one lane is some sort of Singularity; in the other, Nightfall. One will win and one will lose. There will be no silver medal. Either we will soon (perhaps before 2050) begin a transformation even more profound than the industrial revolution, which may make most of our current problems irrelevant, or we will stagger into a collapse like no other.

This means that the next forty years will be the most important in history. What the world needs to do is to prevent Nightfall is not really a mystery. The top priority is to avoid all-out nuclear war, and the way to do that is for the great powers to reduce their nuclear arsenals. The second priority is to slow down 'global wierding' (the fate of Kyoto, etc.). Here things are going less well.

The most effective way to hold back Nightfall for another forty years may be by enmeshing states more deeply with non-state organizations, getting governments to surrender some of their sovereignty in return for solutions that they might be unable to reach independently. In the twenty-first century we must, first, restructure political geography to make room for the kinds of global institutions that might slow down war and global weirding; then we must use the time that buys to carry out a new revolution in energy capture, shattering the fossil-fuel ceiling. Carrying on burning oil and coal like we did in the twentieth century will bring on Nightfall even before the hydrocarbons run out.

---

5 Ian Morris, *Why the West Rules—for Now: The Patterns of History and What They Reveal About the Future* (Profile Books 2010).

For the Singularity to win, we need to keep the dogs of war on a leash, manage global weirding, and see through a revolution in energy capture. Everything has to go right. For Nightfall to win only one thing needs go wrong. The odds look bad.

As we set course to deal with the challenges that Morris presents, we need to recall that the United Nations universal norms on human rights represent the best thinking of humanity at the present stage of its development about how each person should live his or her life, and about how communities should coexist and cooperate nationally and internationally.

Governing the World is another important new book, by Professor Mark Mazower of Columbia University. Published by Penguin in 2012, it has many insights that are sobering. We are, Mazower thinks, living in a time of extreme confusion about the purpose and durability of international institutions. We have moved from an era that had faith in the idea of international institutions to one that has lost it. While internationalism originated as an expression of Western political philosophies and Great Power needs, 'it is clearly now moving beyond that into something much more multicentered and fissiparious.' 'Today our very vocabulary for understanding where we stand in the world is hostage to confused thought and poorly articulate premises. What is "governance"? Who speaks for "civil society"? Is there such a thing as an NGO?'

He considers that the institutions of international governance stand in urgent need of renovation. 'Yet the fundamental nineteenth century insight that effective internationalism rests on effective nationalism remains pertinent.' Now we are on the verge of a new era, and as Western predominance approaches an end, there is much hand-wringing. But, the mere fact that some states are gaining strength as others lose it says little. China, for example, has much to gain and little of any consequence to lose from participating in a system designed to favour leading nations. Like any great power, it will use these institutions to further its own ends, but like its predecessors, it will not always prevail. There is no need to think that the shift in the global balance need of itself mark the end of the international institutions established in the Anglo-American ascendancy.

The rising powers, China above all, have little liking for the IMF, at least in its older incarnation, and attach much greater importance to the idea of preserving sovereignty and some space for domestic political discretion. If their influence grows, the institutions the United States created may be brought back under new direction to the principles that originally animated them. A broader array of voices and perspectives will enrich the rather rigid forms of economic thinking that have predominated since the 1970s.

Getting the institutional architecture right will require fundamental change. In the current crisis, politicians have essentially acted as underwriters, essential but subordinate to the dictates of communities of financial market makers they hesitate to contradict. More generally, the politicians have become policy-makers who listen in the first place to private interests and their lobbyists and try to adjudicate among them. Time will show whether they are any longer capable of governing.

Twentieth century total wars had been fought by states that had mobilized entire societies around shared perils and experiences, and by creating models of equity, solidarity and sacrifice, they had transformed public attitudes in ways that had endured into peacetime. 'Without a comparable transformation in our own views about the nature of government, the public good and the role of the state, without our developing a new kind of faith in our own collective capacity to shape the future, there is no real incentive for our politicians to change.'

To the nineteenth century internationalists, the future had conjured up a new dispensation for mankind, a dispensation they had looked up to with a confidence based upon their control over the universe of facts. Hence Bentham's vision of a perfect system of law that depended on the accumulation of all useful knowledge. To twentieth century institution builders, the future could be planned and tackled with foresight on behalf of entire communities and nations, perhaps even for the world as a whole. Today, 'where the primacy of the fact is challenged by the Web', the future, more important than ever, has been privatized, monetized, and turned into a source of profit. An entire corporate sector is dedicated to commodifying and modelling it. Our financial markets in general take the future as the determinant of present values in a way that simply was not true a century ago. This money-driven individualistic future has crowded out an older vision of what the public good might look like.

In the ongoing atomisation of society, citizens and classes have both vanished as forces for change and given way to a world of individuals, who come together as consumer of goods or information, and who trust the Internet more than they do their political representatives or the experts they watch on television. Governing institutions today have lost sight of the principle of politics rooted in the collective values of a *res publica*, even as they continue to defend the 'civilization of capital.' Professor Mazower concludes:

> As for the rituals of international life, these are now well-established. The world's heads of state flock annually to the UN General Assembly. There are discussions of reform and grandiose declarations of global targets,

and businessmen make their pilgrimage to Davos, seeking to confirm through this triumph of corporate sponsorship that a global ruling elite exists and that they belong to it. Our representatives continue to hand over power to experts and self-interested self-regulators in the name of efficient global governance while a sceptical and alienated public looks on. The idea of governing the world is becoming yesterday's dream'![6]

3 The Need for New Political Thinking

In his highly regarded book, *Western Political Theory in Face of the Future*, Professor Dunn laments, 'We palpably do not know what we are doing.'[7] In October 2013, Oxford University's Oxford Martin Commission for Future Generations published a report calling for a radical shake-up to deliver progress on climate change, reduce economic inequality, improve corporate practices and address the chronic burden of disease. Its recommendations included the creation of a coalition to counteract climate change, to fight communicable disease, end discrimination against future generations by revising discounting methods and adjusting them to take account of the uncertainties, risks and ethical implications for the long-term.[8] Professor Ian Goldin, Director of the Oxford Martin School and Vice-Chair of the Commission, said on the launching of the report: 'Failure to address long-term issues exposes current generations to unacceptable instability and risk; it threatens our ability to build a sustainable, inclusive and resilient future for all.'

For a number of years, Professor Andrew Dobson has been making the case for new political thinking. He advocates 'Ecologism', which makes the Earth as physical object the very foundation-stone of political intellectual edifice, arguing that its finitude is the basic reason why infinite population and economic growth are impossible and why, consequently, profound changes in our social and political behaviour need to take place. Political ecologists stress that consumption of material goods by individuals in 'advanced industrial countries' should be reduced, and that human needs are not best satisfied by continued economic growth as we understand it today.

What sets ecologism apart from political ideologies such as liberalism, conservatism, and socialism, Dobson contends, is its focus on the relationship

---

6 Mark Mazower, *Governing the World: The History of an Idea* (Penguin 2012) 427–28.
7 John Dunn, *Western Political Theory in Face of the Future* (Canto 1979).
8 Now for the Long Term. The Report of the Oxford Martin Commission for Future Generations, Oxford Martin School, Oxford University, 16 October 2013.

between human beings and the non-human natural world. No other modern political ideology, it is contended, has this concern. There are three principal thoughts related to the limits to growth thesis that have come to be of prime importance to the radical green position. They are: first, that technological solutions (i.e. solutions formulated within the bounds of present economic, social and political practices) will not in themselves bring about a sustainable society; second, that the rapid rates of growth aimed for (and often achieved) by the industrialised and industrialising societies have an exponential character, which means that dangers stored up over a relatively long period of time can very suddenly have a catastrophic effect; and third, that the interaction of problems caused by growth means that such problems cannot be dealt with in isolation—i.e. solving one problem does not solve the rest, and may even exacerbate them.

A central question is whether a sustainable society can be brought about through the use of existing state institutions and political ideologies. Liberalism, it is argued, does not provide an answer. Since the guiding idea of political ecology is that this is an ecological place rather than an evolutionary place. With the restoration of the ecological idea in politics, battle with the evolutionary view of political progress (liberalism) has once again been joined. Conservatism, it is contended, is interested in conserving and preserving the past, whereas ecologism is interested in conserving and preserving for the future. Herein lies a signal difference between the conservative and ecological political imaginations. Socialism, for its part, it is added, identifies capitalism as the source of the ills of contemporary society. Political ecologists are much more likely to refer to 'industrialism' as the problem.

One of the reasons the green movement considers itself to 'beyond left and right' is because it believes that the traditional spectrum of opposition between socialism and capitalism is inscribed in a more fundamental context of agreement: a 'super-ideology' called 'industrialism.' Ecologists stress the similarities between capitalist and socialist countries in that they are both considered to believe that the needs of their respective populations are best satisfied by maximizing economic growth. Ecologism envisages a post-industrial future that is quite distinct from that with which we are most generally acquainted. While most post-industrial futures revolve around high-growth, high-technology, expanding services, greater leisure, and satisfaction conceived in material terms, ecologism's post-industrial society questions growth and technology, and suggests that the Good Life will involve more work and fewer material objects. Fundamentally, ecologism takes seriously the universal condition of the finitude of the planet and asks what kinds of political, economic and social practices are possible and desirable.

Professor Gregory Claeys, Professor of Political Thought at the University of London and a prolific writer on political ideas, has argued that we need a new political theory in which we create a new notion of the common good built on the preservation of the natural world. We need to create rights of nature, for forests and animals, that proscribe undue exploitation such as overfishing or destruction of the rain forests. We need a new contract theory, revising our notion of a social contract built on the preservation of individual rights, in light of the need to make preservation of the natural world a key priority. Our priority must be for the protection of nature as well as human beings.

Popular sovereignty, he continues, is not, as such, the highest good but our collective survival is. We need to persuade the majority of this. Market theory should not be decisive. Rebuilding the forests, replenishing fish stocks, reducing pollution and creating alternative energy forms all can involve markets, and can be made profitable where the public provides financial incentives to develop such resources and penalties for those who continue the process of exploitation.

Overpopulation, he adds, is such a central part of the green argument that we must necessarily combat any ideology, secular or religious, that either deliberately or incidentally promotes large families. We must construct a new vision of the future. In this regard, the triumphalist cry of victory by the free market ideal over central planning may be misplaced and premature.

We have, he laments, virtually no models of international organizations upon which to try to imagine the implementation of such policies. We must be ready to deal with the growing wars over scarce resources, notably water and arable land; the movement of large populations seeking such resources, and the conflicts again that would ensue in such a case. The longer we wait to act, the more difficult will be the solution and the less likely the success. We can achieve utopia, but we will have to work hard for it. What will arrive if we do nothing is too unpleasant to contemplate further.[9]

4   Human Rights Strategies of Governance

We think that human rights strategies of governance offer a way of addressing the new threats and challenges in a manner consistent with respect for the integrity, dignity and rights of individuals, groups, and peoples. The International Bill of Human Rights, consisting of the Universal Declaration ('UDHR')

---

9 Professor Claes advances these views in his course on Modern Political Ideas offered in the International Programme of the University of London.

and the two International Covenants, prescribes core standards of human rights for the conduct of governance in all countries, and the Universal Periodic Review process watches over the way in which each government is giving effect to its human rights obligations.

The rights in the International Covenant on Civil and Political Rights ('ICCPR') are to be respected and protected immediately. This also applies to some economic, social and cultural rights, particularly the right not to be discriminated against. In respect of other rights in the International Covenant on Economic, Social and Cultural Rights ('ICESCR'), Governments are to take measures in good faith to implement them progressively in light of the resources available and with the benefit of international cooperation.

By taking the rights in the UDHR and in the two International Covenants as their point of departure, Governments can pursue policies and strategies of governance that are best calculated to meet the needs of the twenty-first century, and to anchor the future political society in the integrity, dignity and freedom of individuals, groups, and peoples. Human rights strategies of governance involve recognizing:

- The supremacy of international human rights law (international customary law, general principles of law and international treaty law) over national law.
- Organs of society nationally, regionally, and internationally, must cooperate in good faith to prevent threats to the existence and security of human kind and the planet.
- Governance in every country of the world must be in accordance with the principles of the UDHR and human rights norms binding upon all governments.
- Regional organizations everywhere must recognize as an inherent part of their mandate to protect human rights recognized in universal and regional norms.
- International organizations everywhere must recognize as an inherent part of their mandate to protect human rights recognized in universal norms. The UN Security Council must respect human rights norms in the course of its work and must act for the protection of human rights in situations or on issues engaging its attention.
- Core norms of international human rights law, particularly norms of *jus cogens*, must be reflected in the constitution of every Member State of the UN.

It is in light of this reasoning that the place of human rights in international constitutional law becomes so important.

5 International Constitutional Law

As part of future-oriented policy and legal thinking, I want to argue for human rights as international constitutional law. To do so, I need to address some gateway issues: Is international human rights law an independent system or is it part of international law? Jan Klabbers, one of the authors of a recent book, *The Constitutionalization of International Law*, thinks that 'international human rights law has become a more or less self-contained system.'[10] On the other hand, the late Professor Ian Brownlie, in his *Principles of Public International Law*, frowned on 'international human rights law' and saw the international law of human rights as part of overall international law. I tend to lean towards this view.

The next gateway issue I need to address is whether there is such a thing as international constitutional law, or the constitutionalisation of international law. The late Professors Ronald St. J. Macdonald and Douglas M. Johnston championed the idea that the UN Charter is international constitutional law. Professor Johnston wrote: '…modern international law can be envisioned idealistically, in ethical and institutional terms, as a collective effort to achieve universal order through the development of constitutional structure and procedure among nations.'[11] Prof. Johnston considered that 'The international law of human rights is the ethical core of world constitutionalism. It is now the focus of numerous monitoring organizations around the world and of several international tribunals.'[12]

Macdonald and Morris considered that the world is no longer governable entirely by resort to the classical system of international law. Even more seriously, it seemed that the purposes and principles of the UN Charter were no longer being served sufficiently in light of new concerns. The text adopted in 1945 did not convey the image of a world tormented by terrorists. Nor did it reflect the most pressing commitments of our time: to democratic governance, to environmental responsibility, and to a freer and more equitable system of world trade. Increasingly, the international law community acknowledges the need to set new priorities in the development of international law.

To this end, they thought it timely to consider the case for strengthening the constitutional framework of norms and institutions established in the second

---

[10] Jan Klabbers, Anne Peters & Geir Ulfstein, *The Constitutionalization of International Law* (Oxford University Press 2009) 2.
[11] Ronald St J. Macdonald & Douglas M. Johnson, *Towards World Constitutionalism* (Martinus Nijhoff 2005) 5.
[12] *Ibid* 19, note 33.

half of the 20th century. The post-Cold War euphoria of the 1990s had virtually evaporated under the stress of new concerns at a time when states comprising the UN system were no longer capable of addressing these challenges. They therefore presented the case for a more 'constitutionalised' system of international law and diplomacy.

6 Human Rights as the Core of International Constitutional Law

The academic world has been probing issues touching on human rights and international constitutional law for some time. In 1987, the Akron Law Review carried the Proceedings of a Symposium held at the School of Law on 13 November 1986 on 'Human Rights as Comparative Constitutional Law.'[13] The International Academy of Constitutional Law, Tunis, in 2000 published a volume, *Constitution et Droit International*, which carried learned presentations on this topic, including by former UN Secretary-General Boutros Boutros-Ghali.[14] More recently a conference was held in France, and the proceedings published under the title, *'Les droits de l'homme: ont-il constitutionalise le monde?.'*[15] Participants referred to elements that might be considered constitutionalisation but, on the whole, left the matter open for the time being.[16]

Jan Klabbers himself recognizes, that 'constitutionalization and constitutionalism themselves are controversial notions'[17] I want to side-step the issue of the constitutionalization of international law as a broader process. I intend to submit that the International Bill of Human Rights, which consists of the UDHR, the ICCPR, and the ICESCR, represent international constitutional law of our world.[18]

How can I support this submission? To begin with, we need to distil our understanding of what we mean by international constitutional law. It embraces those norms of public international law that regulate the governance of the world community nationally, regionally and internationally. Human rights are a

---

13 Jacob WF Sundberg (ed), 'Proceedings of a Symposium held at the School of Law on 13 November 1986 on "Human Rights as Comparative Constitutional Law"' (1987) 20(4) Akron L Rev 1.
14 (2000) 8 Recueil des Cours (*Constitution et Droit International*).
15 Stéphanie Shennette-Vauchez, 'Les droits de l'homme: ont-il constitutionalise le monde?', Coll. Droit de la convention européenne des droits de l'homme, Colloque N 1.
16 Stephanie Hennette-Vauchez et Jean-Marc Sorel (eds), Les droits de l'homme ont-ils constitutionnalise le monde? (Bruylant 2011).
17 *Ibid* 6.
18 See, generally, Bertrand G Ramcharan, 'The Legal Status of the International Bill of Human Rights' (1986) 55 NJIL 366.

part of international constitutional law. There are other parts dealing, for example, with issues of international security, for example Chapters 6 and 7 of the UN Charter. The essential rationale of international constitutional law is to highlight structures and strategies of governance nationally, regionally and internationally.

The sources of international law, as is well known, include treaties, custom, and general principles of law, and judges and renowned publicists can help us clarify what the law is in cases of doubt. Treaties contain contractual obligations that may grow into international customary law. International customary law might further rise into norms of *jus cogens*. I cannot make the case that the UDHR and the two international covenants as a whole represent international customary law or norms of *jus cogens*, although particular provisions might well do so.

In identifying constitutional norms of international human rights law, the protection of humanity and human life must be our starting point. This raises issues of the right to life. The sustainability of life must be our next principle, raising issues of sustainable development and the right to development. The protection of endangered human species is the next principle, raising issues of the rights of minorities and indigenous populations. Cooperation and dialogue must be our next principle, raising rights issues such as the duty to cooperate in good faith. The principle of humanity, a core tenet of international law provides an indispensable foundation for us to build on. The prohibitions of state violence such as torture are likewise foundation elements. So are freedom of conscience and belief; freedom of opinion and expression; the Responsibility to Protect; norms of *jus cogens*; and the principle of equality.

The opening article of the UDHR proclaims that all human beings are born free and equal in dignity and rights and should act towards one another in a spirit of brotherhood and sisterhood. In the Charter of the United Nations, all Member States committed themselves to upholding human rights and fundamental freedoms at home, without discrimination, and to cooperate for their realization in all countries.

The United Nations proclaimed the UDHR as a common standard of achievement for all peoples. It affirms that the will of the people shall be the basis of the authority of governments. Spelling out the content of the UDHR in greater detail, a series of international covenants or treaties has been accepted by Member States containing obligations of result or of conduct. The International Convention on the Rights of the Child has been ratified or acceded to by 193 Member States, the ICCPR by 167 States.

There is a solid body of jurisprudence from human rights treaty bodies and from other authoritative sources on the content of human rights obligations. Under various treaties there are reporting procedures, petitions procedures, and some inter-state complaint procedures. Under the Universal Periodic Review process, which began in 2008, every Member State comes before the Human Rights Council once every four and a half years to explain what it is doing to implement its human rights obligations under the various international human rights instruments. Experiences are shared and recommendations offered and sometimes accepted and implemented.

The 1993 Vienna World Conference on Human Rights affirmed that the universality of human rights is beyond question. In the Millennium Declaration, the leaders of the world committed themselves to specified human rights values to guide their conduct in the twenty-first century. In the World Summit outcome document of 2005, Heads of State and Government reaffirmed 'that our fundamental values, including freedom, equality, solidarity, tolerance, respect for all human rights, respect for nature and shared responsibility, are essential to international relations.' In the same World Summit outcome document, world leaders declared the following: 'We recommit ourselves to actively protecting and promoting all human rights, the rule of law and democracy and recognize that they are interlinked and mutually reinforcing and that they belong to the **universal and indivisible core values** and principles of the United Nations...' They further reaffirmed 'the solemn commitment of our States to fulfill their obligations to promote universal respect for and the observance and protection of all human rights and fundamental freedoms for all in accordance with the Charter, the UDHR and other instruments relating to human rights and international law. The universal nature of these rights is beyond question.'

The world leaders affirmed that each individual State has the responsibility to protect its population from genocide, war crimes, ethnic cleansing and crimes against humanity. This responsibility entails the prevention of such crimes, including their incitement, through appropriate and necessary means. 'We accept that responsibility and will act in accordance with it. The international community should, as appropriate, encourage and help States to exercise this responsibility and support the United Nations in establishing an early warning capability.'

We have seen earlier above that the world leaders, in affirming the universality of human rights and the obligations of governments, invoked the Charter, the UDHR and other instruments relating to human rights and international law. The Declaration on Principles of International Law and Friendly Relations among States of 1970, codified the human rights obligations of Member States of the UN under the UN Charter. Every State, under international law, has specific legal obligations under norms of *jus cogens*, norms of international customary law, norms under general principles law common to the major legal systems, and under particular treaties that they have subscribed to.

The key question to be asked in a discussion of human rights as international constitutional law is the following: If Governments have repeatedly proclaimed these legal and policy commitments are they not under an obligation to make them part of their constitutional and legal orders? We submit that they are, and that this is the essence of human rights as international constitutional law. Concretely we need to build on the International Bill of Human Rights highlighting, in particular:

- The Right to Life
- The Right to Security
- The Right to Dignity
- The Right to Equality
- The Right to Liberty
- The Right to Humane Treatment
- The Right to Diversity
- The Right to Protection
- The Right to Democracy
- The Right to the Rule of Law

This is the core of human rights as international constitutional law. We need dynamic, rather than static, thinking. Classical legal reasoning will not suffice. After the Second World War, the Institute of International Law commissioned from the late Prof. Charles de Visscher a report on 'The Fundamental Rights of Man as the Basis for the Restoration of International Law.' After considering this report, the Institute adopted a resolution with the same title. Fundamental Human Rights must now be the bedrock in shaping the world that is coming. In short, Human Rights must provide the foundations of international constitutional law. We have no other choice!

The UN's role in shaping the future world is greatest in the human rights jurisprudence it has developed to help build a world of human dignity and progress based on respect for human rights. At the forefront of this work has been the UN Human Rights Committee, which monitors the implementation of the ICCPR. The Human Rights Committee is in the process of humanizing sovereignty. The Committee insists that governments are not at liberty to act as they see fit but must conform to international human rights standards. The Human Rights Committee held in a landmark case that the foremost United Nations organ, the Security Council, must comply with international human rights norms when its actions affect individuals. This is a breath-taking decision of the Human Rights Committee in the case of *Sayadi and others v. Belgium* (2008). In that case, Belgium argued that it was shielded from scrutiny because it was acting to implement a Security Council resolution. 'No', the Committee replied; Belgium must comply with its human rights obligations, which took precedence. The Security Council cannot act in breach of human rights.

The Human Rights Committee has insisted that even in times of public emergency there can be no excuses for violating fundamental rights such as the right to life or not to be tortured. In a time when human rights are being flouted in the name of acting against terrorism, the Human Rights Committee holds aloft the banner of international human rights law and insists that no Government is above the law. Among the legal precepts developed by the Human Rights Committee are the following:

- Governments are legally bound to take reasonable and appropriate measures to protect people within their jurisdiction or control.
- The law must strictly control and limit the circumstances in which a person may be deprived of his or her life by the authorities of the State.
- A State, by invoking the existence of exceptional circumstances, cannot evade the obligations it has undertaken under international human rights law by ratifying the Covenant.
- A situation in which the functions and competences of the judiciary and the executive are not clearly distinguishable or where the executive is able to control of direct the judiciary is incompatible with the notion of an independent and impartial judiciary.
- Governments are under a legal obligation to ensure that remedies for violations are effective. Expedition and effectiveness are particularly important in the adjudication of cases involving torture.
- Where violations have taken place Governments must take measures to ensure that similar violations do not take place in the future.
- Governments should take specific and effective measures to prevent the disappearance of individuals and establish effective facilities and procedures to investigate thoroughly by an appropriate and impartial body, cases of missing and disappeared persons.
- Being subjected to incommunicado detention in an unknown location constitutes cruel and inhuman treatment.
- Women and men are entitled to equal treatment in the application of laws.

7 Conclusion

We would conclude this essay with the following submissions, grounded in the belief that human rights represent international constitutional law:

- National constitutional arrangements must be designed, and periodically reviewed, so as to ensure implementation, in good faith, of international human rights obligations.
- International human rights law must take precedence over national law. This is the principle of the supremacy of international law.
- National courts must be empowered to implement international human rights norms.
- International organizations must recognize as an inherent part of their mandate to protect human rights recognized in universal norms. The UN Security Council must respect human rights norms in the course of its work and must act for the protection of human rights in situations or on issues engaging its attention.
- Regional organizations everywhere must recognize as an inherent part of their mandates to protect human rights recognized in universal and regional norms.
- Norms of *jus cogens* must be incorporated within the constitutional and legal orders of every State.
- The core of the UDHR and the ICCPR should be part of the constitutional and legal orders of every State.
- The duty to cooperate, codified in the UN Declaration on Principles of Friendly Relations and Cooperation, should be reflected in the constitutional and legal orders of States.
- Organs of society nationally, regionally, and internationally, must cooperate in good faith to prevent threats to the existence and security of humankind and the planet.
- The duty to cooperate in respect of the Responsibility to Protect should be reflected in the national constitutional order of every State.
- Norms of *jus cogens* and of international customary law should be incorporated into the legal orders of every Member State.
- Every Government must be able to show that it has in place an adequate and effective national protection system.
- Governance in every country of the world must be in accordance with the principles of the UDHR and human rights norms binding upon all governments.

CHAPTER 15

Human Rights in Foreign Policy: Can Realism be Liberalized?

David P. Forsythe

'[T]here is permanent contradiction between human rights and the foreign policy of a state, even in France...One cannot decide the foreign policy of a country only as a function of human rights. To lead a country obviously distances one from a certain Utopianism.'[1]

One narrative has it that World War II proved so profoundly shocking that the victorious powers were determined not to repeat past mistakes. This negative learning produced the United Nations with a more authoritative Security Council ('UNSC'). It also produced for the first time a broad international law of human rights that would produce democratic, rights-protective, and hence peaceful states.[2] Presumably, then, an expanded liberal internationalism was supposed to curtail dangerous developments based on narrow nationalism and its foreign policy derivative, realism.[3]

I challenge this narrative, arguing that policy decisions in the 1940s reflected mostly a continuation of the nation-state system based on narrow nationalism

---

[1] Bernard Kouchner, quoted in The *New York Times* (10 December 2008) at <www.nytimes.com/2008/12/11/world/europe/11france.html> accessed 27 January 2015.

[2] Parallel to the present essay is the question of the validity of the democratic peace theory, namely that consolidated liberal democracies do not often war on each other. The present analysis remains focused on whether there is evidence that states, whether democratic or not, take at least some internationally recognized human rights seriously.

[3] On realism and liberalism, I follow the typology found in Steven W. Hook U.S. *Foreign Policy: The Paradox of World Power* (2nd ed, CQ Press 2008) 68 and *passim*. Realism is state centric and sees states and their leaders as self-interested, focused on national power, pessimistic about the workings of the state system, prioritizing national independence and security. It reflects a narrow nationalism in that what animates policy is concern for one's own interests. Liberalism is not state centric but sees states and their leaders as willing to compromise for the common good in international institutions, giving great saliences to law and human rights, optimistic that international organization can mitigate the dangers of the state system, willing to delegate authority to muscular international institutions. It is thus based on cosmopolitan values. Other views exist as well, such as neo-conservatism and neo-Marxism, which will not be addressed in this short essay. There is no agreement on how to characterize different types of nationalism, including how to recognize and label a blend of narrow nationalism and cosmopolitanism.

but modified by a realist scheme of Great Power management through the UNSC. Structural realism still dominated foreign policy decisions because the insecurity of states was not solved after 1945, as before. Human rights were formally recognized but not very important outside of Western Europe. For key national policy makers after the world war, universally recognized human rights were little more than window dressing. In other words, realists continued to dominate, being more influential than the liberal internationalists who failed to control the most important developments. Narrow nationalism did not yield easily to cosmopolitan values, at least in part because the security dilemma remained for states. There was no centralized power to guarantee their security, so they had to prioritize that subject. Bernard Kouchner, the French politician and activist for human rights and humanitarian affairs, belatedly recognized this fact as per the opening quote.

I suggest that from the beginning of the UN era through contemporary times, a key struggle sometimes affecting the development of policy has been the continuing liberal internationalist effort to get states to take human rights norms seriously. There HAS been more attention to internationally recognized human rights over time, but not to the extent of consistently replacing the narrow, self-interested policies of the major states. Thus, realism as a reflection of narrow nationalism continues to dominate policy, even if liberal internationalism is more important than it once was. In other words, realism has been slightly liberalized, but mostly on issues seen as secondary by the Great Powers.

1 Brief Historical Observations to 1991

Immediately after World War II, endorsement of the new human rights norms was not matched by state willingness to accept significant 'sovereignty costs' and other inconveniences. Most states wanted to be associated with the new human rights norms in a general way but wanted to preserve their freedom of policy-making when it came to implementing the new norms. Stephan Krasner has written about the norm of state sovereignty as 'organized hypocrisy.'[4] In many ways circa 1945 the discourse on human rights was also organized hypocrisy.

Mention of human rights in the UN Charter was less a matter of genuine commitment to cosmopolitan principle and more a matter of being trapped in the nationalistic rhetoric of war time propaganda. Having issued the Atlantic

---

4 Stephen D. Krasner, *Sovereignty: Organized Hypocrisy* (Princeton University Press 1999).

Charter in 1941 with its promises of personal rights and freedoms for all, the United States and Britain then felt obligated, in the face of demands to take the promises seriously, not to brazenly abandon those principles after the war. Without doubt, Britain as led by Churchill did not believe in ending the British Empire and recognizing full national and personal rights for Indians, Kenyans, etc. In fact, far from being committed to universal human rights, Britain engaged in racism and even torture to try to hold onto entities like Kenya (and also Aden).[5] British racist views were also in evidence in the overthrow of Mossadeq in Iran, with London demeaning Iranians as inferior and incompetent, unworthy of fair treatment and adequate compensation for work in the oil industry.[6] Equal autonomy and respect were hardly guidelines for British policies toward the non-Western world for some decades after the 1948 Universal Declaration of Human Rights.

As for Roosevelt ('FDR'), his typical inconsistency and juggling of competing ideas was evident. On the one hand he seemed to buy into the notion that the protection of human rights within nations was necessary for international peace and security. FDR interacted with H.G. Wells and was familiar with Wells' views on the importance of human rights for world peace.[7] On the other hand, early American planning for the United Nations organization as a concert of Great Powers to manage the peace did not emphasize human rights.[8] Just as FDR saw Stalin as one who could be counted on to help manage things after World War II, so FDR's policies in various conferences from 1943 to early 1945 skipped the subject of human rights. Meetings in Moscow, Tehran, and the Dumbarton Oaks conference in Washington to plan for the future did not address human rights. Only later and in a peripheral and vague way were human rights mentioned in the draft UN Charter. While some NGOs and Latin American diplomats had some role in this additive process at the San Francisco Conference that approved the final Charter draft, the U.S. government (under Truman from the spring of 1945) did not change its view that Charter language on human rights should be general rather than specific and aspirational rather than judicially enforceable. After all, the United States in the 1940s still manifested both Jim Crow laws discriminating against African-Americans and

---

5 The UK finally admitted to torture in places like Kenya in the 1950s. See Alan Cowell, 'Britain to Compensate Kenyans for Colonial-Era Torture', *New York Times* (13 June 2013) at <http://www.nytimes.com/2013/06/07/world/europe/britain-colonial-torture-kenya.html?_r=0 > accessed 27 January 2015.

6 Stephen Kinzer, *Overthrow: America's Century of Regime Change From Hawaii To Iraq* (Henry Holt 2006).

7 Jan Herman Burgers, 'The Road to San Francisco: The Revival of the Human Rights Idea in the Twentieth Century' (1992) 14(4) HRQ 447.

8 Samuel Moyn, *The Last Utopia: Human Rights in History* (Harvard University Press 2010).

powerful southern Senators committed to maintaining the American version of Apartheid. The leaders of key nations mostly saw the UN Charter in 1945 as a realist document giving the victorious major powers unfettered rights through the Security Council to do what was necessary to keep the post-war peace.[9] Human rights was a weak tack-on. There was not much 'learning' on this point from the Second World War, certainly not for Stalin and Churchill, and not even for FDR and Truman.

Another dimension of U.S. foreign policy post-1945 is relevant. While some German and Japanese leaders were prosecuted at Nuremburg and Tokyo, other enemy elites who had been implicated in war crimes were brought to the United States to work on national security projects with a view to the coming Cold War. The view of Robert Jackson and others that international criminal law could be used to legalize and pacify international relations was never pursued with singleness of purpose. Eventually the U.S. focus on German war crimes was dropped in order to get Adenauer elected and Germany embedded in NATO.[10] Similar developments occurred in Japan, as attention to war crimes yielded to efforts to align Japan with U.S. security policy. So U.S. views on international criminal justice were dependent on shifting calculations of self-interest, especially pertaining to security. Legalities to defend human rights were to be advanced when convenient and jettisoned when not. National political calculation based on self-interest remained primary. Legal considerations, including on human rights, remained secondary and dependent on those prior realist judgments.[11]

To take one final set of developments, as is well known the 1948 Universal Declaration of Human Rights was not immediately binding, being a General Assembly resolution. According to Eleanor Roosevelt, who was kept on a short leash by the realists in the State Department, it was a statement of aspirations. Truman did not think the Universal Declaration of Human Rights important enough to mention in his memoirs. (And thus we still do not have direct evidence concerning what he thought about the Declaration's endorsement of socio-economic rights, which the U.S. government as a whole basically ignored, then and now, even while twisting arms in support of the Declaration's passage in 1948.)[12] Later, there was no UN human rights court for binding adjudication

---

9   See especially John Gerard Ruggie, *Winning the Peace: America and World Order in the New Era* (Columbia University Press 1996) Ch 2.
10 Peter Maquire, *Law and War: An American Story* (Columbia University Press 2000).
11 See further especially Werner Levi, *Law and Politics in the International Society* (Sage 1976) regarding politics as primary and law as secondary.
12 Mary Ann Glendon, without evidence, surmises that E. Roosevelt persuaded Truman to support the Declaration even with its mention of socio-economic rights: *A World Made New: Eleanor Roosevelt and the Universal Declaration of Human Rights* (Random House 2001).

of the numerous human rights treaties. The Genocide Treaty did not bind consenting states to precise and sure action even in the face of attempted group destruction, and states like the United States reserved against the Article requiring adjudication by the International Court of Justice of unresolved genocide disputes. Much human rights talk was not accompanied by real commitment to human rights protection.

Moreover, in general from 1945 the United States, the most powerful state, sought to endorse a sometimes liberal international law for others while preserving a zone of autonomy for itself.[13] It saw itself as a leader for human rights and rationalized its Cold War policies as defending freedom and the free world. In fact, however, in the strategic struggle with the Soviet Union it displayed many realist traits by, inter alia, manipulating elections, overthrowing elected leaders, aligning with autocrats, etc. It consistently refused to accept most norms of internationally recognized human rights as controlling at home, especially through U.S. Court decisions, with one or two exceptions pertaining to refugee law or the laws of armed conflict.[14]

If one looks at the International Convention on Civil and Political Rights, one finds actually that most of the rights mentioned can be suspended in times of national emergency which threatens the life of the nation. Only a few rights are written as absolute and not subject to emergency derogation. Among these few are the rights to legal personhood, right to life, freedom from torture and cruelty, freedom from slavery, freedom from ex post facto laws. Despite the weaknesses in the Convention's terms, the U.S. Senate, in giving advice and consent for ratification, blocked the use of the treaty in U.S. courts while stipulating that its terms required no standards beyond the U.S. Constitution. This type of initial analysis confirms the view that much of the time national security (often very broadly defined to mean national interests or even national convenience) is trump, not human rights, in foreign policy—even by liberal democracies.[15]

---

13   Shirley V. Scott, *International Law, US Power: The United States' Quest for Legal Security* (CUP 2012). She praises the effectiveness of the United States in pursuing of double standards, trying to advance law for others while exempting itself.

14   The 1951 Refugee Convention through its 1967 Protocol is considered in the United States as a self-executing treaty subject to adjudication in US courts. With regard to the 1949 Geneva Conventions, the Congress has passed implementing legislation on several key points such as war crimes, and US court cases do exist providing binding interpretations of certain treaty provisions.

15   The analysis here also suggests that the argument for 'Asian values' and a short list of 'true' human rights finds support in the structure of the ICCPR, even as the 'Asian values' argument has faded from diplomatic controversy. There is reason for this fade, given (1) its

2 From 1991

If we fast-forward to more recent times and the post-Cold War situation, we find that the new legal edifice of human rights arguably reached a theoretical milestone in 2005 when a UN summit of state leaders endorsed the principle of R2P: the responsibility to protect. According to two paragraphs in a long statement of international standards, if a sovereign state caused or allowed genocide, crimes against humanity, major war crimes, or ethnic cleansing, other states had a duty to respond in accordance with international law.[16] State sovereignty, meaning national supremacy of legal authority, was not absolute but contingent on governmental performance. If national policy transgressed international standards, national claims to independent policy making could be overridden. This diplomatic statement of principle came on the heels of the resumed practice of international criminal courts starting in 1993–1994 and featuring from 1998–2000 a permanent International Criminal Court with subject matter jurisdiction over genocide, crimes against humanity, and major war crimes. Logically ethnic cleansing is subsumed under crimes against humanity (systematic attack on the civilian population). This new criminal law spoke to the same foundational point as R2P: claims to national sovereign prerogative could not be used as a shield to permit gross violations of human rights. Without doubt there was some normative progress. But what of enforcement or implementation?

2.1 After 1991: The Case of Somalia-Rwanda

Toward the end of 1992 the Soviet Union was gone and a smaller, weaker Russia was not a hegemonic competitor with the United States. China had not developed its economic and military capabilities that it would later. So the United States was unchallenged as global hegemon. The George H.W. Bush Administration, in charge of a vast military machine with global reach, having no evident strategic adversaries, and having lost the November 1992 elections, was pressed by particularly media coverage to do something about Somalia. Given the absence of effective government in Mogadishu, or actually any government, and with the countryside plagued by contesting militias, massive starvation

---

articulation by autocrats, and (2) its rejection by East Asian states like Japan, South Korea, and others.

16   A/Res/60/1, paras 138 and 139, out of total of 178. See further Gareth Evans, *The Responsibility to Protect: Ending Mass Atrocities Once and For All* (Brookings 2008).

ruled. This was a matter of unintended famine, not the more usual concern with intentional repression and oppression by public authorities. The situation was one of almost exclusively humanitarian concern to outsiders, there being little perception of strategic importance. Even neighboring Kenya was only slighted affected by civilians fleeing the disaster.

The elder Bush Administration was persuaded to deploy troops to guarantee the delivery of humanitarian assistance for a combination of reasons: (1) it was being pressed to act on several fronts and Somalia seemed more 'do-able' than the Balkans where Washington feared a quagmire; (2) the militias interfering with relief were more bandits than political actors, and more than one Somali political figure quietly gave consent to outside intervention; (3) the global Red Cross network had a workable delivery system in place and only needed adequate protection to make it effective; and (4) there was broad support in the UN Security Council for action. In sum, the elder Bush team responded to pressure for action by choosing the lesser of two evils: Somalia looked relatively easy to manage, which hopefully would take pressure off for a more dangerous action in Bosnia.[17] George H.W. Bush, being a realist, was not prone to humanitarian crusading. He had left Saddam Hussein in place in Iraq after the 1991 Gulf War.

Without covering every twist and turn of subsequent policy-making, one can say that the incoming Clinton Administration, naively wanting to focus on domestic issues almost exclusively, contributed to a series of almost absent-minded decisions in which the goals of outside intervention in Somalia expanded while the capability of both U.S. and UN (separate) forces were reduced. Everyone on the international side also underestimated the independent nature and viciousness of key Somali actors. Hence when in 1993 the U.S. moved from humanitarian relief to coercive state building with a snatch and seize operation directed against the clan leaders of the Aidid faction, a battle erupted that cost the lives of 18 American military personnel (with another 80 wounded). The nation back home was 'treated' to the spectacle of a dead American soldier being dragged through the street by Somali crowds. It did not help matters in Washington that trapped American soldiers had been rescued by a UN relief force.

There was an immediate clamor in the country and Congress for a rapid pullout of the U.S. presence in Somalia. Some commentators noted perfectly accurately that the loss of 18 Americans was not much of a cost for a great power to pay for a foreign venture, and that similar casualties were often sustained

---

17   Jon Western, *Selling Intervention and War, The Presidency, the Media, and the Public* (Johns Hopkins University Press 2005).

just in military training exercises.[18] Nevertheless, the Clinton Administration, ever sensitive to domestic public opinion, especially in its first term, moved quickly to scale back U.S. (and UN) involvement in Somalia. With no strategic rationale to justify American loss of life, the effort to move from humanitarian relief to state building was basically abandoned. The major food crisis had been managed, and so the Somalis were basically left to their feuding fate—which remained the state of play for some fifteen years. Washington, having deployed some 20,000 troops in Somalia, then virtually turned its back on the place until the issue of al-Qaeda-like militants resurfaced circa 2006.

'Saving strangers'[19] did not prove sustainable when costs turned out to be higher than expected and when self-interest in the form of strategic calculation offered no rationale for staying the course. The fiasco of outside intervention in Somalia was to have devastating consequences for Rwanda.

Long standing tensions and conflict between radical Hutus and Tutsi in Rwanda exploded into large scale violence in 1994. Coming on the heels of the 1993 controversy in Somalia, the first and sustained reaction by both UN and US leaders was to look the other way and avoid further involvement. Key UN leaders feared for the future of UN security operations if another major controversy erupted, and key members of the Clinton foreign policy team were still under domestic attack for missteps in Somalia. Therefore proposals to expand the existing UN peacekeeping operation (UNAMIR) into a pro-active enforcement operation were rejected both in New York and Washington.[20]

Contributing to a hands-off policy by outsiders was the fact that Hutu militants seized, killed, and mutilated 10 Belgian soldiers on loan to the existing UN peacekeeping mission, UNAMIR. The reaction by Belgium, a former colonial power in Rwanda, was not to accept responsibility for the overall situation and increase international efforts for law, order, and judicial punishment but to encourage a political retreat. Belgium had no strategic interests in the Great Lakes region of Africa. Brussels removed its remaining troops four days after it suffered fatalities. UNAMIR continued to exist but was irrelevant to the unfolding genocide which took some 800,000 lives. The slaughter was terminated only when Tutsi paramilitary forces invaded from Uganda and put the radical Hutus to flight. France was actually linked to the radical Hutus in several ways and aided in the flight of some of the genocidaires.

---

18   Edward N. Luttwak, 'Where Are the Great Powers?' (1994) 73(4) Foreign Affairs 26.
19   See further Nicholas J. Wheeler, *Saving Strangers: Humanitarian Intervention in International Society* (OUP 2000).
20   Michael J. Barnett, *Eyewitness to a Genocide* (Cornell University Press 2002).

The only Western forceful intervention that occurred was to extract Western personnel from the violence. While the Western states paid large sums of dollars to care for (Hutu) refugees mainly in Zaire as managed by the UN refugee office ('UN High Commissioner for Refugees'), none of them were prepared to expend any significant effort to stop the 1994 killings. After the fact they were willing to first create and then pay for a criminal court (International Criminal Tribunal for Rwanda) to prosecute for genocide, and second to apologize for irresolute action in the face of the well-reported killings. As with the Armenian genocide circa 1915, the facts at the time were well known, but no outside state wanted to place its military in harm's way to 'save strangers.' What UNHCR chief Sadako Ogata wrote about her experiences concerning Rwanda and elsewhere has broad application: 'The international response to humanitarian crisis situations is largely determined by the degree of strategic interests held by the major states.'[21]

2.2 The Case of Bosnia-Kosovo

The elder Bush had handed off Somalia to Bill Clinton; he did the same regarding Bosnia. The Bush Administration had indicated that with regard to the breakup of former Yugoslavia from 1991, while the CIA had accurately predicted a bloodbath, the United States' view was that it did not have a (strategic) dog in that fight.[22] Various factions of the former federation might be tearing themselves apart, but Washington considered the affair a European problem. As noted above, the Bush team considered the Western Balkans a potential quagmire. But the (West) Europeans could not muster the collective will to act decisively to restore a humane order even in the center of Europe. They could only agree to have the UNHCR and the Red Cross network try to provide civilian relief, and to deploy a UN peacekeeping force (UNPROFOR) even though there was no peace to keep.

The Clinton Administration was slow to strike a different pose. First seeking to avoid foreign policy crises as noted, then preoccupied with Somalia and Rwanda, inter alia, the Clinton team dithered. As a substitute for compelling

---

21 Sadako Ogata, *The Turbulent Decade: Confronting the Refugee Crises of the 1990s* (Norton 2005) 318.
22 Secretary of State James Baker's 1991 comment to this effect was widely reported in the media. See, eg, Mark Danner, 'The US and the Yugoslav Catastrophe,' *New York Review of Book* (New York, 20 November 1997) available at <http://www.markdanner.com/articles/62/print> accessed 27 January 2015.

action it agreed via the UN Security Council to create the first international criminal court since the 1940s, the International Criminal Tribunal for Yugoslavia in 1993. Against the drumbeat of media coverage of particularly Serb atrocities, it inched toward more and more coercive action against the dominant and brutal Serbs. Permitting the occasional air strike against Serb militias operating in Bosnia, and then organizing a Croat-Bosnian alliance to check Serb advances, its piecemeal tough policies and threats finally brought the Serb ultimate leader Slobadan Milosevic to the bargaining table. The 1995 Dayton Accord resulted and put an end to much of the violence that had included intentional attacks on civilians, brutal concentration camps, and holding UN Blue Helmets hostage as human shields against anticipated Western air strikes as authorized by the UN. Periodic coercion and the bulldog diplomacy of Richard Holbrook finally brought an end to the horrors. None in the West had acted with dispatch on the basis of a moral imperative to end the Balkan suffering. But at least the West showed more concern for the Balkans compared to Africa. And finally the piecemeal actions, taken partially with a view to not getting too far out ahead of domestic public opinion, paid off.[23]

Four years later events in Kosovo resumed the dilemma of what to do about brutal Serb policies intended to suppress a restless ethnic Albanian majority in the province ruled from Belgrade. The Clinton team, feeling remorse about its delay in responding to Milosevic's maneuvers in Bosnia, and observing ethnic cleansing of the province which reminded of Nazi policies in the 1930s and 1940s, decided to act by 1999. But it was hamstrung by lack of domestic enthusiasm for intervention and lack of Russian cooperation in the UN Security Council. Clinton responded by seeking legitimacy for intervention through the collective action of NATO rather than from UNSC endorsement, and by conducting a high altitude bombing campaign which avoided Western casualties which had torpedoed involvement in Somalia and Rwanda. That type of military action, avoiding Western boots on the ground and pilots shot down and/ or taken captive, no doubt increased civilian 'collateral damage.' But the six week bombing campaign, when combined with belated Russian quiet diplomacy, did cause Milosevic to shift course. He was eventually indicted by the ICTY, arrested by the government in Belgrade because of significant Western pressure, and made to stand trial for atrocities. He died during judicial proceedings. Kosovo eventually declared independence from Serb Yugoslavia.[24]

---

23 A useful perspective is provided by Richard Holbrooke, *To End a War* (Random House 1998).
24 On Clinton's concern to act in Kosovo but hamstrung by lack of domestic support for costly intervention, see Ryan Hendrickson, *The Clinton Wars: Congress, the Constitution, and War Powers* (Vanderbilt University Press 2002).

Bosnia and Kosovo showed that Western intervention, while not always expeditious, could make a difference in stopping atrocities. The key decisions were taken in Washington and other Western capitals, not by UN officials in New York. And those foreign policy decisions were carefully crafted to ensure lack of effective opposition from the numerous domestic critics. Particularly in the United States, even regarding European rather than African atrocities, it still was not popular to pay human costs to protect the rights of 'others.' The 'Clinton wars' in the Western Balkans did not have firm congressional or popular support. If the Administration avoided American casualties there was policy space, based on a permissive deference, for limited intervention. Regarding Europe in the 1990s, the Western democracies did indeed say 'never again,' but only after other options had been tried and only when costs were kept low. In Bosnia effective intervention occurred only after the genocidal massacre at Srebrenica. One Dutch fatality in its Foxbat contribution to UNPROFOR caused the Dutch government to retreat from any effort to seriously impede Serb atrocities. In Kosovo Western intervention occurred only after considerable ethnic cleansing. One is reminded of the comment attributed to Winston Churchill: the Americans can be counted on to do the right thing—after having tried all other options. The West European record was no better and, absent U.S. leadership, would have been worse.

2.3 The Case of Libya-Syria

During the period 1999–2012 much changed in international relations but not the dynamics of international response to atrocities—as demonstrated by the twin Middle Eastern crises of Libya and Syria. The Arab spring, featuring popular demands and street demonstrations for fundamental political change, originated in Tunisia and spilled over into Egypt—with lesser effects in Bahrain and elsewhere. This democratic awakening produced major violence in Libya and Syria. The international response, led by the Western democracies, was more consequential in the former rather than the latter (as of the time of writing). The difference lay in Western perceptions about the costs of intervention.

In Libya, the pariah Kaddafi regime found itself without important allies and without a muscular national military establishment since the dictator had intentionally fragmented his security forces to prevent a coup. It also faced fairly coherent opposition forces based in the eastern region. In a deviation from the Balkan record, Britain and France took the lead in pressing for forceful intervention, the Obama Administration agreed as long as there was burden sharing, and the Russians and Chinese lent their diplomatic support in the

UN Security Council for forceful protection of civilians but not regime change. Therefore an air campaign was launched against Kaddafi's security forces. As led by half of NATO and four Arab states, the air attacks were obviously linked to rebel causes and became a matter of forceful regime change on the pattern of the Kosovo intervention.

While successful in the sense of weakening Kaddafi forces and leading to the capture and killing of the dictator and the collapse of his regime, the intervention had two downsides. First, the Chinese and Russians defected from the diplomatic coalition favoring international action, which had consequences for Syria. Second, the international action was again limited in the sense of avoiding Western high costs. In particular, the West was not inclined to undertake the type of prolonged and grassroots administration which had followed the air attacks in Kosovo. In any event the Libyan rebels were opposed to any type of outside occupation and administration, or even to allowing the International Criminal Court to have jurisdiction over suspected Libyan war criminals. In the instability that followed Kaddafi's demise, weapons flowed to various non-state actors in the region which lead to increased terrorism and the destabilizing of Mali and other parts of the Maghreb. Kaddafi was removed, but neither Libya nor the region was liberal and stabilized. That outcome would have required a much more intrusive and lengthy involvement than NATO states desired.

In Syria as in Libya, peaceful protests and demands for political change were met by bloody resistance. In Syria the Bashar al-Assad regime had important allies, particularly Russia and Iran but also Iraq. It also had a sophisticated air defense system, chemical weapons, and a relatively cohesive and loyal military establishment (with some defections to the rebel side). UNSC endorsement for forceful intervention was impossible due particularly to the policies of China and Russia which were still smarting from de facto regime change in Libya. Russia in particular had much invested in the Assad regime and seemed to relish blocking any Western consideration of deep involvement. It was also the case that the militant opposition was fragmented, with some militias unsympathetic to liberal politics, religious tolerance, and the state of Israel. Therefore outside intervention was correctly seen as more complicated with higher costs.

France, the former colonial power, along with particularly Britain, did not advocate the same sort of intervention they had pushed in Libya but did move toward extensively arming some of the rebel militias. The Obama Administration, fearing another quagmire in the Middle East and wanting to focus greatly on Asia, first adopted a relative hands-off policy, then moved toward non-lethal assistance to various rebel factions along with increased training of those militia in Jordan and Turkey. Belatedly the Obama team provided lethal assistance to selected rebel groups. Washington eventually sought a negotiated solution in tandem with Moscow, both fearing an outcome that might favor Islamic (Sunni) extremists. The central point for this situation (that continued to play out at the time of writing) was that the anticipated costs for Western decisive intervention were seen as much higher than in Libya. Also, if one assumed the fall of the Assad regime, the follow-on situation was much harder to predict, with considerable probability of a new illiberal regime that would be anti-Western and anti-Israel. While various Sunni Arab regimes were firmly opposed to Assad, an Alawite figure backed by Shi regimes in Iran and Iraq (and Shia Hezbollah in Lebanon), Western governments were more ambivalent about how to respond to the situation.

The early stages of the Syrian violence in 2011–2012 reminded roughly of the Spanish civil war in the 1930s. Then the Fascists states intervened on the side of the Franco rebels and the Soviet Union intervened for the elected government, while the Western democracies did not come to the aid of the Republican government (which had radical communist elements within). In Syria, some outside parties intervened (Russia, Iran, Hezbollah) while the Western democracies did not to any comparable extent. Over time the Western more-powerful states inched toward covert intervention not only to bring down Assad but also to counter the illiberal militias. At home in the Western democracies, while some political figures called for more intervention, most congressional and public opinion was on the side of minimizing direct and costly involvement, as had been the case for the 'Clinton wars' in the Western Balkans. The American public, having endured two prolonged armed conflicts in Afghanistan and Iraq, was not in the mood for yet another ground war. It was obvious that President Obama was cautious about Syria, notwithstanding his warning that use of chemical weapons would carry serious consequences.

3   Conclusion

The cases covered above show several cross cutting points: (1) that key decisions about implementing a response to atrocities still reside at the national, not international, level (the role of particularly the UNSC, and sometimes a regional organization, is important for diplomatic and legal considerations, but national decisions control these bodies); (2) these national decisions greatly hinge on perceived national self-interest, in particular anticipated national costs (when costs are seen as high, response to atrocities is less certain and less forceful); (3) even when outside intervention occurs in the face of anticipated or actual atrocities, that intervention still reflects a desire by key nation-states to minimize costs (often the intervention occurs without full domestic support in key democratic states and only in ways that do not trigger legislative and popular push back).

Some other cases could have been chosen that give a slightly more optimistic evaluation of third party response to atrocities. They do not, however, undercut the main point already developed, namely that in cases where costs are anticipated as high, outside response will be slow and limited—or maybe absent. The British engaged in belated unilateral intervention in Sierra Leone in 2000 in order to terminate the civil war there which was characterized by horrific attacks on civilians. The Australians, under a UN mandate, deployed military force in East Timor in 1999 in order to curtail atrocities—and limit unwanted war refugees. The French, again under a UN mandate, took forceful action in Ivory Coast in 2010 in order to implement the outcome of democratic elections and to curtail attacks on civilians. And so on, as per the French in Mali and Central African Republic. But in none of these cases, or others that might be cited, did outside parties contemplate costly expenditure of blood and treasure, and such costly involvement did not develop.

The emphasis here on a forceful response to atrocities should not be understood as ruling out the diplomatic option. One of the points to be made about R2P is that its authors understand the new principle as encouraging early diplomatic involvement in a situation, and that R2P means much more than simply forceful intervention.[25] Thus the authors of R2P stress the importance of UN or even private diplomacy—e.g., by the International Crisis Group, in an effort to deal with anticipated or actual gross violations of human rights. They might point to events in Kenya where those suspected of encouraging ethnic violence in the past have been dealt with in an international process featuring diplomatic and judicial measures—with reduced violence as a result. In Kenya, however, the national leaders who became defendants in the ICC process were effective at mobilizing domestic and international support in order to hamstring judicial efforts to hold them accountable for past incitement to violence. Their first line of defense was to mobilize narrow nationalism in Kenya in order to undercut cosmopolitan values and institutions.[26]

---

[25] See further Gareth Evans, *The Responsibility to Protect: Ending Mass Atrocity Crimes Once and For All* (Brookings 2008).

[26] ICC proceedings against Uhuru Kenyatta and William Ruto floundered as the defendants bribed and intimidated witnesses, stirred up local opposition, and appealed to the fears of other African leaders. As in many nations, the human rights discourse was for others, not for home consumption.

The central point developed here remains. Trying to institutionalize the protection of universal human rights through decisive foreign policy has yet to overcome the collective action problem. International norms are still interpreted and implemented most importantly by national policy-makers who operate primarily with a view to self-interest. Where national costs of enforcing human rights are seen as high, protecting the right of 'others' to be free from atrocities is not the overriding priority. As a practical political matter, humanitarian concern as an international moral imperative does not trump national concern with anticipated costs. Some national leaders do seek to find a way to obstruct atrocities abroad; they are not completely indifferent to the sufferings of strangers—at least sometimes. But they are often seriously constrained by the more parochial, less cosmopolitan views of domestic legislative and popular opinion.

One can try to mesh broad humanitarian concern with conceptions of national interest. One can try to liberalize nationalism, making it less parochial or narrow even if not fully cosmopolitan.[27] One can carefully calculate strategies to bring maximum pressure on national policy makers to be more even-handed in human rights matters.[28] Yet action based primarily on Great Power self-interest continues to be a reality, resulting in the debilitating double standards that tend to delegitimize the international human rights system, as human rights matter only in some situations but not in others. What can be said about a system in which atrocities produce intrusive action in Kosovo but not Rwanda, in Libya but not Syria? Future research should examine the extent to which various actors can push states to a more even-handed record on protecting rights.

---

27   See further Emile M. Hafner-Burton, *Making Human Rights A Reality* (Princeton University Press 2013); and its review by the present author in the Human Rights Quarterly Fall volume, 2013.

28   See, eg, Alison Brysk, *Speaking Rights to Power: Constructing Political Will* (OUP 2013).

PART 4

Essays on Self-Determination

CHAPTER 16

West Papuan Self-determination: New Indigenous Rights or Old-fashioned Genocide?

Catherine J. Iorns Magallanes

1   Introduction

At the turn of the millennium Roger S. Clark expressed his sincere disappointment that for nearly twenty-four years, the international community had turned a blind-eye to the illegal occupation of East Timor by Indonesia. He was particularly 'offended by the positions and actions of states such as Australia, New Zealand and the United States,' and regretted the fact that perhaps 200,000 lives could have been saved had a 'firm stand' been taken from the outset.[1] Regrettably, East Timor (now Timor-Leste) was not the only non-self-governing territory to fall under Indonesia's jurisdiction: the indigenous peoples of West Papua have also been under Indonesian rule since 1962–63.[2] Despite Timor-Leste achieving independence in 2002, and despite a steady stream of human rights

---

1   Roger S Clark, 'East Timor, Indonesia, and the International Community' (2000) 14 Temp Intl & Comp LJ 75, 75. In 1975, the Republic of Indonesia violated United Nations doctrine and international law by invading the Portuguese colony against the will of the local, indigenous population. For Clark's comprehensive outline of how the occupation contravened international law, see Roger S Clark, 'The "Decolonization" of East Timor and the United Nations Norms on Self-Determination and Aggression' (1980–81) 7 Yale J World Pub Ord 2. For New Zealand's role in this affair see Maire Leadbeater, *Negligent Neighbour: New Zealand's complicity in the invasion and occupation of Timor-Leste* (Craig Potton Publishing 2006).

2   Many titles have been used to identify the territory throughout history (Dutch New Guinea, West Irian, Irian Jaya, Papua, West Papua). West Papua has been used throughout this chapter because this is the name favoured by the majority of indigenous Papuans. In the same vein, the indigenous people of West Papua are referred to as Papuan. Although this is a Malay term, it has long been appropriated by the indigenous population of West Papua. As of 2003, Indonesia has divided the territory of West Papua into two provinces, Papua and the other called West Papua which, as Danilyn Rutherford speculates, makes it more difficult for non-experts to follow proceedings, Danilyn Rutherford, 'Review of *An Act of Free Choice: Decolonization and the Right to Self-Determination in West Papua* by Pieter Drooglever' (2010) 90 *Indonesia* 173 ('Rutherford, 'Review of Drooglever''), 174 n 4. For a brief comment on the political act of using the name West Papua, including the definition of 'Irian' as an acronym of 'ikut Republik Indonesia anti-Nederland' (join the Republic of Indonesia against the Dutch),

and environmental abuses occurring in West Papua since Indonesia's takeover over half a century ago, there has been little international effort to address the plight of the Papuans.[3] The same states that Roger Clark singled out in 1975 in relation to East Timor have been equally inert over the situation in West Papua.[4] Importantly, the territory remains outside the United Nation's decolonisation agenda.

However, there is increasing international awareness of the environmental damage and the severe human rights violations still occurring in West Papua. International sympathy increasingly lies with the Papuans, even if not the wherewithal to advance the wishes of the Papuan people at the UN. While there are clear legal, political and practical difficulties in advancing the West Papuan cause, this chapter reminds us—in the same vein as Clark did for East Timor—that the Papuans are still a colonised and oppressed people. Arguing for the exercise of a Papuan right to self-determination probably poses the most such difficulties, but it is increasingly supported by other international human rights laws. I suggest that most important for the international

---

see S Eben Kirksey and J A D Roemajauw, 'The Wild Terrorist Gang: The Semantics of Violence and Self-Determination in West Papua' (2002) 30(2) Oxford Development Studies 189.

3   For example, on a visit to Wellington in February 2013, exiled Papuan campaigner Benny Wenda and human rights lawyer Jennifer Robinson were denied an audience at Parliament: 'McCully Must Listen To West Papuans Not Just Indonesia' Press Release (New Zealand Green Party, 12 Feb 2013), at <http://pacific.scoop.co.nz/2013/02/mccully-must-listen-to-west-papuans-not-just-indonesia> accessed 29 August 2014. In October 2013, Australian Prime Minister Tony Abbott criticised Papuan activism in Australia, suggesting the 'situation in West Papua is getting better, not worse': Jason MacLeod, 'Australia "Blind And Deaf" On Papua' *New Matilda* (Australia, 4 Oct 2013), at <https://newmatilda.com/2013/10/04/australia-blind-and-deaf-papua> accessed 29 August 2014; Selpius Bobii, 'We Live In Terror, Mr Abbott' *New Matilda* (Australia, 23 Oct 2013), at <https://newmatilda.com/2013/10/23/we-live-terror-mr-abbott> accessed 17 April 2015. In contrast, Vanuatu and the Melanesian Spearhead Group are leading the lobby to the United Nations on West Papua's behalf: Godwin Ligo, 'PM: Vanuatu is the Only Hope for West Papua' *Vanuatu Daily Post* (Vanuatu, 10 March 2014), at <http://pidp.eastwestcenter.org/pireport/2014/March/03-11-06.htm> accessed 29 August 2014 ('Ligo, 'PM: Vanuatu is the Only Hope for West Papua'').

4   The New Zealand Government, however, has been recently applauded for deciding against implementing the Eastern Indonesia Community Policing Programme: see 'Indonesia scraps NZ police training programme for Papua' (Radio New Zealand, 20 May 2014), at <http://www.radionz.co.nz/international/pacific-news/244930/indonesia-scraps-nz-police-training-programme-for-papua> accessed 29 August 2014. The Green Party of Aotearoa New Zealand were critics of the scheme that they termed 'Aid that Kills', see 'Greens call for end to "Aid that Kills" Press Release (New Zealand Green Party, 25 Jan 2014), at <https://www.greens.org.nz/press-releases/greens-call-end-aid-kills> accessed 17 April 2015.

community to address are the claims of severe human rights violations in West Papua, particularly the claims of genocide. Hopefully, West Papuan self-determination will follow.

2   Colonisation

As most commentators acknowledge, West Papua's recent history reads as a sorry tale of repression and injustice.[5] Anthropologist Jan Pouwer neatly sorted post-contact West Papuan history into three analytical fields: colonisation (c.1500–1944), decolonisation (1945–1962), and re-colonisation (after 1962).[6] Ever since the territory was effectively re-colonised by Indonesia in 1962–63, the indigenous Papuans—who at the time had been assured independence was in their grasp by the Dutch—have instead been systematically denied a multitude of fundamental human rights and, to employ an often used cliché, have become strangers in their own land. More than this, if recent estimates are to be believed, since 1962–63 some 500,000 Papuans have died as a direct result of the Indonesian occupation.[7]

Officially known as Indonesia's easternmost province, the territory of West Papua consists of the western half of the Pacific island of New Guinea, the second-largest island landmass in the world. West Papua's eastern border follows the 141st meridian which cuts the island in half, dividing the territory from its Melanesian neighbours, the now independent state of Papua New Guinea. Ethnically Melanesian and predominantly Christian, the indigenous Papuans have much stronger ties to their neighbours in the East than to their mostly Muslim, Asian neighbours to the West.[8] The Dutch and British agreement to

---

5   Two of the original texts to expose the history of the territory are: *West Papua: The Obliteration of a People* (2nd ed, TAPOL 1984) ('TAPOL, *West Papua*'); Robin Osborne, *Indonesia's Secret War: The Guerrilla Struggle in Irian Jaya* (Allen & Unwin 1985) ('Osborne, *Indonesia's Secret War*').

6   Jan Pouwer, 'The Colonisation, Decolonisation and Recolonisation of West New Guinea' (1999) 34(2) JPH 157.

7   Jennifer Robinson, 'UN's Chequered Record in West Papua' *Al Jazeera* (London, 21 March 2012), at <http://www.aljazeera.com/indepth/opinion/2012/03/201232172539145809.html> accessed 29 August 2014.

8   Because of the large number of West Papuan refugees (roughly 10,000) in Papua New Guinea and a heightened military presence along the border, West Papuan affairs have become a political issue in Papua New Guinea despite the PNG Government traditionally distancing itself from the dispute. For an older discussion on the relationship between the two territories see Terence Wesley-Smith, 'Lost Melanesian Brothers: The Irian Jaya Problem and its Implications for Papua New Guinea' (1987) 10(3) Pacific Studies 27.

bisect the island in 1848 has been described by historian and anthropologist Chris Ballard as 'one of colonial cartography's more arbitrary' boundaries.[9] Divorced from the British (Australian) and German colonies to the east, West New Guinea (as it was then labelled) became subsumed by the Netherlands East Indies and its future became tied to that of the rest of the Indonesian archipelago.

The colonial status of West New Guinea is important because it informs the basis of modern Indonesian claims on the territory. The preliminary point needs to be made that, despite its formal status as a Dutch colony since the nineteenth century, a large proportion of the indigenous population of West Papua were only ever under nominal colonial rule.[10] Estimates suggest only five per cent of the colony was effectively administered prior to the Second World War.[11] On account of its size, diversity, and distance from Jakarta (then called Batavia), Dutch colonial administration over West New Guinea was, for the most part, *laissez faire*, and the long arm of the colonial state fell short of most Papuans.[12] In the words of Dutch historian Pieter Drooglever, 'New Guinea was not an easy region in which to set up and administer colonial rule,'[13] hence most colonial duties were left to the Sultan of Tidore, a vassal state of the Netherlands East Indies.[14] In 1898, the Dutch set up an administrative centre for West New Guinea at the office of the Dutch Resident at Ternate in the Moluccas.[15] However, this was only nominal and anything more than 'token

---

9   Chris Ballard, 'Blanks in the Writing: Possible Histories for West New Guinea' (1999) 34(2) JPH 149.
10 The first Dutch settlement was erected at Fort Dubus in 1828 as a strategic ploy to prevent other imperial powers claiming territory in the vicinity of their colony: John Saltford, *The United Nations and the Indonesian Takeover of West Papua 1962–1969: The Anatomy of Betrayal* (Routledge Curzon 2003) ('Saltford, *The United Nations and the Indonesian Takeover of West Papua 1962–1969: The Anatomy of Betrayal*') 1.
11 Greg Poulgrain, 'Delaying the "Discovery" of Oil in West New Guinea' (1999) 34(2) JPH 206 ('Poulgrain, "Delaying the 'Discovery' of Oil in West New Guinea"').
12 Anton Ploeg, 'Colonial Land Law in Dutch New Guinea' (1999) 34(2) JPH 191.
13 Pieter Drooglever, *An Act of Free Choice: decolonization and the right to self-determination in West Papua*, Theresa Stanton, Maria van Yperen & Marjolijn de Jager (trans) (Oneworld Publications 2009) ('Drooglever, *An Act of Free Choice*') 25.
14 TAPOL, *West Papua* (n 5) 10. But even then, the Tidorese administration was limited to a handful of coastal settlements on the Bird's Head Peninsula. There is little to suggest that Papuans ever recognised the authority of the Sultan either. See Saltford, *The United Nations and the Indonesian Takeover of West Papua* (n 10) 2.
15 Saltford, *The United Nations and the Indonesian Takeover of West Papua 1962–1969: The Anatomy of Betrayal* (n 10) 2. Note this meant that the territory was still being administered from elsewhere.

settlement' by the Dutch in West Papua was delayed until well into the twentieth century.[16]

In the early 1900s, the Dutch parliament seriously considered whether the future administration of West New Guinea should be separated from that of the rest of its Asian Empire. Proponents of this view argued that because West New Guinea was part of 'Polynesia' not Asia, it made sense to administer it in a different fashion.[17] However, the push for separate administrations did not succeed and the territory continued to be administered as part of the rest of the Empire. Crucially, as Saltford notes, 'this arrangement led Indonesia at independence to claim that the territory was an integral part of the Republic.'[18] Indonesian claims rested on the doctrine of *uti possidetis juris* ('that territorial boundaries of post-colonial states should match those of the colonial territories that they replaced'), as well as further historic—that is, pre-European—claims over the territory reaching back to the seventh century. These justifications trumped Papuan independence wishes at the UN as Indonesian representatives were able to convince the members that West New Guinea was always an inherent part of the Dutch East Indies.[19]

After a brief period of Japanese occupation during World War II, independence leader and inaugural President, Sukarno, quickly began to express his vision for a post-colonial state. In 1945, he proclaimed his belief that 'the national state is only Indonesia in its entirety.'[20] Sukarno's vision was that the new Republic would follow the colonial boundaries of the Dutch East Indies, as well as the pre-colonial area of the Srivijaya and Majapahit empires which arguably included Timor-Leste and West Papua.[21] Sukarno envisaged the new Republic stretching from Aceh in the east to West Papua in the west, or more precisely from the island of Sabang to the Merauke region bordering Papua

---

16 TAPOL, *West Papua* (n 5) 11.
17 Saltford, *The United Nations and the Indonesian Takeover of West Papua 1962–1969: The Anatomy of Betrayal* (n 10) 2.
18 Ibid.
19 Ibid 8.
20 Sukarno's *Pantja Sila* (Five Principles) speech on 1 June 1945, in Clark, 'The "Decolonization" of East Timor and the United Nations Norms on Self-Determination and Aggression' (n 1) 20, n 79.
21 The Buddhist kingdom of Srivijaya originated in Sumatra in the seventh century and was replaced by the Hindu Majapahit kingdom which was established in 1292 and was based on Java. For a discussion on how far-reaching these Empires actually were in relation to the outlying islands of the archipelago see Clark, 'The "Decolonization" of East Timor and the United Nations Norms on Self-Determination and Aggression' (n 1) 20–21 n 80.

New Guinea.[22] This nationalist rhetoric also imbues modern day justifications for the ongoing Indonesian presence in West Papua. Western support for Papuan independence is regularly viewed as an attack on the territorial integrity of the Republic.

Interestingly, the Indonesian claims to West Papua were enunciated without reference to the potential productivity of West Papua's natural resources. According to historian Greg Poulgrain, the existence of large oil reserves found by geologists connected to the American oil industry prior to the Japanese invasion in World War Two were deliberately hidden from Sukarno, thus 'played no part in his nationalistic quest.'[23] Therefore rather than for any economic reason, anthropologist Danilyn Rutherford suggests West Papua was sought after because it was essential to Sukarno's 'vision of Indonesia as a nation-state that transcended religion, race, ethnicity, and class.'[24] In public, the rhetoric surrounding the dispute was that Indonesia would liberate the Papuans from their Dutch colonial overlords, it was framed as 'a defiant act of *de*colonization.'[25] In private, the motivation for possessing West Papua was less altruistic: Sukarno is reported to have said, with reference to West Papua, that 'a nation always needs an enemy.'[26] His biographer believed West Papua provided Sukarno with 'a means of diverting popular attention from domestic discontents.'[27]

The war for liberation from the Dutch lasted until late 1949, with the Hague Agreement of November 1949, where the Netherlands agreed to officially cede sovereignty of the Netherlands East Indies to the Indonesian Republic. However, despite Indonesia's obvious designs on the territory, West New

---

22   Osborne, *Indonesia's Secret War* (n 5) 20.

23   Poulgrain, 'Delaying the "Discovery" of Oil in West New Guinea' (n 11) 205, 207–08.

24   Danilyn Rutherford, *Laughing at Leviathan: Sovereignty and Audience in West Papua* (University of Chicago Press 2012) ('Rutherford, *Laughing at Leviathan: Sovereignty and Audience in West Papua*') 29.

25   Tracey Banivanua-Mar, ' "A Thousand Miles of Cannibal Lands": Imagining Away Genocide in the Re-Colonization of West Papua' (2008) 10(4) J Genocide Res 583, 585 ('Banivanua-Mar, "'A Thousand Miles of Cannibal Lands': Imagining Away Genocide in the Re-Colonization of West Papua"'). For a clear enunciation of Indonesia's anti-colonial aims see Oejeng Soewargana, *West Irian: An Essential Part of Indonesia* (Indonesian Army Information, 1960) 11–12. For example, 'The argument of "self-determination" given by the Netherlands Government in further prolonging their colonial domination in Asia in a new form of course, aroused the wrath of the Asian and African countries which had just recently gained their independence.' *Ibid* 11. According to Robin Osborne, *West Irian: An Essential Part of Indonesia* was a brochure printed by the Indonesian embassy in Canberra for circulation in Australia: Osborne, *Indonesia's Secret War* (n 5) 20.

26   J D Legge, *Sukarno: A Political Biography* (Archipelago Press 2003) 276.

27   *Ibid* 276.

Guinea fell outside the Hague Agreement and the Dutch clung to the territory, somewhat irrationally, until 1962.[28] The post-War period under Dutch rule was crucial for the creation of a Papuan identity. If we are to accept Pieter Drooglever's thesis that the driving force behind Dutch colonialism in West Papua from the turn of the twentieth century was 'to turn savages into people', it is arguable that much more was achieved in this thirteen year window than in the previous half century of colonial intrusion.[29] The substantial gaps in colonial administration throughout the island were being filled as the Netherlands followed a plan which would result in granting West Papua independence in December 1970. It was during these years of accelerated Dutch tutelage that a West Papuan parliament was formed. In addition to this, a national anthem was adopted and the Morning Star was installed as the national flag. Unfortunately, all did not go to plan and today the name 'West Papua' cannot be uttered in public, nor can the Morning Star be flown. The Morning Star has become a potent symbol of resistance and independence today. Every year pro-independence Papuans celebrate the 1st of December as a de facto independence day where the flag is defiantly raised, and the national anthem sung, despite the constant threat of a military crack-down.

The Dutch may have clung feverishly to their last colonial outpost, but Jakarta had the Americans on their side. Relations were incredibly fraught between the two nations after Sukarno called for the mobilisation of all Indonesians to liberate the territory in December 1961. In January 1962 the Battle of Arafura Sea took place where the Dutch and Indonesian navies clashed off the coast of West Papua, and by August, Indonesian paratroopers had been dropped into the territory. Ultimately, American geo-political interests forced an agreement between the two sides. Wary of allowing the Indonesians to fall into hands of the Soviet-bloc, in August 1962 the Kennedy administration brokered what is known as the New York Agreement where administration would initially be ceded to the UN Temporary Executive Authority (UNTEA) before control would be passed to Indonesia in 1963. It needs to be noted that no Papuan voices were present or represented when this deal was made. Once again, West Papua was the 'plaything of foreign powers.'[30] As Saltford puts it, 'it was the Papuans who had most to lose from the settlement. They played no part in the negotiations, but they would be the ones who would have to live

---

28 President Dwight D Eisenhower and political scientist Arend Lijphart both labelled Dutch covetousness of the colony as a 'fetish': Rutherford, *Laughing at Leviathan* (n 24) 70.
29 Commissioner L M F Plate in Drooglever, *An Act of Free Choice* (n 13) 763.
30 The phrase is from *The Neglected Genocide: Human Rights Abuses against Papuans in the Central Highlands, 1977–1978* (Asian Human Rights Commission 2013) ('Asian Human Rights Commission, *The Neglected Genocide*') 3.

with the consequences.'[31] The consequences were Indonesian rule: it took only nine months from the signing of the New York Agreement for full control to be assumed by an impatient Jakarta.

Future President Suharto was behind the military takeover and, from the outset, the Papuans—who had predominantly sided with the Dutch—were treated every bit like the enemy Sukarno had earlier envisioned. The military was swift to suppress any Papuan protest, with reports stating that between 1963 and 1969 some 30,000 Papuans were killed.[32] The contest for sovereignty was finalised with the 1969 'Act of Free Choice', commonly referred to as the 'Act of No Choice' by the indigenous people.[33] It was meant to be a plebiscite carried out according to international practice; however, merely just over 1000 Papuans, out of an indigenous population of approximately one million, participated in 'a form of public deliberation.'[34] The result was a vote to remain under Indonesian rule, but the participants were reportedly under obvious duress.[35] The Act has been denounced widely by commentators and those involved. John Saltford, an expert in the period 1962–1969, has described it as 'a crudely orchestrated charade.'[36] In 2001, one key UN actor involved in the Act, Chakravarthi Narasimhan, retrospectively labelled it a 'sham' and a 'white-wash.'

Although the charade was never officially sanctioned by the United Nations, it also was never condemned. Anxious to avoid international criticism, the UN acknowledged the result of the plebiscite and quickly discarded the whole affair, turning their back on the right of Papuans to self-determination.[37] Cold

---

31   Saltford, *The United Nations and the Indonesian Takeover of West Papua* (n 10) 14.
32   Robinson, 'UN's Chequered Record in West Papua' (n 7).
33   Denise Leith, *The Politics of Power: Freeport in Suharto's Indonesia* (U of Hawai'i P 2003) 13.
34   Rutherford, 'Review of Drooglever' (n 2) 180.
35   See Saltford, *The United Nations and the Indonesian Takeover of West Papua 1962–1969: The Anatomy of Betrayal* (n 10) 158–177. The man in charge of overseeing the Act from the Indonesian side, Brigadier-General Ali Murtopo, apparently threatened to cut out the 'accursed tongues' of the Papuans if they did not vote for integration. Jim Elmslie & Camellia Webb-Gannon, 'A Slow-Motion Genocide: Indonesian rule in West Papua' (2013) 1 Griffith J of L & Human Dignity 142 ('Elmslie & Webb-Gannon, 'A Slow-Motion Genocide: Indonesian rule in West Papua") 157.
36   John Saltford, 'Reflections on the New York Agreement, the Act of Free Choice and developments since' in Peter King, Jim Elmslie & Camellia Webb-Gannon (eds), *Comprehending West Papua* (Centre for Peace and Conflict Studies, University of Sydney 2011) ('King et al., *Comprehending West Papua*') 197.
37   Saltford, *The United Nations and the Indonesian Takeover of West Papua 1962–1969: The Anatomy of Betrayal* (n 10) 175.

War politics entailed Western support for the anti-Communist President Suharto, which was more important than West Papuan self-determination. Today, in the era of free-trade deals and international security fears, most nations are loathe to challenge Indonesia over West Papua because of similar self-interested concerns.

3 Resource Extraction: Freeport Mining

West Papua is Indonesia's most resource-rich province, and like many other Pacific islands, it has been a site for extensive resource exploitation. Unfortunately, in addition to living under oppressive Indonesian rule, the indigenous Papuans have also witnessed extensive degradation of their environment due to the intensive resource extraction of large multinational corporations working in concert with the Indonesian Government. As Peter King has sarcastically pointed out, if it was not for 'the prospective tax and royalty billions to be collected from Freeport copper and gold, BP gas, BHP nickel prospects and prospective paper mills in Papua, Indonesia would arguably be better off without her two troublesome Papuan provinces.'[38] However, the reality is that these incentives are very much alive, Jakarta benefits enormously from West Papuan natural resources, and the Indonesian economy is reliant upon the continued access to these resources on preferential terms. The present situation is far removed from the official position of the Dutch in the 1940s who argued that the incorporation of West Papua into Indonesia would burden the Indonesians because there was a dearth of economically productive natural resources in the territory for the Indonesians to utilise.[39]

Even though West Papua was not originally sought after for its natural resources, it did not take long for these to become the focal point of Jakarta's interest in the region. Under President Suharto (1967–1998), the exploitation of West Papuan resources became a key pillar of Government policy. This was made all too clear in the lead up to the Act of Free Choice, when, according to Jim Elmslie and Camellia Webb-Gannon, the Papuans were informally told by the Indonesians involved in the exercise that Indonesia 'was not interested in them, but in their land.'[40] It soon became apparent that foreign industry also

---

[38] Peter King, 'Self-determination and Papua: The Indonesian Dimension', in King et al. (eds), *Comprehending West Papua* (n 36) 158.

[39] Poulgrain, 'Delaying the "Discovery" of Oil in West New Guinea' (n 11) 205–06.

[40] Elmslie & Webb-Gannon, 'A Slow-Motion Genocide: Indonesian rule in West Papua' (n 35) 157.

paid scant attention to the customary title holders of the land as they moved into the region once 'stable' rule had been established. As Denise Leith has remarked, for the first three decades of its operation Freeport 'cared nothing for the landowners' rights and little for their concerns.'[41] The most well-known of these companies is Freeport-McMoRan which received its first mining Contract of Work from Suharto's New Order regime in 1967 to begin extracting copper and gold reserves at Ertsberg (Dutch for 'Ore Mountain') in the western central highlands of West Papua, home to the Amungme, and now more commonly referred to as Grasberg after the discovery of a second, gigantic, orebody adjacent to the fast-depleting mountain in 1987.[42]

Freeport's role in West Papuan history has been well documented, as has its contribution to Indonesia's record of human rights violations.[43] The scale of the operation was and is enormous. The gold deposit and mine is the largest in the world and the copper mine one of the largest and the world's most profitable.[44] Freeport accounts for 88% of West Papua's non-oil exports.[45] It contributed $33 billion to the Indonesian economy between 1992 and 2004.[46] However, increased production meant an almost exponential increase in waste, which flowed directly into the Agabagong River and out to the Arafura Sea. In 1972 there was 7,500 metric tonnes per day, in 1993 there were 66,000 mt per day,

---

41   Leith, *The Politics of Power* (n 33) 8.
42   Chris Ballard, *Human Rights and the Mining Sector in Indonesia: A Baseline Study* (Mining, Minerals and Sustainable Development Project of the International Institute for Environment and Development 2001) 23. The orebody was originally identified by a Dutch geologist in 1936 but World War Two and subsequent turmoil in the region caused the delay in development.
43   The most substantial study is by Denise Leith, *The Politics of Power* (n 33). Also see Chris Ballard, 'The Signature of Terror: Violence, Memory, and Landscape at Freeport', in Bruno David & Meredith Wilson (eds), *Inscribed Landscapes: Marking and Making Place* (U of Hawai'i P 2002) 13–26; Adérito de Jesus Soares, 'The Impact of Corporate Strategy on Community Dynamics: A Case Study of the Freeport Mining Company in West Papua, Indonesia' (2004) 11 Intl J on Minority and Group Rights 115; Joanna Kyriakakis, 'Freeport in West Papua: Bringing Corporations to Account for International Human Rights Abuses Under Australian Criminal and Tort Law' (2005) 31 Monash U LR 95; Patricia O'Brien, 'The Politics of Mines and Indigenous Rights: A Case Study of the Grasberg Mine in Indonesia's Papua Province' (2010) 11 Georgetown J of Intl Affairs 47.
44   Leith, *The Politics of Power* (n 33) 3.
45   Ballard, *Human Rights and the Mining Sector in Indonesia* (n 42) 23.
46   Jane Perlez & Raymond Bonner, 'Below a Mountain of Wealth, a River of Waste' *The New York Times* (New York, 27 December 2005), at <http://www.nytimes.com/2005/12/27/international/asia/27gold.html?pagewanted=all&_r=0> accessed 29 August 2014.

and by 1998 there were 220,000 mt per day.[47] Freeport estimates that by the time the ore has all been mined, they will have produced six billion tonnes of waste in total, a figure which is more than double the earth excavated for the Panama Canal.[48] As a result, almost 90 square miles of once pristine wetlands below the mine have been severely degraded, and the fish stocks have all but disappeared.[49]

Mining operations have not only produced a colossal amount of waste, but have also been largely responsible for the continued militarisation of the region on account of the interdependent and self-reinforcing nature of the relationship between the Indonesian military and the mining company.[50] Unlike the explicitly nationalist Sukarno, one of Suharto's key priorities was the attraction of foreign investment.[51] Freeport was the first foreign company to sign a contract with Suharto's Government; the company's expertise and capital was desperately needed to drive the Indonesian economy via the exploitation of West Papuan resources. Because of this, Freeport maintained a position of privilege for the duration of Suharto's New Order regime.[52] The relationship was mutually re-enforcing: 'In return for its services at such a critical time, Freeport's needs were fulfilled by an eager Jakarta: it got a highly favourable contract, the riches of Ertsberg, and the military to protect it.'[53]

However, by the 1990s (aided by the birth of the internet), Freeport's activity came under increasing scrutiny from both Indonesian and international NGOs.[54] This publicity forced Freeport to start taking the indigenous

---

47   Ballard, *Human Rights and the Mining Sector in Indonesia* (n 42) 23.
48   Perlez & Bonner, 'Below a Mountain of Wealth, a River of Waste' (n 46).
49   Perlez & Bonner, 'Below a Mountain of Wealth, a River of Waste' (n 46).
50   On this relationship see 'Freeport and TNI' in Leith, *The Politics of Power* (n 33) 220–47.
51   Soares, 'The Impact of Corporate Strategy on Community Dynamics' (n 43) 121.
52   Ballard writes '…its strategic importance to the state exceeds its monetary value. In recognition of its wealth and status as the first symbol of foreign investment confidence in the New Order government, the Freeport mine has been declared one of ten "national assets"', Ballard, *Human Rights and the Mining Sector in Indonesia* (n 42) 3.
53   Leith, *The Politics of Power* (n 33) 14. The relationship between the military and Freeport is best outlined in Perlez & Bonner, 'Below a Mountain of Wealth, a River of Waste' (n 46). The journalists have found that between 1998 and 2004 Freeport provided Indonesia military and police with nearly $20 million.
54   The Indonesian Forum on the Environment (Wahana Lingkungan Hidup Indonesia; WALHI) began its public campaign against Freeport at the beginning of the decade and was joined by the Australian Council for Overseas Aid (ACFOA) in 1995 who released a report *Trouble at Freeport: Eyewitness Accounts of West Papuan Resistance to the Freeport-McMoRan Mine in Irian Jaya, Indonesia, and Military Repression: June 1994–February 1995*: Leith, *The Politics of Power* (n 33) 5–6.

inhabitants of the area—the Amungme and Kamoro *sukus* (tribes)—seriously, and the company sought to ameliorate some of the social problems their enterprise had created. The post-Suharto era has seen greater efforts to curb corruption in the extractive industry sector, and in Freeport's operations in particular. A number of laws and policies were introduced to prevent the continued degradation of the environment, and decision making on resource matters has been devolved to provincial and local governments to a greater extent.[55] Yet, although there may be grounds for some optimism, Jakarta's continued blasé attitude toward enforcing environmental regulations needs to be addressed before the environmental sustainability of mining operations can be achieved.[56]

Moreover, until the Papuans are taken seriously by Jakarta, there is still little chance that the high rate of human rights violations that have plagued the area will be addressed. Chris Ballard has suggested that the 'long-term causes of human rights abuse relate to the broader social and political climate in Indonesia, which sets the terms for human rights observance.'[57] Meanwhile James Anaya has identified 'natural resource extraction and other major development projects in or near indigenous territories as one of the most significant sources of abuse of the rights of indigenous peoples worldwide.'[58] The presence of these industries, Anaya argues, runs counter to the self-determination of indigenous peoples.[59] It is no accident that the mining region features heavily in some of the most depressing statistics of the region. For example, it is estimated that 160 people were killed by the military between 1975 and 1997 in the mine area,[60] while the nearby town of Timika has the second highest rate of HIV/AIDS in West Papua.[61] The Amungme, and other indigenous peoples of the Timika area, have been continually shut out from receiving any benefits from the extraction of their customary land and suffer increasing hardship on account

---

55   Ballard, *Human Rights and the Mining Sector in Indonesia* (n 42) 15.
56   For more precise policy recommendations see Ballard, *Human Rights and the Mining Sector in Indonesia* (n 42) 45 and O'Brien, 'The Politics of Mines and Indigenous Rights' (n 43) 54.
57   Ballard, *Human Rights and the Mining Sector in Indonesia* (n 42) 43.
58   UNGA 'Report of the Special Rapporteur on the Rights of Indigenous Peoples: Extractive Industries Operating Within or Near Indigenous Territories' (July 2011) UN Doc A/HRC/18/35, 18.
59   'Report of the Special Rapporteur on the rights of indigenous peoples' (n 58) 18.
60   Perlez & Bonner, 'Below a Mountain of Wealth, a River of Waste' (n 46). Ballard puts the number at 200 and notes they were all mostly unarmed civilians. Ballard, *Human Rights and the Mining Sector in Indonesia* (n 42) 27.
61   O'Brien, 'The Politics of Mines and Indigenous Rights' (n 43) 52.

of the exploitative practices of the mining operation.[62] Ballard has poignantly written that 'Mining in the Amungme landscape has thus been quite literally an assault upon the body of Amungme belief and the foundations of Amungme identity.'[63] An examination of the latest central government scheme, MIFEE, tends to suggest that Jakarta still has a long way to go before Papuan human rights are to be respected.

4   Modern Land-grabbing for Food Production

The Merauke Integrated Food and Energy Estate ('MIFEE') is the most recent example of an Indonesian project in West Papua causing significant environmental degradation and interfering with indigenous Papuan ways of living. Focused on intensifying food production to supply both Indonesian and foreign markets, MIFEE was launched in August 2010 with the backing of substantial overseas investment.[64] Government conduct in relation to the project is worth exploring because it is perhaps the most compelling illustration of the type of neo-colonialism in the name of 'development' that has been a reoccurring theme of more recent Indonesia administrations. Although couched in altruistic terms, like the mining operations at Grasberg, the proceeds of such economic development accrue to foreign and Indonesian corporate investors and to the Indonesian Government, rather than to West Papua or its indigenous communities.

Merauke, a regency in Southeastern Papua near the Papua New Guinea border, was chosen by the Government as an ideal location for setting aside 1.6 million hectares for the ambitious crop scheme which is part of Jakarta's Masterplan for the Acceleration and Expansion of Indonesia's Economic Development. The plan involves clearing the land, much of which was or is still

---

62   Only 20–26% of workers at the mine are indigenous Papuans: O'Brien, 'The Politics of Mines and Indigenous Rights' (n 43) 52.
63   Ballard, 'The Signature of Terror' (n 43) 18.
64   Paul Barber & Rosa Moiwend, 'Internet Advocacy and the MIFEE Project in West Papua', in King et al. *Comprehending West Papua* (n 36) 40. According to the Indonesian President, Merauke would 'Feed Indonesia, then feed the world.' Selwyn Moran, 'MIFEE: The Stealthy Face of Conflict in West Papua' (*Asian Human Rights Commission*, 19 July 2012), at <http://www.humanrights.asia/opinions/columns/AHRC-ETC-022-2012> accessed 29 August 2014. For a list of key companies involved in the MIFEE project see 'Three years of MIFEE (part 1): a growing movement against plantations in West Papua', (*awas MIFEE*, 23 October 2013), at<http://www.farmlandgrab.org/post/view/22730-three-years-of-mifee-a-growing-movement-against-plantations-in-west-papua> accessed 29 August 2014.

forested, to make way for the production of sugar, rice, corn, palm oil, soybeans and beef. Although the region is home to the indigenous Malind, both local and central Government declared the area to be uninhabited and thus suitable for transformation into agricultural land.

The United Nations Declaration on the Rights of Indigenous Peoples clearly states that States must:

> consult and cooperate in good faith with the indigenous peoples concerned through their own representative institutions in order to obtain their free and informed consent prior to the approval of any project affecting their lands or territories and other resources, particularly in connection with the development, utilisation or exploitation of mineral, water or other resources.[65]

Indeed, Indonesia has ratified several international norms and instruments which entail the right of indigenous peoples to free, prior and informed consent[66] and has implemented this in a number of national and provincial legal frameworks.[67] However, the Malind 'have simply been ignored': no consultation with the indigenous inhabitants of the land was made prior to implementation.[68]

A number of NGOs have criticised the project. An opinion piece for the Asian Human Rights Commission describes: 'Companies are moving in to colonize the land for their plantations, cheating and coercing local people to give up their land.'[69] A joint report by the Forest Peoples Programme, Pusaka, and Sawit Watch has concluded that Jakarta's food policy, exemplified by MIFEE is fundamentally misguided. They argue that the scheme 'is not just failing to

---

65 Article 32(2) in Forest Peoples Programme. 'A sweetness like unto death: Voices of the Indigenous Malind of Merauke, Papua' (*Pusaka and Sawit Watch, Forest Peoples Programme*, 2013) 44, at <http://www.forestpeoples.org/sites/fpp/files/publication/2013/10/asweetnessundodeathmifeeindonesiaenglish2.pdf> accessed 29 August 2014.

66 These also include the United Nations Covenant on Civil and Political Rights; The United Nations Covenant on Economic, Social and Cultural Rights; the United Nations Convention on the Elimination of All Forms of Racial Discrimination; the United Nations Convention on Biological Diversity; and the Voluntary Guidelines on the Responsible Governance of Tenure of Land, Fisheries and Forests in the Context of National Food Security. Forest Peoples Programme et al., 'A sweetness like unto death' (n 65) 44.

67 See 'A sweetness like unto death' (n 65) 45.

68 Paul Barber and Rosa Moiwend, 'Internet Advocacy and the MIFEE Project in West Papua' (n 64) 42.

69 Moran, 'MIFEE' (n 64).

promote local farmers, it is actually undermining local self-sufficiency and local food security, generating poverty for local people and denying their rights to their lands, livelihoods and to a future built on the[sic] own cultures and institutions.'[70] Papuan objections to the scheme are summarised by a protest sign sighted at Yowied Village in Tubang District: 'There is not so much land around Yowied Village. Our lives are dependent on what our environment can provide. Where will the future generations go?'[71] As Terence Wesley-Smith pointed out in 1987, despite West Papua's low population density, 'it is not the case that there are large areas of potentially productive land lying idle.' For instance, only approximately a third of West Papua is habitable, while Papuan systems of agriculture and hunting-and-gathering activities rely on large areas of bush land. Taken alongside the transmigration policies of central Government, MIFEE's ambitious land appropriation can be interpreted as directly dispossessing Papuans from their land, and destroying the cultural practices of the Malind population. The scheme may well be advertised as part of an economic 'masterplan,' but from the Papuan perspective, it looks like another part of Jakarta's masterplan of extreme indigenous marginalisation. The death of those who are critical of the government suggests that Jakarta's intentions are indeed more sinister than they appear.[72]

5   Autonomy

Perhaps unsurprisingly, with so much at stake (and so much to criticise), Indonesia prefers that media not report on what happens in West Papua. Strict press censorship prevails and foreign media are barred from entering West Papua. Unfortunately, journalists are also increasingly being imprisoned, tortured, killed and/or simply 'disappeared.'[73] Alex Perrottet and David Robie,

---

70   'A sweetness like unto death' (n 65) 52.
71   'Three years of MIFEE (part 1)' (n 64).
72   For example, Ardiansyah Matrai'is was a journalist who was critical of the scheme and was found dead, tied to a tree in the middle of a river, with signs of having been tortured. Wesley-Smith, 'Lost Melanesian Brothers' (n 8) 32. See also Alex Perrottet & David Robie, 'Pacific Media Freedom 2011: A status report' (2011) 17(2) Pacific Journalism R 148, 179–180 (also in (2012) 1(3) Pacific Journalism Monographs), at <http://www.pjreview.info/sites/default/files/articles/pdfs/PJR17_2_pacific%20media%20freedom2011.pdf> accessed 29 August 2014. The police concluded that it was a case of suicide. *ibid* 180.
73   See, eg, Perrottet & Robie, 'Pacific Media Freedom 2011' (n 72) 178–181. 'Threats and actual violence against journalists are commonplace in Papua', *ibid* 179. Journalists and environmental defenders are the groups most targeted this way worldwide. See, eg, UNHRC

specialists in Pacific media, have declared that the Pacific's 'most serious case of media freedom violations' occur in West Papua by a large margin.[74] However, the situation inside the territory was not always this oppressive. Papuan fortunes underwent a brief respite after the fall of Suharto's New Order regime in 1998. Under President B.J. Habibie and his successor, Abdurrahman Wahid, Papuans were granted some measures of autonomy. In 2000, Wahid permitted the formation of a Papuan council and the Morning Star flag was even allowed to be raised (as long as it was of a smaller size and fixed at a lower height than an Indonesian one). The name for the territory, Irian Jaya (Victorious Irian), was revoked and replaced by the more agreeable Papua. Such was the relative level of freedom, and expression of pro-independence feeling, during this period that commentators frequently label it the 'Papuan spring'.

Of course, there was more behind Jakarta's loosening grip than first meets the eye.[75] These autonomy measures, enshrined in the Special Autonomy Law (2001), were introduced in the wake of Timor-Leste's independence and therefore were the result of a desire to reduce pro-independence sentiment in West Papua by the devolution of most government affairs to the Papuan provincial government.[76] Richard Chauvel argues that a fundamental distrust of Papuan politicians from Jakarta meant Special Autonomy was never going to succeed. He has discovered that devolution under Special Autonomy was deliberately limited and very little changed in practical terms.[77]

'Report of the Special Rapporteur on the situation of human rights defenders Margaret Sekaggya' (21 Dec 2011) UN Doc A/HRC/19/55. See also 'Deadly Environment: The Dramatic Rise in Killings of Environmental and Land Defenders 1 January 2002–31 December 2013' *Global Witness* (London, 2014), at <http://www.globalwitness.org/deadlyenvironment> accessed 29 August 2014.

74   Perrottet & Robie, 'Pacific Media Freedom 2011' (n 72) 153.

75   Another less savoury feature of Special Autonomy is Jakarta's policy of *pemekaran* or administrative expansion which has seen West Papua carved into a multitude of smaller units since 1999 in what has been judged to be 'divide-and-rule' tactics. See 'Carving up Papua: more districts, more trouble' (Institute for Policy Analysis of Conflict 9 Oct 2013), at <http://file.understandingconflict.org/file/2013/10/IPAC_Carving_Up_Papua_More_Districts,_More_Problems.pdf> accessed 29 August 2014.

76   See Laurence Sullivan, 'Challenges to Special Autonomy in the Province of Papua, Republic of Indonesia' *State Society and Governance in Melanesia* (Discussion Paper, State Society and Governance in Melanesia, Australian National University, 2003), at <https://digitalcollections.anu.edu.au/bitstream/1885/42059/2/sullivan.pdf> accessed 29 August 2014.

77   Richard Chauvel, 'Filep Karma and the fight for Papua's future' *Inside Story* (Melbourne, 6 April 2011), at <http://inside.org.au/filep-karma-and-the-fight-for-papuas-future> accessed 10 February 2015.

Unfortunately, this period of relative freedom was swiftly curtailed and political activity was once again criminalised. The assassination of the self-proclaimed leader of the pro-independence Papua Presidium Council (PDP), Theys H. Eluay, in November 2001 effectively crushed any groundswell of optimism that may have been emerging. The assassination—again shrouded in mystery—made it obvious that Special Autonomy of the Indonesian variety did not approximate self-determination. The raising of the Morning Star flag is currently illegal, as the continued imprisonment of Papuan civil servant Filep Karma from 2004 reminds us.[78]

Indonesian crack-downs have not dented pro-independence feeling, however. A new indigenous Government, the Papuan People's Council (Majelis Rakyat Papua, MRP), has been formed and in 2010 judged special autonomy to be a failure and declared their intention to 'give it back.'[79] A 20,000 strong protest followed to which Jakarta has stayed firm, declaring special autonomy is 'final.'[80] Historically, West Papua's anti-Indonesia independence movements have been characterised by factionalism, but there is a sense that the feeling in West Papua amongst the indigenous population is a lot more uniform. From leaked Indonesian military documents which found their way to the University of Sydney's West Papua Project, there appear to be real signs that 'West Papuan nationalism is spread throughout civil society.' The authors of the report show that the desire for self-determination has not dampened in the face of increased repression: 'the younger generation of Papuan leaders is now stridently demanding the rights to which they are entitled by Indonesian law, albeit increasingly as a non-violent, civil resistance movement.'[81]

6   Self-determination and Genocide

At one level, the argument for Papuan self-determination is straightforward. Self-determination and decolonisation have been on the United Nations' agenda since it began in 1945. A wave of decolonisation accordingly swept

---

78   Karma is still serving his 15 year sentence. See Chauvel, 'Filep Karma and the fight for Papua's future' (n 77).
79   Rutherford, 'Review of Drooglever' (n 2) 182.
80   Though other groups, most notably Papuan religious leaders, have advocated for proper implementation and adherence to the Special Autonomy laws. See 'Joint Statement by Papuan Religious Leaders' (2005) 9 Australian Indigenous Law Reporter 122.
81   Jim Elmslie & Camellia Webb-Gannon with Peter King, 'Anatomy of an Occupation: The Indonesian Military in West Papua' (West Papua Project at the Centre for Peace and Conflict Studies, University of Sydney, August 2011) 2.

through the Pacific from the 1960s onwards. While the application of the various rules was far from uniform,[82] and there are a still a number of Pacific territories that remain involuntarily non-self-governing,[83] the rules ostensibly still apply, as shown in the self-determination of East Timor resulting in independent statehood as late as 2002.

However, at another level, West Papua is a more complex case than many others, given the historic legacy, the level of foreign multinational complicity, and the extreme levels of marginalisation experienced by the Papuan population. Despite the urgency of the situation, there has certainly been insufficient political or legal will to resolve the issue. Indonesia has benefited from the international privileging of the inviolability of territorial boundaries. In international fora Indonesia relies upon the 'statist, realist and rationalist paradigm of international law and relations' that I have previously argued is in urgent need of overturning elsewhere.[84] States appear reluctant to intervene in West Papua, perhaps in case a precedent is set for secession and independent statehood, despite—or perhaps because of—the fact that it has already occurred in the case of East Timor. And, this is despite the more recent developments on indigenous self-determination in international law which focus less on secession and more on alternative constitutional arrangements within states, such as via regional autonomy and similar structures.[85]

---

82   Akihisa Matsuno, 'West Papua and the Changing Nature of Self-Determination' in King et al. *Comprehending West Papua* (n 36) ('Matsuno, "West Papua and the Changing Nature of Self-Determination"') 178.

83   At present, France controls Wallis and Futuna, New Caledonia and French Polynesia. The United States controls Guam, Hawaii and American Samoa. Chile controls Rapa Nui. And New Zealand controls Tokelau.

84   Catherine Iorns, 'Indigenous Peoples and Self Determination: Challenging State Sovereignty' (1992) 24 CWRJIL 199 ('Iorns, 'Indigenous Peoples and Self Determination: Challenging State Sovereignty") 346.

85   See eg, the United Nations Declaration on the Rights of Indigenous Peoples (adopted 13 September 2007) UNGA Res 61/295 and comments on it, such as S James Anaya, 'The Right of Indigenous Peoples to Self-Determination in the Post-Declaration Era' in Claire Charters & Rodolfo Stavenhagen (eds) *Making the Declaration Work: The United Nations Declaration on the Rights of Indigenous Peoples* (International Workgroup for Indigenous Affairs 2009) 184, at <http://www.iwgia.org/iwgia_files_publications_files/making_the_declaration_work.pdf> accessed 29 August 2014. See also, 'Report on the Rights of Indigenous Peoples' (International Law Association Report of the 75th Conference, Sofia, Bulgaria, 2012) 503, 506–512; and 'Interim Report on the Rights of Indigenous Peoples' (International Law Association Report of the 74th Conference, The Hague, 2010) 834, 846–50; both reports also separately available at <www.ila-hq.org/en/committees/index.cfm/cid/1024> accessed 29 August 2014.

There is a growing chorus of support for Papuan self-determination among NGOs, legal experts, and other scholars.[86] Not unusually, it is at the level of civil society where agitation is the most enthusiastic. Renowned linguist and veteran activist Noam Chomsky has criticised the West's complicity in the atrocities in West Papua.[87] South African Archbishop Desmond Tutu has lent his support to the movement, expressing solidarity with the Papuans and urging the UN to take action.[88] Former Vanuatu Prime Minister Moana Carcasses Kalosil has lobbied the UN to investigate human rights abuses inside West Papua.[89] The International Parliamentarians for West Papua (IPWP) and the International Lawyers for West Papua (ILWP) are two of the more promising vehicles for progress to be made on the issue given their proximity to state power. Melinda Janki, chair of the ILWP, stresses that Special Autonomy is not self-determination and implores the international community not to support the former.[90] Valmaine Toki's recent report for the United Nations Permanent Forum on Indigenous Issues recommended that West Papua should urgently be reinstated on the list of Non-Self-Governing Territories.[91] Toki believes such urgency is needed due to the ongoing 'severe human rights violations' in the territory.[92]

Ultimately, of all the arguments that could be made in favour of self-determination for the Papuan population, the most convincing is undoubtedly the serious allegations of genocide committed by the Indonesian state. I have previously echoed the doubts of legal experts who point out the ridiculousness of waiting 'for some arbitrary amount of suffering to be endured before a right

---

86 See eg, 'Open Letter: Access to West Papua' (Conference attendees, *Comprehending West Papua*, University of Sydney, 27 Feb 2011), at <http://www.andreasharsono.net/2011/02/open-letter-access-to-west-papua.html> accessed 29 Aug 2014.

87 Noam Chomsky, 'West Papua Independence' (2013) interview video available at, at <http://freewestpapua.org/2013/12/12/noam-chomsky-speaks-out-on-west-papua/> accessed 29 Aug 2014.

88 'West Papua: Nobel Prize Desmond Tutu calls on UN to act' (Unrepresented Nations and Peoples Organisation, 26 Feb 2004), at <http://www.unpo.org/article/435> accessed 29 Aug 2014.

89 'Vanuatu PM raises West Papua in Geneva' *Scoop* (New Zealand, 10 March 2014), at <http://www.scoop.co.nz/stories/WO1403/S00159/vanuatu-pm-raises-west-papua-in-geneva.htm> accessed 29 Aug 2014; Ligo, 'PM: Vanuatu Is The Only Hope For West Papua' (n 3).

90 Melinda Janki, 'West Papua: Special Autonomy Is Illegal Under International Law', Indigenous Peoples Issues & Resources, 20 January 2011 at <http://indigenouspeoplesissues.com/index.php?option=com_content&view=article&id=8522:west-papua-special-autonomy-is-illegal-under-international-law&catid=32&Itemid=65> accessed 29 Aug 2014.

91 'Study on Decolonization of the Pacific Region' United Nations Economic and Social Council (2013) UN Doc E/C.19/2013/12, 12.

92 Ibid 12.

to secession is recognized.'[93] Similarly, while setting out a convincing case for the inherent genocidal qualities of settler colonialism, Banivanua-Mar also argues that debates over 'whether the killings, massacres, disappearances and structural marginalization of West Papuans amounts to genocide in the legal sense' are 'potentially diversionary', suggesting that these kinds of debates 'run the risk of setting up taxonomies of genocide', and become altogether too cold and clinical, 'amorphous and malleable', effectively silencing the lived experiences of the victims.[94] However, in the case of West Papua this discussion is salient given the inability of international actors to act thus far despite being aware of a litany of historical injustices. Precisely because of the need to appropriately frame the seriousness of the situation for international audiences, Elmslie and Webb-Gannon state that the issue of genocide or not is 'no moot point', they instead believe 'it is perhaps the most pressing contemporary issue.'[95] The Sydney scholars are not alone in this contention; for instance, far from seeing it as fruitless, the Japanese scholar Matsuno has observed a shift in the international framing of self-determination. No longer so concerned with 'original legality alone', Matsuno has found that, more weight is placed on the 'current situation of functioning morality within state borders.'[96] If this holds, suddenly the reporting of human rights abuses by the Indonesian regime and international industry becomes central to the fate of the Papuans.

There have been conflicting assessments of whether the treatment described amounts to genocide under international law. There have been several reports cataloguing the abuses suffered and assessing the claims of genocide; their conclusions differ. For example, in 2004 a team of Yale University researchers produced a substantial report cataloguing case after case (at times in graphic detail) of Indonesian abuses in West Papua and then applied to it the international law of genocide.[97] The researchers were satisfied that the Papuans satisfy

---

93 Iorns, 'Indigenous Peoples and Self Determination' (n 84) 323.
94 Banivanua-Mar, 'A Thousand Miles of Cannibal Lands' (n 25) 586.
95 Elmslie & Webb-Gannon, 'A Slow-Motion Genocide: Indonesian rule in West Papua' (n 35) 156. The framing of the problem is discussed by Akihisa Matsuno in Marni Cordell, 'Does West Papua Have a Publicity Problem?' *New Matilda* (Australia, 3 March 2011), at <https://newmatilda.com/2011/03/03/does-west-papua-have-publicity-problem> accessed 29 Aug 2014.
96 Matsuno, 'West Papua and the Changing Nature of Self-Determination' (n 82) 178. Matsuno cites three recent examples of self-determination in Kosovo, South Sudan and East Timor to support his argument.
97 Elizabeth Brundige et al., *Indonesian Human Rights Abuses in West Papua: Application of the Law of Genocide to the History of Indonesian Rule* (Allard K. Lowenstein International Human Rights Clinic, Yale Law School, April 2004).

the 'group' element of the 1948 Genocide Convention, as well as the 'act' element, and that 'there can be little doubt that the Indonesian government has engaged in a systematic pattern of acts that has resulted in harm to—and indeed the destruction of—a substantial part of the indigenous population of West Papua.'[98] However, the researchers could not confidently state that the conduct of the Indonesian government constituted genocide because of the inability to identify the 'requisite intent or *mens rea*', despite suggesting that a strong argument could be made for it based on learned inference.[99] Because of these self-proclaimed doubts, Pieter Drooglever warns against using the conclusions of the Yale University group as evidence for genocide. Although he admits the gross violence and injustice identified by the group is correct, like them he does not think it can be justifiably labelled genocidal.[100]

On the other hand, the Asian Human Rights Commission investigated the killings that took place in 1977–78 in the Papuan Central Highlands, where the Indonesian military killed 'up to tens of thousands' of Papuans, and in 2013 concluded that the 'clear pattern of mass violence' in this affront alone constituted genocide under the Genocide Convention.[101] They termed it 'the neglected genocide.' Some academics have addressed the Yale report and found the limited conclusions 'unsatisfactory.'[102] For example, Elmslie & Webb-Gannon have few qualms about ascribing genocidal intent onto the Indonesian Government's acts and policies. The unfettered military administration, the extensive transmigration policy, the encouragement of foreign industry which exploits and degrades customary natural resources, and the suppression and demonization of the pro-independence faction of the population (which is a majority of Papuans) all paint a picture of undeniable intent.[103] Further, these policies have not been carried out in a haphazard or erratic fashion, nor is there much evidence of settler-Papuan conflict. Rather, 'Papuans have been killed by Indonesian soldiers and police following orders' under the policy of the Indonesian state since the beginning of their military occupation in 1962–63 to 'destroy those West Papuans who have opposed Indonesian rule.'[104] Elmslie and Webb-Gannon argue that it is impossible to escape the conclusion of intent.[105]

---

98   Ibid 74.
99   Ibid 74.
100 Drooglever, *An Act of Free Choice* (n 13) 761.
101 Asian Human Rights Commission, *The Neglected Genocide* (n 30) 2.
102 Elmslie & Webb-Gannon, 'A Slow-Motion Genocide: Indonesian rule in West Papua' (n 35) 155. For their appraisal of other studies on this question see 153–55.
103 Ibid 156–59.
104 Ibid 155.
105 Ibid 158.

7 Conclusion

I suggest that Roger Clark would be as disappointed at the international inattention to the situation in West Papua as he was for East Timor in the 1970s. The oppression today occurs on more fronts than it used to, such that Papuan independence advocates are up against not only re-colonisation by Indonesia but also the neo-colonial trans-national resource industries.[106] The many vested interests of the resource industries undoubtedly assists with the inattention by other states.

On the other hand, today there are even more internationally accepted human rights and other relevant standards and procedures applicable to the situation than there were in the 1970s, which makes it easier to argue that claimed breaches of such standards must be addressed. It is arguable that many such standards have been breached in the case of West Papua. For example, the international community has formally recognised indigenous rights to lands and territories, to resources, to the free, prior and informed consent of indigenous peoples before removing access to any of these lands and resources, and other related rights in the 2007 UN Declaration on the Rights of Indigenous Peoples including self-determination, even if that is largely expected to be exercised internally. I have already mentioned that the large-scale resource extraction on indigenous territories worldwide has been identified by the UN Special Rapporteur on the Rights of Indigenous Peoples as preventing the exercise of indigenous self-determination by taking away the lands and natural resources which they depend upon, physically and culturally. So it is tempting to argue that the West Papuan situation is simply an example of this and thereby to argue for a development of the parameters of the international law right to indigenous self-determination—perhaps one which also specifically addresses the current conflict with the increasingly-recognised right of development in international law—and to apply it to West Papua.

However, I suggest that the situation in West Papua appears to have gone beyond this and that the international community must address the claims of genocide as a basis for the application of traditional self-determination. Foreign interference has created the situation in West Papua, and its continuing presence has exacerbated the conflict. Members of the international community must continue to advocate for a just solution, including at least investigation of the claims of genocide. In addition, the military occupation needs to end as soon as possible if a West Papuan future is going to be realised. Most international

---

106   Historian Tracey Banivanua-Mar states that West Papua is a 'transnational colony'. Banivanua-Mar, 'A Thousand Miles of Cannibal Lands' (n 25) 594.

legal arguments in relation to West Papua focus on the legal and historical basis for self-determination. However, these arguments are ultimately superfluous in the face of what has and continues to unfold on the ground. It has been put bluntly: 'There is no argument that justifies genocide—not even territorial integrity.'[107] Given the tremendous power deficits operating in the region between coloniser and colonised, the onus to act rests on the international community.*

---

107   Elmslie & Webb-Gannon, 'A Slow-Motion Genocide: Indonesian rule in West Papua' (n 35) 162.

*   Thanks are due to my research assistant Nicholas Hoare (MA (Hist) Well.) who provided much of the material for this chapter.

CHAPTER 17

'Professor Clark, What Can We *Do* about the Western Sahara'?

Suzannah Linton*

1   Introduction

Roger, in his celebrated career as an inspirational teacher of international law, must have faced many challenging questions from students roused to indignation by his lectures revealing global injustice, double standards, abuse of power and human cruelty. He will surely have faced this one from an outraged student: 'Professor Clark, what can we *do* about the Western Sahara'? Roger would have been able to point the student to his fine 2007 publication on the Western Sahara and his splendid earlier publications on East Timor.[1] These works were often part of a common endeavour with other kindred spirits engaged in outstanding and inspiring scholarship that helped to establish the illegality of the aggression against East Timor and Western Sahara. But, as the International Court of Justice ('ICJ') in *Namibia* observed, 'the qualification of a situation as

---

*   Thanks to Gerry Simpson, Arsalan Al Mizory and Jesus Verdu Baeza for helpful comments.
1   Roger's formidable works include 'Western Sahara and the United Nations Norms on Self-Determination and Aggression' in Karin Arts & Pedro Pinto Leite (eds), *International Law and the Question of Western Sahara* (IPJET 2007) ('Clark, 'Western Sahara and the United Nations Norms on Self-Determination and Aggression''); 'Obligations of Third States in the Face of Illegality: Ruminations inspired by the Weeramantry Dissent in the Case Concerning East Timor', in Antony Anghie & Garry Sturgess (eds), *Legal Visions of the 21st Century: Essays in Honour of Judge Christopher Weeramantry* (Kluwer 1998); 'East Timor and An International Criminal Court' in Pedro Pinto Leite (ed), *The East Timor Problem and the Role of Europe* (IPJET 1998); 'Public International Law and Private Enterprise: Damages for a Killing in East Timor' (1996) 3 AJHR 21; 'The "Decolonization" of East Timor and the United Nations Norms on Self-Determination and Aggression' in Pedro Pinto Leite (ed), *International Law and the Problem of East Timor* (CIIA & IPJET 1995); 'Some International Law Aspects of the East Timor Affair' (1992) 5 LJIL 265; 'Timor Gap: The Legality of the "Treaty on the Zone of Cooperation in an Area Between the Indonesian Province of East Timor and Northern Australia"' (1992) Pace Ybk Intl L 69, reprinted in Peter Carey & G Carter Bentley (eds), *East Timor at the Crossroads: Forging of a Nation* (Cassell 1995); 'The "Decolonization" of East Timor and the United Nations Norms on Self-Determination and Aggression' (1980) 7 Yale J World Pub Ord 2.

illegal does not by itself put an end to it. It can only be the first, necessary step in an endeavour to bring the illegal situation to an end.'[2]

My paper commemorates Roger's ground-breaking work by addressing the question of what we can *do* about the Western Sahara, in 2015. There is no need for me to critique what Roger and others have so ably established, but it will help to begin with a brief statement about the law and facts relating to the Western Sahara that are, to my mind, convincingly proven. This setting of the framework will then enable me to engage with the core question of what we can *do*, in the year 2015, when the Western Sahara remains occupied and its people continue to be denied the right to self-determination. With Spain and Morocco still being obstructive, supported in their intransigence by certain Security Council members amid widespread indifference, with illusions about the abilities of the United Nations ('UN') in this matter shattered most recently by the High Commissioner for Human Rights,[3] and the European Union ('EU') joining in to exploit the natural resources of the occupied territory, what can we *do*? What alternative approaches can be employed, in the words of the ICJ, to 'bring the illegal situation to an end'?

2 The Cup of the Western Sahara Runneth over with the Froth of International Law

Since 1975,[4] the Saharawi have been a people who have been forcibly denied their right to self-determination in a political sense, and in an economic sense through the non-consensual exploration and exploitation of the natural resources of their territory.[5] This dispossessed people live today either under Moroccan

---

2   *Legal Consequences for States of the Continued Presence of South Africa in Namibia* (*South West Africa*) *notwithstanding Security Council Resolution 276 (1970)* (Advisory Opinion) [1971] ICJ Rep 16 ('*Namibia Advisory Opinion*'), para 111.
3   High Commissioner Pillay visited Morocco in May 2014, and in her remarks at a press conference made no mention of the occupation of the Western Sahara, referring to the territory as if it were lawfully part of Morocco. See Navi Pillay, 'Opening remarks by UN High Commissioner for Human Rights' (Press conference, Rabat, 29 May 2014), at <http://www.ohchr.org/EN/NewsEvents/Pages/DisplayNews.aspx?NewsID=14652&LangID=E> accessed 1 February 2015.
4   It was in 1966 that the United Nations first called on Spain to hold a referendum in 'Spanish Sahara', see UNGA Res 2229 (XXI) (20 December 1966) 'Question of Ifni and Spanish Sahara' UN Doc A/RS/2229 (XXI) ('UNGA Res 2229 (XXI)'). Morocco first entered the territory in November 1975, taking full control in 1978.
5   For a legal assessment of the mineral exploitation in the Western Sahara, see 'Letter dated 29 January 2002 from the Under-Secretary-General for Legal Affairs, the Legal Counsel, addressed to the President of the Security Council', UN Doc S/2002/161 ('Correll Opinion').

occupation, in the liberated east of the Western Sahara, in the Polisario[6]-controlled camps in Algeria or as part of a global diaspora. Some 260,000 are said to be living in the so-called free areas to the east of the territory, and in the refugee camps.[7]

The Western Sahara is still a non-self-governing territory.[8] *De jure*, its Administering Power remains Spain, whose attempt to abandon her responsibilities in 1975 does not have any legal implications.[9] *De facto*, its Administering Power is the country that has occupied and controlled it since 1975, Morocco.[10] Even before the invasion and occupation, the ICJ found no evidence 'of any legal tie of territorial sovereignty' between Morocco and the Western Sahara such as could affect the established right of its people to self-determination.[11]

---

6 This is the Spanish abbreviation of the leading Saharawi political group, Frente Popular de Liberación de Saguía el Hamra y Rio de Oro (translated as 'Popular Front for the Liberation of Saguia el-Hamra and Rio de Oro').

7 See 'Periodic Report of the Sahrawi Arab Democratic Republic to the African Commission on Human and Peoples Rights containing all the outstanding Reports in accordance with Article 62 of the Charter' (October 2011), at <http://www.achpr.org/files/sessions/55th/state-reports/2nd-2002-2012/periodic_report_sahrawi_eng.pdf> accessed 24 May 2014.

8 It remains on the UN's list of non-self-governing territories, albeit the Administering Power section is now empty, with a note stating 'On 26 February 1976, Spain informed the Secretary-General that as of that date it had terminated its presence in the Territory of the Sahara and deemed it necessary to place on record that Spain considered itself thenceforth exempt from any responsibility of any international nature in connection with the administration of the Territory, in view of the cessation of its participation in the temporary administration established for the Territory. In 1990, the General Assembly reaffirmed that the question of Western Sahara was a question of decolonization which remained to be completed by the people of Western Sahara.' See <http://www.un.org/en/decolonization/nonselfgovterritories.shtml> accessed 24 May 2014.

9 See 'Declaration on Principles of International Law Concerning Friendly Relations and Cooperation Among States' (24 October 1970) UN Doc A/RES/2625 (XXV) ('UNGA Res 2625 (XXV)'); Correll Opinion (n 5) paras 6–8, confirming that Spain could not transfer its responsibilities as Administering Power.

10 UNGA Res 2625 (XXV) (n 9) sets out the well-established customary rule that 'No territorial acquisition resulting from the threat or use of force shall be recognized as legal.' UNGA Res 3314 (XXIX) (14 December 1974) 'The Definition of Aggression' UN Doc A/S/3314 (XXIX) ('UNGA Res 3314 (XXIX)') took this forward. See too, *Legal Consequences of the Construction of a Wall in the Occupied Palestinian Territory* (Advisory Opinion) [2004] ICJ Rep 136 ('*Palestine Advisory Opinion*'), para 87. In relation to the Western Sahara, UNSC Res 380 (6 November 1975) UN Doc S/RES/380 (1975) calls on Morocco 'immediately to withdraw' and UNGA Res 34/37 (21 November 1979) refers to Morocco's occupation of the territory.

11 *Western Sahara* (Advisory Opinion) [1975] ICJ Rep 12 ('*Western Sahara Advisory Opinion*'), para 162.

The act of aggression of 1975 continues to exist as a violation of international law for so long as Morocco occupies the territory.[12]

Institutionally, the United Nations has general responsibilities in relation to self-determination, it being among the core purposes of the institution; there are also three specific chapters in the Charter devoted to promoting and protecting the interests of dependent peoples.[13] The nature of the right to self-determination creates obligations *erga omnes*,[14] and the international community as a whole is obliged to respect and ensure the entitlement of the Saharawi to a process whereby they may freely determine their political status, and to ensure that they are able freely to 'pursue their economic, social and cultural development', as well as to safeguard and guarantee their inalienable rights to their natural resources.[15] In the context of determining their future political status, the Saharawi should be enabled to choose between full independence and the creation of a new State; association with an existing independent State; or integration into an existing independent State.[16]

Furthermore, all UN member States have been normatively engaged in this matter through the Charter, as well as in customary international law. General Assembly Resolution 2625 (XXV) is, in this area of self-determination, widely regarded as being either a statement of customary law or evidencing the elements of customary law.[17] There are also duties of non-recognition as elaborated

---

12   See Charter of the United Nations (entered into force 24 October 1945), 1 UNTS XVI ('UN Charter') art 2(4); UNGA Res 2625 (XXV) (n 9); UNGA Res 3314 (XXIX) (n 10).
13   UN Charter (n 12) Chapter XI, XII, XIII.
14   *Palestine Advisory Opinion* (n 10), paras 155–56; *Case Concerning East Timor (Portugal v Australia)* [1995] ICJ Rep 90, para 29; *Western Sahara Advisory Opinion* (n 11) paras 54–59; *Namibia Advisory Opinion* (n 2) paras 52–53.
15   See inter alia, UNGA Res 1514 (XV) (14 December 1960) 'Declaration on the Granting of Independence to Colonial Countries and Peoples' UN Doc A/RES/1514 (XV); UNGA Res 1541 (XV) (15 December 1960) 'Principles which should guide Members in determining whether or not an obligation exists to transmit the information called for under Article 73 e of the Charter' UN Doc A/4684 (1960) 66 ('UNGA Res 1541 (XV)').
16   UNGA 1541 (XV) (n 15). However, independence and integration with Morocco are the options that were actually on offer through the UN Settlement Plan.
17   See Clark, 'Western Sahara and the United Nations Norms on Self-Determination and Aggression' (n 1). The ICJ in *Nicaragua* used this resolution as evidence of *opinio juris* in relation to the use of force and non-intervention as customary rules, see *Military and Paramilitary Activities in and against Nicaragua (Nicaragua v United States of America)* (Merits) [1986] ICJ Rep 14, paras 188, 202. In the *Palestine Advisory Opinion* (n 10) para 87, the ICJ described the provision in the resolution—on the principle of excluding the acquisition of territory by use of force—as a reflection of customary international law.

by the ICJ in *Namibia*.[18] Third party States are also to be guided by the court's Advisory Opinion on the *Wall*, which found there to be an obligation to work towards cessation of acts of illegality with reference to the Israeli wall.[19] It confirmed that third States are under 'an obligation not to render aid or assistance' in maintaining that illegality and that States parties to the 1949 Geneva Conventions 'are under an obligation, while respecting the United Nations Charter and international law, to ensure compliance by Israel with international humanitarian law as embodied in that Convention.'[20]

Under the UN Charter, both Spain as the *de jure* Administering Power, and Morocco as the *de facto* Administering Power, are bound to prioritise the interests of the Saharawi, and 'accept as a sacred trust the obligation to promote to the utmost, within the system of international peace and security established by the present Charter, the well-being of the inhabitants of these territories.'[21] The two States are also obliged to safeguard the natural resources of the Western Sahara, the implementation of which would include protection against exploitation and plundering from private actors such as corporations.[22] As the Correll Opinion makes clear, economic activities in the Western Sahara must not adversely affect the interests of the Saharawi, being the peoples of the protected territory, but must be directed towards assisting them in the exercise of their right to self-determination and protecting their 'inalienable rights' to their natural resources now and in the future from plunder and exploitation.[23] Morocco, as the occupying power of the Western Sahara, is also bound by international norms applying to occupied territories, notably relevant parts of

---

18   *Namibia Advisory Opinion* (n 2) paras 122–4.
19   *Palestine Advisory Opinion* (n 10) para 159.
20   *Ibid* 136, 187–89. For an authoritative assessment of the implications, see James Crawford SC 'Third Party Obligations with respect to Israeli Settlements in the Occupied Palestinian Territories' (24 January 2012) ('Crawford Opinion on Israeli Settlements'), at <http://www.tuc.org.uk/sites/default/files/tucfiles/LegalOpinionIsraeliSettlements.pdf> accessed 6 June 2014, paras 71–109.
21   UN Charter (n 12) art 73.
22   Correll Opinion (n 5) para 25, addressing the issue of offshore petroleum exploration concessions granted by Morocco to private corporations: 'while the specific contracts which are the subject of the Security Council's request are not in themselves illegal, if further exploration or exploitation activities were to proceed in disregard of the interests and wishes of the people of Western Sahara, they would be.' Also see Hans Correll, 'The legality of exploring and exploiting natural resources in Western Sahara' in Neville Botha et al., *Multilateralism and International Law with Western Sahara as a Case Study* (VerLoren van Themaat Centre, University of South Africa 2010).
23   Correll Opinion (n 5).

Geneva Convention IV and the Regulations annexed to the Hague Convention of 1907.[24] It is also subject to international law rules on use of force, and aggression.[25]

The normative extravaganza cited above has been nothing but froth for the Saharawi.[26]

The Western Sahara illustrates realism in action: the triumph of might over right, how what international law views as fundamental is easily sacrificed to the interests of States. It presents a vision of international law and its universe as utterly lacking substance. There is nothing there. Or is that too harsh, too simplistic? What we can *do* about this miserable failure, what can we *do* about the Western Sahara, in the year 2015?

3   Remedial Exceptionalism: Froth Busting?

My argument, set out in the following pages, is that the Western Sahara is now to be regarded as an exceptional case in the way that Kosovo is increasingly viewed, and that should condition the way that we respond in order to 'bring the illegal situation to an end.' Flowing from this, I contend that self-determination in the Western Sahara now needs to be exercised without the United Nations and Morocco, and we need to develop a flexible approach to

---

24   Geneva Convention relative to the Protection of Civilian Persons in Time of War (adopted 12 August 1949, entered into force 21 October 1950) 75 UNTS 287; Convention (IV) Respecting the Laws and Customs of War on Land and its Annex: Regulations concerning the Laws and Customs of War on Land (adopted 18 October 1907, entered into force 26 January 1910) 187 CTS 227; 1 Bevans 631.

25   UNGA Res 2625 (XXV) (n 9).

26   We can here recall the statement in the Aaland Islands Opinion from almost a hundred years ago:

>   The fact must, however, not be lost sight of that the principle that nations must have the right of self-determination is not the only one to be taken into account. Even though it be regarded as the most important of the principles governing the formation of States, geographical, economic and other similar considerations may put obstacles in the way of its complete recognition. Under such circumstances, a solution in the nature of a compromise, based on an extensive grant of liberty to minorities, may appear necessary according to international legal conception and may even be dictated by the interests of peace.

Report of the International Committee of Jurists entrusted by the Council of the League of Nations with the task of giving an advisory opinion upon the legal aspects of the Åaland Islands question, League of Nations Council Document B7 21/68/106 (1921) ('Åaland Islands Report'), 2–3.

the process by which the Saharawi are to make their choices as part of the exercise of self-determination.

An influential use of the notion of exceptionalism warranting differential treatment can be found in the report of UN Special Envoy to Kosovo, Martti Ahtisaari:

> Kosovo is a unique case that demands a unique solution… In unanimously adopting resolution 1244(1999), the Security Council responded to Milosevic's actions in Kosovo by denying Serbia a role in its governance, placing Kosovo under temporary United Nations administration and envisaging a political process designed to determine Kosovo's future. The combination of these factors makes Kosovo's circumstances extraordinary.[27]

Why was/is Kosovo unique? The Ahtisaari quote cites to Security Council Resolution 1244 and the international presence in Kosovo since 1999, to the exclusion of the sovereign, Serbia. Several other examples shining light on to the reasoning of States are useful in developing the argument for exceptionalism in the Western Sahara. Canada referred to Kosovo's history of war and criminality, and the role of the UN and other international organisations in administering the territory and providing for its security, and 'the ongoing role that international organizations such as the European Union will play in assisting Kosovo with its transition to full independence.'[28] Costa Rica referred to the crimes of the past, the will of the people and the absence of other solutions.[29] Switzerland pointed out that this was not ideal, but it was the most suitable of the options (pointing out that 'in view of the circumstances of this particular case, Switzerland's recognition of the independence of Kosovo does not constitute a precedent').[30] Sweden observed Kosovo's assurance that it will establish a democratic and multi-ethnic state that secures the rights of the minorities and the protection of the cultural heritage and that it also accepts continued international supervision of Kosovo, the international presence in

---

27 Report of the Special Envoy of the Secretary-General on Kosovo's future status, Letter from the Secretary-General addressed to the President of the Security Council (26 March 2007) Annexes I-XII UN Doc S/2007/168.

28 Full text at <http://www.international.gc.ca/media/aff/news-communiques/2008/385954.aspx?lang=en> accessed 2 June 2014.

29 Full text at <http://www.rree.go.cr/ministerio/index.php?stp=131&langtype=espanol&SID=> accessed 2 June 2014.

30 Full text at <http://www.eda.admin.ch/eda/en/home/recent/media/single.html?id=17497> accessed 2 June 2014.

the territory based on UN Security Council Resolution 1244 and the unique history, as well as the EU's position that 'Kosovo is a sui generis case that cannot be deemed to have any effect as a precedent.'[31]

The notion of exception is not actually new, it draws from the Canadian Supreme Court's *Quebec* ruling which itself was inspired by the Aaland Islands Report.[32] It is coming to be more widely accepted that in an exceptional situation where a people have been denied the right to exercise their right to self-determination internally in a non-colonial situation, and have faced particularly serious violations of fundamental rights, they may be entitled to secede.[33] However, we are here not even dealing with secession, the Western Sahara requires even less violence to fundamental concepts and rules than Kosovo. I would argue that after decades of the Saharawi being denied the right to self-determination, subjected to foreign domination and many human rights violations, and made the victim of international power politics, the Western Sahara situation must be treated as exceptional if it is to be resolved. Three points can be made to illustrate that there is no other feasible option. Firstly, a free and fair process of exercising the act of free choice through a UN process has been put off for decades and the political blockages appear insurmountable. Secondly, the original Saharawi population who would have been entitled to vote further to the UN's Settlement Plan are dying out, and there is a new demography flowing from population movement from Morocco into the occupied territory.[34] Thirdly, the international community has been shifting towards internal arrangements within Morocco, forcing the Saharawi into negotiations on autonomy or

---

31   Full text at <http://www.government.se/sb/d/10358/a/99714> accessed 2 June 2014.
32   Åaland Islands Report (n 26).
33   However, neither the ICJ in *Kosovo* nor the Canadian Supreme Court in *Quebec* actually endorsed the theory known as 'remedial secession' as an extension of the right to self-determination.
34   It is pertinent to revisit UNGA Res 2229 (XXI), which 'invited' Spain to ensure that only the 'indigenous people of the Territory participate in the Referendum' (n 4). For the Settlement Plan, see UNGA (XLVI) 'Report of the Secretary-General' (1991) UN Doc S/22464/1991. In this plan, an identification commission would update a 1974 census carried out by the Spanish, which identified 73,497 indigenous Saharawis. Also, 'Report of the United Nations Visiting Mission to Spanish Sahara' (1975) in 'Report of the Special Committee on the Situation with Regard to the Implementation of the Declaration on the Granting of Independence to Colonial Countries and Peoples' UN Doc A/10023/Add.5, Annex. For a succinct overview of the tortuous voter registration efforts, see <http://www.un.org/en/peacekeeping/missions/minurso/background.shtml> accessed 2 June 2014. 84, 251 applicants were found eligible to vote out of 147, 249 identified, with another 2, 130 found eligible to vote after appeals.

other arrangements within that kingdom.[35] It seems that the present situation can only be resolved if one looks 'outside of the box', and recognises it as having become an exceptional situation justifying novel approaches.

In my view, the Western Sahara is not appropriately to be seen in terms of 'earned sovereignty', which is broadly understood to mean managed devolution, in a post-colonial situation, of sovereign authority and functions from a State to a sub-State entity.[36] This recalls Morocco's offer of autonomy for the Western Sahara, and is no real option.[37] However, it does seem reasonable to argue that on a moral level, the Saharawi have now earned an entitlement to be treated differently. This takes us back to Kosovar exceptionalism. Buchanan's remedial rights justification theory, providing 'a remedy of last resort for persistent and grave injustices', provides a more intellectually coherent argument than merely claiming that the Western Sahara is a special case.[38] Buchanan's point is that exceptional circumstances may justify exceptional responses such as recognition of a remedial right to secession, an act which has traditionally been viewed with great concern for its impact on territorial sovereignty.[39] It provides a justification for an otherwise illegal response, but one that is rooted in the illegality committed against the group by the parent State.[40] Aware of

---

[35] From 2000, the Secretary-General began to speak of reviewing the situation, and from Envoy Baker onwards, the UN seemed to shift towards favouring Morocco's autonomy approach, see UNGA 'Report of the Secretary-General on the situation concerning Western Sahara' (17 February 2000) UN Doc S/2000/131. See also *infra* n 37.

[36] See for example International Crisis Group, 'Intermediate Sovereignty as a Basis for Resolving the Kosovo Crisis' ICG Balkans Report no. 46 (9 November 1998), at <http://www.crisisgroup.org/~/media/files/europe/kosovo.pdf> accessed 1 February 2015; Paul R Williams & Francesca Jannotti Pecci, 'Earned Sovereignty: Bridging the Gap between Sovereignty and Self-Determination' (2004) 40 SJIL 347 and Michael P Scharf, 'Earned Sovereignty: Juridical Underpinnings' (2012) 31 Denv J Int'l L & Pol'y 373.

[37] The 'Moroccan Initiative for Negotiating an Autonomy Statute for the Sahara Region' UNGA (LXII) (11 April 2007) full text available at <http://www.map.ma/en/dossier/moroccan-initiative-negotiating-autonomy-statute-sahara-region> accessed 1 February 2015. In his General Assembly Report in April of 2004 UN Secretary-General Kofi Anan confirmed that Morocco no longer accepted the Settlement Plan, and would accept nothing but negotiations about the autonomy of Western Sahara in the framework of Moroccan sovereignty. See UNGA 'Report of the Secretary-General' (23 April 2004) UN Doc S/2004/325.

[38] Allen Buchanan, *Justice, Legitimacy and Self-determination: Moral Foundations for International Law* (OUP 2003) ('Buchanan, *Justice, Legitimacy and Self-determination*') 217.

[39] Ibid; Allen Buchanan, *The Morality of Political Divorce: Fort Sumter to Lithuania and Quebec* (Westview Press 1991); Allen Buchanan, 'Theories of Secession' (1997) Phil & Public Aff 26(10) 31.

[40] Buchanan, *Justice, Legitimacy and Self-determination* (n 38) 217–21.

the potentially destabilising implications, Buchanan attempts to limit his theory justifying remedial secession to three cases: (1) 'large-scale and persistent violations of basic individual human rights'; (2) 'unjust taking of a legitimate state's territory'; (3) 'a state's persistent violation of an intrastate autonomy agreement.'[41]

Points (1) and (2) seem well established here. In this regard, the Western Sahara has two interesting features. Firstly, while the territory remains on the list of non-self-governing territories, it has also been recognised as a State by a number of other States. Made in 1975 on 27 February, POLISARIO's unilateral declaration of the establishment of the SADR led to recognition, albeit patchy and shifting, by a not-insignificant number of States.[42] The SADR is also a member State of the African Union.[43] Secondly, the territory has been unlawfully occupied by Morocco without the Saharawi having had a chance to determine their future. This is therefore not about secession, but about decolonisation and ensuring the right to self-determination, as well as ending an act of aggression that has been internationally tolerated since 1975. It is axiomatic that self-determination should ideally be exercised 'within the framework of sovereign States and consistent with the maintenance of the territorial integrity of those States.'[44] However, I do not see territorial integrity issues presently arising in the Western Sahara. If it is an issue of concern at all, it is more likely the territorial integrity of Spain, the negligent *de jure* Administering Power, that is engaged and not that of the illegal occupier. In 1975, to quote the ICJ, Morocco had never had 'any tie of territorial sovereignty' over the Western Sahara; since then it has not gained good title, even if the UN has continually deferred to it as it were a sovereign with legitimate territorial issues. Morocco has no business dictating anything about the referendum or proposing an autonomy plan or determining the fate of the territory; it should not be continued to allowed to derive 'special advantage resulting from aggression.'[45]

Drawing from the remedial approach, I would argue that repairing the situation in the Western Sahara only needs limited and carefully circumscribed

---

41   Ibid, 218–22.
42   According to the London representative of the Polisario, the most reliable information about the recognition of the SADR is the listing at <http://www.arso.org/03-2.htm> accessed 29 June 2014, although it does not include the recognition by South Sudan [email on file with the author]. From this list, it appears that there have been 83 recognitions in one form or another, but that 35 of these States have frozen or cancelled such recognition and of these, 5 have 're-instated' their recognition.
43   It was admitted as a member State of the Organisation of African Unity in 1982.
44   *Reference re Secession of Quebec* (1998) 2 SCR 217.
45   UNGA Res 3314 (XXIX) (n 10).

exceptions to two fundamental rules of international law: the right to self-determination and the prohibition of aggression. In relation to the aggression, the blockage has been political—international apathy and willingness to appease Morocco despite her continuing breaches of international law. In relation to self-determination, the blockage is also political and to do with the norm's secondary rules, *inter alia*, on the mechanics of the process of self-determination.[46] The international community has been tunnel-visioned about the referendum being a UN-led process, with Morocco involved. But why should it be? Why should Morocco be an essential partner; it is after all the occupying power, and its vested interest in a certain result has been allowed to thwart the rights of the Saharawi all these years. Can a consultation not be held without the UN and Morocco, but with substitute international management and supervision?

In *Western Sahara*, the ICJ stressed that the essence of self-determination is that the people with the entitlement must be allowed freely to express their will to determine their political future.[47] Consultation is an 'inescapable imperative', wrote Judge Nagendra Singh in his declaration.[48] The Security Council had, until 2007, affirmed the importance of a referendum in the Western Sahara.[49] Consistency with this requires a process that is representative, democratic, free and fair; it must also respect the fact that the choice vests in the Saharawi people, held by the Court to have the right to self-determination. Even so, in *Western Sahara*, the Court acknowledged there were two situations where consultations would not be required: where a certain population does not constitute a 'people' entitled to self-determination, and where there are 'special circumstances' rendering such consultation unnecessary.[50] What are these 'special

---

46 See Caitriona Drew, 'The Meaning of Self-Determination: "the Stealing of the Sahara" Redux?' in Karin Arts & Pedro Pinto Leite (eds), *International Law and the Question of Western Sahara* (IPJET 2007), on the relationship between the process and substance of self-determination.

47 *Western Sahara Advisory Opinion* (n 11) paras 58–59. UNGA Res 1514 (n 15); 'Factors Which Should Be Taken Into Account In Deciding Whether A Territory Is Or Is Not A Territory Whose People Have Not Yet Attained A Full Measure Of Self-Government' (27 November 1953) UN Doc A/RES/742 (VIII). Also see the International Covenant on Civil and Political Rights (adopted 16 December 1966, entered into force 23 March 1976) 999 UNTS 171 and the International Covenant on Economic, Social and Cultural Rights (adopted 16 December 1966, entered into force 3 January 1976) 993 UNTS 3.

48 *Western Sahara Advisory Opinion* (n 11) Declaration of Judge Nagendra Singh, para 81.

49 The last call was in UNSC Res 1754 (30 April 2007) 'The situation concerning Western Sahara' UN Doc S/RES/1754 (2007).

50 *Western Sahara Advisory Opinion* (n 11) para 59.

circumstances'? Kosovo has not had a referendum, and the ICJ has famously held that the unilateral declaration of independence there did not violate a rule of international law, there being no such rule.[51] I would argue that what is essential is a free and genuine expression of the will of the peoples of the territory. There is nothing in international law that requires the participation of the UN. The organisation's close involvement in acts of self-determination is commonly authorised by the Security Council or asked for by the State concerned, but has never been a pre-requisite in international law.[52] Further, there is nothing in international law that requires the participation of the occupying power, Morocco, or Spain, the negligent Administering Power that has abandoned her 'sacred duty' since 1975. The three should be regarded as 'impediments' to Saharawi self-determination, to borrow from the ICJ in its *Wall* Advisory Opinion.[53]

The requirement of holding a public consultation that is compliant with international law appears to be capable of being met in the Western Sahara in three situations: (1) within the Polisario part of the Western Sahara, the so-called free zone; (2) in the camps that they control in Algeria, assuming it is done with that State's consent; and (3) around the world, assuming there is international assistance with allowing the diaspora to vote. Obviously, a consultation of the Saharawi is not going to be possible in relation to the occupied area, given Morocco's obstruction. Here is where exceptionalism and the remedial rights theory can come in too—this may be the extent of the self-determination that is possible. The practical reality may determine that unless they are allowed to travel out to cast their vote, those Saharawi residing inside the Moroccan-occupied territory just cannot be included in the 'self-determination unit' participating in a referendum. Continuing to force Saharawi self-determination to be held perpetually captive to the occupying power's demands is not just recognising an illegality, contrary to the principle affirmed by the ICJ in *Namibia*, *East Timor* and the *Wall*, but also allows the wrongdoer to benefit from his wrongdoing (*ex injuria jus non oritur*) and frustrates the rights of an entire people.

---

51   The ICJ in the *Western Sahara Advisory Opinion* (n 11) did note that there have been examples where the General Assembly has accepted self-determination without a referendum. Ifni was such case, an example of a 'colonial enclave.'

52   A 1983 UN publication acknowledges a lack of uniformity in this area, and that UN participation can vary from situation to situation, see UN Department of Political Affairs, Trusteeship and Decolonisation, 'Decolonisation No 19' (December 1983).

53   *Palestine Advisory Opinion* (n 10) para 159.

Given the failures of the UN in this matter, MINURSO should be freed of its mandate in relation to the public consultation.[54] Every effort must be made to ensure that the alternative process of choosing is organised, managed and conducted in a free, fair and regular manner.[55] The immediate candidate, in terms of international organisations, would be the African Union of which SADR is a member State. It has, of course, a long history of attempting to resolve this situation, rooted in respect for the right to self-determination.[56] Within that, African States such as South Africa that have, without self-interest, championed the rights of the Saharawi, would be countries to look to for leadership. East Timor's experience of a referendum could be particularly instructive, and it has long been in solidarity with the Saharawi's right to determine their future. At time of writing, self-organised referenda have a very bad press. But, even before the Crimean farce, there was the notorious example of the fraudulent 'Act of Free Choice' in what was Dutch New Guinea, known today as either West Papua or West Irian, and that was glossed over by the UN.[57] On the other hand, Southern Sudan's referendum was successfully organised, conducted and managed by the Southern Sudan Referendum Commission, a domestic

---

54 UNSC Res 690 (29 April 1991) UN Doc S/RES/690 (1991) approved the Secretary-General's implementation plan for the Western Sahara, and MINURSO was established to give effect to it. The plan was for the Special Representative of the Secretary-General to have sole and exclusive responsibility over all matters relating to a referendum in which the people of Western Sahara would choose between independence and integration with Morocco.

55 What happens beyond the referendum is beyond the scope of this paper, but in my view, if the vote is for independence, there will have to be some kind of international presence to secure liberated Western Sahara, strengthen the capacity for self-governance that Polisario has already developed, and to work towards the return of the occupied lands in the west, as well as the return of refugees and diaspora Saharawi. This is an area where the doctrine of 'earned sovereignty' may factor in to guide the international community in deciding on when that administration should end.

56 See for example, OAU Assembly of Heads of State and Government resolutions AHG/Res.92 (XV) and AHG/114 (XVI). Its Implementation Committee had recommended, inter alia, the appointment of an impartial interim administration with all necessary powers to organise and conduct the referendum. This formed the basis of the UN's Settlement Plan. UNSC Res 658 (27 June 1990) UN Doc S/RES/658 envisaged the Organisation of African Unity (as it then was) working in cooperation with the UN in organising and supervising the Referendum.

57 See Pieter Drooglever, *An Act of Free Choice: Decolonisation and the Right to Self-Determination in West Papua* (Oneworld Publications 2009). This is an English translation of his ground-breaking 2005 book published in Dutch, *Een Dad Van Vrije Keuze: De Papoea's va westelijk Nieuw-Guinea en de grenzen van het zelfbeschikkingsrecht* (Uitgeverij Boom 2005).

body created by the Southern Sudan Referendum Act of 2009.[58] The official Abyei referendum, promised for 2011 in the Comprehensive Peace Agreement of 11 July 2008 between the Government of Sudan, the National Congress Party and the Sudan People's Liberation Movement/Army remains in abeyance—the stumbling blocks are several, some are *déjà vu*: the question of who it is who is eligible to vote and arguments about the criteria to be used where one of the two groups is nomadic.[59] My point is that having the UN involved is not necessary, and it is also no guarantee that the process will meet the standards of process required.

One could also argue that there is an alternative based on exceptionalism in the Western Sahara: comprehensive international recognition of the SADR as a sovereign State may be warranted because of the 'special circumstances' of the Western Sahara. Even granting an alleged 'lowering of the standards' of statehood in a decolonisation situation, the reality is obvious: the SADR does not today meet the usual 'objective' conditions for statehood. SADR's only genuine exercise of governmental power is in the liberated part of the territory where there is little to govern, and its exercise of authority in the Algerian camps is subject to the consent and control of Algeria. But, recognition in practice remains an unprincipled political affair that is truly within the sovereign's discretion. We still seem to be in the position that Sir Hersch Lauterpacht described in 1947: 'recognition of states is not a matter governed by law but a question of policy.'[60] Even so, it seems that the declaratory approach has become more pronounced over time, and seems to be borne out more and more in the practice of States.[61] Polisario issued a unilateral declaration of independence announcing the creation of the SADR on 27 February 1976, leading to a degree of recognition by States, presumably influenced by the harsh reality of abandonment by the territory's *de jure* Administering Power and

---

58   See <http://unmis.unmissions.org/Portals/UNMIS/Referendum/SSRC%20FAQ.pdf> accessed 24 May 2014.
59   There, too, a much-criticised informal referendum has been held, involving just the Ngok Dinka community. See Tshaba Tjemolane & Amanda Lucey, 'The referendum in Abyei is an ongoing challenge for the African Union' (*Institute for Security Studies*, 2 December 2013), at <http://www.issafrica.org/iss-today/the-referendum-in-abyei-is-an-ongoing-challenge-for-the-african-union> accessed 6 June 2014.
60   Hersch Lauterpacht, *Recognition in International Law* (first published CUP 1947, Grotius Classic Reprint 2013) ('Lauterpacht, *Recognition in International Law*') 1.
61   James Crawford, *The Creation of States in International Law* (2nd edn, OUP 2006) ('Crawford, *The Creation of States in International Law*') 23–25; James Crawford, *Brownlie's Principles of Public International Law* (8th edn, OUP 2012) 144–51.

immediate invasion and occupation by Morocco.[62] If no referendum is possible, could this unilateral declaration not now be regarded as an exercise of self-determination? Can we argue, post Kosovo, that there is an emerging *duty* to recognise in such exceptional cases? It seems clear that renewed interest in recognition of the SADR, and ultimately full membership of international organisations most notably the UN, could actually serve constitutive purposes which would seem to be essential for taking the Western Sahara situation forward.[63] The territory already enjoys legal personality as a non-self-governing territory, as a State in the eyes of recognising-States, and as a member State of the African Union. However, if the majority of States take up recognition of the SADR along the lines of what has been done with Kosovo, and are prepared to engage in substantial legal and diplomatic relations with it, the attributes of statehood that flow could create a dynamic that can facilitate resolution of the situation that is principled and in accordance with international law.

4 More Froth-Busting: Towards a 'Responsibility Approach'

In his legal opinion on the matter of the produce from Israeli settlements in the Occupied Palestinian Territories, Professor Crawford concluded that:

> Unfortunately, the present reality of the political situation in Palestine is such that it is unlikely that any adverse legal ramifications will result from States or private entities continuing to engage with the unlawful settlements. [...] Regrettably, the political will does not seem to exist at present to enforce principles of international law in respect of the settlements.[64]

This implicitly challenges us to work to create political spaces within which changes can take place. Changed political realities are, after all, how East Timor came to have its 1999 referendum that led to statehood. Out of ravaged Kosovo has come an entity that has at time of writing been recognised as a State by 108

---

62   In *Kosovo*, the ICJ found that there is nothing in International Law that would render the unilateral declaration in itself illegal. On relevant State practice, see Crawford, *The Creation of States in International Law* (n 61) 557–62.

63   See James Crawford, 'Introduction', in Lauterpacht, *Recognition in International Law* (n 60); also Thomas D Grant, *The Recognition of States: Law and Practice in Debate and Evolution* (Greenwood Publishing Group 1999).

64   Crawford Opinion on Israeli Settlements (n 20) para 139.

countries, because it has come to be seen as an exceptional situation.[65] Palestine has always been special, and following on from its admission to the United Nations as a non-member State, is now entering into treaties as a State and is being recognised by more and more States.[66] Western Sahara now needs to be recognised as an exceptional situation justifying a different approach.

Parallel and complementary to the remedial exceptionalism approach suggested in this paper, I would also argue that it is time to engage with a more robust 'responsibility approach' as a way of changing the political dynamic. Diplomacy has clearly been the preferred approach since the invasion and occupation of the Western Sahara began in 1975. The results have been the catalogue of violations of international law that were highlighted in the early part of this paper. A change of approach must now be seen as imperative, and the law of responsibility—whether State, international organisation, corporation or individual—needs to be viewed as part of the arsenal to 'bring the illegal situation to an end.' The 'responsibility approach' has become feasible as the law has become more coherent and clearly defined thanks to the International Law Commission's Articles on the Responsibility of States for Internationally Wrongful Acts[67] and the Articles on the Responsibility of International Organisations,[68] jurisprudence from international courts and tribunals, developments at the International Criminal Court in relation to the crime of aggression, as well as State practice as illustrated through domestic court proceedings.

Space constraints mean that I can here only highlight one possibility that should be part of a 'responsibility approach': recourse to the Court of Justice of the EU, challenging the fishing agreements between the EU and the Kingdom of Morocco, as set out in the Fisheries Partnership Agreement of 2006 ('FPA'), and its 2013 Protocol.[69] These permit, for a generous fee, the European fishing

---

65   Data from <http://www.kosovothanksyou.com> accessed 6 June 2014.
66   On 29 November 2012, the General Assembly adopted UNGA Res 67/19 (LXVII) (29 November 2012) UN Doc A/RES/67/19 granting Palestine the status of non-member observer in the General Assembly. Since then, it has, *inter alia*, acceded to the seven universal human rights treaties.
67   ILC, 'Articles on Responsibility of States for Internationally Wrongful Acts adopted by the International Law Commission at its 53rd session' (3 August 2001) 53 UN GAOR Supp 10, 43, UN Doc A/56/83 (2001).
68   ILC, 'Draft Articles on the Responsibility of International Organizations adopted by the International Law Commission at its 63rd session' (3 June 2011).
69   On 22 May 2006, the Council approved the Fisheries Partnership Agreement between the European Community and the Kingdom of Morocco, OJ l L141; see also the Protocol between the European Union and the Kingdom of Morocco setting out the fishing opportunities and financial contribution provided for in the Fisheries Partnership

fleet to have access to the waters off the coast of the Western Sahara by virtue of a provision referring to the 'the waters falling within the sovereignty or jurisdiction of the Kingdom of Morocco.'[70] Pertinent here are UN General Assembly Resolutions 48/46 of 10 December 1992 and 49/40 of 9 December 1994, underscoring how

> exploitation of the marine and other natural resources of colonial and Non-Self-Governing Territories by foreign economic interests...is a threat to the integrity and prosperity of those Territories.[71]

It bears mentioning that the agreement with Morocco has been politically divisive and that it came under repeated challenge in the Parliament.[72] Even so, it was eventually approved in December 2013.[73] Two legal opinions were rendered by the Parliament's Legal Service about the FPA—in 2006 and in 2009—and both considered the agreement's lack of express reference to the Western Sahara. The 2006 opinion took the view that the EU could enter into the FPA provided Morocco shared the benefits of relevant off-shore fishing with the people of the Western Sahara, while the 2009 opinion underscored the obligation to ensure that economic activities of this nature are carried out for the benefit of the people of a non-self-governing territory, in

---

Agreement between the European Union and the Kingdom of Morocco (16 December 2013), OJ L349/1.

[70] The SADR itself has a document called Law No 03/2009 (21 January 2009) Establishing The Maritime Zones of The Saharawi Arab Democratic Republic, at <http://www.sadroiland-gas.com/petroleg.htm> (accessed 24 May 2014). It has declared an Exclusive Economic Zone of 200 nautical miles off the Western Sahara coastline. See generally Western Sahara Resource Watch, at <http://www.wsrw.org> accessed 24 May 2014.

[71] Note that the UNGA Res 50/33 (L) (6 December 1995) 'Activities of Foreign Economic and Other Interests Which Impede the Implementation of the Declaration on the Granting of Independence to Colonial Countries and Peoples in Territories Under Colonial Domination' UN Doc A/RES/50/33 (1995) distinguishes between economic activities that can benefit such people and those that are detrimental to them.

[72] European Parliament, Amendment 17, A6-0163/17, recording the proposal to add the words 'i.e. in the waters lying exclusively to the north of latitude 27'40/N, as laid down in international law'; 'EU lawmakers block Morocco-Western Sahara fishing deal' (Radio Netherlands Worldwide,14 December 2011), at <http://www.rnw.nl/africa/bulletin/eu-lawmakers-block-morocco-western-sahara-fishing-deal> (accessed 24 May 2014).

[73] EU Business, 'EU Parliament approves Morocco Fisheries Deal' (*EU Business*, 11 December 2013), at <http://www.eubusiness.com/news-eu/morocco-economy.s26> (accessed 24 May 2014).

accordance with their wishes, and noted that the lack of evidence that this was in fact the case.[74]

What would one base a case against the EU on?[75] While the Community is not bound directly by the UN Charter, *Kadi* makes clear that the court will review EU actions on the basis of the Treaty establishing the European Union itself, and 'fundamental rights forming an integral part of the European Union legal order.'[76] The EU must respect international law in the exercise of its powers— the Court of First Instance held, in *Yusuf and Al Barakaat* that the EU 'may not infringe the obligations imposed on its Member States by the Charter of the United Nations or impede their performance' of such obligations, and also that the EU 'is bound, by the very Treaty by which it was established, to adopt all the measures necessary to enable its Member States to fulfil those obligations.'[77] A robust argument for violation of Article 73 of the UN Charter could be founded on the fact that the FPA, involving exploitation of the rich fishing waters off the Western Sahara, was not entered into in consultation with the indigenous people of the territory, and the EU failed to provide for an effective mechanism that ensures that the benefits of the agreement would benefit the Saharawi. As UN Legal Counsel Corell advised in 2002 in relation to oil-reconnaisance and evaluation activities in areas off the shores of the Western Sahara

---

[74] 'The currently negotiated Partnership Fisheries Agreement between the EU and the Kingdom of Morocco—compatability with International Law' (Opinion of the European Parliament Legal Service 6664/06, 22 February 2006); Opinion of the European Parliament Legal Service (13 July 2009) cited in Armin Steinbach, 'The Western Sahara Dispute: A Case for the ECJ?' (2011–2012) 18 Columbia Journal of European Law (CJEL) 415 ('Steinbach, 'The Western Sahara Dispute: A Case for the ECJ?") at 419.

[75] I am encouraged in this approach by a passing remark in Professor Crawford's Opinion to the Trade Unions Congress on the responsibilities of States or private entities engaged in operations within the Israeli settlements in the Occupied Palestinian Territories. One of the issues considered there was EU law, and he referred to the EU and the Western Sahara, observing that there that '[t]here is no doubt that the FPA, like its predecessor agreements, contravenes the right to self-determination of the people of Western Sahara and well as the principle of non-recognition; yet there have to date been no legal repercussions for any State party', see Crawford Opinion on Israeli Settlements (n 20) para 131, footnotes omitted. For a wide ranging EU Law discussion, see Steinbach, 'The Western Sahara Dispute: A Case for the ECJ' (n 74).

[76] See *Kadi v Council and Commission* (Judgment) [2005] ECR 11–3649, Case T-315/01 paras 192, 203–04; Joined ECJ cases, *Commission, Council, UK v Yassin Abdullah Kadi* (Judgment) [2013] C-584/10 P, C-593/10 P and C-595/10 P paras 97–101.

[77] *Yusuf and Al Barakaat International Foundation v Council and Commission* [2005] ECR 11–3533 Case T- 306/01 paras 259 et seq.

while the specific contracts which are the subject of the Security Council's request are not in themselves illegal, if further exploration or exploitation activities were to proceed in disregard of the interests and wishes of the people of Western Sahara, they would be.[78]

Other limbs of a claim could involve the EU's responsibilities in relation to self-determination, unjust enrichment under the Treaty on the Functioning of the European Union as well as the UN Convention on the Law of the Sea.[79] However, in its practice, the court sets the burden of proof high in such matters, requiring that the complaint show that the EU breached its obligations to individuals 'in a sufficiently serious manner', that harms be quantifiable and that there must be a causal link between the EU's actions and the damages suffered.[80] Steinbach argues that going to the court for an annulment of the FPA would probably fail on procedural grounds, and an action for damages in this matter is fraught with significant difficulties (although pessimistic, he believes 'no clear prediction can be made how the Court would assess such a claim').[81] It seems to me to be a risk worth taking.

Finally, there are two routes that I have not recommended but which should be mentioned. In reflecting on the way forward with a 'responsibility approach', I did consider the wisdom of a return to the ICJ to seek an Advisory Opinion on the implications of the failure of the international community to respect an obligation that the court declared in 1975 was specifically owed *erga omnes* to the people of the Western Sahara. Although the Court's Advisory Opinions on the *Wall* and *Kosovo* were non-binding, and ignored by Israel and Serbia, they galvanised the Kosovar and Palestinian causes internationally. However, with the Western Sahara and the record of the last few decades, the law is perfectly clear, and an effort like this seems likely to be seized upon as an excuse to delay things further.

And, it will be observed that I have not advocated the return to armed resistance, although it would be understandable if the Saharawi were to do so. If it were to happen, this would be presented by them as a just war, a war of national liberation, and we would have a return to the issue of the 'right to

---

78 Correll Opinion (n 5) para 25.
79 Treaty on the Functioning of the European Union (2007) (consolidated version) 2012 OJ C326/47; UN Convention on the Law of the Sea 1982 (entered into force 1 December 2009) UNTS Vol 1833, A-31363.
80 *Odigitria AAE v. Council of the European Union and of the European* Communities [1996] ECR I-6129.
81 Steinbach, 'The Western Sahara Dispute: A Case for the ECJ?' (n 74) 438.

resist.'[82] SADR is a party to the African Charter of Human and Peoples Rights, which enshrines 'the unquestionable and inalienable right to self-determination.'[83] Following from this core concept are significant provisions rooted in Africa's wars of liberation, acknowledging the right of a people denied these rights, through colonisation or oppression, to free themselves 'from the bonds of domination by resorting to any means recognised by the international community', and the corresponding 'right' of such peoples to seek the assistance of member States in 'their liberation struggle against foreign domination.'[84] As Wilson has pointed out, international law in the 1960s began to favour rebels fighting for self-determination, and even if States did not 'openly agree that liberation movements had the authority to resort to force if self-determination was denied, at least they had begun to condemn the use of force by the colonial power, but not the liberation movement.'[85] The Saharawi may also call upon a chain of General Assembly resolutions, of questionable force, about the rights of oppressed peoples to resist and defend themselves using force.[86]

---

82 See UNGA Res 2649 (XXV) (30 November 1970) 'The importance of the universal realization of the right of peoples to self-determination and of the speedy granting of independence to colonial countries and peoples for the effective guarantee and observance of human rights' UN Doc A/S/2649 (XXV). In UNGA Res 34/37 (XXXIV) (21 November 1979) 'Question of Western Sahara' UN Doc A/34/37 (1979), the General Assembly deplored the Moroccan occupation, affirmed the right of the Saharawi to self-determination as well as 'the legitimacy of their struggle to ensure the enjoyment of that right.'

83 African Charter on Human and Peoples' Rights (entered into force 21 October 1986) (1982) 21 ILM 58 ('African Charter') art 20. SADR became a party on 2 May 1986. Also see the Preamble to the Charter of the Organisation of African Unity (entered into force 13 September 1963) 479 UNTS 39.

84 African Charter (n 83) arts 21, 22.

85 Heather Wilson, *International Law and the Use of Force by National Liberation Movements* (Clarendon Press 1988) 111.

86 See for example, UNGA Res 2708 (XXV) (14 December 1970) 'Implementation of the Declaration on the Granting of Independence to Colonial Countries and Peoples' UN Doc A/RES/2708 (XXV) (73:5:22), where the General Assembly reaffirmed 'its recognition of the legitimacy of the struggle of the colonial peoples and peoples under alien domination to exercise their right to self-determination and independence by all means at its disposal' and UNGA Res 3103 (XXVIII) (12 December 1973) 'Basic Principles of the Legal Status of the Combatants Struggling Against Colonial and Alien Domination and Racist Regimes' UN Doc A/RES/3103 (XXVIII) (83:13:19) which reaffirmed 'the legitimacy of peoples' struggle for liberation from colonial and foreign domination and alien subjugation by all available means, including armed struggle.' Also relevant are UNGA Res 1514 (XV) (n 14) and UNGA Res 2625 (XXV) (n 9).

Let us hope, dear Professor Clark, we will one day stop citing the Western Sahara as a showcase example of the froth of international law and the weakness of global governance in the area of international peace and security, and that somewhere on the horizon is a time when students will ask instead for the story of how the long-frustrated hopes of a people in the desert finally came true.

PART 5

Essays on International, Transnational and Comparative Criminal Law

CHAPTER 18

Forks in the Road: Personal Reflections on Negotiating the Kampala Amendments on the Crime of Aggression

Christian Wenaweser and Stefan Barriga

1 Introduction

Much has been written about the 2010 Kampala amendments to the Rome Statute of the International Criminal Court ('ICC') on the crime of aggression, in particular by Roger Clark. In fact, Roger was one of the few authors who wrote about the crime of aggression even before the 2010 Review Conference adopted the amendments by consensus, and in doing so contributed actively to the negotiation process as an academic.[1] This contribution is only surpassed by his contribution as a State representative for Samoa during the negotiations. True to form, however, his authority as a negotiator stemmed mainly from his impressive credentials as an academic, and perhaps also from his impressive voice. 'I don't need a microphone' was on several occasions his response to unresponsive sound equipment, and indeed, people listened. What they heard was always a sharp analysis of the intricate legal issues under discussion, often coupled with concrete proposals on how to get out of this and that conundrum, and always based on firm conviction and belief. His views had tremendous impact on the manner in which the negotiating text on the crime of aggression evolved over the years. Roger was a fixture of the long and arduous negotiating process leading to the Review Conference, not missing a single negotiation since 2003. Just as important as his substantive contribution,

1 Here are only some of his contributions: Roger S Clark, 'Rethinking Aggression as a Crime and Formulating Its Elements: The Final Work-Product of the Preparatory Commission for the International Criminal Court' (2002) 15 LJIL 859; Roger S Clark, 'The Crime of Aggression and the International Criminal Court' in Jose Doria et al (eds), *The Legal Regime of the International Criminal Court. Essays in Honour of Professor Igor Blsishchenko* (Martinus Nijhoff 2009); Roger S Clark, 'Negotiating Provisions Defining the Crime of Aggression, its Elements and the Conditions for ICC Exercise of Jurisdiction Over it' (2009) 20 EJIL 1103; Roger S Clark, 'Amendments to the Rome Statute of the International Criminal Court Considered at the First Review Conference on the Court, Kampala, 31 May-11 June 2010' (2010) 2 GoJIL 689.

however, was his unshakable belief in what we were doing. When most people were full of doubt about the prospects of success, such thoughts never seemed to even have entered Roger's mind: he was simply always ready to make the next step, until there was no other step to make.

The successful conclusion of the negotiations is owed in no small part to Roger Clark. This goes to show that in any intergovernmental negotiation process, individuals and their decisions matter. Of course, legal precedent, power relationships, alliances and group dynamics are important. But there is something deeply human and at times almost whimsical that again and again influences a negotiation—who happens to represent a certain country at a certain moment in time, how these individuals are able to communicate with each other, how they assess what others are really thinking, and what strategic conclusions they draw from that.

We experienced these factors vividly during the roughly seven years during which we led this negotiation process, from 2003 to 2010: Christian as Chair of the Special Working Group on the Crime of Aggression and later as President of the Assembly of States Parties (and the 2010 Review Conference), and Stefan as his legal advisor. In fact, there were many occasions where we ourselves were faced with difficult judgment calls, especially as we produced new versions of the negotiation text and background papers. Add a bracket here, or not, focus on one issue but not another, dare to come up with a compromise proposal, now or later, or not at all. There were many forks in the road that led from Rome to Kampala.[2] Here, we would like to reflect upon some of the more significant such moments, with a focus on the endgame in Kampala.

2   A Problem from Rome

The Rome Conference in 1998 began under the most daunting of circumstances. The draft forwarded for consideration by the Diplomatic Conference was full of square brackets indicating disagreement. Pretty much all the core issues—role of the Security Council, independence of the Prosecutor, complementarity, even sentencing issues—were open and agreement on all of them seemed difficult at best. The inclusion of the crime of aggression can be added to this list: there was relatively easy agreement among States that the three 'core crimes' (genocide, crimes against humanity and war crimes) should fall

---

[2]   The whole negotiation history from Rome to Kampala is reflected in Stefan Barriga and Claus Kreß (eds), *The Travaux Préparatoires of the Crime of Aggression* (CUP 2012) ('Barriga and Kreß (eds), *The Travaux Préparatoires of the Crime of Aggression*'), in particular 333–724.

within the jurisdiction of the Court, despite significant open questions concerning their definitions. On the crime of aggression, however, the room was divided as to whether it should be included in the Statute at all. Some argued that the crime of aggression not only belonged among the most serious crimes under international law, but even that it was the supreme crime under international law, much along the lines argued by Chief Justice Robert Jackson at the International Military Tribunal in Nuremberg.[3] Others pointed out that the crime was inherently political in nature and therefore very different from the three core crimes, that there was no binding definition of a crime of aggression, and that the world had changed significantly since WW II: the majority of armed conflicts were now intra-State conflicts, while aggression by a State committed against another was the rare exception. For many, the crime of aggression was just an additional complication in these very challenging negotiations and a distraction from getting the overall job on the treaty done. This led even countries like Liechtenstein to advocate against including the crime of aggression and focusing on the overall task of concluding the Rome Statute instead. There was, however, strong pressure for inclusion, not least by the German delegation led by the late Hans-Peter Kaul, who was later to become one of the first ICC judges.[4] So by way of compromise, the crime was included in the jurisdiction of the Court, while the task of finding agreement on a definition and provisions for the exercise of jurisdiction was relegated to a review conference to be held seven years after entry into force of the Rome Statute.[5]

3 Progress in Princeton

Discussions on the crime of aggression continued after Rome in the framework of the Preparatory Commission set up to prepare for the entry into force of the

---

[3] See 'Judicial Decisions, International Military Tribunal (Nuremberg), Judgment and Sentences' (1947) 41 AJIL 186.

[4] Hans-Peter Kaul passed away on 21 July 2014 after a period of serious illness, which led him to resign from the ICC with effect from 1 July 2014. For his view of the Rome negotiations see Hans-Peter Kaul, 'Der Beitrag Deutschlands zum Völkerstrafrecht' in Christoph Safferling & Stefan Kirsch (eds), *Völkerstrafrechtspolitik* (Springer 2014), 72–82.

[5] Accordingly, art 5(1) of the 1998 Rome Statute mentions the crime of aggression as one of the crimes over which the Court has jurisdiction, but art 5(2) states: 'The Court shall exercise jurisdiction over the crime of aggression once a provision is adopted in accordance with articles 121 and 123 defining the crime and setting out the conditions under which the Court shall exercise jurisdiction with respect to this crime. Such a provision shall be consistent with the relevant provisions of the Charter of the United Nations.'

Statute.[6] Given the urgency of the other tasks at hand, such as the drafting of the Rules of Procedure and Evidence and other important documents required for the Court to start its operations, there was little time assigned to those discussions. Some progress was made in the form of a Coordinator's paper, which mainly helped structure future discussions. The negotiation mandate was carried over to the Special Working Group on the Crime of Aggression, which started its work in September 2003, and which delivered a very advanced draft of the amendments in February 2009, with few, albeit some major, outstanding issues that remained to be resolved.

The negotiation phase between 2003 and 2009 came to be known as the 'Princeton Process', named after the venue of a series of informal meetings that we organized at Princeton University in New Jersey, in collaboration with the Liechtenstein Institute on Self-Determination at the Woodrow Wilson School ('LISD').[7] These meetings proved to be extraordinarily effective, thanks in no small part to the welcoming atmosphere created by our gracious host, LISD Director Wolfgang Danspeckgruber. Delegates, academics and civil society experts engaged in open and interactive discussions on many of the vexing issues, and over time found agreements on many of them. They included, for example, agreement that a determination by the Security Council that an act of aggression took place would not be binding on the ICC, to safeguard the due process rights of the accused. We also agreed that all three of the Rome Statute's existing trigger mechanisms should apply to the crime of aggression (Security Council referral, State Party referral, *proprio motu* investigation). And most importantly, we came to an agreement on the definition of the crime of aggression, which was adopted at the last session of the Special Working Group in February 2009. Many times, it was Roger Clark's voice of reason that steered us toward a solution, especially when dealing with general concepts of criminal law and legislative drafting. For lack of space, we cannot delve into the details of these issues here, but will focus on the final round of negotiations in Kampala.

4 Drama in Kampala

Tensions concerning the crime aggression were quite high before the Review Conference began. Concerns that Kampala may become an 'aggression

---

6 All important documents of the Preparatory Commission's work from 1999 to 2002 are reproduced in Barriga and Kreß (eds), *The Travaux Préparatoires of the Crime of Aggression* (n 2) 333–414.

7 All major documents from the Princeton Process are reproduced in Barriga and Kreß (eds), *The Travaux Préparatoires of the Crime of Aggression* (n 2) 421–708.

conference' and thus inevitably a tense affair had been alleviated, at least somewhat, by the addition of a 'stocktaking' exercise: the Review Conference would also look at how the ICC and States Parties were doing on the biggest challenges facing the Court in its daily work (cooperation, complementarity, peace and justice, victims). This would be a largely cooperative and constructive exercise, which would be crucial to create a positive atmosphere.[8] Nevertheless, the aggression discussions dominated the talk before Kampala. True, the Princeton Process had resulted in an agreement on the definition of the act and crime of aggression,[9] but very big questions remained. How could the starkly opposing views on the role of the Security Council be brought together? Would it be possible, if those efforts failed, to agree on a 'definition only' solution, i.e. to write the definition into the Statute and leave the provisions governing the role of the Council to a later stage? Many were also anxious about the role the US would play at the Conference. Despite repeated invitations, US delegations had not taken part in any ICC-related activities for eight years and therefore also missed the Princeton Process. The prospect of a difficult and controversial vote in particular caused much anxiety.

The final showdown in the negotiations took place from 31 May to 11 June 2010 at Munyonyo Resort on the shores of Lake Victoria, on the outskirts of Kampala. Most delegations stayed directly at this hotel, which had the great advantage of creating a campus-like atmosphere. Physical proximity among the negotiators meant that it was much easier for everyone to talk to and bounce off ideas each other and share latest developments in between official meetings, even at breakfast or after hours. People knew where to find each other.[10]

---

8   For an overview of the content of these discussions, see Review Conference of the Rome Statute of the International Criminal Court: Kampala, 31 May—11 June 2010, Official Records, RC/11, in particular Annexes V(a)—V(d), 77–119.

9   The Princeton Meetings began in June 2004. The fifth and last Princeton Meeting took place in June 2009. The final non-paper of the Princeton Process is reprinted in Barriga and Kreß (eds), *The Travaux Préparatoires of the Crime of Aggression* (n 2) 677–84.

10 In one instance, proximity went a bit too far though. On his second day into the conference, Stefan noticed that his hotel room was adjacent to a suite that was used by the US delegation for its own meetings, separated only by a wooden door. When sitting at this desk in his room, he could hear much of the conversation on the other side, whether he wanted to or not. It was a surreal situation, finding himself eavesdropping, unintentionally, on the delegation of the country that leads the world in global spying. After agonizing for several hours about how to deal with this situation (Should he use this unexpected access to privileged information to help advance the negotiation process? Wouldn't the US delegation sooner or later find out, and consider the Conference President, whom he

The Question of State Consent

Negotiations in Kampala were scheduled to last for two weeks, and no time was lost. Consultations began in the format of the Working Group on the Crime of Aggression, chaired by H.R.H. Prince Zeid Ra'ad Zeid Al-Hussein. One of the big outstanding questions was the question of aggressor State consent, in other words, whether the amendments should require some type of consent by the alleged aggressor State before the Court could proceed with an investigation regarding a crime of aggression. This highly political question was closely linked to the highly technical question as to which amendment procedure should be applied. The latter was a rather puzzling question to which the Rome Statute simply did not provide a clear-cut answer. The issue provided fertile ground for creative compromise proposals. Most prominent among them was the so-called ABS proposal, submitted by the delegations of Argentina, Brazil and Switzerland.[11] Representatives of these three countries had for several weeks prior to the Review Conference worked on a proposal so innovative and daring, they could not even be sure that the solution devised therein would be acceptable to their own masters had it really been up for formal adoption. Some aspects of the non-paper were in line with the stated positions of these (and many other) delegations: for example, it provided that a determination by the Security Council that a State committed aggression against another should not be a *conditio sine qua non* for an investigation by the Court, thereby rejecting the longstanding and forceful demand by permanent members of the Council. But the paper sought to make this proposition palatable to the permanent members of the UN Security Council ('P-5') with an intriguing trade-off. The Court's jurisdiction over the crime of aggression based upon Security Council referrals (which did not raise difficult questions of State consent) would become effective after the very first ratification of the amendments. In turn, the Court's other two triggers (State referral, *proprio motu* investigation) would only become effective after ratifications by 7/8 of States Parties. The logic behind the compromise was to begin with the less controversial part, and to delay what was difficult to accept for the P-5 to the very distant future. It was a risky proposition. How long would it take until an amendment on the crime

---

advised, to be compromised? What if he would misunderstand what he overheard and draw wrong conclusions?), he decided to move to another room. His vacated room did not stay empty for long though; apparently the Head of the US delegation moved in soon afterward, probably delighted about the coincidence of having a room available right next door.

11   The so-called ABS paper is reproduced in Barriga and Kreß (eds), *The Travaux Préparatoires of the Crime of Aggression* (n 2), 740–42.

of aggression would be ratified by 7/8 of States Parties? At the time of the Review Conference, this would have translated to 100 required ratifications out of 114 States Parties, giving a mere 15 States Parties the power to prevent the operationalization of this part of the deal forever.

The ABS proposal was ultimately not adopted in Kampala, but it had several elements that we could work with and that paved the ground for a final compromise. Most importantly, the ABS proposal introduced the idea of devising different rules for Security Council referrals on the one hand and State referrals/*proprio motu* investigations on the other. There was an inherent logic to that, because Security Council referrals do not rely on State consent, which had been such a controversial issue. Indeed, we had ourselves for some time pondered the idea of splitting the existing procedural provisions on exercise of jurisdiction along those lines. But, we had not dared to take that step, because we did not want to be misunderstood to give preferential treatment to Security Council referrals. After all, a separate draft article on Council referrals would quickly reveal that the procedure based on this trigger was much more straightforward than the procedure based on State referrals and *proprio motu* investigations, which could reinforce arguments that the latter two triggers should be abandoned altogether. However, with the same structural approach coming from countries like Argentina, Brazil and Switzerland, not countries suspected of favoritism of the Security Council, the decision to split the draft articles in the negotiating text along these lines was quick and easy.

Splitting the draft articles was a useful improvement to the structure of the text, but did not bridge the gap on the substantive question of State consent. The question was highly polarizing, with roughly half of the delegations in favor of such a requirement, and roughly half of them against.[12] The ABS proposal belonged to the latter camp, which was more interested in protecting the interests of the presumed victims of aggression than the sovereignty of the alleged aggressor State. But what exactly was the meaning of consent? Different expressions of consent were conceivable, though most delegations simply had in mind that any alleged aggressor State should have ratified the aggression amendments.

But then Canada joined the creative drafting movement and came up with an innovative proposition of its own: indeed, the consent of the alleged

---

[12] In March 2010, Prince Zeid Ra'ad Zeid Al-Hussein conducted an informal 'roll-call' inter alia on the question of state consent, which revealed a roughly even split among delegations. The result was not formally recorded, but is reflected in S. Barriga, 'Negotiation the Amendments on the Crime of Aggression' in Barriga and Kreß (eds), *The Travaux Préparatoires of the Crime of Aggression* (n 2) 3, 45 note 238.

aggressor State should be required, but not in the form of ratification of the amendments. Instead, an ad-hoc expression of consent of the States involved, including States that had not even ratified the Rome Statute in the first place, would suffice.[13] It was a strongly consent-oriented proposal, but it did set the bar significantly lower and sparked further discussion about possible compromises. Having delegations representing largely opposite camps in the negotiations issuing compromise ideas is a godsend for anyone charged with facilitating such a process. We asked these delegations to sit together and figure out whether there was any way for them to come up with a joint paper. It was a very long shot, given the remaining major gap between the two approaches. So, they locked themselves in for many hours, and to our great surprise and delight, came out with a common position (here referred to as CABS paper).[14] The compromise among these delegations, who already before had ventured so far from their original positions, looked as follows: 1) the Court's exercise of jurisdiction would only begin five years after the amendments enter into force for any State Party; 2) the Security Council would not serve as an exclusive jurisdictional filter (more on that issue below); 3) the Court's jurisdiction in case of State referrals and *proprio motu* proceedings would be consent-based, but based on an opt-out approach. By default, there would be jurisdiction over an alleged aggressor State Party to the Rome Statute, unless that State Party would opt out. And jurisdiction regarding non-States Parties to the Rome Statute would be entirely excluded.

This was not the first time that an opt-out approach was suggested as the solution to the vexing question of State consent: we had included this option in past Chair's discussion papers.[15] But up until that moment, roughly 48 hours before the end of the Review Conference, delegations had simply not felt enough pressure to engage in a real give-and-take. The opt-out approach was indeed one of the few conceivable positions in between the two extremes that had cancelled each other out for so long: full and active prior consent by the alleged aggressor State versus no consent. While the opt-out approach was positioned in between these two extremes, it certainly was not at the midpoint. It was much closer to the position of the consent-oriented delegations, since it excluded non-States Parties entirely and since opting out was—at least

---

13   The Canadian proposal is reproduced in Barriga and Kreß (eds), *The Travaux Préparatoires of the Crime of Aggression* (n 2) 753.

14   The CABS paper is reproduced in Barriga and Kreß (eds), *The Travaux Préparatoires of the Crime of Aggression* (n 2) 772.

15   See 2009 Chairman's Non-Paper on the Exercise of Jurisdiction, reprinted in Barriga and Kreß (eds), *The Travaux Préparatoires of the Crime of Aggression* (n 2) 688.

legally—extremely easy to do. It could be described as a passive-consent approach that limited jurisdiction to States Parties only. The CABS paper made waves all around the Munyonyo Resort. The delegations involved in its drafting worked hard to convince others that this was the only way out, and the feedback was generally positive, with mostly smaller concerns about technical issues. We therefore included the opt-out approach into the next version of the negotiating text.[16]

That was, however, easier said than done. The CABS delegations had done a great job designing a policy compromise on the question of State consent that could probably find the support of the room, given how far we had come. But the paper did not explain how this approach could be squared with the Rome Statute's provisions on amendments. The crux of the matter was how such an approach would relate to the second sentence of article 121(5), which states, simply put, that the Court shall not exercise jurisdiction in respect of States Parties that do not accept an amendment regarding the definition of a crime. Many delegations had argued that there was no way around the simple statement made in that sentence, and that therefore any State Party that would not ratify the amendments would simply not be subject to the Court's jurisdiction over the crime of aggression. In other words, the second sentence seemed to indicate a strict opt-in approach, not an opt-out. That was the so-called 'negative understanding' of that sentence, which we had been discussing in the negotiations for several years.[17] Was there a way around that in light of the emerging consensus on an opt-out system? Was a 'positive understanding' of that sentence possible?

We spent much of the night of 9 to 10 June pondering this question as we prepared the next version of the negotiating text. After many conversations with legal experts from different delegations, we came to the conclusion that the legal key for an opt-out approach was to read article 121(5) in the context of other provisions of the Rome Statute, including articles 5 and 12. We therefore emphasized that States Parties to the Rome Statute had already opted into the Court's jurisdiction over the crime of aggression, precisely by ratifying the Statute in its original version. The first paragraph of article 12 of the Rome Statute states that any party to the Rome Statute 'accepts the jurisdiction of the Court with respect to crimes referred to in article 5', which explicitly includes the crime of aggression. States Parties have thus already accepted jurisdiction

---

16 See 2010 President's First Paper, reprinted in Barriga and Kreß (eds), *The Travaux Préparatoires of the Crime of Aggression* (n 2) 774–78.

17 See for example the 2005 Princeton Report, reprinted in Barriga and Kreß (eds), *The Travaux Préparatoires of the Crime of Aggression* (n 2) 450, paras 5–17.

over the crime of aggression, despite the fact that this crime was yet to be defined by way of an amendment. Our approach was thus to stress the unique position of the crime of aggression in the Rome Statute (which was 'half-in, half-out'), for which, as article 5(2) highlights, we had to devise a jurisdictional solution *sui generis*. The next two versions of the negotiating text[18] therefore added additional references to article 12(1)—alluding to the already given acceptance of jurisdiction—and to article 5(2), which emphasizes that the provision on the crime of aggression should also include conditions for the exercise of jurisdiction, which were therefore for the Review Conference to decide. The text also deleted the references to the alternative 'negative' or 'positive' understanding of the second sentence of article 121(5), because the answer to the question of its effects was now contained in the opt-out clause. Of course an opt-out clause only makes sense if the default position is 'in'! Otherwise, the system would first require States Parties to opt in, and then allow them to opt out—an entirely absurd approach in this context, and one that no delegation ever advocated for during and prior to Kampala.

Our attempt at squaring the circle between the amendment provisions and the opt-out approach met with great interest, and many delegations gave us concrete suggestions on how to get it done. The delegation of Japan, however, was not convinced that it was legally possible to create a true opt-out system under article 121(5). Instead, Japan suggested that we would first have to amend the amendment procedures. Given how much headache the existing ambiguous and contradictory provisions had given us over the past years, that was not a bad approach in principle. But it had two major flaws: first, with only 48 hours left until the end of the Conference, such a drastic change of course would have been a non-starter for the negotiations; and second, amending the amendment procedures would have required ratifications by 7/8 of States Parties. The new amendment provisions would therefore come into effect only many years into the future, and possibly never. We thus had to stick to our approach of trying to reconcile the competing forces of existing provisions of the Rome Statute. We were convinced that this was possible, especially if the decision was ultimately taken by consensus. On Thursday, 10 June, the penultimate day of the Review Conference, at 11.30 p.m. we presented the fine-tuned version of this approach to the room. No delegation voiced any objection to this paper, which identified only one issue as still outstanding: the role of the Security Council in case of State referrals and *proprio motu* investigations (draft article 15 *bis*).

---

18   2010 President's First Paper and 2010 President's Second Paper, reprinted in Barriga and Kreß (eds), *The Travaux Préparatoires of the Crime of Aggression* (n 2) 774–82, 782–86.

The Role of the Security Council

The role of the Security Council in determining the existence of an act of aggression by one State against another, and its consequences for the criminal law case against the leader responsible for such an act, had been the big conundrum from the beginning. The gap between the existing positions was fundamental, and there was no obvious way of bridging it. Separating the triggers was an important step in reaching consensus, but it did not by itself solve this conceptual disagreement. The permanent members of the Security Council in particular insisted on the exclusive competence of the Council to make a determination that an act of aggression had been committed, while the vast majority of States felt that the Council's competence was primary rather than exclusive and that there should be alternative avenues for prosecuting the crime of aggression that safeguarded the judicial independence of the Court.

An opening came, rather unexpectedly, from a delegate of one of the permanent members, well into the second week of negotiations. In a bilateral consultation with Christian, that delegate indicated that a Council determination may not be necessary in the case of a Security Council referral. While seemingly not that significant with respect to the practical application of this trigger, the concession was nevertheless groundbreaking. After all, the P-5 position had been an absolute one and often been presented as the only one compatible with the UN Charter. But now it appeared imaginable to have situations where the Court could investigate crimes of aggression without a Council determination. Very surprised at first, Christian quickly consulted with the most active P-5 delegations who expressed doubts that the approach would be helpful, but received no objections. The next Chair's paper,[19] produced on 10 June, therefore contained not only a split of the triggers into draft articles 15 *bis* and 15 *ter*, but also indicated that in the course of investigations based on a Security Council referral, the Court would not have to wait for the Council to make a determination of an act of aggression—after all, the request for an investigation would have emanated from the Council in the first place. While there was some buyer's regret expressed privately by permanent members, the approach was of course embraced by all other delegations and soon led to a clean draft article 15 *ter*.

That left only one question to be solved, as mentioned above: what should the Security Council's role be in cases where it did *not* refer a situation to the Court? Two alternatives were on the table. Under Alternative 1, the Court could only proceed with an investigation into a crime of aggression where the Security Council had already determined the existence of an act of aggression. Under

---

[19] See 2010 President's Second Paper, reprinted in Barriga and Kreß (eds), *The Travaux Préparatoires of the Crime of Aggression* (n 2), 782–86.

Alternative 2, inaction by the Security Council would not be the end of the investigation, but instead the Court's own judges could authorize the investigation after a six-months waiting period.

Breakthrough on the Final Day

The table was thus set for the endgame on Friday. After the conference, we found out that this was a time when the blogosphere was spreading gloom of imminent failure and how it was impossible to bring the divergent positions together in a consensus. So, when many were wondering whether we would put a package to a recorded vote (considered crazy or not feasible by most, also because of a possible lack of quorum on the last day of the conference), we were entirely focused on forging a consensus. The last non-paper would be decisive. We kicked around several ideas, but settled for the obvious: letting the cat out of the bag on the two other triggers, since the vast majority of delegations strongly preferred Alternative 2. We had been of the view for a long time that a comprehensive package could only be possible if this approach was to be adopted, but during all those years we had been given no signs of compromise on the part of the P-5. The compromise on 15 *ter* had opened the door a crack, so now it was time to put our foot in. Clearly, this was another big step for the P-5: if 15 *ter* had been a compromise at the conceptual level, each of the permanent members still had full control in practice. If an unwelcome investigation into a crime of aggression seemed possible, preventing a referral was an easy way out. That, of course, did not apply to the other triggers. We therefore added several elements to draft article 15 *bis* to make Alternative 2 more acceptable: first, the Court organ to authorize the investigation would not be a Pre-Trial Chamber (composed of three judges), but the Pre-Trial Division in its entirety (composed of six judges), an entity that does not otherwise have any competence under the Rome Statute. This gave the authorization particular significance and spread it out over several players. Second, we referenced article 16, the famous deferral competence of the Council. This of course applies anyway, but we felt giving it special emphasis here would be helpful. Third, we proposed to add a provision that would delay the Court's exercise of jurisdiction by at least seven years. This included a requirement for a separate decision by States Parties to activate the Court's jurisdiction—thereby adding the notion that, at least procedurally, the last word was not spoken in Kampala.

We put this idea on paper during the early hours of Friday morning, the last day of the Conference.[20] Then, we convened a very informal meeting of the

---

20   See 2010 President's Preliminary Compromise Proposal, reprinted in Barriga and Kreß (eds), *The Travaux Préparatoires of the Crime of Aggression* (n 2) 789.

main stakeholders to test the idea. It was the only time we used this format to discuss a proposal, and we did it because it was late in the game and truly crunch time. Concessions are made more easily with fewer people watching. Every other paper had been discussed in informal plenary, after extensive preparations through bilateral and other meetings, but there was simply not enough time to do this again. We had managed to line up some of our closest supporters to speak in favor of the non-paper as a reasonable compromise, but we knew of course that the key was with the P-5. So we started the meeting and braced for impact, expecting that this would be the moment where our compromise proposal would blow up in our face, courtesy of the permanent members. Happily, we were wrong.

After a very positive and supportive tone had been set by the first few speakers, the US requested the floor. Head of Delegation Harold Koh gave an extensive and detailed presentation of the US position and how it was anchored in the UN Charter, but in the second half of his intervention also indicated that the non-paper was something the US could work with. While not a State Party, the US had the biggest delegation in Kampala and also one of the most influential voices on the crime of aggression, with significant sway over the position of other P-5. The US intervention proved crucial: the rest of the interventions ranged from reluctantly to openly supportive, as good an outcome as we could have wished for. This meeting was the real breakthrough in Kampala. Some were looking to uncork the bottles to celebrate, and it was only early afternoon. But it turned out that we had another serious problem.

Activation: The Last Hurdle

The Friday morning non-paper provided for delayed activation of the Court's exercise of jurisdiction by seven years. This was an approach we had for long considered as potentially helpful in countering the argument that the Court was not ready to investigate a crime of this complexity. A cooling-off period after the difficult negotiations in Kampala would certainly be helpful for everybody. But our non-paper provided for automatic activation of the regime under 15*ter* (*Security Council referrals*), while the 15*bis* provisions (State referrals, *proprio motu* investigations) would require States Parties to take an active decision to that effect. To our mind, this was in line with the fact that the Security Council trigger was the less controversial regime, but also with the fact that the ABS paper itself had foreseen that the activation of the Security Council trigger (requiring one single ratification) would be much easier than the activation of the two other triggers (requiring ratifications by seven-eighth of States Parties). To our surprise, it was primarily Brazil that vigorously opposed our approach to activation and demanded that both triggers be treated the same way.

In the late afternoon, direct negotiations between interested delegations over this aspect finally failed, and there was a concrete risk that the package might fail over what we considered to be a smaller issue, at least in comparison to the question of the role of the Security Council that we had just tentatively solved. Positions became more and more entrenched in the course of these discussions though and also more ideologically charged. Some delegations started linking the question of the activation mechanism to the issue of Security Council reform, a toxic ingredient for any multilateral negotiation.

We therefore had to step in once again. We decided quickly to have the activation requirement apply to both regimes in the same way. Clearly, the ABS group was not willing to accept anything else, and the P-5 could probably live with this equal treatment, as long as the threshold for activation was high enough. Throughout the evening, discussions focused on the question of the threshold. The P-5 position was that the activation decisions should be decided by consensus, thereby giving a *de facto* veto to each State Party. The opposing view was that a simple majority should suffice, if indeed an activation decision was necessary at all. Discussions were getting very tense as the day was rapidly approaching its end. The positive atmosphere of the early afternoon was almost squandered, and there was an increasing sense of confusion especially among those who had not been involved in the small group meeting in the morning; they had been waiting for an informal plenary for many hours now. After intense rounds of bilaterals, we produced our final compromise proposal, which again sought to provide a middle ground: both triggers would require an activation decision to be taken by States Parties, no earlier than 1 January 2017, by the same majority as is required under the Rome Statute for the adoption of amendments, i.e. two-thirds of all States Parties.[21]

While all the major stakeholders had been consulted on this solution, there was a significant last-minute push for the consensual threshold, but in the end there was a nod from all the States Parties, or at least no objection.

There was, however, a last moment of drama. When Christian proposed the draft amendments in their entirety for formal adoption, the delegate of Japan requested the floor. Tensions in the room rose, as the Head of Delegation of Japan proceeded with his statement,[22] which was strongly critical of the approach contained in the draft on the question of amendment procedures. When he used the phrase 'it is with a heavy heart', most people in the room

---

21   The President's Final Compromise Proposal is reprinted in Barriga and Kreß (eds), *The Travaux Préparatoires of the Crime of Aggression* (n 2) 804.

22   For the statement of Japan see 2010 Explanations of Position, reprinted in Barriga and Kreß (eds), *The Travaux Préparatoires of the Crime of Aggression* (n 2) 810.

thought that consensus had failed in the last minute, after all. But the statement was simply an explanation of position, pretty much along the lines agreed the day before in a bilateral meeting. We had certainly expected the statement to occur not before, but after formal adoption of the amendments (as many States took the floor after the deed was done), and normally we would have double-checked with Japan before convening the formal plenary. In the last-minute chaos over the question of activation, however, we simply forgot, to the detriment of many shocked delegates who erroneously came to believe that Japan would proceed to break consensus. Moments later, the gavel fell and the amendments were adopted by consensus.

5 Conclusion

Being at the helm of the negotiations on the crime of aggression from 2003 to 2010 has without a doubt been the most challenging and most rewarding task we have been faced with in our professional lives. For most observers, as well as for many participants, finding agreement on the crime of aggression seemed as elusive as a number of other hopeless negotiations, such as the search for a general definition of terrorism in international law. The reward lay not only in the ultimately successful conclusion of the process, but also in the process itself. What made the negotiations on the crime of aggression, despite the pressures and the politics, particularly enjoyable and productive, was the camaraderie and mutual trust that we developed over time. Being able to hold a number of rounds negotiations in summer-camp like atmosphere in Princeton, and to some extent in Kampala, was an important factor in that regard. Even more important was to have the right mix of people at the right time—especially people like Roger Clark, who influenced the process not because of the size of the country he represented, but because of his towering presence as a true expert on the subject matter.

Being supported by a diverse group of representatives from different countries made the task of steering a negotiation process through fundamental differences of opinion somewhat less impossible. It allowed us to act with greater confidence as we proposed to the group, time and again, how to move forward on the many strands of our negotiation, through countless non-papers, background papers, Chair's papers and so on. Many ideas and proposals needed to be tested, and many decisions had to be made. Through all this, we tried not to lose sight of the fact that in any multilateral process, the Chair is never fully in control, and that too much hesitation can make a complicated situation even worse. Or as Yogi Berra put it: 'When you come to a fork in the road, take it!'

CHAPTER 19

The Elusive Essence of Crimes against Humanity

Margaret M. deGuzman

1 Introduction

Although crimes against humanity have been prosecuted in national and international fora for over sixty years, both the normative foundations and the definitional elements of this category of crimes remain unclear. Unlike war crimes and genocide, crimes against humanity are not yet the subject of a dedicated international convention. Crimes against humanity are defined in the Rome Statute of the International Criminal Court ('Rome Statute'), but that treaty stipulates that it should not be construed as limiting the progressive development of international law.[1] However, a convention on crimes against humanity may be adopted in the near future. A group of international experts has been working to promote such a convention;[2] and, in July 2014, the International Law Commission ('ILC') decided to begin working on draft articles that will form the basis for a convention.

For a convention to strengthen the law of crimes against humanity, rather than entrench current ambiguities, the ILC and the broader international community must clarify the conceptual underpinnings of these crimes. This chapter seeks to contribute to that process by elucidating a tension between the twin goals animating the definition of crimes against humanity. One purpose of creating a category of crimes called 'crimes against humanity' is to identify crimes that 'shock the conscience of humanity' so that the international community can express that shock through prosecution and punishment. At the same time, the definition seeks to distinguish crimes against humanity from 'ordinary' crimes that are subject only to national jurisdiction. These two goals are related and, indeed, are generally conflated. It is the gravity

---

1   See Rome Statute of the International Criminal Court (signed 17 July 1998, entered into force in force 1 July 2002) 2187 UNTS 38544 ('ICC') art 10 ('Nothing in this Part shall be interpreted as limiting or prejudicing in any way existing or developing rules of international law for purposes other than this Statute.') ('Rome Statute').
2   The effort is led by Professor Leila Sadat at the Washington University School of Law and is described in Leila Sadat (ed), *Forging a Convention for Crimes Against Humanity* (CUP 2011) ('Sadat, *Forging a Convention for Crimes Against Humanity*').

of the crimes—humanity's shock—that is usually cited to justify international jurisdiction.

However, these two goals are distinct and potentially in tension. The need to delimit international jurisdiction in contrast to national jurisdiction suggests the definition should include clear limitations. This goal is often cited to support a requirement that crimes against humanity be committed in furtherance of a state or organizational policy. Such a policy element helps to distinguish crimes against humanity from 'ordinary crimes' because states are unlikely to prosecute crimes in which they are complicit. In contrast, the goal of articulating which crimes 'shock the conscience of humanity' favors a broader definition. Many people are reluctant to agree that only crimes committed by governments or similar organizations pursuant to policies shock humanity's conscience. Moreover, if crimes against humanity are defined broadly, they are better able to adjust to the evolution of humanity's conscience over time.

Roger Clark's work on crimes against humanity hints at the distinction between the goals of delimiting international jurisdiction, and of encompassing all crimes that shock humanity's conscience. In analyzing the definition of crimes against humanity, Professor Clark labels two of the elements 'jurisdictional'. These are the Nuremberg Charter's requirement that crimes against humanity be committed in connection with armed conflict and the Rome Statute's requirement of an 'attack' against a civilian population. Professor Clark asserts that these elements do not constitute substantive limitations on the concept of crimes against humanity, but merely restrict the jurisdictions of the particular courts adjudicating such crimes.[3]

Professor Clark's assertion that some elements of crimes against humanity are jurisdictional rather than substantive does not reflect the majority position. Most of the commentary on crimes against humanity assumes that the questions of jurisdiction and substance are inextricable. That is, that each of the elements of crimes against humanity tells us both what crimes merit the label 'crimes against humanity' and what crimes warrant international adjudication.[4]

---

3   Roger S Clark, 'History of Efforts to Codify Crimes Against Humanity' in Sadat, *Forging a Convention for Crimes Against Humanity* (n 2) ('Clark, 'History of Efforts''); Roger S Clark, 'Crimes Against Humanity at Nuremberg' in George Ginsburgs & Vladimir Nikolaevich Kudriavtsev (eds), *The Nuremburg Trial and International Law: Issue 42* (Martinus Nijhoff 1990) 195–96; Roger S Clark, 'Crimes Against Humanity and the Rome Statute of the International Criminal Court' in George Ginsburgs et al (eds), *International and National Law in Russia and Eastern Europe: Essays in Honor of George Ginsburgs* (Martinus Nijhoff 2001) 152.

4   See eg, Robert Dubler, 'What's in a Name? A Theory of Crimes Against Humanity' (2008) 15 Austl J Int'l L 85, 95 ('As part of this process, in 1994, the Security Council adopted the test of a 'widespread or systematic attack against any civilian population' for a crime against

In Professor Clark's view, on the other hand, neither the Nuremberg Charter's requirement of a link to armed conflict nor the ICC Statute's element of an 'attack against a civilian population' expresses the essence of crimes against humanity. Those elements serve merely to limit the reach of the relevant courts.

Professor Clark has not advanced a theory of the 'essence' of crimes against humanity; nor will this short essay undertake that task. Instead, this essay seeks to extend Professor Clark's intuition that the essence of crimes against humanity, whatever it may be, is broader than the appropriate jurisdictional reach of particular courts. The essay begins by reviewing the development of the law of crimes against humanity to demonstrate the competing pulls of the two goals over time. It then assesses the debate over the policy element in the scholarship, showing that each side's position is driven by an emphasis on one of the two goals. The essay concludes by arguing that in light of the different kinds of courts that adjudicate crimes against humanity a convention on crimes against humanity should be driven more by the need to capture broadly the crimes that shock humanity's conscience than by that of limiting the jurisdiction of any particular court.

2 Jurisdiction and Shockingness (Gravity) in the Evolution of the Definition of Crimes against Humanity

When crimes against humanity were first codified in the Nuremberg Charter, the goal was not to identify particularly shocking crimes—although the Nazi crimes obviously qualified—but rather to justify the tribunal's jurisdiction. This was accomplished by linking crimes against humanity to war crimes, over which jurisdiction was already established under international law.[5] The

---

humanity in times of peace. Viewed in its historical context, this test was intended to describe both the international crime and the nature of the internal atrocity to which the Security Council felt compelled and entitled to respond under Chapter VII'); David Luban, 'A Theory of Crimes Against Humanity' (2004) 29 Yale J Int'l Law 85, 93 ('Crimes against humanity are international crimes committed by politically organized groups acting under color of policy, consisting of the most severe and abominable acts of violence and persecution, and inflicted on victims because of their membership in a population or group rather than their individual characteristics.').

5 See Charter of the International Military Tribunal (8 Aug 1945) 82 UNTS 279 (IMT) art 6(c) (defining crimes against humanity as 'murder, extermination, enslavement, deportation, and other inhumane acts committed against any civilian population, before or during the war; or persecutions on political, racial or religious grounds in execution of or in connection with any crime within the jurisdiction of the Tribunal, whether or not in violation of the domestic law of the country where perpetrated').

Nuremberg Charter's definition therefore does not contain the 'gravity elements' that became central to later definitions, in particular the requirement of a widespread or systematic attack.[6] Moreover, the Nuremberg judges did not always treat crimes against humanity as more serious than war crimes for sentencing purposes.[7]

When the ILC started work on the Draft Code of Offenses Against the Peace and Security of Mankind ('Draft Code') its initial focus remained on the goal of distinguishing such crimes from national crimes. The Commission identified the 'political' nature of the crimes as their defining characteristic.[8] The 1954 Draft Code defined crimes against humanity as: 'Inhuman acts...committed against any civilian population on social, political, racial, religious or cultural grounds by the authorities of a State or by private individuals acting at the instigation or with the toleration of such authorities.'[9] The commentary to the Draft Code notes that the purpose of this political element is to ensure that inhuman acts committed by private individuals are not considered international crimes.[10]

In the early 1980's, however, the ILC changed its approach to crimes against humanity, deciding that it is not the political nature of the crimes that matters but their special gravity.[11] This shifted the focus from crafting a definition of crimes that states would not prosecute because they are responsible or complicit, to identifying crimes that the international community considers particularly horrific. The ILC struggled for many years to determine what crimes fit this description.[12] The 1991 Draft Code replaced 'crimes against humanity'

---

[6] The Charter does require that the crimes be committed against a civilian 'population,' which arguably implies a notion of scale. See Clark, 'International and National' (n 3) 152.

[7] Micaela Frulli, 'Are Crimes Against Humanity More Serious than War Crimes?' (2001) 12 EJIL 329, 343.

[8] International Law Commission, 'Report of the International Law Commission on its 3rd Session' (16 May – 27 July 1951) UN Doc A/CN.4/48 para 58(a) ('The Commission first considered the meaning of the term 'offences against the peace and security of mankind', contained in Resolution 177 (II). The view of the Commission was that the meaning of this term should be limited to offences which contain a political element and which endanger or disturb the maintenance of international peace and security.').

[9] International Law Commission, 'Report of the International Law Commission to the General Assembly' (1954) UN Doc A/CN.4/SER.A/1954/Add. 1 para 50.

[10] Ibid 150.

[11] 'First Report on the Draft Code of Crimes against the Peace and Security of Mankind, by Mr. Doudou Thiam, Special Rapporteur'(1986) UN Doc A/CN.4/364 para 37.

[12] See, eg International Law Commission, 'Report of the International Law Commission on the Work of its 36th Session' (7 May-27 July 1984) UN Doc A/39/10 paras 34, 63 (noting the

with 'systematic or mass violations of human rights' in an effort to capture the gravity element of the crimes.[13] Since the definition no longer required the involvement of a state, the distinction between crimes against humanity and 'ordinary' crimes was now less stark. To determine what crimes crossed the line under this definition, it was necessary to apply the ambiguous concepts of scale and systematicity, and a broader range of crimes were likely to qualify.

By the time the ILC issued it final Draft Code in 1996, however, it had reinstated the 'political' element, although now the element had become optional. Crimes against humanity were defined as inhumane acts 'committed in a systematic manner or on a large scale and instigated or directed by a Government or by any organization or group.'[14] Given that a 'government' is necessarily an 'organization or group' the inclusion of that term in the definition is superfluous. What the mention of 'government' suggests is that the ILC remained torn between the goals of ensuring a strict differentiation between international and national crimes and that of capturing the range of crimes that shock humanity's conscience.

When crimes against humanity were defined in the statute of the *ad hoc* International Criminal Tribunal for Former Yugoslavia ('ICTY') there was apparently little thought given to establishing a strict distinction between such crimes and 'ordinary' crimes or to emphasizing their gravity. The definition mirrors that of the Nuremberg Charter, omitting both the requirement of state action and of a widespread or systematic attack.[15] Instead, the nexus with armed conflict was included in an effort to satisfy the principle of legality, although the judges quickly concluded that this no longer reflected customary international law.[16] The lack of attention to delineating jurisdiction or establishing gravity through the definition makes sense because neither of these issues was contested in that situation. The crimes committed in former Yugoslavia

---

difficulty of developing criteria for seriousness and concluding that seriousness is a function of many different factors).

13   International Law Commission, 'Report of the International Law Commission on the Work of its 43rd Session' (29 April – 19 July 1991) UN Doc A/46/10, 103 ('ILC Report of 1991').

14   International Law Commission, 'Report of the International Law Commission on the Work of its 48th Session' (6 May – 26 July 1996) UN Doc A/51/10, 47.

15   Statute of the International Criminal Tribunal for the former Yugoslavia (adopted 25 May 1993) UN Doc S/25704 art 5 ('The International Tribunal shall have the power to prosecute persons responsible for the following crimes when committed in armed conflict, whether international or internal in character, and directed against any civilian population....').

16   See *Prosecutor v. Tadic* (Decision on the Defense Motion for Interlocutory Appeal on Jurisdiction) IT-94-1 (2 Oct 1995) para 141.

were widely acknowledged to be exceptionally serious and there was no legitimate national government to contest the tribunal's jurisdiction.

When crimes against humanity were defined for the purpose of the International Criminal Tribunal for Rwanda ('ICTR'), the nexus to armed conflict was replaced with the requirement that the crimes take place in the context of a 'widespread or systematic attack against a civilian population.'[17] Indeed, the ICTY judges ultimately read this requirement into that Tribunal's statute as well,[18] although both tribunals have interpreted the requirement broadly.[19] They have also rejected the requirement in the ICC Statute that crimes against humanity be committed pursuant to a policy.[20] Again, this makes sense because the scope of the tribunals' jurisdiction is well established and they therefore have little incentive to maintain a strict distinction between crimes against humanity and crimes under national law.

When the Rome Statute was negotiated, it became much more important to distinguish crimes against humanity from 'ordinary' crimes. Since the ICC was to have prospective jurisdiction, many states felt that the Court's subject matter jurisdiction should be restricted in ways that protected their sovereignty. Such concerns were central to the inclusion in the Rome Statute of the requirement that crimes against humanity be committed in connection with 'a State or organizational policy.'[21]

---

17   Statute of the International Criminal Tribunal for Rwanda (adopted 8 Nov 1994) S/Res/955 art 3.

18   *Prosecutor v. Tadic* (Judgment) IT-94-1-A (15 July 1999) para 248 ('The Appeals Chamber agrees that it may be inferred from the words 'directed against any civilian population' in Article 5 of the Statute that the acts of the accused must comprise part of a pattern of widespread or systematic crimes directed against a civilian population and that the accused must have known that his acts fit into such a pattern.').

19   See *Prosecutor v. Kunarac et al* (Judgment) IT-96-23-T & IT-96-23/1-T (22 Feb 2001) para 431 ('Only the attack, not the individual acts of the accused, must be 'widespread or systematic'. A single act could therefore be regarded as a crime against humanity if it takes place in the relevant context.'); *Prosecutor v. Ndindabahizi* (Judgment) ICTR-2001-71-1 (15 July 2004) para 477 ("[S]ystematic' refers to an organized pattern of conduct, as distinguished from random or unconnected acts committed by independent actors.').

20   *Prosecutor v. Kunarac et al* (Judgment) IT-96-23 (12 June 2002) para 98; *Prosecutor v. Semanza* (Judgment) ICTR-97-20-A (20 May 2005) para 269.

21   Rome Statute (n 1) art 7; see also Darryl Robinson, 'Crimes Against Humanity: Reflections on State Sovereignty, Legal Precision and the Dictates of the Public Conscience' in Flavia Lattanzi & William A Schabas (eds), *Essays on the Rome Statute of the International Criminal Court, Volume I* (Editrice il Sirente 1999) 141.

3   The Debate over the Breadth of Crimes against Humanity

The debate that has ensued about the meaning of the policy element evidences the tension between the goals of restricting jurisdiction and of giving voice to humanity's conscience. Some of the ICC's judges have interpreted the policy requirement narrowly, asserting that crimes against humanity must be strictly distinguished from 'ordinary' crimes. In dissenting from the decision to authorize investigation in the Kenya situation, Judge Kaul argued that the policy must be that of a state or a 'state-like' organization.[22] According to Judge Kaul, the threat posed by an inhumane state policy 'is so fundamentally different in nature and scale' that it 'elevates [the] crimes to the international level.'[23] Other ICC judges have indicated that the policy must be formally adopted and disseminated. The Pre-Trial Chamber in the *Gbagbo* case adjourned the confirmation hearing, asking the prosecutor to produce additional evidence showing that the policy to commit the crimes was formalized.[24] Likewise, in the *Mbarushimana* case, the Pre-Trial Chamber adopted a strict view of the purpose that must be behind the policy, holding that retaliatory targeting does not qualify.[25]

Many ICC judges, however, have taken a broader view of what constitutes a crime against humanity. The majority of the Pre-Trial Chamber in the Kenya situation held that crimes against humanity can be committed not only by states and state-like organizations, but also by any organization that 'has the capability to perform acts which infringe on basic human values.'[26] A Trial Chamber confirmed this approach in the *Katanga* judgment, holding that the term 'organization' simply requires sufficient coordination to be able to carry out an attack.[27] The Appeals Chamber in the *Gbagbo* case rejected the idea that the policy must be formalized, asserting that: 'an attack which is planned,

---

22   *Situation in the Republic of Kenya* (Decision Pursuant to Article 15 of the Rome Statute on the Authorization of an Investigation into the Situation in the Republic of Kenya) ICC-01/09 (31 March 2010) Dissenting Opinion of Judge Hans-Peter Kaul para 66 ('*Situation in the Republic of Kenya*').

23   Ibid para 60.

24   *Prosecutor v. Gbagbo* (Decision Adjourning the Hearing on the Confirmation of Charges Pursuant to Article 61(7)(c)(i) of the Rome Statute) ICC-02/11-01/11-432 (3 June 2013) para 44.

25   *Prosecutor v. Mbarushimana* (Decision on the Confirmation of Charges) ICC-01/04-01/10-465-Red (16 Dec 2011) para 265; see also Darryl Robinson, 'Crimes Against Humanity: A Better Policy on "Policy"' in Carsten Stahn (ed), *The Law and Practice of the International Criminal Court* (OUP 2014) 1 (discussing the decision) ('Robinson, 'A Better Policy'').

26   *Situation in the Republic of Kenya* (n 22) para 90.

27   *Prosecutor v. Katanga* (Judgment) ICC-01/04-01/07-3436 (7 March 2014) para 1120.

directed or organised—as opposed to spontaneous or isolated acts of violence—will satisfy the policy criterion, and that there is no requirement that the policy be formally adopted.'[28] These decisions suggest that many ICC judges are less concerned with establishing a strict distinction between crimes against humanity and national crimes, than with ensuring that this category of crimes is adequately broad to cover all possible shocks to humanity's conscience.

The scholarship on crimes against humanity reflects a similar divide over the appropriate breadth of the definition that can be traced to differing emphases on the two central goals. Since the adoption of the Rome Statute, some scholars have taken the position that the policy requirement is an essential element of crimes against humanity and should be interpreted narrowly to include only the policies of states or state-like organizations.[29] Cherif Bassiouni, an eminent scholar who chaired the Working Group that drafted the ICC definition, has even controversially asserted that the drafters' intent was to limit the kinds of organizations capable of committing crimes against humanity to those that bear the characteristics of a state.[30]

Scholars who support a strictly construed policy requirement tend to emphasize the importance of distinguishing crimes against humanity from ordinary crimes. They argue that the key function of this category is to capture crimes that states are unwilling or unable to prosecute. It is this 'impunity gap' that justifies international jurisdiction. According to William Schabas:

> Over the decades, a principal rationale for prosecuting crimes against humanity as such has been the fact that such atrocities generally escape

---

28 *Prosecutor v. Gbagbo* (Judgment on the Appeal of the Prosecutor Against the Decision of Pre-trial Chamber I of 3 June 2013 entitled 'Decision Adjourning the Hearing on the Confirmation of Charges Pursuant to Article 61(7)(c)(i) of the Rome Statute') ICC-2/11-01/11 (16 Dec 2013) para 215. See also *Prosecutor v. Ntaganda* (Decision Pursuant to Article 61(7)(a) of the Rome Statute on the Charges of the Prosecutor Against Bosco Ntganda) ICC-01/04-02/06 (9 June 2014) para 19.

29 See for example, M Cherif Bassiouni, *Crimes Against Humanity: Historical Evolution and Contemporary Application* (CUP 2011) 50; William A Schabas 'State Policy as an Element of International Crimes' (2008) 98 J Crim L & Criminology 953 ('Schabas, 'State Policy as an Element of International Crimes'').

30 M Cherif Bassiouni, *The Legislative History of the International Criminal Court: Introduction, Analysis, and Integrated Text Vol. I* (Transnational 2005) 151–152; but see Charles Chernor Jalloh, 'What Makes a Crime against Humanity a Crime against Humanity?' (2013) 23 Am U Int'l L Rev 381 ('Jalloh, 'What Makes a Crime against Humanity a Crime against Humanity?'') (arguing that the legislative history on this point is unclear).

prosecution in the State that normally exercises jurisdiction, under the territorial or active personality principles, because of the State's own involvement or acquiescence.[31]

Professor Schabas adds that 'individual crimes committed in isolation from abstract entities are of little or no interest at the international level.'[32]

Proponents of the narrower version of crimes against humanity are not committed to capturing all crimes that shock humanity's conscience in the definition. They point out that, as a general matter, it is usually states and state-like organizations that are capable of committing crimes that are sufficiently serious to shock humanity's conscience.[33] While they acknowledge that there may be exceptions, their view is that, in the words of Claus Kreß, 'it is legitimate for the definition of a crime to deal with the typical case.'[34] Some scholars support the state policy requirement on the philosophical grounds that crimes against humanity shock humanity's conscience in a particular way; in David Luban's words they represent 'politics gone cancerous.'[35] Such scholars also seem motivated, at least in part, by a desire to distinguish crimes against humanity from national crimes.[36]

In contrast, other scholars take a broader view of the definition of crimes against humanity. They argue that the ICC should interpret the policy requirement loosely to including any kind of policy, whether formalized or not, and any kind of 'organization', whether or not it has the characteristics of a state.[37]

---

31 Schabas, 'State Policy as an Element of International Crimes' (n 29) 974.
32 *Ibid* 982.
33 See, eg, Klaus Kreß, 'On the Outer Limits of Crimes against Humanity: The Concept of Organization within the Policy Requirement: Some Reflections on the March 2010 ICC Kenya Decisions' (2010) 23 LJIL 855 ('Kreß, 'On the Outer Limits of Crimes against Humanity'') 866.
34 *Ibid* 866.
35 David Luban, 'A Theory of Crimes against Humanity' (2004) 29 Yale J Int'l L 85 ('Luban, 'A Theory of Crimes against Humanity''), 117; see also Richard Vernon, 'What is Crime against Humanity?' (2002) 10 J Pol Phil 231 (making a similar argument).
36 Luban, 'A Theory of Crimes against Humanity' (n 35) 120 ('Great depravity by itself does not distinguish crimes against humanity from the cruelest deeds that municipal systems criminalize.').
37 See, eg, Robinson, 'A Better Policy' (n 25) 2–3 (asserting that 'there is ample customary law authority for a policy element, if it is understood as a modest threshold'); Leila Nadya Sadat, 'Crimes Against Humanity in the Modern Age' (2013) 107 AJIL 334, 376 (suggesting that the policy element should be interpreted as a minimal threshold); Robert Cryer et al, *An Introduction to International Criminal Law and Procedure* (CUP 2010) 240 ('For those jurisdictions that apply a policy element, the policy element must be interpreted in accordance with the previous jurisprudence as a modest threshold that excludes random action.').

Some argue that future definitions of crimes against humanity, including in any convention, should omit the requirement altogether.[38]

These scholars are not satisfied with defining crimes against humanity in reference to 'the typical case.' Instead, they highlight the ways in which crimes not committed by states and state-like organizations can shock humanity's conscience. They point out, for instance, that a single terrorist is capable of poisoning a city's water supply,[39] and that technology increasingly enables various kinds of groups to coordinate violence in ways that do not mimic the behavior of states.[40] Charles Jalloh notes that tribes may not constitute 'state-like organizations' but may nonetheless be capable of the kinds of crimes that shock humanity.[41] Advocates of the broader approach also assert that a formal policy of a state or state-like organization is not the only way to distinguish crimes against humanity from national crimes. In particular, they argue that such crimes may also be distinguishable by the magnitude of the harm they inflict, as reflected in the 'widespread' alternative requirement in many definitions.[42]

Darryl Robinson has staked out a position somewhere between these two groups. Professor Robinson argues that the idea of 'widespread' harm is not sufficient to distinguish crimes against humanity from 'ordinary' crimes because it encompasses situations where states have a high rate of unconnected serious crimes.[43] He rejects the arguments of some scholars that the requirement of an 'attack' sufficiently screens out such situations, on the grounds that the term 'attack' lacks precision.[44] At the same time, he believes that the kind of strictly defined policy that some of the ICC jurisprudence has required makes the crimes too difficult to prove, and excludes crimes that should qualify from the definition.[45] As such, he argues that a widely defined

---

38   See Charles Chernor Jalloh, '(Re)defining Crimes Against Humanity' in Larry May & Elizabeth Edenberg (eds), *Just Post Bellum and Transitional Justice* (CUP 2013) 118; Matt Halling, 'Push the Envelope – Watch it Bend: Removing the Policy Requirement – Extending Crimes Against Humanity' (2010) 23 LJIL 827, 827 ('Halling, 'Push the Envelope"); Guenael Mettraux, 'The Definition of Crimes Against Humanity and the Question of a 'Policy' Element' in Sadat, *Forging a Convention for Crimes against Humanity* (n 2).

39   Kai Ambos & Steffen Wirth, 'The Current Law of Crimes Against Humanity: An Analysis of UNTAET Regulation 15/2000' (2002) 13 Crim LF 1, 17.

40   See eg, Jalloh, 'What Makes a Crime against Humanity a Crime against Humanity?' (n 38) 417.

41   *Ibid* 430.

42   See Charles Chernor Jalloh, *The Sierra Leone Special Court and its Legacy* (CUP 2013) 213.

43   Robinson, 'A Better Policy' (n 25) 3.

44   *Ibid* 4.

45   *Ibid* 27.

policy of a broadly defined organization is required to justify international jurisdiction.[46]

In resolving this debate, the drafters of a convention on crimes against humanity should recognize that the different positions reflect divergent beliefs about the goals that should animate the definition of crimes against humanity. Those advocating the more stringent policy requirement focus on establishing a clear distinction between crimes against humanity and 'ordinary' crimes. Although they acknowledge that establishing this distinction via the policy element may exclude some crimes that shock humanity's conscience, they are willing to bear that cost to gain the benefits of a clear distinction. They emphasize that a clear distinction protects state sovereignty and encourages states to join regimes governing crimes against humanity.[47]

Those advocating a broader definition, on the other hand, are more concerned with ensuring that all of the crimes that shock humanity's conscience are included than with establishing a clear distinction between such crimes and crimes under national jurisdiction. They admit that states are usually willing, and at least as able as international courts, to prosecute crimes in which the state is not complicit. Nonetheless, in the minority of cases where crimes that shock humanity's conscience occur without state complicity and no state is willing and able to prosecute, the international community should have the ability to step in.[48]

4 Conclusion: Defining Crimes against Humanity for an International Convention

The drafters of an international convention on crimes against humanity should privilege the goal of capturing the range of crimes that may shock humanity's conscience over that of establishing a clear distinction between international and national crimes. First, it is particularly important for an international convention

---

46 Ibid 7.
47 Kreß, 'On the Outer Limits of Crimes against Humanity' (n 33) 861 ('The existence of sovereignty interests which militate in favor of confining the use of the international criminal law instrument to certain forms and constellations of human rights violations is rather obvious.'); M Cherif Bassiouni, *Crimes Against Humanity in International Criminal Law* (2nd Rev Ed, Kluwer Law Int'l 1999) 243, 246 (arguing that without a state policy requirement there would be too much uncertainty about what constitutes a crime against humanity).
48 Leila Sadat grounds her recommendation for a broad definition in empirical data showing that crimes against humanity are likely to be central to the work of the ICC. See Leila Nadya Sadat, 'Crimes Against Humanity in the Modern Age' (2013) 107 AJIL 334.

to avoid creating an impunity gap. It is impossible to predict what future crimes the international community may wish to condemn as crimes against humanity, making it essential that the definition be sufficiently broad. Moreover, the definition will govern prosecutions of crimes against humanity not only in international courts, but also in national courts and perhaps 'hybrid'[49] courts as well. National communities may, legitimately, have different visions of what crimes constitute crimes against humanity; and such differences should be accommodated by a broad international definition. Finally, leaving the definition broad will enable it to evolve as the norms of the international community change.

While it is important to protect state sovereignty by limiting the reach of international courts and tribunals, this can be accomplished in ways other than adopting restrictive definitions of international crimes. For courts that are created to address particular situations, whether *ad hoc* tribunals or hybrid courts, the international community can be careful to create the institutions only for situations where the legitimacy of supra-national adjudication is beyond dispute. With regard to the ICC, the international community can develop mechanisms to ensure that the Court only becomes involved in situations that merit international involvement. To some extent, such mechanisms already exist. As Allison Danner notes, the ICC prosecutor is more accountable to the international community than is commonly acknowledged.[50] If states are not satisfied with existing accountability mechanisms, however, they can institute additional safeguards, such as requiring outside approval before the ICC may engage in particular situations.[51]

A broad definition will require either omitting the Rome Statute's policy requirement from the convention or specifying that it should be interpreted broadly.[52] The group of international experts that has been working to promote a convention on crimes against humanity concluded that modifying the Rome Statute definition would be a mistake.[53] Many states have already implemented

---

49 Hybrid courts, such as the Special Court for Sierra Leone, have elements of international and national courts.

50 See Allison Marston Danner, 'Enhancing the Legitimacy and Accountability of Prosecutorial Discretion at the International Criminal Court' (2003) 97 AJIL 510.

51 See Alexander KA Greenawalt, 'Justice without Politics? Prosecutorial Discretion and the International Criminal Court' (2006) 39 NYU J of Int'l L and Politics 583, 664–70 (suggesting a system of deference to political bodies under some circumstances).

52 Robinson has suggested amending the ICC's Elements of Crimes to clarify the policy element. See Robinson, 'A Better Policy' (n 25) 28.

53 Sadat, 'Forging a Convention' (n 2) 58 ('Such a treaty should retain the definition of the ICC's article 7 in order to build on the consensus already existing between 114 States that are ICC States Parties').

the Rome Statute's definition in their national laws, and changing the definition at this stage would generate confusion and conflict in the law. The better course therefore is for the drafters of the convention to specify that the policy element can be satisfied by virtually any kind of organization and policy. The element's purpose is essentially to exclude the kinds of unconnected individual crimes that most people agree do not constitute crimes against humanity.

The convention on crimes against humanity should thus reflect Professor Clark's view that the 'substance' of these crimes is not as restricted as the appropriate reach of particular courts. As to what that 'substance' entails, the convention is unlikely to resolve that difficult question.

CHAPTER 20

Towards a New Global Treaty on Crimes Against Humanity

*Leila Nadya Sadat**

On 17 July 2014, an historic, but little-noticed, event occurred: The United Nations International Law Commission ('ILC') voted to move the topic of a new treaty on crimes against humanity to its active agenda and appoint a Special Rapporteur.[1] The expectation is that the Rapporteur will prepare, and the Commission will debate, a complete set of Draft Articles which will be sent to the United Nations General Assembly in due course. This could lead to the adoption of a new global treaty on crimes against humanity, filling a normative gap that has persisted for nearly seventy years.

This essay asks why, and whether, the international community should finally codify crimes against humanity in an international convention, particularly given its recent inclusion in the Statute of the International Criminal Court ('ICC'). It considers the normative foundations and practical application of crimes against humanity by international and national courts, and how a new treaty might strengthen both the preventive and punishment dimensions of national and international responses to these crimes. It is a particularly appropriate contribution to a festschrift in honor of Roger Clark, as his work on the Nuremberg trials[2] was some of the very earliest reading I did on the subject in 1992, when the notion of a permanent international criminal court was just a dream, and one could not have imagined the court we have today, nor the progress that has been made in the fight against impunity.

---

* I am grateful to Madaline George, Ashley Hammett and Douglas Pivnichny for their superb assistance. Nothing in this essay represents or should be construed as representing the views of the ICC Prosecutor or any organ of the Court.
1 International Law Commission, 'Daily Bulletin' (18 July 2014), at <http://legal.un.org/ilc/sessions/66/jourchr.htm> accessed 30 January 2015. The Rapporteur's charge is to prepare a First Report on the subject, which will begin the process of proposing Draft Articles to the Commission for its approval. The First Report would normally be circulated within the Commission and discussed at its next session in summer 2015.
2 Roger S Clark, 'Crimes Against Humanity at Nuremberg', in George Ginsburgs & V N Kudriavtsev (eds) *The Nuremberg Trial and International Law* (Kluwer 1990).

1   Crimes against Humanity and Customary International Law

The concept of crimes against humanity emerged as a response to inhumane acts that transgressed the bounds of 'civilized' behavior, even when committed by a government or Head of State, and particularly if carried out on a massive scale. Over time, they have become a residual category, addressing atrocities that cannot be categorized either as war crimes (because they address evils not within the purview of the laws of war or because they take place outside of armed conflict) or as genocide within the meaning of the Genocide Convention of 1948, because they do not represent the intentional destruction of one of the four groups (racial, religious, national or ethnic) it protects. They are controversial because they not only describe as *immoral* certain acts of government (and, later, non-state actors) but label them *criminal*—depriving the officials and other perpetrators accused of such crimes of defenses they might wield as a function of state sovereignty. Moreover, released from their original moorings through the development of customary international law and their codification in the Rome Statute for the ICC, they have now come to represent attacks carried out not only during inter-state conflict, but in intra-state armed conflict, or even peace time, as well, as discussed below, and attacks by State and non-State actors.[3]

It was not until World War II that a serious effort to set out the specific parameters of 'crimes against humanity' in an international agreement occurred.[4] 'Crimes against humanity' were specifically included in the Charters of the International Military Tribunals at Nuremberg[5] and Tokyo[6] after a great deal of negotiation which focused much more on the aggressive war and war crimes charges. In early drafts, what became crimes against humanity were referred to as 'atrocities and persecutions and deportations on political, racial

---

3   Rome Statute of the International Criminal Court (adopted 17 July 1998, entered into force 1 July 2002) 2187 UNTS 90 ('Rome Statute') art 7(2)(a). Some of the early writings on crimes against humanity insisted that they were autonomous from war crimes and crimes against peace. See eg Eugene Aroneanu, *Le crime contre l'humanité* (Dalloz 1961) 20–21.
4   There were earlier references to the term in the 19th Century and in the three-power declaration issued condemning the massacre of the Armenians in 1915. See Clark, 'Crimes Against Humanity at Nuremberg' (n 2) 177–78.
5   Agreement for the Prosecution and Punishment of Major War Criminals of the European Axis, and Establishing the Charter of the International Military Tribunal (adopted 8 August 1945, entered into force 8 August 1945) 82 UNTS 279 ('IMT Charter').
6   Charter of the International Military Tribunal for the Far East (adopted 19 January 1946, entered into force 19 January 1946, amended 26 April 1946) (1946) TIAS 1589 ('IMFTE Charter').

or religious grounds.'[7] It was not until the London conference and the signing of the Charter on 8 August 1945 ('London Charter') that the term 'crimes against humanity' appeared. A note by Robert Jackson indicated that the intention was to make sure that 'we are reaching persecution, etc., of Jews and others in Germany as well as outside of it, and before as well as after commencement of the war.'[8] Apparently, Sir Hersch Lauterpacht proposed the addition to the text at a meeting with Robert Jackson, during which he put forward the idea of presenting the case against the accused under the three principal headings we know today: crimes against peace, war crimes and crimes against humanity.[9] This ensured the entry of the term 'crimes against humanity' into the international legal lexicon, and perhaps obscured the fact that this was in many ways the most revolutionary of the charges upon which the accused were indicted and convicted, given that its foundations in international law were so fragile.[10]

The proceedings at Nuremberg did not themselves focus greatly on crimes against humanity; the Tokyo trials even less so. Article 6(c) of the London Charter defined them as:

> Namely, murder, extermination, enslavement, deportation, and other inhumane acts committed against any civilian population, before or during the war, or persecutions on political, racial or religious grounds in execution of or in connection with any crime within the jurisdiction of the Tribunal whether or not in violation of the domestic law of the country where perpetrated.[11]

---

[7] United States Department of State, 'Revised Draft of Agreement and Memorandum Submitted by American Delegation, June 30, 1945', *Report of Robert H Jackson, United States Representative to the International Conference on Military Trials, London 1945* (Publication 3080, 1949) 119, 121.

[8] United States Department of State, 'Notes on Proposed Definition of "Crimes", Submitted by American Delegation, July 31, 1945', *Report of Robert H Jackson, United States Representative to the International Conference on Military Trials, London 1945* (Publication 3080, 1949) 394.

[9] Elihu Lauterpacht, *The Life of Sir Hersch Lauterpacht* (CUP 2010) 272; See also Philippe Sands, 'My Legal Hero: Hersch Lauterpacht', *The Guardian* (London, 11 November 2010), at <http://www.theguardian.com/law/2010/nov/10/my-legal-hero-hersch-lauterpacht> accessed 31 January 2015; Martti Koskenniemi, 'Hersch Lauterpacht and the Development of International Criminal Law' (2004) 2 JICJ 810, 811; Philippe Sands, 'Twin Peaks: The Hersch Lauterpacht Draft Nuremberg Speeches' (2013) 1 CJICL 37, 37.

[10] The other was the crime of waging an aggressive war. Professor Clark discusses the negotiating history in detail. See Clark, 'Crimes Against Humanity at Nuremberg' (n 2) 180–90.

[11] IMT Charter (n 5) art 6(c). The definition in the IMFTE Charter was similar, but removed the reference to persecution on 'religious grounds': IMFTE Charter (n 6) art 5(c).

Although the indictment charged twenty of the twenty-two defendants at Nuremberg with crimes against humanity, it was not very specific as to what crimes the accused had committed which fell within that rubric. The Prosecution's theory was essentially that the accused, by debasing the 'sanctity of man in their own countries...affront[ed] the International Law of mankind'[12] and in all but two cases in which crimes against humanity were charged, the crimes against humanity charges were brought in parallel with war crimes charges and often charges of crimes against peace. The judgment of the Tribunal was similarly non-specific, acknowledging that crimes against humanity were somehow different than war crimes, but providing little interpretative guidance as to their elements. The preoccupation of the Tribunal as regards these charges was evidently the 'Final Solution', and Hitler's attempted extermination of European Jews. The two accused, Julius Streicher and Baldur von Schirach, who were found guilty only of crimes against humanity, were convicted of 'incitement to murder and extermination' on the basis of virulently anti-Jewish propaganda (Streicher) and of deporting Jews from Vienna (von Schirach).[13] As Roger Clark notes in his assessment of the judgment, the 'core of the concept of Nazi crimes against humanity' was terror and persecution—including mass murder and concentration camps—'directed at political opponents and Jews'.[14] As he notes, however, this relatively cautious approach to the London Charter seems attributable more to the Tribunal's focus upon its own jurisdiction and interpretation of the Charter than an attempt to 'make a pronouncement about the concept of crimes against humanity in general.'[15]

Following the trials, the principles embodied in the IMT Charter and Judgment were adopted by the General Assembly in 1946,[16] and codified by the International Law Commission in 1950 which largely retained the Nuremberg definition.[17] In this way, crimes against humanity were transformed from rhetorical flourish to a category of offences condemned by international law for which individuals could be tried and punished. During the same period, the

---

12 Egon Schwelb, 'Crimes Against Humanity' (1946) 23 BYBIL 178, 198–99, citing Sir Hartley Shawcross, 'Closing Address' (Nuremberg Tribunal, 26 July 1946).
13 'Judicial Decisions: International Military Tribunal (Nuremberg) Judgment and Sentences, October 1, 1946' (1947) 41 AJIL 172, 296, 310–11 ('IMT Judgment').
14 Clark, 'Crimes Against Humanity at Nuremberg' (n 2) 195.
15 Ibid.
16 'Affirmation of the Principles of International Law Recognized by the Charter of the Nuremberg Tribunal' UNGA Res 95 (1) (11 December 1946) UN Doc A/64/Add.1, 188.
17 'Documents of the Second Session Including the Report of the Commission to the General Assembly' (1950) 2 UNYBILC 374.

Geneva Conventions of 1949 on the laws of war were adopted,[18] as was the Genocide Convention, covering a certain narrow category of crimes against humanity.[19] No comprehensive treaty on crimes against humanity was ever proposed or negotiated, however, and customary international law often continued to link it to the commission of crimes against peace or war crimes, a requirement that was not definitively removed until 1998, when the Rome Statute for the ICC finally permanently abolished the linkage, thereby acknowledging its autonomous nature.

Crimes against humanity under customary international law percolated into the legal systems of a handful of countries that had domesticated the crime, such as Canada, France, and Israel, and certain elements of their prohibition could be found in new international instruments prohibiting torture and apartheid.[20] Israel prosecuted Adolf Eichmann,[21] and France conducted a series of trials relying essentially upon Article 6(c) of the Nuremberg Charter, convicting not only Klaus Barbie, the infamous 'Butcher of Lyon', but two French participants in the Vichy regime.[22] However, these cases were the

---

18   Geneva Convention (I) for the Amelioration of the Condition of the Wounded and Sick in Armed Forces in the Field (adopted 12 August 1941, entered into force 21 October 1950) 75 UNTS 31 (First Geneva Convention); Geneva Convention (II) for the Amelioration of the Condition of the Wounded and Sick and Shipwrecked Members of Armed Forces at Sea (adopted 12 August 1949, entered into force 21 October 1950) 75 UNTS 85 (Second Geneva Convention); 1949 Geneva Convention (III) Relative to the Treatment of Prisoners of War (adopted 12 August 1949, entered into force 21 October 1950) 75 UNTS 135 (Third Geneva Convention); Geneva Convention (IV) Relative to the Protection of Civilian Persons in Time of War (adopted 12 August 1949, entered into force 21 October 1950) 75 UNTS 85 (Second Geneva Convention) UNTS 287 (Fourth Geneva Convention).

19   Convention on the Prevention and Punishment of the Crime of Genocide, (adopted 9 December 1948, entered into force 12 January 1951) 78 UNTS 277 (Genocide Convention).

20   See International Convention on the Suppression and Punishment of the Crime of Apartheid (adopted 30 November 1973, entered into force 18 July 1976) 1015 UNTS 243; Convention against Torture and Other Cruel, Inhuman or Degrading Treatment or Punishment (adopted 10 December 1984, entered into force 26 June 1987) 1465 UNTS 85; Organization of American States, Inter-American Convention to Prevent and Punish Torture (adopted 9 December 1985, entered into force 28 February 1987) OASTS 67; Council of Europe, European Convention for the Prevention of Torture and Inhuman or Degrading Treatment or Punishment (adopted 26 November 1987, entered into force 1 February 1989) ETS 126.

21   *Attorney General of the State of Israel v Adolf Eichmann* (1994) 36 ILR 5, affd 36 ILR 277.

22   See eg Leila Sadat Wexler, 'The Interpretation of the Nuremberg Principles by the French Court of Cassation: From Touvier to Barbie and Back Again' (1994) 32 Colum J Transnat'l L 296.

exception, not the rule, and all involved a link to World War II. Latin American jurisprudence on crimes against humanity has only more recently begun truly to develop, notably in Peru, Argentina and most recently Ecuador, following decades of sweeping amnesty laws, and a lack of political will or domestic codification under which to prosecute these crimes.[23] But even though the commission of mass atrocities continued apace during the second half of the twentieth century,[24] there was little accountability imposed upon those ostensibly responsible, whether government officials or military leaders, rebels, insurgents or low-level perpetrators.[25] And, there was no talk of a new convention on crimes against humanity, although the ILC continued to work on defining the crime under customary international law.[26]

---

23 Jo-Marie Burt, 'Challenging Impunity in Domestic Courts: Human Rights Prosecutions in Latin America' in Félix Reátegui (ed) *Transitional Justice: Handbook for Latin America* (Brasilian Amnesty Commission, Ministry of Justice 2011) 285. Many human rights violations in Latin America are charged as something other than 'crimes against humanity,' however reference and discussion of such has found its way into various judgments, including that of former Peruvian president Alberto Fujimori. Jo-Marie Burt, 'Guilty as Charged: The Trial of former Peruvian President Alberto Fujimori for Grave Violations of Human Rights' (2009) 3 IJTJ 384, 398–99. Moreover, Argentina has successfully prosecuted former Generals for crimes against humanity committed in the 1970s and 1980s, while Ecuador is currently proceeding with its first crimes against humanity trial. For a comprehensive analysis of the codification of crimes against humanity in Latin American states, see Ramiro García Falconí, 'The Codification of Crimes Against Humanity in the Domestic Legislation of Latin American States' (2010) 10 IntCLR 453.

24 A recent study suggested that from 1945 to 2008, between 92 and 101 million persons were killed in 313 different conflicts, the majority of whom were civilians. In addition to those killed directly in these events, others died as a consequence, or had their lives shattered in other ways—through the loss of property, victimization by sexual violence, disappearances, slavery and slavery-related practices, deportations and forced displacements and torture. M Cherif Bassiouni, 'Assessing Conflict Outcomes: Accountability and Impunity' in M Cherif Bassiouni (ed), *The Pursuit of International Criminal Justice: A World Study on Conflicts, Victimization, and Post-Conflict Justice* (Intersentia 2010) 6.

25 In 1989, the Cold War ended with the fall of the Berlin Wall and this began to change. The International Criminal Court project, which had lain fallow, was restarted with the introduction of a resolution into the General Assembly by Trinidad and Tobago, leading a coalition of 16 Caribbean nations, and the continuation of work on the Draft Code of Crimes at the International Law Commission. See 'Report of the Commission to the General Assembly on the work of its Forty-Eighth Session' (1996) 2 UNYBILC 15; see also Leila Nadya Sadat, *The International Criminal Court and the Transformation of International Law: Justice for the New Millennium* (Martinus Nijhoff 2002).

26 The ILC took up the question of crimes against humanity as part of its work on the Draft Code of Crimes Against the Peace and Security of Mankind which was finalized in 1996,

2   What Difference Could a Treaty Make?

The absence of a comprehensive treaty on crimes against humanity did not mean that international law did not prohibit their commission. The Statute of the International Court of Justice ('ICJ') identifies the sources of international law as including not only 'international conventions' but 'international custom, as evidence of a general practice accepted as law' and 'general principles of law recognized by civilized nations.'[27] While treaties are listed first, in Article 38(1)(a), followed by custom (paragraph (b)), and then general principles (paragraph (c)), it has been generally understood that the order in which the sources of law are listed in Article 38 does not establish a strict hierarchy amongst them, but instead are listed in the order in which a judge would typically consult them in addressing a particular legal question.[28] Thus, to the extent crimes against humanity remained part of customary international law but were not codified in an international convention (other than the 1945 Nuremberg Charter), they could still presumably be the basis for future prosecutions or a basis of State responsibility. At the same time, the absence of a clear definition, and the crime's continued linkage to other offenses (crimes against peace and war crimes), made it a clumsy rubric at best, and incomplete and ineffective at worst. Moreover, under the legality principle, which requires crimes to be defined prior to prosecution and also requires them to be defined to a certain level of particularity, it is not clear that prosecuting an individual for violating customary international law—without a clear Statute defining it—is consistent with modern understandings of human rights law. Indeed, when the ILC considered *not* defining the crimes in the Rome Statute, but simply listing them, the nearly unanimous response of commentators was that this would violate the principle of legality.[29]

---

but never adopted. 'Report of the International Law Commission on the Work of its Forth-Eighth Session' (1996) 2 UNYBILC 17, 45.

[27]   Statute of the International Court of Justice (adopted 26 June 1945, entered into force 24 October 1945) 33 UNTS 993 art 3(1).

[28]   See eg Ian Brownlie, *Principles of Public International Law* (7th edn, OUP 2008) 5.

[29]   The International Law Commission took the position that the draft statute was primary an 'adjectival and procedural instrument,' and therefore did not define the crimes. UNGA Draft Statute for the International Criminal Court, Report of the International Law Commission UN GAOR 49th Sess Supp 16, UN Doc A/49/10 (1994). This position was criticized by most experts, and ultimately the Preparatory Committee for the Court and later the Diplomatic Conference assumed the task of setting out complete definitions of the three crimes currently in the Court's jurisdiction. See eg Leila Sadat, 'The Proposed Permanent International Criminal Court: an Appraisal' (1996) 29(3) Cornell Int'l L J 665, 667.

Thus, while customary international law remains important to international criminal law, the practice with respect to this sub-specialty has been to adopt treaties defining crimes and imposing obligations upon States to enact penal legislation, to prevent the crimes (in some cases), to extradite or try the offenders and to cooperate with each other in the apprehension, trial and even serving of the accused's sentence. There are now more than 318 international criminal law conventions, covering twenty-four general categories of international crime including terrorism, drug trafficking, hostage taking, aircraft hijacking, environmental crimes, non-applicability of statutes of limitations, apartheid, genocide, torture, unlawful use of weapons, aggression, piracy, bribery, environmental protection, corruption, destruction of cultural property and theft of nuclear materials, each one of which contains some combination of definitional provisions, provisions for interstate cooperation and other provisions related to the enforcement of the treaty itself.[30]

A few examples may be useful to illustrate the difficulties engendered by the absence of a treaty covering crimes against humanity. In the 1990s, when war broke out in the former Yugoslavia, and the Rwandan genocide took place, the international community once more reached for the Nuremberg precedent only to find that it had failed to finish that project. This made the task of elaborating statutes for the two new ad hoc Tribunals difficult and complex. The uncertainty in the law was evidenced by the texts of the Statutes for the International Criminal Tribunals for the former Yugoslavia ('ICTY') and Rwanda ('ICTR') adopted by the Security Council in 1993 and 1994 respectively. Although similar in many respects, they contained different and arguably contradictory definitions of crimes against humanity. The ICTY Statute, for example, included a link to armed conflict whereas the ICTR Statute did not. Conversely, the ICTR Statute required a persecutory or discriminatory element in its chapeau, which the ICTY Statute did not. These substantive and potentially important variations in the definition of the crime were difficult to square with the idea of universal international crimes under customary international law.[31] Cherif Bassiouni underscored this problem in an important but

---

30 Jordan J Paust, M Cherif Bassiouni, et al., *International Criminal Law: Cases and Materials* (4th ed, Carolina Academic Press 2013) 17–18.
31 *See, eg* UNSC Res 827 (1993) UN Doc S/RES/827 (ICTY Statute); UNSC Res 955 (1994) UN Doc S/RES/955 (ICTR Statute); Agreement for the Prosecution and Punishment of the Major War Criminals of the European Axis (adopted 8 August 1945, entered into force 8 August 1945) 8 UNTS 270 (IMT Statutes for Tokyo); and Control Council Law No. 10, Punishment of Persons Guilty of War Crimes, Crimes against Peace and Humanity (1946) 3 Official Gazette of the Control Council for Germany also differed slightly from the Nuremberg definition.

little-noticed article, in which he lamented the 'existence of a significant gap in the international normative proscriptive scheme, one which is regrettably met by political decision makers with shocking complacency.'[32]

At the international level, then, the absence of a clear definition led to some difficulties in the elaboration of the Statutes for the ad hoc international criminal tribunals.[33] Equally problematic was the inability to use national or hybrid mechanisms to pursue accountability under universal jurisdiction. A case in point is the Cambodian 'genocide.'[34] From 1975 to 1979, the Khmer Rouge regime killed an estimated 1.7 to 2.5 million Cambodians, out of a total population of seven million.[35] For the most part, individuals were killed, tortured, starved or worked to death by the Khmer Rouge not because of their appurtenance to a particular racial, ethnic, religious or national group—the four categories to which the Genocide Convention applies—but because of their political or social classes, or the fact that they could be identified as intellectuals.[36] While theories have been advanced suggesting ways that the Genocide Convention applied to these atrocities[37] and the Co-Prosecutors in Case 2/2 at the Extraordinary Chambers in the Courts of Cambodia (ECCC) have argued that some groups were exterminated *qua* groups—such as the Cham Muslims and the Vietnamese[38]—most experts agree that:

---

32   M Cherif Bassiouni, '"Crimes Against Humanity": The Need for a Specialized Convention' (1994) 31(3) Colum J Transnat'l L. 457, 457.

33   The Statute of the Special Court for Sierra Leone is not identical to either the ICTY, the ICTR or the ICC Statute, although it was adopted in 2002. See Statute of the Special Court for Sierra Leone, U.N.-Sierra Leone, art 2, (adopted 16 January 2002, entered into force 12 April 2002) 2178 UNTS 149, which provides that the Court

shall have the power to prosecute persons who committed the following crimes as part of a widespread or systematic attack against any civilian population: a. Murder; b. Extermination; c. Enslavement; d. Deportation; e. Imprisonment; f. Torture; g. Rape, sexual slavery, enforced prostitution, forced pregnancy and any other form of sexual violence; h. Persecution on political, racial, ethnic or religious grounds; i. Other inhumane acts.

34   Gareth Evans, 'Crimes Against Humanity and the Responsibility to Protect' in Leila Nadya Sadat (ed) *Forging a Convention for Crimes Against Humanity* ('Sadat, *Forging a Convention*').

35   Cf Craig Etcheson, *After the Killing Fields: Lessons from the Cambodian Genocide* (Praeger 2005) 118–120.

36   Cf Samantha Power, *A Problem From Hell: America and the Age of Genocide* (Harper Perennial 2002) 87–154.

37   See Hurst Hannum, 'International Law and Cambodian Genocide: The Sounds of Silence' (1989) 11 HRQ 82 (describing the mass atrocities in Cambodia as an 'auto genocide').

38   *Prosecutor v. Nuon, Ieng, Khieu & Ieng* (Closing Order) (2010) Extraordinary Chambers in the Courts of Cambodia paras 1336–42, 1343–49 <http://www.eccc.gov.kh/sites/default/files/documents/courtdoc/D427Eng.pdf> accessed 31 January 2015.

> [F]or all its compelling general moral authority the Genocide Convention had absolutely no legal application to the killing fields of Cambodia, which nearly everyone still thinks of as the worst genocide of modern times. Because those doing the killing and beating and expelling were of exactly the same nationality, ethnicity, race and religion as those they were victimizing—and their motives were political, ideological and class-based...the necessary elements of specific intent required for its application were simply not there.[39]

This raised problems at the ECCC, as Prosecutors were forced to rely upon crimes against humanity, and in the absence of a treaty had to prove that it did not violate the legality principle to indict the accused on that ground for their conduct in the 1970s, a laborious task given its lack of codification.[40] Likewise, prior to the ECCC's establishment, when Pol Pot was subsequently arrested in Cambodia in 1997, he could not be tried for genocide. Cambodia could not muster the political will, and other countries lacked the legal infrastructure required. Although many countries such as the Netherlands and Denmark could exercise universal jurisdiction over genocide, torture, terrorism and hijacking, they could not do so over crimes against humanity because no treaty existed setting out a definition of the offense and modalities of inter-state cooperation, including procedures for extradition.[41] Pol Pot died one year later, at the age of 73.[42]

39　Evans, 'Crimes Against Humanity and the Responsibility to Protect' (n 34) 3.
40　*Prosecutor v. Nuon & Khieu* (Case 002/01 Judgment) (2014) Extraordinary Chambers in the Courts of Cambodia paras 16,-17, 411, 416, 426, 435–36 <http://www.eccc.gov.kh/sites/default/files/documents/courtdoc/2014-08-07%2017:04/E313_Trial%20Chamber%20Judgement%20Case%20002_01_ENG.pdf> accessed 31 January 2015. The ECCC addressed each of the crimes against humanity alleged—murder, extermination, persecution on political grounds, and 'other inhumane acts'—and determined that each was recognized 'as a crime against humanity under customary international law by 1975').
41　David Scheffer, *All the Missing Souls: A Personal History of the War Crimes Tribunals* (Princeton UP 2013) 347–49.
42　'Cambodia Tribunal Convicts Khmer Rouge Leaders' *Newsmax* (United States, 7 August 2014), at <http://www.newsmax.com/Newsfront/Cambodia-Khmer-Rouge-Verdict/2014/08/07/id/587422/> accessed on 18 August 2014). The Extraordinary Chambers in the Court of Cambodia have tried three individuals since its establishment in 2003. See Agreements between the United Nations and The Royal Government of Cambodia Concerning the Prosecution Under Cambodian Law of Crimes Committed during the Period of Democratic Kampuchea (adopted 6 June 2003, entered into force 29 April 2005) 43 UNTS 2329.

Likewise, although the *Pinochet* case is often referred to as an example of the power of universal jurisdiction with respect to international crimes, the decision of the House of Lords in *Pinochet III* is more a testament to the requirement of a treaty-based definition of international crime and jurisdiction. The Law Lords, in considering the legality of Pinochet's potential extradition from the UK to Spain for crimes he had allegedly committed in Chile, limited extradition to the crime of torture, committed after the entry into force of the Torture Convention for the UK, Spain and Chile.[43] Without the existence of a treaty—the Torture Convention in this particular case—the *Pinochet* case would not have been successfully prosecuted. Unfortunately, the limitations imposed by the Lords' reliance upon the entry into force of the Torture Convention for all three countries meant that virtually all of the most serious crimes could not be considered.[44] Likewise, in *Belgium v. Senegal*, the ICJ found that Senegal had an obligation to either try or extradite former Chadian leader Hissène Habré who was indicted by the Belgian investigating judge 'as the perpetrator or co-perpetrator, *inter alia* of serious violations of international humanitarian law, genocide, crimes against humanity and war crimes,' but not under customary international law, only under the express provisions of Articles 6 and 7 of the Torture Convention so providing, which applied as both States were parties.[45]

Finally, the case of *Bosnia v. Serbia*[46] evidenced the difficulty created by gaps in States' responsibility for the commission of crimes against humanity. Because the jurisdiction of the ICJ is based on a compromissory clause in the Genocide Convention, the Court's discussion—which centered upon whether the atrocities committed in Bosnia constituted genocide—missed the point. Despite the 200,000 deaths, estimated 50,000 rapes, and 2.2 million people

---

43 *R v. Bow Street Metropolitan Stipendiary Magistrate, Ex parte Pinochet Ugarte (No 3)* [2000] 1 AC 147.
44 *Ibid* 175–76, 179, 188.
45 Questions relating to the *Obligation to Prosecute or Extradite (Belgium v Senegal)* Judgment [2012] ICJ Rep 422, 450 ('[A]ny State party to the Convention may invoke the responsibility of another State party with a view to ascertaining the alleged failure to comply with its obligations *erga omnes partes,* such as those under Article 6, paragraph 2, and Article 7, paragraph 1, of the Convention, and to bring that failure to an end.'). Senegal ultimately opted to try Habré before a special court created for that purpose. 'Senegal: Hissène Habré Court Opens' *Human Rights Weekly* (New York, 8 February 2013), at <http://www.hrw.org/news/2013/02/08/senegal-hissene-habre-court-opens> accessed 31 Jan 2015.
46 *Case Concerning the Application of the Convention on the Prevention and Punishment of the Crime of Genocide (Bosnia & Herzegovina v Serbia & Montenegro)* [2007] ICJ Rep 91 ('*Bosnia & Herzegovina v Serbia & Montenegro*').

forcibly displaced as a result of the Serb ethnic cleansing campaign, genocide was held to have been proven only in the massacre of some 8,000 Muslim men and boys in Srebrenica in July 1995.[47] Although the Court recognized that crimes against humanity had been committed, it could not address them. Had a global treaty on crimes against humanity equipped the ICJ with jurisdiction, the Court could have more fully addressed Bosnia's allegations.[48]

The latter example raises one more difficulty engendered because crimes against humanity do not have their own convention—and that is a tendency to 'overuse' the Genocide Convention because it is the only tool available. This ranges from confusing rhetoric and anger on the part of victim's groups who insist that the wrongs done to them constituted 'genocide', to overly technical discussions by governments and the international community as to whether a particular atrocity constitutes 'genocide' or not, which could give rise to a duty to prevent, not just a requirement of punishment,[49] and to disappointment when an atrocity turns out to be 'only' a crime against humanity, as opposed to a genocide, which implicitly downgrades the significance of crimes against humanity as a legal and sociological category.

From the above examples, we see that the absence of a global treaty on crimes against humanity leads to several categories of difficulties: (1) an impunity gap, in which individuals are unable to be prosecuted or are prosecuted only with difficulty at both the national and international levels; (2) a State responsibility gap, because the definition of crimes against humanity is uncertain and no compromissory clause exists to permit litigation before the ICJ regarding their commission; (3) a situation of definitional uncertainty leading to difficult questions regarding whether a particular atrocity was or was not a crime against humanity; and (4) a downgrading of crimes against humanity and overuse of the Genocide Convention as a legal tool.

---

47   Ibid 297.
48   Article 26 of the Proposed Convention grants such jurisdiction. See 'Proposed International Convention on the Prevention of Crimes Against Humanity' in Appendix 1 in Sadat, *Forging a Convention* (n 34) Appendix 1 (Proposed Convention). The same can also be said for the actions brought to the Court by Croatia and Serbia. See *Case Concerning the Application of the Convention on the Prevention and Punishment of the Crime of Genocide (Croatia v Serbia)* [2008] ICJ Rep 118.
49   See eg Power, *A Problem From Hell* (n 36); *Bosnia & Herzegovina v Serbia & Montenegro* (n 46) para 427 (stating '[t]he obligation on each contracting State to prevent genocide is both normative and compelling. It is not merged in the duty to punish, nor can it be regarded as simply a component of that duty.').

3 Codification of Crimes against Humanity in the ICC Statute: Necessary but Not Sufficient

With the adoption of the ICC Statute in 1998, crimes against humanity were at last defined and ensconced in an international convention. I had the pleasure of working with Roger Clark on the ICC's establishment, before, during and after the Rome Conference, and there is no doubt that adoption of the ICC Statute was a watershed moment in International Law. He served on the ILA Committee on the ICC that I had the honor to chair and participated in the negotiations as legal adviser to the government of Samoa. He was an active participant in the negotiations, and an influential voice. I learned a great deal from him, and was always grateful for his advice on technical issues in the Statute and the practice of the United Nations. In terms of crimes against humanity, the ICC definition is similar to earlier versions, but differs in important respects, such as the requirement that crimes against humanity be committed 'pursuant to a State or organizational policy',[50] and the absence of any linkage to armed conflict. The addition of the policy element continues to elicit controversy, because the ad hoc tribunals rejected that element as a matter of customary international law.[51] Of course, the ICC Statute *by its own terms* did not purport to represent customary law, but only law defined for the purposes of the Statute itself,[52] suggesting that perhaps it is possible for 'Rome

---

50   Rome Statute (n 3) art 7(2)(a).

51   *Prosecutor v. Kunarac* (Judgment) 2002 <http://www.icty.org/x/cases/kunarac/acjug/en/kun-aj020612e.pdf> accessed 31 January 2015 para 98. The appeals chamber noted that there was some 'debate' in the jurisprudence of the Tribunal on the question whether a policy or plan constitutes an element of crimes against humanity (para 98 note114). The *Kunarac* appeals chamber decision effectively ended the debate. See also *Prosecutor v. Vasiljević* (Judgment) 2002 <http://www.icty.org/x/cases/vasiljevic/tjug/en/vas021129.pdf> accessed 31 January 2015 para 36; *Prosecutor v. Naletilić and Martinović* (Judgment) 2003 <http://www.icty.org/x/cases/naletilic_martinovic/tjug/en/nal-tj030331-e.pdf> accessed 31 January 2015 para 234; *Prosecutor v.* Blaškić (Judgment) 2004 <http://www.icty.org/x/cases/blaskic/acjug/en/bla-aj040729e.pdf> accessed 31 January 2015 paras 100, 120, 126; *Prosecutor v. Krnojelac* (Judgment) 2002 <http://www.icty.org/x/cases/krnojelac/tjug/en/krn-tj020315e.pdf> accessed 31 January 2015 para 58; *Prosecutor v. Semanza* (Judgment) 2003 <http://www.ictrcaselaw.org/docs/doc37512.pdf> accessed 31 January 2015 para 329; *Prosecutor v. Kajelijeli* (Judgment and Sentence) 2003, <https://www1.umn.edu/humanrts/instree/ICTR/KAJELIJELI_ICTR-98-44A/KAJELIJELI_ICTR-98-44A-T.pdf> accessed 31 January 2015 para 827.

52   See eg Rome Statute art 7(1) ('For the purpose of this Statute, "crime against humanity" means…'). Whether it has *subsequently* come to represent customary international law is the subject of some debate: see Guénaël Mettraux, 'The Definition of Crimes Against Humanity and the Question of a "Policy" Element' in Sadat, *Forging a Convention* (n 34) 142; Kai

law' to be different than customary international law outside the Rome Statute.[53] At the same time, given that the ICC Statute applies to nationals of ICC Non States Parties through the possibility of referral by the Security Council, as well as the Court's territorially based jurisdiction, most have concluded that it is difficult to support the notion of different versions of crimes against humanity law existing inside and outside the ICC Statute, and have suggested that the ICC definition has ultimately come to represent customary international law.[54]

If so, perhaps the ICC Statute is sufficient to fill the gaps identified in the preceding sections flowing from the absence of a treaty on crimes against humanity? Certainly, the negotiation of the ICC Statute arguably solved the question of definitional uncertainty and clearly gave crimes against humanity an autonomous status, definitively delinking it from war crimes against genocide. But, the other gaps and difficulties identified in Part II remain. First, the ICC Statute applies only to cases to be tried before the ICC, that is to a handful of perpetrators from the limited number of cases that fall within the jurisdiction of that court. Unlike the ad hoc tribunals, the ICC has a very broad mandate to not only assist with punishment but also works towards prevention of atrocity crimes, in situations scattered all over the world. Given the Court's small size and limited resources, it has had to be very judicious about limiting the number of cases per situation. This will leave many potential perpetrators outside the reach of the ICC Statute, and other mechanisms will be required to bring them to book.

Second, the ICC Statute does not require States to adopt implementing legislation on the crimes within the Statute, although many have done so and the Statute assumes that they have an obligation to do so.[55] A recent study suggests that thirty-four percent of ICC States Parties do not have legislation on crimes against humanity; the percentage is much higher for non-states parties.[56] Moreover, the ICC Statute provides no vehicle for inter-State cooperation, leaving gaps in mutual legal assistance, extradition and other aspects of the

---

Ambos, 'Crimes Against Humanity and the International Criminal Court' in Sadat, *Forging a Convention* (n 34) 279.

[53] Leila Sadat, 'Custom, Codification and Some Thoughts About the Relationship Between the Two: Article 10 of the ICC Statute' (2000) 35 DePaul LR 909.

[54] Leila Nadya Sadat, 'Crimes Against Humanity in the Modern Age' (2013) 107 AJIL 334, 372–74.

[55] Rome Statute, (n 3) 'Preamble' cl 6.

[56] Arturo J Carrillo & Annalise K Nelson, 'Comparative Law Study and Analysis of National Legislation Relating to Crimes Against Humanity and Extraterritorial Jurisdiction' (2014) 46 Geo Wash Int'l LR 8, 8, 9.

horizontal cooperation needed for the prosecution of atrocity crimes across State borders.

Third, the ICC Statute does not provide for State responsibility but only addresses the possible criminal responsibility of individuals, and does not explicitly impose an obligation upon States to prevent as well as punish crimes against humanity. A new treaty could do so, along the lines of the Genocide Convention, and consistently with the Responsibility to Protect doctrine.[57]

Finally, although 122 States have ratified the ICC Statute at time of writing, many remain outside the system. Just as many of these jurisdictions—like Russia, India and the United States—have ratified the Genocide and Geneva conventions,[58] it is not impossible to imagine that they would support and ultimately ratify a new convention on crimes against humanity. The House of Delegates of the American Bar Association ('ABA') recently adopted—unanimously—a resolution calling for federal legislation and for the United States to take the lead in negotiating a new treaty on crimes against humanity.[59] Although the United States Senate has historically been resistant to the adoption of new treaties addressing human rights, the ABA's vote—and the government's response thus far—suggests that at least in principle the United States might take a positive negotiating position to any new treaty. Interested States could support a crimes against humanity convention, thereby agreeing to the treaty definition of the crime, agree upon the need to prevent, punish and cooperate regarding it, but still take the time they need to become comfortable with the adjudicative jurisdiction of the ICC.

Although it has recently been proposed that a new inter-State mutual legal assistance convention be adopted covering all of the crimes in the ICC Statute,[60] that effort has not received much attention largely because it fills only one of the gaps identified above (inter-State cooperation) and, additionally, is not a realistic alternative for States not party to the ICC Statute, given that they may not have incorporated the ICC crimes into their national legislation and may not, therefore, be in a position to cooperate with other States on questions of mutual legal assistance. It also would not address many of the critical

---

57   *The Responsibility to Protect: Report of the International Commission on Intervention and State Sovereignty* (ICISS 2001).
58   A complete list of ratifications of the Genocide and Geneva Conventions are available at <https://treaties.un.org/> accessed 31 January 2015.
59   American Bar Association Resolution 300 (adopted 18 August 18 2014), at <http://www.americanbar.org/news/reporter_resources/aba-2014-annual-meeting/2014-annual-meeting-house-of-delegates-resolutions/300.html> accessed 30 January 2015.
60   UNGA Draft Res (28 March 2013), 'International Cooperation in the Fight Against the Crime of Genocide, Crimes against Humanity and War Crimes', UN Doc E/CN.15/2013/L.5.

subsidiary elements required for the effective prosecution of atrocity crimes: the non-applicability of Statutes of limitation, the lifting of immunities, setting out modes of liability, and other provisions essential to establishing a comprehensive regime for the prevention and punishment of crimes against humanity.

4   A New Treaty for Crimes against Humanity?: The Crimes against Humanity Initiative and the Task Now before the ILC

A   *The Work of the Crimes against Humanity Initiative*

Concerned about the problems of continued impunity for the commission of atrocity crimes, in 2008, the Whitney R. Harris World Law Institute at Washington University School of Law launched the Crimes Against Humanity Initiative, with three primary objectives: (1) to study the current state of the law and sociological reality as regards the commission of crimes against humanity; (2) to combat the indifference generated by an assessment that a particular crime is 'only' a crime against humanity (rather than a 'genocide'); and (3) to address the gap in the current law by elaborating the first-ever comprehensive specialized convention on crimes against humanity.[61]

The Initiative progressed in phases, each building upon the work of the last. In 2011, the first edition of *Forging a Convention for Crimes Against Humanity* was published, which included a major study of issues that needed to be considered if a new treaty was to be elaborated, as well as a model text of a *Proposed International Convention for the Prevention and Punishment of Crimes Against Humanity* in English and in French.[62] The work was overseen by a Steering Committee of distinguished experts.[63]

During Phase II of the Initiative, papers written by leading experts were presented and discussed at a conference held at Washington University School of

---

[61]   Leila Nadya Sadat, 'A Comprehensive History of the Proposed International Convention on the Prevention and Punishment of Crimes Against Humanity' in Sadat, *Forging a Convention* (n 34) xxiii–iv.

[62]   'Proposed Convention' in Sadat, *Forging a Convention* (n 34) 359. The Proposed Convention can also be found on page 403 in French and on page 503 in Spanish. These texts, as well as Arabic, Chinese, German and Russian translations, are also available at <http://www.crimesagainsthumanity.wustl.edu> accessed 31 January 2015.

[63]   The Steering Committee is composed of Professor M Cherif Bassiouni, Ambassador Hans Corell, Justice Richard Goldstone, Professor Juan Mendez, Professor William Schabas and Judge Christine Van den Wyngaert.

Law on 13–14 April 2009, and then revised for publication.[64] They addressed the legal regulation of crimes against humanity and examined the broader social and historical context within which they occur. Each chapter was commissioned not only to examine the topic's relationship to the elaboration of a future treaty, but to serve as an important contribution to the literature on crimes against humanity in and of itself. Professor Clark contributed a wonderful essay on the history of efforts to codify crimes against humanity.[65]

The papers ranged from technical discussions of specific legal issues such as modes of responsibility, immunities and amnesties, enforcement and gender crimes to broader conceptual treatments of earlier codification efforts, the definition of the crime in the Rome Statute and customary international law, and the phenomenon of ethnic cleansing. Several of the papers contrasted the ICC and ad hoc tribunal definition of crimes against humanity and were very helpful to the discussions as the drafting effort progressed; the same can be said for the many other contributions which addressed specific topics such as crimes against humanity and terrorism, universal jurisdiction, and the Responsibility to Protect.

In discussing the scholarly work, more questions were raised than answered. What was the social harm any convention would protect? Atrocities committed by the State, or a broader concept that would include non-State actors? Would a new legal instrument prove useful in combating atrocity crimes? How would any new instrument interact with the Rome Statute for the ICC? As the initial scholarly work was undertaken, a preliminary draft text of the Convention, prepared by Cherif Bassiouni, was circulated to participants at the April meeting to begin the drafting process. As the *Initiative* progressed, nearly 250 experts were consulted, many of whom submitted detailed comments (orally or in writing) on the various drafts of the proposed convention circulated, or attended meetings convened by the Initiative either in the United States or abroad. Between formal meetings, technical advisory sessions were held during which every comment received—whether in writing or communicated verbally—was discussed as the draft convention was refined. The *Proposed Convention* went through seven major revisions (and innumerable

---

64   One paper was commissioned subsequent to the April meeting based upon the emphasis in that meeting on inter-state cooperation as a principal need to adopt the Convention: Laura M Olson, 'Re-enforcing Enforcement in a Specialized Convention on Crimes Against Humanity: Inter-State Cooperation, Mutual Legal Assistance, and the *Aut Dedere Aut Judicare* Obligation' in Sadat, *Forging a Convention* (n 34) 323.

65   Roger S Clark, 'History of Efforts to Codify Crimes Against Humanity: From the Charter of Nuremberg to the Statute of Rome' in Sadat, *Forging a Convention* (n 34) 8.

minor ones) and was approved by the members of the Steering Committee in August 2010 in English.

The *Proposed Convention* has begun, not ended, the debate. Elaborated by experts without the constraints of government instructions (although deeply cognizant of political realities), it is a platform for discussion by States, the International Law Commission, civil society and academics with a view to the eventual adoption of a United Nations Convention on the Prevention and Punishment of Crimes Against Humanity. The *Proposed Convention* builds upon and complements the ICC Statute by retaining the ICC's definition of crimes against humanity but has added robust interstate cooperation, extradition and mutual legal assistance provisions in Annexes 2–6. Universal jurisdiction was retained (but is not mandatory), and the Rome Statute served as a model for several additional provisions, including Articles 4–7 (Responsibility, Official Capacity, and Non-Applicability of Statute of Limitations) and with respect to final clauses. Other provisions draw upon international criminal law and human rights instruments more broadly, such as the recently negotiated Enforced Disappearance Convention, the Terrorist Bombing Convention, the Convention Against Torture, the United Nations Conventions on Corruption and Organized Crime, The European Transfer of Proceedings Convention, and the Inter-American Criminal Sentences Convention, to name a few.[66]

Yet although the drafting process benefited from the existence of current international criminal law instruments, the creative work of the Initiative was to meld these and our own ideas into a single, coherent model convention that establishes the principle of state responsibility as well as individual criminal responsibility (including the possibility of responsibility for the criminal acts of legal persons) for the commission of crimes against humanity. Thus, Article 1 of the *Proposed Convention* reads:

Article 1 Nature of the Crime

> Crimes against humanity, whether committed in time of armed conflict or in time of peace, constitute crimes under international law for which there is individual criminal responsibility. In addition, States may be held responsible for crimes against humanity pursuant to principles of States responsibility for internationally wrongful acts.[67]

---

66   A complete list can be found in the table at the back of the Proposed Convention in Sadat, *Forging a Convention* (n 34) 398–401, 445–48.
67   Proposed Convention (n 48) art 1.

The *Proposed Convention* innovates in many respects by attempting to bring prevention into the instrument in a much more explicit way than predecessor instruments, by including the possibility of responsibility for the criminal acts of legal persons, by excluding defences of immunities and statutory limitations, by prohibiting reservations, and by establishing a unique institutional mechanism for supervision of the Convention. Echoing its 1907 forbearer, it also contains its own 'Martens Clause' in the Preamble, as follows:

> Declaring that in cases not covered by the present Convention or by other international agreements, the human person remains under the protection and authority of the principles of international law derived from established customs, from the laws of humanity, and from the dictates of the public conscience, and continues to enjoy the fundamental rights that are recognized by international law...[68]

Elaborating the 27 articles and six annexes of the treaty was a daunting challenge, and one that could not have been accomplished without the dedication and enthusiasm of many individuals.[69] The effort has been well-rewarded; in 2010, more than 75 experts endorsed the objectives of the Initiative in a Declaration adopted on 12 March 2010, in Washington, D.C., as did the Prosecutors of the world's international criminal courts and tribunals in the *Kigali Declaration of the Fifth Colloquium of Prosecutors of the International Criminal Tribunals* adopted on 13 November 2009, and the *Fourth Chautauqua Declaration* adopted on 31 August 2010.[70] The *Proposed Convention* has now been translated into

---

[68] Ibid 'Preamble' cl 13.

[69] I am particularly grateful to M Cherif Bassiouni for his extraordinary efforts in leading the drafting effort and his service as a member of the Initiative's Steering Committee, and equally grateful to the other members of the Steering Committee for their leadership. Each member brought tremendous energy and expertise to the project, guiding its methodological development and conceptual design, and carefully reading, commenting upon and debating each interim draft of the Proposed Convention extensively. As with all such projects, many supported, and continue to support, the effort, without being on the front pages of it, so to speak. Their contributions are noted in 'Preface and Acknowledgments', in Sadat, *Forging a Convention* (n 34) xxvi–viii.

[70] 'Declaration on the Need for a Comprehensive Convention on Crimes Against Humanity' reprinted in Sadat, *Forging a Convention* (n 34) 579; 'Kigali Declaration of the Fifth Colloquium of Prosecutors of International Criminal Tribunals' reprinted in Sadat, *Forging a Convention* (n 34) 588; 'The Fourth Chautauqua Declaration' in Sadat, *Forging a Convention* (n 34) 591.

Arabic, Chinese, German, Russian and Spanish, and continues to attract discussion and debate.[71]

B   *The International Law Commission Moves Forward*

The ILC first included the topic of crimes against humanity on its long-term work program in 2013 on the basis of a report prepared by Professor Sean Murphy.[72] The report identified four key elements that a new convention should have: a definition adopting Article 7 of the Rome Statute; an obligation to criminalize crimes against humanity with national legislation; robust interstate cooperation procedures; and a clear obligation to prosecute or extradite offenders.[73] The report also emphasized how a new treaty would complement the Rome Statute.[74]

In autumn 2013, States had an opportunity to comment on the Commission's decision to include the topic in its long-term work program at the General Assembly Sixth Committee. Many States commented favorably on the prospect of a new crimes against humanity convention. Slovenia, for example, stated that 'all efforts should be directed at filling this gap.'[75] Austria, the Czech Republic, Italy, Norway, Peru, Poland and the United States also welcomed the decision.[76] A major focus was the importance of ensuring a new treaty complements the Rome Statute, as the comments of Malaysia and the United

---

71   For a list of the Initiative's activities, see <http://crimesagainsthumanity.wustl.edu/> accessed 31 January 2015.

72   Report to the International Law Commission, Report of the Working Group on the Obligation to Extradite or Prosecute (aut dedere aut judicare) (22 July 2013) UN Doc. A/CN.4/L.829.

73   *Ibid* para 8.

74   *Ibid* paras 9–13.

75   UNGA Sixth Committee (68th Session) 'Statement by Mr. Borut Mahnič' (30 October 2013) 8.

76   UNGA Sixth Committee (68th Session) 'Statement by Gregor Schusterschitz' (28 October 2013), Agenda item 81, 5; UNGA Sixth Committee (68th Session) 'Statement by Mr. Petr Válek' (29 October 2013), Agenda item 81, 3; UNGA Sixth Committee (68th Session) 'Statement by Min. Plenipotentiary Andrea Tiriticco' (29 October 2013), Agenda item 81, 5; UNGA Sixth Committee (68th Session) 'Statement on behalf of the Nordic Countries by Mr. Rolf Einar Fife' (28 October 2013), Agenda item 81, 3–4; UNGA Sixth Committee (68th Session) 'Intervención de la Misión Permanente del Perú' (29 October 2013), Agenda item 81, 2; UNGA Sixth Committee (68th Session) 'Statement by Ambassador Ryszard Sarkowicz' (30 October 2013), Agenda item 81,5; UNGA Sixth Committee (68th Session) 'Statement by the United States' (2013), Agenda item 81, 4.

Kingdom, for example, made clear.[77] Some States questioned the need for a new treaty. For example, Iran stated that it 'does not seem that...there is a legal loophole to be filled through the adoption of a new international instrument.'[78] Other states questioning the need for a treaty included France, Malaysia, Romania and Russia.[79]

In May 2014, prior to the Commission's July session, the Proposed Convention was the basis of an Experts' Meeting held at the Villa Moynier in Geneva bringing together international justice experts and members of the ILC. Participants discussed the need for a new convention, its potential content and the process of building support amongst states. These discussions are summarized in a report published on 17 July 2014.[80] Participants noted the long involvement of the Commission on the subject of crimes against humanity and commented upon the progressive stance of the Commission in de-linking crimes against humanity from armed conflict in its formulation of the Nuremberg Principles. In paragraph 123 of its commentary to *Principles of International Law recognized in the Charter of the Nürnberg Tribunal and in the Judgment of the Tribunal*, the ILC noted 'that [crimes against humanity] may take place also before a war in connection with crimes against peace.'[81] It was also observed that the ILC was nearing completion of its work on the obligation to extradite or prosecute (*aut dedere aut judicare*), and was therefore in an excellent position to take up the question of a new convention on crimes against humanity.

Following this meeting, the ILC voted, on 18 July 2014, to add the topic of crimes against humanity to its active agenda and appointed Professor Murphy as Special Rapporteur. The Rapporteur will prepare draft articles for discussion

---

77 UNGA Sixth Committee (68th Session) 'Statement by Ms. Sarah Khalilah Abdul Rahman' (30 October 2013), Agenda item 81, 1, para 3; UNGA Sixth Committee (68th Session) 'Statement by Mr. Jesse Clarke' (28–30 October 2013) Agenda item 81, 5.

78 UNGA Sixth Committee (68th Session) 'Statement by Professor Djamchid Momtaz' (5 November 2013) Agenda item 81, 7.

79 UNGA Sixth Committee (68th Session) 'Statement by Mrs. Edwige Belliard' (28 October 2013) Agenda item 81, 2; UNGA Sixth Committee (68th Session) 'Statement by Ms. Sarah Khalilah Abdul Rahman', (28–30 October 2013), Agenda item 81, 76; UNGA Sixth Committee (68th Session) 'Statement by Mrs. Alina Orosan' (October 2013) Agenda item 79, 5; UNGA Sixth Committee (68th Session) 'Statement by the Representative of the Russian Federation' (2013) Agenda item 79, 6 (2013).

80 Leila Nadya Sadat & Douglas J Pivnichny, *Fulfilling the Dictates of Public Conscience: Moving Forward with a Convention on Crimes Against Humanity* (Whitney R Harris World Law Institute 17 July 2014) ('Geneva Report').

81 'Report of the International Law Commission on the work of its second session', UN Doc A/1316 para 123 reprinted in (1950) 2 UNYBILC 364, UN Doc A/CN.4/SER.A/1950/Add.1.

by the Commission, and comment by States.[82] Under the ILC's Statute, it can suggest further study at that point, depending upon government reaction; or the convening of a diplomatic conference to negotiate a new treaty.[83] The work could be completed in as little as four years; or could take considerably longer, depending upon the enthusiasm of governments (or not).[84]

5   Conclusion

The Nuremberg legacy suggests that to meet the challenges of a world in which the commission of atrocity crimes is but too common, three elements are required: rules, institutions and enforcement. Rules that govern human behavior, and institutions to assist with the formulation, the application and the enforcement of those rules. Although the ICC is an important step forward in the prevention and punishment of atrocity crimes, without national enforcement, it will have less impact than one might hope for.

When beginning the *Crimes Against Humanity Initiative*, it was daunting to ask both whether it would make a difference, and whether it represented the right step forward. While concerns remain regarding the content of any new treaty that might be negotiated as well as the relationship of any new convention with the Rome Statute, the absence of a global treaty on crimes against humanity means that we are effectively depriving our strongest institutions—national governments—of the tools they need to comprehensively address this most ubiquitous of crimes. It also leaves significant enforcement gaps, and the law may remain unclear, particularly with respect to Rome Non-State Parties. The work of the *Initiative* over the past seven years, as well as the decision taken by the ILC, suggests that the time has come at last to remedy this normative and enforcement gap in international law.

---

[82] International Law Commission, 66th Session 'Provisional Summary Rec of the 3227th Meeting' UN Doc A/CN.4/SR.3227.

[83] Statute of the International Law Commission, arts 16, 17, GA Res 174 (II), UN GAOR, 2nd Sess, UN Doc A/RES/175(II) (21 Nov 1947).

[84] Geneva Report (n 79) para 79.

CHAPTER 21

Challenges in Applying Article 8 of the Rome Statute

Tim McCormack*

1   **The Esteemed Representative of Samoa**

It is a pleasure for me to write in honour of Roger Clark, whom I first met in November 1993. Gerry Simpson and I had travelled to New York to join the Australian Government Delegation to the Sixth Committee of the UN General Assembly for discussions on the International Law Commission's Draft Code of Crimes against the Peace and Security of Mankind. Gerry and Roger had met each other earlier in London and in The Hague at meetings of the International Platform of Jurists for East Timor (IPJET) and had obviously enjoyed each other's company. Roger invited Gerry and I to travel from New York City to Camden, New Jersey to deliver a guest lecture to his JD class at Rutgers University Law School. In classic Roger style, delivering the lecture was insufficient and Gerry and I were not only hosted for dinner but also as overnight guests at Roger's home.

    I instantly warmed to Roger, as so many people do. We share an Antipodean heritage and that was a mutual cause of celebration from the outset, but I also appreciated his genuine warmth, his laconic sense of humour, his laid-back informality and his enthusiasm for our shared intellectual interests. Gerry and I met up with Roger again in 1998 at the Diplomatic Conference in Rome to negotiate the terms of the Rome Statute. As the esteemed representative of Samoa he was thoroughly immersed in the details of the draft text and his revelling in the historic significance of the moment was both infectious and inspiring.

---

*   The views expressed here are those of the author alone and do not necessarily represent the views of the Office of the Prosecutor of the International Criminal Court. The author is deeply grateful for the insightful comments of Bridget Dunne, Madeleine Summers and Natalia Jevglevskaja on an earlier draft of this chapter. Both Bridget and Madeleine served as research assistants to Tim McCormack in the Office of the Prosecutor at the International Criminal Court and are outstanding ambassadors for the Tim Hawkins Memorial Scholarship. Natalia is a PhD candidate at the Melbourne Law School. All three are great researchers and delightful people and Tim is enormously privileged to work with them.

Since the Rome Conference, Roger has regularly returned to successive meetings of the Preparatory Committee and, following entry into force of the Statute, to annual meetings of the Assembly of States Parties. The story of how a professor of international law came to represent the Pacific Island nation of Samoa is a wonderful and enduring testament to Roger's approach to teaching and of the friendships he has formed with many of his former students. Which of his academic colleagues has ever been close to being trusted to represent a foreign government in multilateral treaty negotiations, not as a once-off but repeatedly and for decades?

Roger is never a passenger in the turbulent multilateral world but constantly suggests, prods, pushes, even pleads for an improvement here or for stronger language there. He contributes beyond the plenary (with his regular interventions from the floor) by writing—for academic journals, for NGOs, and for the multilateral process. His writing is never an end in itself. It is never from the perspective of needing to maintain his publication record. Instead, Roger is constantly reflecting on how to make a more meaningful contribution. Even post-retirement from his stellar professorial career, Roger continues to care—and that is not something that can be said of all our professional colleagues.

Roger cares about the International Criminal Court ('ICC') and has worked hard for its institutional success. He has written extensively on many aspects of the Rome Statute and still advocates for reform of many of its provisions. I offer this chapter in tribute to him confident in the assurance that he will be interested in the content and gratified by the sentiment accompanying it.

2   Structure of Article 8 and Characterisation of the Conflict

One glaring feature of Article 8 of the Rome Statute is its sheer bulk. Containing as it does a total of 53 substantive offence provisions, Article 8 dwarfs all other articles in the Rome Statute. Although there was nothing controversial about the inclusion of an article on war crimes in the Statute of the ICC, it is perhaps unsurprising, given the voluminous detail of the provision, that negotiation of Article 8 took some time.[1]

---

1 See Herman von Hebel & Darryl Robinson, 'Crimes Within the Jurisdiction of the Court' in Roy S Lee (ed), *The International Criminal Court: The Making of the Rome Statute—Issues, Negotiations, Results* (Kluwer Law International 1999). The authors explain some of the preparatory discussions leading to the Rome Diplomatic Conference which exposed disagreements about the scope and content of the war crimes jurisdiction of the Rome Statute. Some of the more complex issues were simply deferred for negotiation in Rome and the authors

It is axiomatic that the key contextual element for any war crime is an armed conflict. While the statement itself is uncontroversial, it does raise a semantic question: why does a war crime require the existence of an armed conflict rather than a war? A war only exists following formal declaration by a State. Consequently, all Four Geneva Conventions of 1949 apply 'to all cases of declared war or of any other armed conflict...even if the state of war is not recognized by one of [the parties to the conflict]'.[2] So, as early as 1949, the international community recognised the importance of extending the scope of application of the Geneva Conventions beyond situations involving formal declarations of war. The application of legal constraints on the conduct of military operations ought not to depend upon the political whims of parties to an armed conflict. The shift of focus from formal declarations of war to the factual reality of armed conflict occurred in a broader contemporary context. In the wording of Article 2(4) of the 1945 United Nations Charter, for example, the prohibition is on resort to military force and not on formal declarations of war.[3] That broader scope of application was itself a reaction to the earlier 1922 Covenant of the League of Nations and the 1928 Kellogg-Briand Pact both of which prohibited resort to war as an instrument of national policy. Member States of the League and States Parties to the Pact were able to evade their treaty obligations by simply not formally declaring war.[4] Extending the scope of application of the Geneva Conventions to situations of armed conflict whether or not war is formally declared, or formally recognised by parties to it, is entirely consistent with the earlier approach taken to the drafting of the scope of Article 2(4) of the UN Charter.

Another semantic question arises then: why are they called war crimes and not armed conflict crimes? Technically it would be more accurate to speak of armed conflict crimes but technical accuracy is not the sole determinate for common parlance. The term 'war crimes' enjoys such widespread familiarity and extensive use that it is difficult to imagine even a concerted campaign for

---

identify a number of these issues and the ways in which disagreements were resolved in the final text of Article 8.

2   See art 2 of the four Geneva Conventions: 1949 Geneva Convention (I) for the Amelioration of the Condition of the Wounded and Sick in Armed Forces in the Field art 2; 1949 Geneva Convention (II) for the Amelioration of the Condition of the Wounded and Sick and Shipwrecked Members of Armed Forces at Sea art 2; 1949 Geneva Convention (III) Relative to the Treatment of Prisoners of War art 2; 1949 Geneva Convention (IV) Relative to the Protection of Civilian Persons in Time of War art 2.

3   United Nations, *Charter of the United Nations* (24 October 1945) 1 UNTS XVI, art 2(4).

4   See, for example, Tim McCormack, 'Anticipatory Self-Defence in the Legislative History of the U.N. Charter' (1991) 25 Israel L Rev 1, 8–15.

'armed conflict crimes' having any chance of success. 'War crimes' has become so entrenched in common parlance that it is used to describe the whole gamut of international crimes—including crimes against humanity, genocide and the crime of aggression—even though none of those other categories of international crime require the existence of an armed conflict as a contextual element.[5] In this chapter, I only use the term 'war crimes' to describe serious violations of international humanitarian law.

The offences in Article 8 of the Rome Statute are structured in four key groupings—two of which, Article 8(2)(a) and (b), cover war crimes in international armed conflicts and the other two of which, Article 8(2)(c) and (e) cover war crimes in non-international armed conflicts. The four groupings follow a consistent structural pattern. Article 8(2)(a) and (c), for example, include specific categories of offences derived from particular provisions of the Four Geneva Conventions of 1949 applicable in international and non-international armed conflicts respectively. Article 8(2)(a) lists grave breaches of the Geneva Conventions derived from the specific provisions of each of the Four Conventions and these grave breaches only apply in international armed conflicts. Article 8(2)(c) lists serious violations of Article 3 common to all Four Geneva Conventions which apply in non-international armed conflicts. Article (8)(2)(b) and (e) contain other serious violations of the laws and customs applicable in international and non-international armed conflicts respectively.

One consequence of the wording of Article 8 is that the Prosecution has to form a view of the legal character of an armed conflict whenever it contemplates charges of war crimes. The text of Article 8 requires the Prosecution to prove the contextual element of the specific offence: either that the offence occurred in the context of an international or a non-international armed conflict depending upon the particular charge selected.

Some have argued for a unitary set of crimes applicable in all armed conflicts irrespective of the legal characterisation of a particular armed conflict.[6] There is a certain appeal in the simplicity of such an approach, and it accords

---

5 It is possible of course for crimes of genocide and crimes against humanity to be committed in the context of an armed conflict and to be charged alongside war crimes proper. On this point see Peter Rowe, 'War Crimes' in Dominic McGoldrick, Peter Rowe & Eric Donnelly (eds), *The Permanent International Criminal Court: Legacy and Policy Issues* (Hart Publishing 2004), 203–204. The distinction I am making is that neither genocide nor crimes against humanity require the existence of an armed conflict. Either crime can be perpetrated in war or in peacetime. War crimes cannot be perpetrated other than in an armed conflict.
6 See James G Stewart, 'Towards a Single Definition of Armed Conflict in International Humanitarian Law: A Critique of Internationalized Armed Conflict' (2003) 850 IRRC 313.

well with questions of principle. The focus of international criminal trial proceedings should be on the alleged conduct of the accused rather than on the legal characterisation of the armed conflict. Dov Jacobs, blogging on the ICC Trial Chamber's characterisation of the armed conflict in the Ituri District of the Democratic Republic of the Congo ('DRC') in its judgment on *Prosecutor v Thomas Lubanga Dyilo* ('*Lubanga*'), for example, has articulated some of the frustration here:

> At the outset, it should be pointed out that this is a generally irrelevant point. Indeed, I believe that the drafters of the ICC Statute, by maintaining the strict dichotomy between international and non-international armed conflicts in the drafting of Article 8 in relation to conduct that is criminalized in both cases, forgot that international criminal law is not international humanitarian law despite their obvious conceptual kinship. The distinction should have only been maintained for conduct that is criminalized only in one of them (generally international armed conflict).
>
> The fact remains that this distinction remains in the Statute and it was therefore necessary to define the nature of the armed conflict because it technically leads to different crimes being prosecuted: 8(2)(b)(xxvi) for an international armed conflict and 8(2)(e)(vii) for a non-international armed conflict.[7]

The Judges of the Trial Chamber themselves acknowledged their own dilemma in the *Lubanga* judgment when discussing the distinction between international and non-international armed conflict:

> It is to be observed at the outset that some academics, practitioners, and a line of jurisprudence from the ad hoc tribunals have questioned the usefulness of the distinction between international and non-international armed conflicts, particularly in light of their changing nature. In the view of the Chamber, for the purposes of the present trial the international/non-international distinction is not only an established part of the international law of armed conflict, but more importantly it is enshrined in the relevant statutory provisions of the Rome Statute

---

7   Dov Jacobs, 'Comments on Lubanga Judgment (Part 3): the Armed Conflict, the Elements of the Crime and a Dissent Against the Dissent' (*Spreading the Jam*, 15 March 2012), at <http://dovjacobs.com/2012/03/15/comments-on-lubanga-judgment-part-3-the-armed-conflict-the-elements-of-the-crime-and-a-dissent-against-the-dissent/> accessed 11 November 2014.

framework, which under Article 21 must be applied. The Chamber does not have the power to reformulate the Court's statutory framework.[8]

The Trial Chamber here is surely correct. Whatever the merits of a unitary list of war crimes applicable in international and non-international armed conflicts alike, the Trial Chamber and the parties to trial proceedings are all bound by the terms of the Statute. There is no ambiguity about the structure of Article 8.

In contrast, the Statute of the International Criminal Tribunal for the Former Yugoslavia Statute ('ICTY Statute') includes much greater flexibility in relation to allegations of war crimes and the characterisation of an armed conflict. Article 2 of the ICTY Statute is precisely equivalent in scope to Article 8(2)(a) of the Rome Statute incorporating grave breaches of the Geneva Conventions. Both the Trial Chamber and the Appeals Chamber of the ICTY in *Prosecutor v Duško Tadić ('Tadić')*[9] affirmed that grave breaches of the Conventions can only be perpetrated in an international armed conflict. But, that is where the commonalities between the ICTY Statute and Article 8 of the Rome Statute end. Article 3 of the ICTY Statute gives jurisdiction over 'other serious violations of the laws and customs of war' without specifying the legal character of the requisite armed conflict. Consequently, the Appeals Chamber, in its decision in the *Tadić* challenge to the jurisdiction of the Tribunal, affirmed that Article 3 of the ICTY Statute extended both to: serious violations of the law (other than grave breaches of the Conventions covered by Article 2 of the ICTY Statute) in international armed conflicts; and also to serious violations in non-international armed conflict. This interpretation of the scope of Article 3 of the ICTY Statute renders the provision the equivalent of, or perhaps even broader than, the scope of Article 8(2)(b), (c) and (e) of the Rome Statute combined.[10]

Article 3 of the ICTY Statute does include some indicative serious violations of the law not otherwise covered by the grave breaches regime in Article 2 but that list is not exhaustive. ICTY Trial Chambers and Appeals Chamber have been free to find a legal basis for a purported offence in either treaty or customary international humanitarian law. I will discuss some of the challenges

---

8   *Prosecutor v Thomas Lubanga Dyilo* (Judgment) ICC-01/04-01/06 (14 March 2012) (*'Lubanga* Trial Judgement') para 539.
9   *Prosecutor v Duško Tadić* (Judgment) IT-94-1-T (7 May 1997); *Prosecutor v Duško Tadić* (Judgment) IT-94-1-A (15 July 1999).
10 *Prosecutor v Duško Tadić* (Decision on the Defence Motion for Interlocutory Appeal on Jurisdiction) IT-94-1-AR72 (2 October 1995) paras 85–93 (*'Tadić* Interlocutory Appeal Decision').

arising from the different approach of the Rome Statute before returning to the contrast with Article 3 of the ICTY Statute.

3 Fewer Offences in Non-International Armed Conflicts

Articles 8(2)(c) and 8(2)(e) Already a Breakthrough But…
Some national delegations in Rome proposed that Article 8 should only grant subject matter jurisdiction to the ICC in respect of war crimes allegedly perpetrated in international armed conflicts on the basis of a lack of explicit treaty criminalisation of serious violations of the law in non-international armed conflicts.[11] That position did not prevail at the Diplomatic Conference. Instead, the sum of Article 8(2)(c) and 8(2)(e) of the Rome Statute constitutes a list of war crimes in non-international armed conflicts unprecedented in its scope.

The grave breaches regime of the 1949 Geneva Conventions applied only to specified violations in international armed conflicts and there was no explicit obligation on States Parties to also criminalise serious violations of Common Article 3—the one provision extending *de minimis* prohibitions to non-international armed conflicts. There were two significant breakthroughs in relation to enforcement in the Geneva Conventions: (1) the hitherto untried obligation on States Parties to penalise grave breaches in their domestic criminal law and to either investigate and try or extradite for trial those alleged to have perpetrated any grave breach; and, (2) the advent of some legal regulation of those armed conflicts not of an international character through Common Article 3. It is perhaps understandable that this second breakthrough was considered significant enough, in and of itself, without extending the scope of the first breakthrough beyond grave breaches of the Conventions to also cover serious violations of Common Article 3. Consequently, though, implementing legislation for many States Parties only achieved what the treaties explicitly required—the criminalisation of grave breaches in international armed conflicts and not serious violations of Common Article 3 in non-international armed conflicts.[12]

---

11 See Herman von Hebel & Darryl Robinson, 'Crimes Within the Jurisdiction of the Court' (n 1) 104–105. At page 105, footnote 87 the authors refer to 'China, India and several other Asian States, several Arab States, the Russian Federation and Turkey' as amongst the minority of States arguing for the exclusion from the Rome Statute of war crimes in non-international armed conflict.

12 One example is the Australian *Geneva Conventions Act 1957* (Cth) which criminalised grave breaches of all Four Geneva Conventions but was silent on serious violations of Common Article 3.

The disparate approach to enforcement of violations of the law in international and in non-international armed conflicts in 1949 was further exacerbated in 1977. This time, instead of a single Article in a broader treaty, Additional Protocol II constituted the world's first multilateral treaty exclusively regulating the conduct of hostilities in non-international armed conflict. That was a significant development in the extension of application of international humanitarian law to non-international armed conflicts.

Additional Protocol I, however, is the much more substantial of the two Additional Protocols. It extends the substantive rules applicable in international armed conflicts to include the regulation of means and methods of warfare and a codification of the law of targeting. Article 85 of Additional Protocol I adds to the list of specific grave breaches in the Four Geneva Conventions and obliges all States Parties to criminalise those additional offences in domestic criminal law. In contrast, Additional Protocol II is silent on any obligation to enforce serious violations in non-international armed conflict. Many States Parties to both Protocols did all that the international law of treaties obliged them to do and nothing more: they added to the list of grave breaches in international armed conflicts and did not criminalise any violations of international humanitarian law in non-international armed conflicts.[13] One legacy of this disparity in approach was uncertainty as to whether war crimes could be perpetrated in non-international armed conflicts or whether serious violations of international humanitarian law only constituted war crimes in international armed conflicts?

The Appeals Chamber of the ICTY profoundly influenced clarification of the customary international law position. In the ICTY's first trial, the accused, Duško Tadić, challenged the jurisdiction of the Tribunal and appealed the adverse finding of the Trial Chamber. Amongst other grounds of the appeal, the accused argued that the Tribunal, if it had jurisdiction at all, only had jurisdiction over war crimes committed in the context of an international armed conflict.[14] As adverted to above, the Appeals Chamber found against the accused and decided that the Tribunal had jurisdiction over any serious violation of international humanitarian law occurring in any armed conflict, whether

---

13   Again by way of example, Australia ratified the two Additional Protocols in 1991 and immediately amended the *Geneva Conventions Act 1957* (Cth). However, the amending legislation only did what the Protocols explicitly obliged States Parties to do. Grave breaches of Additional Protocol I (in international armed conflicts) were penalised but the legislation was silent on serious violations of Additional Protocol II (in non-international armed conflicts).

14   *Tadić* Interlocutory Appeal Decision (n 10) para 65.

international or non-international.[15] That finding was facilitated in part by the drafting of the ICTY Statute. Whereas Article 2 provided for grave breaches of the Geneva Conventions, Article 3 of the Statute provided for violations of the laws and customs of war. The Appeals Chamber found that grave breaches of the Geneva Conventions are a particular category of serious violations of international humanitarian law which are specified in the text of the Four Geneva Conventions. Because the Conventions themselves only apply to international armed conflicts, those grave breaches, referred to in Article 2 of the ICTY Statute, can only be perpetrated in an international armed conflict. In contrast, however, serious violations of the laws and customs of war referred to in Article 3 of the ICTY Statute can occur in any armed conflict regardless of its legal characterisation including in non-international armed conflicts.[16]

By the time of the Rome Diplomatic Conference in 1998, any lingering uncertainty about war crimes in non-international armed conflicts had evaporated. The drafting of Article 3 of the ICTY Statute and the interpretation of its scope by the ICTY Appeals Chamber in *Tadić*, as well as the drafting of Article 4 of the ICTR Statute (covering Violations of Article 3 Common to the Geneva Conventions and of Additional Protocol II, there being no question that the armed conflict in Rwanda was non-international in its legal character), had clarified the state of customary international criminal law. Article 8(2)(e) of the Rome Statute is the particular source of unprecedented development of the explicit extension of individual criminal liability in non-international armed conflicts, given that the offences in Article 8(2)(c)(i)–(iv)—serious violations of Common Article 3 of Geneva Conventions—were previously included in Article 4 of the ICTR Statute.

Disparate List of Offences in International and Non-International Armed Conflicts

Despite the unquestionable significance of Articles 8(2)(c) and 8(2)(e), however, it is also glaringly obvious that the ICC's subject matter jurisdiction over war crimes in a non-international armed conflict is substantially more restricted than it is for international armed conflicts. After all, the combined total of war crimes in Articles 8(2)(a) and (b) is 34,[17] and in Articles 8(2)(c) and (e) only 19.[18] That differential of 15 more offences in international armed conflicts can only

---

15   *Ibid* para 94.
16   *Ibid* paras 89–93.
17   Arts 8(2)(a)(i)–(viii) and 8(2)(b)(i)–(xxvi).
18   Arts 8(2)(c)(i)–(iv) and 8(2)(e)(i)–(xv).

mean that the Prosecution is more limited in the charges it can lay in the context of non-international armed conflicts.

In fact, the differential of 15 offences was even more pronounced before the Review Conference of States Parties to the Rome Statute in Kampala, Uganda in 2010. Prior to the Conference Article 8(2)(e) contained only 12 provisions and was silent on the Court's jurisdiction over the use of particular weapons in non-international armed conflicts. It was successfully argued in Kampala that there was no legitimate reason to allow the Court to try an individual for an alleged use of dum-dum bullets, poisoned weapons or asphyxiating gases in an international armed conflict but not also in a non-international armed conflict. Those three provisions, already listed in Article 8(2)(b)(xxvii)–(xix) now also appear in Article 8(2)(e)(xiii)–(xv) in precisely the same order and with precisely the same wording as the corresponding provisions in Article 8(2)(b). It is perhaps regrettable that States Parties did not take the opportunity afforded by the Kampala Conference to undertake a more comprehensive stocktake of other provisions included in Article 8(2)(b) but omitted from Article 8(2)(e).

Some indicative examples of key omissions in Article 8(2)(e) will follow. These examples demonstrate that the weight of the disparity in ICC subject-matter jurisdiction falls upon civilian populations in the context of non-international armed conflicts. Given the prevalence of non-international armed conflicts in the world generally, and amongst the situations currently before the Court specifically, the relative lack of accountability for offences against civilians in such conflicts is potentially damaging and profoundly disconcerting.

Attacks on Civilians, Civilian Objects and Disproportionate Military Force

The first five war crimes in Article 8(2)(b)(i)–(v) all involve harmful attacks on civilians and civilian property in international armed conflicts. It is telling that only two of these provisions have a corresponding offence in Article 8(2)(e). The two corresponding offences are: 'intentionally directing attacks against the civilian population' (8(2)(b)(i) and 8(2)(e)(i)); and 'intentionally directing attacks against...a humanitarian assistance or peacekeeping mission' (8(2)(b)(iii) and 8(2)(e)(iii)). The three offences in international armed conflicts which are absent from the Court's jurisdiction in non-international armed conflicts are: 'intentionally directing attacks against civilian objects' (8(2)(b)(ii)); intentionally launching a disproportionate military attack (8(2)(b)(iv); and 'attacking or bombarding...[undefended] towns, villages, dwellings or buildings' (8(2)(b)(v)).

One explanation for the omission of these three offences from Article 8(2)(e) is that Additional Protocol II does not explicitly include the prohibitions. Article 13(2) of Additional Protocol II prohibits directing attacks against the civilian population but Additional Protocol II makes no explicit reference to a prohibition on directing attacks against civilian property or of disproportionate attacks. In contrast, Article 52(1) of Additional Protocol I explicitly prohibits attacks on civilian objects and both Articles 51(5)(b) and 57(2)(iii)(b) explicitly prohibit disproportionate military attacks. However, the explicit inclusion of the prohibitions in Additional Protocol I but not in Additional Protocol II, is hardly a justification for including the offences in Article 8(2)(b) and omitting them from Article 8(2)(e). Explicit inclusion in Additional Protocol II was never the sole criterion for replication of an Article 8(2)(b) offence in Article 8(2)(e). A number of Article 8(2)(e) offences are not explicitly included in Additional Protocol II including, for example: directing attacks against…a humanitarian assistance or peacekeeping mission (8(2)(e)(iii)); forced pregnancy and enforced sterilization (8(2)(e)(vi)); ordering the displacement of the civilian population (8(2)(e)(viii)); killing or wounding treacherously a combatant adversary (8(2)(e)(ix)); declaring that no quarter shall be given (8(2)(e)(x)); and the three categories of prohibited weapons added at the Kampala Review Conference in 2010 (8(2)(e)(xiii)–(xv)).

Belgium claimed that the proposed amendments to the Rome Statute to replicate the list of prohibited weapons in non-international armed conflicts were aimed at:

> standardizing rules regarding situations of international armed conflict and situations of non international armed conflict by adding in the list of the article 8, paragraph 2, e) the use of three sort of weapons (poison and empoisoned weapons, asphyxiating, poison or other gases and all analogous liquids, materials or devices and bullets which expand or flatten easily in the human body) already listed in the article 8, paragraph 2, b).[19]

The Belgian proposal gained popular support amongst States Parties to the Rome Statute. The ICRC response to the proposal at the 2009 Assembly of States Parties resonated with many delegations: 'what is inhumane and consequently proscribed in international armed conflict cannot but be inhumane and inadmissible in a non-international armed conflict'.[20] A similar sentiment

---

19 See 'Draft Amendments to the Rome Statute on War Crimes', International Criminal Court, Assembly of States Parties, 29 September 2009, at <http://iccreviewconference.blogspot.com.au/2010/05/prohibited-weapons-and-belgian.html> accessed 27 January 2015.
20 This statement is quoted in Coalition for the International Criminal Court blog-post on the Belgian weapons proposal, at <http://iccreviewconference.blogspot.com.au/2010/05/prohibited-weapons-and-belgian.html> accessed 27 January 2015.

led Roger Clark, reflecting on the adoption of the Belgian proposal at the Review Conference, to affirm that '[t]he distinctions between rules of all kinds applicable in international and non-international armed conflict are slowly disappearing'.[21]

The same rationale for extending the list of prohibited weapons to non-international armed conflicts is also applicable to attacks on civilian objects, disproportionate attacks and attacks on undefended towns and villages. The ICRC has certainly formed the view that each of these three identified offences are prohibited at customary international law in both international and non-international armed conflicts.[22] The ICRC's conclusions in relation to the scope of these three Rules are substantiated by other relevant treaty law provisions (various Protocols to the Certain Conventional Weapons Convention, Protocol II to the Hague Convention on Cultural Property), the scope and the interpretation of the ICTY Statute and also the inclusion of the Rules in national military law manuals which explicitly extend the application of the Rules to non-international armed conflicts. There is no logical reason why Article 8(2)(e) of the Rome Statute should not replicate corresponding provisions to those already contained in Article 8(2)(b)(ii), (iv) and (v).

The non-inclusion of these offences in non-international armed conflicts raises potentially serious implications for the Office of the Prosecutor. In the *Mbarushimana* Confirmation of Charges proceedings, for example, the Prosecution asserted the existence of a non-international armed conflict in the Kivus District of the DRC. It alleged that Mbarushimana was responsible for, *inter alia*, multiple counts of the war crime of intentionally directing attacks against the civilian population or against individual civilians not taking a direct part in hostilities in violation of Article 8(2)(e)(i) of the Rome Statute.[23] In relation to the specific allegations of an attack on the village of Busurungi and surrounding villages on or about 9–10 May 2009, evidence confirmed the knowledge of the FDLR (Forces démocratiques de libération du Rwanda—the

---

21 Roger Clark, 'Amendments to the Rome Statute of the International Criminal Court Considered at the First Review Conference on the Court, Kampala, 31 May—11 June 2010' (2010) 2 GoJIL 689, 707.

22 See ICRC *Customary International Humanitarian Law*, Rule 7 'The Principle of Distinction Between Civilian Objects and Military Objectives'; Rule 14 'Proportionality in Attack'; and Rule 37 'Open Towns and Non-Defended Localities'. The ICRC claims that all three Rules of customary international humanitarian law apply in both international and non-international armed conflicts.

23 *Prosecutor v Callixte Mbarushimana* (Decision on Confirmation of Charges) ICC-01/04-01/10 (16 December 2011) paras 108–22 ('*Mbarushinana*, 'Decision on Confirmation of Charges').

non-state armed group Mbarushimana was involved with) of the location of several DRC Military (Forces Armées de la République Démocratique du Congo—hereinafter FARDC) positions 'within and on the outskirts of the village of Busurungi' and also co-located amongst the dwellings of the civilian population. In circumstances where evidence confirms the presence of military personnel and military objects in the area attacked, the Prosecution would normally consider charging the war crime of disproportionate military force. Certainly the Defence in *Mbarushimana* sought to argue that the attack on Busurungi was planned as a military assault on an enemy stronghold and that any civilians killed in the attack were coincidental 'collateral damage'.[24]

Given the lack of a war crime of disproportionate military force in Article 2(e) of the Rome Statute, the only possible charge here is Article 8(2)(e)(i)—the war crime of intentionally directing attacks against the civilian population. The ICC Pre-Trial Chamber in *Mbarushimana* took a flexible approach to the interpretation of the scope of the offence. Paragraph 142 of the Decision on Confirmation of the Charges states that:

> In the view of the Chamber, the war crime of attacking civilians pursuant to article 8(2)(e)(i) of the Statute does not presuppose that the civilian population is the sole and exclusive target of the attack. The crime may be perpetrated in any of the two following scenarios: (i) when individual civilians not taking direct part in the hostilities or the civilian population are the sole target of the attack or (ii) when the perpetrator launches the attack with two distinct specific aims: (a) a military objective, within the meaning of articles 51 and 52 of the Protocol Additional to the Geneva Conventions of 12 August 1949 ("the AP I"); and simultaneously, (b) the civilian population or individual civilians not taking direct part in the hostilities. The latter scenario must be distinguished from situations where, in violation of the principle of proportionality, a disproportionate attack is intentionally launched with the specific aim of targeting a military objective, with the awareness that incidental loss of life or injury to civilians will or may occur as a result of such an attack. In such a case, the targeting of the civilian population is not the aim of the attack but only an incidental consequence thereof.[25]

It is not immediately obvious where the demarcation lies between the Pre-Trial Chamber's scenario (ii) and a disproportionate attack. Presumably, applying

---

24   *Ibid* para 141.
25   *Ibid* para 142 (footnotes omitted).

the same analysis to a disproportionate attack it could be said that the crime can be perpetrated in one of two scenarios:

> when a legitimate military objective is the sole target of the attack but with the awareness that incidental loss of life or injury to civilians will or may occur as a result of the attack; or
> when the perpetrator launches the attack with two distinct specific aims: a military objective; and, simultaneously, the civilian population or individual civilians not taking direct part in hostilities.

In the context of an international armed conflict where both crimes (intentionally directing an attack against civilians (Article 8(2)(b)(i)) and launching an attack with disproportionate military force (Article 8(2)(b)(iv)) are available, the overlap between the second scenario for both crimes may actually constitute something approximating a total eclipse. This is in large part because Article 8(2)(b)(iv) requires the Prosecution to prove a higher threshold, that the expected loss of civilian life and/or damage to civilian property is '*clearly excessive*'. Articles 51(5)(b), 57 (2)(a)(iii) and 57(2)(b) of Additional Protocol I of 1977 only require that the expected loss of civilian life and/or damage to civilian property be 'excessive in relation to the concrete and direct military advantage anticipated'. Given this elevated requirement in Article 8(2)(b)(iv) of the Rome Statute, it will only be in unusual circumstances in which the nature and quantity of ordnance deployed is so overwhelming that it will be possible for the Prosecution to prove the war crime of disproportionate military force. Of course, in non-international armed conflicts, the Prosecution will be dependent upon Trial and Appeals Chambers following the same approach as the Pre-Trial Chamber in *Mbarushimana*, because the war crime of disproportionate military force is simply not included in Article 8(2)(e) of the Rome Statute.

In the *Mbarushimana* decision on the Confirmation of the Charges, the Pre-Trial Chamber applied its test for intentionally directing attacks against the civilian population to the FDLR attack on Busurungi to the evidence presented by the Prosecution and decided that:

> there are substantial grounds to believe that the attack on Busurungi and surrounding villages on or about 9–10 May 2009 was launched by the FDLR with the aim of targeting both military objectives (FARDC positions in the village and surroundings) and the civilian population or individual civilians not taking direct part in the hostilities. The Chamber is further satisfied that the FDLR soldiers who took part in the attack were aware of the civilian status of the victims and intended to attack the civilian

population or individual civilians not taking direct part in the hostilities since they were considered enemies. The Chamber therefore finds substantial grounds to believe that the war crimes of attacking civilians under article 8(2)(e)(i) of the Statute and murder under article 8(2)(c)(i) of the Statute were committed by the FDLR troops in Busurungi and surrounding villages on or about 9–10 May 2009.[26]

The Pre-Trial Chamber in *Mbarushimana* followed the decision of the Pre-Trial Chamber on Confirmation of the Charges in *Katanga and Ngudjulo*[27] and the approach of both Pre-Trial Chambers was affirmed by the Trial Chamber in the *Katanga* Judgment.[28] Given this willingness of both Chambers to uphold the offence of intentionally attacking civilians in circumstances where military objectives are also attacked, one might query whether a separate war crime of disproportionate force in Article 8(2)(e) is necessary. However, there is as yet no decision from the ICC Appeals Chamber on this jurisprudence and, in the absence of a definitive Appeals Chamber ruling, it is possible that some future ICC Trial Chamber may disagree with the Judgment in *Katanga*.

None of this particular case law deals with the lack of specific war crimes in Article 8(2)(e) of intentionally attacking civilian objects and/or civilian property and intentionally attacking undefended towns and villages. It is not difficult to imagine factual scenarios in the context of a non-international armed conflict in which these omissions from Article 8(2)(e) prove problematic for the laying of charges and for any possibility of accountability for those responsible. Given that all three offences are already prohibited in customary international law regulating non-international armed conflicts, all uncertainty could readily be removed by amendment to Article 8(2)(e) adding corresponding offences to those already listed in Articles 8(2)(b)(ii), (iv) and (v).

Using Human Shields and Starvation of the Civilian Population

Two other offences against the civilian population omitted from the Court's jurisdiction in non-international armed conflicts are 'utilizing the presence of a civilian or other protected person to render certain points, areas or military forces immune from military operations' (use of human shields—Article 8(2)(b)(xxiii)) and 'intentionally using starvation of civilians as a method of warfare by depriving them of objects indispensable to their survival, including

---

26 *Ibid* para 151.
27 *Prosecutor v Germain Katanga and Mathieu Ngudjolo Chui*, (Decision on the Confirmation of Charges) ICC-01/04-01/07 (30 September 2008) para 273.
28 *Prosecutor v Germain Katanga* (Judgment) ICC-01/04-01/07 (7 March 2014).

wilfully impeding relief supplies as provided for under the Geneva Conventions' (Article 8(2)(b)(xxv)).

Article 23 of Geneva Convention III and Article 28 of Geneva Convention IV both prohibit the use of protected persons (prisoners of war and civilians under foreign military occupation respectively) 'to render certain points or areas immune from military operations'. Article 51 of Additional Protocol I, dealing with the protection of the civilian population generally, includes an explicit prohibition on the use of human shields. Article 51(7) states that

> [t]he presence or movements of the civilian population or individual civilians shall not be used to render certain points or areas immune from military operations, in particular in attempts to shield military objectives from attacks or to shield, favour or impede military operations. The Parties to the conflict shall not direct the movement of the civilian population or individual civilians in order to attempt to shield military objectives from attacks or to shield military operations.

In contrast, Additional Protocol II is silent on the use of civilians to shield military objectives, and so the disparity in the Rome Statute between international and non-international armed conflicts reflects a pre-existing disparity in the relevant treaty law.

Despite this disparate treaty law reality, the International Committee of the Red Cross ('ICRC') Customary International Humanitarian Law Study asserts that the use of human shields is prohibited in both international and non-international armed conflicts.[29] To substantiate the assertion in respect of non-international armed conflicts, the ICRC concedes the lack of an explicit prohibition on the use of human shields in Additional Protocol II but points to the obligation in Article 13(1) that 'the civilian population and individual civilians shall enjoy general protection against the dangers arising from military operations' as sufficiently broad to cover the specific practice. The ICRC also explains that the use of human shields is often associated with hostage-taking involving the forced placement of hostages in close physical proximity to military objectives and Article 4(2)(c) of APII explicitly prohibits hostage-taking. Additionally, deliberate use of civilians to shield military objectives is inconsistent with the rule on distinction and in violation of 'the obligation to take feasible precautions to separate civilians and military objectives'.

---

29 See 'Rule 97. Human Shields' (*International Committee of the Red Cross Customary International Humanitarian Law Database*), at <https://www.icrc.org/customary-ihl/eng/docs/v1_rul_rule97> accessed 29 January 2015.

Drawing on general principles from treaty law rather than explicit provisions in other contexts is never the strongest line of argument and the ICRC does not rely on this source of authority alone. The military manuals of several States extend the prohibition on the use of human shields to non-international armed conflicts and the national legislation of at least eight States criminalises the use of human shields in both international and non-international armed conflicts. The use of human shields in several non-international armed conflicts has been condemned by several States and by the UN, and the ICRC has not been able to identify any contrary state practice (such as examples of an acceptance of the lawfulness of the use of human shields in non-international armed conflict). Given the ICRC's substantiation of its assertion of the customary law rule, there is no justifiable reason for Article 8(2)(e) not to include this particular offence.

Although the ICC has not yet dealt with an allegation of the use of human shields, it is patently obvious that the omission of this offence from Article 8(2)(e) is potentially problematic. The overwhelming majority of the armed conflict situations under consideration by the Office of the Prosecutor involve non-international armed conflicts. Any allegation of the use of human shields in any of those situations cannot be prosecuted for want of an offence in Article 8(2)(e). There are situations involving allegations of the use of human shields which are not currently within the Court's jurisdiction, but which at some future stage may fall within in. Israel, for example, routinely accuses Hamas of perpetrating the war crime of using civilians to shield military positions in Gaza.[30] If, hypothetically, the ICC gained jurisdiction over acts committed on the physical territory of Palestine, including Gaza, the Prosecutor could only investigate the allegations of use of human shields if she was satisfied that the situation was an international armed conflict. In such circumstances, so much effort would have to be expended first on determining the legal characterization of the conflict between Israel and the Palestinians rather than on the substantive evidence to determine whether or not the allegations could be substantiated.

The second offence is the war crime of starvation of the civilian population. The explicit criminalisation of the prohibition on starvation dates back to 1919 in the aftermath of the First World War. The Allied Commission on Responsibility for the War included starvation in its list of 32 war crimes—violations of the established laws and customs of war—for which defendants from the defeated

---

[30] See, for example, 'Hamas' Use of Human Shields is a War Crime' (*Israel Defense Forces Blog*, 7 August 2014), at <http://www.idfblog.com/blog/2014/07/14/hamas-use-human-shields-war-crime/> accessed 29 January 2015.

Central Powers could be held accountable.[31] As with all the other offences included in Article 8(2)(b) but omitted from Article 8(2)(e) above, Additional Protocol I codifies the prohibition on starvation of the civilian population in international armed conflicts. Article 54(1) articulates the prohibition unambiguously: 'starvation of civilians as a method of warfare is prohibited'. Importantly, and distinct from all other omissions from Article 8(2)(e) referred to above, Article 14 of Additional Protocol II codifies the prohibition in almost precisely the same unambiguous terms in non-international armed conflicts: 'starvation of civilians as a method of combat is prohibited.'

Given the explicit inclusion of the prohibition on starvation in Article 14 of Additional Protocol II in virtually identical terms to the articulation of the prohibition in Additional Protocol I, it is difficult to understand the rationale for omission of starvation as a war crime in non-international armed conflicts in the Rome Statute. The ICRC confidently asserts that the customary law prohibition extends to international and non-international armed conflicts alike. Article 14 of Additional Protocol II is obviously important to substantiate the assertion but the ICRC also draws upon additional sources including relevant national legislation, military manuals and case law.[32]

There have been no allegations before the ICC to date of starvation used as method of warfare although it is entirely possible that there may be in the future. If such evidence emerges in the context of the investigation of alleged ICC war crimes in a non-international armed conflict, it will be extremely frustrating to be precluded from laying charges for want of subject matter jurisdiction—particularly given the strong legal basis for criminalisation of the offence in non-international armed conflicts.

4 Advantages in Non-International Armed Conflict Offences

The broader range of offences in international armed conflicts may well provide the Prosecution with greater confidence in pursuing charges where there is a possibility of successfully characterizing the conflict as an international armed conflict. Concomitantly, the prosecution strategy in a non-international

---

31 Commission on the Responsibility of the Authors of the War and on Enforcement of Penalties, 'Report Presented to the Preliminary Peace Conference 29 March 1919' (1920) 14(1) AJIL 95, 115–16.

32 See 'Rule 53. Starvation as a Method of Warfare' (*International Committee of the Red Cross Customary International Humanitarian Law Database*), at <https://www.icrc.org/customary-ihl/eng/docs/v1_rul_rule53> accessed 29 January 2015.

armed conflict context may well be stymied or more limited as a result of the narrower range of offences under Article 8(2)(c) and (e). However, the quantitative disparity of offences between international and non-international armed conflicts is not the entire story. Sometimes, where equivalent offences exist in both international and non-international armed conflicts, qualitative differences in their elements can expose the fallacies of an assumption that the international armed conflict offence always allows broader scope for prosecution. The stand-out example is the war crime of child soldiering.

Article 8(2)(b)(xxvi) and Article 8(2)(e)(vii) are drafted in identical terms but for one key difference. Aside from the application of the former to international armed conflict, and the latter to non-international armed conflict, the difference is that Article 8(2)(b)(xxvi) requires the Prosecution to prove that children under the age of fifteen were conscripted or enlisted into 'national armed forces', whereas 8(2)(e)(vii) only requires that children under the age of fifteen were conscripted or enlisted into 'armed forces or groups'.

Given that an international armed conflict only exists where two or more States are opposed to each other, the wording of Article 8(2)(b)(xxvi) seems readily explicable. One could imagine that the drafters simply assumed that the conscription or enlistment of children in an international armed conflict would only be into 'national armed forces' of a party to the conflict. However, as Michael Cottier explains, the insertion of the qualifier 'national' in Article 8(2)(b)(xxvi) represented a carefully crafted compromise. Several Arab States had expressed concerns that the phrase 'armed forces' without qualification could be applied to the *intifadah* and to Palestinian children under 15 joining it. The preferred phrase was 'regular armed forces'. However, several other delegations strongly opposed any such narrowing of scope. 'National armed forces' is the resulting balance of those opposing positions but it is not clear what constitutes national armed forces or, in particular, what forces might be excluded from the scope of the qualifier.[33]

Perhaps in most cases of international armed conflict, this particular element of the offence of child soldering will be relatively straightforward to establish. However, it is well known that the law applicable to international armed conflicts applies to factual situations other than those involving fighting between the military forces of two states. One such situation involves a non-State armed group operating under the overall control of a State (or even opposing non-State armed groups each operating under the overall control of

---

[33] Michael Cottier, 'Article 8' in Otto Triffterer (ed), *Commentary on the Rome Statute of the International Criminal Court: Observers' Notes, Article by Article* (2nd ed, CH Beck, Hart, Nomos 2008), 473.

a State). Another possible situation could involve a paramilitary organization that is aligned with a national military but not strictly part of it, and which recruits child soldiers. Another alternative factual situation might involve military occupation by the forces of a foreign State. What if there is an armed conflict in part of the territory under occupation between non-States armed groups not otherwise connected to the occupation? Which is the appropriate charge if evidence substantiates the conscription or enlistment of child soldiers into one or both non-State armed groups while the occupation is continuing?

The Prosecution had argued at the confirmation of charges stage of proceedings against *Thomas Dyilo Lubanga*[34] that the legal character of the armed conflict in the Ituri District of the DRC was non-international. The Pre-Trial Chamber disagreed and characterised the situation as an international armed conflict. The Chamber determined that an armed conflict is 'international in character if it takes place between two or more States; this extends to the partial or total occupation of another State, whether or not the said occupation meets with armed resistance'.[35] The Chamber relied heavily on the International Court of Justice findings in the *Democratic Republic of the Congo v. Uganda* case, namely that Ugandan Government Forces were engaged in a military occupation of part of the Ituri District of the DRC and that, consequently, the situation constituted an international armed conflict.[36]

In finding against the Prosecution on the legal characterisation of the armed conflict in Ituri, the Pre-Trial Chamber explicitly stated that there was no need for the Prosecution to reframe the charges against the accused because the corresponding offences of child soldering (Article 8(2)(b)(xxvi) and 8(2)(e)(iv)) 'criminalise the same conduct, whether it is committed in the context of an armed conflict of an international character or in the context of an armed conflict not of an international character'.[37] The Pre-Trial Chamber was surely correct—that the two corresponding provisions criminalise the same conduct of 'conscripting or enlisting' children under 15 years of age or 'using them to actively participate in hostilities' irrespective of the legal characterisation of the conflict. However, the Pre-Trial Chamber chose not to discuss the potential problem for the Prosecution arising from the Chamber's determination that

---

34 *Prosecutor v Thomas Lubanga Dyilo* (Decision on the Confirmation of Charges) ICC-01/04-01/06 (29 January 2007) ('*Lubanga*, Decision on the Confirmation of Charges').
35 *Ibid* para 209.
36 *Armed Activities on the Territory of the Congo (Democratic Republic of the Congo v. Uganda)* (Judgment) [2005] ICJ Rep 59, para 175.
37 *Lubanga*, Decision on the Confirmation of Charges (n 34) para 204.

Uganda's military occupation of part of the Ituri District would require the Prosecution to prove the elements of Article 8(2)(b)(xxvi)—including that the UPC (Lubanga's non-State armed group the *Union des Patriotiques Congolais*) constituted 'national armed forces'.

Can a non-State armed group ever constitute 'national armed forces'? Perhaps, if the non-State armed group exercises effective authority and control over physical territory, that might allow a Chamber to determine that the non-State armed group is operating effectively as a 'quasi-State'. But any such determination is presumably dependent upon the particular factual situation, and it is not difficult to conceive of international armed conflict situations in which non-State armed groups engaged in the conscription of young children do not exercise effective authority and control over any physical territory. The Pre-Trial Chamber in *Lubanga* accepted that a *Tadić*-type situation, where a non-State armed group (in the *Tadić* Case, the Bosnian Serb Forces) operates under the 'overall control' of a State (in the *Tadić* Case, Serbia), also constitutes an international armed conflict.[38] Given this contingency, it is entirely possible that a future Trial Chamber, faced with a non-State armed group operating under the 'overall control' of another State but which does not exercise effective authority over any physical territory, will find that the Prosecution has failed to discharge its duty to prove that children under 15 were conscripted or enlisted into 'national armed forces'.

This potential pitfall was avoided in the *Lubanga* case because the Prosecution was able to demonstrate that the armed conflict in which the UPC was engaged in Ituri occurred outside the physical territory under the military occupation of Ugandan Government forces and did not involve any non-State armed groups operating under the control of States. In its judgment in the Case, the Trial Chamber analysed the identity and character of the parties to the armed conflict in question and found that the protracted armed conflict involved the UPC fighting against other non-State armed groups, none of which operated under the 'overall control' of a State.[39] Furthermore, the Trial Chamber found that:

> the Ugandan military occupation of Bunia airport does not change the legal nature of the conflict between the [various]...rebel groups since this conflict, as analysed above, did not result in two states opposing each

---

38   *Ibid* paras 210–11.
39   *Lubanga* Trial Judgment (n 8) paras 552–63.

other, whether directly or indirectly, during the time period relevant to the charges.[40]

The Trial Chamber changed the legal characterisation of the factual situation and found that the armed conflict in Ituri was of a non-international character. The Prosecution's obligation then was to prove that *Lubanga* was criminally responsible for conscripting or enlisting children under 15 into an 'armed force or group' and not into 'national armed forces'. Given the nature of the UPC, this element of the war crime of child soldering was significantly easier to prove than would have been the case had the Trial Chamber decided not to over-rule the Pre-Trial Chamber's characterisation of the conflict.

5   Options for Reform

The call to eliminate the legal characterisation of the conflict—that if there is an armed conflict it is irrelevant what type of armed conflict it is—and to replace Article 8 with a unitary set of war crimes over which the ICC has jurisdiction in all armed conflicts, is appealing on multiple levels. Such an outcome would simplify the investigation of alleged offences and bring clarity to the parties to proceedings, as well as to the Trial and Appeals Chambers. But substantial obstacles to that outcome persist. Politically, many States have no desire to remove the distinction, preferring instead to maintain a higher threshold for non-international armed conflicts to ensure that domestic situations of tension and civil disturbance remain unregulated by international law, and within the exclusive sovereign jurisdiction of the State. Legally, the unitary set of rules approach ignores those aspects of international armed conflicts not applicable to non-international armed conflicts including military occupation, neutrality, combatant status and entitlement to prisoner-of-war protection. These legal issues will always be utilised by those desirous of maintaining the distinction.

In the absence of political will to remove the distinction altogether, the Assembly of States Parties could take either of two options to rectify the glaring omissions in the scope of war crimes subject-matter jurisdiction in non-international armed conflicts. The first option would be to follow the Kampala Review Conference precedent and extend the list of offences in Article 8(2)(e), thereby reducing the current disparity between Article 8(2)(b) and 8(2)(e) offences. Such an approach would not constitute a wholesale restructuring of

---

40   *Ibid* 565.

Article 8 and has the advantage of extending the Kampala precedent. The same *rationale* for extending the list of prohibited weapons applies *mutatis mutandis* to attacks on civilian property, disproportionate military force, starvation as a method of warfare, and so on.

The second option for the Assembly of States Parties would be to retain Article 8(2)(a) and 8(2)(c) representing, as both provisions do, the explicit treaty regimes of offences applicable in international and non-international armed conflicts respectively, but then replacing Articles 8(2)(b) and 8(2)(e) with a provision more akin to Article 3 of the ICTY Statute—other serious violations of the laws and customs of war. Such a provision could include an exhaustive list of offences, which would be consistent with the overall approach to the current Article 8. Alternatively, such a provision could be modelled on Article 3 of the ICTY Statute by featuring an indicative list of offences, leaving it to the Prosecution to argue that a war crime not included in the indicative list exists in treaty and/or in customary international humanitarian law in either international or non-international armed conflicts to the satisfaction of the Trial Chamber. This is the approach of Article 3 of the ICTY Statute and, consequently, the ICTY has contributed some important jurisprudence on the laws and customs of war.

Any of these approaches to reform of Article 8 would rectify the current disparity of coverage of offences between international and non-international armed conflicts. Maintenance of the *status quo* risks a future trial scenario involving a non-international armed conflict in which the Prosecution is precluded from laying charges for want of subject matter jurisdiction. In such a situation it may take a Pre-Trial, Trial or Appeals Chamber declaring the facts unregulated by Article 8(2)(e) to act as a catalyst for change. The approach to the Kampala amendments to Article 8(2)(e) was proactive, and it would be a pity not to emulate the motivation behind that important precedent by undertaking a comprehensive reform of the list of offences in non-international armed conflicts.

CHAPTER 22

Perpetrators (Article 25 (3) of the ICC Statute)

Thomas Weigend

The first case prosecuted in the International Criminal Court ('ICC') has finally been resolved. On 1 December 2014, the Appeals Chamber affirmed the conviction and sentence of Thomas Lubanga Diylo for co-perpetrating the war crime of conscripting child soldiers in violation of Article 8 (2) (e) (vii) ICC Statute. The decision of this case (and others before the ICC) significantly hinged on the question to what extent and under what conditions acts of other persons can be attributed to the defendant. Since international crimes typically are not committed by lone offenders but by more or less coordinated groups, the question of attribution of the acts of others is a key issue of international criminal law. Article 25(3)(a)–(d) of the ICC Statute[1] aims at providing guidelines for resolving this issue, but—as was to be expected—the interpretation of these provisions has proved to be highly controversial. In the *Lubanga* case, the ICC Appeals Chamber noted that

> the question of whether an accused 'committed' a crime—and therefore not only contributed to the crime committed by someone else—cannot only be answered by reference to how close the accused was to the actual crime and whether he or she directly carried out the incriminated conduct.

---

[1] Art 25(3)(a)–(d) ICC Statute reads:
In accordance with this Statute, a person shall be criminally responsible and liable for punishment for a crime within the jurisdiction of the Court if that person:
(a) Commits such a crime, whether as an individual, jointly with another or through another person, regardless of whether that other person is criminally responsible;
(b) Orders, solicits or induces the commission of such a crime which in fact occurs or is attempted;
(c) For the purpose of facilitating the commission of such a crime, aids, abets or otherwise assists in its commission or its attempted commission, including providing the means for its commission;
(d) In any other way contributes to the commission or attempted commission of such a crime by a group of persons acting with a common purpose. Such contribution shall be intentional and shall either:
  (i) Be made with the aim of furthering the criminal activity or criminal purpose of the group, where such activity or purpose involves the commission of a crime within the jurisdiction of the Court; or
  (ii) Be made in the knowledge of the intention of the group to commit the crime; [...]

Rather, what is required is a normative assessment of the role of the accused person in the specific circumstances of the case.[2]

These few sentences—vague and open-ended as they may appear at first sight—are the result of a trip over a minefield of difficult legal questions related to the compromise statement on perpetratorship and accomplice liability in Article 25(3)(a)–(d) ICC Statute. In this article, I will limit myself to touching upon a few of the more general issues which lie at the basis of the Appeals Chamber's statement. It gives me special pleasure to contribute these lines to a volume honouring Roger S. Clark—distinguished scholar, esteemed diplomat and old friend, who has contributed in so many ways to promoting the cause of international criminal law.

1 Perpetrators and Accessories

(1) *A General Distinction?*

The first question that needs to be answered is whether one should distinguish among various categories of participants in a criminal enterprise, or whether it is preferable to apply a unitary model[3] and treat alike anyone who makes a causal contribution to a criminal offence, dealing with individual differences only at the level of sentencing.

Strong arguments have been raised in favour of a unitary approach to criminal liability, in particular with regard to international crime. Roger Clark has remarked that it would miss the point to consider the 'big fish' who order or instigate their subordinates to commit core crimes as mere 'secondary' parties.[4] In a similar vein, Judge Fulford has argued that 'there is no proper basis for

---

2 *Prosecutor v Lubanga* (Judgment on the appeal of Mr Thomas Lubanga Dyilo against his conviction) ICC-01/04-01/06 A 5 (1 December 2014) ('*Lubanga Appeals Judgment*'), para 473.

3 Hans Vest, 'Problems of Participation—Unitarian, Differentiated Approach, or Something Else?' (2014) 12 JICJ 295 ('Vest, 'Problems of Participation—Unitarian, Differentiated Approach, or Something Else?"') at 306 correctly pointed out that the term 'unitarian' model is ambiguous in that it can mean (a) a categorical leveling of all forms of participation in a crime or (b) an equalization only of sentencing ranges for perpetrators and accomplices. I will use the term in the more comprehensive sense, indicating a lack of distinction among categories of perpetrators and accomplices.

4 Roger S Clark, 'Drafting a General Part to a Penal Code: Some Thoughts Inspired by the Negotiations on the Rome Statute of the International Criminal Court and by the Court's First Substantive Law Discussion in the Lubanga Diylo Confirmation Proceedings' (2008) 19 Crim LF 519, 544.

concluding that ordering, soliciting or inducing a crime (Article 25(3)(b)) is a less serious form of commission than committing it 'through another person' (Article 25(3)(a)).'[5] According to Judge Fulford, the concepts of participation as set out in Article 25(3)(a)–(d) ICC Statute 'will often be indistinguishable in their application vis-à-vis a particular situation', and were therefore not intended to be mutually exclusive.[6] In a forceful plea for introducing unitary perpetrator liability, James G. Stewart maintains that 'what matters...is that the assailant made a substantial causal contribution to a prohibited harm while harbouring the mental element necessary to make him responsible for that crime.'[7] Stewart would consequently regard as perpetrators all those who directly or indirectly 'contribute to a crime'.[8] Any further distinction, Stewart thinks, would only lead to confusion and would appear 'esoteric to ordinary citizens.'[9] To the extent that there exists a moral difference between perpetration and complicity, this difference, according to Stewart, 'may as well feature at the sentencing stage, along with other relevant factors.'[10]

Various chambers of the ICC have, however, interpreted Article 25(3) ICC Statute as an embodiment of a model that distinguishes between perpetrators and accomplices.[11] As the Appeals Chamber succinctly put the matter in the *Lubanga* Appeals judgment:

> ...under this provision [Art. 25(3)], an individual can be held criminally responsible for either *committing* a crime (sub-paragraph (a)) or for *contributing* to the commission of a crime by another person or persons in one of the ways described in sub-paragraphs (b) to (d). This indicates that the Statute differentiates between two principal forms of liability,

---

5   *Prosecutor v Lubanga* (Trial Chamber Judgment) ICC-01/04-01/06 (14 March 2012), *Separate Opinion of Judge Adrian Fulford* ('*Lubanga, Separate Opinion of Judge Fulford*') para 8.

6   *Ibid* para 7. For a similar argument, see Kai Ambos, *Internationales Strafrecht* (3rd ed, CH Beck 2014) para 7/13 (claiming that Art 25 (3) ICC Statute represents a functional unitary system as also exists in Austrian criminal law).

7   James G Stewart, 'The End of "Modes of Liability" for International Crimes' (2012) 25 LJIL 165 ('Stewart, 'The End of "Modes of Liability" for International Crimes") 207.

8   *Ibid* 208.

9   *Ibid* 212.

10 *Ibid* 207.

11 See, eg, *Prosecutor v Katanga and Chui* (Decision on Confirmation of Charges) ICC 01/04-01/07 (30 September 2008) ('*Katanga and Chui, Decision on Confirmation of Charges*') para 486; *Prosecutor v Katanga* (Judgment) ICC 01/04-01/07 (7 March 2014) ('*Katanga Trial Judgment*') paras 1383–1385.

namely liability as a perpetrator and liability as an accessory. In the view of the Appeals Chamber, this distinction is not merely terminological; making this distinction is important because, generally speaking and all other things being equal, a person who is found to commit a crime him- or herself bears more blameworthiness than a person who contributes to the crime of another person or persons. Accordingly, it contributes to a proper labelling of the accused person's criminal responsibility.[12]

It is difficult to find fault with this argument as a matter of statutory law. The structure of Article 25(3)(a)–(d) ICC Statute clearly indicates a categorical distinction between perpetrators and 'mere' accomplices. Whereas Article 25(3)(a) holds personally responsible, without imposing further conditions, those who 'commit' a crime, Article 25(3)(b) and (c) require for liability that a crime has in fact been committed or has been attempted—presumably by a person other than the instigator or aider. Article 25(3)(d) likewise requires that a crime has been committed or attempted by 'a group' to whose activity the defendant has contributed.[13] The criminal responsibility of the types of offenders listed in Article 25(3)(b)–(d) is thus accessorial; they may be punished only if someone else commits or at least attempts to commit an offence.

One may have doubts about the wisdom of introducing a strict distinction between perpetrators and accomplices, especially where some types of accomplices (those guilty of ordering or instigating) are difficult to distinguish from some types of perpetrators (indirect perpetrators acting though a responsible other person). But, the alternative—treating alike everyone who contributes to the commission of a crime—is not very attractive either. As a matter of doctrine, a unitary system would lead to an awkward dependence on murky borderlines: the difficult distinction between causal and non-causal contributions, or (still more difficult) between necessary and merely substantial causal contributions would then become the sole criterion for a person's responsibility. As a matter of policy, one should not underestimate the significance of fair labelling, especially when a crime emanates from a group of persons. Declaring every member of the group to be equally guilty as a perpetrator

---

12   *Lubanga Appeals Judgment* (n 2) para 462 (citations omitted).
13   A distinction between perpetrators and accessories is also implied in Art 25(3)(f) ICC Statute: a person can be punishable for an attempt only if he or she attempted to *commit* a crime; an attempt to order a crime or to aid in its commission is thus not punishable. See Andreas Herzig, 'Die Tatherrschaftslehre in der Rechtsprechung des Internationalen Strafgerichtshofs' (2013) Zeitschrift für internationale Strafrechtsdogmatik 189 ('Herzig, 'Die Tatherrschaftslehre in der Rechtsprechung des Internationalen Strafgerichtshofs'') 198.

of the crime may appear unfair not only to the defendants but also to the general public.[14]

Regardless of doctrinal niceties, the difference between committing a crime and helping another person to commit a crime seems to be well-grounded in public consciousness across jurisdictions. In some common law jurisdictions, a less radical 'semi-unitary' approach can be found: they distinguish between perpetrators (who with their own hands perform all requisite material elements of a crime) and persons involved in a joint (criminal) enterprise. As is well known, the notion of a Joint Criminal Enterprise as the basis for criminal responsibility has been adopted by the ad-hoc tribunals for former Yugoslavia and Ruanda.[15] But even this approach appears deficient in that it lets the crucial distinction between perpetrators and mere participants in a criminal enterprise turn on the rather bland empirical criterion on who does or does not pull the trigger.[16] If we expect the criminal law not only to determine who will be punished and who will be acquitted but also to allocate and express degrees of responsibility, then we will need to make the difficult distinction between those who are mainly responsible (perpetrators) and those who participate in the crime in a less blameworthy fashion (accomplices). If we frame the issue in this way, it is clear that the distinction is not an empirical or logical but a normative one: we do not distinguish between direct or immediate causal contributions and 'remote' ones but allocate greater or lesser responsibility. Resolving normative issues typically is not a matter of simple yes/no decisions, but of difficult distinctions and debatable outcomes. But that is the price of attempting to do justice to different types of participating in a crime.

Does it matter whether the distinction between degrees of responsibility is made on the level of guilt or on the level of sentencing (as the 'unitarians' prefer)? From a pragmatic viewpoint, there is nothing to be gained by distinguishing among various types of criminal responsibility on the basis of quaint expressions (such as are to be found in Article 25(3)(a)–(c) ICC Statute) and by trying to interpret them by employing equally quaint 'theories'. It might indeed 'free up considerable capacity, save donors' resources,

---

14   See Gerhard Werle & Florian Jeßberger, *Principles of International Criminal Law* (3rd ed, OUP 2014) ('Werle & Jeßberger, *Principles of International Criminal Law*') margin note 509; Elies van Sliedregt, *Individual Criminal Responsibility in International Law* (OUP 2012) ('van Sliedregt, *Individual Criminal Responsibility in International Law*') 154; Vest, 'Problems of Participation—Unitarian, Differentiated Approach, or Something Else?' (n 3) 300–02.

15   Starting with *Prosecutor v Tadic* (Appeals Chamber Judgment) IT-94-1-A (15 July 1999) paras 172 et seq.

16   Cf van Sliedregt, *Individual Criminal Responsibility in International Law* (n 14) 131 et seq.

and hasten trials'[17] at international tribunals to shift the issue of personal responsibility for a group crime completely to the black box of sentencing; and Rule 145(1)(c) of the ICC Rules of Procedure and Evidence offers a handle for taking the 'degree of participation' of each convicted defendant into account when determining his or her sentence. But, there are two arguments against this easy solution to the problem. First, the distinction between the main culprits and the figures at the margin of a multi-person criminal enterprise is not an individual but a categorical one; it goes to the *type* of guilt, not just to the measure of individual blame. Second, the problem of establishing criteria for greater or lesser individual responsibility does not disappear when it has been shifted to sentencing;[18] it may only be better concealed (and remain unresolved) amidst a host of other individual sentencing considerations. For example, as long as there is no agreement on whether a person who provides a necessary instrument for committing a crime is equally or less blameworthy than those who actually carry out the criminal act, the sentencing judge cannot come to a rational conclusion as to the sentencing factor 'degree of participation' with regard to that defendant. We thus have to do the hard work of developing criteria for allocating (relative) responsibility regardless of where in the criminal process the relevant determination will be made.

(2) *A Hierarchy among Types of Participation?*

There has been some discussion on whether the sequence of types of responsibility in Article 25(3)(a)–(d) ICC Statute reflects a (descending) gradation, so that perpetrators under Article 25(3)(a) carry the greatest blame, and aiders of group crime under Article 25(3)(d) are the least blameworthy. The existence of such a gradation was first asserted by Gerhard Werle,[19] and there is some language in support of this concept in the *Lubanga* trial judgment of ICC Trial Chamber I.[20] However, Trial Chamber II has clearly rejected

---

17 The quotation is from Stewart, 'The End of "Modes of Liability" for International Crimes' (n 7) 217.
18 Cf Kai Ambos, *Treatise on International Criminal Law Vol I* (OUP 2013) ('Ambos, *Treatise on International Criminal Law Vol I*') 146.
19 See Gerhard Werle, 'Individual Criminal Responsibility in Article 25 ICC Statute' (2007) 5 JICJ 953, 956–957. Ambos, *Treatise on International Criminal Law Vol I* (n 18), at 146–47. seems to follow that view. Vest, 'Problems of Participation—Unitarian, Differentiated Approach, or Something Else?' (n 3) at 303, 305, supports the notion of a (limited) 'hierarchy' between principals and accomplices but not among the variants of accomplice liability under Art 25(3)(b), (c) and (d).
20 *Prosecutor v Lubanga* (Trial Chamber Judgment) ICC-01/04-01/06 (14 March 2012) ('*Lubanga* Trial Judgment') para 996 (referring to the relationship between Art 25(3)(a)

the existence of a 'hiérarchie de culpabilité' in the *Katanga* trial judgment of 2014.[21]

The argument in favour of a 'hierarchical' system is indeed not very strong. In his latest statement, Werle suggests that the differentiation in terminology and the placement into separate categories in Article 25(3) ICC Statute 'would not have any practical effect if it were not taken into account in sentencing matters.'[22] That, however, is a circular argument. It is exactly the question whether the sequence of types of participation in Article 25(3) reflects a substantive ordering that would need to be given 'practical effect.' Given the fact that the only relevant sentencing provision (Rule 145(1)(c) of the RPE) does not refer to any statutory gradation but only to 'the degree of participation of the convicted person', the issue remains a theoretician's headache: one may well concede to Werle that 'the particular mode of participation may serve as an indicator of the degree of criminal responsibility'[23] as long as Werle recognizes the possibility that an individual aider and abettor may, considering the concrete weight and importance of her contribution, receive a more severe sentence than the perpetrator whom she assisted. Or, put in the words of Trial Chamber II:

> Il n'existe pas de corrélation automatique entre le mode de responsabilité et la peine. Ceci démontre bien que l'auteur d'un crime n'est pas toujours considéré comme étant moralement plus répréhensible que le complice.[24]

2 How to Distinguish between Perpetrators and Accomplices

Since Article 25(3)(a)–(d) ICC Statute, as we have seen, rests on the assumption that there exists a categorical difference between perpetrators and accomplices, it is necessary to distinguish between these two groups. The Statute,

---

and (d)). See also *Prosecutor v Mbarushimana* (Decision on the Confirmation of Charges) ICC-01/04-01/10 (16 December 2011) para 279.

21 *Katanga Trial Judgment* (n 11) para 1386. See also *Lubanga, Separate Opinion of Judge Fulford* (n 5) para 9; *Prosecutor v Chui* (Trial Chamber Judgment) ICC-01/04-02/12 (18 December 2012), Concurring Opinion of Judge Christine Van den Wyngaert ('*Chui, Concurring Opinion of Judge Van den Wyngaert*') paras 22–24; van Sliedregt, *Individual Criminal Responsibility in International Law* (n 14) 108–09 (pointing out that persons who order or solicit the commission of crimes can be more blameworthy than those who carry them out).

22 Werle & Jeßberger, *Principles of International Criminal Law* (n 14), margin note 519.

23 Ibid.

24 *Katanga Trial Judgment* (n 11) para 1386.

however, only lists types of participants without defining their roles; and some of the types bear a close resemblance to each other but are placed in different categories. This state of affairs has led to a desperate search for 'the' criterion for distinguishing between perpetrators and accomplices. Building on a string of decisions by various chambers of the ICC,[25] the *Lubanga* Appeals Chamber sums up the result of this search:

> The most appropriate tool for conducting such an assessment is an evaluation of whether the accused had control over the crime, by virtue of his or her essential contribution to it and the resulting power to frustrate its commission, even if that essential contribution was not made at the execution stage of the crime.[26]

This tool, which has been called 'control theory',[27] has remained controversial even within the ICC[28] but seems to have been accepted by the great majority of the judges. 'Control theory' has also been applied by the *Lubanga* Appeals Chamber. The Chamber starts out by explaining the need to find an *objective* element that distinguishes perpetrators from accomplices.[29] The Chamber then adopts the view that an 'essential' (i.e., indispensable) contribution is the hallmark of a perpetrator; by contrast, an accomplice may provide a 'substantial' contribution but still lacks 'control' in that she is not in a position to frustrate the perpetration of the crime by withholding her contribution.[30]

---

[25] The groundwork was laid in *Prosecutor v Lubanga* (Decision on the Confirmation of Charges) ICC-01/04-01/06 (9 January 2007) ('*Lubanga Decision on Confirmation of Charges*') paras 327–41.

[26] *Lubanga Appeals Judgment* (n 2) para 473.

[27] For a recent assessment, see Jens D Ohlin, Elies van Sliedregt & Thomas Weigend, 'Assessing the Control-Theory' (2013) 26 LJIL 725 ('Ohlin et al., 'Assessing the Control-Theory"); for a thorough critique, see Lachezar Yanev & Tijs Kooijmans, 'Divided Minds in the Lubanga Trial Judgment: A Case against the Joint Control Theory' (2013) 13 Int'l Crim L Rev 789.

[28] See in particular *Lubanga, Concurring Opinion of Judge Fulford* (n 5) paras 6–12; *Chui, Concurring Opinion of Judge Van den Wyngaert* (n 21), paras 22–30.

[29] *Lubanga Appeals Judgment* (n 2) para 468.

[30] *Lubanga Trial Judgment* (n 20) paras 997–99, 1006. Trial Chamber II followed the same approach in the *Katanga Trial Judgment* (n 11) paras 1389–91. Trial Chamber II emphasized the notion that the Statute needs to be interpreted in a way that consistently affords a space of application to each component of Art 25(3)(a)–(d) as well as of art 30 ICC Statute; *ibid* at 1395. In the view of Trial Chamber II, the 'control' test meets this requirement.

The 'control' criterion is useful in that it permits courts to apply a one-issue test that will often provide a clear answer. That test also has a plausible normative basis: as a general rule, the law may *ceteris paribus* place greater blame on those who can determine whether or not the offence comes to fruition than on those who have no such power. The 'control' criterion has the further advantage of reaching beyond 'immediate' causation: it extends perpetrator liability to high-ranking personnel who do not dirty their hands by spilling blood but give orders to subordinates, knowing that their orders will be carried out. Furthermore, the 'control' test avoids the pitfall of the Joint Criminal Enterprise doctrine, which spreads the blame too far by treating alike every member of a conspiracy regardless of the importance of his or her role in carrying out the criminal plans of the group.

Yet, the 'control' test may in fact be less reliable than it appears to be. As Judge Fulford has pointed out, the determination whether a person 'controlled' the commission of a crime requires a hypothetical examination of what would have happened if the actor's contribution had been withheld.[31] The uncertainties involved and the necessarily speculative character of this hypothetical thought operation increase where a larger group of participants are involved: if A had not provided the plan for a criminal operation, would B have made that plan? Would B's plan have been as prone to success as A's plan was? If C had not provided the weapons used in a massacre, might D have sent equally effective weapons? Or would the same victims have been killed at the same time with more primitive weapons that were already available to the group? 'Control' theory also can lead to difficult problems concerning the identity of a crime: If participant E abandons a common design to attack a civilian population and his retreat leads to the postponement of the attack by a week, is the later attack still the same war crime as the one that E had helped plan?

Two further objections have been raised against 'control' theory. First, it has no basis in the ICC Statute or in customary international law but has been

---

31 Cf *Lubanga, Concurring Opinion of Judge Fulford* (n 5) para 17: 'It will largely be a matter of guesswork as to the real consequence for the particular crime if the accused is (hypothetically) removed from the equation, and most particularly it will not be easy to determine whether the offence would have been committed in any event.' See also Jens David Ohlin, 'Searching for the Hinterman' (2014) 12 JICJ 325 ('Ohlin, 'Searching for the Hinterman'") at 329–30. It has been suggested that the problem of hypothetical second-guessing could be reduced by assessing the essential character of a contribution *ex ante*: if the common plan provides for an essential role for A, then A is a perpetrator, regardless of whether his contribution actually proved indispensable when the plan was carried out; see Ohlin et al., 'Assessing the Control-Theory' (n 27) 731.

imported arbitrarily from German doctrine;[32] second, the 'control' criterion is relevant only under the condition that Article 25(3) ICC Statute provides a hierarchical ranking of types of participation.[33] I find neither objection persuasive. As for the legal basis of 'control' theory,[34] this 'theory' is not more than a device for the interpretation of one aspect of Article 25(3)(a)–(d) ICC Statute. Any court is free to devise tools or test questions for the interpretation of the law, and it is not necessary to find a source for such aids in customary international law. Nor are international courts precluded from considering or even adopting arguments and ideas developed in national jurisdictions.[35]

As to the necessity of the 'control' criterion, Judge Van den Wyngaert has argued that

> if there is no hierarchical arrangement between these concepts [i.e., principals and accessories], principals can be just as blameworthy as accessories. If this is true, then why go to such theoretical lengths to divide principals and accessories at all?[36]

This argument, plausible as it appears at first sight, conflates two separate issues. Even if we agree that the catalogue of types of participation in Article 25(3)(a)–(d) ICC Statute does not signify a descending categorical hierarchy of blameworthiness, this does not absolve us of the need to distinguish between perpetrators and accomplices, for the reasons set out above (1.1.). Judge Van den Wyngaert in fact implicitly accepts the need for a distinction by suggesting, in the context of joint perpetration, that only a 'direct' contribution to the performance of the *actus reus* will suffice for perpetratorship.[37] That is a

---

32 *Lubanga, Concurring Opinion of Judge Fulford* (n 5) para 10.
33 *Katanga Trial Judgment* (n 11), *Minority Opinion of Judge Christine Van den Wyngaert* ('*Katanga, Minority Opinion of Judge Van den Wyngaert*') para 281.
34 For an analysis of the doctrinal similarities with German '*Tatherrschaftslehre*', see Thomas Weigend, 'Perpetration through an Organization: The Unexpected Career of a German Legal Concept' (2011) 9 JICJ 91 ('Weigend, 'Perpetration through an Organization: The Unexpected Career of a German Legal Concept'').
35 See *Lubanga Appeals Judgment* (n 2) para 470: 'The Appeals Chamber considers it appropriate to seek guidance from approaches developed in other jurisdictions in order to reach a coherent and persuasive interpretation of the Court's legal texts. This Court is not administrating justice in a vacuum, but, in applying the law, needs to be aware of and can relate to concepts and ideas found in domestic jurisdictions.' See also Herzig, 'Die Tatherrschaftslehre in der Rechtsprechung des Internationalen Strafgerichtshofs' (n 13) 199.
36 *Katanga, Minority Opinion of Judge Van den Wyngaert* (n 33) para 281.
37 *Chui, Concurring Opinion of Judge Van den Wyngaert* (n 21) paras 44–48.

sensible (if debatable[38]) approach but implies that a distinction must be made between principals and accessories to a crime. And when Judge Van den Wyngaert suggests, in her *Katanga* minority opinion, that one should follow 'the ordinary meaning of the language of article 25(3) of the Statute in light of its object and purpose',[39] this too implies a distinction between perpetrators and accessories: the content and language of Article 25(3) clearly make such a distinction, even though accomplices may in individual cases be as blameworthy as perpetrators.

Before we take another look at the 'control' criterion, let us consider possible alternatives. Various approaches for identifying perpetrators have been suggested, but on balance they do not fare better than the 'control' test. Treating as a perpetrator everyone who has an 'operative link' to the commission of the crime by making a 'causal' contribution, as proposed by Judge Fulford,[40] casts the net too wide; and limiting perpetratorship to persons who are 'directly' involved in the performance of the *actus reus*, as suggested by Judge Van den Wyngaert,[41] introduces a criterion that is normatively dubious[42] and is difficult to apply consistently in critical cases.[43]

Another alternative is to make the distinction turn not on objective but on *subjective* criteria: Jens David Ohlin has recently proposed that *intention* should be the distinguishing mark of perpetratorship. According to his theory, a perpetrator must share 'a bona fide joint intention with the other co-perpetrators',[44] which means that the perpetrator must 'desire' the offence to be committed.[45]

---

38   For criticism, see Ohlin et al., 'Assessing the Control-Theory' (n 27) 729–30.
39   *Katanga, Minority Opinion of Judge Van den Wyngaert* (n 33) para 281.
40   *Lubanga, Separate Opinion of Judge Fulford* (n 5) para 16.
41   *Chui, Concurring Opinion of Judge Van den Wyngaert* (n 21) paras 44–48.
42   A division of labour between co-perpetrators is a typical feature of joint perpetration; it is therefore not very useful to withhold the label of 'perpetrator' from those whose contribution, according to the common plan, is a bit further removed from the performance of the *actus reus*. In cases of perpetration 'through another person', the 'directness' criterion would be even more difficult to apply.
43   *Chui, Concurring Opinion of Judge Van den Wyngaert* (n 21) para 47 proposes a broad interpretation of 'directness': 'Sometimes the means used to commit the material elements of a crime inherently require planning and coordination (eg an air raid by a bomber squadron). In all those cases the distinctive feature of what constitutes a direct contribution is that it is an intrinsic part of the actual execution of the crime.' The concept of 'intrinsic part' considerably relaxes the 'directness' requirement, thus leaving a broad margin of appreciation to the judges in each individual case.
44   Ohlin, 'Searching for the Hinterman' (n 31) 338. See also Jens D Ohlin, 'Joint Intentions to Commit International Crimes' (2011) 11 Chi J Int'l L 693, 721.
45   Ohlin, 'Searching for the Hinterman' (n 31) 341.

This theory is reminiscent of the *animus* theory that German courts have espoused since the late 19th century: the German Imperial Court had proclaimed that those who have the mind of a perpetrator (*animus auctoris*) are perpetrators, whereas those who think of themselves as mere associates (*animus socii*) are deemed accomplices.[46] The virtue of this theory is its extreme flexibility: since a person's *animus* at the time of the crime can only be attributed in hindsight, the distinction between perpetrators and accomplices is left to the practically unreviewable discretion of the trial court. But it is difficult to understand why, of two individuals who jointly contribute in identical ways to the commission of a crime, one should be treated as a perpetrator because he acted with 'intention', whereas his co-defendant who foresaw but did not desire the outcome is convicted as a mere accomplice.[47]

Does the lack of viable alternatives mean that the 'control' test remains as the optimal solution for separating principals from accessories? We have seen that the criterion of the 'indispensability' of a person's contribution is less than precise when applied to group crime. And this criterion may, if applied as broadly as by the *Lubanga* Trial Chamber,[48] over-extend the label of perpetratorship to persons who were far removed from the center of the harmful conduct. It may therefore be useful to treat 'control' as one (strong) indicator of principal liability but to add other indicators, such as the close temporal proximity of the person's contribution to the *actus reus* of the offence, and/or a strong subjective interest of the individual in the success of the criminal enterprise.[49] Having a broader array of indicators rather than a one-dimensional test makes the application of the law more difficult, but it permits the court to develop a more nuanced jurisprudence as to what are the proper characteristics of a perpetrator in contrast to an accomplice.

---

46   *Reichsgericht*, Judgment of 7 January 1881, 3349/80, published in (1881) 3 Entscheidungen des Reichsgerichts in Strafsachen 181. For further German case law, see references in Ohlin et al, 'Assessing the Control-Theory' (n 27) 733 n 35.

47   Ohlin, 'Searching for the Hinterman' (n 31) 336 argues that 'mental elements—especially volitional ones—represent the defendant's desire to bring about a state of affairs in the world. As such, these volitional elements represent a moral choice, a decision for which agents will be called to account by their social communities and the criminal law.' This may well be correct—but a similar moral choice is also made by the person who acts with (mere) knowledge or even recklessness as to the forbidden result; and we are generally 'called to account' for what we do, not for what we think. In the end, Ohlin seems to accept a combination of objective ('control') and subjective ('intention') factors as requirements for perpetratorship; *ibid*, at 341. This is close to the solution proposed here.

48   Cf *Lubanga Trial Judgment* (n 20) para 1356.

49   For a more detailed anaysis, see Ohlin et al., 'Assessing the Control-Theory' (n 27) 732–34.

3 Joint Perpetration and Indirect Perpetration

In the final part of this paper, I will add a few remarks on the concepts of joint and indirect perpetration. Not surprisingly, these two forms of perpetration have led to much debate among the judges of the ICC and beyond. Since international crime is group crime, the commission of an offence 'as an individual' by a single offender is bound to be exceptional. Since groups as such are not punishable under the ICC Statute,[50] it is the interpretation of joint and indirect perpetration that determines the reach of the law to members of the group.

(1) *Joint Perpetration*

Joint perpetration has two main elements: an agreement or common plan which will result in the commission of a crime, and an essential contribution by each co-perpetrator. In addition, co-perpetrators must act with *mens rea*, that is, they must be aware of the common plan as well as of their role in it, and they must intend or foresee any result which is a material element of the offence.[51] It appears beyond dispute that the common plan need not be spelled out but can be implicit, and further that the criminal aspect of the planned conduct need not be specifically intended by the co-perpetrators as long as they are aware, as minimally required by Article 30 (2) ICC Statute, that the material elements of the offence in question will be fulfilled in the ordinary course of events.[52]

It is with regard to the requirement of an objective contribution that 'control' theory plays a decisive role. The element of an 'essential' contribution clearly is not to be understood in a naturalistic sense requiring 'that a person actually carry out directly and personally the incriminated conduct in order to

---

50 For possible reasons for the concentration of international criminal tribunals on individual criminal responsibility, see Shachar Eldar, 'Exploring International Criminal Law's Reluctance to Resort to Modalities of Group Responsibility' (2013) 11 JICJ 331. The most convincing doctrinal explanation of this phenomenon is international criminal law's expressive function, which demands a distinctive analysis of individual guilt rather than an across-the-board declaration of responsibility of a whole group (*ibid*, at 344–45).

51 Cf *Lubanga Trial Judgment* (n 20) para 1018; *Lubanga Appeals Judgment* (n 2) paras 335–46, 473.

52 *Lubanga Appeals Judgment* (n 2) paras 446–51. The Appeals Chamber is right in criticizing the Lubanga Pre-Trial and Trial Chambers for having couched the requisite *mens rea* in terms of 'taking a sufficient risk'; *ibid*, paras 442, 449. Each co-perpetrator must know not only that there is a *risk* that the material elements may be fulfilled but that this is almost certain (to the extent that one can predict future events).

be a co-perpetrator'.[53] But as has been mentioned above, it is not sufficient, according to ICC case law, that a person only make a 'substantial' contribution to the common plan; instead, the contribution has to be 'essential' in the sense that the crime would not have been the same without it.[54] An 'essential' contribution can, however, be made not only at the execution stage of the crime, but also at the planning or preparation stage.[55] This extension may lead to a very broad understanding of co-perpetration: as long as the common plan is itself deemed 'essential' to the crime as it was carried out, anyone who participated in devising the plan is liable as a perpetrator, even if he has no role in the actual realisation of the plan.

A contested issue concerns the combination of co-perpetration and indirect perpetration ('through another person').[56] This situation may occur where two or more military leaders join forces in a military operation and bring together their respective troops, knowing that the soldiers will commit crimes. Whereas some judges have recognized this combination as one way in which each leader makes an 'essential' contribution to the commission of an offence,[57] Judge Van den Wyngaert maintains that adding a fourth type of perpetratorship to the three types listed in Article 25(3)(a) ICC Statute would violate the principle of legality.[58] She asserts that under the majority interpretation a defendant can be held responsible for the conduct of the physical perpetrator of a crime, even though the defendant neither exercised any direct influence over this person nor shared any intent with him.[59] But this phenomenon is nothing but the effect of the doctrine of joint perpetration: if two military leaders make a common plan to jointly commit an offence by employing the

---

53 *Lubanga Appeals Judgment* (n 2) para 466.
54 *Lubanga Decision on Confirmation of Charges* (n 25) para 347; *Lubanga Trial Judgment* (n 20) paras 993, 999–1001.
55 *Lubanga Appeals Judgment* (n 2) para 469.
56 For discussions of this issue, see Boris Burghardt & Gerhard Werle, 'Die mittelbare Mittäterschaft—Fortentwicklung deutscher Strafrechtsdogmatik im Völkerstrafrecht?' in René Bloy et al. (ed), *Gerechte Strafe und legitimes Strafrecht: Festschrift für Manfred Maiwald zum 75. Geburtstag* (Duncker & Humblot 2010) 849; Jernej Letnar Cernic, 'Shaping the Spiderweb: Towards the Concept of Joint Commission through Another Person under the Rome Statute and Jurisprudence of the International Criminal Court' (2011) 22 Crim LF 539; Stefan Wirth, 'Co-Perpetration in the Lubanga Trial Judgment' (2012) 10 JICJ 971, 980; Ohlin et al., 'Assessing the Control-Theory' (n 27) 734–37.
57 See *Katanga and Chui Decision on Confirmation of Charges* (n 11) para 493.
58 *Chui, Concurring Opinion of Judge Van den Wyngaert* (n 21) paras 61–64; see also *Katanga, Minority Opinion of Judge Van den Wyngaert* (n 33) para 278.
59 *Chui, Concurring Opinion of Judge Van den Wyngaert* (n 21) para 61.

armed forces under the command of each leader, their acts can be mutually attributed. Hence the orders that A gives to his troops are attributed to B, and vice versa. This means that A is treated as if he had ordered B's troops to commit the crimes in question; and if that ordering fulfils the requirements of indirect perpetration, then A is responsible as an indirect perpetrator for the acts done by B's troops. 'Indirect co-perpetration' is thus not a novel form of perpetration unforeseen by Article 25(3)(a) ICC Statute but only a special variant of co-perpetration.

(2) *Indirect Perpetration*

Article 25(3)(a) ICC Statute defines committing a crime 'through another person' as one type of principal responsibility. This is, by itself, not extraordinary because most legal systems recognize the fact that a perpetrator can make use of an innocent agent, for example, a child or an insane person, to carry out the physical *actus reus* of an offence.[60] The ICC Statute's definition is rather unusual, however, in that it makes perpetration 'through another person' include the case that 'that other person is criminally responsible'. This means that 'perpetration through another person' is regarded as an independent type of principal responsibility, not a mere fallback position for cases which would otherwise fall between the cracks of perpetration and accomplice liability. Perpetration 'through' a criminally responsible agent is, moreover, a concept particularly well suited to international criminal law, because it reflects a typical situation of group crime: leaders commit crimes by making use of an armed group or a powerful bureaucracy under their command.

Since its early decisions, the ICC has grappled with the question what requirements must be met in order to hold the leader of a group responsible for committing criminal acts 'through' his subordinates. In 2008, Pre-Trial Chamber I in the Decision on the Confirmation of Charges against Katanga and Chui elaborated the notion of 'control over an organised apparatus of power'.[61] Relying heavily on German legal doctrine, Pre-Trial Chamber I proclaimed that a leader may be held responsible for the acts of his subordinates if he has command power in a hierarchical organisation that is composed of sufficient subordinates to guarantee that the superior's orders will be carried out, if not by one subordinate, then by another; the actual executor of the order is then merely a replaceable 'cog in the wheel'.[62] Deviating from German

---

[60] For a comparative overview, see van Sliedregt, *Individual Criminal Responsibility in International Law* (n 14) 90–91.
[61] *Katanga and Chui Decision on Confirmation of Charges* (n 11) paras 500 et seq.
[62] *Ibid* paras 512, 516.

doctrine, Pre-Trial Chamber I extended the concept of perpetration through an organisation to situations where 'a leader secures automatic compliance via his control of the apparatus...through intensive, strict, and violent training regimens'.[63]

The consequences of a finding that a person was a leader in such an organisation have never become entirely clear. Is it a sufficient or a necessary condition for holding a leader liable for acts carried out by his subordinates, or is it merely an indicator of the leader's actual dominance of his subordinates? In her Concurring Opinion in the judgment acquitting Matthieu Ngudjolo Chui, Judge Van den Wyngaert opposed the notion that control over an organisation could be 'a constitutive element of criminal responsibility under Article 25(3)(a)'.[64] In 2014, Trial Chamber I, in convicting Germain Katanga, still relied on the concept of 'contrôle sur l'organisation.'[65] The Chamber also retained the criterion of the fungibility of individual members of the organisation but noted that 'les modalités de contrôle sur les individus peuvent être de plus en plus diversifiées et sophistiquées et qu'il s'avère singulièrement difficile d'appréhender et de comprendre la nature et la dynamique interne des organisations criminelles contemporaines.'[66] Moreover, the Chamber emphasized that control through an organisation is not the only way in which perpetration through another person can be realized.[67] Rather, in the view of the Trial Chamber,

> le seul critère indispensable (...) est que l'auteur indirect exerce, d'une façon ou d'une autre y compris, le cas échéant, au sein d'une organisation, un contrôle sur le crime commis par l'intermédiaire d'une autre personne.[68]

This means that perpetration through another person can be attributed only to leaders who actually make use of their authority within the organization, with the aim that subordinates carry out the crime in question.[69] Although Judge Van den Wyngaert may have over-interpreted this statement when she claims that the *Katanga* Trial Chamber had 'rejected' the idea that the so-called

---

63   *Ibid* para 518.
64   *Chui, Concurring Opinion of Judge Van den Wyngaert* (n 21) para 52.
65   *Katanga Trial Judgment* (n 11) paras 1403–1404.
66   *Ibid* para 1411.
67   *Ibid* para 1406.
68   *Ibid*.
69   *Ibid* para 1412.

'*Organisationsherrschaft*' doctrine is a constitutive element of 'indirect perpetration' in the sense of article 25(3)(a) ICC Statute,[70] it is safe to say that the *Katanga* Trial Chamber has moved toward a less doctrinal and more flexible application of the doctrine. What counts is not the identification of certain characteristics of an organization, but the fact that the defendant was in a position to determine whether the crime was to be committed—either because his personal influence on the direct perpetrator was such that the latter would carry out his orders without question, or because the group was organised in a way that made certain that the defendant's orders would be followed. It is thus 'interpersonal control'[71] (however it may have been brought about) that is the hallmark of perpetration 'through another person',[72] and control over an organisation is only one of several possible means to exert control over the physical perpetrator.[73]

4   A General Concept of Perpetration?

Even this brief survey has shown that the 23 words of Article 25(3)(a) ICC Statute raise a host of difficult questions. Do they express or at least imply a normatively consistent notion of 'perpetration' which sets principal actors apart from lesser participants in a criminal enterprise? I doubt that this is the case. It is not evident that a person who commits a crime 'through' another responsible agent should be categorically different from a person who 'orders' the commission of a crime (Article 25(3)(b)), and even 'assisting' in the commission of a crime (Article 25(3)(c)) may not be very different from committing that crime 'jointly with another'. By adopting a list of traditional concepts taken from different jurisdictions, the authors of the ICC Statute took the path of least resistance but left it to those who seek to interpret the Statute (that is, most prominently the judges of the Court) to make sense of the various categories of participants in a crime. The authors of the Statute were wise enough not to make penalties depend on the categorization of a person's contribution as perpetration or 'mere' complicity. But, they still left ample opportunity for devising consistent ways of distinguishing those who are 'central' to the commission of a crime from those who contribute at the

---

70   *Katanga, Minority Opinion of Judge Van den Wyngaert* (n 33) para 279 note 70.
71   See van Sliedregt, *Individual Criminal Responsibility in International Law* (n 14) 170.
72   Cf Weigend, 'Perpetration through an Organization: The Unexpected Career of a German Legal Concept' (n 34) 109; Ohlin et al., 'Assessing the Control-Theory' (n 27) 737–38.
73   *Katanga, Minority Opinion of Judge Van den Wyngaert* (n 33) para 279 note 70.

periphery. In applying this distinction, we may be well-advised not to rely too much on theoretical constructs borrowed from one or the other national jurisdiction. It might instead be one guideline for interpretation to restrict use of the label of 'perpetrator' to those who are responsible as leaders for the collective commission of the most serious crimes of international concern (cf. Article 1 ICC Statute).

CHAPTER 23

The Limited Reach of Superior Responsibility

Shane Darcy*

The doctrine of superior responsibility is firmly embedded in the fabric of international criminal law. As a seemingly broad mode of criminal liability, it has not, however, yielded the results that one would expect from a form of liability that allows military commanders or civilian superiors to be held responsible for the acts of subordinates which they fail to prevent or punish. Its apparent potential to hold the most senior leaders to account for allowing international crimes to be committed has not been fulfilled. Superior responsibility has generated controversy from its inception, for several reasons, including its theoretical reach to the top of military and political chains of command and authority.[1] Justice Frank Murphy of the United States Supreme Court reacted to the first application of command responsibility, in *Yamashita*, by warning that 'the fate of some future President of the United States and his chiefs of staff and military advisers may well have been sealed by this decision.'[2] There is no question that such high-ranking individuals can no longer evade responsibility simply by virtue of their official position, while international criminal law also generates liability for such persons where they order, plan or instigate the commission of international crimes.[3] Key differences between superior responsibility and such other modes of liability—which are codified separately in the Rome Statute of the International Criminal Court—are that superior responsibility addresses omissions, and involves a lower *mens rea* standard than the general requirement that crimes be committed with 'intent and knowledge.'[4] That is to say, high-ranking officials may be criminally responsible for failing to prevent or punish crimes committed by their subordinates, even where they did not intend that such offences be committed or have full knowledge of their commission. Yet, despite the broadening of criminal liability

---

* Thanks to Abby Satterfield for her research assistance.
1 See eg 'Commission on the Responsibility of the Authors of the War and on the Enforcement of Penalties: Report Presented to the Preliminary Peace Conference, March 19, 1919' (1920) 14 AJIL 95, 121, 143.
2 *In re Yamashita* 327 US 1 (1946) 28 ('*In re Yamashita*').
3 Rome Statute of the International Criminal Court (adopted 17 July 1998, entered into force 1 July 2002) 2187 UNTS 90 ('Rome Statute') arts 25, 27.
4 *Ibid* art 30.

that superior responsibility entails, practice before international criminal tribunals and elsewhere reveals that the doctrine has not been applied as successfully, as often, or as high up the chain of command as one might expect. This essay seeks to consider why this is the case, paying particular attention to the legal requirements of the doctrine and their application by international and national tribunals.

Trials before international criminal tribunals have often, but not exclusively, involved the prosecution of the most senior persons responsible for international crimes.[5] Such a focus has been explicitly mandated at times: the Nuremberg Tribunal, for example, tried the 'major war criminals of the European Axis',[6] while the Statute of the Special Court for Sierra Leone envisaged prosecution of 'persons who bear the greatest responsibility for serious violations.'[7] The completion strategy of the *ad hoc* Tribunals involved a focus on the 'most senior leaders',[8] reflecting the judges' view that 'the major objectives of the Security Council are in large part not fulfilled if only low-level figures rather than the civilian, military and paramilitary leaders who were allegedly responsible for the atrocities are brought before the Tribunals for trial.'[9] The Rome Statute does not contain any limitation regarding seniority, although the Prosecutor's policy has been to focus on 'the most serious crimes and on those who bear the greatest responsibility for these crimes.'[10] Before turning to the application of superior responsibility in the context of such trials, it is worth considering how political considerations have had a significant influence on whether the most senior leaders are put on trial in the first place.[11]

---

5   For a statistical overview, see Alette Smeulers, Barbora Hola & Tom van den Berg, 'Sixty-Five Years of International Criminal Justice: The Facts and Figures' (2013) 13 Int'l Crim LR 1 ('Smeulers et al., 'Sixty-Five Years of International Criminal Justice: The Facts and Figures'') 25–29.

6   Agreement for the Prosecution and Punishment of the Major War Criminals of the European Axis, and Charter of the International Military Tribunal (adopted 8 August 1945, entered into force 8 August 1945) art 1.

7   Statute of the Special Court for Sierra Leone (adopted 16 January 2002, entered into force 12 April 2002) 2178 UNTS 138 ('Statute of the Special Court for Sierra Leone') art 1.

8   See UNSC Res 1503 (28 August 2003) UN Doc S/Res/1503.

9   'Report of the Expert Group to Conduct a Review of the Effective Operation and Functioning of the International Tribunal for the Former Yugoslavia and the International Criminal Tribunal for Rwanda' UN Doc S/2002/597 (2000) para 96.

10 Report on Prosecutorial Strategy (International Criminal Court, Office of the Prosecutor, 14 September 2006) 5.

11 See generally Jackson Nyamuya Maogoto, *War Crimes and Realpolitik: International Justice from World War I to the 21st Century* (Lynne Rienner 2004); Robert Cryer, *Prosecuting International Crimes; Selectivity and the International Criminal Law Regime* (CUP 2005).

The Treaty of Versailles envisaged the trial of the German Kaiser before an international tribunal 'for a supreme offence against international morality and the sanctity of treaties',[12] although Wilhelm II was given asylum in the Netherlands and never faced trial.[13] Cherif Bassiouni considers that despite the express provision in the treaty, the Allies 'did not intend to prosecute a royal monarch' at a time when many European heads of state were also royals.[14] After the Second World War, the 'major war criminals' tried by the Tokyo Tribunal excluded the Japanese Emperor, as the United States had 'exempted him from prosecution and worked to avoid implicating him personally during the trials', in order to advance its geopolitical interests with Japan.[15] Political factors have also played a role in senior trials before contemporary international criminal justice mechanisms. Slobodan Milošević had been instrumental in Bosnian peace negotiations, but just prior to his arrest, he had become 'a direct obstacle to Western policy.'[16] Both he and Charles Taylor, former heads of state, were tried '*after* key international players had determined that their usefulness to the political process had ended.'[17] Radovan Karadžić claimed that he had been promised immunity from prosecution by the United States for his cooperation in peace efforts, although the alleged offer was not viewed by the ICTY Appeals Chamber as a barrier to prosecution.[18]

Similar political influences manifest themselves at a national level, especially in the context of prosecutions on the basis of universal jurisdiction. Proceedings under Ireland's Geneva Conventions Act 1962, for example, must be initiated or consented to by the government's lawyer, the Attorney General. Clive Baldwin, a senior legal advisor for Human Rights Watch has commented in the British context that:

> The UK has a dismal record of holding senior political and military figures criminally responsible for serious crimes of their forces—it seems the last time this happened was in 1651, during the English Civil War. [...]

---

12 Treaty of Versailles (adopted 28 June 1919) art 227.
13 M Cherif Bassiouni, 'The Perennial Conflict between International Criminal Justice and *Realpolitik*' (2006) 22 Ga St U LR 541, 551.
14 Ibid.
15 David Bosco, *Rough Justice: The International Court in a World of Power Politics* (OUP 2014) ('Bosco, *Rough Justice: The International Court in a World of Power Politics*') 26.
16 Ibid 63.
17 Ibid 126.
18 See *Prosecutor v Karadžić* (Decision on Karadžić's Appeal of Trial Chamber Decision on Alleged Holbrooke Agreement) IT-95-5/18-AR73.4 (12 October 2009).

ultimate power over individual prosecutions still rests with the Attorney General, a politician and member of the government. It is hardly surprising that no politician has ever been investigated when a member of the government can block prosecutions.[19]

Attempts to prosecute high-ranking foreign State officials in countries such as Belgium, Spain and the United Kingdom have led to the assumption of greater political control over any exercise of universal jurisdiction by national courts.[20] It is telling that in the context of the United States opposition to the International Criminal Court, a Bush administration official admitted that its concern was less the trial of soldiers by an international court, but rather that the Court might pursue 'top public officials—President Bush, Secretary Rumsfeld, Secretary Powell—they are at the heart of our concern.'[21] While political factors can provide an explanation as to why leadership trials are held, or not, they do not account for the limited reach of superior responsibility in the context of such prosecutions. The answer may lie in the requirements of this mode of liability, as elaborated and applied by various courts and tribunals.

The codification of superior responsibility in Additional Protocol I to the 1949 Geneva Conventions brought some clarity to the scope and elements of the doctrine, because even though the relevant provision was 'based on the Yamashita case',[22] the infamous Second World War case had left much uncertainty and controversy in its wake.[23] The Japanese General was prosecuted by a United States Military Commission, and subsequently executed, for failing 'to

---

19   Clive Baldwin, 'Why the ICC Needed to Reopen the Iraq Abuse Case' *The Huffington Post* (London, 19 May 2014), at <http://www.huffingtonpost.co.uk/clive-baldwin/why-the-icc-needed-to-reo_b_5349894.html> accessed 9 February 2015.
20   Fannie Lafontaine, 'Universal Jurisdiction—the Realistic Utopia' (2012) 10 JICJ 1277; 'The Principle and Practice of Universal Jurisdiction: PCHR's work in the occupied Palestinian territory' (Palestinian Centre for Human Rights 2010), at <http://pchrgaza.org/files/Reports/English/pdf_spec/PCHR-UJ-BOOK.pdf> accessed 9 February 2015.
21   Bosco, *Rough Justice: The International Court in a World of Power Politics* (n 15) 79, citing Elizabeth Becker, 'On World Court, US Focus Shifts to Shielding Officials' *The New York Times* (New York, 7 September 2002).
22   Michael Bothe, Karl Josef Partsch & Waldemar A Solf, *New Rules for Victims of Armed Conflict: Commentary on the Two 1977 Protocols Additional to the Geneva Conventions of 1949* (Martinus Nijhoff 1982) 525.
23   See generally Richard L Lael, *The Yamashita Precedent: War Crimes and Command Responsibility* (Scholarly Resources Inc 1982); Allan A Ryan, *Yamashita's Ghost: War Crimes, MacArthur's Justice, and Command Responsibility* (UP of Kansas 2012).

discover and control the criminal acts' of his subordinates.[24] Article 86(2) of the Protocol reads:

> The fact that a breach of the Conventions or of this Protocol was committed by a subordinate does not absolve his superiors from penal or disciplinary responsibility, as the case may be, if they knew, or had information which should have enabled them to conclude in the circumstances at the time, that he was committing or was going to commit such a breach and if they did not take all feasible measures within their power to prevent or repress the breach.[25]

Superiors are not automatically liable for the acts of their subordinates and three key elements are required under the Protocol for the doctrine's successful application: a superior-subordinate relationship, actual knowledge or information pointing to criminal activities by subordinates, and a failure to stop or punish such offences. These requirements, which will be looked at in turn, are also present in the superior responsibility provisions of the statutes of the various international criminal tribunals, albeit with some minor modifications.[26]

The existence of a superior-subordinate relationship is essential for the doctrine's operation. In theory, it extends to all persons up the chain of command. The authoritative *Commentary on the Additional Protocols* observes, in relation to the corresponding duty of commanders under Article 87, that:

> There is no member of the armed forces exercising command who is not obliged to ensure proper application of the Conventions and the Protocol. As there is no part of the army which is not subordinated to a military commander at whatever level, this responsibility applies from the highest level of the hierarchy, from the Commander-in-Chief down to the common soldier who takes over as head of the platoon to which he

---

24 'Trial of General Tomoyuki Yamashita' in *Law Reports of Trials of War Criminals*, vol 4 (United Nations War Crimes Commission 1948) 1 (*'Trial of General Yomoyuki Yamashita'*) 35.

25 Protocol Additional to the Geneva Conventions of 12 August 1949, and Relating to the Protection of Victims of International Armed Conflicts (adopted 8 June 1977, entered into force 7 December 1978) 1125 UNTS 3 (Protocol I) art 86(2).

26 See Statute of the International Criminal Tribunal for the Former Yugoslavia (adopted 25 May 1993) ('ICTY Statute') art 7(3); Statute of the International Criminal Tribunal for Rwanda (adopted 8 November 1994) ('ICTR Statute') art 6(3); Statute of the Special Court for Sierra Leone (n 7) art 6(3); Rome Statute (n 3) art 28.

belongs at the moment his commanding officer has fallen and is no longer capable of fulfilling the task.[27]

For superiors to be responsible, however, the relationship must entail the exercise of effective control over subordinates. In *Čelebići*, one of the key superior responsibility cases before the ICTY, the Trial Chamber held that the formal existence of a superior-subordinate relationship is insufficient in and of itself: 'Instead, the factor which determines liability for this type of criminal responsibility is the actual possession, or non-possession, of powers of control over the actions of subordinates.'[28] This mode of liability thus applies to '[a]ll superiors in a chain of command who exercise effective control.'[29] Superior responsibility, the ICTR has noted, is 'predicated upon the power of the superior to control or influence the acts of subordinates',[30] although the ability to influence alone would not be sufficient. Judges at the International Criminal Court have explained that effective control would not seem to 'accommodate any lower standard of control such as the simple ability to exercise influence over forces or subordinates, even if such influence turned out to be substantial.'[31] The Rome Statute expressly requires 'effective command or control' on the part of military commanders, and 'effective authority and control' in the case of non-military superiors, whereas this element had been effectively read in by the judges of the *ad hoc* tribunals. In *Ntaganda*, the Pre-Trial Chamber held that a superior-subordinate relationship existed between the accused, a military commander, and both troops and civilians over whom he exercised command and control.[32] In the case of the latter, he had the capacity to order them to 'engage in hostilities.'[33]

---

27   Yves Sandoz, Christophe Swinarski & Bruno Zimmermann (eds), *Commentary on the Additional Protocols of 8 June 1977 to the Geneva Conventions of 12 August 1949* (Martinus Nijhoff 1987) 1019.
28   *Prosecutor v Zejnil Delalic* et al. (Trial Judgment) IT-96-21-T (18 November 1998) ('*Delalic* Trial Judgment') para 370.
29   Paola Gaeta et al., *Cassese's International Criminal Law* (OUP 2013) ('Gaeta et al., *Cassese's International Criminal Law*') 187.
30   *Prosecutor v Bagilishema* (Trial Judgment) ICTR-95-1A-T (7 June 2001) para 37.
31   *Prosecutor v Bemba Gombo* (Decision on the Confirmation of Charges) ICC-01/05/-01/08 (15 June 2009) ('*Bemba Gombo* Confirmation of Charges Decision') para 415.
32   *Prosecutor v Ntaganda* (Decision on the Confirmation of Charges) ICC-01/04-02/06 (9 June 2014) ('*Ntaganda* Decision on the Confirmation of Charges') para 166.
33   Ibid.

Establishing the existence of effective control is a key requirement, without which any modern prosecution based on superior responsibility will fail.[34] Liability for a superior can only arise for offences occurring during the time when such effective control existed. The *Bemba* Pre-Trial Chamber considered that effective control must have existed from at least the time that subordinates were about to commit crimes.[35] The ICTY Appeals Chamber has similarly held that liability for superiors does not arise for crimes committed 'before the accused assumed command over the subordinate.'[36] The law as it stands would seem to rule out the criminal liability of successors for crimes committed by subordinates while under the effective control of their predecessors.[37] The upshot of this emphasis on effective control is a limitation on which superiors can be held to account under the doctrine:

> In practical terms, command responsibility is not taken to extend as far up the chain of command as might logically be implied, that is to commanders in chief, and is generally confined to officers in some meaningful supervisory capacity.[38]

The Appeals Chamber of the ICTY included amongst indicators of effective control, the ability to issue command orders to the subordinates in question, the exercise of disciplinary authority thereover, and influence over promotions and terminations.[39] The presence of effective control is treated as a matter of evidence, more than of substantive law, and 'whether a given form of authority possessed by a superior amounts to an indicator of effective control depends on the circumstances of the case.'[40] Recent practice shows that a significant number of contemporary superior responsibility prosecutions have not succeeded

---

34 *Prosecutor v Perišić* (Appeal Judgment) IT-04-81-A (28 February 2013) ('*Perišić* Appeal Judgment') para 87.

35 *Bemba Gombo* Confirmation of Charges Decision (n 31) para 419.

36 *Perišić* Appeal Judgment (n 34) para 87.

37 See David Akerson & Natalie Knowlton, 'President Obama and the International Criminal Law of Successor Liability' (2009) 37 Denver J Intl L & Pol'y 615. See also Joakim Dungel & Shannon Ghadiri, 'The Temporal Scope of Command Responsibility Revisited: Why Commanders Have a Duty to Prevent Crimes Committed after the Cessation of Effective Control' (2010) 17 U C Davis J Intl L & Pol'y 1.

38 Nomi Bar-Yaacov, 'Command Responsibility' in Roy Gutman, David Rieff & Anthony Dworkin (eds), *Crimes of War* (2nd ed, WH Norton 2007) 117, 118.

39 *Perišić* Appeal Judgment (n 34) para 97. See also *Prosecutor v. Strugar* (Appeal Judgment) IT-01-42-A (17 July 2008) ('*Strugar* Appeal Judgment') paras 195, 253.

40 *Strugar* Appeal Judgment (n 39) para 254.

because of the absence of a superior-responsibility relationship entailing effective control.[41] This element has been described as 'the major obstacle to the application of command responsibility.'[42]

Liability for superiors exercising effective control is based on their failure to either prevent subordinate crimes or to punish them afterwards, even if the actions of these subordinates were pursuant to orders from above. As a United States Military Tribunal put it in the *High Command* case:

> Under basic principles of command authority and responsibility, an officer who merely stands by while his subordinates execute a criminal order of his superiors which he knows is criminal, violates a moral obligation under International Law. By doing nothing he cannot wash his hands of international responsibility.[43]

There has been a debate as to whether superior responsibility is a mode of liability or a crime itself, and although a dereliction of duty offence may exist in national military law, under international criminal law, guilty superiors are convicted under this doctrine for the crimes committed by their subordinates.[44] Criminal responsibility under the Statutes of the *ad hoc* Tribunals arises because 'the superior failed to take the necessary and reasonable measures to prevent such acts or to punish the perpetrators thereof.'[45] It is clear from the jurisprudence that this element does not present a superior with alternative options, but rather two distinct obligations covering prevention and punishment.[46] Judicial bodies must assess whether a superior was in fact in a position to fulfil these obligations. In *Čelebići*, the ICTY explained that a superior can

---

41   See for example *Prosecutor v Kordić & Čerkez* (Appeal Judgment) IT-95-14/2-A (17 December 2004) para 913; *Perišić* Appeal Judgment (n 34) para 119; *Prosecutor v Blaškić* (Appeal Judgment) IT-95-14-A (29 July 2004) para 421.

42   Beatrice I Bonafé, 'Finding a Proper Role for Command Responsibility' (2007) 5 JICJ 599 ('Bonafé, 'Finding a Proper Role for Command Responsibility'') 608.

43   'United States of America v Wilhelm von Leeb et al' in *Trials of War Criminals before the Nuernberg Military Tribunals under Control Council Law No. 10* vol 11 (United States Government Printing Office 1953) 462, 512.

44   See for example *Prosecutor v Krnojelac* (Appeal Judgment) IT-97-25-A (13 September 2003) para 171 ('an accused is not charged with the crimes of his subordinates but with his failure to carry out his duty as a superior to exercise control'); Gaeta et al., *Cassese's International Criminal Law* (n 29) 191–192.

45   ICTY Statute (n 26) art 7(3).

46   *Prosecutor v Bagilishema* (Trial Judgment) ICTR-95-1A-T (7 June 2001) para 49; *Prosecutor v Strugar* (Trial Judgment) IT-01-42-T (31 January 2005) ('*Strugar* Trial Judgment') para 373.

only be held criminally responsible 'for failing to take such measures that are within his material possibility.'[47] After the Second World War, General Yamashita was convicted for having 'failed to provide effective control of your troops as was required by the circumstances',[48] even though questions were raised about his capacity to maintain order given the strength of both armed resistance against Japanese forces and the United States military assault on the Philippines.[49] Justice Röling, the Dutch judge at the International Military Tribunal for the Far East, emphasised the necessary element of power, alongside knowledge and duty, for criminal responsibility to arise for omissions by superiors,[50] although the Tokyo Tribunal held that members of the Japanese cabinet could be liable even where they were powerless to prevent atrocities.[51]

The Rome Statute's formulation makes reference to the power of a superior in relation to three requirements: preventing subordinate crimes, repressing such acts and ensuring that subordinates are held to account:

> The superior failed to take all necessary and reasonable measures within his or her power to prevent or repress their commission or to submit the matter to the competent authorities for investigation and prosecution.[52]

Article 28 also seems to impose a causative link between the superior's failings and the crimes committed by subordinates. It refers to crimes having occurred 'as a result' of a superior failing to exercise proper control over subordinates. The *Bemba* Pre-Trial Chamber addressed the seeming logical inconsistency in Article 28 that crimes might have been caused by a failure to punish after the fact. The Pre-Trial Chamber clarified that the requirement of causation applies only to a superior's duty to prevent crimes. It also observed that 'a commander's past failure to punish crimes is likely to increase the risk that further crimes will be committed in the future.'[53] Echoing Kai Ambos, the Pre-Trial Chamber found that the necessary causative link is established where it is shown that the failure of the superior to exercise their duty increased the risk

---

47   *Delalic* Trial Judgment (n 28) para 395.
48   *Trial of General Tomoyuki Yamashita* (n 24) 35.
49   See comments by Murphy, *In re Yamashita* (n 2) 35.
50   'Opinion of Justice Röling' in Neil Boister & Robert Cryer (eds), *Documents on the Tokyo International Military Tribunal* (OUP 2010) 679 ('Boister & Cryer, *Documents on the Tokyo International Military Tribunal*'), 706.
51   'Judgment of the International Military Tribunal for the Far East' in Boister & Cryer (n 50) 71, 82–84.
52   Rome Statute (n 3) art 28(2)(c).
53   *Bemba Gombo* Confirmation of Charges Decision (n 31) paras 423–24.

of subordinate crime.[54] Overall, the omission element of this mode of liability is exacting, requiring that superiors failed to take measures within their power to deal with subordinate crimes, and also with a contributory aspect whereby their omission increased the risk of offences.

The mental element has always been 'the most troublesome issue' for superior responsibility.[55] It was controversial when the doctrine was mooted after the First World War. The United States representative on the 1919 Commission on the Responsibility of the Authors of the War and the Enforcement of Penalties had been 'unalterably opposed' to a form of liability where a commander might be 'punished for the acts of others without proof being given that he knew of the commission of the acts in question or that, knowing them, he could have prevented their commission.'[56] The *mens rea* was contentious when the doctrine was first applied by war crimes tribunals, with *Yamashita* seen as having been convicted 'with no proof of knowledge other than what would be inadmissible in any other capital case or proceeding under [the United States'] system, civil or military.'[57] Writing in 1973, before any international codification of superior responsibility, Roger Clark perceptively identified that a lower mental element, a gross negligence test, was needed in order to make the command structure more responsive to the goal of minimising the loss of human life during wartime.[58] Imposing responsibility for war crimes could contribute to achieving such a humanitarian goal, because of the 'deterrent and educative effects of punishment.'[59] Commenting on the application of command responsibly in the context of prosecutions for the My Lai massacre, Clark considered that reliance on an actual knowledge standard would in effect amount to 'an invitation to the commander to see and

---

54 *Ibid* para 426. See Kai Ambos, 'Superior Responsibility' in Antonio Cassese, Paola Gaeta & John R W D Jones (eds), *The Rome Statute of the International Criminal Court: A Commentary* vol 1 (OUP 2002) 823, 860; *Prosecutor v Bemba Gombo* (Amicus Curiae Observations) ICC-01/05/-01/08 (20 April 2009) ('*Bemba Gombo* Amicus Curiae Observations') paras 30–47; *Ntaganda* Decision on the Confirmation of Charges (n 32) para 174. See also Darryl Robinson, 'How Command Responsibility Got So Complicated: A Culpability Contradiction, Its Obfuscation and a Simple Solution' (2010) 13 MJIL (2010) 1 ('Robinson 'How Command Responsibility Got So Complicated: A Culpability Contradiction, Its Obfuscation and a Simple Solution'').
55 Gary D Solis, *The Law of Armed Conflict* (CUP 2009) ('Solis, *The Law of Armed Conflict*') 402.
56 'Commission on the Responsibility of the Authors of the War' (n 1) 143.
57 *In re Yamashita* (n 2) 53 (Justice Rutledge).
58 Roger S Clark, 'Medina: An Essay on the Principles of Criminal Liability for Homicide' (1973) 5 Rutgers Camden LJ 59, 78.
59 *Ibid*.

hear no evil.'[60] These observations point to the tension that arises between the pursuit of such humanitarian goals by holding commanders to account under superior responsibility and the principle of personal culpability.

Hugo Grotius wrote that rulers exercising authority over others 'may be held responsible for the crime of a subject if they know of it and do not prevent it when they could and should prevent it.'[61] Superior responsibility does not require actual knowledge and entails an exception to the general mental element standard of 'intent and knowledge' as set out in the Rome Statute. Additional Protocol I referred to superiors who knew or 'had information which should have enabled them to conclude' of subordinate wrongdoing, while the statutes of the *ad hoc* tribunals similarly specified that superiors would be liable if they 'knew or had reason to know' of offences. Article 28 of the Rome Statute not only incorporates a less than actual knowledge standard, it also provides different *mens rea* requirements for military and civilian superiors:

> That military commander or person either knew or, owing to the circumstances at the time, should have known that the forces were committing or about to commit such crimes; [...]
> The superior either knew, or consciously disregarded information which clearly indicated, that the subordinates were committing or about to commit such crimes;

As Roger Clark has noted, these provisions entail a negligence standard for military commanders, and something 'akin to recklessness' for civilian superiors.[62] He was undoubtedly correct in predicting that the mental element under the Rome Statute 'will be the subject of both confusion and controversy.'[63]

The *mens rea* requirements for superior responsibility have been subject to considerable judicial scrutiny at the *ad hoc* tribunals, and while the judges at the International Criminal Court have only addressed this occasionally, their

---

60 *Ibid.*
61 Hugo Grotius, *De Jure Belli ac Pacis Libri Tres* Book 2, Chapter XXI, Francis W Kelsey (trans) (first published 1646, Carnegie Endowment for International Peace, Division of International Law 1925) 523.
62 Roger S Clark, 'Drafting a General Part to a Penal Code: Some Thoughts Inspired by the Negotiations on the Rome Statute of the International Criminal Court and by the Court's First Substantive Law Discussion in the Lubanga Dyilo Confirmation Proceedings' (2008) 19 Crim LF 519, 550.
63 Roger S Clark, 'The Mental Element in International Criminal Law: The Rome Statute of the International Criminal Court and the Elements of Offences' (2001) 12 Crim LF 291, 326, footnote? 117.

approach can already be distinguished from that of the other tribunals. The prevailing standard at the Tribunals has been that espoused in *Čelebići*, where the requirement of 'had reason to know' meant that a superior would be criminally responsible when put on notice of subordinate crimes:

> This information need not be such that it by itself was sufficient to compel the conclusion of the existence of such crimes. It is sufficient that the superior was put on further inquiry by the information, or, in other words, that it indicated the need for additional investigation in order to ascertain whether offences were being committed or about to be committed by his subordinates.[64]

The *Bemba* Pre-Trial Chamber, however, held that the Rome Statute supported a lower knowledge standard, one of negligence, alongside actual knowledge.[65] Amnesty International, in an *amicus curiae* to the Pre-Trial Chamber, had specifically made the argument that Article 28 incorporates a negligence standard.[66] The Chamber found that the 'should have known' standard puts a more 'active duty' on commanders to know how their troops are behaving, to inquire 'regardless of the availability of information at the time on the commission of the crime.'[67]

The Court's interpretation of the Rome Statute is correct and is very much in keeping line with Roger Clark's earlier observations that an actual knowledge standard might encourage a hands-off approach by superiors. In the proceedings against Captain Medina in relation to My Lai, an actual knowledge was applied, despite the law allowing for a lower *mens rea*. Clark saw the hypocrisy, given that this approach was 'much more generous' to Medina, a United States national, than the rules that had been applied to Yamashita.[68] Telford Taylor, the former Nuremberg prosecutor, felt that this approach 'virtually dictated acquittal' and then immunized those higher up the chain of command; 'for if the company captain, within earshot of the killings and in radio communications with the guilty unit, could not be found liable, how could colonels and generals overhead in helicopters?'[69]

---

64 *Delalic* Trial Judgment (n 28) para 393.
65 *Bemba Gombo* Decision on Confirmation of Charges (n 31) para 429.
66 *Bemba Gombo* Amicus Curiae Observations (n 54).
67 *Bemba Gombo* Decision on Confirmation of Charges (n 31) para 434.
68 Clark, 'Medina: An Essay on the Principles of Criminal Liability for Homicide' (n 58) 71–72.
69 Telford Taylor, 'The Course of Military Justice', *The New York Times* (New York, 2 February 1972) 39.

There is no question that commanders are required to ensure that their subordinates observe international humanitarian law, but it can be fairly asked whether negligent superiors who should have known of wrongdoing, but do not, should be criminally responsible for those acts (international crimes) which they neither ordered nor necessarily intended. It has been suggested that a commander 'assumes the risk of criminality if he does not properly emplace mechanisms to ensure compliance with the laws and customs of warfare.'[70] Such mechanisms are of course necessary, but it is debatable as to whether a failure to establish them should be a basis for criminal liability. Article 86 of Additional Protocol I, it bears repeating, referred to superiors being open to 'penal or disciplinary responsibility.' Negligent superiors would perhaps be best dealt with by national disciplinary systems. Darryl Robinson's comments on the causal contribution of superiors are relevant here:

> international institutions mandated to deal with the persons most responsible for the most serious crimes need not be pre-occupied with derelictions that did not contribute to even a single core crime. The commander may be liable under national laws for her dereliction of duty, but we should not treat her as party to serious international crimes in which she is not implicated.[71]

In both *Bemba* and *Ntaganda*, Pre-Trial Chambers of the International Criminal Court have acknowledged the negligence standard for military commanders under Article 28, but have in fact relied upon the actual knowledge standard in confirming the charges against the accused.[72]

At the International Criminal Court, prosecutions on the basis of Article 28 are very uncommon. At the time of writing, charges on this basis have been laid against just two of the thirty persons against whom proceedings have been initiated before the permanent court. The arrest warrants issued for Jean-Pierre Bemba Gombo and Bosco Ntaganda had plead only modes of liability

---

70   Michael A Newton & Casey Kuhlman, 'Why Criminal Culpability Should Follow the Critical Path: Reframing the Theory of Effective Control' (2010) 40 Netherlands Ybk Int'l L 3 ('Newton & Kuhlman, 'Why Criminal Culpability Should Follow the Critical Path: Reframing the Theory of Effective Control") 70.
71   Robinson 'How Command Responsibility Got So Complicated: A Culpability Contradiction, Its Obfuscation and a Simple Solution' (n 54) 58.
72   *Bemba Gombo* Decision on Confirmation of Charges (n 31) para 489; *Ntaganda* Decision on the Confirmation of Charges (n 32) para 167.

under Article 25,[73] but on the suggestion of the pre-trial judges in *Bemba*, the Prosecutor filed revised charges based on Article 28, as an alternative, alongside other modes of liability.[74] The *Bemba* Pre-Trial Chamber treated Article 28 as a fallback, holding at the confirmation of charges stage that it only need examine alleged criminal responsibility under this rubric should substantial grounds for believing such responsibility existed under Article 25 not be established.[75] Superior responsibility has been much more prominent in trials before the *ad hoc* tribunals. According to Bonafé, of the 99 individuals that had faced trial before the ICTY and ICTR by April 2007, over half (54) were prosecuted on the basis of superior responsibility.[76] However, only ten were convicted by that time under this mode of liability, excluding those who had pleaded guilty.[77] Over the life of the *ad hoc* tribunals, there have been very few convictions based on command responsibility alone.[78] At the time of writing, almost half of all ICTY indictees have been charged on the basis of superior responsibility (77), with only five having been successfully convicted when charged on that basis alone.[79] Twenty-one accused have been acquitted of the Article 7(3) charges, twenty-three acquitted under Article 7(3), but convicted under Article 7(1), and fifteen have been convicted under both articles. Although some cases are not yet complete, and others have been transferred to national jurisdictions, the statistics show that only around 30% of ICTY superior responsibility indictments have resulted in convictions.

In modern international criminal law, superior responsibility is said to comprise 'one of the forms of liability that is least likely to lead to successful

---

[73] See *Prosecutor v Bemba Gombo* (Warrant of Arrest) ICC-01/05/-01/08 (23 May 2008); *Prosecutor v Ntaganda* (Warrant of Arrest) ICC-01/04-02/06 (22 August 2006); *Prosecutor v Ntaganda* (Decision on Prosecutor's Application under art 58) ICC-01/04-02/06 (12 July 2012).

[74] *Prosecutor v Bemba Gombo* (Decision Adjourning the Hearing pursuant to art 61(7)(c)(iii)) ICC-01/05/-01/08 (3 March 2009) paras 42–49. See also *Prosecutor v Ntaganda* (Document Containing the Charges) ICC-01/04-02/06 (10 January 2014) paras 147–151.

[75] *Bemba Gombo* Decision on Confirmation of Charges (n 31) paras 342, 402–403.

[76] Bonafé, 'Finding a Proper Role for Command Responsibility' (n 42) 602.

[77] Ibid.

[78] See for example *Strugar* Trial Judgment (n 46); *Strugar* Appeal Judgment (n 39); *Prosecutor v Hadžihasanović and Kubura* (Trial Judgment) IT-01-47-T (15 March 2006); *Prosecutor v Hadžihasanović and Kubura* (Appeal Judgment) IT-01-47-A, (22 April 2008); *Prosecutor v Delić* (Trial Judgment) IT-04-83-T (15 September 2008).

[79] These figures were compiled on the basis of publicly available information on the website of the ICTY. Thanks to Abby Satterfield for her research assistance in this regard.

convictions.'[80] This is remarkable, given the prominence of the doctrine in the Statutes and jurisprudence of various international tribunals, not to mention the immense scholarship to which it has given rise. But it may explain why the Prosecutor of the International Criminal Court has shown little enthusiasm for pursuing accused persons under the modes of liability in Article 28. The low conviction rate for those charged under superior responsibility is a result of the stringent application of the doctrine's requirements, especially effective control, as well as a preference for using other modes of liability which involve direct participation.[81] The ICTY Appeals Chamber explained with regard to the latter:

> The provisions of Article 7(1) and Article 7(3) of the Statute connote distinct categories of criminal responsibility. Where both Article 7(1) and Article 7(3) responsibility are alleged under the same count, and where the legal requirements pertaining to both of these heads of responsibility are met, a Trial Chamber should enter a conviction on the basis of Article 7(1) only, and consider the accused's superior position as an aggravating factor in sentencing.[82]

The stricter application of the various elements brings the doctrine into line with the principle of personal culpability, but of course makes securing a conviction more onerous. It is argued that the effective control requirement in particular, as elaborated by international courts, 'may allow non-state actors to escape criminal culpability' because of their non-traditional structures.[83]

The limited success or indeed reliance on superior responsibility can also be explained by looking at the sentences of those convicted. Empirical evidence demonstrates that at the ICTY, the average sentence has been lower for those convicted under Article 7(3), and where convictions have been based solely on command responsibility, sentences have been 'the lowest...and rather lenient.'[84] While abuse of a superior position is the most commonly cited aggravating factor by sentencing judges, they have handed down lower

---

80   Bonafé, 'Finding a Proper Role for Command Responsibility' (n 42) 602.
81   Ibid 611–15.
82   *Prosecutor v. Kordić and Čerkez* (Appeal Judgment) IT-95-14/2-A (17 December 2004) para 34.
83   Newton & Kuhlman 'Why Criminal Culpability Should Follow the Critical Path: Reframing the Theory of Effective Control' (n 70) 9. See however Sandesh Sivakumaran, 'Command Responsibility in Irregular Groups' (2012) 10 JICJ 1129.
84   Uwe Ewald, '"Predictably Irrational"—International Sentencing and its Discourse against the Backdrop of Preliminary Empirical Findings on ICTY Sentencing Practices' (2010) 10 Int'l Crim LR 365, 394.

sentences for those convicted under superior responsibility because such persons have not been active participants in criminal activity.[85] Such persons are clearly neither the architects nor the driving force behind the commission of international crimes. Those convicted under superior responsibility were generally mid to low-level military commanders,[86] with civilian superiors being shown to 'rarely possess formal powers of control similar to those of military commanders.'[87] Although the overwhelming majority of convicted perpetrators before international criminal tribunals have been military rather than civilian,[88] command responsibility has not proven to be the most suitable vehicle for holding such persons to account.

Superior responsibility as a legal doctrine first came into existence in the context of the post-Second World War war crimes prosecutions, and its first international codification was in Additional Protocol I, an instrument specifically addressed to situations of armed conflict. Its *raison d'etre* would seem to be to hold military commanders responsibility for war crimes perpetrated by their subordinates. Although Article 28 of the Rome Statute covers both civilian and political leaders, and does not the limit the types of crimes to which the doctrine applies, both law and practice certainly indicate that military commanders are its primary target, and war crimes its main subject matter.[89] Convictions based on superior responsibility for crimes against humanity or genocide are a rarity,[90] while, as Roger Clark correctly predicted, the doctrine could and should not be applied to the crime of aggression.[91] The latter can only be committed by persons 'in a position effectively to exercise control over

---

85 Barbara Holá, Catrien Bijleveld & Alette Smeulers, 'Consistency of international sentencing: ICTY and ICTR Case Study' (2012) 9 Euro J Criminology 539, 543, 547. See also Barbara Holá, Alette Smeulers & Catrien Bijleveld, 'International Sentencing Facts and Figures: Sentencing Practice at the ICTY and ICTR' (2011) 9 JICJ 411, 429–430.
86 Bonafé, 'Finding a Proper Role for Command Responsibility' (n 42) 616.
87 *Ibid* 609.
88 For a statistical overview, see Smeulers et al., 'Sixty-Five Years of International Criminal Justice: The Facts and Figures' (n 5) 26.
89 Bonafé, 'Finding a Proper Role for Command Responsibility' (n 42) 616.
90 See for example *Prosecutor v Ntagerura, Bagambiki and Imanishimwe* (Trial Judgment) ICTR-99-46-T (25 February 2004); *Prosecutor v Ntagerura, Bagambiki and Imanishimwe* (Appeal Judgment) ICTR-99-46-A (7 July 2006).
91 Roger S Clark, 'Rethinking Aggression as a Crime and Formulating Its Elements: The Final Work-Product of the Preparatory Commission for the International Criminal Court' (2002) 15 LJIL 859, 885–886; Roger S Clark, 'Negotiating Provisions Defining the Crime of Aggression, its Elements and the Conditions for ICC Exercise of Jurisdiction Over It' (2009) 20 EJIL 1103, 1109.

or to direct the political or military action of a State.'[92] But even in the context of war crimes, superior responsibility is not proving to be suited to trying senior military or political leaders before international tribunals.

While superior responsibility is featuring less and less in international criminal trials, given that reckless or negligent superiors are not seen as bearing the greatest responsibility for international crimes, that is not to say that such persons should escape disciplinary or criminal responsibility nationally, as required by Additional Protocol I. The International Committee of the Red Cross considers that state practice has established superior responsibility as part of customary international law applicable to both international and non-international armed conflicts.[93] This is undoubtedly true, but the evidence cited includes primarily international jurisprudence, the statutes of international tribunals, national legislation and military manuals. That only a few national cases are presented in the Committee's study demonstrates the limited application of superior responsibility nationally. Clive Baldwin found no evidence that authorities in the United Kingdom 'ever applied' command responsibility,[94] while Gary Solis observed that 'there rarely is a trial of a U.S. commander for command-responsibility-based charges.'[95] The concern expressed by United States Supreme Court Justice Murphy in 1946 over 'the boundless and dangerous implications' of command responsibility is no longer merited.[96] Even the more sensible, modern version of the doctrine, one which addresses many of the concerns raised by superior responsibility's earliest incarnation, has not been widely applied in domestic systems, despite the unquestionable prevalence of violations. The reasons may lie more in questions of power and politics after all, than of law.

---

92 ICC Assembly of States Parties Res RC/Res.6 'The crime of aggression' (11 June 2010) art 8*bis*(1).
93 Jean-Marie Henckaerts & Louise Doswald-Beck, *Customary International Humanitarian Law, Volume I: Rules* (CUP 2005) 558–561.
94 Clive Baldwin, 'Why the ICC Needed to Reopen the Iraq Abuse Case' (n 19).
95 Solis, *The Law of Armed Conflict* (n 55) 404.
96 *In re Yamashita* (n 2) 28.

CHAPTER 24

Possession as a Criminal Offence and the Function of the Mental Element: Reflections from a Comparative Perspective

Kai Ambos

Roger Clark is well known these days for his writings on international criminal law and human rights, as well as his participation in the ICC negotiations as a representative of Samoa. There was however another life of Roger Clark, some decades ago, at the beginning of his academic career, when he dealt with the nitty gritty questions of criminal law doctrine. Roger's 1966 LLM thesis at the University of Wellington analysed the highly technical theme of 'Defences to offences of strict liability'. In a later article in the New Zealand Law Journal, drawing from his thesis,[1] Roger inquired into the similarly complex topic of possession offences, commenting on two seminal English cases and some further case law. Roger's analysis focused on the concept of possession and the requisite mental requirements for the respective offences. There are, of course, many problems surrounding these offences, but I will limit myself here to a theoretical inquiry into the structure, rationale and concept of these offences, including their subjective side. I will draw on the relevant Anglo-American and German writings on the matter. It should be clear after my analysis that this is yet another topic where these two legal traditions fully ignore each other, even though a mutual exchange could be fruitful given their strikingly similar approaches and findings.

My little inquiry will be structured as follows: I will first inquire into the structure and rationale of 'possession offences', and highlight some of the ensuing conceptual problems. I will then take a closer look at the concept of possession with regard to the conduct requirement in criminal law and the functions accorded to the mental element. Finally, I will propose a concept of possession offences compatible with a liberal system of criminal law.

---

1   Roger Clark, 'Strict Liability Offences of Possession' (1967) New Zealand LJ 182 ('Clark, 'Strict Liability Offences of Possession'").

1 Structure, Rationale and some Problems of Possession Offences

Possession offences criminalise the mere possession of things or objects. There exists a wide variety of these offences.[2] This variety calls for a nuanced treatment and a classification or categorization. One quite straightforward, rather naturalist classification focuses on the dangerousness of the objects possessed. These may be dangerous *per se*, for example guns, illicit drugs, obscene materials or certain chemical substances;[3] or they may be *per se* neutral or innocuous, for example certain tools which are normally used for a totally licit purpose, e.g. repairing one's bicycle, but could also be used for a criminal purpose, e.g. a burglary.[4] Given this possible double use, we could call this second category of objects 'dual-use objects'. The nature of the object influences the rationale of criminalisation. At first sight, only the criminalization of the possession of dangerous objects can be justified. Here, the rationale for criminalisation can be seen in the dangers or risks inherent in these objects and the legislator's aim to control them in order to limit their inherent danger by criminally prohibiting their possession.[5] Thus, such possession offences

---

2 See for example, Andrew Ashworth & Lucia Zedner, 'Prevention and Criminalization: Justifications and Limits' (2012) 15 New Cr L Rev 542 ('Ashworth & Zedner, "Prevention and Criminalization: Justifications and Limits"'), 545–555 (England); Markus D Dubber, 'Policing Possession: The War on Crime and the End of Criminal Law' (2001) 91J Crim L & Criminology 829 ('Dubber, "Policing Possession: The War on Crime and the End of Criminal Law"'), 834–835, 856–857; Markus D Dubber, 'The Possession Paradigm: The Special Part and the Police Power Model of the Criminal Process', in Robin Antony Duff & Stuart Green (eds), *Defining Crimes: Essay on the Special Part of Criminal Law* (OUP 2005) 91 ('Dubber, "The Possession Paradigm"'), 96–97 (USA, New York); Ken Eckstein, *Besitz als Straftat* (Duncker & Humblot 2011) ('Eckstein, "Besitz als Straftat"') 39 ff (Germany); Gudrun Hochmayr, *Strafbarer Besitz von Gegenständen* (Manz 2005) ('Hochmayr, Strafbarer Besitz von Gegenständen') 6 ff (Austria, Germany, Switzerland).
3 On dangerous objects see also Eckstein, *Besitz als Straftat* (n 2) 70–72; Hochmayr, *Strafbarer Besitz von Gegenständen* (n 2) 51 (with a view to the legal interest [*Rechtsgut*] violated).
4 For the same distinction Nuria Pastor Muñoz, 'Besitz- und Statusdelikte: eine kriminalpolitische und dogmatische Annäherung' (2006) 153 Goltdammer's Archiv für Strafrecht 793 ('Pastor Muñoz, 'Besitz-und Statusdelikte: eine kriminalpolitische und dogmatische Annäherung"'), 797–98 (structure a and b cases). *Los delitos de posesión y los delitos de estatus: una aproximación políticocriminal y dogmática*, (Atelier 2005).
5 In a similar vein Pastor Muñoz, 'Besitz-und Statusdelikte: eine kriminalpolitische und dogmatische Annäherung' (n 4) 799; see also Friedrich-Christian Schroeder, 'Besitz als Straftat' (2007) 2 Zeitschrift für internationale Strafrechtsdogmatik 444 ('Schroeder, 'Besitz als Straftat''), 448 right column ('Quelle von Gefahren'); for a parallel to offences of (abstract) endangerment see also Hochmayr, *Strafbarer Besitz von Gegenständen* (n 2) 150.

normally pursue purposes of prevention,[6] they aim to avoid greater harm or harm that may arise from the uncontrolled possession and use of the respective objects.[7] In contrast, the possession of neutral objects can or should only be criminalized if something else—in addition to the mere possession—justifies such a criminalization, that is, the illicit use of the respective object for the commission of an offence. An example would be where the burglar uses certain tools for a burglary. We will return to this necessary limitation below.

The criminalization of the possession of *per se* neutral objects raises various problems. First, it entails a change in focus from the non-dangerous object to the dangerous possessor. The danger arises when the person comes to be in possession of the object. It turns the criminal law of possession into a law on (allegedly) dangerous possessors, a new law on vagrancy,[8] operating as a form of 'discretionary social control' of allegedly dangerous individuals.[9] From this perspective, possession offences are part and parcel of a 'criminal justice turned police system' which invokes possession offences to 'police', that is to target, stigmatise and incapacitate certain 'dangerous' or 'antisocial' members of society.[10] Thus, from the perspective of the repression-prevention dichotomy

---

[6] In the same vein Ashworth & Zedner, Prevention and Criminalization: Justifications and Limits (n 2) 546; more specifically, in favour of security as a justification for the criminalization of the possession of firearms, see Victor Tadros, 'Crimes and Security' (2008) 71 Mod L Rev 71 940, at 943–946.

[7] In favour as this approach facilitates early police intervention, see Andrew P Simester and others, *Simester and Sullivan's Criminal Law* (5th edn, Hart 2013) ('Simester and others, *Simester and Sullivan's Criminal Law*') 81–82.

[8] Dubber, 'Policing Possession: The War on Crime and the End of Criminal Law' (n 2) 836 ('possession has replaced vagrancy as the sweep offense of choice'), 859 ('paradigmatic offense in the current campaign to stamp out crime by incapacitating as many criminals as we can get our hands on'), 908 ('offense designed and applied to remove dangerous individuals even before they have had an opportunity to manifest their dangerousness in an ordinary inchoate offense'), 908ff.

[9] George P Fletcher, *Rethinking Criminal Law* (OUP reprint 2002) ('Fletcher, *Rethinking Criminal Law*') 202ff.

[10] Dubber, 'The Possession Paradigm' (n 2) 97 ('Possession…functions like a modern sweep offense that sweeps far wider than the original sweep offense, vagrancy, as every day there are far more criminal possessors than there are vagrants and packs a far greater punch, with maximum penalties for possession alone extending to life imprisonment without the possibility of parole, without mentioning the substantial possession enhancements for other crimes, as contrasted with the overnight jailings followed by a more or less formal order to "get out of town" once common for those deemed vagrants'); on the characteristics of the possessor with regard to status, dangerousness see *ibid* 113–14; on the match of dangerous person and object see *ibid* 116.

drawing the line between backward-looking criminal law and forward-looking police law, possession offences rather belong to the latter creating a police-like liability for a dangerous state of being and turning possessors into spoilers.[11] Of course, modern legislators cannot state this openly. They cannot criminalize objects that are per se neutral on the grounds that they are possessed by dangerous individuals. It is for this reason that they criminalize the possession of these objects right away, notwithstanding the ensuing danger of over-criminalization.

This criminalization operates, secondly, on the basis of double presumptions with regard to the dangerousness of the possessor and with regard to the possible occurrence of other (previous or subsequent) offences. As to the possessor, the presumption about the person's dangerousness fills the absence of dangerousness in the respective object. Take the above mentioned example of certain dual-use objects: the criminalization of their possession rests on the potential for their being used for criminal purposes which, in turn, rests on the presumed dangerousness of the possessor. Such a presumption, however, can only be considered legitimate if there exist reliable objective indicia for the possessor's dangerousness, for example, a preparatory criminal act or his membership in a criminal organization.[12] Otherwise, the criminalization constitutes an illegitimate presumption amounting to a 'Verdachtsstrafe', a punishment on the basis of a mere suspicion.[13] The distinction between a legitimate and illegitimate presumption runs along the lines of the classical dichotomy between manifest versus subjective criminality.[14] Under the former concept, a

---

11 See from a German perspective Otto Lagodny, *Strafrecht vor den Schranken der Grundrechte* (Mohr 1996) ('Lagodny, *Strafrecht vor den Schranken der Grundrechte*') 323, 336 ff ('polizeirechtliche[r] Zustandsstörerverantwortlichkeit').

12 See Pastor Muñoz, 'Besitz- und Statusdelikte: eine kriminalpolitische und dogmatische Annäherung' (n 4) 800–02 (arguing that in these 'structure c, d and e' cases the offender's 'manifestation of subjective dangerousness' ['Äußerung der subjektiven Gefährlichkeit'] violates the 'personal conditions of security' as part of a concept of normative security as an essential pillar of our society [translation from German by the author]).

13 In the same vein, see Cornelius Nestler, 'Rechtsgüterschutz und Strafbarkeit des Besitzes von Schußwaffen und Betäubungsmittel', in Institut für Kriminalwissenschaften (ed), *Vom unmöglichen Zustand des Strafrechts* (P Lang 1995) 65 ('Nestler, 'Rechtsgüterschutz und Strafbarkeit des Besitzes von Schußwaffen und Betäubungsmittel'''), 68; Eckstein, *Besitz als Straftat* (n 2) 261–63 (regarding some possession offences); Ken Deiters, 'Buchbesprechung Eckstein' (2004) 151 *Goltdammer's Archiv für Strafrecht* 58 ('Deiters, "Buchbesprechung Eckstein"'), 61; Pastor Muñoz, 'Besitz-und Statusdelikte: eine kriminalpolitische und dogmatische Annäherung' (n 4) 800, 803 (for her 'structure b' cases).

14 Fletcher, *Rethinking Criminal Law* (n 9) 200.

dangerous object is necessary to manifest criminality and sinister implications,[15] while subjective criminality only relies on the possessor's dangerousness to justify criminalization. Of course, the exact line between a legitimate and illegitimate presumption is difficult to draw since it is predicated on the nature and intensity of the objective manifestation of the possessor's dangerousness.[16] As to other previous or subsequent offences, the said presumption may operate backwards or forwards. Take for example the possession of drugs where, on the one hand, 'the anticipating conduct of import, manufacture, purchase', and, on the other, the subsequent conduct of 'use, sale, or export' is co-criminalized.[17]

This brings us to another important feature of possession offences, namely that they either follow the logic of anticipatory criminalisation (*Vorverlagerung*) or of the criminalisation of subsequent conduct (*Nachverlagerung*).[18] Most possession offences follow the first logic in that the possession as such does not cause harm or violate any *Rechtsgut* (relevant legal interest).[19] From the perspective of the harm principle, possession offences can therefore be characterised as 'harmless'[20] albeit not necessarily 'resultless'[21] offences. From the perspective of the *Rechtsgut*-principle, a phase preceding and following the

---

15 See for example s 5.06 (2) MPC (presumption of criminal purpose from possession of weapon).

16 See also Pastor Muñoz, 'Besitz-und Statusdelikte: eine kriminalpolitische und dogmatische Annäherung' (n 4) 803 (admitting that it is difficult to determine 'when a conduct unambiguously affirms the manifestation of subjective dangerousness…' [translation from German by the author]).

17 Dubber, 'Policing Possession: The War on Crime and the End of Criminal Law' (n 2) 907.

18 See Pastor Muñoz, 'Besitz-und Statusdelikte: eine kriminalpolitische und dogmatische Annäherung' (n 4) 798–805.

19 For a comparative analysis of the concepts of harm and *Rechtsgut,* see Kai Ambos, 'The Overall Function of International Criminal Law: Striking the Right Balance between the Rechtsgut and the Harm Principles' (2014) 3 Crim Law and Philos 8 ('Ambos, 'The Overall Function of International Criminal Law: Striking the Right Balance between the Rechtsgut and the Harm Principles'").

20 Dubber, 'Policing Possession: The War on Crime and the End of Criminal Law' (n 2) 861, 926; Dubber, 'The Possession Paradigm' (n 2) 91, 99; more nuanced Fletcher, *Rethinking Criminal Law* (n 9) 198 (no proof 'that the defendant intended to harm anyone with the material possessed.').

21 Imprecise as to the distinction between harm and result Dubber, 'The Possession Paradigm' (n 2) at 99 putting 'result' and 'harm' on an equal footing. This is incorrect since 'harm' is only one possible 'result' of a human conduct or the commission of an offence. In other words, 'result' is an umbrella term encompassing 'harm'. In case of possession offences, one may well argue that the 'result' is the very possession brought about by a

violation of the respective legal interest can be distinguished.[22] Thus, possession offences usually criminalize, as already noted above, possession with a view to prevent future harm or a violation of a legal interest. Exceptionally, though the criminalization finds its rationale in the non-perpetuation of harm already caused or of an ongoing violation of a legal interest. The possession offence here follows the logic of the classical criminalization of the *auxilium post delictum*, for example in the case of receiving stolen goods.[23] The underlying rationale, being to prevent the perpetuation of the wrongful deprivation of property,[24] is entirely legitimate and as such recognised in many legal systems.[25] A more specific example is the possession of child pornography. Here the criminalisation aims, *inter alia*, to prevent the abuse of children in the production of the pornographic material by deterring users and thus reducing the demand and removing the economic incentive for the producers.[26]

The logic of anticipatory criminalisation of harmless neutral objects will run counter to the concepts of harm and *Rechtsgut* since the respective possession offences do neither entail the causation of harm nor the violation of legal interests. Otherwise, when criminalizing the possession of dangerous objects, possession offences aim to prevent, as the so-called endangerment offences,[27] risk to harm or legal interests. Here again, it is difficult to draw the line between risks that are sufficiently concrete or sufficiently proximate to the harm, and those that are too abstract or too remote from the harm. Take the case of gun possession. While a gun is, as such, a dangerous object (it may be used to injure or kill someone) and thus presents a risk to harm, it may be safely stored away and used by its rightful owner only for lawful purposes.

---

previous act (eg drug possession as a result of drug acquisition) while this result is usually not harmful as such; see also *infra* note 48 with main text.

22   Eckstein, *Besitz als Straftat* (n 2) 81–83, 256–57 (*Vor- und Nachverletzungsphase*).

23   See Stuart P Green, 'Thieving and Receiving: Overcriminalizing the Possession of Stolen Property' (2011) 14 New Cr L Rev 35 ('Green, 'Overcriminalizing the Possession of Stolen Property'').

24   Green, 'Overcriminalizing the Possession of Stolen Property' (n 23) 37.

25   See for example ss 257 and 259 German Criminal Code as well as—representing the Spanish and Portuguese-speaking systems—art 298 Spanish Penal Code, arts 194–195 Peruvian Penal Code and art 180 Brazilian Penal Code (*receptación* and *receptação*).

26   Pastor Muñoz, 'Besitz-und Statusdelikte: eine kriminalpolitische und dogmatische Annäherung' (n 4) 804; Eckstein, *Besitz als Straftat* (n 2) 67–69.

27   They constitute insofar at least abstract endangerment offences (*Gefährdungsdelikte*), for a discussion see Dubber, 'The Possession Paradigm' (n 2) 99–101.

Thus, gun possession may be considered legitimate or illegitimate, depending on the concrete circumstances of the case, the characteristics of the gun and, perhaps most importantly, the underlying assumptions and values of the society concerned. In any case, critics rightly point out that possession offences anticipate criminalisation even beyond attempt liability.[28] This is because they do not require a restricting conduct element ('substantial step', 'physical proximity' or any other limiting criterion).[29] In this sense, possession offences constitute 'doubly inchoate offences',[30] anticipating liability in a double way, not only with regard to actual harm or a violation of a legal interest, but even before the attempt stage.

2   Possession, Conduct and the Mental Element

Criminal responsibility is predicated on human conduct, meaning there has to be an act or omission.[31] To be imputed to a person, the criminal result of a specific *actus reus* must have been caused by this person, by his or her conduct. The ensuing conduct requirement is generally accepted in German criminal law.[32] It is also recognized in common law, traditionally under the name of

---

28   See Dubber, 'Policing Possession: The War on Crime and the End of Criminal Law' (n 2) 908 ('one step farther from the actual infliction of personal harm than ordinary inchoate offenses like attempt'); see also Andrew Ashworth & Jeremy Horder, *Principles of Criminal Law* (7th edn, OUP 2013) ('Ashworth & Horder, *Principles of Criminal Law*') 98.

29   For a comparative perspective, see Kai Ambos, *Treatise on International Criminal Law, Volume I* (OUP 2013) ('Ambos, *Treatise on International Criminal Law, Volume I*') 245ff.

30   Dubber, 'Policing Possession: The War on Crime and the End of Criminal Law (n 2); similarly Nestler, Rechtsgüterschutz und Strafbarkeit des Besitzes von Schußwaffen und Betäubungsmittel' (n 13) 67.

31   On the rationale and concept of omission as a 'non-act' see Ambos, *Treatise on International Criminal Law, Volume I* (n 29) 180ff.

32   Lagodny, *Strafrecht vor den Schranken der Grundrechte* (n 11) 322–323; Eberhard Struensee, 'Besitzdelikte', in Erich Samson (ed), *Festschrift für G. Grünwald zum siebzigsten Geburtstag* (Nomos 1999) ('Struensee, Besitzdelikte') 713, 714–15; Hochmayr, *Strafbarer Besitz von Gegenständen* (n 2) 53; Ken Eckstein, 'Grundlagen und aktuelle Probleme der Besitzdelikte—EDV, EU, Strafrechtsänderungsgesetze, Konkurrenzen' (2005) 117 Zeitschrift für die gesamten Strafrechtswissenschaften 107 ('Eckstein, 'Grundlagen und aktuelle Probleme der Besitzdelikte—EDV, EU, Strafrechtsänderungsgesetze, Konkurrenzen"') 110; Schroeder, Besitz als Straftat (n 5) 448 left column.

the—too limited—act requirement,[33] in modern terms it is viewed as either a conduct,[34] control[35] or action[36] requirement.

Possession offences are difficult to reconcile with this requirement[37] as possession expresses a relationship of domination or control between a person

---

[33] Wayne R La Fave, *Criminal Law* (5th ed, West/Thomson 2010) ('La Fave, *Criminal Law*') 320–326; Paul H Robinson, *Fundamentals of Criminal Law* (2nd ed, Little, Brown 1995) 250–260 (with various references); for a 'normative defence' see Michael S Moore, *Act and Crime—The Philosophy of Action and its Implications for Criminal Law* (OUP 1993) ('Moore, *Act and Crime—The Philosophy of Action and its Implications for Criminal Law*') 46 ff; crit Douglas Husak, *Philosophy of Criminal Law* (Rowman & Littlefield 1987) ('Husak, *Philosophy of Criminal Law*') 79 ff (but, apparently, equating 'act' and 'actus reus'); Douglas Husak, 'The alleged act requirement in criminal law', in John Deigh & David Dolinko (eds), *The Oxford Handbook of the Philosophy of Criminal Law* (OUP 2011) ('Husak, 'The alleged act requirement in criminal law'') 107 (arguing, *inter alia*, that the basic issue of this requirement of the meaning of an act has not been clarified, 108–16). However, a plausible normative concept of an act (or action) exists, for example Roxin's concept of the act as the socially relevant expression of personality ('Persönlichkeitsäußerung', cf. Claus Roxin, *Strafrecht. Allgemeiner Teil I* (4th edn, C H Beck 2006) ('Roxin, *Strafrecht. Allgemeiner Teil I*') § 8 margin number 44–75) or Duff's, in fact quite similar, concept of 'action' as a 'social phenomenon' based on interaction with the world and actualised practical reasoning (Robin Antony Duff, *Answering for Crime* (Hart 2007) ('Duff, *Answering for Crime*') 99–100). See also P.C. Busato, 'Una crítica a los delitos de posesión a partir del concepto de acción significativa. Conexiones entre el *civil law* y el *common law* en las tesis de Tomás Vives Antón y George Fletcher', Revista Penal 35 (2015), 8 ff.

[34] See s 2.01(1) Model Penal Code ('A person is not guilty...unless his liability is based on a conduct...'); see Husak, 'The alleged act requirement in criminal law' (n 33) 116 (correctly arguing that the MPC contains a conduct requirement).

[35] Husak, *Philosophy of Criminal Law* (n 33) 81, 97 ff; Husak, The alleged act requirement in criminal law (n 33) 108 ff (proposing a requirement of control or competence on the basis of the ability to behave reasonably, 116–22). However, the control criterion suffers from vagueness and imprecision, as admitted by Husak himself (Husak, 'The alleged act requirement in criminal law' (n 33) 121–122; crit also Duff, *Answering for Crime* (n 33) 101 and *passim*). In addition, the 'control' requirement is nowadays employed as a concept distinguishing modes of participation in comparative and international criminal law (cf Kai Ambos, 'A Workshop, a Symposium and the Katanga Trial Judgment of 7 March 2014' (2014) 12 JICJ 219, 226–28).

[36] Duff, *Answering for Crime* (n 33) 101 ff (replacing the act requirement by 'a more modest "action presumption"' [101] which requires, in line with his concept of action, 'an actualization of the results of practical reasoning in a way that has an impact on the world' [107] and differs, essentially for this actualization, from the act requirement [106–07 with examples]; it is also 'limited' in that it accepts responsibility for proper omissions [112–13]). The problem with this requirement is, of course, that it is hard to prove that a certain action is the result of the 'actualization of the results of practical reasoning' for one cannot know the reasoning of the agent taking place in his internal sphere.

[37] But see Markus D Dubber & Mark Kelman, *American Criminal Law: Cases, Statutes, and Comments* (2nd edn, Foundation Press 2008) ('Dubber & Kelman, *American Criminal Law:*

and a thing.[38] If this thing is dangerous, the said relationship constitutes a 'threat unit'.[39] Possession is static instead of dynamic, 'a state of being, a status'.[40] Possession in criminal law also refers, objectively, to a relationship of domination or control coupled with, subjectively, a will to possess (*Herrschaftswille*).[41] The possessor may exercise actual (effective) or potential (possible) control over the particular object. Accordingly, we can speak of 'actual' or 'constructive' possession;[42] given the importance of the relationship of the person with the object, the traditional imputation is turned into one 'from object to person...'[43]

This nature of possession has important theoretical implications. Possession does not constitute conduct.[44] Neither can one read—contrary to the

---

Cases, Statutes, and Comments') 252–53 (arguing that with the increasing number of possession statutes the act requirement was no longer an issue).

38   Struensee, Besitzdelikte (n 32) 716; Eckstein, *Besitz als Straftat* (n 2) 17; Hochmayr, *Strafbarer Besitz von Gegenständen* (n 2) 54 ('Zuteilungsrelation' [quoting A. Kaufmann]).

39   Dubber, 'The Possession Paradigm' (n 2) 114.

40   Dubber & Kelman, *American Criminal Law: Cases, Statutes, and Comments* (n 37) 253; see also Eckstein, *Besitz als Straftat* (n 2) 17 ('statischer Zustand'); Schroeder, 'Besitz als Straftat' (n 5) 448–449 ('Zustand'); Hochmayr, *Strafbarer Besitz von Gegenständen* (n 2) 63.

41   See extensively Eckstein, *Besitz als Straftat* (n 2) 94 ff, 239–40; also Schroeder, 'Besitz als Straftat' (n 5) 448 left column; contra Hochmayr, *Strafbarer Besitz von Gegenständen* (n 2) 79–81, 135, 146 (focusing on the mere objective presence of the respective object in the private sphere of the respective person).

42   La Fave, *Criminal Law* (n 33) 328–29; Dubber, 'The Possession Paradigm' (n 2) 115–116.

43   Dubber, 'The Possession Paradigm' (n 2) 116.

44   Struensee, 'Besitzdelikte' (n 32) 716; Eckstein, *Besitz als Straftat* (n 2) 209–10, 220–25 (absence of act in particular in case of the so-called 'aufgedrängter Besitz' [imposed possession]), 226; Eckstein, Grundlagen und aktuelle Probleme der Besitzdelikte—EDV, EU, Strafrechtsänderungsgesetze, Konkurrenzen (n 32) 112; Hochmayr, *Strafbarer Besitz von Gegenständen* (n 2) 53 (but ultimately tracing it back to a [previous] conduct in line with the prevailing view, *infra* note 46); Dubber, 'The Possession Paradigm' (n 2) 103 (only 'constructive conduct offence'); Pastor Muñoz, 'Besitz-und Statusdelikte: eine kriminalpolitische und dogmatische Annäherung' (n 4) 797 (against reformulation as an act, but in favour of omission); in a similar vein previously Gerald Grünewald, 'Anmerkung' (1986) 6 Strafverteidiger 243, 245; also Husak, 'The alleged act requirement in criminal law' (n 33) 111, argues that possession is no act but takes this as an argument against the act requirement although this requirement only formulates a normative proposition. The incompatibility with the conduct requirement does not, however, make possession offences incompatible with the requirement of legality (*nullum crimen sine lege*) as enshrined in art 103 (2) of the German *Grundgesetz* which provides that 'An act may be punished only if it was defined by a law as a criminal offence before the act was committed.' The *Bundesverfassungsgericht* has insofar correctly held that the term '*Tat*' ('act') in this provision does not predetermine the quality of the incriminated conduct (*Bundesverfassungsgericht,*

prevailing view in Anglo-American[45] and German doctrine[46]—an implicit conduct element in possession offences by referring to the earlier act of bringing about possession of the object or to a subsequent omission such as failure to dispose of the object.

As to the former, the positive act element, there are, in fact, three kinds of positive acts which may co-exist with possession: the previous acquisition of the object, the active maintaining or even defending of the possession of the object, and the use of the object.[47] However, these acts cannot be put on an

---

Decision of 16 June 1994, in Neue Juristische Wochenschrift 47 (1994), 2412 right column; *Bundesverfassungsgericht* Decision of 6 July 1994 in (1995) 48 Neue Juristische Wochenschrift 248 right column; conc. Eckstein, *Besitz als Straftat* (n 2) 234–235; Pastor Muñoz, 'Besitz- und Statusdelikte: eine kriminalpolitische und dogmatische Annäherung' (n 4) 797; but see also Lagodny, *Strafrecht vor den Schranken der Grundrechte* (n 11) 321–335 (seeing a constitutional incompatibility since possession offences do not presuppose human conduct as required by art 103 (2) *Grundgesetz* and are thus 'not suitable' [*ungeeignet*] in the sense of the constitutional proportionality test (on this test see Ambos, "The Overall Function of International Criminal Law: Striking the Right Balance between the Rechtsgut and the Harm Principles" (n 19) at fn 32 ff).

45 See s 2.01(4) MPC (referring to previous procuring and the subsequent ability to terminate possession); see also La Fave, *Criminal Law* (n 33) 327; Moore, *Act and Crime—The Philosophy of Action and its Implications for Criminal Law* (n 33) 21 (arguing that 'either the act of taking possession or...the omission to rid oneself of possession' is punished) and 22 (possession 'defined so as to include an act or an omission'); Simester and others, *Simester and Sullivan's Criminal Law* (n 7) 81; Dubber, 'The Possession Paradigm' (n 2) 115; also Husak, 'The alleged act requirement in criminal law' (n 33) 114 (referring to procurement and receipt as 'prior conduct' including omission [albeit this is usually subsequent to the possession!]).

46 See the German legislator's reasoning with regard to drug possession, Bundestags-Drucksache 6/1877, 9 (arguing that it is not a state ['Zustand'] but a causal conduct that is punished, namely the 'bringing about and maintenance ['Herbeiführung oder Aufrechterhaltung'] of this state' [sic!]); also *Bundesverfassungsgericht*, Decision of 16 June 1994, in (1994) 47 Neue Juristische Wochenschrift 2412, at 2413 left column; id., Decision of 6 July 1994, in (1995) 48 Neue Juristische Wochenschrift 248 left column. See also Eckstein, *Besitz als Straftat* (n 2) 18, 124, 141ff., 224, 226, 239–40, 264; Hochmayr, *Strafbarer Besitz von Gegenständen* (n 2) 54–55, 64–65, 85 ff (positive act), 96 ff (omission), 145; Walter Gropp, 'Besitzdelikte und periphere Beteiligung', in G. Dannecker and others (eds), *Festschrift für Harro Otto zum 70. Geburtstag* (Carl Heymanns 2007) 249, 251; Jörg Eisele, 'Vorbemerkungen zu den §§ 13ff.', in Adolf Schönke & Horst Schröder, *Strafgesetzbuch* (29th edn, Beck 2014) ('Eisele, 'Vorbemerkungen zu den §§ 13 ff"') margin number 42; crit Schroeder, 'Besitz als Straftat' (n 5) 448 right column.

47 See Struensee, 'Besitzdelikte' (n 32) 716–18.

equal footing with the possession itself: they either precede it, and may then result in possession[48] (acquisition); or they follow the actual possession (maintenance and use). In addition, they are usually criminalized separately.[49] The paradigmatic example in this respect constitutes drug possession. It is, on the one hand, preceded by several previous acts (cultivation, acquisition, import etc.) and, on the other, followed by subsequent acts (distribution, trafficking etc.). Furthermore, one can note that the reading of a positive act into possession offences does not sit well with one of the primary purposes of these offences, namely the facilitation of criminal prosecution by lowering evidentiary requirements, in particular by removing the need to adduce proof of the unlawful acquisition (a positive act!) of the object.[50] In fact, if a possession offence is traced back to any previous act of acquisition or otherwise, this act constitutes an element of the possession offence and must be proved. Thus, the legislative purpose would be undermined.[51] On the other hand, if proof of a positive act is not required, how can a positive act then be part of possession in the first place?[52]

While it seems, at first sight, more plausible to read an omission element into possession by referring to the possessor's refusal to terminate his

---

48 Insofar as a possession offence can be qualified as a result crime, see Lagodny, *Strafrecht vor den Schranken der Grundrechte* (n 11) 326 (state of possession as sub-case of result offence); Hochmayr, *Strafbarer Besitz von Gegenständen* (n 2) 63ff., 146 (seeing, a result [*Erfolg*] in the safekeeping [*Gewahrsam*] of a thing brought about by the previous act and connected to the temporal element of permanency in the sense of the concept of a *Dauerdelikt* [permanent offence], thereby turning a possession offence, similar to an offence of deprivation of liberty, into a '*Erfolgs-Dauerdelikt*'); T. Walter, 'Vorbemerkungen zu den §§ 13 ff', in Heinrich Wilhelm Laufhütte and others (eds), *Strafgesetzbuch. Leipziger Kommentar. Volume 1* (12th edn, De Gruyter 2006) margin number 36; see also Eckstein, *Besitz als Straftat* (n 2) 213–215, 264 (seeing a 'result' in the maintenance of possession, at 226); see previous comment (n 21).

49 See Lagodny, *Strafrecht vor den Schranken der Grundrechte* (n 11) 325 (arguing that acquisition of drugs is criminalized separately); Schroeder, 'Besitz als Straftat' (n 5) 448 right column; crit Hochmayr, *Strafbarer Besitz von Gegenständen* (n 2) 86 (arguing that this is not always the case).

50 See the explicit reasoning of the German legislator with regard to drug possession Bundestags-Drucksache 6/1877 (n 46) 9; see also Moore, *Act and Crime—The Philosophy of Action and its Implications for Criminal Law* (n 33) 21–22.

51 In the same vein see Lagodny, *Strafrecht vor den Schranken der Grundrechte* (n 11) 318; Eckstein, 'Grundlagen und aktuelle Probleme der Besitzdelikte—EDV, EU, Strafrechtsänderungsgesetze, Konkurrenzen' (n 32) 111.

52 See Struensee, 'Besitzdelikte' (n 32) 717.

possession,[53] this view is, ultimately, also unconvincing. Omission is the opposite of action, it is non-action, the absence of action or a failure to act.[54] If possession is action, or as previously described, effective control over an object, it is nonsensical and highly artificial to define it in a negative way as non-action, or the refusal to terminate the effective control.[55] Nevertheless, if one does read an omission element into possession, a host of problems arise. First, it is unclear how the termination of possession is to take place.[56] The law on possession, at least in German-speaking jurisdictions, is silent on the matter.[57] If one wants to prevent the danger allegedly attached to an object, it simply does not make sense to allow any form of termination even one which leads to the loss of the object or risk-creation.[58] Secondly, criminal liability for omission is predicated upon a duty to act.[59] This raises the controversial and complex question where this duty shall be derived from in case of possession offences. If one conceives these as conduct offences (in the form of separate

---

53 See for the mainstream view eg Appeals Court (Oberlandesgericht) of Zweibrücken, Decision of 18 December 1985, in (1986) 39 Neue Juristische Wochenschrift 2841–2 (defendant blamed for possession of a gun since 'he fails to terminate his possession…'); see also the second part of s 2.01(4) Model Penal Code: 'aware of his control for a sufficient period to have been able to terminate his possession', which implies that the possessor once aware of his (unlawful) possession is under a duty to dispose of the object. Also see American Law Institute, *Model Penal Code and Commentaries. Part 1. General Provisions §§ 1.01 to 2.13* (American Law Institute 1985) 224 ('An actor who is aware of his control of the thing possessed for a period that would enable him to terminate control has failed to act in the face of a legal duty imposed by the law that makes his possession criminal.'). For scholarly discussion, see also Pastor Muñoz, 'Besitz-und Statusdelikte: eine kriminalpolitische und dogmatische Annäherung' (n 4) 797 (possessor's competence for possession); on the categorization as separate offences of omission see *infra* note 61.
54 Ambos, *Treatise on International Criminal Law, Volume 1* (n 29) 180.
55 Even a more radical view, see Struensee, 'Besitzdelikte' (n 32) 719 ('absurd' and not covered by the 'literal meaning').
56 See Lagodny, *Strafrecht vor den Schranken der Grundrechte* (n 11) 327; Struensee, 'Besitzdelikte' (n 32) 720.
57 Lagodny, *Strafrecht vor den Schranken der Grundrechte* (n 11) 327; Hochmayr, *Strafbarer Besitz von Gegenständen* (n 2) 105.
58 In this sense however J. Scheinfeld, 'Buchbesprechung Festschrift Grünwald' (2007) 154 *Goltdammer's Archiv für Strafrecht* 721, 725; Lagodny, *Strafrecht vor den Schranken der Grundrechte* (n 11) 328–332 (discussing possibilities of termination of possession and considering that only a duty to return the object appears as reasonable although it does not exempt from punishment); see also Hochmayr, *Strafbarer Besitz von Gegenständen* (n 2) 105ff.
59 Ambos, *Treatise on International Criminal Law, Volume 1* (n 29) 183–84.

offences of omission),[60] one may find this duty in the omission element, in the description of the conduct itself.[61] This is consistent with the linguistic English approach.[62] Otherwise, one would have to look for an extra-legal obligation to act.[63] Thirdly, one would have to prove that the possessor had the possibility to dispose of the object, namely that he knew of its existence and, in addition, was aware of his duty to get rid of it.[64] This, again, would undermine the legislator's purpose of facilitating the proof of the offence.[65]

This leaves us with the mental element in possession, its functions and precise meaning. First, the mental element has been invoked to overcome the incompatibility with the conduct requirement by redefining possession as an 'act' if the possessor is aware of its possession. Thus, Section 2.01 (4) of the Model Penal Code ('MPC') defines possession as 'an act...if the possessor *knowingly* procured or received the thing possessed or was *aware* of his control thereof...'.[66] Of course, the MPC's naturalistic conception of an act as a *voluntary* bodily movement[67] and the Commentary on this provision make clear that the mental element does not primarily, or at least not exclusively, serve

---

60 See Eckstein, *Besitz als Straftat* (n 2) 169–70; Hochmayr, *Strafbarer Besitz von Gegenständen* (n 2) 96ff. (at 100); Eisele, Vorbemerkungen zu den §§ 13 ff (n 46). German doctrine distinguishes between a separate (genuine, proper) offence of omission ('*echtes Unterlassungsdelikt*') where the duty to act is statute-based and an 'improper' offence of omission ('*unechtes Unterlassungsdelikt*') with extra-legal duties to act (*Garantenstellung* and *pflicht*), see Ambos, *Treatise on International Criminal Law, Volume I* (n 29) 186–88.
61 Lagodny, *Strafrecht vor den Schranken der Grundrechte* (n 11) 327.
62 Ambos, *Treatise on International Criminal Law, Volume I* (n 29) 185.
63 On such obligations see Ambos, *Treatise on International Criminal Law, Volume I* (n 29) 184–85.
64 See also Struensee, 'Besitzdelikte' (n 32) 720 (indicating that there is no case law making such findings as to the mental state of the possessor).
65 See also Lagodny, *Strafrecht vor den Schranken der Grundrechte* (n 11) 318, 331, 332; Eckstein, *supra* note 32, 111.
66 Emphasis added. For criticism of this provision (if taken literally) Husak, 'The alleged act requirement in criminal law' (n 33) 112.
67 Cf s 2.01 (1) and (2) both referring to 'voluntary' act(s); in the same vein Moore, *Act and Crime—The Philosophy of Action and its Implications for Criminal Law* (n 33), 39–40, 44–46 ('simple bodily movement...caused by volition'). This corresponds to the naturalistic, causal concept of act once defended within the classical theory of crime of the late 19th and early 20th century (cf Roxin, *Strafrecht. Allgemeiner Teil I* (n 33) § 8 margin number 10–16) long overcome by modern German doctrine. In line with this view voluntariness is not a further requirement of an act but implicit in any human act, that is, non-voluntary movements are, by definition, no acts (in the same vein Robin Antony Duff, 'Action, the act requirement and criminal liability', in John Hyman & Helen Steward (ed), *Agency and*

here to transform possession into an act but serves to reaffirm the voluntariness of the possession.[68] This brings us right back to the subjective side of the concept of possession already defined above,[69] namely the will to possess the object. Indeed, nobody can possess a thing 'without a minimum of discernible voluntary involvement.'[70] Thus, the most basic subjective ingredient of possession is voluntariness as expressed by a minimum will to possess and a maximum will to dominate the thing possessed.

This explains Lord Parker's statement in *Lockyer v. Gibb*, where he made the very concept of possession dependent upon the possessor's awareness regarding the thing possessed for 'a person cannot be said to be in possession of some article which he or she does not realize is…in some place over which she has control.'[71] In *Warner*, albeit a confusing decision with a *ratio decidendi* difficult to identify,[72] the House of Lords followed *Lockyer* insofar as it read a mental ingredient into the term possession itself (with regard to the otherwise strict liability offence of drug possession) while refusing to read this requirement, as Lord Reid did, into the offence as a whole.[73]

Their Lordships there distinguished further between general knowledge as to the possession of 'the thing itself' ('something')—which they considered necessary—and more precise knowledge as to its nature, qualities or contents—which they considered as unnecessary.[74] While this distinction may at first glance appear artificial and of little practical value[75]—if only for the fact that proof of such a nuanced knowledge requirement is hardly pos-

---

Action (CUP 2004) 69). On the importance of voluntariness see also Husak, 'The alleged act requirement in criminal law' (n 33) 119.

68   'An actor who knowingly procures or receives the thing possessed has, *of course*, engaged in a *voluntary* act that can serve as the predicate for criminal liability.' (American Law Institute, *Model Penal Code and Commentaries. Part 1. General Provisions §§ 1.01 to 2.13* (American Law Institute 1985), 224 [emphasis added]).

69   See (n 41) with main text.

70   Eckstein, *Besitz als Straftat* (n 2) 239 ('Minimum an erkennbarer Willensbeteiligung').

71   *Lockyer v. Gibb* [1966] All ER 2, 655; quoted according to Clark, 'Strict Liability Offences of Possession' (n 1) 182 right column.

72   Crit Ashworth & Horder, *Principles of Criminal Law* (n 28) 98; Simester and others, *Simester and Sullivan's Criminal Law* (n 7) 163; David Ormerod, *Smith & Hogan's Criminal Law* (13th edn, OUP 2011) 173 ('Ormerod, *Smith & Hogan's Criminal Law*').

73   Ormerod, *Smith & Hogan's Criminal Law* (n 74) 173; Ashworth & Horder, *Principles of Criminal Law* (n 28) 98; Simester and others, *Simester and Sullivan's Criminal Law* (n 7) 163.

74   See Simester and others, *Simester and Sullivan's Criminal Law* (n 7) 162 (quoting Lord Pearce summarizing the law).

75   Crit Simester and others, *Simester and Sullivan's Criminal Law* (n 7) 163 ('fictional, artificial…').

sible—it actually draws our attention to the issue of the precise contents of the mental element of possession. After all, it is, arguably, the most important (third) function of the mental element to bring possession offences into line with the culpability or fault principle. Indeed, the MPC's possession definition, providing for subjective requirements, can be seen as a culpability provision,[76] albeit leaving the more precise definition of the mental element open. This definition is the core part of a liberal concept of possession to be developed in the following section.

3   A Liberal Concept of Possession Liability

If, as we have said previously,[77] possession is a state of being (*Zustand*) modelled on the relationship between person and object, we can also say that possession offences punish this state as such[78] and can be classified as offences criminalising states of being (*Zustandsdelikte*).[79] So far so good but how can

---

76   See Husak, 'The alleged act requirement in criminal law' (n 33) 115.
77   See notes 41 ff and main text.
78   Eckstein, *Besitz als Straftat* (n 2) 226.
79   See Eckstein, *Besitz als Straftat* (n 2) 170, 225 (defining 'Zustandsdelikte', on the one hand, as 'offences of commission and genuine omission plus x', and on the other, as a new, autonomous form of criminal liability, besides offences of commission and omission, and opposed to conduct/act-based offences); Eckstein, 'Grundlagen und aktuelle Probleme der Besitzdelikte—EDV, EU, Strafrechtsänderungsgesetze, Konkurrenzen' (n 32) 113, 141; concurring Lampe, *infra* note 90; Schroeder, Besitz als Straftat (n 5) 448–49; *contra* Eisele, 'Vorbemerkungen zu den §§ 13 ff' (n 46) and especially Hochmayr, *Strafbarer Besitz von Gegenständen* (n 2) 133ff. She argues in particular, on the basis of her concept of an 'Erfolgs-Dauerdelikt' (*supra* n 48), that under Eckstein's concept criminalization in cases of 'imposed possession' [*aufgedrängter Besitz*] is broader since the possessor has, unlike in her approach (102–105), no time to deliberate [*Überlegungsfrist*] with a view to the termination of the possession (136–138) and thus, ultimately, the mere intent not to terminate it, i.e., the mere thought [*reine Gedankenstrafe*] is punished (142–143). Yet, this critique is unconvincing. Apart from being incompatible with possession as a state instead of a conduct, Hochmayr's concept of an *Erfolgs-Dauerdelikt* does not provide for limiting criteria of criminalisation in itself. The requirement of an *Überlegungsfrist* in cases of imposed possession does not follow conceptually from Hochmayr's approach but is a mere proposition which can equally applied to these cases under Eckstein's approach. Also, it would have to be proven that the possessor did not have the intent or will to terminate the possession (see also Eckstein, 'Grundlagen und aktuelle Probleme der Besitzdelikte—EDV, EU, Strafrechtsänderungsgesetze, Konkurrenzen' (n 32) 112). This would presuppose that, in objective terms, it was actually possible for him to do so.

these offences be reconciled with the fundamental principles of a liberal criminal law, in particular the principles of legality and culpability?[80]

As to legality we have already referred above to the case law of the German Constitutional Court according to which possession offences do not violate the legality principle of the German *Grundgesetz*.[81] Indeed, the legality principle cannot be interpreted as imposing on the legislator too rigid guidelines as to the nature and quality of the incrimination as long as it complies with the substantive rules of the principle: its requirements of *lex praevia, certa, stricta* and *scripta*. The legality principle does not contain a different standard for possession offences. Just as with all other offences, the penal prohibition must exist at the time of the commission (*lex praevia*) in a written form (*lex scripta*), in a clear and unambiguous manner (*lex certa*) and must not be applied to a similar conduct by analogy (*lex stricta*).[82]

Since legality does not provide for a different standard, the real test is if these offences comply with the culpability requirement. Culpability is hereby understood in a normative sense: as a principle that premises punishment on the blameworthiness of the agent's wrongful conduct, i.e., as a distinct concept of blameworthiness going beyond mere mental states, with excuses operating as its negation.[83] Normative culpability goes (far) beyond the mere psychological (descriptive, empirical) elements of the subjective side of the *Tatbestand*, i.e. intent (purpose, will etc.) and knowledge (awareness). In common law parlance, culpability goes beyond the (psychological) fault element, the classical mens rea in the narrow sense and, also, the French *élément moral*.[84] In fact, it

---

Hochmayer downplays the objective and subjective control criteria proposed by Eckstein (*supra* notes 88 and 89 with main text).

80   See Ambos, *Treatise on International Criminal Law, Volume 1* (n 29) 87 ff; Kai Ambos, *Treatise on International Criminal Law, Volume 11* (OUP 2014) 287–88 (in addition to legality and culpability on fairness and proportionality as further fundamental principles).

81   See (n 44) and main text.

82   See Ambos, *Treatise on International Criminal Law, Volume 1* (n 29) 90 with further references.

83   On such a normative theory of guilt in English legal thinking Fletcher, *Rethinking Criminal Law* (n 9) 499–500; George Fletcher, *The Grammar of Criminal Law* (OUP 2007) 319ff.

84   See Kai Ambos, 'Zur Entwicklung der französischen Straftatlehre' (2008) 120 Zeitschrift für die gesamte Strafrechtswissenschaft 181, 187–91, 194–95; in French: 'Réflexions sur la théorie francaise de l'infraction pénale du point de vue allemand' in Jocelyne Leblois-Happe (ed), *Vers un nouveau procès pénal?* (Société de Législation comparée 2008) 147–62; in Spanish, 'Observaciones a la doctrina francesa del hecho punible desde la perspectiva alemana', *InDret* (Revista para el análisis del derecho), at <http://www.indret.com/pdf/556_es.pdf> accessed 10 November 2014.

does not speak to the naturalistic concept of intent and knowledge at all—as wrongly implied by Section 2.02 MPC claiming to define the 'General requirements of culpability'. It focuses instead on blame, moral responsibility, reproach so serious to deserve punishment, i.e., normative, value-based concepts (what has been called, not very fortunately, *mens rea* in the broad sense).[85]

If one sees possession offences, as defended in this paper, as non-conduct offences criminalizing certain states of being, it is inconsistent to invoke previous conduct to bring these offences into line with the culpability principle.[86] Instead, an autonomous, culpability-based and restrictive interpretation of these offences is required. It follows from the above considerations on the mental element that the will to possess and a minimum awareness as to the thing possessed are the necessary ingredients of any definition of the mental element of possession.[87] For it is only the existence of such a subjective minimum standard that enables the possessor to exercise the personal control of the thing possessed (as the objective constitutive element of possession),[88] and thus justifies the imputation from object to person mentioned above.[89] This minimum standard is the starting point for the discussion of the more concrete questions, in particular with regard to the minimum degree of the mental element requirement (full awareness and will *versus* allowing for a lower negligence standard) and with regard to the contents of the cognitive requirement as to the duty13) to terminate the possession (awareness of *general* possibility to act as opposed to *concrete* possibility).[90]

---

85 On *mens rea* in the narrow and broad sense (purpose/knowledge and recklessness/negligence) see P Robinson, 'Mens rea' in Joshua Dressler (ed), *Encyclopedia of Crime & Justice* (2nd edn, Macmillan 1995).

86 But see Eckstein, *Besitz als Straftat* (n 2) 139–40 (even invoking the 'act accessoriety' [Handlungsakzessorietät] of possession); therefore rightly criticized by Deiters, 'Buchbesprechung Eckstein' (n 60; for a rebuttal see Eckstein, 'Grundlagen und aktuelle Probleme der Besitzdelikte—EDV, EU, Strafrechtsänderungsgesetze, Konkurrenzen' (n 32) 115.

87 In a similar vein, see Eckstein, *Besitz als Straftat* (n 2) 240, 242–43, 265 (but including negligent possession, 'Besitzfahrlässigkeit').

88 This can be much better expressed in German with the concept of 'personale Beherrschung' or 'Beherrschbarkeit' (see Eckstein, *Besitz als Straftat* (n 2) 239; Eckstein, 'Grundlagen und aktuelle Probleme der Besitzdelikte—EDV, EU, Strafrechtsänderungsgesetze, Konkurrenzen' (n 32) 114; E.-J. Lampe, 'Buchbesprechungen' (2001) 113 Zeitschrift für die gesamten Strafrechtswissenschaften 885, 895).

89 See (n 43) and main text.

90 For the former, see Hochmayr, *Strafbarer Besitz von Gegenständen* (n 2) 126, for the latter see Struensee, Besitzdelikte (n 32) 720; for a discussion see Hochmayr, op cit 125–27.

In any case, minimum awareness is a prerequisite of another, albeit more objective, constitutive element of any possession offence: the personal exercise of control of the possessor over its objects. This, in turn, presupposes that the possessor has, pursuant to *Warner*,[91] the opportunity to discover the relevant object. Thus, personal exercise of control means actual, not merely potential exercise of control.[92] A further objective limitation may follow from the (legitimate) cause of the possession: any possession which is the result of lawful activity by the prosecutorial authorities (and exceptionally even private citizens). An example would be the confiscation of drugs or the disarming of a wrongful possessor; this cannot be prohibited and, thus, cannot properly be the object of criminalization.[93] Similarly, a (short) possession to pre-empt danger or harm from occurring is justified and thus cannot be subject to punishment.[94]

Of course, these restrictions do not suffice to reconcile the criminalization of the possession of neutral or dual-use objects with the culpability principle. As already argued above,[95] criminalization in these cases rests on the presumed criminal use of the object(s) and the implicit dangerousness of the possessor. In addition to reliable 'hard' evidence of this dangerousness, criminalization is predicated on the proof of the possessor's intent to use the respective object(s) in a criminal fashion.[96] In fact, this intent to use, as a specific purpose of possession, links the possession to a conduct and thus marks the difference to a pure possession offence.[97]

---

91 See Ormerod, *Smith & Hogan's Criminal Law* (n 74) 173–74, 916; Simester and others, *Simester and Sullivan's Criminal Law* (n 7) 162. For criticism on the use of this element for an expansion of responsibility in *Lewis*, see Ashworth & Horder, *Principles of Criminal Law* (n 28) 98; Simester and others, *Simester and Sullivan's Criminal Law* (n 7) 163; Ormerod, *Smith & Hogan's Criminal Law* (n 74) 174.

92 Simester and others, *Simester and Sullivan's Criminal Law* (n 7) 164.

93 The current law grants defences in these situations, see eg the EU Directive 2011/92/EU of 13 December 2011 (on the criminalization of, *inter alia*, the possession of child pornography), recital 17 (the term 'without right' provides for a defence in cases of 'legitimate possession' of authorities in order to conduct criminal proceedings) or the common law defence of innocent possession (Dubber & Kelman, *American Criminal Law: Cases, Statutes, and Comments* (n 37) 269–70).

94 Hochmayr, *Strafbarer Besitz von Gegenständen* (n 2) 88 ff, 91 ('Gewahrsam zur Gefahrenbeseitigung').

95 *Ibid* (n 12) and main text.

96 See also Fletcher, *Rethinking Criminal Law* (n 9) 199–200; Ormerod, *Smith & Hogan's Criminal Law* (n 74) 916 (with regard to fraud but for a broader application).

97 See also Lagodny, *Strafrecht vor den Schranken der Grundrechte* (n 11) 334–35. Duff, *Answering for Crime* (n 33) 114, speaks insofar of 'active possession' as possession plus the intent to do something, for example, to retain an illegal drug; a further intended end corresponds to his actualization of the results of one's practical reasoning (see n 36).

CHAPTER 25

Of War-Councils and War-Mongering: Considering the Viability of Incitement to Aggression

Gregory S. Gordon*

1   Introduction

In representing Samoa as part of the Preparatory Commission for the International Criminal Court in reference to the crime of aggression, Roger Clark took an expansive view of the potential scope of liability and submitted a proposal that 'raised the question whether there should be liability under the Rome Statute for direct and public incitement to aggression.'[1] The proposal was tabled and incitement was not ultimately incorporated into the aggression amendments adopted at the Kampala Review Session in 2010.[2] In the meantime, as a normative matter, regardless of the Rome Statute's final text, Professor Clark's question remains unanswered: should incitement to aggression have been included in the Kampala Amendments? This paper analyzes that question and concludes it should have—but with important limitations on the scope of the crime.

So why include incitement to aggression and what kind of limitations would be implicated? To answer those questions, we must first consider that, in relation to incitement, aggression-related discourse can theoretically be bifurcated between what we may refer to as 'war-council' speech and 'war-mongering'

---

*   The author would like to thank Professor Roger Clark for all his great insights during the drafting of this paper.
1   Michael G Kearney, *The Prohibition of Propaganda for War in International Law* (OUP 2007) ('Kearney, *The Prohibition of Propaganda for War in International Law*') 240. Kearney refers to Dr Clark's proposal as being submitted as part of the Special Working Group on the Crime of Aggression. However, the proposal was submitted as part of the Tenth Session of the Preparatory Commission in July 2002. See Preparatory Commission of the International Criminal Court, Elements of the Crime of Aggression, Proposal Submitted by Samoa, 21 June 2002 at <http://daccess-dds-ny.un.org/doc/UNDOC/GEN/N02/438/52/PDF/N0243852.pdf?OpenElement> accessed 20 July 2014.
2   International Criminal Court, Assembly of State Parties, 31 May-11 June 2010, Resolution RC/Res.6, U.N. Doc. RC/Res.6 (11 June 2010) ('Kampala Amendments'), at <http://www.icc-cpi.int/iccdocs/asp_docs/Resolutions/RC-Res.6-ENG.pdf> (resolution adopting aggression amendments to the Rome Statute).

speech. Regarding the former, it is important to consider that aggression is a leadership-oriented crime with an *in personam* jurisdiction limited to an individual exercising control over the political or military action of a State. However, such an individual, even if the most powerful dictator, is not capable of carrying out himself the multitude of simultaneous and multi-level tasks necessary to plan and launch a modern aggressive war. He will operate within some sort of bureaucratic framework and/or military hierarchy that will necessarily require communication with other government/military officials as part of such an enterprise. Such communications essentially represent 'councils of war' conducted in the relatively insular corridors of power. With respect to such 'war-council' aggression speech, the utility of any corollary incitement provision is questionable—those who would act—the controllers of the government/military apparatus—need no exhorting as they monopolize agency.

Related to this, and in contrast to the other ICC core crimes, war-council-related aggression conduct (necessarily entailing internal government discussions) is inextricably linked with speech. So it may appear somewhat redundant or superfluous to criminalize speech that would trigger other such speech. As a result, in order to capture the inchoate potential of the offense, 'attempt to commit aggression' would seem to criminalize effectively essayed but unrealized projects of illegitimate state-initiated armed violence against other states. Moreover, unlike the other core crimes, any theoretical 'inciting' speech connected to war-council aggression conduct does not as directly entail dehumanization or marginalization of an out-group being targeted for violence or inhumane treatment. Thus, the unique power of speech in relation to mass atrocity—its capacity to demean and objectify the other—is not as directly implicated with regard to war-council aggression.

But the other variety of aggression-related discourse that a theoretical incitement crime implicates, 'war-mongering,' is quite different. It entails government leaders conditioning their citizens to support illegal war campaigns through speeches and mass media. It is not always a *sine qua non* for perpetrating the crime of aggression (as war-council conduct is) but, in cases of controversial war campaigns, it is sometimes needed to assure sufficient troop morale and civilian cooperation. And, it empirically entails speech dehumanizing the enemy population. Further, it has historically been recognized as an offense. So, criminalizing it via incitement makes more sense and, indeed, fills in important gaps within the aggression offense's definitional and operational framework. Thus, the crime of direct and *public* incitement to commit aggression, the public element implicitly excluding 'war-council' communication, is certainly viable.

This paper is divided into four parts. Part 2 will trace the origins of aggression as an offense in international law and show how it was eventually defined at Kampala in 2010. Part 3 will examine aggression's individual conduct elements in relation to incitement. Finally, Part 4 will consider the viability of an incitement to aggression offense and demonstrate why such a crime in relation war-council discourse is doctrinally problematic but may be feasible in relation to war-mongering communication. Given aggression's role as the breeding ground for the other core ICL crimes, qualifiedly including it within the envelope of incitement achieves the proper balance between sound policy and doctrinal coherence.

2   The Origins and Formulation of the Aggression Offense

The modern crime of aggression traces its roots to violations of one half of the older doctrine of 'just war' (the part dealing with the right to go to war as opposed to right conduct in war)—history's pre-twentieth century version of *jus ad bellum*. Guidelines for what constituted a 'just war' were developed over the millennia and, from a Western perspective, originated from religious thinkers such as St. Augustine and Thomas Aquinas. By the seventeenth century, Dutch philosopher Hugo Grotius distilled this learning into seven required elements: (1) just cause; (2) 'right authority' (i.e., a legitimate sovereign to initiate the war); (3) 'right intention' on the part of the parties using force; (4) that the resort to force be proportional; (5) that force be a last resort; (6) that war be undertaken with peace as its goal (not for its own sake); (7) and that there be a reasonable *hope of success*.[3] In the absence of these criteria, the state engaged in theoretical criminal conduct but there were no positive law consequences other than the self-help remedy of reprisal.[4]

That began to change in the twentieth century. The modern *jus ad bellum* regime was launched with the 1919 League of Nations Covenant, which restricted in three ways the right of members to resort to war: (1) imposing a three-month cooling off period after issuance of a Council report, arbitral award, or judicial decision; (2) precluding recourse to war before the dispute

---

[3] Karma Nabulsi, 'Just and Unjust War' in Roy Gutman, David Rieff & Anthony Dworkin (eds) *Crimes of War: What the Public Should Know* (2nd ed, W W Norton & Co 2007) 276.

[4] *See* Harry D. Gould, 'What Happened to Punishment in the Just War Tradition' in Eric A. Henize & Brent J. Steele (eds), *Ethics, Authority, and War: Non-State Actors and the Just War Tradition* (Palgrave Macmillan 2009) 73–75 (discussing just war theory, punishment and reprisal).

had been submitted to the League Council, arbitration, or adjudication for settlement; and (3) making war a matter not just of domestic concern but of international concern by mandating that any circumstance that threatened to disturb international peace be submitted to one of three dispute resolution agencies.[5] The Locarno Treaties of 1925 added additional legal impediments to waging war in Europe by setting out stipulations between Germany and her neighbors that they would not attack one another, except in cases of self-defense.[6] That legal framework was bolstered again by the 1928 Kellogg-Briand Pact, or Treaty of Paris, which was entered into by over sixty nations, including the great powers of the United States, France, the United Kingdom, the Soviet Union, Japan, as well as Germany.[7] The agreement sought to outlaw war but it contained no enforcement mechanism, which ultimately neutered it.[8] And various acts of aggression in the 1930s led to the Second World War and a reassessment of jus ad bellum in its aftermath.

World War II was a watershed event in the history and development of the crime of aggression. For purposes of bringing the major Nazi war criminals to justice, the victorious Allied Powers established the International Military Tribunal at Nuremberg ('IMT'). Article 6 of the IMT Charter provided for prosecution of three core crimes: war crimes, crimes against humanity and crimes against peace. The latter, contained in subsection (a) and the basis for the first charge against the defendants, consisted of the 'planning, preparation, initiation or waging of a war of aggression, or a war in violation of international treaties, agreements or assurances, or participation in a common plan or conspiracy [to do so].'[9] Article 6 also provided that conspiracy to commit any of the core crimes gave rise to criminal liability. But, the IMT held that the Charter

---

5 Christopher R Rossi, 'Jus Ad Bellum in the Shadow of the 20th Century' (1994) 15 NYL Sch J Int'l & Comp L 49, 71–72.

6 Alberto L Zuppi, 'Aggression as International Crime: Unattainable Crusade or Finally Conquering the Evil?'(2007) 26 Penn St Int'l L Rev 1 ('Zuppi, 'Aggression as International Crime"), 8 n28.

7 Zuppi, 'Aggression as International Crime', The Kellogg-Briand Pact, 1928, <http://history.state.gov/milestones/1921-1936/Kellogg> accessed 4 June 2014.

8 Roger D Scott, 'Getting Back to the Real United Nations: Global Peace Norms and Creeping Interventionism' (1997) 154 Mil L Rev 27, 34.

9 Charter of the International Military Tribunal, 8 August 1945, art 6, 82 UNTS 279, 280, at<http://www.yale.edu/lawweb/avalon/imt/proc/imtconst.htm> accessed 20 July 2014. Unfortunately, 'war of aggression' is left entirely undefined and the provision provides no insight as to the scope, if any, of individual responsibility. *See* Roger S Clark, 'Nuremberg and the Crime against Peace' (2007) 6 Wash U Global Stud L Rev 527, 529 (reviewing the negotiations that led to the drafting of the crimes against peace provision in the IMT Charter).

supported a conspiracy count only with respect to crimes against peace. In the end, the Tribunal found twelve defendants guilty of crimes against peace and eight guilty of conspiracy to commit crimes against peace.[10] Based on substantially similar language in its Charter, which included conspiracy as a component of crimes against peace, the International Criminal Tribunal for the Far East ('IMTFE') in Tokyo convicted twenty-four Japanese defendants for the same crime.[11]

In the initial post-IMT/IMTFE period, with the onset of the Cold War as a backdrop, little doctrinal progress was made in terms of defining the crime of aggression. Without furnishing additional insights into its meaning, the international community nevertheless continued to stress the illegal nature of aggression. For example, barring cases of self-defense, the 1945 U.N. Charter, in Articles 1 and 2(4) respectively, prohibited aggression and the threat or use of force against the territorial integrity or political independence of any state.[12] And the 1950 Principles of International Law Recognized in the Charter of the Nuremberg Tribunal and in the Judgment of the Tribunal, formulated by the International Law Commission (ILC), confirmed that the act of planning, preparing, initiating, or waging a war of aggression constitutes a crime against peace giving rise to individual criminal responsibility.[13]

In 1954, the ILC advanced the doctrinal project somewhat by adopting its Draft Code of Offences against the Peace and Security of Mankind.[14] Article 2, paragraph 1 of the Code declared as criminal 'any act of aggression, including the employment by the authorities of a State of armed force against another State for any purpose other than national or collective self-defence or in pursuance of a decision or recommendation of a competent organ of the United Nations.'[15]

The big doctrinal breakthrough, however, came twenty years later. In 1974, the U.N. General Assembly adopted Resolution 3314, which laid the Rosetta

---

10   Noah Weisbord, 'Conceptualizing Aggression' (2009) 20 Duke J Comp & Int'l L 1, 2 n 3.
11   *Ibid*.
12   UN Charter art 1 (declaring that among the purposes of the UN is 'the suppression of acts of aggression or other breaches of the peace…'); art 2 (prohibiting the 'threat or use of force against the territorial integrity or political independence of any state…'). *But see* art 51 ('Nothing in the present Charter shall impair the inherent right of individual or collective self-defence…').
13   Principles of International Law Recognized in the Charter of the Nuremberg Tribunal and in the Judgment of the Tribunal, Principle VI(a), 5 UN GAOR Supp (No. 12) at 14, UN Doc A/1316 (1950).
14   Zuppi, 'Aggression as International Crime' (n 6) 17.
15   *See* (1954) 1 Y B Int'l L Comm'n 123, UN Doc A/1858, A/2162 A/CN.4/85.

Stone for the current modern definition of aggression. Meant to guide the Security Council in the exercise of its peace and security mandate, Article 1 of Resolution 3314, consistent with the notion of illegal use of force set forth in Article 2(4) of the UN Charter, defines 'aggression' as 'the use of armed force by a State against the sovereignty, territorial integrity or political independence of another State, or by any other manner inconsistent with the Charter of the United Nations.'[16]

Article 3 of Resolution 3314 then went on to describe the following as constituting acts of aggression, despite no declaration of war, the list being non-exhaustive (per Article 4):

(a) The invasion or attack by the armed forces of a State of the territory of another State, or any military occupation, however temporary, resulting from such invasion or attack, or any annexation by the use of force of the territory of another State or part thereof;
(b) Bombardment by the armed forces of a State against the territory of another State or the use of any weapons by a State against the territory of another State;
(c) The blockade of the ports or coasts of a State by the armed forces of another State;
(d) An attack by the armed forces of a State on the land, sea or air forces, or marine and air fleets of another State;
(e) The use of armed forces of one State which are within the territory of another State with the agreement of the receiving State, in contravention of the conditions provided for in the agreement or any extension of their presence in such territory beyond the termination of the agreement;
(f) The action of a State in allowing its territory, which it has placed at the disposal of another State, to be used by that other State for perpetrating an act of aggression against a third State;
(g) The sending by or on behalf of a State of armed bands, groups, irregulars or mercenaries, which carry out acts of armed force against another State of such gravity as to amount to the acts listed above, or its substantial involvement therein.[17]

Some twenty-four years later, delegates negotiating the International Criminal Court Statute in Rome included aggression within Article 5 as a crime within

---

16   Definition of Aggression, art 1, UNGA Res 3314 (XXIX), Annex, UN Doc A/RES/3314(XXIX) (14 December 1974).
17   *Ibid* arts 3 & 4.

the jurisdiction of the Court.[18] But they failed to define the offense, or provide any other details regarding its function, choosing instead to defer consideration of those details to a mandatory Review Conference scheduled seven years hence.[19] This was followed by a series of Preparatory Commissions (1999–2002), Special Working Groups (2003–2009) and informal gatherings held at Princeton University (2004–2007) to flesh out the details regarding aggression in advance of the planned 2010 Review Conference in Kampala, Uganda.[20]

The Review Conference was held from 31 May to 10 June 2010. During this time, the Assembly of States Parties adopted a resolution that included a definition of the crime of aggression and a regime covering operationalization of the offense.[21] Aggression was defined in new article 8 *bis* of the Statute, which reads:

1. For the purpose of this Statute, 'crime of aggression' means the planning, preparation, initiation or execution, by a person in a position effectively to exercise control over or to direct the political or military action of a State, of an act of aggression which, by its character, gravity and scale, constitutes a manifest violation of the Charter of the United Nations.
2. For the purpose of paragraph 1, 'act of aggression' means the use of armed force by a State against the sovereignty, territorial integrity or political independence of another State, or in any other manner inconsistent with the Charter of the United Nations. Any of the following acts, regardless of a declaration of war, shall, in accordance with United Nations General Assembly resolution 3314 (XXIX) of 14 December 1974, qualify as an act of aggression: [containing the same list as contained in Article 3 of Resolution 3314].[22]

The key doctrinal developments in 8 *bis* are embodied in paragraph 1, which creates and assigns individual criminal responsibility—in contrast to state

---

18   Rome Statute of the International Criminal Court, UN Doc A/CONF.183/9 (1998) ('Rome Statute') art 5.
19   Beth Van Schaack, 'Negotiating at the Interface of Power and Law: The Crime of Aggression' (2011) 49 Colum J Transnat'l L 505, 512.
20   *Ibid*.
21   Françoise Bouchet-Saulnier, *The Practical Guide to Humanitarian Law* (Doctors Without Borders/Médecins Sans Frontières (MSF) 2014) ('Bouchet-Saulnier, *The Practical Guide to Humanitarian Law*') 16.
22   Kampala Amendments (n 2) art 8 *bis*.

liability—for commission of the aggression offense.[23] Paragraph 1 also requires that, going beyond the 1974 GA definition of aggression, any such act of aggression constitutes 'by its character, gravity and scale' a 'manifest violation of the Charter of the United Nations.' This so-called 'threshold clause' 'ensures that only very serious and unambiguously illegal instances of a use of force by a State can give rise to individual criminal responsibility of a leader of that State under the Statute.'[24]

Related to the leadership element of the crime, the Kampala Amendments also added Article 25(3 *bis*).[25] Article 25 sets forth different categories of participation in an offense that give rise to individual criminal responsibility.[26] Paragraph 3 *bis* provides that, in relation to the crime of aggression, Article 25 'shall apply only to persons in a position effectively to exercise control over or to direct the political or military action of a State.'[27] Thus, the new provision seeks to confirm that the leadership clause contained in Article 8 *bis* applies to secondary perpetrators—accomplices will be found liable only if they too fulfil the leadership requirement.[28]

Finally, as part of the Kampala Amendments, Annex II effected changes to the ICC's Elements of Crimes to include elements for the aggression offense.[29] Those elements include:

1. The perpetrator planned, prepared, initiated or executed an act of aggression.
2. The perpetrator was a person in a position effectively to exercise control over or to direct the political or military action of the State which committed the act of aggression.
3. The act of aggression—the use of armed force by a State against the sovereignty, territorial integrity or political independence of another State, or in any other manner inconsistent with the Charter of the United Nations—was committed.

---

23   Bouchet-Saulnier, *The Practical Guide to Humanitarian Law* (n 21) 17.
24   Handbook on Ratification and Implementation of the Kampala Amendments to the Rome Statute of the ICC ('*Ratification Handbook*') 8, at <http://crimeofaggression.info/documents/1/handbook.pdf> accessed 7 June 2014.
25   Kampala Amendments (n 2) art 25(3 *bis*).
26   Rome Statute (n 18) art 25.
27   Kampala Amendments (n 2) art 25(3 *bis*).
28   *Ratification Handbook* (n 24) 16.
29   Kampala Amendments (n 2) Annex II.

4. The perpetrator was aware of the factual circumstances that established that such a use of armed force was inconsistent with the Charter of the United Nations.
5. The act of aggression, by its character, gravity and scale, constituted a manifest violation of the Charter of the United Nations.
6. The perpetrator was aware of the factual circumstances that established such a manifest violation of the Charter of the United Nations.[30]

3 Aggression's Individual Conduct Elements and Incitement

A   *The Individual Conduct Elements*

To understand the potential range of individual incitement liability connected to the aggression offence, one must first consider the *actus reus* elements of aggression as well as the legal nature of incitement itself. Regarding the former, the language of Article 8 *bis* of the Rome Statute offers important preliminary insights. That provision states that individual liability for the 'crime of aggression' means 'the planning, preparation, initiation or execution, by a person in a position effectively to exercise control over or to direct the political or military action of a State....'[31] But what in particular is meant by the words 'planning, preparation, initiation or execution'? Unfortunately, the Nuremberg and Tokyo Tribunals provided little guidance.[32] But the plain meaning of the words are nevertheless revelatory. Carrie McDougall notes that 'planning' is likely to consist primarily of 'revealing in meetings during which plans for a use of force are formulated.'[33] She notes that 'preparation' could include:

> Acts such as creating the necessary military or economic capacities to commit acts of aggression (such as acquiring weapons for the specific purpose of committing an act of aggression, amassing troops on a border ready for a preemptive strike, or liquidating state assets to fund a state war machine), or political and diplomatic manoeuvers (such as forming

---

[30] Ibid.
[31] Kampala Amendments (n 2) art 8 *bis*.
[32] See Carrie McDougall, *The Crime of Aggression under the Rome Statute of the International Criminal Court* (Cambridge University Press 2013) ('McDougall, *The Crime of Aggression under the Rome Statute of the International Criminal Court*') 187 (noting that the Nuremberg and Tokyo precedents provide little guidance in terms of the meaning of planning, preparation, initiation or execution/waging).
[33] Ibid.

military alliances with the specific aim of enhancing military might for a planned act of aggression or the making of high-level diplomatic representations in order to conceal a State's real intention and thereby gain the military advantage of surprise).[34]

'Initiation' is self-explanatory and means, according to the IMTFE, 'commencing the hostilities.'[35] Muhammed Aziz Shukri has reasoned that 'initiating' an act of aggression is tantamount to 'the decision to commit the act of aggression'[36]—in other words, 'the decision taken immediately before the actual use of force, not a general decision to act aggressively that might be taken in the planning stage.'[37] Moreover, given the leadership requirement embedded in Art. 8 *bis*, 'such decisions are necessarily limited to those taken at the strategic, as opposed to the tactical, level....'[38]

Finally, as Stefan Barriga notes, conduct related to 'execution' is typically within the realm of the soldier. But in reference to the typical activity of a leader in the context of modern warfare, it could, for example, refer to an upper tier official executing 'a devastating act of armed force by a simple push of a button.'[39] McDougall observes that '"execution" will be read as encompassing all substantive strategic acts undertaken after the initiation of an act of aggression to secure the continuation and success of the aggressive act.'[40]

B   Incitement

The Oxford English Dictionary defines 'incitement' as 'the action of provoking unlawful behaviour or urging someone to behave unlawfully.'[41] Similarly,

---

34   *Ibid* at 187–88.
35   R J Pritchard & Sonia N Zaide (eds), *The Tokyo War Crimes Trial* (Garland Publishing 1981) vol. 20, at 48448–48449 ('IMTFE Judgment').
36   Muhammed Aziz Shukri, 'Individual Responsibility for the Crime of Aggression' in Roberto Bellini (ed), *International Criminal Justice: Law and Practice from the Rome Statute to Its Review* (Ashgate 2013) 528.
37   McDougall, *The Crime of Aggression under the Rome Statute of the International Criminal Court* (n 32) at 188.
38   *Ibid*.
39   Stefan Barriga, 'Against the Odds: The Results of the Special Working Group on the Crime of Aggression' in Stefan Barriga *et al* (eds), *The Princeton Process on the Crime of Aggression, 2003–2009* (Lynne Rienner Publishers 2009) 7.
40   McDougall, *The Crime of Aggression under the Rome Statute of the International Criminal Court* (n 32) at 189.
41   Oxford University Press, Oxford Dictionaries Online, <http://www.oxforddictionaries.com/definition/english/incitement> accessed 26 June 2014.

Black's Law Dictionary describes 'incitement' as 'the act or an instance of provoking, urging on, or stirring up...the act of persuading another person to commit a crime...' As these definitions suggest 'incitement is a speech act.'[42] In his seminal treatise *On Liberty*, John Stuart Mill indicated incitement consists of a speech intended by the speaker to provoke lawless action in a context conducive to such action being taken—in other words, when the urging of action is direct.[43] Moreover, Mill would consider such speech to be incitement regardless of whether it actually provoked the intended criminal conduct.[44] In other words, as elucidated by Glanville Williams, incitement is an inchoate crime:

> An inciter is one who counsels, commands or advises the commission of a crime. It will be observed that this definition is much the same as that of an accessory before the fact. What, then, is the difference between the two? It is that in incitement the crime has not (or has not necessarily) been committed, whereas a party cannot be an accessory in crime unless the crime has been committed. An accessory before the fact is party to consummated mischief; an inciter is guilty only of an inchoate crime.[45]

International law has incorporated these elements into its definition of incitement, which has applied almost exclusively to the offence of direct and public incitement to commit genocide. Arising from cases adjudicating guilt in the planned mass slaughter of the Tutsi in 1994, the International Criminal Tribunal for Rwanda issued a series of groundbreaking judgments defining incitement.[46] This jurisprudence broke the offence down into the following

---

42 Raphael Cohen-Almagor, 'Boundaries of Freedom of Expression before and after Prime Minister Rabin's Assassination' in Raphael Cohen-Almagor (ed), *Liberal Democracy and the Limits of Tolerance: Essays in Honor and Memory of Yitzhak Rabin* (University of Michigan Press 2000) ('Cohen-Almagor, 'Boundaries of Freedom of Expression before and after Prime Minister Rabin's Assassination'') 82.

43 John Stuart Mill, *On Liberty* (2nd ed Ticknor and Fields 1863) 107–08. *See also* Cohen-Almagor, Boundaries of Freedom of Expression before and after Prime Minister Rabin's Assassination (n 42) 82.

44 Cohen-Almagor, 'Boundaries of Freedom of Expression before and after Prime Minister Rabin's Assassination' (n 42) 82.

45 Glanville Williams, *Criminal Law* (2nd ed, Steve & Sons 1961) 612.

46 *See Prosecutor v. Akayesu*, Case No. ICTR 96-4-T, Judgment (2 September 1998) (ICTR's first incitement decision finding liability based on defendant's urging Hutu militia to slaughter town's Tutsi population); *Prosecutor v. Kambanda*, Case No. ICTR 97-23-S, Judgment and Sentence (4 September 1998) (incitement charge against Prime Minister of rump genocide regime based in part on his congratulating génocidaires who had already

elements: (1) public; (2) direct; (3) *mens rea*; and (4) speech content. In *Prosecutor v. Akayesu*, the ICTR held that, in the context of the crime of direct and public incitement to commit genocide, speech could be deemed 'public' if addressed to 'a number of individuals in a public place' or to 'members of the general public at large by such means as the mass media, for example, radio or television.'[47] And, the communication could satisfy the 'direct' criterion if, when considering the language 'in the light of its cultural and linguistic content...the persons for whom the message was intended immediately grasped the implication thereof.'[48] The requisite *mens rea* (element (3) above) bifurcates into a dual intent: (a) to provoke another to commit genocide, and (b) to commit the underlying genocide itself.[49] Significantly, given its inchoate nature as discussed above, causation is not a required element—put another way, to make out a prima facie case, the prosecutor need not prove the incitement resulted in genocide.

Incitement's most complex and problematic feature involves its core defining element—'speech content.' In formulating this criterion, the ICTR had labored to distinguish between legitimate exercise of free speech (regardless of how offensive) and corrosion of such words into criminal advocacy. The jurisprudence has suggested four analytic criteria to establish whether speech could be characterized as either lawful expression or illicit advocacy: *text* (involving a parsing and exegetical interpretation of the key words in the speech);[50] *purpose* (embracing on one end of the spectrum, clearly lawful goals, such as historical research or distribution of news, and, on the other end,

---

killed and analogizing Tutsis to dogs drinking Hutu blood); *Prosecutor v. Ruggiu*, Case No. ICTR 97-32-I, Judgment and Sentence (1 June 2000) (Belgian RTLM announcer's incitement conviction based on broadcast of euphemisms, such as 'go to work,' idiomatically understood by listeners as calls for mass murder); *Prosecutor v. Niyitegeka*, Case No. ICTR 96-14-T, Judgment and Sentence (16 May 2003) (Rwandan minister's use of bullhorn directly after massacre to thank killers for 'good work' considered incitement); *Prosecutor v. Nahimana, Barayagwiza, & Ngeze*, Case No. ICTR 99-52-T, Judgment and Sentence (3 December 2003) (finding radio and print media executives guilty of incitement in connection with establishment of RTLM and dissemination of its genocidal broadcasts as well as founding and publishing of anti-Tutsi newspaper *Kangura*); *Prosecutor v. Bikindi*, Case No. ICTR-01-72-T, Judgment (2 December 2008) (extremist Hutu tunesmith's liability based on code-word calls for murder directly before massacre, not on hate songs written before the genocide and disseminated by others).

47   *Prosecutor v. Akayesu*, Case No. ICTR 96-4-T, *ibid* para 556.
48   *Ibid* paras 557–58.
49   *Ibid* para 560.
50   *Prosecutor v. Nahimana, Barayagwiza, & Ngeze* (n 46) para 1001.

clearly unlawful ends such as explicit exhortations to violence);[51] *context* (circumstances surrounding the speaker's text—such as contemporaneous large-scale interethnic violence, as well as the speaker's tone of voice);[52] and the *relationship* between the speaker and the subject (the analysis should be more speech-protective when the speaker is part of a minority criticizing either the government or the country's majority population).[53]

With reference to the last criterion, it should be pointed out that incitement has empirically involved persons in positions of authority urging subordinates or segments of the population at large to engage in attacks against innocents. The ICTR cases again are illustrative—political leaders persuading subordinates (e.g., Mayor Jean-Paul Akayesu urging *Interahamwe* militia to kill local Tutsis[54] or Prime Minister Jean Kambanda exhorting the public at large to murder Tutsis[55]); radio announcers urging listeners to victimize Tutsis (e.g., broadcaster Georges Ruggiu whipping up violent impulses in Hutus on the RTLM airwaves);[56] and celebrities trying to inspire violence among fans (pop music star Simon Bikindi prodding Hutu civilians on a bullhorn to murder Tutsis).[57] In the military context, officers encourage subordinates to commit illegal violence against persons *hors de combat*.[58]

One other point about the incitement crime in international law bears mention. One of its prominent features is its projection of hatred toward and dehumanization of intended victims to anaesthetise would-be perpetrators to extreme and large-scale violence. In the genocide context, the ICTR cases are rife with examples. Mayor Jean-Paul Akayesu, in encouraging militia members to kill Tutsis, referred to the latter as 'cockroaches.'[59] In conditioning the population for mass murder, Prime Minister Jean Kambanda analogized Tutsis to dogs drinking Hutu blood.[60] Pop singer Simon Bikindi referred to Tutsis as 'snakes' in urging Interahamwe militia to kill them. Incitement to commit war

---

51 *Ibid* paras 1000–1006.
52 *Ibid*.
53 *Ibid* para 1006.
54 *Prosecutor v. Akayesu*, Case No. ICTR 96-4-T (n 46) para 674.
55 *Prosecutor v. Kambanda*, Case No. ICTR 97-23-S (n 46) para 39(viii).
56 *Prosecutor v. Ruggiu*, Case No. ICTR 97-32-I (n 46) paras 44(iii), (iv).
57 *Prosecutor v. Bikindi*, Case No. ICTR-01-72-T (n 46) para 5 (2 December 2008).
58 See Gregory S 'Gordon, 'Formulating a New Atrocity Speech Offense: Incitement to Commit War Crimes", (2012) 43 Loy U Chi L J 281 ('Gordon, 'Formulating a New Atrocity Speech Offense: Incitement to Commit War Crimes"), 284–88 (demonstrating instances of incitement to commit war crimes).
59 *Prosecutor v. Akayesu*, Case No. ICTR 96-4-T (n 46) para 674.
60 *Prosecutor v. Kambanda*, Case No. ICTR 97-23-S (n 46) para 39(viii).

crimes is no different.[61] In my scholarship, I have pointed out that military commanders have referred to would-be murder victims (such as civilians and prisoners of war) as crocodiles, dogs, pigs, fish and insects.[62]

C The Relationship between Aggression and Incitement

In light of these considerations, how can one best situate any potential relationship between aggression and incitement? Does it make sense to criminalize incitement to aggression? Given the range of relevant aggression conduct considered above—planning, preparing, initiating, and executing—as well as aggression's leadership component, incitement (i.e. advocating illegal conduct) would seem to apply in two key contexts: (1) urging persons within the leadership apparatus to participate in conduct that contributes to the planning, preparation, initiation or execution of acts of aggression; and (2) advocating to lower level officials or soldiers or to members of the public at large to execute the leaders' plans for aggression.

The first type of urging—in other words, something that would fit into the definition of 'incitement'—seems to contemplate meetings and/or discussions within the cadre of government or military high-level decision-makers. The IMT explained that this group could be rather large in scope:

> Hitler could not make aggressive war by himself. He had to have the **cooperation** of statesmen, military leaders, diplomats, and businessmen...[63]

And certainly, any advocacy toward committing acts of aggression in this context could be more pronounced in a leadership framework less dictatorial than Nazi Germany. Such advocacy would take place in councils of government or military within the more sequestered corridors of power.[64] It is submitted that

---

61 *Prosecutor v. Bikindi*, Case No. ICTR-01-72-T (n 46) para 268.
62 Gordon, 'Formulating a New Atrocity Speech Offense: Incitement to Commit War Crimes' (n 58) 284–288.
63 Judgment, *United States v. Goering* et al., International Military Tribunal, 1 October 1946, *Nazi Conspiracy and Aggression: Opinion and Judgment* (1947) ('IMT Judgment'), at 223 (emphasis added).
64 *See, eg*, Jack O'Connell, *King's Counsel: A Memoir of War, Espionage, and Diplomacy in the Middle East* (W W Norton & Company 2011) 119 ('The Egyptian government made the formal decision to attack Israel in a secret high-level meeting in October 1973...'); Paul R Gregory, *Lenin's Brain and Other Tales from the Secret Soviet Archives* (Hoover Institution Press 2008) 125 ('The actual [Soviet] decision to invade Afghanistan was made at a meeting [attended by politburo members] held in Brezhnev's country house...'); Gregory D Koblentz, *Living Weapons: Biological Warfare and International Security* (Cornell

this sort of 'behind closed door' advocacy for aggression should be referred to as 'war-council' incitement.

The second kind of advocacy is directed toward persons outside of the leadership cadre who are nevertheless essential to the prosecution of acts of aggression. At the 1945 negotiations in London for the IMT Charter, Chief U.S. Prosecutor Robert Jackson alluded to this kind of incitement in the following colloquy with British representative Sir David Maxwell Fyfe:

> SIR DAVID MAXWELL FYFE: Mr. Justice Jackson, just to clarify the discussion, could your point be fairly put this way: that you want the entering into the plan to be made a substantive crime?
> MR. JUSTICE JACKSON: Yes. The knowing **incitement** and planning is as criminal as the execution.[65]

The IMT indictment specified the kind of incitement to which Justice Jackson referred. It 'ascribed…criminal responsibility to the defendants with regard to…propaganda intended to directly incite to specific wars of aggression.'[66] And, responsibility for such propaganda factored into the convictions of crimes against peace for IMT defendants Rudolf Hess, Wilhelm Keitel, and Alfred Rosenberg.[67] The IMTFE judgment focused even more on individual criminal responsibility for this variety of incitement to commit aggression. For example, the Tribunal found Sadao Araki guilty of crimes against peace in large part for advancing 'the Army policy to prepare for wars of aggression by…speeches and by control of the press, inciting and preparing the Japanese people for war.'[68] The IMTFE found Kingoro Hashimoto guilty on similar grounds, specifying that he incited 'the appetite of the Japanese people for the possessions of Japan's neighbours, by inflaming Japanese opinion for war to secure these possessions….'[69] It is submitted that this sort of 'appeal to the public' advocacy for aggression should be referred to as 'war-mongering' incitement.

University Press 2011) 47 ('During the second week of January [1991,] Saddam Hussein held a high-level meeting to discuss the status of Iraq's chemical and biological weapons and plans on how they could be used').

65 Robert H Jackson, *Report of Robert H. Jackson, United States Representative to the International Conference on Military Trials* (Dept of State 1945) 376.
66 Kearney, *The Prohibition of Propaganda for War in International Law* (n 1) 35.
67 *Ibid* 38.
68 IMTFE Judgement (n 35) 1146–47.
69 *Ibid* 1152.

4   The Viability of an Incitement to Aggression Offense

In light of the above considerations, does it make sense to criminalize incitement to aggression within the context of the Rome Statute? That depends on the category of incitement. The arguments for criminalizing 'war-council' incitement are not terribly compelling. First of all, as formulated in the Rome Statute, aggression is a leadership-focused crime limited to an individual exerting control over a country's political or military operations. As established above, though, such an individual depends on others to handle the myriad undertakings involved in initiating and sustaining acts of aggression in modern times.

Although the defendant will facilitate actions within the framework of a leadership cadre and while this likely implies a range of communication entailing persuasion, such persuasion does not bear the traditional indicia of incitement. First, although persons within the leadership core may be in superior-subordinate relationships, they are all part of the same team and are, by virtue of their jobs, working in cooperation to plan, prepare, initiate and execute acts of aggression. By virtue of their respective leadership roles, they are all subject to the ICC's *in personam* jurisdiction. So, the value of any attendant incitement provision is doubtful—those who would act—the controllers of the government/military apparatus—need no exhorting as they are in many senses a single corporate entity and therefore monopolize agency.

Additionally, unlike genocide or war crimes, for instance, advocacy speech in the war-council context does not as directly involve demonization of the intended victims. Decisions made within the leadership clique imply consensus through facilitated group discussion, not frenzied soap-box oratory. While deficits in consensus-building may entail negative references to the intended objects of aggression, it would seem any such aspersions would rarely, if ever, degrade to the base level of dehumanization. As a result, the distinctive power of inciting speech to inspire mass atrocity is not sufficiently at issue in the war-council aggression context.

Finally, war-council-related aggression—conduct necessarily entailing internal government/military discussions in the planning, preparation, initiation and execution stages—is indissolubly connected to speech in the first place. It represents group action and group action is only possible through communication by members within the group. So it may seem rather unnecessary or gratuitous to criminalize speech that merely generates other such speech. Consequently, in cases of inchoate conduct within the war-council aggression context, from a policy perspective, 'attempt to commit aggression' better satisfies any justice concerns.

The same is not true for incitement in the war-mongering context. The speech involved there does bear the traditional hallmarks of incitement. In the first place, it involves state officials employing inflammatory rhetoric to mold opinion and agitate for action among the public at large or the rank-and-file military to back acts of aggression. While, in contrast to war-council discourse, it may not always be a necessary component of an aggression campaign, in instances of more divisive government conduct, it may be needed to promote *esprit de corps* and morale among soldiers and/or cooperation and sacrifice among civilians.

Moreover, such speech empirically seeks to vilify and dehumanize the targeted enemy. In this regard, reference to Article 20 of the International Covenant on Civil and Political Rights ('ICCPR') is instructive.[70] ICCPR Article 20(1) prohibits 'any propaganda for war' and its twin provision in subsection (2) makes illegal 'any advocacy of national, racial or religious hatred that constitutes incitement to discrimination, hostility or violence.' That the two sub-provisions are paired together is no coincidence. Article 20's drafting history reveals certain delegates perceived the prohibition against war propaganda to include 'the dissemination of slanderous rumours which undermined relations between States, and incitement to national, racial, or religious hatred.'[71] Thus, war propaganda was linked in the drafting history to incitement to national, racial, or religious hatred. In fact, Michael Kearney posits that '"war propaganda" represented a composite of different forms of incitement to violence...'.[72] Consistent with this, one commentator has noted that ICCPR Article 20(1) seeks to prohibit 'individuals from vilifying other individuals.'[73]

And, even apart from ICCPR Article 20(1), other commentators have noticed the similarities between the traditional nature and contours of incitement and war-mongering. For example, Parvesh Singla observes:

> Propaganda is a powerful weapon in war; it is used to dehumanize and create hatred toward a supposed enemy...by creating a false image in the

---

70 International Covenant on Civil and Political Rights (adopted 19 December 1966, entered into force 23 March 1976) 999 UNTS 171, art 5(2).

71 Kearney, *The Prohibition of Propaganda for War in International Law* (n 1) at 116 (one delegate, the USSR, sought a combined provision for 'prevention of war propaganda, incitement to enmity among nations, racial discrimination, and dissemination of slanderous rumour.').

72 *Ibid* 117.

73 Sarah Joseph, 'A Rights Analysis of the Covenant on Civil and Political Rights' (1999) 5 J Int'l Legal Stud 57, 74.

mind. This can be done by using derogatory or racist terms...or by making allegations of enemy atrocities.[74]

So, criminalizing war-mongering speech via incitement to aggression is more feasible and desirable from a policy perspective. And, if the offense were styled as direct and *public* incitement to commit aggression, the public element would implicitly exclude 'war-council' communication, making it viable within the normative framework of the Rome Statute.[75] The elements of the crime would be roughly consistent with incitement to genocide—direct, public, a *mens rea* consistent with the target crime, and a parsing of the text to determine if the speech represents permissible expression or criminal advocacy. In other words, any divergences from incitement to genocide would owe to any differences in the target crime.

Nevertheless, one can anticipate certain arguments against inclusion of an incitement to aggression provision. As a threshold matter, it could be contended that inchoate offenses in relation to the crime of aggression are not possible given the Elements of the Crimes in relation to aggression adopted as part of the Kampala Amendments. In particular, the third element provides that 'The act of aggression...was committed.'[76] In other words, it could be argued that the State act of aggression must have already been committed before any individual criminal responsibility could attach to leaders. But this argument has no merit. The ICC Elements of Crimes for other offenses are phrased in the same way. For instance, one of the common elements for crimes against humanity is that 'The conduct was committed as part of a widespread or systematic attack directed against a civilian population.' And yet inchoate crimes can be committed in reference to crimes against humanity—for example, Article 25(3)(f) would permit prosecution of attempted crimes against humanity.[77]

Similarly, it has been suggested that inchoate versions of aggression, given their incomplete nature, may not satisfy the gravity admissibility criterion found i Articles 17 and 53 of the Rome Statute. McDougall observes that 'given

---

74 Parvesh Singla, *The Manual of Life: Understanding Counter-Terrorism* (WordPress 2002) 9.
75 This contrasts with my other incitement scholarship where I have otherwise advocated eliminating the 'public' element of the crime. See Gregory S Gordon, *Atrocity Speech Law* (OUP *forthcoming 2015*) (arguing that the 'public' element of incitement should be eliminated from the incitement to genocide offense as 'private' incitement can be just as potent as 'public,' depending on the surrounding circumstances).
76 Kampala Amendments (n 2) Annex II.
77 McDougall, *The Crime of Aggression under the Rome Statute of the International Criminal Court* (n 32) 200–01.

the gravity threshold employed by the OTP, and the Rome Statute's requirement that the Court's jurisdiction be limited to the most serious crimes of concern, it is difficult to see the point [of whether inchoate aggression is a viable crime] ever coming before the judges of the Court to determine.' This argument is flawed for the same reason as the previous one—the Rome Statute implicitly allows for the gravity of inchoate crimes by deeming them prosecutable through Article 25 (attempt at (3)(f) and incitement to commit genocide at (3)(e)).

However, even assuming the Statute's criminalization parameters are not enough to allay this concern, we can certainly imagine a scenario where justice would demand prosecution of an inchoate crime linked to aggression. For example, imagine a regime whose recently prepared act of aggression has not been carried out. Imagine also that the regime has committed acts of aggression in the past (and perhaps individuals in that regime have been prosecuted for those acts). If the regime had been planning future acts of aggression that were stymied for any number of reasons, we may very well wish to prosecute those of its members who had been verbally grooming its citizens to participate in the illegal use of armed force.

Another potential argument is that the crime is redundant. In other words, speaking to the public or subordinates to garner support for successfully committing an act of aggression is implicitly part of 'preparing' to commit an act of aggression. There is therefore no need to have a separate 'incitement' offense. But this does not take into account the fact that 'verbal support for aggressive acts is…likely to be insufficient to meet the definition of either planning or preparation.'[78] As a result, a separate offence of incitement would permit prosecution of verbal conduct used to rouse public opinion against a targeted enemy and raise support and morale for the planned act of aggression.

Free speech advocates may object to the proposed crime based on fears of it chilling legitimate expression, regardless of how repugnant the speech. But this objection is similarly unavailing. Incitement to aggression, as proposed herein, can only be prosecuted if sufficiently 'direct' within a context demonstrating the speech could imminently and realistically contribute to the perpetration of the target crime. Moreover, given the gravity of aggression itself—considered the poisonous tree of crimes bearing the fruit of atrocity in the form of genocide, crimes against humanity and war crimes—any potential chilling effect is significantly outweighed.

---

78   *Ibid*, 188. *See also* Sascha Mueller, 'The Crime of Aggression under German Law' (2008) 6 NZ YBIL 183, 189 (In reference to the German domestic law against aggression, 'due to the severity of punishment [for preparatory acts] incitement or verbal support…do not meet this requirement.').

5 Conclusion

Among other things, the empirical link between aggression and mass atrocity makes clear the epochal nature of the 2010 Kampala achievement. Defining aggression and operationalizing it within the Rome Statute, assuming the necessary ratifications and adoption, will go a long way toward eliminating the scourge of illegal war. But, that is likely not enough. There are ancillary pockets of aggression-related criminality that may be implicated and failing to deal with them could prove fatal. One of those is incitement to commit aggression. As this essay has demonstrated, incitement within the aggression framework theoretically arises in two different instances. The first is in the 'war-council' context, when elite-tier leaders gather to design and effectuate acts of aggression—such speech does not really amount to traditional incitement and its use by individuals in cases of unrealized acts of aggression can be adequately punished as attempt. The second theoretical instance of such speech is the 'war-mongering' context, when leaders appeal to lower-level subordinates or the public at large to garner necessary support for aggressive designs. Policy and history suggest this latter variety of incitement be criminalized as 'direct and public incitement to commit aggression.' With modifications taking into account differences in the target offenses, the elements of this crime would track those of incitement to genocide. Such a doctrinal formulation should allay free speech concerns while criminalizing an often indispensable aspect of preparation for acts of aggression. In raising the issue of aggression and incitement all those years ago, it turns out Roger Clark's doctrinal and policy instincts were spot on—the war-mongering variety of incitement should indeed be criminalized. And so as we celebrate in this volume Dr. Clark's great achievements in the area of international law, we can only hope his instincts will eventually prove prophetic.

CHAPTER 26

Individual Criminal Responsibility: Of 'Dog's Law', Offending against Sound Popular Feeling, Semi-colons and Commas

Kenneth J. Keith*

This paper, written in tribute to a great scholar and friend for more than 50 years, draws on his wide interests in the principles of criminal law, international law and legal process and on the human values underlying them. It also gives attention to some of the lawyer's crafts, especially in the careful drafting of texts and the use of possibly relevant sources and evidences of the law. The paper focuses on individual criminal responsibility, particularly by reference to the principles of non-retroactivity and the certainty of criminal law. A notable American criminal law scholar some years ago brought both principles together in 'the principle of legality': 'a limitation on penalisation...effected by the required prescription and application of specific rules'.[1]

1 'Dog's Law'

The story may begin in the late 18th century with the beginnings of the movements for the codification of law, particularly with Jeremy Bentham, responsible, among many other things, for the addition of the words 'codification' and 'international law' to the English language. In his article on William Blackstone's *Commentaries on English Law*[2] and in his other writings, he expressed his hostility to judge-made law. In 1792, in *Truth versus Ashhurst*, he responds in these terms to the proposition stated by Mr Justice Ashhurst that 'Everyman has the means of knowing all the laws he is bound by'.

---

* Many thanks to David McKeever for outstanding research assistance and comment and not only with this paper.

1 Jerome Hall, *General Principles of Criminal Law* (Bobs-Merrill Company 1947) 19; also Jerome Hall, 'Nulla poena sine lege' (1937) 47 YLJ 2, 165.

2 Reissue of Jeremy Bentham, *A Comment on the Commentaries and a Fragment on Government* (1776), edited by James H Burns & Henry LA Hart (Athlone Press 1977).

> Do you know how [the judges] make [the common law]? Just as a man makes law for his dog. When your dog does anything you want to break him of, you wait until he does it, and then you beat him for it. This is the way you make laws for your dog: and this is the way judges make law for you and me. They won't tell you beforehand what it is he *should not do*—they won't so much as allow of his being told: they lie by till he has done something which they say he should *not have done*, and then they hang him for it.

He goes on to say that the French have had enough of this dog-law; they are turning it as fast as they can into statute law, and. nor do they ever make a law without doing all they can think of to let every creature among them know of it, or, as an inscription in the Palais des Invalides in Paris puts it, the Napoleonic Code was to provide 'justice égale et intelligible pour tous'.

The general process of codification in the 19th century had particular application to the criminal law, notably in the common law world with Macaulay preparing the Indian Criminal Code in 1835–1837 (enacted only in the wake of the Indian Mutiny in 1857 and applicable, with amendments, to this day in Pakistan, Bangladesh, Myanmar, Sri Lanka, Malaysia, Singapore and Brunei), R S Wright's for Jamaica in 1877 (following the 1865 uprising, not enacted there but adopted elsewhere in the Caribbean), James Fitzjames Stephens in 1878, not enacted in England and Wales as intended, but forming the basis of Canadian Criminal Code of 1892 and the New Zealand Code of 1893,[3] and Samuel Griffiths for Queensland in 1899 (also adopted in Nigeria, Cyprus and Palestine).[4] Codes, including criminal codes, were also enacted in the United States in the late 19th century as a result, in part at least, of the efforts of David Dudley Field who was also a prime mover in the setting up in 1873 of the Institut de Droit International (the reform of international law being too important to be left to governments) and the International Law Association

---

[3] Professor I D Campbell, Roger's mentor in criminal law, had this to say in 1966 about the state of the essentially uncodified English criminal law: 'What a lamentable story it is! I refer...to the dismal state of criminal jurisprudence in England: a condition from which one might well have expected it to be extricated by now, but which, on the contrary, recent decisions of high authority have tended to worsen rather than cure' (see his review of Smith J C and B Hogan, *Criminal Law*, 1965, in (1966) 2 NZULR 233).

[4] On these processes generally, see B. Wright, 'Macaulay's Indian Penal Code: Historical Context and Originating Principles', in Wing Cheong Chan et al (eds), *Codification, Macaulay and the Indian Penal Code: The Legacies and Modern Challenges of Criminal Law Reform* (Ashgate 2011) 19–55; Barry Wright, 'Criminal Law Codification and Imperial Projects: The Self-Governing Jurisdiction Codes of the 1890s' (2008) 12 Legal History 19.

(originally called the Association for the Reform and Codification of the Law of Nations).

Three features of that codification effort are relevant: the express rejection of common law crimes, the emphasis on specificity of definition, along with proper notice, and the careful articulation of 'parties to crimes', that is, of those who in addition to the principal perpetrator of a crime, may be held guilty. The 'parties' provision was often made applicable to all crimes in the code and at the same time it replaced the confusing and complex common law.

The Stephen model stated that everyone is a party to and guilty of an offence who actually commits it; does anything for the purpose of aiding any person to commit the offence; abets any person in committing the offence; or counsels or procures any person to commit the offence.[5] It also provides for liability in respect of actions taken in relation to a common intention to prosecute an unlawful purpose and for accessories after the fact.[6] Essentially the same provisions are still to be found in the relevant criminal codes in force well over a century later.[7]

An associated principle or presumption of interpretation developed by the judges and reflected in some Interpretation Acts calls for criminal statutes to be strictly construed.[8] Careful specificity in the drafting of an international crime is also to be seen in the nineteenth century in a very early international criminal convention—the Convention for the Protection of Submarine Telegraph Cables of 1884. That convention made it a 'punishable offence to break or injure a submarine cable, wilfully or by culpable negligence, in such a manner as might interrupt or obstruct telegraphic communication.' Two years later, 'doubts having been raised as to the meaning of the word "wilfully"...it is understood [declared a Protocol] that the provision...does not apply to cases of breakage or injury caused incidentally or of necessity in the repair of a cable,

---

5   See Part IV of the 1880 Bill (sect 72). Stephen's earlier digest, which was a first step towards his drafting of a code, had expressly distinguished between principals in the first and second degree (see James Fitzjames Stephen (ed), *A Digest of the Criminal Law (Crimes and Punishments)* (4th edn, Macmillan and Co 1887) 30–32 (arts 35–38)).
6   Sects 73–74.
7   See eg George P Fletcher, *Rethinking Criminal Law* (Little, Brown 1978) ch 8.5–8.8.
8   On the development of this principle, see Livingston Hall, 'Strict or Liberal Construction of Penal Statutes' (1935) 48 Harvard L Rev 748. For a modern illustration, see art 22(2) of the 1998 Rome Statute of the International Criminal Court, under which 'The definition of a crime shall be strictly construed and shall not be extended by analogy. In case of ambiguity, the definition shall be interpreted in favour of the person being investigated, prosecuted or convicted.'

when all precautions have been taken to avoid such breakage or injury'.[9] That convention, along with others which limited criminal jurisdiction to the flag state, was cited by France in the Permanent Court of International Justice ('PCIJ') in the *Lotus* case in support of its argument that only the flag state has jurisdiction over offences committed on the high seas—a matter on which our honorand comments in his contribution on that case to the UN AudioVisual Library on International Law.[10]

The particular specification of those who are to be criminally responsible as parties to be found in many national criminal codes in the 19th and 20th centuries has been matched in major multilateral treaties establishing criminal offences adopted over the last 50 years or more: treaties relating to genocide, hijacking, offences at sea, narcotics, the protection of UN and Associated Personnel, terrorist bombings, mercenaries, the International Criminal Court ('ICC'), nuclear terrorism, financing terrorism, disappearances, corruption and international organised crime. Related provisions have been included in the agreements and Security Council resolutions establishing ad hoc tribunals. A number of those provisions have some common features, such as attempts, threats and participating as an accomplice. In some, as appropriate, those who organise or direct the crime are made liable and in three cases elements of common purpose or participation in an organised criminal group have been introduced. Those provisions and the variations between them are considered later. For the moment it is enough to note first the care that had evidently been exercised by those, including lawyers as legislators or assistants to legislators, who prepared those provisions and, second, the very clear affirmation of the principle against retroactive criminal liability and penalty included in the Universal Declaration of Human Rights, the Third and Fourth Geneva Conventions of 1949,[11] the International Covenant on Civil and Political Rights (the principle is non-derogable even in national emergencies), the Statute of the ICC and regional human rights treaties. Another important element is that the Hague Regulations of 1899 and 1907, the Geneva Conventions of 1949 and the 1977 Protocols forbid collective punishments, yet again emphasising individual responsibility.

---

9 Declaration, Explanatory of Articles II and IV, of the Plenipotentiaries of the Signatory Governments of the Convention for the Protection of Submarine Cables of 14 March 1884, adopted 1 December 1886.

10 This and other lectures on a range of topics are available via <http://www.un.org/law/avl/> accessed 1 February 2014.

11 Arts 99 and 67, respectively.

2 Sound Popular Feeling

What of the work of lawyers as counsel and judges? Rulings of the PCIJ, the Nuremberg Tribunal and the International Criminal Tribunal for former Yugoslavia provide answers, as do related rulings of national courts.

The first case concerns the replacement in 1935 in the penal law of Danzig, a free city under the protection of the League of Nations, of the provision to the effect that

> Article 2.—An act is only punishable if the penalty applicable to it has been prescribed by a law in force before the commission of the act.

By the following

> Article 2.—Any person who commits an act...which is deserving of penalty according to the fundamental conceptions of a penal law and sound popular feeling shall be punished [...].

The new decree was headed 'Creation of Law by the Application of Penal Laws by Analogy'. The PCIJ was asked whether that new law was consistent with the Constitution of Danzig. 'No' was its answer.[12] The penal law was no longer equally clear both to the judge and the accused. Criminality would now depend entirely upon the appreciation of the situation by the Public Prosecutor and the Judge. 'Sound popular feeling is a very elusive standard', varying from man to man. Further, the Constitution of Danzig endowed the Free City with a form of government under which the State organs were being kept within the confines of the law (*Rechtstaat*, a State governed by the rule of law). While the fundamental rights in the Constitution were not absolute they may be restricted by law which

> must itself specify the conditions of such restriction, and, in particular, determine the limit beyond which an act can no longer be justified as an exercise of a fundamental liberty and becomes a punishable offence. It must be possible for the individual to know, beforehand, whether his acts are lawful or liable to punishment.[13]

---

12   *Consistency of certain Danzig legislative decrees with the constitution of the Free City* PCIJ Rep Series A/B No 65.
13   *Ibid* 57.

That decree had been promulgated by the National Socialist Party dominated Government which had recently taken control of the Free City. In its German manifestation that Party had enacted a similar law in that country.[14]

3   The Semi-colon and the Comma

The next case, decided only a decade later, is that of the Nuremberg Tribunal where again real caution is to be observed in the preparation of the Agreement establishing the Tribunal and setting out its law, and then in some of the rulings made by the Tribunal.

The London Agreement of 8 August 1945 gave the Nuremberg Tribunal jurisdiction over three crimes: crimes against peace, war crimes, and crimes against humanity. The last was defined, initially, in this way:

> (c) Crimes against humanity: namely, murder, extermination, enslavement, deportation, and other inhumane acts committed against any civilian population, before or during the war; or persecutions on political, racial or religious grounds in execution of or in connection with any crime within the jurisdiction of the Tribunal, whether or not in violation of the domestic law of the country where perpetrated.

On 6 October 1945, the very day on which the indictment was issued, a protocol was signed in Berlin to remove 'a discrepancy' between the text in the Russian language and the texts in English and French. The consequence was that in the English text the semi-colon after the words 'before and during the war' was replaced by a comma and a comparable change was made to the French text. Our honorand has carefully examined the process leading to that change.[15] That change meant that the inhumane acts were crimes within the jurisdiction of the Tribunal only if connected to one of the other crimes. Consistently with that change, Count 4 in the indictment, relating to crimes against humanity, began with a temporal limitation:

---

[14]   I have discussed this case in Kenneth Keith, 'The International Court of Justice and Criminal Justice' (2010) 59 ICLQ 895.

[15]   Roger S Clark, 'Crimes against Humanity' in George Ginsburgs & Vladimir Nikolaevich Kudriavtsev (eds), *The Nuremberg Trial and International Law* (Martinus Nijhoff 1990), 177–99.

All the defendants committed Crimes against Humanity during a period of years preceding 8 May 1945 in Germany and in all those countries and territories occupied by the German armed forces since 1 September 1939 and in Austria and Czechoslovakia and in Italy and on the High Seas. (emphasis added.)

That this limiting connection was a material element of the crime was confirmed by the Tribunal.[16]

The modes of liability applicable to all three crimes before the Nuremberg Tribunal were stipulated at the end of Art. 6 of the Charter: 'leaders, organizers, instigators and accomplices participating in the formulation or execution of a common plan or conspiracy to commit any of the foregoing crimes are responsible for all acts performed by any persons in execution of such plan'. The Tribunal clarified the scope of conspiracy liability:

The Prosecution says, in effect, that any significant participation in the affairs of the Nazi Party or Government is evidence of a participation in a conspiracy that is in itself criminal. Conspiracy is not defined in the Charter. But in the opinion of the Tribunal the conspiracy must be clearly outlined in its criminal purpose. It must not be too far removed from the time of decision and of action. The planning, to be criminal, must not rest merely on the declarations of a party program, such as are found in the 25 points of the Nazi Party, announced in 1920, or the political affirmations expressed in Mein Kampf in later years. The Tribunal must examine whether a concrete plan to wage war existed, and determine the participants in that concrete plan.[17]

The Tribunal was also careful to distinguish modes of liability from substantive offences. Art. 6(a) of the IMT Charter defined:

---

[16] *Judgment of the International Military Tribunal at Nuremberg, 1 October 1946*, reproduced in (1947) 41 AJIL 172 ('*Nuremberg Judgment*') 249. This requirement was retained in art 5 of the Statute of the International Criminal Tribunal for Yugoslavia (though on the position under customary international law at the time, see the *obiter* statement in *Prosecutor v Tadić* (Appeal Judgment) IT-94-1 (2 October 1995) ('*Tadić Appeal Judgment*') paras 140–141), but not in the definition of crimes against humanity in the Statute of the International Criminal Tribunal for Rwanda (art 3), the 1996 International Law Commission Draft Code of Crimes against the Peace and Security of Mankind (art 18), or the Rome Statute of the International Criminal Court (art 7).

[17] *Nuremberg Judgment* (n 16) 222.

> Crimes against Peace: namely, planning, preparation, initiation or waging of a war of aggression, or a war in violation of international treaties, agreements or assurances, or participation in a common plan or conspiracy for the accomplishment of any of the foregoing;

There was no reference to either common plan or conspiracy in sub-paragraphs (b) or (c) (war crimes and crimes against humanity, respectively). Count 1 of the Indictment charged 'common plan or conspiracy' as a discrete crime, however, and the Prosecution argued that conspiracy to commit war crimes or crimes against humanity was a self-standing crime under the Charter. The Tribunal categorically rejected this argument:

> In the opinion of the Tribunal these words [at the end of Art. 6] do not add a new and separate crime to those already listed. The words are designed to establish the responsibility of persons participating in a common plan. The Tribunal will therefore disregard the charges in Count One that the defendants conspired to commit War Crimes and Crimes against Humanity, and will consider only the common plan to prepare, initiate, and wage aggressive war.[18]

The strict, textual approach of the Nuremberg Tribunal on this issue was recalled by the US Supreme Court in its 2006 decision in *Hamdan v Rumsfeld*, where a majority of that Court dismissed a charge of conspiracy on the basis that it was not known in the law of war.[19] In a 2012 decision, the D.C. Court of Appeals quashed the conviction of the same defendant for material support for terrorism, on the basis that the relevant domestic legislation must be interpreted consistently with the principle of non-retroactivity in criminal law, and

---

18   *Ibid* 224 (see, to similar effect, *In re Brandt and others (The Medical Trial)*, 20 August 1947, 14 ILR 296).

19   *Salim Ahmed Hamdan, Petitioner v Donald H. Rumsfeld, Secretary of Defense et al*, 548 US 557 (2006), 47–48, per Stevens J; see discussion in Michael J Kelly & Timothy L McCormack, 'The Nuremberg Trial and the Subsequent Development of International Law', in David A Blumenthal & Timothy L McCormack, *The Legacy of Nuremberg: Civilising Influence of Institutionalised Vengeance?* (Martinus Nijhoff 2008), 109–112. This finding of the Nuremberg Tribunal was also recalled by the ILC in its Commentary on principles of individual criminal responsibility under its 1996 Draft Code of Crimes against the Peace and Security of Mankind (UN International Law Commission, *Yearbook of the International Law Commission 1996, Volume 2, Part 1* (United Nations Publications 2005) 21, para 13).

the offence in question did not exist in the international law of war at the material time.[20]

The same careful approach to the scope of liability was also seen in the Nuremberg Tribunal's handling of its power to declare as criminal any organization of which an individual defendant was a member. The Tribunal noted that the combined effect of Art. 9 of the IMT Charter and Control Council Order No. 10 was that

> A member of an organization which the Tribunal has declared to be criminal may be subsequently convicted of the crime of membership and be punished for that crime by death. This is not to assume that international or military courts which will try these individuals will not exercise appropriate standards of justice. This is a far reaching and novel procedure. Its application, unless properly safeguarded, may produce great injustice.[21]

The Tribunal stated that the Charter gave it a discretion here, one which did not permit arbitrary action, 'but should be exercised in accordance with well-settled legal principles, one of the most important of which is that criminal guilt is personal, and that mass punishments should be avoided.'[22] It continued as follows:

> [a] criminal organization is analogous to a criminal conspiracy in that the essence of both is cooperation for criminal purposes. There must be a group bound together and organized for a common purpose. The group must be formed or used in connection with the commission of crimes denounced by the Charter. Since the [Tribunal's] declaration with respect to the organizations and groups will, as has been pointed out, fix the

---

[20] In response to the 2006 decision of the Supreme Court, the US Congress had passed the Military Commissions Act of 2006 which specifically identified the crimes which the military commissions (set up to prosecute members of Al-Qaeda and the Taliban) had the authority to try—including material support for terrorism and conspiracy. Hamdan was prosecuted under the new legislation, acquitted of conspiracy but convicted of material support. On appeal against conviction, a three-judge panel of the Court of Appeal (DC Circuit) quashed his conviction (*Hamdan v United States of America*, DC Circuit, No. 11–1257, 16 October 2012, at 16–17 on non-retroactivity and 24–25 on the offence of material support). The U.S government has since requested the rehearing, by the full court, of the related case of *Al-Bahlul v United States*.

[21] *Nuremberg Judgment* (n 16), 250.

[22] *Ibid* 251.

criminality of its members, that definition should exclude persons who had no knowledge of the criminal purposes or acts of the organization and those who were drafted by the State for membership, unless they were personally implicated in the commission of acts declared criminal by Article 6 of the Charter as members of the organization. Membership alone is not enough to come within the scope of these declarations.[23]

The Tribunal called for an amendment to the Control Council Law to prescribe limitations on the punishment of membership in those groups declared to be criminal. Turning to the facts, the Tribunal declared as criminal certain members of the leadership corps of the Nazi party, the Gestapo and SD, and the SS.[24] In each case, however, it limited this finding to the part of the organisation constituted by those members who became or remained members with knowledge that it was being used for the commission of acts declared criminal by Article 6 of the Charter, or who were personally implicated as members of the organization in the commission of such crimes; it excluded those who ceased being members before the outbreak of the war.

This paper earlier recalled the principles prohibiting retroactive criminal law and requiring criminal law to be certain (which may be see together as the principle of legality) and the practice of the drafters of International criminal conventions in the spelling out of parties to offences. The variations in that drafting may be seen as one piece of evidence of the proposition stated in 2003 by Antonio Cassese, based on his extensive scholarly and practical experience, that international criminal law was still to attain the degree of sophistication seen in national legal systems and was still rudimentary.[25]

4 Joint Criminal Enterprise

Those principles and those varying drafting practices, noted earlier, are important for an assessment of the third decision considered in this paper—that

---

23   Ibid 251.
24   Ibid 252–67. The Tribunal rejected the Prosecution's arguments that the SA, Reich Cabinet, and the General Staff and High Command should be declared criminal (ibid 267–272).
25   Antonio Cassese, *International Criminal Law* (OUP 2003) 135. This characterisation of international criminal law was retained in the second edition of this work, published in 2008 (at 32, note 1), and also in the most recent edition, revised by a number of commentators (Antonio Cassese, Paola Gaeta, Laurel Baig, Mary Fan, Christopher Gosnell & Alex Whiting, *Cassese's International Criminal Law* (3rd edn, OUP 2013) 4–5).

given by an Appellate Chamber of the International Criminal Tribunal for Former Yugoslavia in 1999 in the _Tadić_ case, the first appeal following a contested trial in that Tribunal. In that appeal the Prosecutor challenged the Trial Chamber's acquittal of Tadić on charges of grave breaches under the Geneva Conventions, violations of the laws and customs of war and a crime against humanity. The facts which the Prosecutor alleged in support of those charges were that armed Serbs including the accused, on or about 14 June 1992, killed five named residents in a village in Prijedor in front of their homes. While the Trial Chamber was satisfied beyond reasonable doubt that the accused was a member of the armed group that entered the village, searched it for men, seized several of them, beat them and then departed with them (actions which were the subject of separate charges on which the accused was convicted) and that after their departure, the five men named in the Indictment were found lying dead in the village,

> this Trial Chamber cannot, on the evidence before it, be satisfied beyond reasonable doubt that the accused had any part in the killing of the five men or any other.[26]

The Trial Chamber explained that nothing was known about the killings or their circumstances, and referred to related events which it said were not relevant to any finding of responsibility. It had earlier reviewed at length the 'considerable evidence regarding the events of 14 June.'[27] The Prosecutor on a cross appeal challenged the reasonable doubt ruling and contended that the Chamber misdirected itself on the applicability of the common purpose doctrine. On the first matter, the Appeal Chamber, after a brief discussion, held that the only reasonable conclusion the Trial Chamber could have drawn was that the armed group to which the Appellant belonged killed the five men.[28] The Appeal Chamber began the next section of its judgment in this way:

> (a) Article 7(1) of the Statute and the Notion of Common Purpose
> 185. The question therefore arises whether under international criminal law the Appellant can be held criminally responsible for the killing of the five men from Jaskici even though there is no evidence that he personally killed any of them. The two central issues are:

---

26   _Prosecutor v Tadić_ (Opinion and Judgment) IT-94-1 (7 May 1997) para 373.
27   _Ibid_ paras 344–72.
28   _Tadić Appeal Judgment_ IT-94-1-A (15 July 1999) paras 178–83.

(i) whether the acts of one person can give rise to the criminal culpability of another where both participate in the execution of a common criminal plan; and
(ii) what degree of *mens rea* is required in such a case.

Article 7(1) of the ICTY Statute provides as follows:

> A person who planned, instigated, ordered, committed or otherwise aided and abetted in the planning, preparation or execution of a crime referred to in articles 2 to 5 of the present Statute, shall be individually responsible for the crime.

In the course of the next 40 paragraphs, the Chamber elaborates the principle of Joint Criminal Enterprise ('JCE') and applies it to the facts of this case, reaching this finding:

> The Trial Chamber erred in holding that it could not, on the evidence before it, be satisfied beyond reasonable doubt that the Appellant had any part in the killing of the five men from the village of Jaskici. The Appeals Chamber finds that the Appellant participated in the killings of the five men in Jaskici, which were committed during an armed conflict as part of a widespread or systematic attack on a civilian population. The Appeals Chamber therefore holds that under the provisions of Article 7(1) of the Statute, the Trial Chamber should have found the Appellant guilty.

The Appeal Chamber did not reach that conclusion by the direct application of Article 7(1) of its Statute but on the basis of participation in the execution of a joint (or common or collective) criminal plan or enterprise or purpose—the adjectives and nouns appear to be used interchangeably. The Chamber begins with the 'basic assumption...of personal culpability', *nulla poena sine culpa*, a principle laid down in constitutions, laws and judicial decisions (but interestingly it makes no reference to its statement in the Universal Declaration of Human Rights, the 1949 Geneva Conventions, the European Convention on Human Rights or the International Covenant on Civil and Political Rights). Rather, puzzlingly, it declares that 'in international criminal law the principle is laid down, inter alia, in Article 7(1) if [its] statute', which it then sets out.

The Appeal Chamber then addresses the question whether participating in a common criminal purpose falls within Article 7(1). It is apparent, says the Tribunal, from Article 7(1) and the crimes over which it has jurisdiction, that jurisdiction appears to extend beyond those who actually commit the crimes.

INDIVIDUAL CRIMINAL RESPONSIBILITY   441

That is plainly so and not merely 'apparent' but that does not extend the jurisdiction of the tribunal beyond the precise terms of the crime as stated in its Statute, for instance of ordering grave breaches of the Geneva Conventions or being complicit in genocide. The notion that persons other than the actual perpetrator are covered, it continues, is spelt out in the Secretary-General's report leading to the establishment of the Tribunal:

> The Secretary-General believes that *all* persons who *participate* in the planning, preparation or execution of serious violations of international humanitarian law in the former Yugoslavia are individually responsible for such violations.[29]

That sentence preceded the text of what became Article 7(1); it will be noted that it is a summary of that provision with 'participate' (which the Chamber emphasises) replacing the six verbs actually included in that provision. But the Chamber gives that sentence a reading which prefers that general word, included in the report proposing the Statute, to the specific terms of the Statute formally adopted by the Security Council as the law of the Tribunal.

> Thus, all those who have engaged in serious violations of international humanitarian law, whatever the manner in which they may have perpetrated, or participated in the perpetration of those violations, must be brought to justice. If this is so, it is fair to conclude that the Statute does not confine itself to providing for jurisdiction over those persons who plan, instigate, order, physically perpetrate a crime or otherwise aid and abet in its planning, preparation or execution. The Statute does not stop there. It does not exclude those modes of participating in the commission of crimes which occur where several persons having a common purpose embark on criminal activity that is then carried out either jointly or by some members of this plurality of persons. Whoever contributes to the commission of crimes by the group of persons or some members of the group, in execution of a common criminal purpose, may be held to be criminally liable, subject to certain conditions, which are specified below.[30]

But the Statute does so 'confine' itself; it does 'stop there' with its six verbs; and it does not include other 'modes of participating' in committing crimes where several persons have a common purpose.

---

29   *Ibid* para 190 (emphasis supplied by the Appeals Chamber).
30   *Ibid.*

The Chamber then concludes that its interpretation is supported not just by the object and purpose of the Statute but also by the very nature of crimes committed in wartime. Although only some of the group may commit the criminal act, the participation of others is often vital. To hold criminally liable only the person who performed the criminal act would disregard the role of those who made the criminal act possible. At that point the Chamber, no doubt recalling the other six verbs in Article 7(1) as well as the extended definitions of the grave breaches and genocide crimes in the Statute, added that to hold the non-perpetrators liable only as aiders and abetters might understate the degree of their criminal responsibility.[31] But the actual extent of their involvement in the criminal activity would, of course, be a matter for sentencing, especially given that the Tribunal's power of sentencing to imprisonment is scarcely constrained by its Statute (Article 24).

The Chamber then called in aid Post World War II decisions on charges of war crime, national law and two international criminal conventions and elaborated what it saw as three distinct categories of collective criminality.

The first category appears to fall plainly within Article 7(1) since it requires (1) voluntary participation in an aspect of the common design such as providing material assistance and (2) an intention to achieve the unlawful result. So too does the second category appear to fall within article 7(1). It requires (1) an organised system to commit war crimes, (2) the accused's awareness of the nature of the system and (3) participation in enforcing it i.e. encouraging, aiding, abetting in realising the common criminal design (the passage quoted from the Belsen case in n.251 is briefer). If the two categories do fall within the scope of article 7(1) what is the purpose of imposing further words on top of its rather clear and long established terms?

It is the third category (JCE III) which has caused controversy[32]—a common design where one of the perpetrators commits an act which, while outside the common design, was nevertheless a natural and foreseeable consequence of the effecting of the common design. This category was supported by decisions of war crimes tribunals, Italian cases and two conventions. I comment on the

---

31   *Ibid* paras 191–92.
32   The latest edition of a leading textbook notes that JCE has generated scholarly criticism as a form of guilt by association and is colloquially referred to as 'just convict everyone' (James Crawford, *Brownlie's Principles of Public International Law* (8th edition, OUP 2012) 678. For various perspectives on JCE liability, see the symposium articles in (2007) 5 JICJ 1.

first and last, the Italian decisions not being readily accessible. (recall Mr Justice Ashhurst.)

The two war crimes trials concerned the killing of prisoners of war who were being marched through hostile crowds. In the first, the charge was that the accused had committed a war crime in that they were concerned in the killing of the POWs. 'Concerned' was the word used in the United Kingdom tribunals as reflecting the longer formula in Control Council Law 10, Article II (2) (which included accessories, those who ordered, and abettors). All seven accused were together throughout the events, and the two military accused refrained from interfering with a crowd which murdered the prisoners. The facts in the second case were similar and the charges were in terms of encouraging, acting, abetting and participating in the killings and assaults. In neither case was a reasoned judgement given and any analysis has to depend on the statements by the Prosecutor, no judge advocate being involved. In none of the statements reproduced by the Appeal Chamber is there any comment supporting the idea of common enterprise. They were both cases of mob violence in which the accused, who were present throughout, failed to meet their responsibilities to the POWs. They appear to plainly fall within the terms of Article II(2) as accessories and abettors.

On the basis of those cases, the Italian cases and its earlier interpretation of the Statute, the Tribunal concludes that the notion of common design as a form of accomplice liability is firmly established in customary international law.[33] It seeks further support from provisions about common purpose included in a terrorism convention and the Statute of the ICC[34]–but those are express provisions, they are exceptional in the 20 or more conventions mentioned earlier, and they were not in force when the alleged offences occurred or even when the decision was given. The Appeal Chamber finally called attention to some national legislation upholding the notion of common purpose—but, again, they are express statutory provisions, several of them in penal codes which deny any role to common law crimes.

---

33   *Tadić Appeal Judgment* (n 16), para 220. Some years later, the presiding judge of that Chamber expressed the contrary view, contending that in fact the customary basis for JCE did not exist at the time of the decision but maintaining that the Chamber was in any event competent to take this action on the basis of 'judicial creativity' (Mohamed Shahabbudeen, 'Judicial Creativity and Joint Criminal Enterprise', in Shane Darcy & Joseph Powderly (eds) *Judicial Creativity at the International Criminal Tribunals* (OUP 2010) 190, 197 and 199–200).

34   *Ibid* paras 221–22.

5   Certainty and Specificity in Defining Criminal Responsibility

It is not my purpose in looking closely at the reasoning on the JCE issue in *Tadić* to deny the role that a common purpose doctrine can play in criminal law. As many penal codes indicate, it may well have a real value. My primary purpose rather is to emphasise that the creation of criminal liability is a matter for the legislator, the treaty maker and not for the judge, national or international. That, to return to the principles I recalled at the outset, is to emphasise the ban on retroactive criminality, the need for specificity in the statement of the crime and the rejection of any idea of collective punishments. The criminal responsibility with which we are concerned is individual. As a distinguished British judge, Lord Wright, said in his foreword to the final volume of the Law Reports of Trials of War Criminals:

> The principle of individual responsibility is a necessary condition of the establishment of a system of law; what the law does is to define that responsibility. It is not content with the formulation of moral rules. It postulates personal sanctions.[35]

Supporting that formulation, that postulation of criminal responsibility are the increasingly recognised principles in international law and practice of broader participation and openness in law-making processes, and indeed ideas of democracy.

My second and much more personal purpose is to attempt to replicate something of our honorand's scholarly skill.[36]

---

[35] XV Law Reports of Trials of War Criminals (HMSO 1949), xv.

[36] See, for example, his 'Accident—or what became of *Kilbride v Lake*', in Roger S Clark (ed) *Essays in Criminal Law in New Zealand* (Sweet and Maxwell 1971), a series of lectures in honour of ID Campbell, whose brilliant essay 'Crime by Omission', rightly appears first in the volume, and his 'Criminal Code Reform in New Zealand? A Martian view of the Erewhon Crimes Act 1961 with some footnotes to the 1989 Bill' (1991) 21 VUWLR 1.

CHAPTER 27

The 2012 Protocol on the Illicit Trade in Tobacco: Signpost to the Future of Transnational Criminal Law?

Neil Boister

1   Introduction

More than two decades ago, Professor Roger Clark pioneered the analysis of harmonising trends in doctrinal development across a range of diverse global crime control treaties (hereinafter 'suppression conventions').[1] His work suggested the application of comparable rules across the sample of treaties he had made and he recommended further analysis.[2] Clark's innovative work did not confront the question of whether the similarities in rules in the suppression conventions suggested a broader system of some kind. Inspired, I recklessly suggested there is a systemic nature to what I called transnational criminal law,[3] although I recognise that the meaning of the concept is not yet settled.[4] Clark did note that little work had been done in order to discover whether there were significant trends towards general principles revealed through the provisions of the suppression conventions.[5] Concerns have long been expressed about the lack of principled protection for individuals subject to transnational

---

1 Roger S Clark, 'Offenses of International Concern: Multilateral State Treaty Practice in the Forty Years Since Nuremberg' (1988) 57 Nordic JIL 49 ('Clark, "Offenses of International Concern: Multilateral State Treaty Practice in the Forty Years Since Nuremberg"').

2 *Ibid* 86.

3 See Neil Boister, 'Transnational Criminal Law?' (2003) 14 EJIL 953 ('Boister, "Transnational Criminal Law"'); Neil Boister, *An Introduction to Transnational Criminal Law* (OUP 2012) 13; Neil Boister, 'The Concept and Nature of Transnational Criminal Law', in Neil Boister & Robert Currie (eds), *The Routledge Handbook of Transnational Criminal Law* (Routledge 2014, 11–26) ('Boister & Currie, *The Routledge Handbook of Transnational Criminal Law*').

4 Sabine Gless & John AE Vervaele, 'Law Should Govern: Aspiring General Principles for Transnational Criminal Justice' (2013) 9 Utrecht Law Review 1 ('Gless & Vervale, "Law Should Govern: Aspiring General Principles for Transnational Criminal Justice"') 2.

5 Clark, "Offenses of International Concern: Multilateral State Treaty Practice in the Forty Years Since Nuremberg" (n 1) 72ff.

criminal law,[6] and recent research has emphasised the need for a set of principles to govern transnational criminal law.[7] Commentators highlight the fact that law does not always govern the application of official power to individuals in the transnational space where states cooperate in the suppression of criminal activity.[8]

This chapter employs selected provisions of a recently developed suppression convention as a vehicle for engaging in some brief reflections on the nature of transnational criminal law and the principles governing it. The instrument in question is the Protocol on the Illicit Trade in Tobacco Products (the 'ITP'),[9] adopted in November 2012 by the fifth Conference of the Parties of the World Health Organisation Framework Convention on Tobacco Control (the 'FCTC'),[10] although not yet in force.

2   The ITP in Brief

The ITP was negotiated to flesh out the general obligations to reduce the illicit trade in tobacco products contained in article 15 of the FCTC.[11] Its substance is concerned with supply chain control. Part III contains provisions on the licensing of the manufacture of and import and export of tobacco products,[12] due diligence obligations on those engaged in the supply chain,[13] provisions for tracking and tracing of tobacco products,[14] and related provisions. Part IV is

---

6   See generally Robert Currie, 'The Protection of Human Rights in the Suppression of Transnational Crime' in Boister & Currie, *The Routledge Handbook of Transnational Criminal Law* (n 3).

7   See, for example, the various articles in the Special Issue: 'Law Should Govern: Aspiring General Principles for Transnational Criminal Justice' (2013) 9 Utrecht Law Review.

8   Gless & Vervale, 'Law Should Govern: Aspiring General Principles for Transnational Criminal Justice' (n 4) 2.

9   See Conference of the Parties to the WHO Framework Convention on Tobacco Control, Draft Protocol to Eliminate Trade in Tobacco Products, FCTC COP/5/6, 11 May 2012.

10   WHO Framework Convention on Tobacco Control (opened for signature 21 May 2003, entered into force 27 February 2005) 2302 UNTS 166.

11   See generally, Neil Boister, 'The (Un-) Systematic Nature of the UN Criminal Justice System: The (Non) Relationship Between The Draft Illicit Tobacco Trade Protocol and The UN Convention Against Transnational Organised Crime' (2010) 21 Crim LF 361; Neil Boister, 'Recent Progress in the Development of a Protocol on the Illicit Trade in Tobacco Products' (2010) 5(1) Asian Journal of WTO and Int'l Health Law Policy 53.

12   Art 6.

13   Art 7.

14   Art 8.

concerned with offences, Part V with international cooperation. Remarkably, a law enforcement agency from a regional organisation, the European Anti-Fraud Office (OLAF), led the development of the ITP.[15] OLAF's experts were highly influential during the negotiations particularly in regard to supply chain control. The provisions in Part III were the most controversial. Some are delicate compromises, and the future of the ITP is uncertain. Opened for signature from 10 January 2013 to 9 January 2014, the ITP has been signed by 53 States and the European Union. It will enter into force after forty states ratify. Only seven states have done so.[16] In contrast, the FCTC was one of the most rapidly ratified treaties.[17] In order to place the ITP within the development of transnational criminal law, it is necessary first to define transnational crime and transnational criminal law.

3 The Definition of Transnational Crime

Gless and Vervaele point out that 'transnational crime' can be defined by way of exclusion, i.e. all those crimes that are neither core international crimes (crimes within the jurisdiction of international criminal tribunals) nor purely national crimes (crimes 'having effects solely within one jurisdiction, or not having an extraterritorial link...and only of prosecutorial interest to a single state').[18] Alternatively, it can be defined by attempting to demarcate crimes that are 'transnational in nature' because they have an (i) extraterritorial (in the sense of some part of the harmful conduct being carried out beyond the territory of a state affected by the harmful conduct) and (ii) cross-border (in the sense of the harmful conduct transiting the boundaries of two or more states) dimension. This approach is reflected in article 3 on the 'Scope of Application' of the United Nations Convention

---

15 See generally, Neil Boister, 'The European Anti-Fraud Office and the Protocol to Eliminate Illicit Trade in Tobacco Products', in Andrew D Mitchell & Tania Voon (eds), *The Global Tobacco Epidemic and the Law* (Edward Elgar 2014) ('Boister, "The European Anti-Fraud Office and the Protocol to Eliminate Illicit Trade in Tobacco Products"') 64.

16 See Status of Ratification, as at 17 April 2015, UN Treaty Collection, <https://treaties.un.org/pages/ViewDetails.aspx?src=TREATY&mtdsg_no=IX-4-a&chapter=9&lang=en> accessed 17 April 2015.

17 Although only adopted in 2003, there are already 178 partes to the FCTC—see Parties to the WHO framework Convention on Tobaccco Control, as at 5 June 2014, <http://www.who.int/fctc/signatories_parties/en/> accessed 6 June 2014.

18 Gless & Vervale, 'Law Should Govern: Aspiring General Principles for Transnational Criminal Justice' (n 4) 2.

against Transnational Organised Crime,[19] which applies the Convention to a range of offences that are

> committed in more than one State; (b)...committed in one State but a substantial part of its preparation, planning, direction or control takes place in another State; (c)...committed in one State but involves an organised criminal group that engages in criminal activities in more than one State; or (d)...committed in one State but has substantial effects in another State.

Although demarcating the zone of criminality in this way does not define transnational criminal law,[20] it does provide some pointers towards such a definition.

Approaches to Defining Transnational Criminal Law

Gless and Vervaele suggest that two distinct approaches can be taken to the definition of transnational criminal law.[21] An 'empirical-inductive' approach defines it as the sum of all of the existing laws applying to transnational crime, both national and international. The alternative 'deductive and normative approach' restricts transnational criminal law to 'those rules and legal instruments that have been specifically created to deal with transnational criminal matters'.[22] They add two further approaches: the inclusion of purely domestic criminal cases where there is some transnational criminal justice activity of a cooperative kind; and, the inclusion of integrated systems for dealing with transnational crime where the point of reference is the region not the nation.[23] The former appears to be an expansion of the empirical inductive approach, the latter a regional species of the deductive normative approach.

In my submission, there is a teleological programmatic element present in the deductive normative approach. It is absent from the empirical inductive approach, which makes the former more suited to defining transnational criminal law. I have argued elsewhere that the label 'transnational criminal law'

---

19 (Opened for signature 16 December 2000 entered into force 29 September 2003) 2225 UNTS 209.
20 Gless & Vervale, 'Law Should Govern: Aspiring General Principles for Transnational Criminal Justice' (n 4) 3.
21 Ibid.
22 Ibid.
23 Ibid 4.

provides a doctrinal match for the criminological term transnational crime.[24] The historical record of the development over the last 150 years or so of suppression conventions from anti-slavery and anti-counterfeiting instruments, via drugs, corruption and organised crime instruments, up to the ITP, indicates a conscious construction of separate regimes of rules that are slowly (and somewhat incoherently) meshing into a 'system' of transnational criminal law. The systemic nature of transnational criminal law does not derive in an orthodox way from a unified ordered hierarchy of rules emanating from a single source of authority, but from a plurality of national norms inter-linked within broad frameworks of international obligations.

The rationale for such a system is found in the perception of growing threats within this zone, and the unification of these threats under the rubric of security from transnational crime.[25] The preamble of the ITP, for example, notes the deep concern of the parties 'that the illicit trade in tobacco products is contributing to the spread of the tobacco epidemic, which is a global problem that calls for effective, appropriate and comprehensive domestic and international responses.'[26] The objective of the ITP is 'to eliminate all forms of the illicit trade in tobacco products.'[27] A link is made to other forms of transnational activity at various places in the ITP, including the rationale that it 'funds transnational criminal activity'.[28]

Yet, I would argue that the aims of the programme are more clearly derivable from the prudential practice of powerful states or groups of states seeking to protect themselves from harmful activity originating elsewhere than from the global community rhetoric found in the joint pronouncements of UN crime control conferences. The level of state commitment to the programme is revealed by the indirect nature of the international treaty obligations in which states parties promise to adopt national criminal laws to suppress particular activities. It illustrates that transnational criminal law is an instrument of a loosely aligned Vattelian society of states where sovereignty and self-interest are the dominant values and laws of coordination the result.[29]

---

24   Boister, 'Transnational Criminal Law?' (n 3).
25   Part VII of the UN Secretary General's, *A More Secure World: Our Shared Responsbility, the High Level Panel Report on Threats, Challenges and Changes* (United Nations 2004), signals out security against transnational crime as a global priority–available at <http://www.un.org/en/peacebuilding/pdf/historical/hlp_more_secure_world.pdf> (accessed 10 June 2014).
26   Para 5.
27   Art 3.
28   Preamble para 13.
29   Boister, 'Transnational Criminal Law?' (n 3) 967–74.

Finally, while transnational criminal law may serve the selective purposes of some states far more than others, it is global. Although it does have regional components, as Ivory puts it, '[t]he challenge is to defend a definition of TCL in more normatively heterogeneous 'spaces' than Europe...'.[30]

4 Principles of Transnational Criminal Law

The suppression conventions that form the backbone of transnational criminal law do not contain a fully worked out set of general principles applicable to all conceivable transnational criminal situations ensuring basic adherence to the rule of law. One reason is that there is no transnational criminal jurisdiction, only many national criminal jurisdictions each with its own principles,[31] and the teleology of state protection that underlies transnational criminal law formally accepts state sovereignty over the *ius puniendi* and the incompatibility of different legal traditions. The ITP, for example, provides in article 16(3):

> Nothing contained in this Protocol shall affect the principle that the description of the unlawful conduct including the criminal offences established in accordance with this Protocol and of the applicable legal defences or other legal principles controlling the lawfulness of conduct is reserved to the domestic law of a Party and that such unlawful conduct including criminal offences shall be prosecuted and sanctioned in accordance with that law.

Principles for individual protection also inevitably give way in the face of the single over-riding goal of the system, a goal patent in the language of the suppression conventions: effective law enforcement. The Preamble of the ITP, for example, speaks of the conviction of the signatories that it 'will be a powerful, effective means to counter illicit trade in tobacco products and its grave consequences.'[32] Nonetheless, it is worth taking a closer look at whether the different components of the suppression conventions—criminalisation and

---

30 Radha Ivory, 'The Right to a Fair Trial and International Cooperation in Criminal Matters: Article 6 ECHR and the Recovery of Assets in Grand Corruption Cases' (2013) 9 Utrecht Law Review 147 ('Ivory, "The Right to a Fair Trial and International Cooperation in Criminal Matters"') 164.

31 Gless & Vervale, 'Law Should Govern: Aspiring General Principles for Transnational Criminal Justice' (n 4) 5.

32 Preamble para 24.

the establishment and enforcement of criminal jurisdiction—reveal any principles.

Principles for Substantive Criminalisation

The suppression conventions have a substantive law-making role. They exist to create similar criminal offences that enable suppression of the particular activity domestically and the articulation of the party's national criminal laws to enable cooperation. It is basic to the global rule of law that the criminalisation of conduct be undertaken by a valid legislative authority.[33] While policy norm diffusion may occur through voluntary embrace of these norms, it may also be deeply coercive and non-transparent both during negotiation of the suppression convention and in the transfer of technical know-how during implementation.[34] The situation becomes confusing when the agent of legal change is a customs organization from a powerful and wealthy regional bloc but operating with an obscure mandate, as in the development of the ITP under the guidance of OLAF. States participated in the diplomatic negotiations and their delegates voted for the ITP, but the ITP is in large degree OLAF's handiwork and was based in substance on the public-private partnership model of the European Commission's anti-contraband and anti-counterfeiting agreements with tobacco companies.[35]

Most of the provisions for criminalization in the suppression conventions embrace the principle of personal guilt as a prerequisite to criminal liability. This is usually indicated by provisions for the material and mental elements of a crime in the definitions of the 'criminal offences' in the conventions. It is debatable whether the suppression conventions provide sufficient legal certainty to support transnational legality. Take the ITP, for example. In terms of article 14(1) states parties are obliged to prohibit as unlawful an extremely detailed range of activities covering the full tobacco supply-chain, as well as a

---

[33] Michiel JJP Luchtman, 'Towards a Transnational Application of the Legality Principle in the EU's Area of Freedom, Security and Justice?' (2013) 9 Utrecht Law Review 11 ('Luchtman, "Towards a Transnational Application of the Legality Principle in the EU's Area of Freedom, Security and Justice?"') 14.

[34] Paulette Lloyd, Beth Simmons & Brandon Stewart, 'Combating Transnational Crime: The Role of Learning and Norm Diffusion in the Current Rule of Law Wave' in Michael Zürn, André Nollkaemper & Randall Peerenboom (eds), *Rule of Law Dynamics: In an Era of International and Transnational Governance* (1st ed, CUP 2012) 164–70.

[35] See Boister (n 15) 67. See, for example, the Agreement with Philip Morris International—see *Anti Contraband and Anti-Counterfeit Agreement and General Release* (9 July 2004), European Commission <http://ec.euorpe.eu/anti_fraud/documents/cigarette-smugg-2004/agreement_2004.pdf> (accessed 1 June 2014).

range of ancillary activities used to avoid enforcement. Only conduct elements are spelled out; no mention is made of mens rea. The latter is explicable by the fact that many of these offences are at most administrative offences in many states. Indeed, because of the failure of states to agree on which of these forms of conduct were serious enough to be worthy of criminalisation, article 14(2) leaves it to each party to decide which of these various forms of conduct to criminalise.[36] Criminalisation triggers international cooperation under Part V of the ITP. The ITP does not provide a clear guide to anyone trying to figure out how they should behave in regard to the supply of tobacco products—they will have to acquaint themselves with the domestic criminal (and in many states administrative) laws of states parties that establish jurisdiction over their conduct.

The suppression conventions normally provide little in the way of principled guidance of punishment other than urging severity, and the ITP is no exception. Principles of proportionality and deterrence are, however, tersely referred to in article 16 which obliges states parties to ensure that individuals held liable for unlawful conduct including crimes 'are subjected to effective, proportionate and dissuasive criminal or non-criminal sanctions, including monetary sanctions.' What is envisaged here is a broad range of potential measures, including administrative sanctions. While practical, the penal nature of administrative sanctions is obscured by their employment without trial by administrative decision. They avoid the *ne bis in idem* rule, impose a milder degree of censure less likely to draw public attention, and involve less formal process and less rigorous standards of proof. Intriguingly article 17 prompts parties to consider adopting measures to authorize their competent authorities to levy an amount proportionate to lost taxes from infringers, i.e. seizure payments of the kind pioneered in the EU's Agreement with Philip Morris International.[37] In addition, article 7(4) permits the 'blocking' of customers stopping business relations with that customer when they are identified as a risk through due diligence reporting by participants in the supply chain. While parties will not have to use these administrative sanctions, they cannot complain if others do, and there is no principled guidance for how they are to be used.

---

36   Boister, 'The (Un-) Systematic Nature of the UN Criminal Justice System…' (n 11) 387.
37   Boister, 'The European Anti-Fraud Office and the Protocol to Eliminate Illicit Trade in Tobacco Products' (n 15) 67.

Principles for Establishing Criminal Jurisdiction

Lex certa is essential to the rule of law. Transnational criminal law should be readily known and available, and certain and clear.[38] Ireland-Piper suggests that it is only reasonable to demand of a person that they be familiar with the criminal laws of states into whose jurisdiction they venture, if that extraterritorial jurisdiction has been established 'for widely recognised crimes, such as those forming the subject of international agreements and treaties.'[39] Then again, it is not clear that the suppression conventions can be relied on to establish a reasonable presumption of consciousness of the wrongfulness of one's conduct under another state's law just because of their status as international agreements. Take the ITP. In addition to the unexceptionable obligations to establish territorial jurisdiction over the criminal offences established in accordance with article 14, under article 26 it permits more controversial extraterritorial jurisdiction using the nationality and the substantial effects principles. A novelty using language borrowed from the UN Convention against Corruption,[40] however, is permission to parties to establish jurisdiction under article 26(2)(a) when 'the offence is committed against that party'. This provision accepts that certain unspecified tobacco offences—most likely those involving revenue or excise fraud—are crimes against the state, and that what appears to be a form of protective jurisdiction should be applied to them. It confirms fiscal self-protection of the state is a legitimate basis for jurisdiction within transnational criminal law, signalling a departure from the strictly security based concept originally associated with this form of jurisdiction. In doing so it raises concerns, in principle, about the sufficiency of the connection required to establish jurisdiction over potential offenders. But, the more fundamental concern about permitting extraterritorial jurisdiction at all in article 26 is that there is no standardised set of criminal offences in the ITP because under article 14 that choice has been left to the states parties.

Another danger of the suppression conventions is that they encourage the prescription of potentially overlapping jurisdiction, without any principles so as to prevent the imposition of an unfair burden on alleged transnational criminals through the prospect of many sequential prosecutions for the same

---

38 Danielle Ireland-Piper, 'Prosecutions of Extraterritorial Conduct and the Abuse of Rights Doctrine' (2013) 9 Utrecht Law Review 68 ('Ireland-Piper, "Prosecutions of Extraterritorial Conduct and the Abuse of Rights Doctrine"') 87.
39 Ibid.
40 Article 42(2)(d), United Nations Convention against Corruption, New York, 31 October 2003 (adopted 31 October 2001 entered into force 14 December 2005) 2349 UNTS 41.

crime. As Vervaele points out *ne bis in idem* is not a global principle.[41] The parties to suppression conventions have never succeeded in establishing a theory of precedence in concurrent jurisdiction. They establish only duties to consult other interested states parties, and the ITP is no exception.[42] What is absent is a more principled guidance awarding exclusive priority to a state, because the centre of gravity of prosecution lies with it[43] unless there is credible evidence that establishing jurisdiction is being used to shield the accused from prosecution elsewhere.

Principles for Enforcing Criminal Jurisdiction

It is also fundamental to the rule of law that the enforcement of criminal jurisdiction against alleged transnational criminals takes place under legal authority. Much of the recent focus on transnational criminal law has explored the potential due process 'protection gaps' that open up in the space between national laws and outside the protection of international human rights law.[44] The suppression conventions create a negative global citizenship in the sense that they impose obligations on individuals not to commit certain crimes against the shared interests of other states, but this citizenship is unbalanced because they give little in the way of positive protection against executive power.

Although it is a principle of the rule of law that all individuals are entitled to a fair trial,[45] there is no basic transnational standard for a 'fair trial' beyond a state's domestic criminal jurisdiction.[46] Standards of fairness differ from state to state and within states depending on whether the process has some extraterritorial element or not.[47] And as Ivory notes, it is difficult to deduce a fair trial principle from the *telos* of transnational criminal law.[48]

---

41 John AE Vervaele, 'Ne Bis in Idem: Towards a Transnational Consitutional Principle in the EU?' (2013) 9 Utrecht Law Review 211, 229.

42 See, for example, art 26(6) of the ITP.

43 See the preliminary presumption in the Eurojust Guidelines, Making the Decision—"Which Jurisdiction Should Prosecute?" Eurojust Annual Report, 2003.

44 Gless & Vervale, 'Law Should Govern: Aspiring General Principles for Transnational Criminal Justice' (n 4) 1–2.

45 Ireland-Piper, 'Prosecutions of Extraterritorial Conduct and the Abuse of Rights Doctrine' (n 38) 88.

46 Gless & Vervale, 'Law Should Govern: Aspiring General Principles for Transnational Criminal Justice' (n 4) 6.

47 Ibid.

48 Ivory, 'The Right to a Fair Trial and International Cooperation in Criminal Matters' (n 30) 164.

Take for example, the ITP. It makes provision inter alia for the sharing of general and enforcement information,[49] the sharing of administrative information for the specific purpose of risk assessment,[50] direct cooperation between law enforcement agencies,[51] the exchange of liaison officers,[52] and special investigative techniques.[53] The most prominent principle in all of these processes is the protection of sovereignty over criminal justice. Article 25 requires all obligations in the ITP to be carried out in a manner consistent with the principles of sovereign equality and territorial integrity and of non-intervention. At a more specific level the *lex loci* rules information exchange[54] and mutual legal assistance.[55]

Protections for individuals are rare. In the ITP's provision on extradition, for example, in terms of article 30(10) all parties guarantee 'fair treatment at all stages of proceedings, including enjoyment of all rights and guarantees provided by the domestic law of the Party in the territory in which that person is present.' There is sporadic protection in administrative or legal assistance. Under article 29(11) of the ITP, for example, requesting parties while under a general duty of speciality when it comes to information sent to them by the requested state, are not prevented 'from disclosing in its proceedings information or evidence that is exculpatory to an accused person.'[56] Some emphasis is placed in the newer suppression conventions on protecting personal data collected by law enforcement agencies. In implementing the ITP, for example, parties 'shall protect personal data of individuals regardless of nationality or residence, subject to national law, taking into consideration international standards regarding the protection of personal data'. Article 8(9)(e) imposes a confidentiality requirement on information exchanged after tracking and tracing requests.[57]

Judicial oversight of administrative action is one of the incidents of the rule of law requirement that the executive act lawfully.[58] In this regard the suppression conventions are silent, even though they encourage the development of

---

49   Arts 20, 21.
50   Art 28(e).
51   Art 27(2).
52   Art 27(1)(e).
53   Art 19.
54   Art 22.
55   Art 29(10).
56   Art 29(11).
57   See also art 32(5).
58   Luchtman, 'Towards a Transnational Application of the Legality Principle in the EU's Area of Freedom, Security and Justice?' (n 33) 14.

elaborate administrations for enforcement. The ITP, for example, has no provision for the supervision of executive action by organisations like OLAF, even though in terms of article 4(e) parties are obliged to cooperate on information exchange with 'relevant regional and international intergovernmental organisations'. More disquieting is that the ITP provides a potential vehicle for tobacco companies to play a role in anti-contraband law enforcement through article 8(1), which makes provision for the establishment some five years after entry into force of the ITP of a

> global tracking and tracing regime, comprising national and/or regional tracking and tracing systems and a global information-sharing focal point located at the Convention Secretariat…accessible to all Parties, enabling Parties to make enquiries and receive relevant information.

As revealed in the negotiations, OLAF's view of how this should work is that the data is collected from the tobacco industry and then sent to a central national point and then from there to the international clearing house.[59] Article 8(5) requires manufacturers to record and store the information and ensure under article 8(6) that it is accessible to the Party. In the EU, at least, the data would be collected on demand from the manufacturers rather than through storing the records of all tobacco movements. Other states parties would be free to set up their own systems and set the level of industry involvement. But critically the ITP fails to stipulate that level of involvement. This model of private involvement in law enforcement echoes the increasing role played by banks in the anti-money laundering regime. Their role in the AML regime increased when it switched from compulsory reporting of onerous amounts of data on their customers to a risk-based approach which vested the discretion to assess and report risk in the banks.[60] As different national regimes for tracking and tracing emerge under the ITP it is possible the tobacco companies will find themselves in a similar position where they are able to make choices about access to information that will affect the course of investigations. For example, article 1(14) of the ITP defines tracking and tracing as 'systematic monitoring and recreation by competent authorities *or any other person* acting on their behalf of the route or movement taken by items through the supply chain, as

---

59 Boister, 'The European Anti-Fraud Office and the Protocol to Eliminate Illicit Trade in Tobacco Products' (n 11) 72.
60 See generally Louis de Koker, 'The 2012 Revised FATF Recommendations: Assessing and Mitigating Mobile Money Intergity Risks within the New Standards Framework' (2013) 8 Washington Journal of Law, Technology & Arts 165, 173.

outlined in Article 8' [my emphasis]. Article 8(12) insists that no obligations assigned to a party be performed or delegated to the tobacco industry, but tracking and tracing is not an obligation assigned exclusively to a state party. Article 1(4) permits parties to contract this monitoring out to the tobacco industry. Article 8(13) requires the Parties to ensure that their competent authorities when participating in the tracking and tracing regime only interact with the tobacco industry to the extent strictly necessary to implement the article. It is difficult to say how effective this safeguard will be.

Some of the ITP's negotiating parties were aware of the risks, hence the inclusion in the preamble of reference to article 5(3) of the FCTC in which the parties specifically emphasized 'the need to be alert to any efforts by the tobacco industry to undermine or subvert strategies to combat illicit trade tobacco products and the need to be informed of activities of the tobacco industry that have a negative impact on strategies to combat illicit trade in tobacco products.'[61] Just how alert parties will be to the potential negative influence of the tobacco industry when the latter has assumed an important role in law enforcement, remains to be seen. Article 4(2) does provide that '[i]n implementing their obligations under this Protocol, Parties shall ensure the maximum possible transparency with respect to any interactions they may have with the tobacco industry.' Assuming (naively) a universally ideal level of transparency, all this will ensure is that government agency dealings with the industry are transparent. It does nothing to open up the workings of the industry itself, which may be shrouded by claims of privacy of business information.

5   Conclusion

Transnational criminal law is used to suppress a range of activities from repugnant conduct *malum in se* such as trading in slaves[62] to actions *malum prohibitum* such as manufacturing tobacco without a license,[63] all because they possess an extraterritorial dimension. If we think of transnational criminal law

---

61   Preambular paras fifteen and sixteen.
62   See art 1(1) and (6) of the 1926 Slavery Convention (signed 25 October 1926 entered into force 9 March 1927) 60 LNTS 253.
63   See art 14(1)(a) of the 2012 Protocol to Eliminate Illicit Trade In Tobacco Products, opened for signature 10 January 2013, available at UNTS, <http://treaties.un.org/doc/source/signature/2012/CN699E.pdf> accessed 13 November 2013.

as a methodological lens,[64] it reveals that alleged criminals are members of multiple normative communities, local, territorial, extraterritorial, and non-territorial in nature.[65] The suppression conventions provide a framework for state intervention in the transnational criminal legal space. These conventions emphasize effectiveness limited only by sovereignty and grant few protections to individuals. However, newer conventions like the ITP are opening up a space for governance within which weakly regulated regional actors such as OLAF can work to influence the activities of state law enforcement agencies (both inside and outside their region) and thus indirectly have an impact on individuals. Conventions like the ITP are also enabling the expansion of transnational normative framework to include 'soft' 'administrative' transnational criminal law which uses administrative and regulatory processes. Their penal nature obscured, these civil processes increase coercive public power, while eroding individual rights and executive accountability. Furthermore, the ITP illustrates that the plural legal space that is transnational criminal law now also potentially provides a space for the activities of private entities. This it has been suggested will reinforce the lack of principled control over the enforcement of transnational criminal law. If the ITP is a signpost to the future of transnational criminal law, it points to a future of fewer principles, not more.

---

64 Peer Zumbansen, 'Defining the Space of Transnational Law: Legal Theory, Global Governance and Legal Pluralism' (2012) 21 Transnational Law & Contemporary Problems 305, 307, 312, 330.

65 Paul Schiff Berman, *Global Legal Pluralism: A Jurisprudence of Law Beyond Borders* (CUP 2012) 11.

PART 6

Essays on and from North America

∴

CHAPTER 28

Roger Clark's Role in the Removal of Capital Punishment from the American Law Institute's Model Penal Code

Ellen S. Podgor

1   Introduction

Roger Clark was instrumental in the removal of the death penalty from the American Law Institute's ('ALI') Model Penal Code. I had the pleasure of submitting with him the original motion to declare the ALI's opposition to capital punishment. Although our motion was submitted prior to the 2007 ALI Annual Meeting, it was at the May 2009 Annual Meeting that a motion removing the capital punishment provision from the Model Penal Code was passed by the membership. The ALI, after a somewhat contentious two-hour meeting, voted that

> [f]or reasons stated in Part V of the Council's report to the membership, the Institute withdraws Section 210.6 of the Model Penal Code in light of the current intractable institutional and structural obstacles to ensuring a minimally adequate system for administering capital punishment.[1]

On 23 October 2009, the ALI 'Council voted overwhelmingly, with some abstentions, to accept the resolution of the capital punishment matter as approved by the Institute's membership at the 2009 Annual Meeting.'[2]

This essay tells the story of Roger Clark's role in the withdrawal of the capital punishment provision in the ALI's Model Penal Code and why it is important. As a partner with Roger Clark in this Motion and presentation to the ALI, admittedly this presentation of events may be somewhat biased.[3]

---

1   American Law Institute, 'Publications Catalog: Model Penal Code', <http://www.ali.org/index.cfm?fuseaction=publications.ppage&node_id=92> accessed 24 June 2014.
2   Ibid.
3   I also co-authored two books with Professor Roger Clark: Edward M Wise, Ellen S Podgor, & Roger S Clark, *International Criminal Law: Cases and Materials* (3d edn, LexisNexis 2009); Ellen S Podgor & Roger S Clark, *Understanding International Criminal Law* (3d edn, LexisNexis 2013).

2 The Model Penal Code & Section 210.6

The ALI 'is the leading independent organization in the United States producing scholarly work to clarify, modernize, and otherwise improve the law.'[4] It is an exclusive organization with a limited membership that includes '4000 lawyers, judges, and law professors of the highest qualifications.'[5] The Institute 'drafts, discusses, revises, and publishes Restatements of the Law, model statutes, and principles of law that are enormously influential in the courts and legislatures, as well as in legal scholarship and education.'[6] One of its premier documents is the Model Penal Code, which was completed by the Institute in 1962. Professor Roger Clark became a member of the Institute in 1982, thus he was not a part of the drafting of the Model Penal Code. He has been, however, an active member of the consultant's group to the recent and ongoing Sentencing Project of the ALI.

The United States has fifty different state criminal law systems with different sets of statutes. Additionally, there is the federal system that offers a United States Code with over 4,500 criminal statutes and an even greater number of regulations with criminal provisions.[7] Although there is no one criminal code for all the different States, many of the basic principles used in these statutes take a consistent approach. This is in part because the ALI's Model Penal Code has had a profound effect on the laws passed within the different state legal systems.

The Model Penal Code's influence can be seen in changes made to state statutes in the 1960s and 1970s.[8] Admittedly, some of the provisions within the

---

[4] See <http://www.ali.org/index.cfm?fuseaction=about.overview> accessed 20 July 2014.
[5] *Ibid.*
[6] *Ibid.*
[7] See 'Reining in Overcriminalization: Assessing the Problem, Proposing Solutions', Hearing Before the Subcomm. on Crime, Terrorism, and Homeland Sec. of the H. Comm. on the Judiciary, 111th Cong. 15 (2010) (statement of Jim E Lavine, President, Nat'l Ass'n of Criminal Def Lawyers), available at <http://judiciary.house.gov/hearings/printers/111th/111-151_58476.PDF> accessed 24 June 2014 ('[A]t least 10,000, and quite possibly as many as 300,000, federal regulations that can be enforced criminally. The truth is no one, including the government, has been able to provide an accurate count of how many criminal offenses exist in our federal code.'); see also Ellen S Podgor, 'Introduction Overcriminalization: New Approaches to a Growing Problem' (2012) 102 J Crim L & Criminology 529; John S Baker, Jr, 'Jurisdictional and Separation of Powers Strategies to Limit the Expansion of Federal Crimes' (2005) 54 American U L Rev 545 (discussing the expansion of federal criminal law).
[8] Paul H Robinson & Markus D Dubber, 'The American Model Penal Code: A Brief Overview' (2007) 10 New Crim L Rev 319 (discussing the history of the Model Penal Code).

Model Penal Code have had a greater influence than others.[9] As noted by Professors Paul H. Robinson and Jane A. Grall, 'American criminal law [...] advanced significantly towards providing such precision, clarity, and rationality, owing in large part to the Model Penal Code.'[10]

Professor Herbert Wechsler was the chief architect and chief reporter on the Model Penal Code, and according to his wife '[h]e considered the Model Code his proudest achievement.'[11] In addition to serving as a model for states revising their criminal statutes, it has had a strong influence in the teaching of criminal law, as it is a rare criminal law class in the United States that does not spend significant time reflecting on the provisions of the Model Penal Code.

When initially drafted, there was consideration given to whether capital punishment should be included in the document. The 1980 Commentaries to the ALI Model Penal Code note that the Reporter favored abolishing capital punishment. The Advisory Committee supported this position with an 18-2 vote, and voted 17-3 that the Institute express itself on this issue. The ALI Council was not convinced about expressing a position against capital punishment. In the end, the Institute voted to not express opinion, placing the section pertaining to the death penalty, Section 210.6, in brackets.[12]

Section 210.6 of the Model Penal Code was titled 'Sentence of Death for Murder: Further Proceedings to Determine Sentence.' Subsection (1) provides the circumstances when death is not an acceptable sentence. These include when there are no aggravating circumstances, substantial mitigating circumstances exist, the defendant enters a plea, he or she is under 18 years of age, the defendant's 'physical or mental condition calls for leniency,' or when some doubt still remains respecting the defendant's guilt. Subsection (2) has two alternative provisions which explain the proceeding and evidence allowed at a capital sentencing hearing. Finally, subsection (3) and (4) offer the aggravating and mitigating circumstances that can be considered in this proceeding.

Although the Institute may have thought that no opinion was being stated with this bracketed provision, courts saw the inclusion of a death penalty provision differently. 'The Commentaries to Section 210.6, published in 1982, stated

---

9   See Gerard E Lynch, 'Towards a Model Penal Code, Second (Federal?): The Challenge of the Special Part' (1998) 2 Buffalo Crim L Rev 297–298.
10 Paul H Robinson & Jane A Grall, 'Element Analysis in Defining Criminal Liability: The Model Penal Code and Beyond' (1983) 35 Stanford L Rev 681, 683.
11 American Law Institute Reporter, 'Herbert Wechsler 1909–2000' (Summer 2000) at <http://www.ali.org/ali_old/R2204_Wechsler.htm> accessed 24 June 2014.
12 American Law Institute, 'Status Report on Capital Punishment' (April 2008) Annex 3, 12 (Letter of Ad Hoc Committee on Death Penalty to Program Committee, 2 October 2007).

that the Supreme Court's decisional law 'amounts to a broad endorsement of the general policy reflected in the Model Code provisions.'[13] It was noted in a report to the ALI that '38 states and the federal government authorize the death penalty, and most have looked for guidance in some way to Section 210.6.'[14] Thus, what was intended to be a non-endorsement of capital punishment in reality became a go-to document for drafting a death penalty statute.

3 The Clark-Podgor Motion

In 2001, the ALI decided to revisit the Sentencing provisions of the Model Penal Code with the drafting of a 'prospectus.'[15] Kevin Reitz, then sole Reporter for this project, made it clear that the death penalty would not be a discussion of the ALI's Sentencing Project. 'Professor Reitz, Director Lance Liebman, and many of the advisors to the current project believed[...]that taking up capital punishment in this project would raise issues different from those being addressed.'[16] The concern was expressed that it 'would decrease the likelihood that [the] work would receive serious attention in states considering reform of their sentencing laws and procedures.'[17] One advisor to the project, Frank Zimring, resigned from the project when it was clear that capital punishment would not be a question considered by the Sentencing Project. He argued that '[t]o ignore the most visible and troubling aspect of American criminal justice is a much greater threat to the legitimacy of the Model Penal Code revision project than to confront it.'[18]

Upon learning that capital punishment was being excluded from the discussion of the Sentencing Project, Professor Clark contacted me and we discussed this troubling omission. What followed was the drafting, mostly by Roger Clark, of the Clark-Podgor Motion that called for the ALI to abolish the death penalty. This motion was intended to be considered as part of the Sentencing Project.

---

13 'Status Report on Capital Punishment' (n 12) Annex 3, 14 (Letter of Ad Hoc Committee on Death Penalty to Program Committee, 2 October 2007) (citing ALI, Model Penal Code and Commentaries, Part II, § 210.6, p. 111 (1980)).
14 Ibid.
15 Franklin E Zimring, 'Zimring, 'The Unexamined Death Penalty: Capital Punishment and Reform of the Model Penal Code" (2005) 105 Columbia L Rev 1396, 1398.
16 'Status Report on Capital Punishment' (n 12) Annex 2, 2 ('Zimring, 'The Unexamined Death Penalty: Capital Punishment and Reform of the Model Penal Code" ALI President Michael Traynor's Letter to Members of the Institute, 10 May 2007).
17 Ibid.
18 Zimring, 'The Unexamined Death Penalty: Capital Punishment and Reform of the Model Penal Code' (n 15) 1396.

It was the ALI that separated the discussion of capital punishment from Sentencing that was the subject of the Sentencing Project, but both Roger Clark and I concurred in this decision in that we did not move immediately to call the question on our motion. Allowing capital punishment to be discussed separately was in no way a statement that capital punishment should not be considered as part of the Sentencing Project. Rather, it was an agreement to let the ALI consider our Motion in further detail.

The Clark-Podgor Motion, filed on 2 April 2007, to be consistent in that it stated, '[t]hat the Institute is opposed to capital punishment.' Accompanying the Motion was a four page Statement in Support of this Motion.[19] It notes the lack of influence that the Model Penal Code's Sentencing provisions have had on 'the bulk of sentencing-code revisions undertaken since the mid-1970s.' In contrast, to the overall sentencing provisions having insignificant influence on U.S. law, the capital punishment provisions have served as a 'paradigm of constitutional permissibility.'[20]

The Statement in Support of the Clark-Podgor Motion to abolish the death penalty provides a glimpse of the civilized world which has abandoned capital punishment. In addition to noting the arguments provided by countries that have abolished the death penalty, it notes that studies have shown that there is no evidence that the 'death penalty rationally serves a legitimate penological intent.'[21] In support of abolishing the death penalty, the Statement in Support of the Clark-Podgor Motion notes the history of the Model Penal Code's Section 210.6 and the position against the death penalty by the initial Advisory Committee of the Model Penal Code. Yet, as discussed in this Supporting Statement, the failure of the Code to pronounce a position against capital punishment resulted in a perception of support.[22]

The Statement in Support of the Clark-Podgor Motion invokes the spirit of the late Professor Norval Morris, who was a life-long abolitionist of capital punishment. The rationale for including this reference here was that the ALI's 2006 Sentencing Project Discussion Draft used as the statement of purposes, the theories coming from Norval Morris. The Sentencing Project Discussion Draft, however, failed to mention the fact that he was opposed to the death penalty.

---

19   Roger S Clark & Ellen S Podgor, Model Penal Code: Sentencing, Motion on Capital Punishment (2 April 2007) <http://www.ali.org/doc/MPC-Motion-Clark%20Podgor-April%202.pdf> accessed 24 June 2014.
20   *Ibid* (citing the 1980 Commentaries of the Model Penal Code).
21   *Ibid*.
22   *Ibid* 3.

The Clark-Podgor Motion ends with Justice Blackmum's dissenting opinion from *Callins v. Collins*,[23] which states:

> From this day forward, I no longer shall tinker with the machinery of death. For more than 20 years I have endeavored—indeed, I have struggled—along with a majority of this Court, to develop procedural and substantive rules that would lend more than the mere appearance of fairness to the death penalty endeavor. Rather than continue to coddle the Court's delusion that the desired level of fairness has been achieved [...] I feel morally and intellectually obligated to concede that the death penalty experiment has failed. It is virtually self-evident to me now that no combination of procedural rules or substantive regulations can ever save the death penalty from its inherent constitutional deficiencies [...] The problem is that the inevitability of factual, legal, and moral error gives us a system that we know must wrongly kill some defendants, a system that fails to deliver the fair, consistent and reliable sentences of death required by the Constitution.[24]

Although normally a motion filed in April 2007 would be voted upon at the May Annual meeting, this was not the case with the Clark-Podgor Motion. At the request of the ALI's President, Michael Traynor, Professor Clark and I agreed to hold our Motion pending the Institute's study of this issue. The initial consideration was given when the ALI had an open forum on the issue of capital punishment at the Annual 2007 Meeting. Both Professor Clark and I were given time at this meeting to start this introductory conversation about the issue of capital punishment.

Roger Clark started by stating how the omission of capital punishment from the Sentencing Project goes to the 'moral legitimacy of the project' and thus to the 'moral legitimacy of our great Institute.'[25] He noted that the Institute in 1962 'deluded itself into thinking it could take no position on this issue.'[26] But, devising 'a set of aggravating and mitigating circumstances and a procedure to go with them' resulted in 'a disaster that succeeded only in giving a patina of constitutional legitimacy to an otherwise irrational process.'[27] He also stressed

---

23   510 U.S. 1141 (1994).
24   *Ibid* 1145–46.
25   'Status Report on Capital Punishment' (n 12) Annex 4, 30 (Transcript of 2007 Annual Meeting, 16 May 2007).
26   *Ibid.*
27   *Ibid.*

how Norval Morris was an opponent of capital punishment. He concluded by stating how taking a position against capital punishment would be in keeping with the Institute's bylaws of 'better adaptation' of law 'to social needs' and 'to secure the better administration of justice.'

My comments following on the heels of Roger Clark were that our Motion was not intended to undermine the Sentencing Project.[28] I argued that the international arena's rejection of the death penalty, the fact that many states had instituted death penalty moratoriums, and the fact that the title of the project was Sentencing, required us to include capital punishment as an aspect of Sentencing Project. Just because some may not adopt the Model Penal Code, or revisions to it, was nothing new for the Model Penal Code, as States in the past had not adopted portions of the Model Penal Code.[29] My presentation focused on capital punishment being a necessary component to the Sentencing Project.

Our comments were followed by those of the ALI Director Lance Liebman and Sentencing Reporter Professor Kevin Reitz.[30] Others from the floor then spoke in favor and against the role that the death penalty should play in the ALI's Sentencing Project.[31]

4   The Meltzer Report

President Traynor thereafter appointed an ad hoc committee 'to advise the Program Committee, the Council, and the Director about alternative ways in which the Institute might respond to the concerns underlying the motion.'[32] This ad hoc committee issued what became known as the Meltzer Report, named after committee chair Daniel Meltzer.[33] After providing a history of the ALI's position on the death penalty, the Report focused on the options of whether a study of the death penalty, either as part of the Sentencing Project or as a separate project, would be a wise course for the Institute.[34] It noted the changed circumstances since 1962, and discussed how Supreme Court

---

28   *Ibid* 30–31.
29   *Ibid* 31.
30   *Ibid* 32.
31   *Ibid* 32–37.
32   'Status Report on Capital Punishment' (n 12) Annex 3, 11.
33   The members of this committee were Christine Durham, Kay Knapp, Gerard Lynch, Myles Lynk, and William Webster.
34   'Status Report on Capital Punishment' (n 12) Annex 3, 11–24.

jurisprudence since 1962 'calls into question the validity of some aspects of Section 210.6.'[35] It mentioned how empirical studies showed how 'the administration of capital punishment is infected by racial discrimination.'[36] It also noted that this was an opportunity for the ALI to provide guidance. The Report stated that, 'some have remarked that if the ALI does not seek to provide a framework for the administration of capital punishment that is preferable to existing practice, it is not clear who else can and will.'[37]

The Meltzer report presented three possible outcomes: call for abolition, withdraw Section 210.6, or revise Section 210.6.[38] While noting the 'opportunity for productive work on capital punishment by the Institute,'[39] the Meltzer Report also noted its concerns. One of these concerns was that '[i]t was uncertain that an ALI project, whatever its outcome, would have influence with respect to so politicized an issue as the death penalty.'[40] One point of agreement within the ad hoc committee noted in the Meltzer Report, was that if the Institute decided to proceed with a project, 'it should be separate from, rather than a part of the ongoing Sentencing Project.'[41]

5   The ALI Program Committee

In November 2007, the ALI followed up the discussion with an electronic forum, allowing members to discuss this issue in more detail. Twenty-one members posted comments on this forum.[42] An additional five comments were submitted separate from the online forum.[43] The forum ended with a thank you from Professor Clark and myself and also a statement that '[w]e continue to believe that this organization, if it is to be true to itself, should deal with the most extreme sentences—death.'[44] We further noted, '[i]t is apparent that there are strong views for proceeding to a vote on our motion, or at least for further consideration to be given to the death penalty in the

---

35   *Ibid* 16.
36   *Ibid* 17.
37   *Ibid* 18.
38   *Ibid* 19.
39   *Ibid* 20.
40   *Ibid* 21.
41   *Ibid* 23.
42   'Status Report on Capital Punishment' (n 12) Annex 5, 39 (listing a summary of the comments made on the electronic forum on 26 November 2007).
43   *Ibid* 42–43.
44   *Ibid* 43.

sentencing project or in another ALI project pertaining specifically to the sentence of death.'[45]

On 30 November 2007, the Program Committee of the ALI met, and in a letter dated 3 December 2007, made a recommendation that '[t]he Institute should take further steps to consider the American law regarding the death penalty and its operation in practice.'[46] Four reasons were given for this recommendation, including that 'some ALI members seek to have the Institute recommend the abolition of the death penalty, and the Institute should give this matter more serious attention than a mere vote on a motion to endorse abolition would provide.'[47] The recommendation called for the drafting of a paper on the death penalty with respect to the ALI, and that the paper would be presented to the Council the following fall and to the 2009 Annual Meeting.[48] The Council agreed in substance to the Program Committee's recommendation but questioned the speed of the timetable outlined by the Committee, suggested that there be more than one author for this study, that there be advisors with death penalty experience assisting, and '[t]hat the President consult with the Executive Committee about presenting this matter to the Institute's membership.'[49]

6 The Steiker Report & Removal of Section 210.6

The ALI, thereafter, appointed Carol S. Steiker, a Harvard University law professor, and Jordan M. Steiker, a Texas University law professor, to write the report. This brother-sister team, with the assistance of an advisory committee, filed their Report on November 2008.[50] It advised against taking a political position regarding the moral and political arguments regarding the death penalty.[51] But it also discussed 'the underlying problems and structural barriers that have

---

45 Ibid.
46 'Status Report on Capital Punishment' (n 12) Annex 6, 45 (Paul L Friedman, Program Chair Letter of 3 December 2007 to ALI—Program Committee Recommendation Regarding the Death Penalty).
47 Ibid.
48 Ibid 46.
49 'Status Report on Capital Punishment' (n 12) Annex 7, 47 (Excerpt of Minutes of Council Meeting on 6–7 December 2007).
50 American Law Institute, 'Report of the Council to the Membership of The American Law Institute on the Matter of the Death Penalty' (15 April 2009) Annex B, 17 <http://www.ali.org/doc/Capital%20Punishment_web.pdf>.
51 Ibid 6.

undermined regulatory efforts.'[52] It stated that the 'difficulties that continue to undermine its administration, and the structural and institutional obstacles to curing those ills forms the basis of our recommendation to the Institute.'[53] Finally it called for the ALI to withdraw Section 210.6 of the Model Penal Code with the following statement, '[i]n light of the current intractable institutional and structural obstacles to ensuring a minimally adequate system for administering capital punishment, the Institute calls for the rejection of capital punishment as a penal option.'[54]

On Tuesday 19 May 2009, the agenda scheduled for a one hour slot the Capital Punishment Report and a vote on the Council Recommendation that the ALI withdraw Model Penal Code § 210.6.[55] The room had an unusually large crowd and it was clear that that the discussion would be intense. Although set to last an hour, in reality, the discussion lasted much longer—over two hours. ALI members attending this meeting were asked to vote on the Institute withdrawing Section 210.6 of the Model Penal Code.[56] The wording of the motion was modified during the discussion, but in the end it passed.[57] It was a historic ALI meeting. On 23 October 2009, the ALI Council approved the resolution to remove Section 210.6 from the Model Penal Code.[58]

7   The Status of the Death Penalty in the United States

In recent years, the use of the death penalty in the United States has significantly declined. In 1997, there were 265 death sentences, in 2002 there were 165 death sentences, in 2007, there were 120 death sentences, and in 2013 the number was down to 79.[59] Since 1973, there have been 140 people released from

---

52   *Ibid* 8.
53   *Ibid* 49.
54   Carol S Steiker & Jordan M Steiker, 'No More Tinkering: The American Law Institute and the Death Penalty Provisions of the Model Penal Code' (2010) 89 Texas L Rev 353, 359.
55   American Law Institute, '86th Annual Meeting: Tentative Agenda' <http://www.ali.org/index.cfm?fuseaction=meetings.annual_schedule09> accessed 24 July 2014.
56   'Report of the Council to the Membership of The American Law Institute on the Matter of the Death Penalty' (n 50) 4.
57   Mark Stichel, American Law Institute, Annual Meeting Blog, 'The Matter of the Death Penalty' (posted 19 May 2009) at <http://www.ali.org/index.cfm?fuseaction=meetings.annual_blog&startrow=21> accessed 24 June 2014.
58   'Publications Catalog: Model Penal Code' (n 1).
59   Death Penalty Information Center, 'Facts about the Death Penalty' (19 June 2014) at <http://www.deathpenaltyinfo.org/documents/FactSheet.pdf> accessed 24 June 2014.

death row premised on evidence of innocence.[60] Yet despite this, the death penalty remains in thirty-two states. A recent report by Richard C. Dieter of the Death Penalty Information Center demonstrated that a minority of two percent of the counties in the United States produce most of the death cases.[61] According to this same report, only nine states executed individuals in 2012.

Although the number of death sentences has declined, many issues still remain. For example, the United States still has not resolved issues related to execution of foreign nationals. A continual problem has been the failure of the United States to provide foreign nationals their consular rights pursuant to Article 36 of the Vienna Convention of Consular Rights.[62] And most importantly, some states still continue to execute individuals for crimes. The United States' position on capital punishment is a marked difference from the International Criminal Court, which has jurisdiction of the most heinous of crimes, yet omits capital punishment from the list of possible punishments for crimes committed.[63] Many other countries in the world have also been aggressive in removing a death penalty option.[64]

Whether the tide has finally turned against the use of capital punishment in the United States is uncertain. It is clear that the ALI was not ready to forcefully voice an opinion against this punishment. The prohibition passed by the ALI was limited solely to the way it was being implemented, with a clear opinion being expressed that a decision on its morality should not be addressed.

---

60 Ibid 2 (citing Staff Report, House Judiciary Subcommittee on Civil & Constitutional Rights, October 1993, with updates from DPIC).

61 Richard C Dieter, 'The 2% Death Penalty: How a Minority of Counties Produce Most Death Cases at Enormous Costs to All' (October 2013) at <http://deathpenaltyinfo.org/documents/TwoPercentReport.pdf> accessed 24 June 2014.

62 See generally Sandra Babcock, 'The Limits of International Law: Efforts to Enforce Rulings of the International Court of Justice in U.S. Death Penalty Cases' (2012) 62 Syracuse L Rev 183.

63 Professor Roger Clark represented the Government of the Independent State of Samoa in the negotiations to create the Court. As a member of the 'Like-Minded Group', Samoa supported the decision not to include capital punishment in the Rome Statute. At the time, Samoa was listed by Amnesty International (which has the best data on the international status of the death penalty) as 'de facto abolitionist.' Although the death penalty was on the books, Samoa had never executed anyone since its independence from New Zealand in 1962. In the course of preparing legislation to give effect to the Rome Statute, Samoa repealed the legislative provision making it theoretically possible.

64 Roger S Clark, 'The Attrition of Capital Punishment Worldwide as the American Law Institute Withdraws its Model Penal Code Provision Recommending How to Do It' (2010) 21 Crim LF 511.

8 Conclusion

I was fortunate to be part of the Clark-Podgor Motion that started the ALI project to consider the question of whether to oppose the death penalty. Although the ALI failed to provide a clear statement in opposition to this form of punishment, the result of the statement provided is that the message is finally sent that the death penalty in its current form in the United States is unacceptable. More importantly, states can no longer reference the Model Penal Code as a document accepting capital punishment. The elimination of Section 210.6 from the Model Penal Code should have happened back in the late 50s and early 60s. Perhaps if the ALI's Council had heeded the advice of its reporter, advisers, and membership, capital punishment in the United States would have progressed more slowly. But that did not happen. If it had then I would not have had the pleasure of being part of the historic moment in the history of the ALI when the Clark-Podgor Motion was presented to the Institute, and when the Institute finally removed its capital punishment provision within the Code. The Clark-Podgor Motion was never passed by the ALI, but without this motion the Sentencing Project might have continued without any recognition of what was really happening with respect to capital punishment sentencing in the United States.

CHAPTER 29

Customary International Law as the Rule of Decision in Human Rights Litigation in the US Courts

Joseph W. Dellapenna

1   Introduction

Roger Clark has devoted a lifetime to the promotion and advancement of the international law of human rights, both in his scholarship[1] and other work.[2] One feature of the legal landscape within which he has worked was the possibility of invoking national court jurisdiction to develop and enforce such rights, including courts in the United States.[3] While the Supreme Court of the United States[4] and Congress[5] have made it more difficult to bring such suits in an American court, that possibility still remains. Such suits, for example, might be sustainable as ordinary tort suits in state or federal court.[6] That possibility

---

1   See, eg Albert P Blaustein, Roger S Clark & Jay A Sigler (eds), *Human Rights Sourcebook* (Washington Institute Press 1987); Roger S Clark, 'Humanitarian Intervention: Help to Your Friends and State Practice' (1983) 13 Ga J Int'l & Comp L 211; Roger S Clark, 'Peacekeeping Forces, Jurisdiction, and Immunity: A Tribute to George Barton' (2012) 43 Victoria U of Wellington L Rev 77; Roger S Clark, 'The Mental Element in International Criminal Law: The Rome Statute of the International Criminal Court' (2001) 12 Crim LF 291.
2   See, eg Roger S Clark and others, *Report of the Outside Observer Mission, Palau Referendum, December 1986* (International League for Human Rights 1987); Roger S Clark, Geoffrey Robertson, & Ousmane Kane, *Report of the Commission of Experts on Reforming Internal Justice at the United Nations* (United Nations 2006).
3   See, eg *Filártiga v Peña-Irala*, 630 F2d 876 ('*Filártiga v Peña-Irala*') 879 2nd Cir. 1980).
4   Most recently in *Kiobel v Royal Dutch Petroleum Corp.*, 133 S. Ct. 1659 (2013) ('Kiobel').
5   See eg 28 USC § 2242(e) (barring suits by aliens detained as a possible enemy combatant from suing on any other basis than a petition for habeas corpus), upheld: Hamad v Gates, 732 F3d 990 (9th Cir 2013), cert denied, 134 S. Ct. 2866; Ameur v Gates, 950 F Supp 2d 905 (ED Va 2013) (dicta allowing suit under international law but finding the torture claims to be barred by the immunity of the US federal government).
6   See eg, Samantar v Yousuf, 560 US 305 (2010) (construing the Foreign Sovereign Immunities Act to allow a suit against a former Minister of Defense of Somalia for human rights abuses); Licci ex rel Licci, Lebanese Canadian Bank, SAL 732 F3d 161 (2d Cir 2013) (allowing suit under state law and the federal Anti-Terrorism Act); Vance v Rumsfeld, 653 F3d 591

leaves the admittedly narrow question of what legal rule courts should apply in deciding litigation in American courts over human rights claims—in other words, what particular rule of law provides the rule of decision in human rights litigation in American courts. While this is a narrow question, it depends upon important issues regarding the role of international law in American courts as well as broader questions regarding the choice of the rule of decision generally in American legal practice. Without a correct resolution of such questions, national courts cannot be an effective tool for enhancing and enforcing internationally based human rights.

2   Choice of Law Generally

I begin with the legal principles that US courts apply to determine the outcome of civil litigation. Today, choice of law in the United States for the most part remains a matter of state law. As a result, three different choice of law theories compete in American courts for acceptance depending on the state in which the court sits:[7]

(7th Cir 2011) (allowing a Bivens claim based on violations of international law that also violated constitutional standards); Estate of Amergi v Palestine Auth'y, 611 F3d 1350 (11th Cir 2010) (allowing ordinary wrongful death claims while disallowing Alien Tort Statute claims); Sexual Minorities Uganda v Lively, 960 F Supp 2d 304 (D Mass 2013) (allowing suit under the Alien Tort Statute and Massachusetts law); Quraishi v Nakhla, 728 F Supp 2d 702 (D Md. 2010) (state law claims are not preempted by federal law), aff'd sub nom al Shimari v Caci Int'l, Inc., 679 F3d 205 (4th Cir). But see In re Terrorist Attacks of Sept. 11, 2011, 714 F3d 118 (2d Cir 2013) (finding that state law claims were not raised adequately after dismissing federal law claims), cert denied, 2014 WL 2921775; Arias v Dyncorp, 517 F Supp 2d 221, 228–229 (D DC 2007) (existence of a claim under the Alien Tort Statute does not preempt state law claims). But see Enahoro v Abubakar, 408 F3d 877, 883–886 (7th Cir 2005) (holding that state-law claims are preempted by the terrorism provisions of the Torture Victims Act), cert denied, 546 US 1175 (2006); Baker v Libya, 775 F Supp 2d 48, 74 (D DC 2011) (holding that state-law claims are preempted by the terrorism provisions of the Foreign Sovereign Immunities Act). See generally Sam Foster Halabi, 'The Supremacy Clause as a Structural Safeguard of Federalism: State Judges and International Law in the Post-Erie Era' (2012) 23 Duke J Comp & Int'l L 63 ('Halabi, "The Supremacy Clause as a Structural Safeguard of Federalism: State Judges and International Law in the Post-Erie Era"'); Julian G Ku, 'The State of New York Does Exist: How the States Control Compliance with International Law' (2004) 82 NCL Rev 457; John T Parry, 'International Law in State Courts: Sovereignty, Resistance, Contagion, and Inevitability' (2012) 20 Willamette J Int'l L & Disp Resol 48; G Edward White, 'A Customary International Law of Torts' (2006) 41 Val UL Rev 755.

7   For the most part, federal courts in the United States apply the choice of law rules of the state in which the court sits. Klaxon Co. v Stentor Elec. Mfg. Co., 313 US 487 (1941). The exceptions

(1) a rule-centered 'vested rights' approach aimed at coordinating competing sovereignties;
(2) a methodology-centered 'interest analysis' aimed at coordinating social policies; and
(3) a new rule-centered 'neoterritorialist' approach aimed at coordinating the parties' expectations.

In the following subsections, I briefly describe each theory, followed by a brief discussion of whether these theories should be applied in a criminal prosecutions and of the constitutional limitations on choice of law.

A   The Vested Rights Approach to Choice of Law

The first *Restatement of Conflicts*[8] summarized the vested rights system of choice of law which is still followed in some states.[9] Under this system, courts first characterize the nature of the suit and then select the jurisdiction under whose law rights of that type 'vest':

(1) for torts, the place where the injury occurred;[10]
(2) for contracts, the place where the contract was made, or where the contract was to be performed;[11] and
(3) for property rights, the location of the property at the time the rights in question vested.[12]

Vested rights, which focused on selecting the state or nation that had sovereign authority over a transaction or event,[13] suffer from apparent rigidity in

---

    to this rule do not include claims set in an international context. Day & Zimmerman v Challoner, 423 US 3 (1975).
8   Restatement of Conflict of Laws (1934) ('Restatement').
9   Symeon C Symeonides, 'Choice of Law in American Courts in 2013: Twenty-Seventh Annual Survey' (2014) 62 Am J Comp L 223 ('Symeonides, 'Choice of Law in American Courts in 2013"), 282.
10 Restatement (n 8) §§ 377, 378.
11 Ibid §§ 332, 358.
12 Ibid § 208.
13 See eg, Alabama Great Southern RR v Carroll, 11 So. 803, 808–809 (Ala. 1892) ('[E]ach sovereignty, state or nation, has the exclusive power to finally determine and declare what act or omissions in the conduct of one to another…shall impose a liability in damages for the consequent injury, and the courts of no other sovereignty can impute a damnifying quality to an act or omission which afforded no cause of action where it transpired.').

formally relying on a single factor to select a single sovereign's law to cover every aspect of a suit. Focusing as it does on sovereignty, the approach arguably is better suited to litigation involving a choice between the laws of different nations. Courts developed a plethora of escape devices (characterization, *renvoi*, public policy, etc.), to avoid the ostensibly inexorable commands of these apparently simple rules in order make the system far less certain than it appears on the surface, and perhaps more just.[14]

B   *Interest Analysis*

Over the past 80 years, American legal scholars have developed choice of law techniques that are both multifactorial and policy sensitive.[15] Their approach is termed 'interest analysis'. Arguably better suited to coordinating policies of states within a federal union, it predominates in the United States today.[16] Interest analysis has many different guises, the best known of which are: Brainerd Currie's 'governmental interest analysis';[17] Robert Leflar's 'choice influencing considerations' (also known as the 'better law' approach);[18] Willis Reese's 'most significant relationship' test (also known as the 'Second Restatement' approach);[19] and Russell Weintraub's 'functional

---

14   See generally Peter Hay, Patrick J Borchers & Symeon C Symeonides, *Conflicts of Law* (5th ed, West Academic Publishing 2010) ('Hay, Borchers & Symeonides, Conflicts of Law') 145–174, 804–807; Russell J Weintraub, *Commentary on the Conflicts of Law* (6th ed, Foundation Press 2010) ('Weintraub, Commentary on the Conflicts of Law') 49–128, 424–443.

15   See eg, David Cavers, 'A Critique of the Choice-of-Law Problem' (1933) 47 Harv L Rev 173.

16   Symeonides, 'Choice of Law in American Courts in 2013' (n 9) 282.

17   Brainerd Currie, *Selected Essays on Conflicts of Laws* (Durham Duke University Press 1963). All modern choice of law theories are deeply indebted to Professor Currie. See generally Hay, Borchers & Symeonides, *Conflicts of Law* (n 14) 27–41, 808–833; Weintraub, *Commentary on the Conflicts of Law* (n 14) 8–9, 449–465; Lea Brilmayer, 'Interest Analysis and the Myth of Legislative Intent' (1980) 78 Mich L Rev 392 ('Brilmayer, "Interest Analysis and the Myth of Legislative Intent"').

18   Robert A Leflar, Luther L McDougal III & Robert L Felix, *American Conflicts Law* (4th ed, Michie Co 1986). See generally Hay, Borchers & Symeonides, *Conflicts of Law* (n 14) 56–62, 835–843; Weintraub, *Commentary on the Conflicts of Law* (n 14) 11–12, 468–472.

19   Willis Reese was the Reporter for the Restatement (Second) of Conflict of Laws (1971) ('Restatement (Second)'). See generally Hay, Borchers & Symeonides, *Conflicts of Law* (n 14) 62–78, 108–113, 843–834; Weintraub, *Commentary on the Conflicts of Law* (n 14) 7–8, 405–407, 529–537.

analysis.'[20] While scholars debate the fine points of these analyses, often with great vehemence,[21] the various forms of interest analysis are actually very similar.

Each version of interest analysis focuses on selecting the governing rule of law for a particular issue, and not, as under vested rights, the governing jurisdiction for the entire litigation.[22] Thus each asks a court to begin by examining the potentially relevant formal rules of law to see if they are in fact different, or if they would lead to a different result in the case. If the potentially relevant rules are not different or if they would all produce the same result if applied to the case, there is in fact *no conflict*. If the potentially relevant rules of law are different and would lead to a different result if applied, a court then examines the policies underlying the formal rules.[23] If the policy of only one potentially relevant rule would be affected by its application, there is a *false conflict*, and the court should apply the only relevant rule of law, described as the law of the only state with an interest in having its law applied.[24] If the policy of more than one potentially relevant rule will be affected, there is a *true conflict*.[25] There might also be cases in which the policies underlying every potentially relevant rule of law would not be affected by non-application of the rule. This last situation has come to be called an *unprovided for case*.[26] Only for true conflicts and unprovided for cases do the several versions of interest analysis posit widely differing ways to resolve the conflict.

Courts have, with few exceptions, not concerned themselves with the fine points of these various versions of interest analysis. Rather, courts have preferred to synthesize elements of the several analyses in an attempt to find the most relevant law for a particular issue in a case.[27] Because the modern

---

20   Weintraub, *Commentary on the Conflicts of Law* (n 14) 62–66, 396–400, 541–553. See also Hay, Borchers & Symeonides, *Conflicts of Law* (n 14) 45–51.

21   See eg, David E. Seidelson, 'Interest Analysis or the Restatement Second of Conflicts: Which Is the Preferable Approach to Resolving Choice-of-Law Problems?' (1988) 27 Duq L Rev 73.

22   See eg, Caruolo v John Crane, Inc., 226 F3d 46, 59 (2nd Cir 2000).

23   See eg, Dym v Gordon, 209 NE2d 792, 794 (NY 1965) (Dym was overruled on other grounds in Tooker v Lopez, 249 NE2d 394 (NY 1969)).

24   Tooker v Lopez, 249 NE2d 394, 395–396, 398 (NY 1969). See generally Hay, Borchers & Symeonides, *Conflicts of Law* (n 14) 810–812; Weintraub, *Commentary on the Conflicts of Law* (n 14) 397.

25   See Hay, Borchers & Symeonides, *Conflicts of Law* (n 14) 812–15.

26   It is by no means clear that 'unprovided for cases' exist. See Larry Kramer, 'The Myth of the Unprovided-for Case' (1989) 75 Va L Rev 1045. The phrase remains widely used in conflicts scholarship. See Hay, Borchers & Symeonides, *Conflicts of Law* (n 14) 815–18; Weintraub, *Commentary on the Conflicts of Law* (n 14) 456–60.

27   See eg, Filetech SA v France Telecom SA, 157 F3d 922, 932 (2nd Cir 1998); Reyno v Piper Aircraft Co., 630 F2d 149, 167 (3rd Cir 1980), rev'd on other grounds, 454 US 235 (1981). See generally Hay, Borchers & Symeonides, *Conflicts of Law* (n 14) 88–93, 869–74.

approaches depend on often virtually unanswerable questions about the nature and weight of competing state policies, the synthesis in most courts features a pronounced bias in favor of plaintiffs in torts—or at least a pronounced bias in favor of the forum's law, which amounts to the same thing if plaintiffs choose a forum because of its favorable law.[28] In contracts cases, the synthesis favored by the courts generally seeks to effectuate the intent of the parties.[29] Courts are particularly likely to follow the law chosen in an express choice-of-law clause.[30]

Depending as it does on imponderables, interest analysis at best is complex, confusing, and highly unpredictable. In an occasional case, a court has favored a foreign, anti-plaintiff law for a tort despite apparent general preference for plaintiff-favoring, forum-favoring rules.[31] Similarly, a contract has been held

---

28   See eg, O'Connor v Lee-Hy Paving Corp., 579 F2d 194 (2nd Cir), cert denied, 439 US 1034 (1978); Rosenthal v Warren, 475 F2d 438 (2nd Cir), cert denied, 414 US 856 (1973); Fisher v Huck, 624 P2d 177 (Or Ct App 1981). See also Brilmayer, 'Interest Analysis and the Myth of Legislative Intent' (n 17); Willis LM Reese, 'American Trends in Private International Law: Academic and Judicial Manipulation of Choice of Law Rules in Tort Cases' (1980) 33 Vand L Rev 717 ('Reese, American Trends in Private International Law') 727–29, 734–37.

29   See eg, Seetransport Wiking Trader Shiffahrtsgesellschaft MBH & Co. v Romania, 123 F Supp 2d 174, 184–85 (SDNY 2000); Falcoal, Inc. v Turkiye Komur Isletmeleri Kurumu, 660 F Supp 1536, 1542 (SD Tex 1987); Bernkrant v Fowler, 360 P2d 906 (Cal 1961). See generally Hay, Borchers & Symeonides, *Conflicts of Law* (n 14) 1129–62; Weintraub, *Commentary on the Conflicts of Law* (n 14) 504–29, 553–68; Reese, 'American Trends in Private International Law' (n 28) 737.

30   Wallace Hardware Co. v Abrams, 223 F3d 382, 397–400 (6th Cir 2000); Fina, Inc. v Arco, 200 F3d 266 (5th Cir 2000); Krock v Lipsay, 97 F3d 640, 645 (2nd Cir 1996); Mazzoni Farms, Inc. v E.I. DuPont de Nemours & Co., 761 So 2d 306, 312 (Fla 2000); Schroeder v Rynel, Ltd., 720 A.2d 1164, 1166 (Me 1998). See also Restatement (Second) (n 19) § 187; Inter-American Convention on the Law Applicable to Contractual Obligations (signed 17 March 1994, entered into force 16 April 1994), OAS Doc OEA/Ser K/XXI.5, art 7, reprinted (1994) 33 ILM 732; Regulation (EC) No, 593/2008 on the Law Applicable to Contractual Obligations, adopted 17 June 2008, OJ L177, 4 July 2008, at 6, arts 11, 12; William J Woodward, Jr, 'Contractual Choice of Law: Legislative Choice in an Era of Party Autonomy' (2001) 54 SMU L Rev 697. For the application of this rule in international contracts, see Patrick J Borchers, 'The Internationalization of Contractual Conflicts Law' (1995) 28 Vand J Transnat'l L 421; Philip A Buhler, 'Forum Selection and Choice of Law Clauses in International Contracts: A United State Viewpoint with Particular Reference to Maritime Contracts and Bills of Lading' (1995) 27 U Miami Inter-Am L Rev 1; Eberhard H Röhm & Robert Koch, 'Choice of Law in International Distribution Contracts: Obstacle or Opportunity?' (1998) 11 NY Int'l L Rev 1.

31   See eg, Offshore Rental Co. v Continental Oil Co, 583 P2d 721 (Cal 1978); Dym v Gordon, 209 NE2d 792 (NY 1965); Casey v Manson Const. Co, 428 P2d 898 (Or 1967).

invalid on dubious grounds in an occasional case despite the usual preference for validity.[32] And, some courts have applied interest analysis to such areas as property or family law, although for these areas courts tend more strongly to stay with the vested-rights system for choice of law.[33] The complexity and uncertainty of interest analysis makes it an ideal 'escape device.' A court can justify using any law it wants without resort to the traditional escape devices,[34] and thus the traditional escape devices have tended to atrophy or even disappear under interest analysis in favor of sometimes transparently result-oriented application of interest analysis—essentially, interest analysis provides an *ad hoc* approach to each case.[35]

C   The Neoterritorialist Approach

Some state courts have rejected interest analysis because of its inherent uncertainty.[36] Some of these courts have chosen to continue to apply the vested rights or 'territorialist' approach despite the rigidities and other difficulties in that system.[37] Other courts and scholars, disillusioned with both vested rights (too rigid) and interest analysis (too whimsical), have developed a third approach that attempts to combine what are arguably the best points of both systems.[38] This new approach is the 'neoterritorialist' approach.

---

32   See eg, Barnes Group, Inc. v C & C Prod., Inc., 716 F2d 1023 (4th Cir 1983); Woods Tucker Leasing Corp. v Hutcheson-Ingram Dev Co., 626 F2d 401 (5th Cir 1980); Lilienthal v Kaufman, 395 P2d 543 (Or 1964).

33   See eg, Carter v Sandberg, 458 A2d 924 (NJ Super 1983) (property); In re Lenherr's Estate, 314 A2d 255 (Pa 1974) (marriage).

34   Compare Tomlin v Boeing Co., 650 F2d 1065 (9th Cir 1981); with Henry v Richardson-Merrell Co., 508 F2d 28 (3rd Cir 1975); and with Heavner v Uniroyal, Inc., 305 A2d 412 (NJ 1973). Also compare Martineau v Guertin, 751 A2d 776 (Vt 2000); with Myers v Langlois, 721 A2d 129 (Vt 1998).

35   Hay, Borchers & Symeonides, *Conflicts of Law* (n 14) 27–41; Weintraub, *Commentary on the Conflicts of Law* (n 14) 396–97, 460–503; Reese, 'American Trends in Private International Law' (n 28) 720–30.

36   See eg, Braxton v Anco Elec., Inc., 409 SE2d 914, 915 (NC 1991); Boudreau v Baughman, 368 SE2d 849, 853–54 (NC 1988).

37   See eg, Spinozzi v ITT Sheraton Corp., 174 F3d 842, 844–45 (7th Cir 1999); Philip Morris Inc. v Angeletti, 752 A2d 200, 231 (Md 2000); BHP Petrol (Americas), Inc. v Texaco Exploration, Inc., 1 P3d 1253 (Wyo 2000).

38   Chila v Owens, 348 F Supp 1207 (SDNY 1972); First Nat'l Bank in Fort Collins v Rostek, 514 P2d 314 (Colo 1973); Neumeier v Kuehner, 286 NE2d 454 (NY 1972); Cipolla v Shaposka, 267 A2d 854 (Pa 1970). See generally David Cavers, *The Choice of Law Process* (University of Michigan Press 1965); Hay, Borchers & Symeonides, *Conflicts of Law* (n 14) 859–69, 874–993;

Under the neoterritorialist approach, courts work out territorially centered rules that are more narrowly drawn than the rules for vested rights. Because the rules are more narrowly drawn, they, like interest analysis, are more sensitive to the policies at stake for particular issues and therefore presumably are more just. Yet, being territorially sensitive, the approach is expected to be more predictable than interest analysis has proven to be. Furthermore, neoterritorialism stresses the expectations of the parties, even in torts cases, rather than guesses about the policies underlying various competing laws.[39] Neoterritorialism localizes these expectations differently for rules meant to regulate conduct ('admonitory rules,' which direct conduct—'admonish'—and therefore turn on where the regulated conduct occurs) and rules meant to allocate the financial consequences of an act or event ('compensatory rules,' which focus on ensuring just compensation for injuries and have turned the relation of the act or event to the domiciles of the parties).[40]

Specific neoterritorialist rules thus far have not been accepted outside the forum that created them.[41] Thus, consensus among champions of neoterritorialism exists only at a high level of generality, particularly as so many rules of law are simultaneously both admonitory and compensatory, as those terms are used in neoterritorialism. Supporters of 'neoterritorialism' thus have felt obliged to accept the possibility of displacing their rules in unspecified cases. A residual interest analysis remains their major escape device.[42]

Weintraub, *Commentary on the Conflicts of Law* (n 14) 449–56, 500–02; Reese, 'American Trends in Private International Law' (n 28) 730–34.

39   First Nat'l Bank in Fort Collins v Rostek, 514 P2d 314 (Colo 1973); Neumeier v Kuehner, 286 NE2d 454 (NY 1972); Cipolla v Shaposka, 267 A2d 854 (Pa 1970). See also Weintraub, *Commentary on the Conflicts of Law* (n 14) 400–402; Erin A O'Hara & Larry E Ribstein, 'From Politics to Efficiency in Choice of Law' (2000) 67 U Chi L Rev 1151; Thomas J Rueter & Joshua H Roberts, 'Pennsylvania's Reasonable Expectations Doctrine: The Third Circuit's Perspective' (2000) 45 Villa L Rev 581. The relevance of the parties' expectations in torts cases is emphatically denied under interest analysis. Tooker v Lopez, 249 NE2d 394, 399 (NY 1969).

40   See Schultz v Boy Scouts of Am., Inc., 480 NE2d 679 (NY 1985). See generally Hay, Borchers & Symeonides, *Conflicts of Law* (n 14) 884–993; Weintraub, *Commentary on the Conflicts of Law* (n 14) 500–02; John T Cross, 'The Conduct-Regulating Exception in Modern United States Choice-of-Law' (2003) 36 Creighton L Rev 425.

41   See eg, Weintraub, *Commentary on the Conflicts of Law* (n 14) 455–56.

42   Anderson v SAM Airlines, 939 F Supp 167 (EDNY 1996); Towley v King Arthur Rinks, Inc., 351 NE2d 728 (NY 1976); Neumeier v Kuehner, 286 NE2d 454, 457–58 (NY 1972).

3   Choosing the Rule of Decision in an International Context

The foregoing discussion of choice of law in the United States leaves open the question of whether there are, or should be, different choice of law rules when one of the contending bodies of law is from a foreign nation or is international law. The American answer to this question, to a surprisingly large extent, is no. While the question of choice of law (and other conflicts of law questions) in other nations is usually set in an international context, so much so that the field of law is often called 'private international law,'[43] the rules elsewhere are not so different from those found in the United States. This should not surprise because, for the most part the entire field of conflicts of law—including choice of law—developed in the United States through the conscious application of principles borrowed from international law to the interstate context.[44] Today, there is considerable controversy over using international legal sources for interpreting the U.S. Constitution,[45] controversy in which Justice Antonin

---

43   See, eg, Richard Frimpong Oppong, 'Private International Law Scholarship in Africa (1889–2009)—A Selected Bibliography' (2010) 58 Am J Comp L 319. One of the major projects for harmonizing conflicts of law globally is the Hague Conference on Private International Law (founded 1893). See Hague Conference on Private International Law, Annual Report (2013). See also Hay, Borchers & Symeonides, *Conflicts of Law* (n 14) at 1–3.

44   See eg, Grover & Baker Sewing Mach. Co. v Radcliffe, 137 US 287, 296–298 (1890) (holding that recognition of a judgment under the full faith and credit clause applicable between states of the United States is determined by international principles of law and not 'municipal' [local] principles of law); Pennoyer v Neff, 95 US 714, 722 (1877) ('[E]xcept as restrained and limited by [the Constituion, States] possess and exercise the authority of independent States, and the principles of public law…are applicable…to them'); D'Arcy v Ketchum, 52 US (11 How) 165, 174–76 (1850) (applying the 'well established rules of international law' to determine when a judgment is entitled to full faith and credit); McElmoyle v Cohen, 38 US (13 Pet) 312, 327 (1839) (applying the principles of international law to determine a choice of law question). See generally Sarah H Cleveland, 'Our International Constitution' (2006) 31 Yale J Int'l L 1 ('Cleveland, Our International Constitution'), 50–54.

45   See Roper v Simmons, 543 US 551, 622–628 (2005) (Scalia, J, with Rehnquist, CJ & Thomas, J, dissenting) (denouncing recourse to international legal sources as a device for interpreting the US Constitution); Lawrence v Texas, 539 US 558, 598 (2003) (Scalia, J, with Rehnquist, CJ & Thomas, J, dissenting) (same); Atkins v Virginia, 536 US 304, 325 (Rehnquist, CJ, with Scalia & Thomas, JJ, dissenting) (same). See also Roger P Alford, 'Misusing International Sources to Interpret the Constitution' (2004) 98 Am J Int'l L 57; Anthony J Bella Jr & Bradford Clark, 'The Law of Nations as Constitutional Law' (2012) 98 Va L Rev 729; Cleveland, Our International Constitution (n 44); Joan L Larsen, 'Importing Constitutional Norms from a 'Wider Civilization': Lawrence and the Rehnquist Court's Use of Foreign and

Scalia has led the charge against such recourse. Yet, even Justice Scalia relies on principles of international law to decide choice of law questions.[46] To consider the role of international law, either as a source of choice-of-law rules or as a source of the substantive law to be applied, one must first consider whether international law or practice directs a particular methodology for choosing the rule of decision in cases and then whether international law provides substantive rules of decision that can be chosen under any relevant choice-of-law methodology.

A   Does International Law Direct Choices of Law?

Among the choice-of-law methodologies currently used in American courts, arguably either the territorialist vested rights theory or the neoterritorialist theory might be considered more appropriate in an international context because of the continuing strong emphasis on territorial sovereignty between nations, while the interest analysis approach would be more appropriate for coordinating policies within a federal union.[47] In fact, however, there is no consensus along these lines, either within the United States or internationally. Increasingly courts in other countries even apply choice-of-law methodologies that are remarkably similar to interest analysis even though they are choosing between the laws of different nations.[48] The situation in the United States is somewhat more complicated but in the end comes out about the same.

International Law in Domestic Constitutional Interpretation' (2004) 65 Ohio St LJ 1283; Christopher Linde, 'The US Constitution and International Law: Finding the Balance' (2006) 15 J Transnat'l L & Pol'y 305; John O McGinnis, 'The Comparative Disadvantage of Customary International Law' (2006) 30 Harv JL & Pub Pol'y 7; Richard A Posner, 'The Supreme Court 2004 Term: Forward: A Political Court' (2005) 119 Harv L Rev 31, 90; Michael D Ramsey, 'The Limits of Custom in Constitutional and International Law' (2013) 50 San Diego L Rev 867 ('Ramsey, The Limits of Customary International Law'); Michael P Socarras, 'International Law and the Constitution' (2011) 4 Fed Cts L Rev 185; Ernest A Young, 'Foreign Law and the Denominator Problem' (2005) 119 Harv L Rev 148.

46   See Sun Oil Co. v Wortman, 486 US 717, 723–25 (1988). See generally Lea Brilmayer, 'Untethered Norms after Erie Railroad Co. v Tompkins: Positivism, International Law, and the Return of the Brooding Governance' (2013) 54 Wm & Mary L Rev 725 ('Brilmayer, Untethered Normas after Erie Railroad Co. v Tompkins: Positivism, International Law, and the Return of the Brooding Governance').

47   Hay, Borchers & Symeonides, *Conflicts of Law* (n 14) 9–27. See also Albert Ehrenzweig, 'Interstate and International Conflicts of Law: A Plea for Segregation' (1957) 41 Minn L Rev 717; Gerhard Kegel, 'Paternal Home and Dream Home: Traditional Conflict Laws and the American Reformers' (1979) 27 Am J Comp L 615.

48   See eg, JH Rayner (Mincing Lane) Ltd. v Department of Trade [1989] 3 All ER 523 (HL); Attorney-General of New Zealand v Ortiz [1983] 2 All ER 93 (HL); A. Co. Ltd. v Republic of

American courts routinely decide choice-of-law questions involving the law of other nations exactly the same way as they decide such choices between laws of different states of the United States.[49] Only in some fairly constrained contexts does federal law or the United States Constitution constrain the choices of rules of decision by state courts. Occasionally, one might almost say randomly, the Supreme Court of the United States will override state choice of a rule of decision on the grounds that the choice interferes with the conduct of foreign relations by the federal government.[50] Perhaps because such interventions are rare, the Court has never articulated a coherent theory about how, or how far, this principle applies.

Beyond the possibility of interference with the conduct of foreign relations, the US Supreme Court at one time was to reverse state choices of rules of decision based on whether a state or nation has legislative jurisdiction, *i.e.*, has jurisdiction to prescribe the law applicable to an action or an event.[51] That question underlies some aspects of each of the choice-of-law methodologies competing for application in American courts. For about 75 years, the Supreme Court has operated on the premise that more than one state or nation has legislative jurisdiction and there is no role for the Court in reviewing choices to apply the law of one or another of such states of nations.[52] Only in the rare case when an American court has chosen to apply the law of a state or nation that lacks legislative jurisdiction will the US Supreme Court intervene.[53]

X, [1994] 1 Lloyd's Rep 111 (QB Div 1993); Attorney General v Wellington Newspapers Ltd., [1989] 2 FSR 691 (NZ 1988). See generally Hay, Borchers & Symeonides, *Conflicts of Law* (n 14) 129–41; Weintraub, *Commentary on the Conflicts of Law* (n 14) 535–37.

49 See, eg, KMW Int'l v Chase Manhattan Bank, 606 F2d 10 (2nd Cir 1979) (Iran); Tramontana v VARIG, 50 F2d 468 (DC Cir 1965) (Brazil), cert denied, 383 US 943 (1966); Victor v Sperry, 329 P2d 728 (Cal Ct App 1958) (Mexico); D'Agostino v Johnson & Johnson, Inc., 628 A2d 305 (NJ 1993) (Switzerland); Edwards v Eire Coach Lines Co., 929 NY 2d 41 (2011) (Ontario); Neumeier v Kuehner, 286 NE2d 454 (NY 1972) (Ontario); Babcock v Jackson, 191 NE2d 279 (NY 1963) (same).

50 See eg, American Ins. Ass'n v Garamendi, 539 US 396 (2003); Zschernig v Miller, 389 US 429 (1968); Banco Nacional de Cuba v Sabbatino, 376 US 398 (1964).

51 See Home Ins. Co. v Dick, 281 US 397 (1930) (striking down the application of Texas law in a Texas court to events in Mexico because Texas did not have legislative jurisdiction).

52 See Pacific Employers Ins. Co. v Industrial Accident Comm'n, 306 US 493 (1939); and Alaska Packers Ass'n v Industrial Accident Comm'n, 294 US 532 (1935). See also Franchise Tax Bd. v Hyatt, 538 US 488 (2003); Sun Oil Co. v Wortman, 486 US 717 (1988); Allstate Ins. Co. v Hague, 449 US 302 (1981).

53 See eg, Phillips Petroleum Co. v Shutts, 472 US 797, 814–23 (1985).

The question of legislative jurisdiction has been addressed more pointedly in international conflicts of law than in the interstate conflicts of law on which most American courts and scholars have focused their attention, particularly as regards the application of public law such as criminal law. Many scholars have asserted over the years that limitations under international litigation regarding legislative jurisdiction ('jurisdiction to prescribe')[54] are fundamentally different from the limitations applied in wholly domestic contexts.

Recourse to the relevant body of international legal principles is made difficult by the different vocabulary used in international law compared to the vocabulary used in American law. In the United States, the international vocabulary has largely been reserved for diplomacy and other international discourse, appearing in American judicial opinions mostly in occasional and rare criminal cases or in quasi-criminal proceedings such as antitrust, and then when the central events occurred outside the United States.[55] These principles are not limited to criminal or quasi-criminal cases, however.[56] The American Law Institute's *Restatement (Third) of the Foreign Relations Law of the United States*[57] describes the four traditional headings of jurisdiction to prescribe recognized in international law as:

---

54 The phrase 'legislative jurisdiction' is used in the Restatement of Conflicts, while the phrase 'jurisdiction to prescribe' is used in the Restatement of Foreign Relations Law. See Restatement (Second) (n 19) § 9 cmt B; Restatement (Third) of Foreign Relations Law § 401 (1987) ('Restatement (Third)).' See generally Willis L.M. Reese, Legislative Jurisdiction (1978) 78 Colum L Rev 1587.

55 Crimes: United States v Pizzarusso, 338 F2d 8 (2nd Cir), cert denied, 392 US 936 (1968); Rivard v United States, 375 F2d 882 (5th Cir 1967), cert denied sub nom Groleau v United States, 389 US 884 (1968). Antitrust: Continental Ore Co. v Union Carbide Co., 370 US 690 (1962); Laker Airways Ltd. v SABENA, 731 F2d 909 (DC Cir 1984); United States v ALCOA, 148 F2d 416 (2nd Cir 1945). See generally Lee M Caplan, 'The Constitution and Jurisdiction over Foreign States: The 1996 Amendment to the Foreign Sovereign Immunities Act in Perspective' (2001) 41 Va J Int'l L 369, 381–93; Andrew L Strauss, 'Beyond National Law: The Neglected Role of the International Law of Personal Jurisdiction in Domestic Courts' (1995) 36 Harv Int'l LJ 373. Some commentators have concluded that international standards apply only to criminal matters. See eg, Gillian Triggs, 'An International Convention on Sovereign Immunity? Some Problems in Application of the Restrictive Rule' (1982) 9 Monash U L Rev 74, 96–98. But see von Dardel v USSR, 623 F Supp 246, 254 (D DC 1985) (applying the principles of international jurisdiction in a civil case), vacated on other grounds, 736 F Supp 1 (D DC 1990).

56 See Sosa v Alvarez-Machain, 542 US 692, 762–63 (2004) (Ginsburg & Breyer, JJ, concurring) (applying international jurisdiction principles to torts); Vivian Grosswald Curran, 'Mass Torts and Universal Jurisdiction' (2013) 34 U Pa J Int'l L 799.

57 Restatement (Third) (n 54) §§ 402, 404, 423.

(1) the territorial principle;
(2) the personality (or nationality) principle;[58]
(3) the protective principle; and
(4) the universality principle.

When the territorial principle is invoked because the subject of the action in question (in the grammatical sense of the word 'subject') is located within the state at the time of the action, jurisdiction to prescribe has long been accepted everywhere; in fact, 'subjective territorial jurisdiction' is considered the primary form of jurisdiction to prescribe in public law.[59] In contrast, states also claim jurisdiction to prescribe because the object of the action (in the grammatical sense of the word 'object') is located in the state—*i.e.,* when the act occurs outside the state but causes a significant effect on persons or property within the state.[60] 'Objective territorial jurisdiction' has been applied broadly, but its application is often controversial and that application evokes the greater part of international jurisdictional controversies.[61]

---

58   Generally referred to as the nationality principle, but in order to make the import of this principle clear, I prefer the term 'personality principle.' Phrasing it this way makes it unnecessary to develop a supposedly separate principle known as the 'passive personality' principle and shows how this principle actually relates to other principles of legislative jurisdiction. For cases listing the passive personality principle as a separate principle, see United States v Pizzarusso, 388 F2d 8, 10 (2nd Cir), cert denied, 392 US 936 (1968); Rivard v United States, 375 F2d 882, 885 (5th Cir 1967), cert denied sub nom; Groleau v United States, 389 US 884 (1968). See the text *infra* at notes 67–76.

59   American Banana Co. v United Fruit Co., 213 US 347, 356 (1909); Restatement (Third), *supra* note 54, § 402(1); Gerhard Kegel & Ignaz Seidl-Hohenveldern (Joseph J Darby trans), 'On the Territorial Principle in Public International Law' (1982) 5 Hastings Int'l & Comp L Rev 245.

60   Strassheim v Daily, 221 US 280, 285 (1911) (dictum); United States v Ricardo, 619 F2d 1124 (5th Cir), cert denied, 449 US 1063 (1980); United States v ALCOA, 148 F2d 416, 443–44 (2nd Cir 1945); Restatement (Third) (n 54) § 403 rep note 3.

61   See eg, Poynter v Commerce Comm'n, [2010] 3 NZ L Rep 300 (NZ Sup Ct). See also Zachary D Clopton, 'Replacing the Presumption against Extraterritoriality' (2014) BUL Rev 1; Monica Hanna & Michael A. Wiseman, 'Discovering Secrets: Trends in US Courts' Deference to International Blocking Statutes and Banking Secrecy Laws' (2013) 130 Banking LJ 692; Danielle Ireland-Piper, 'Extraterritorial Criminal Jurisdiction: Does the Long Arm of the Law Undermine the Rule of Law?' (2012) 13 Melb J Int'l L 122; Edward J Krauland & Anthony Rapa, 'Between Scylla and Charybdis: Identifying and Managing Secondary Sanctions Risk Arising from Commercial Relationships with Iran' (2014) 15 Bus LJ 3; Chris Noonan, 'Bad Poynter: International Cartels and Territorial Jurisdiction' (2013) 19 NZ Bus LQ 138; Dan Jerker B. Svantesson, 'The Extraterritoriality of EU Data Privacy

These controversies are not actually over the basic concept of objective territorial jurisdiction, but rather over a narrower class of claims to exercise jurisdiction to prescribe. No state disputes a claim of jurisdiction based upon an action abroad that causes a serious tangible effect in the state claiming legislative jurisdiction.[62] When the effect in the forum is intangible or insubstantial, however, states sometimes will go to extreme lengths to block such claims of legislative jurisdiction.[63] Attempts to ameliorate the resulting controversy by asserting objective territorial jurisdiction only if an effect was intended by the actor[64] have failed to solve the problem because they misconstrue its nature. The controversy only partly concerns fairness to the defendant; it centers on the clash of important social policies between the state (nation) where the action occurred and the state (nation) where the effect was felt—on the propriety of the application of the forum state's substantive law to the act.[65] At times, the US Supreme Court has tended to assert the national interest without

---

Law: Its Theoretical Justification and Its Practical Effects on US Businesses' (2014) 50 Stan J Int'l L 53.

[62] See eg, United States v Villamonte-Marquez, 462 US 579 (1983); United States v Columba-Colella, 604 F2d 356, 358–59 (5th Cir 1979); Rivard v United States, 375 F2d 882 (5th Cir 1967), cert denied sub nom Groleau v United States, 389 US 884 (1967).

[63] See eg, The [British] Protection of Trading Interests Act, 1980, c 11; Kay Bushman, 'The British Protection of Trading Interests Act of 1980: An Analysis' (1980) J Int'l L & Econ 253; Alan Vaughan Lowe, 'Blocking Extraterritorial Jurisdiction: The British Protection of Trading Interests Act' (1981) 75 Am J Int'l L 257. Despite the objections of the British government to US claims to apply objective territorial jurisdiction to anti-trust claims, the British have applied their criminal law to crimes no more tangible than attempted fraud where the targeted property was located in England. DPP v Stonehouse, 1978 AC 55 (HL); Regina v Baxter, [1972] 1 QB 1. See also Diamond v Bank of London & Montreal Ltd., [1979] 1 QB 333. British courts also have refused to apply their law to fraud in England if the targeted property was locatee abroad. Regina v Governor of Pentonville Prison, 71 Crim App 241 (1980); Regina v Tirado, 59 Crim App 80 (1974).

[64] United States v Ricardo, 619 F2d 1124 (5th Cir), cert denied, 449 US 1063 (1980); United States v Baker, 609 F2d 134 (5th Cir 1980); United States v ALCOA, 148 F2d 416 (2nd Cir 1945). See also F. Hoffman-La Roche Ltd. v Empagran SA, 542 US 155 (2004); People v Blume, 505 NW2d 843 (Mich 1993).

[65] See Restatement (Third) (n 54) §§ 403, 414–16. Compare Laker Airways Ltd. v SABENA, 731 F2d 909 (DC Cir 1984); with British Airways Bd. v Laker Airways Ltd., [1983] 1 QB 142, vacated, [1984] 3 WLR 413 (HL). See generally Paul Schiff Berman, 'A Pluralist Approach to International Law' (2007) 32 Yale J Int'l L 301, 316–19 (discussing the clash of policies involved in conflicts between applicable laws and judgments in the international legal system, with particular emphasis on the conflicts created by differing laws and policies applicable to the internet).

regard to the concerns of or effects on other nations.[66] Often, other nations protest this approach,[67] yet they also apply the same approach themselves.[68] The most recent decisions from the US Supreme Court have ameliorated these clashes by imposing a strong reading of the presumption against the extraterritorial application of US statutes.[69]

Jurisdiction to prescribe based on the nationality of the actor (the 'active personality' principle) is another basis that has long been recognized everywhere.[70] Claims of jurisdiction to prescribe based upon the nationality of the person acted upon (the 'passive personality' principle) are almost universally

---

66   Hartford Fire Insurance Co. v California, 509 US 764, 798–99 (1993).
67   For example, Prime Minister Margaret Thatcher repeatedly and personally intervened with President Ronald Reagan about the case of Laker Airways Ltd. v SABENA, 731 F2d 909 (DC Cir 1984), until the US government brokered a settlement. Geoffrey Smith, Reagan and Thatcher 141–44, 164–65 (WW Norton 1991). See generally Hannah L Buxbaum, 'Jurisdictional Conflict in Global Antitrust Enforcement' (2004) 16 Loy Consumer L Rev 365; Alexander Layton & Angharad M. Perry, 'Extraterritorial Jurisdiction: European Responses' (2004) 26 Hous J Int'l L 309.
68   See eg, The Wood Pulp Case, [1988] ECR 5193 (Eur Ct Justice Case 89/85, 1988).
69   See eg, Morrison v National Australia Bank Ltd., 561 US 247 (2010); Serra v Lapin, 600 F3d 1191, 1197–1200 (9th Cir 2010); Arc Ecology v US Dep't Air Force, 411 F3d 1092 (9th Cir 2005). See also Carlos M Vázquez, 'Things We Do With Presumptions: Reflections on Kiobel v Royal Dutch Petroleum' (2014) 89 Notre Dame L Rev 1719.
70   See eg, State v Bacon, 112 A 682 (Del 1920); Hanks v State, 13 Tex Ct App 289, 305 (1882); Commonwealth v Gaines, 4 Va (2 Va Cas) 172, 173 (1819); Ex parte McNeely, 14 SE 436 (W Va. 1892). See generally Restatement (Third) (n 54) § 402(2); Model Penal Code § 1.03(1)(f), (2) (1962); Hay, Borchers & Symeonides, *Conflicts of Law* (n 14) 336–39; Weintraub, *Commentary on the Conflicts of Law* (n 14) 209–211; Mark D Rosen, '"Hard" or "Soft" Pluralism?: Positive, Normative, and Institutional Considerations of States' Extraterritorial Powers' (200&) 51 St LULJ 713, 719–22 ('Rosen, 'Hard' or 'Soft' Pluralism?'); Mark D Rosen, 'Extraterritoriality and Political Heterogeneity in American Federalism' (2002) 150 U Pa L Rev 855, 871–76 ('Rosen, Extraterritoriality and Political Heterogeneity in American Federalism'). For American cases applying federal law to US citizens while abroad, see Steele v Bulova Watch Co., 344 US 280, 282 (1952); United States v Blackmer, 284 US 421(1932); United States v Bowman, 260 US 94 (1922); United States v McVicker, 979 F Supp 2d 1154 (D Ore 2013); United States v Martinez, 599 F Supp 2d 784, 800 (WD Tex 2009); United States v Clark, 435 F3d 1100 (9th Cir 2006), cert denied, 549 US 1343 (2007). For American cases applying state law to the state's citizens while outside the state, see Skiriotes v Florida, 313 US 69 (1941); Felton v Hodges, 374 F2d 337 (5th Cir 1967); F/v American Eagle v State, 620 P2d 657 (Alaska 1980); People v Weeren, 607 P2d 1279 (Cal 1980); Commonwealth v Gaines, 4 Va. (2 Va Cas) 172 (1819); State v Mueller, 171 N.W2d 414 (Wis 1969).

rejected.[71] Even countries, like France, that routinely assert passive personality jurisdiction object vehemently when other countries assert this jurisdiction against their nationals.[72] For at least a century, the American government consistently opposed the passive personality theory.[73] One federal court expressly rejected the principle as applicable in the United States.[74] In response to the growing problem of international terrorism, however, the executive branch embraced the theory of passive personality in the mid-1980s.[75] Subsequently Congress enacted anti-terrorism statutes that appear to be based on the passive personality principle.[76]

---

71 See generally The SS Lotus (France v Turkey), PCIJ Rep Series A No. 10; Restatement (Third) (n 54) § 402 comment e; Geoffrey R Watson, 'The Passive Personality Principle' (1993) 28 Tex Int'l LJ 1 ('Watson, The Passive Personality Principle') 14–30.

72 See generally Eric Cafritz & Omar Tene, 'Article 113–117 of the French Penal Code: The Passive Personality Principle' (2003) 41 Colum J Transnat'l L 585.

73 The Cutting Case 1887 (1888) For Rel 751, reported in 2 John Bassett Moore (1906) Digest of International Law 228. See also Restatement (Third) (n 54) § 402; Watson, The Passive Personality Principle (n 71) 4–9.

74 United States v Columba-Colella, 604 F2d 356, 360 (5th Cir 1979). See also Zenith Radio Corp. v Matsushita Elec. Indus. Co., 494 F Supp 1161, 1179 n38 (ED Pa 1980), aff'd on other grounds, 723 F2d 319 (3rd Cir 1983), rev'd on other grounds, 475 US 574 (1986).

75 Abraham D Sofaer, 'Fighting Terrorism through Law' (1985) 85 State Dep't Bull 38, 41–42. See also Office of Legal Counsel, Memorandum for the Attorney General: Applicability of Federal Criminal Laws and the Constitution to Contemplated Lethal Operations against Shaykh Anwar al-Aulaqi, 16 July 2010, at <https://www.aclu.org/sites/default/files/assets/2014-06-23_barron-memorandum.pdf> accessed 13 October 2014. See generally Watson, The Passive Personality Principle (n 71) 9–10.

76 See 18 USC § 32 (the Sabotage Act); 18 USC § 1203 (the Hostage Taking Act); 18 USC § 2331 (the Anti-Terrorism Act); 28 USC § 1605A (the Foreign Sovereign Immunities Act). See generally Terry Richard Kane, 'Prosecuting International Terrorists in United States Courts: Gaining the Jurisdictional Threshold' (1987) 12 Yale J Int'l L 294; David Kris, 'Recent Development and Legislation: Interpreting 18 USC § 2331 under US and International Law' (1990) 27 Harv J Legis 579; Watson, 'The Passive Personality Principle' (n 71) 10–13, 30–46. The war on terror has generated more support for the application of the passive personality principle. See eg, William P Hoye, 'Fighting Fire with... Mire? Civil Remedies and the New War on State-Sponsored Terrorism' (2002) 12 Duke J Comp & Int'l L 105, 110; Christopher C Joyner, 'Countering Nuclear Terrorism: A Conventional Response' (2007) 18 Eur J Int'l L 225, 239; Jackson Nyamuya Maogoto, 'Countering Terrorism: From Wigged Judges to Helmeted Soldiers—Legal Perspectives on America's Counter-Terrorism Responses' (2005) 6 San Diego Int'l LJ 243, 259; Alexander J Urbelis, 'Rethinking Extraterritorial Prosecution in the War on Terror: Examining the Unintentional Yet Foreseeable of Extraterritorially Criminalizing the Provision of Material Support to Terrorists and Foreign Terrorist Organizations' (2007) 22 Conn J Int'l L 313; Andrew S Williams,

Changing executive and legislative attitudes toward the passive personality principle have led American courts to begin to apply the passive personality principle where authorized by statute.[77] Several federal courts recently have accepted the general legitimacy of the passive personality principle in *dicta*.[78] How far these courts will apply the principle in other contexts or whether the executive branch will accept its application against the United States remains unclear.[79] The presumption that, absent express language to the contrary, acts of Congress are intended to have effect only within the territory of the United States is perhaps enough to answer the question in the negative.[80] In international terms, the different treatment given acts where a claim of jurisdiction is based on the location of the effect or on the person affected reflects both the greater likelihood of a defendant being surprised by a claim to apply the law of the victim's state (suppose one is involved in a traffic accident in the United

---

'The Interception of Civil Aircraft over the High Seas in the Global War on Terror', (2007) 59 AFL Rev 73, 126.

[77] United States v Rezaq, 134 F3d 1121, 1133 (DC Cir), cert denied, 525 US 834 (1998); United States v Morin, 80 F3d 124 (4th Cir 1996). See generally Abraham Abramovsky, 'Extraterritorial Jurisdiction: The United States' Unwarranted Attempt to Alter International Law in United States v Yunis' (1990) 15 Yale J Int'l L 121.

[78] See United States v Yousef, 327 F3d 56, 96–97 (2d Cir), cert denied, 540 US 933 (2003); Biton v Palestinian Interim Self-Gov Auth'y, 510 F Supp 2d 144 (D DC 2007). In many cases, passive personality was given as an alternative holding when jurisdiction was also justified on less contentious grounds. See United States v Neil, 312 F3d 419, 422 (9th Cir 2002); United States v Hill, 279 F3d 731, 739–40 (9th Cir 2002); United States v MacAllister, 160 F3d 1304, 1308 n9 (11th Cir 1998), cert denied, 528 US 853 (1999); United States v Felix-Gutierrez, 940 F2d 1200, 1205–06 (9th Cir 1991), cert denied, 508 US 906 (1993); United States v Benitez, 741 F2d 1312, 1316 (11th Cir 1984); United States v Marino-Garcia, 679 F2d 1373, 1381 (11th Cir 1972); Price v Libya, 110 F Supp 2d 10, 12–13 (D DC 2000), rev'd on other grounds, 294 F3d 82 (DC Cir 2002); United States v bin Laden, 92 F Supp 2d 189, 221–22 (SDNY 2000); Goldberg v USB AG, 690 F Supp 2d 92, 108–111 (EDNY 2010); United States v Martinez, 599 F Supp 2d 784, 800 (WD Tex 2009); United States v Roberts, 1 F Supp 2d 601, 606–07 (ED La 1998); United States v Layton, 509 F Supp 212, 216 (ND Cal 1981), appeal dismissed, 645 F2d 681, cert denied, 452 US 972 (1981).

[79] Rejecting application of the passive personality principle when not authorized by statute: Neely v Club Med. Mgt. Services, Inc., 63 F3d 166, 185 n17 (3rd Cir 1995); United States v Vasquez-Velasco, 15 F3d 833, 841 n7 (9th Cir 1994). Accepting application of the passive personality principle when asserted by a foreign state as a basis for extradition: In re Ahmad, 726 F Supp 389, 398–99 (EDNY 1989), aff'd on other grounds sub nom Ahmad v Wigin, 910 F2d 1063 (2nd Cir 1990); In re Extradition of Demjanjuk, 612 F Supp 544, 558 (ND Ohio 1985) (alternate holding).

[80] Kiobel (n 4); Argentina v Amerada Hess Shipping Corp., 488 US 428, 440–41 (1989). See also Vázquez (n 69).

States with a car that turns out to be driven by a French citizen), and the lesser degree of intrusion into the interests of a state by an act affecting an absent national compared to an act intruding into the territory of the state and thereby threatening to affect the whole community.

The last two headings of jurisdiction to prescribe—the protective principle and the universality principle—turn upon the nature of the act in question rather than on the location or effect of the action or the citizenship of the persons involved. Under the protective principle, a state is justified in exercising jurisdiction when an act strongly affects significant interests of the state regardless of where the act occurs or by whom it is done, generally involving threats to the integrity or security of the state itself. Examples include attacks on a state's officials, espionage against a state, counterfeiting a state's currency, perjury to a state official, or other interference with government operations.[81] American courts have stretched the protective principle to justify the arrest of non-nationals on the high seas aboard foreign-flagged vessels or aircraft when they are engaged in drug smuggling on the basis that this was a threat to the 'national interest.'[82] Congress also has authorized the extraterritorial application

---

81   Restatement (Third) (n 54) § 402(3). See eg, Strassheim v Daily, 221 US 280 (1911); United States v Ayesh, 702 F 3d 162 (4th Cir), cert denied, 133 S Ct. 1619 (2013); United States v Felix-Gutierrez, 940 F2d 1200, 1206 (9th Cir 1991), cert denied, 508 US 906 (1993); United States v Benitez, 741 F2d 1312, 1316 (11th Cir 1984), cert denied, 471 US 1137 (1985); Persinger v Iran, 729 F3d 835, 843 n12 (DC Cir), cert denied, 469 US 881 (1984); McKeel v Iran, 722 F2d 582, 588–589 (9th Cir 1983), cert denied, 469 US 880 (1984); In re Marc Rich. & Co., 707 F2d 663, 666 (2d Cir), cert denied, 463 US 1215 (1983); United States v Khalje, 658 F2d 90, 92 (2d Cir 1981); United States v Birch, 470 F2d 808, 811 (4th Cir 1972), cert denied, 411 US 931 (1973); United States v Pizzarusso, 388 F2d 8, 9–10 (2nd Cir), cert denied, 392 US 936 (1968); Diaz Marin v United States, 352 F2d 174 (5th Cir 1965); Rocha v United States, 288 F2d 545, 549 (9th Cir), cert denied, 366 US 948 (1961); United States v Hamdan, 801 F Supp 2d 1247, 1269 (Ct Mil Comm'n Rev 2011), rev'd on other grounds, 696 F3d 1238 (DC Cir 2012); United States v Campbell, 798 F Supp 2d 293, 308 (D DC 2011); United States v bin Laden, 92 F Supp 2d 189, 195 (SDNY 2000); United States v Zehe, 601 F Supp 196, 198 n3 (D Mass 1985); United States v Layton, 509 F Supp 212, 216 (ND Cal 1981) (alternative holding), appeal dismissed, 645 F2d 681, cert denied, 452 US 972 (1981); Hanks v State, 13 Tex App 289 (1882). See Ian Brownlie, *Principles of Public International Law* (5th ed, Clarendon Press 1998) ('Brownlie, 5th ed Principles of Public International Law') 307; Iain Cameron, *The Protective Principle of International Criminal Jurisdiction* (Dartmouth Publishing 1994).

82   See eg, United States v Lawrence, 727 F3d 386, 395 (5th Cir 2013), cert denied, 134 S Ct 1340 (2014); United States v Ibarguen-Mosquera, 634 F3d 1370, 1378–1379 (11th Cir 2011); United States v Saac, 632 F3d 1203, 1211 (11th Cir), cert denied sub nom Renegifo v United States, 132 S Ct 139 (2011); United States v Cardales-Luna, 632 F3d 731, 747 (4th Cir), cert denied, 132 S Ct 573 (2011). See also United States v Banjoko, 590 F2d 1278, 1281 (11th Cir 2009)

of a law criminalizing conspiracies to destroy property with explosives—an outgrowth of the war on terror. This statute has been upheld by a court on the basis that it is an application of the protective principle.[83] Whether the international community will accept such broad readings of the protective principle remains an unsettled question.[84]

The universality principle allows jurisdiction over acts universally viewed as heinous, and the actor is subject to punishment by any state that obtains custody of the actor, although arguably the law to be applied is international law rather than the law of any particular state.[85] Controversy is also characteristic

---

(applying the protective principle to stowing away on a US-bound ship); State v Flores, 188 P3d 706, 712–13 (Ariz 2008) (applying state law under the protective principle to the solicitation of illegal immigrants in Mexico as an alternative holding). But see United States v Perlaza, 493 F3d 1149, 1161–1162 (9th Cir 2006) (declining to apply the protective principle to drug smuggling absent a statutory basis in US law).

83   United States v Reumayr, 530 F Supp 2d 1210, 1222 (DNM 2008).

84   One early decision from the United States took note to the narrow compass the protective principle in international practice. United States v Yunis, 681 F Supp 896, 903 n14 (D DC 1988), aff'd on other grounds, 924 F2d 1086 (DC Cir 1990). Whether this remains true is not clear.

85   War crimes, crimes against humanity, or crimes against peace: In re Yamashita, 327 US 1 (1946); Abelesz v Magyar Nemzeti Bank, 692 F3d 661, 676 (7th Cir 2012); Sarei v Rio Tinto, PLC, 671 F3d 736, 787 (9th Cir 2011), cert denied, 133 S Ct 1995 (2013), Daliberti v Iraq, 97 F Supp 2d 38, 54 (D DC 2000); Flatow v Iran, 999 F Supp 1, 23 (D DC 1998), execution refused, 67 F Supp 2d 535 (D Md 1999), aff'd mem sub nom Flatow v Alavi Fndtn., 225 F3d 653 (4th Cir 2000); Charter of the International Military Tribunal (1945) 59 Stat 1544; Convention on the Prevention and Punishment of Genocide (adopted 9 December 1948, entered into force 12 January 1951) 78 UNTS 277; Attorney-General of Israel v Eichmann (1962) 36 ILR 277. See also Jillian Blake, 'Should Domestic Courts Prosecute Genocide? Examing the Trial of Efraín Ríos Montt' (2014) 39 Brook J Int'l L 563; Brilmayer, Untethered Normas after Erie Railroad Co. v Tompkins: Positivism, International Law, and the Return of the Brooding Governance (n 46); Nidal Nabil Jurdi, 'The Domestic Prosecution of the Crime of Aggression after the International Criminal Court Review Conference: Possibilities and Alternatives' (2013) 14 Melb J Int'l L 129; Pierre N Leval, 'Distant Genocides' (2013) 38 Yale J Int'l L 231; Michael P Scharf, 'Universal Jurisdiction and the Crime of Aggression' (2012) 53 Harv Int'l LJ 357. Air or sea piracy: Ex parte Quirin, 317 US 1 (1942); United States v Ali, 718 F3d 929 (DC Cir 2013: United States v Shibin, 722 F3d 233 (4th Cir 2013), cert denied, 134 S Ct 1935 (2014); United States v Belfast, 611 F3d 783, 810–813 (11th Cir 2010), cert denied, 131 S Ct 1511 (2011); United States v Lei Shi, 525 F3d 729 (9th Cir), cert denied, 555 US 934 (2008); United States v Rezaq, 134 F3d 1121, 1131–1132,1133 n6 (DC Cir), cert denied, 525 US 834 (1998); United States v Yunis, 924 F2d 1086, 1091 (DC Cir 1991); Convention on the High Seas (opened for signature 29 April 1958, entered into force for the US 30 September 1962), 13 UST 2312, TIAS no. 5200, 450 UNTS 82 arts 14–22; 22 USC §152; Convention for the

of such claims of jurisdiction. In accepting or opposing extraterritorial forms of jurisdiction, a state must balance the achievement of its own or other states' substantive policies against the risk of surprise in exercising jurisdiction over people acting abroad in the reasonable belief that they can be held accountable only under the law of the state where they act or of which they are citizens, in a forum to which they have significant ties.[86]

A thoughtful analysis by an American judge would use the international standards on jurisdiction to prescribe to determine which nations have legislative jurisdiction, and therefore which nation's laws might be applied consistent the constitutional limitations on choice of law.[87] Certainly more than one nation could have legislative jurisdiction over a human rights violation under the international standards. For example, if an American citizen tortures an

---

Suppression of Unlawful Seizure of Aircraft, (opened for signature 16 December 1970, entered into force for the US 14 October 1971), 22 UST 1641, TIAS no 7192 (1971); Convention for the Suppression of Unlawful Acts against the Safety of Civil Aviation (opened for signature 23 September 1971, entered into force for the US 26 January 1973) 24 UST 564, TIAS no 7570 (1973), 49 USC §§ 1301(38), 1472. See also Samuel Shnider, 'Universal Jurisdiction over 'Operation of a Pirate Ship': The Legality of the Evolving Piracy Definition in Regional Prosecutions' (2013) 38 NCJ Int'l L & Com Reg 473. Attacks on diplomats: von Dardel v USSR, 623 F Supp 246, 254 (D DC 1985), vacated on other grounds, 736 F Supp 1 (D DC 1990); Convention on the Prevention and Punishment of Crimes against Internationally Protected Persons (opened for signature 14 December 1973, entered into force for the US 20 February 1977) 28 UST 1975, TIAS no 8532 (1977); 18 USC §§ 1116, 1201.

Rejecting universal jurisdiction: In re Terrorist Attacks of Sept. 11, 2011, 714 F3d 118 (2d Cir 2013) (declining to apply universal jurisdiction to terrorism), cert denied, 2014 WL 2921775; United States v Yousef, 327 F3d 56, 106–8 (2d Cir) (same), cert denied, 540 US 933 (2003); United States v Perlaza, 493 F3d 1149, 1161–1162 (9th Cir 2006) (declining to apply the universal jurisdiction to drug smuggling); United States v Carvajal, 924 F Supp 2d 219, 241–42 (D DC 2013) (same). But see Flatow v Iran, 999 F Supp 1, 14 (D DC 1998) (applying universal jurisdiction to terrorism), execution refused, 67 F Supp 2d 535 (D Md 1999), aff'd mem. sub nom. Flatow v Alavi Fndtn., 225 F3d 653 (4th Cir 2000). See generally Restatement (Third) (n 54) § 404; Brownlie, 5th ed *Principles of Public International Law* (n 81) 307–08; Stephen Macedo et al (eds), *The Princeton Principles on Universal Jurisdiction* (Princeton University Program in Law and Public Affairs 2001); Nahal Kazemi, 'Justifications for Universal Jurisdiction: Shocking the Conscience Is Not Enough' (2013) 49 Tulsa L Rev 1.

86   World-Wide Volkswagen Corp. v Woodson, 444 US 286, 291–95 (1980); Kulko v Superior Ct, 436 US 84, 92–98 (1978); Shaffer v Heitner, 433 US 186, 207–09, 214–16 (1977); McGee v International Life Ins. Co., 355 US 220, 223 (1957); International Shoe Co. v Washington, 326 US 310, 319–20, 323 (1945). See also Restatement (Third) (n 54) §§ 403, 421(1), 431(1); Ingrid Wuerth, 'Pinochet's Legacy Reassessed' (2012) 106 Am J Int'l L 731.
87   See eg, Phillips Petroleum Co. v Shutts, 472 US 797, 814–23 (1985).

Afghan citizen in a 'black jail' in a third country, a large number of nations could claim legislative jurisdiction and thus each of these nations could claim to have its law applied. The United States would have legislative jurisdiction because of the 'active personality' (nationality) principle, Afghanistan could claim jurisdiction under the passive personality principle, and the third country could claim jurisdiction under the subjective territoriality principle. In addition, a good many nations could claim jurisdiction to prescribe under the universality principle. Only modest changes to the hypothetical case could bring in the objective territorial and protective principles as well. And within this broad range of choices, it is hard to imagine a case in which the Constitution would actually override a choice to use the law of one interested nation rather than another.[88] As Justice Robert Jackson, in a speech 40 years ago, best summarized the constitutional limits on choice-of-law: 'We [the Supreme Court] will adopt no rule, permit a good deal of overlapping and confusion, but interfere now and then, without imparting to the bar any reason by which the one or the other course is to be guided or predicted.'[89] Of course, lower courts can choose to use the international standards in doing their own analysis of the choice-of-law question—whether in terms of vested rights, interest analysis, or neoterritorialism. If they do not refer to the international standards but nonetheless choose to apply a body of law from a source that has legislative jurisdiction under those standards, even if that is not likely to be the one that most or all international tribunals would choose, their choice will not be set aside on appeal.

B   *Applying Customary International Law as the Rule of Decision*

The foregoing discussion has been cast in terms of choosing the rule of decision from the laws of one or another nation or state. This neglects that an important potential source of the rule of decision—particularly in human rights litigation—could be international law itself.[90] This possibility could arise even in cases in which a court's competence to try the case is not based on international law.[91]

---

88   See eg, Sun Oil Co. v Wortman, 486 US 717 (1988); Allstate Ins. Co. v Hague, 449 US 302 (1981).

89   Robert H Jackson, 'Full Faith and Credit-the Lawyer's Clause of the Constitution' (1945) 45 Colum L Rev 1, 26.

90   See eg, Abebe-Jira v Negewo, 72 F3d 844, 847–48 (11th Cir), cert denied, 519 US 830 (1996); Filártiga v Peña-Irala (n 3) 880–90.

91   See eg, Liu v Republic of China, 892 F2d 1419, 1428–30 (9th Cir), cert denied, 497 US 1058 (1990); Flatow v Iran, 999 F Supp 1, 18 (D DC 1998), execution refused, 67 F Supp 2d 535 (D Md 1999), aff'd mem sub nom Flatow v Alavi Fndtn., 225 F3d 653 (4th Cir 2000).

It has long been a common understanding in American jurisprudence that customary international law is part of 'our law'—a special form of US federal common law.[92] Apparently the first American federal case to apply customary international law as the rule of decision was decided in 1796.[93] A state court applied customary international law in a decision in 1784 (before there were federal courts or any concept of federal common law).[94] A statute (the Alien Tort Statute) has been on the books since 1789, conferring competence on federal courts to hear suits between 'aliens for tort only, committed in violation of the law of nations.'[95] Thus this premise should be taken as firmly established in American law.[96] Notwithstanding the firm pedigree for this premise, voices have been raised to challenge the status of customary international law as federal common law (as opposed to state common law) in recent decades.[97] Today

---

92   Banco Nacional de Cuba v Sabbatino, 376 US 398, 425 (1964); Oliver Am. Trading Co. v Mexico, 264 US 440 (1924); The Paquete Habana, 175 US 677, 700 (1900); Hilton v Guyot, 159 US 113, 163 (1895); New York Life Ins. Co. v Hendren, 92 US 286 (1875); The Nereide, 13 US (9 Cranch) 388, 423 (1815); Chisholm v Georgia, 2 US (2 Dall) 419, 474 (1793). For the classic analysis of this premise, see Edwin Dickinson, 'The Law of Nations as Part of the National Law of the United States' (1952) 101 U Pa L Rev 26.

93   Ware v Hylton, 3 US (3 Dall) 199 (1796).

94   Respublica v de Longchamps, 1 U S (1 Dall) 113, 119 (Pa 1784).

95   28 USC § 1350.

96   See Restatement (Third) (n 54) §§ 111 to 115.

97   See Jack L Goldsmith & Eric A Posner, *The Limits of International Law* (OUP 2005); Curtis Bradley, Jack L Goldsmith & David H Moore, 'Sosa, Customary International Law and the Continuing Relevance of Erie' (2007) 120 Harv L Rev 869; Saikrishna Prakash, 'The Constitutional Status of Customary International Law' (2006) 30 Harv JL & Pub Pol'y 65; Ramsey, *The Limits of Customary International Law* (n 45); Paul B Stephen, 'Courts, the Constitution, and Customary International Law: The Intellectual Origins of the Restatement (Third) of Foreign Relations Law of the United States' (2003) 44 Va J Int'l L 33; Philip Trimble, 'A Revisionist View of Customary International Law' (1986) 33 UCLA L Rev 665; Arthur Mark Weisburd, 'State Courts, Federal Courts, and International Cases' (1995) 20 Yale J Int'l L 1; Ernest A Young, 'Sorting out the Debate over Customary International Law' (2002) 42 Va J Int'l L 365. These revisionist arguments have evoked strong responses. Mark A. Chinen, 'Game Theory and Customary International Law: A Response to Professors Goldsmith and Posner' (2001) 23 Mich J Int'l L 43; William S Dodge, 'Customary International Law and the Question of Legitimacy' (2007) 120 Harv L Rev F 1; David Golove, 'Leaving Customary International Law Where It Is: Goldsmith's and Posner's The Limits of International Law' (2006) 34 Ga J Int'l & Comp L 333; Ryan Goodman & Derek Jinks, 'Filártiga's Firm Footing: International Human Rights and Federal Common Law' (1997) 66 Fordham L Rev 463; Andrew T Guzman, 'The Promise of International Law' (2006) 92 Va L Rev 533; Jun-Shik Hwang, 'A Sense and Sensiblity of Legal Obligation: Customary International Law and Game Theory' (2006) 20 Temple Int'l & Comp. LJ 111;

this premise is also caught up in the efforts to redefine the relationship of the United States to the global community and to international law generally.[98]

There are several rationales for the recent questioning of the reality of customary international law as actually American, or at least federal, common law, at least in cases involving the rights and liabilities of private parties. First, customary international law nearly always was used to constrain the actions of federal or state government officials in the conduct of their duties[99] and to guide courts in interpreting acts of Congress with international effects as well as treaties.[100] Most of these cases involved the territorial reach of laws or other technical matters; for more substantive issues, such as the protection of human rights, American courts seem to have felt far less bound by international standards, at least until recently.[101]

Harold Hongju Koh, 'Is International Law Really State Law?' (1998) 111 Harv L Rev 1824; Gerald Neuman, 'Sense and Nonsense about Customary International Law: A Response to Professors Bradley and Goldsmith' (1997) 66 Fordham L Rev 371; Beth Stephens, 'Federalism and Foreign Affairs: Congress's Power to 'Define and Punish...Offenses against the Law of Nations'' (2000) 42 Wm & Mary L Rev 447; Beth Stephens, 'The Law of Our Land: Customary International Law as Federal Law after Erie' (1997) 66 Fordham L Rev 393; Jon M Van Dyke, 'The Role of Customary International Law in Federal and State Court Litigation' (2004) 26 U Haw L Rev 361; Carlos Vazquez, 'Customary International Law as US Law: A Critique of the Revisionist and Intermediate Positions and a Defense of the Modern Position' (2011) 86 Notre Dame L Rev 1495.

98 See David L Sloss, Michael D Ramsey & William S Dodge (eds), *International Law in the US Supreme Court: Continuity and Change* (CUP 2011).

99 See eg, In re Yamashita, 327 US 1 (1946); The Paquete Habana, 175 US 677 (1900); United States v Cordero, 668 F2d 32, 36 (1st Cir 1981); Rodriguez-Fernandez v Wilkinson, 654 F2d 1382, 1388–90 (10th Cir 1981); Nguyen Da Yen v Kissinger, 528 F2d 1194, 1201 n13 (9th Cir 1975); Bergman v de Sieyes, 170 F2d 360 (2nd Cir 1948); Tarros SpA v United States, 982 F Supp 2d 325, 337–338 (SDNY 2013).

100 See eg, United States v Villamonte-Marquez, 462 US 579 (1983); McCulloch v SN de Marineros de Honduras, 372 US 10 (1963); Lauritzen v Larsen, 345 US 571 (1953); Spiess v C. Itoh & Co., 643 F2d 353, 356 (5th Cir 1981); Ralpho v Bell, 569 F2d 607 (DC Cir 1977); Karadzole v Artukovic, 247 F2d 198, 204–06 (9th Cir 1957), vacated on other grounds, 355 US 383 (1958); United States v ALCOA, 148 F2d 416, 443–444 (2nd Cir 1945); The Over the Top, 5 F2d 838, 842–43 (D Conn 1925); In re Mark C.H., 906 NS2d 419, 432–34 (Surrog Ct 2010) Restatement (Third) (n 54) § 114.

101 See eg, Fiallo v Bell, 430 US 787 (1977); Kleindienst v Mandel, 408 US 753 (1972). But see Oyama v California, 332 US 633, 649–50 (1948) (Black & Douglas, JJ, concurring) 673 (Murphy & Rutlege, JJ, concurring); Filártiga v Peña-Irala (n 3) 880–85; United States v Toscanino, 500 F2d 267, 277–79 (2nd Cir 1974); Lareau v Manson, 507 F Supp 1177, 1187 n9 (D Conn 1980), modified on other grounds, 651 F2d 96 (2nd Cir 1981).

American courts rarely used customary international law as a rule of decision in litigation between private parties. Historically, the Alien Tort Statute itself was virtually ignored, to the point that Judge Friendly once called it a 'legal Lohengrin.'[102] Even when cases under the Alien Tort Statute became more common after 1976, the court often did not use customary international law as the rule of decision despite the fact that a violation of international law is a prerequisite to cases under the act.[103] Courts in only a handful of cases did apply customary international law as the rule of decision under the Alien Tort Statute.[104] In the face of this, no wonder few courts applied customary international law when the court's competence to hear a case was established on some other basis.

One might have expected American courts to turn to international law under the Foreign Sovereign Immunities Act[105] when it came into effect in 1976, if only because of the statute's stated aim that US law relative to the immunity of foreign states is to be consistent with international standards.[106] Several American courts have relied on customary international law to resolve their jurisdiction or the immunity of the foreign state.[107] One court even applied customary international law to the merits of a non-commercial tort

---

102   ITT v Vencap, 519 F2d 1001, 1015 (2nd Cir 1975). Before 1976 (when the Foreign Sovereign Immunities Act, 28 USCA §§1602–03, came into effect), the Alien Tort Statute was successfully invoked as the basis of judicial competence in only four cases. Ardra v Clift, 195 F Supp 857, 859 (D Md 1961); Pauling v McElroy, 164 F Supp 390, 393 (D DC 1958), aff'd mem, 278 F2d 252 (DC Cir), cert denied, 364 US 835 (1960); Bolchos v Darrell, 3 F Cas 810 (D SC 1795) (No 1, 607); Moxon v Fanny, 17 F Cas 942, 948 (D Pa 1793) (No 9,895).

103   See eg, Estate of Amergi v Palestine Auth'y, 611 F3d 1350 (11th Cir 2010); Abdullahi v Pfizer, Inc., 562 F3d 163 (2nd Cir 2009), cert denied, 130 S Ct 3541 (2010); Taveraz v Taveraz, 477 F3d 767 (6th Cir 2007); Filártiga v Peña-Irala, 630 F2d 876, 879 (2nd Cir 1980); Mehinovic v Vuckovic, 198 F Supp 2d 1322, 1357–60 (ND Ga 2002).

104   Iwanowa v Ford Motor Co., 67 F Supp 2d 424, 441–445 (D NJ 1999); Beanal v Freeport-McMoran, Inc., 969 F Supp 362, 369–377 (ED La 1997), aff'd on other grounds, 197 F3d 161 (5th Cir 1999); Xuncax v Gramajo, 886 F Supp 162, 179–81 (D Mass 1995) (dictum); Forti v Suarez-Mason, 672 F Supp 1531, 1539–40 (ND Cal 1987), further order, 694 F Supp 707 (ND Cal 1988). See generally Carlos M Vásquez, 'Alien Tort Claims and the Status of Customary International Law' (2012) 106 Am J Int'l L 531.

105   28 USC §§ 1602–11.

106   Id., § 1602.

107   See eg, Fulwood v Germany, 734 F3d 72, 78 (1st Cir 2013); Persinger v Iran, 690 F2d 1010, 1018 (DC Cir 1982), op withdrawn & replaced on other grounds, 729 F2d 835 (DC Cir), cert denied, 469 US 881 (1984); Liu v Republic of China, 642 F Supp 297, 304–05 (ND Cal 1986), aff'd on other grounds, 892 F2d 1419 (9th Cir 1989), cert denied, 497 US 1058 (1990); Morel de Letelier v Chile, 488 F Supp 665, 673 (D DC 1980).

claim under the Immunities Act.[108] That approach is more justifiable regarding property taken in violation of international law where Congress's withdrawal of immunity itself refers to international law, whether customary or otherwise.[109] In general, however, courts remain unwilling to apply international law as a rule of decision in suits against foreign states under the Foreign Sovereign Immunities Act[110] or even to refer the basic questions of jurisdiction and immunity to international law.[111]

In 1980, two decisions appeared to give new life to customary international law as a rule of decision. Both cases involved political murders by officials of South American governments—the clearest denial of internationally protected human rights if courts were prepared to abandon the traditional notion that international law did not apply to the behavior of a government to its own citizens.[112] In

---

108   Von Dardel v USSR, 623 F Supp 246, 253–59 (D DC 1985), vacated on other grounds, 736 F Supp 1 (D DC 1990). See also Forti v Suarez-Mason, 672 F Supp 1531, 1540 (ND Cal 1987), further order, 694 F Supp 707 (N.D. Cal. 1988). On non-commercial torts, see 28 USC § 1605(a)(5); Joseph W Dellapenna, Suing Foreign States and Their Corporations (2nd ed, BNA Books 2003) ('Dellapenna, Suing Foreign States and Their Corporations') §§ 7.25 to 7.29.

109   28 USC § 1605(a)(3). See Dellapenna, Suing Foreign States and Their Corporations (n 108) § 7.19. For cases applying customary international law in this context, see e.g Austria v Altmann, 541 US 677 (2004); Cassirer v Spain, 616 F3d 1019, 1034–1037 (9th Cir 2010), cert denied, 131 S Ct 1057 (2011); Agudas Chasidel Chabad of US v Russian Fed., 528 F3d 934, 943–946 (DC Cir 2008); Siderman de Blake v Argentina, 965 F2d 699, 711–12 (9th Cir 1992), cert denied, 507 US 1017 (1993); West v Multibanco Comermex, SA, 807 F2d 820, 831–832 (9th Cir), cert denied, 482 US 906 (1987). But see McKesson Corp. v Iran, 672 F3d 1066, 1075–1078 (DC Cir 2012) (applying customary international law to find that it did not apply), cert denied, 133 S Ct 1582 (2013).

110   See eg, Frolova v USSR, 761 F2d 370 (7th Cir 1985); Tel-Oren v Libya, 726 F2d 774 (DC Cir), cert denied, 469 US 811 (1984); Wyle v Bank Melli, 577 F Supp 1148, 1163–64 (ND Cal 1983). But see Mortimer Off Shore Services, Ltd. v German Fed. Rep., 615 F3d 97, 109–10 (2d Cir 2010).

111   See eg, Certain Underwriters at Lloyd's, London v Libya, 811 F Supp 2d 53, 72 (D DC. 2011) (considering the terrorism exception to immunity); de Csepel v Hungary, 808 F Supp 2d 113, 143 (D DC 2011) (considering the expropriation exception to immunity), rev'd on other grounds, 714 F3d 591 (DC Cir 2013).

112   For the traditional rule, see: Dreyfus v von Finck, 534 F2d 24, 31 (2nd Cir), cert denied, 429 US 835 (1976); Tablaclera Severiano Jorge, SA v Standard Cigar Co., 392 F2d 706 (5th Cir) cert denied, 393 US 924 (1968); Pons v Cuba, 294 F2d 925, 926 (DC Cir 1961), cert denied 368 US 960 (1962); Jafari v Iran, 539 F Supp 209, 215 (ND Ill. 1982); Present v US Life Ins. Co., 232 A.2d 863, 873 (NJ Super 1967). A variation on this old notion is the idea that international environmental law does not apply to intra-national pollution that violates only the rights of the citizens of the country where the pollution occurs. Flores v Southern Peru Copper Corp., 414 F3d 233 (2d Cir 2003).

the first case, *Morel de Letelier v. Chile*,[113] Judge Joyce Hens Green invoked customary international law to conclude that the acts of Chile were clearly illegal, and therefore not within the discretionary function exception to the withdrawal of immunity for non-commercial torts. This can be dismissed as a rather vague and hesitant reliance on customary international law, which Green ignored when she reached the merits of the claim. The murders took place in the District of Columbia, and thus its laws could be, and were, easily applied as the rule of decision.[114] Judge Green herself even appears to have repudiated whatever use she made of customary international law in the *Morel de Letelier* case barely a year later.[115]

While Judge Green's opinion recognized some role for international law under the Immunities Act, just what role she envisaged for international law was not at all clear. The second 1980 decision seemed much clearer, but it did not involve a foreign state or an agency or instrumentality. In *Filártiga v. Pena-Irala*[116] the defendant had been Inspector General of Police in Asuncion, Paraguay. Plaintiffs alleged that the defendant was responsible for the torture-murder of a seventeen-year-old boy. The father and the sister of the boy brought suit under the Alien Tort Statute when they found Pena in Brooklyn after he overstayed his visitor's visa.[117] One could hardly have designed a more sympathy evoking set of facts for upholding the court's competence and finding liability, and yet the only possible bases of competence—the Alien Tort Statute and federal question competence[118]—both required a finding that there had been a violation of international law by Pena. Judge Eugene Nickerson dismissed the proceeding for lack of competence.[119]

The Court of Appeals for the Second Circuit reversed through a unanimous opinion from Judge Irving Kaufman that was praised by most commentators.[120]

---

113   488 F Supp 665, 673 (D DC 1980). See also Liu v Republic of China, 892 F2d 1419, 1431 (9th Cir 1989), cert denied, 497 US 1058 (1990); Persinger v Iran, 690 F2d 1010, 1017–19 (DC Cir 1982), op. withdrawn & replaced on other grounds, 729 F2d 835 (DC Cir), cert denied, 469 US 881 (1984). See generally Dellapenna, Suing Foreign States and Their Corporations (n 108) § 7.27.

114   Morel de Letelier, 502 F Supp 259, 266–267 (D DC 1980).

115   Tel-Oren v Libya, 517 F Supp 542, 545–550 (D DC 1981), aff'd, 726 F2d 774 (DC Cir), cert denied, 469 US 811 (1984).

116   630 F2d 876 (2nd Cir 1980).

117   *Ibid* 878–79. Peña-Irala was subsequently deported.

118   28 USC §§ 1331, 1350. Federal question competence could be sustained on the theory that international law is part of the federal common law. Filártiga v Peña-Irala (n 3) 886.

119   Filártiga v Peña-Irala (n 3) 879–80.

120   See eg, William d'Zurilla, 'Individual Responsibility for Torture under International Law' (1981) 56 Tul L Rev 186; James Paul George, 'Defining Filártiga: Characterizing International

Kaufman read the emerging concepts of international human rights law expansively, finding that the right to be free from official torture was violated.[121] While Kaufman used this conclusion to uphold the court's competence under the Alien Tort Statute, he was careful to avoid the question of whether Paraguayan law or international law would provide the rule of decision.[122] He hinted that neither the doctrine of *forum non conveniens* nor the Act of State doctrine would bar the suit.[123]

Judge Green, having relied on international law in deciding the immunity issue in *Morel de Letelier*, went on in *tel-Oren v. Libya*[124] to decide that the international law of human rights does not create a 'specific right to a private claim.' Because of this conclusion, she dismissed the case for lack of competence based on the Alien Tort Statute or on a federal question.[125] Her decision was affirmed *per curiam* by a unanimous panel, but the panel divided hopelessly over their reasons.[126] Judge Harry Edwards concluded that political terrorism was not a violation of international law,[127] and therefore the court was without competence based on either the Alien Tort Statute or on a federal question.[128] Judge Robert Bork concluded that political terrorism probably violated international law,[129] but that international law did not provide a private right of action except for those few situations in which a private right of action was possible in 1789—when the Alien Tort Statute was enacted.[130] Finally, Judge

---

Torture Claims in United States Courts' (1984) 3 Dick J Int'l L 1; 'Symposium, Filártiga v Pena-Irala' (1981) 11 Ga J Int'l & Comp L 307; Symposium, 'The Future of Human Rights in the World Order' (1981) 9 Hofstra L Rev 337.

121 Filártiga v Peña-Irala (n 3) 880–85. See also Abebe-Jira v Negewo, 72 F3d 844, 847–48 (11th Cir), cert denied, 519 US 830 (1996).

122 Filártiga v Peña-Irala (n 3) 887–90. Judge Kaufman concluded that the conduct in question was unlawful under Paraguayan law. Id. at 889–890. But see Abebe-Jira v Negewo, 72 F3d 844, 848 (11th Cir) (suits under the Alien Tort Claims Act are governed by federal common law fashioned to remedy violations of international law), cert denied, 519 US 830 (1996).

123 Filártiga v Peña-Irala (n 3) 889–90. See also Abebe-Jira v Negewo, 72 F3d 844, 848 (11th Cir), cert denied, 519 US 830 (1996).

124 517 F Supp 542, 549–50 (D DC 1981), aff'd, 726 F2d 774 (DC Cir 1984), cert denied, 469 US 811 (1985).

125 517 F Supp 548–49.

126 726 F2d 774 (DC Cir 1984), cert denied, 469 US 811 (1985).

127 726 F2d 795–96.

128 *Ibid* 777–96.

129 *Ibid* 805–08.

130 *Ibid* 801–20. See also Curtis Bradley, 'Customary International Law and Private Rights of Action' (2000) 1 Chi J Int'l L 421; Anthony D'Amato, 'What Does Tel-Oren Tell Lawyers?

Roger Robb concluded that the claim was not justiciable as a political question properly left to other branches of government to resolve.[131]

Perhaps a partial explanation of why American judges are wary of embracing customary international law as the rule of decision under the Immunities Act may be found in the risk that this will require them to examine and possibly apply a body of customary international law termed 'cogent rules,' 'peremptory norms,' or *jus cogens*.'[132] Peremptory norms remain a limited set of rules accepted by the international community relating to activities so universally condemned that the activities are never legal; the rules are so basic and express such fundamental values that a state cannot deviate from the norm except when authorized by another rule of general international law also having a peremptory character.[133] While this is an apparent contradiction to the usual understanding of what constitutes customary international law, such norms emerged in the second half of the twentieth century as a response to the egregious crimes against peace and crimes against humanity in World War II and thereafter, occuring with distressing frequency.[134] Examples include genocide, slavery, murder, torture, prolonged arbitrary detention, and racial discrimination, at

---

Judge Bork's Concept of the Law of Nations Is Seriously Mistaken' (1985) 79 Am J Int'l L 92; Harold Hungdah Koh, 'Transnational Public Law Litigation' (1991) 100 Yale LJ 2347, 2382–86; Kenneth Randall, 'Federal Questions and the Human Rights Paradigm' (1988) 73 Minn L Rev 349, 397–99; Joseph Modeste Sweeney, 'A Tort only in Violation of the Law of Nations' (1995) 18 Hastings Int'l & Comp L Rev 445.

131 Tel-Oren, 726 F2d 823–27.
132 See eg, Rosenberg v Lashkar-e-Taiba, 980 F Supp 2d 336, 343–44 (EDNY 2013); Devi v Silva, 861 F Supp 2d 135, 142 (SDNY 2012).
133 Vienna Convention on the Law of Treaties (adopted 22 May 1969, entered into force 27 January 1980) 1155 UNTS 331, arts 53, 64; The Barcelona Traction Co. (Belgium v Spain) [1970] ICJ Rep 3, 32; Restatement (Third) (n 54) § 102 comment k. See also Alvarez-Machain v United States, 331 F3d 604, 612–14 (9th Cir 2003), rev'd on other grounds, 542 US 692 (2004); Princz v Germany, 26 F3d 1166, 1173 (DC Cir 1994), cert denied, 513 US 1121 (1995); Siderman de Blake v Argentina, 965 F2d 699, 714–15 (9th Cir 1992), cert denied, 507 US 1017 (1993); Committee of US Citizens Living in Nicaragua v Reagan, 859 F2d 929, 940 (DC Cir 1988); In re World War II Era Japanese Forced Labor Litigation, 164 F Supp 2d 1160, 1168–69 (N.D. Cal.2001), rev'd on other grounds sub nom. Deutsch v Turner Corp., 324 F3d 682 (9th Cir), cert denied sub nom Tenney v Mitsui & Co., 540 US 820 (2003).
134 Steven Fogelson, 'Note, The Nuremburg Legacy: An Unfulfilled Promise' (1990) 63 S Cal L. Rev 833. On whether the 'new' customary international law actually is different from 'traditional' customary international law, see Fernando Téson, *A Philosophy of International Law* (Westview Press 1998); Jack Goldsmith & Eric Posner, 'Understanding the Resemblance between Modern and Traditional Customary International Law' (2000) 40 Va J Int'l L 639.

least when these are performed by or under the responsibility of a state.[135] What quickly becomes striking in researching peremptory norms is that the concept, so widely supported in judicial *dicta*, international agreements, and the writings of legal scholars has found so little application in state practice.'[136] Some American courts seem to have applied instead the law of the state in which the court sits to such claims rather than international law.[137] Several

---

135   Military & Paramilitary Activities in Nicaragua (Nicaragua v United States) [1986] ICJ Rep 14, 100–01; Hostages in Tehran (United States v Iran) [1980] ICJ Rep 3; Advisory Opinion on Reservations to the Convention of Genocide [1951] ICJ Rep 15, 21, 24, 29–30. For applications by American courts, see Beanal v Freeport-McMoran, Inc., 197 F3d 161, 165–69 (5th Cir 1999); United States v Matta-Ballesteros, 71 F3d 754, 763–65 (9th Cir), amended, 98 F3d 1100 (9th Cir 1996), cert denied, 519 US 1118 (1997); Kadic v Karadzic, 70 F3d 232, 244–46 (2nd Cir 1995), rehearing denied with op, 74 F3d 377 (2nd Cir), cert denied, 518 US 1005 (1996); Trajano v Marcos, 978 F2d 493, 498–500 (9th Cir 1992), cert denied sub nom Marcos-Manotoc v Trajano, 508 US 972 (1993), further appeal sub nom In re Estate of Marcos Human Rts. Litigation, 25 F3d 1467 (9th Cir 1994), cert denied sub nom Estate of Marcos v Hilao, 513 US 1126 (1995), injunction dissolved after remand sub nom In re Estate of Marcos Human Rts. Litigation, 94 F3d 539 (9th Cir), judgment for damages aff'd, 103 F3d 767 (9th Cir 1996), amended judgment aff'd sub nom. Sison v Estate of Marcos, 165 F3d 36 (9th Cir 1998); Siderman de Blake v Argentina, 965 F2d 699, 716–17 (9th Cir 1992), cert denied, 507 US 1017 (1993); Committee of US Citizens Living in Nicaragua v Reagan, 859 F2d 929, 941 (DC Cir 1988); tel-Oren v Libya, 726 F2d 774, 781 (DC Cir) (Edwards, J., concurring), cert denied, 469 US 811 (1984); Filártiga v Peña-Irala (n 3). See also Regina v Bartle ex parte Pinochet [1998] 4 All ER 897 (H.L.), reprinted in (1998) 37 ILM 1302, [1999] 2 All ER 97 (HL), reprinted in (1999) 38 ILM 581. See generally Peter Baehr, *Human Rights: Universality in Practice* (Palgrave Macmillan 2002); Steven Ratner & Jason Abrams, *Accountability for Human Rights Atrocities in International Law: Beyond the Nuremberg Legacy* (Oxford University Press 1977); Restatement (Third) (n 54) §§ 404, 702; Hurst Hannum, 'The Status of the Universal Declaration of Human Rights in National and International Law' (1996) 25 Ga J Int'l L 287; 'Symposium, The International Criminal Court: Consensus and Debate on the International Adjudication of Genocide, Crimes against Humanity, War Crimes, and Aggression' (1999) 32 Cornell Int'l LJ 431. For intensive critiques of these theories, see Tony Evans (ed), *Human Rights Fifty Years on: A Reappraisal* (Manchester University Press 1998); J Shand Watson, *Theory and Reality in the International Protection of Human Rights* (Transnational Publishers 1999); Curtis Bradley & Jack Goldsmith, 'Pinochet and International Human Rights Litigation' (1999) 97 Mich L Rev 2129; Ulf Linderfalk, 'The Effect of Jus Cogens Norms: Whoever Opened Pandora's Box, Did You Ever Think of the Consequences?' (2007) 18 Eur J Int'l L 853.

136   Ian Sinclair, *The Vienna Convention on the Law of Treaties* 18 (2nd ed, Manchester University Press 1984). See eg, Devi v Silva, 861 F Supp 2d 135, 142 (SDNY 2012) (finding that jus cogens did not apply).

137   Liu v Republic of China, 892 F2d 1419, 1428–30 (9th Cir), cert denied, 497 US 1058 (1990); Flatow v Iran, 999 F Supp 1, 18 (D DC 1998), execution refused, 67 F Supp 2d 535 (D. Md. 1999), aff'd mem. sub nom Flatow v Alavi Fndtn., 225 F3d 653 (4th Cir 2000).

American courts have avoided taking a position on this question by simply applying the Torture Victim Protection Act of 1991,[138] which prohibits most of these international crimes and arguably provides the rule of decision even without recourse to customary international law.[139]

Where all this leaves customary international law as a possible rule of decision in litigation under the Immunities Act or otherwise is not clear. If customary international law is part of federal law, it must be applied as the rule of decision in place of any other arguably relevant rule of law unless displaced by some other rule of federal law.[140] These cases unquestionably involve a federal interest in controlling external relations, and are inappropriate for application of idiosyncratic notions drawn from the laws of various states, either of the United States or of the world community. The uncertainty of the four judges who passed on the *tel-Oren* claims highlights the widespread confusion and doubt about the content of customary international law—especially the international law of human rights.[141] This uncertainty and its potential to result in confusion is by itself enough to suggest that American courts will be cautious in applying customary international law.[142] And it is settled law that customary international law cannot override a contrary federal statute.[143]

---

138   28 USC § 1350 note, § 2.
139   Beanal v Freeport-McMoran, Inc., 197 F3d 161, 165–66 (5th Cir 1999); Abebe-Jira v Negewo, 72 F3d 844, 848 (11th Cir), cert denied, 519 US 830 (1996); Kadic v Karadzic, 70 F3d 232, 243–244 (2nd Cir 1995), rehearing denied with op., 74 F3d 377 (2nd Cir), cert denied, 518 US 1005 (1996); Trajano v Marcos, 978 F2d 493, 500 n.18 (9th Cir 1992), cert denied sub nom. Marcos-Manotoc v Trajano, 508 US 972 (1993), further appeal sub nom In re Estate of Marcos Human Rts. Litigation, 25 F3d 1467 (9th Cir 1994), cert denied sub nom Estate of Marcos v Hilao, 513 US 1126 (1995), injunction dissolved after remand sub nom In re Estate of Marcos Human Rts. Litigation, 94 F3d 539 (9th Cir), judgment for damages aff'd, 103 F3d 767 (9th Cir 1996), amended judgment aff'd sub nom Sison v Estate of Marcos, 165 F3d 36 (9th Cir 1998). See generally Russell Weintraub, 'Establishing Incredible Events by Credible Evidence: Civil Suits for Atrocities that Violate International Law' (1996) 62 Brook L Rev 753, 767–70.
140   See Dellapenna, Suing Foreign States and Their Corporations (n 108) § 8.7.
141   See generally Restatement (Third) (n 54) §§ 701 to 722. Also consider the differing views on the legality and standards of review for expropriations of property: Banco Nacional de Cuba v Sabbatino, 376 US 398, 426–37 (1964); Restatement (Third), *supra*, § 712.
142   Sosa v Alvarez-Machain, 542 US 692, 725 (2004); Mamani v Berzain, 654 F3d 1148, 1155 n.9 (11th Cir 2011); Serra v Lapin, 600 F3d 1191, 1196–97 (9th Cir 2010); Garcia v Chapman, 911 F Supp 2d 1222, 1233 (SD Fla 2012); Commissioner of Correction v Coleman, 38 A3d 84, 108–12 (Conn 2012).
143   See eg, TMR Energy Ltd. v State Property Fund of Ukraine, 411 F3d 296, 302 (DC Cir 2005); Wang v Ashcroft, 320 F3d 130, 142 n18 (2nd Cir 2003). One court has held, however, that

Even granting that US courts are to apply customary and other international law accepted by the United States, or perhaps by a clear consensus of nations, many cases would have to be decided to develop precise contours for this law.[144] Confronted with this daunting prospect, and the tradition of deference to executive prerogatives in the conduct of foreign relations,[145] courts anomalously held that basing competence on an allegation of a violation of international law does not require the court to apply international law as the rule of decision.[146] Nor is the desire to find a 'neutral body of law' likely lead a court to apply international law, customary or otherwise.[147] Instead, a bare

---

Congress cannot extend customary international law by statute. United States v Bellaizac-Hurtado, 700 F3d 1245 (11th Cir 2012).

[144] Looking to consensus appears to be the thrust of the more recent cases. Banco Nacional de Cuba v Sabbatino, 387 US 398, 426–37 (1964); Filártiga v Peña-Irala (n 3) 881–84; Dreyfus v von Finck, 534 F2d 24, 30–31 (2nd Cir), cert denied, 429 US 835 (1976); Centre for the Independence of Judges v Mabey, 19 Bankr 635, 646–648 (D. Utah 1982); tel-Oren v Libya, 517 F Supp 542, 545–50 (D DC 1981), aff'd, 726 F2d 774 (DC Cir), cert denied, 469 US 811 (1984). See also Restatement (Third) (n 54) §§ 101 to 103, 132. On the primacy of US view on international law in US courts, see Restatement (Third), *supra*, §§ 1(a); 135.

[145] American Ins. Assoc. v Garamendi, 539 US 396 (2003); Mexico v Hoffman, 324 US 30 (1945); Ex parte Peru, 318 US 578 (1943); United States v Pink, 315 US 203 (1942); United States v Belmont, 301 US 324 (1937); United States v Curtiss-Wright Export Corp., 299 US 304 (1936); Konowaloff v Metropolitan Museum of Art, 702 F3d 140, 145–46 (2d Cir), cert denied, 133 S. Ct. 2837 (2013); el-Shifa Pharmaceutical Indus. Co. v United States, 607 F3d 836 (DC Cir 2010), cert denied, 131 S Ct 997 (2011); In re Assicurazioni Generali, SpA, 592 F3d 113, 117–19 (2nd Cir), cert denied, 131 S Ct 698 (2010); Gonzalez-Vera v Kissinger, 449 F3d 1260 (DC Cir 2006), cert denied, 549 US 1206 (2007); Hwang Geum Joo v Japan, 413 F3d 45 (DC Cir 2005), cert denied, 546 US 1208 (2008); Ye v Zemin, 383 F3d 620 (7th Cir 2004) (holding that the presidential determination of who is entitled to head-of-state immunity is binding on the courts), cert denied, 544 US 975 (2005). See generally Lewis S. Yelin, 'Head of State Immunity as Sole Executive Lawmaking' (2011) 44 Vand J Transnat'l L 911; Andrew T Winkler, 'The International Zone of Twilight: Enforcing Customary International Law by Executive Order' (2014) 31 Wis Int'l LJ 854.

[146] For a persuasive argument that this anomaly requires the court to apply international law as the rule of decision under the Alien Tort Statute, see Jeffrey Hadley Louden, 'Note, The Domestic Application of international Human Rights Law: Evolving the Policies' (1981) 5 Hastings Int'l & Comp L Rev 161 ('Louden, Note, The Domestic Application of international Human Rights Law: Evolving the Policies'), 181–89. In Huynh Thi Anh v Levy, 586 F2d 625, 630 (6th Cir 1978), the court suggested that the failure to apply international law as the rule of decision should oust the court of its competence under the Alien Tort Statute.

[147] Louden, 'Note, The Domestic Application of international Human Rights Law: Evolving the Policies' (n 146) 185–89.

majority of the Supreme Court of the United States seems intent on giving the most restrictive reading possible to the scope and effect of international law when it would enable litigation before an American court, whether in the form of treaties[148] or as international customary law.[149] The Supreme Court and lower American courts have, however, embraced customary international if it would serve to preclude litigation before American courts.[150] There is considerable debate in the law reviews over the virtues of this practice and the related executive policies of turning away from customary international law.[151]

---

148   See eg, United States v Alvarez-Machain, 504 US 655 (1992) (holding that the existence of an extradition treaty between Mexico and the United States does not preclude the kidnapping of a suspect as an alternative to extradition because kidnapping is not expressly excluded); Gross v German Found. Indus. Initiative, 549 F Supp 2d 605 (3rd Cir 2008) (construing the U.S.-German joint statement creating the foundation as not authorizing private rights of action), cert denied, 556 US 1236 (2009); Cornejo v San Diego Cty., 504 F3d 853 (9th Cir 2007) (construing the Vienna Convention on Consular Relations as not creating private rights of action); Natural Resources Defense Council v Environmental Prot. Agency, 464 F3d 1 (DC Cir 2006) (holding that the Montreal Protocol is not 'law' for the United States). But see Jogi v Voges, 480 F3d 822, 831–35 (7th Cir 2005) (construing the Vienna Convention on Consular Relations as creating private rights of action).

149   See eg, Sosa v Alvarez-Machain, 542 US 692, 725 (2004) (allowing the application of customary international law under the Alien Tort Statute only if the proposed cause of action 'rest on a norm of international character accepted by the civilized world and defined with a specificity comparable to the features of the 18th-century paradigms [that the Supreme Court has] recognized'). See also Hamdan v United States, 696 F3d 1238, 1250–52 (DC Cir 2012) (concluding that providing material support for terrorism is not an international crime); Velez v Sanchez, 693 F3d 308, 315–24 (2d Cir 2012) (holding that the degree of exploitation of the plaintiff's labor did not amount to slavery or other violations of customary international law); Flomo v Firestone Nat. Rubber Co., 643 F3d 1013 (7th Cir 2011) (same); People v Myles, 274 P.3d 413, 445–46 (declining to determine whether defendant's trial violated standards for a fair trial as found in customary international law), cert denied, 133 S. Ct. 256 (2012).

150   See Habyarimana v Kagame, 696 F3d 1029 (10th Cir 2012) (applying the customary international law of head-of-state immunity to bar the suit), cert denied, 133 S. Ct. 1607 (2013); Doe v Roman Catholic Diocese of Galveston-Houston, 408 F Supp 2d 272 (S.D. Tex. 2005) (same).

151   See David J Bederman, 'Acquiescence, Objection and the Death of Customary International Law' (2010) 21 Duke J Comp & Int'l L 31; Curtis Bradley & Mitu Gulati, 'Withdrawing from International Custom' (2010) 120 Yale LJ 202; Rachel Brewster, 'Withdrawing from International Custom: Choosing between Default Rules' (2010) 21 Duke J Comp & Int'l L 47; William S Dodge, 'After Sosa: The Future of Customary International Law in the United States' (2009) 17 Willamette J Int'l L & Disp Resol 21; Paul R Dubinsky, 'International Law in the Legal System of the United States' (2010) 58 Am J Comp L 455; Halabi, The

4 Conclusion

With strong voices on the Supreme Court and in Congress increasingly against the globalization of American law, the barriers to litigation involving international human rights claims are actually growing.[152] In light of this reality, customary international law will probably remain more of an unrealized possibility lurking in the background rather than a real presence on the choice-of-law scene. Just like the constitutional limits on choice of law,[153] American courts are only likely to apply customary international law erratically and without much predictability rather than as a coherent and comprehensive source of rules of decision in human rights cases or most any other kind of case.[154] American courts will continue to resort to customary international law as an alternative ground for decisions also based on the application of the forum's or a plaintiff-favoring law.[155] In such decisions, resort to customary international

---

Supremacy Clause as a Structural Safeguard of Federalism: State Judges and International Law in the Post-Erie Era (n 6); Joseph Keller, 'Sovereignty vs. Internationalism and Where the United States Should Find International Law' (2005) 24 Penn State Int'l L Rev 353; Donald J Kochan, 'The Political Economy of the Production of Customary International Law: The Role of Non-Governmental Organizations in US Courts' (2004) 22 Berkeley J Int'l L 240; Chin Leng Lim & Olufemi Elias, 'Withdrawing from Custom and the Paradox of Consensualism in Customary International Law' (2010) 21 Duke J Comp & Int'l L. 143; John O McGinnis & Ilya Somin, 'Should International Law Be Part of Our Law?' (2007) 59 Stan L Rev 1175; Gwynne Skinner, 'Customary International Law, Federal Common Law, and Federal Court Jurisdiction' (2010) 44 Val UL Rev 825; Carlos Vazquez, 'Withdrawing from International Custom: Terrible Food, Small Portions' (2011) 120 Yale LJ 269; Penny M Venetis, 'The Broad Jurisprudential Significance of Sosa v Álvarez-Machain: An Honest Assessment of the Role of Federal Judges and Why Customary International Law Can Be More Effective Than Constitutional Law for Redressing Serious Abuses' (2011) 21 Temp Pol & Civ Rts L Rev 41.

152 See notes 4 and 5, *supra*.
153 See Roberts, *supra* note 89, at 26.
154 See eg, Institute of Cetacean Research v Sea Shepard Conservation Soc., 725 F3d 940, 947 (9th Cir 2013) (applying customary international law to decide that piracy is a crime, but otherwise ignoring that body of law).
155 See eg, First Nat'l City Bank v BANCEC, 462 US 611, 622–23, 626–28, 633–34 (1983) Asociacion de Reclamantes v Mexico, 735 F2d 1517, 1522–24 (DC Cir 1984); cert denied, 470 US 1051 (1985); Persinger v Iran, 690 F2d 1010, 1017–19 (DC Cir 1982), op. withdrawn & replaced on other grounds, 729 F2d 835 (DC Cir), cert denied, 469 US 881 (1984); M.C. v Bianchi, 782 F Supp 2d 127, 130–32 (ED Pa 2011). For a case that seems actually to have applied customary international law as the rule of decision, see Banco Nacional de Cuba v Chase Manhattan Bank, 658 F2d 875, 887–94 (2nd Cir 1981).

law might only be a makeweight for the decision not to apply the foreign state's law, rather than an independent basis of decision. Yet as several courts have suggested that even if customary international law is not an independent basis for decisions on the merits, it can be a persuasive guide to interpreting other possible rules of decision.[156]

---

[156] See eg, Ozaltin v Ozaltin, 708 F3d 355, 358 n.4 (2d Cir 2013); Aquamar SA v Del Monte Fresh Produce NA, Inc., 179 F3d 1279, 1294–95 (11th Cir 1999).

CHAPTER 30

Human Rights Treaties in and beyond the Senate: The Spirit of Senator Proxmire

Jean Galbraith

The second time I met Roger Clark, he stood on a chair and sang *Waltzing Matilda*. The occasion was a party celebrating Roger's forty years of teaching at Rutgers-Camden. As the toasts that evening made clear, Roger had become an institution within Rutgers. Everyone knew his hearty New Zealand accent, tracked his running, noted his love of music so pluralist that it included the unofficial Australian anthem, and, above all, acknowledged his devotion to the moral imperatives that underlie international humanitarian and human rights law.

In tribute to Roger, this essay explores issues related to the ratification of human rights treaties in the United States. For supporters, the picture at first is a bleak one. In 1995, Louis Henkin wrote a famous piece in which he suggested that the process of human rights treaty ratification was haunted by 'the ghost of Senator Bricker'—the isolationist Senator who in the 1950s had waged a fierce assault on the treaty power, especially with regard to human rights treaties.[1] Since that time, Senator Bricker's ghost has proved even more real. Professor Henkin's concern was with *how* the United States ratified human rights treaties—with the packet of reservations, declarations, and understandings ('RUDs') attached by the Senate in giving its advice and consent. Today, the question is not *how* but *whether*. It is now twenty years since the United States ratified a major human rights treaty.

Yet one common theme that arches across U.S. foreign relations law is the power of the dialectic. 'A Hamilton may be matched against a Madison;'[2] 'Professor Taft is counterbalanced by Theodore Roosevelt;'[3] and the great Supreme Court decisions of *Youngstown* and *Curtiss-Wright* stand in tension with one another.[4] So too in the Senate. The ghost of Senator Bricker may be on the prowl. But opposing him is the spirit of the Senator Proxmire, the late

---

1   Louis Henkin, 'Editorial Comment, U.S. Ratification of Human Rights Conventions: The Ghost of Senator Bricker' (1995) 89 AJIL 341 ('Henkin, 'Editorial Comment, U.S. Ratification of Human Rights Conventions'') 341.
2   *Youngstown Sheet & Tube Co. v. Sawyer* 343 U.S. 579, 635 n1 (1952) (Jackson, J, concurring).
3   *Ibid* (adding that '[i]t even seems that President Taft cancels out Professor Taft').
4   Harold Hongju Koh, 'Why the President (Almost) Always Wins in Foreign Affairs: Lessons of the Iran-Contra Affair' (1988) 97 Yale LJ 1255, 1306–09.

internationalist who for many years led a lonely campaign to keep the Genocide Convention on the Senate's agenda. His spirit is one with whom Roger would enjoy a conversation.[5] For unlike Senator Bricker, Senator Proxmire believed that the United States should be responsive to international human rights norms. His tenacity ultimately helped lead to the ratification of the Genocide Convention, thirty-nine years after President Truman had signed it.

The spirit of Senator Proxmire embodies two trends in relation to unratified human rights treaties. The first is simply that efforts towards Senate advice and consent for at least some of these treaties persist and persist. While no Senator today can match Senator Proxmire's tenacity, the treaties' supporters keep on trying. The second trend—less direct, but even more interesting—is that unratified human rights treaties are nonetheless influencing the shape of law in the United States. As scholars have documented, these treaties are affecting administrative action, state and local legislation, and judicial interpretation. The most high-profile example is the Supreme Court's citation to unratified human rights treaties in the course of constitutional interpretation. In essence, these uses of unratified human rights treaties are advancing Senator Proxmire's goal of having the United States be responsive to human rights norms, although not doing so through his preferred means of treaty ratification.

There is an intriguing parallel between how isolationists and internationalists have used what might be considered second-best legal tools in order to pursue their goals. Just as Senator Bricker did not achieve a constitutional amendment limiting the treaty power but his spiritual descendants used RUDs to similar effect, so advocates of human rights treaties are failing to achieve their ratification yet making them count in other ways. In both cases, opponents have cried foul. Professor Henkin viewed the use of certain RUDs as bordering on unconstitutional, and those wary of international influences view uses of unratified human rights treaties as inappropriate dodges around the constitutional process for treaty advice and consent. But in both cases, the practice has embraced half-measures.

1   Human Rights Treaties in the Senate from 1995 to 2014

In the early 1990s, the United States seemed on the cusp of abandoning its longstanding aloofness to human rights treaties. In 1992, the United States

---

5   For an example of Roger's fondness for conversation with friendly ghosts, see Roger S Clark, 'The International Criminal Law System' (2010) 8 NZJ Publ Int'l L 27 ('Clark, 'The International Criminal Law System'') 27.

ratified the International Covenant on Civil and Political Rights ('ICCPR') and in 1994 it ratified the Convention on the Elimination of All Forms of Racial Discrimination ('CERD') and the Convention against Torture ('CAT'). Writing in 1995, Professor Henkin observed that ratification of the Convention on the Elimination of All Forms of Discrimination against Women ('CEDAW') was 'expected in 1995' and added that the United States 'might adhere to several [other human rights treaties] before long.'[6]

Professor Henkin's predictions were overly optimistic. CEDAW did not receive ratification in 1995 and nor has any major human rights treaty since. CEDAW remains formally before the Senate, as do the American Convention on Human Rights and the International Covenant on Economic, Social and Cultural Rights ('ICESCR').[7] In addition, in 2012 the Obama Administration transmitted the Convention on the Rights of Persons with Disabilities ('CRPD') to the Senate. But since 1994, the only Senate resolutions of advice and consent on human rights treaties have involved treaties dealing with discrete issues of children's rights. Thus, in 2002, the Senate advised and consented to the first two optional protocols to the Convention on the Rights of the Child, one of which deals with children in armed conflict and the other of which deals with the sexual exploitation of children.[8] (As to the actual Convention on the Rights of the Child, the United States signed it in 1995, but to date the President has not transmitted it to the Senate for advice and consent.)

Three things are particularly notable about the failure of human rights treaties to make it through the Senate. First, this failure comes despite the willingness of supporters of these treaties to accept RUDs that limit the treaties'

---

6 Henkin, 'Editorial Comment, U.S. Ratification of Human Rights Conventions' (n 1) 341. The process by which the United States joins international agreements varies depending on what constitutional process the United States considers appropriate and on whether signature/ratification/accession is called for under international law. For purposes of this essay, I focus on the approach employed to date in the context of human rights treaties. This is that the President signs the treaty; the President then transmits the treaty to the Senate for advice and consent; the Senate advises and consents, implementing legislation is passed if deemed necessary (although this could theoretically happen after ratification as well), and then the President ratifies the treaty on behalf of the United States. There is no certainty that a treaty will progress from any one step to the next step.

7 This information, as well as information about other pending treaties before the Senate, can be found on the THOMAS Treaties database maintained by the Library of Congress, at <http://thomas.loc.gov/home/treaties/treaties.html> accessed 11 June 2014.

8 148 Cong Rec. 10683–85 (18 June 2002). Since 1995, the Senate has also advised and consented to a number of treaties that, though classified as belonging to areas like arms control, labor, organized crime, and private international law, nonetheless have human rights dimensions.

practical effects. Second, this failure is part of a broader trend in treaty non-ratification, although the trend is particularly strong with regard to human rights treaties. And third, despite everything, some human rights treaties remain meaningfully, not simply formally, on the Senate's agenda.

During the advice and consent process for human rights treaties in the early 1990s, there was debate over how willing supporters of human rights treaties should be to accept RUDs in order to get the treaties through the Senate. Scholars raised concerns about the validity of some of these RUDs under international and U.S. constitutional law.[9] Ultimately, however, the treaties approved in the early 1990s came with significant RUDs. As Curtis Bradley and Jack Goldsmith have argued, these RUDs 'helped break the logjam in domestic politics that had prevented U.S. ratification of any of the major human rights treaties.'[10]

Today, the inclusion of RUDs for the ratification of any human rights treaties seems a given, although the executive branch may push back on the addition of specific RUDs. Yet despite this, even the human rights treaties with the most support—CEDAW and the CRPD—have not received advice and consent. Following hearings on CRPD in late 2013, for example, the ranking Republican member on the Senate Foreign Relations Committee announced that he could not support it, saying that he was 'uncertain that even the strongest RUDs would stand the test of time.'[11]

The failure of human rights treaties to make it through the Senate is part of a broader trend. Since the 1994 election cycle, the slightest whiff of controversy has usually been enough to doom a treaty. In the decade from 2000 through 2010, for example, only one treaty received the Senate's advice and consent where there were any recorded 'no' votes.[12] Part of this is due to the stiffness of the two-thirds requirement, and part of it is due to the procedural difficulties of getting to a floor vote.[13] Where disputed treaties have made it through the Senate, it has

---

9   See Curtis A Bradley & Jack L Goldsmith, 'Treaties, Human Rights, and Conditional Consent' (2000) 149 U Pa L Rev 399 ('Bradley & Goldsmith, 'Treaties, Human Rights, and Conditional Consent") 401 note 4 (citing sources).

10   Ibid 459.

11   'Corker: Advocating for U.S. Disabilities Rights Abroad Should Not Come at the Expense of the Constitution' (Press Release 20 December 2013) <http://www.corker.senate.gov/public/index.cfm/2013/12/corker-advocating-for-u-s-disability-rights-abroad-should-not-come-at-the-expense-of-the-constitution> accessed 11 June 2014.

12   This was the New START Treaty. Jean Galbraith, 'Prospective Advice and Consent' (2012) 37 Yale J Int'l L 247, 287.

13   Ibid 296. For a discussion and explanation of how the procedural hurdles to treaty ratification are higher in the United States than in most other countries in the world, see Oona

been because of deep engagement by the executive branch from the President down, as with the New START Treaty under the Obama Administration and earlier with the Chemical Weapons Convention under President Clinton. This engagement has not seemed as powerful in the human rights context.

The ghost of Senator Bricker would doubtless applaud these developments. The particular legal mechanism most called for by Senator Bricker in the early 1950s, when he served in the Senate as a Republican from Ohio, was a constitutional amendment that would have limited the extent to which treaties could deal with issues outside of Congress's powers under Article I of the Constitution and the extent to which treaties could be self-executing.[14] Senator Bricker was unsuccessful in getting such an amendment through the Senate, let alone any further. But, as Professor Henkin observed in his famous essay, Senator Bricker would likely have approved of the inclusion of RUDs regarding federalism and non-self-execution, as these effectively reach his desired result with regard to the particular treaties to which they are attached.[15]

Even more to the point, Senator Bricker would doubtless have rejoiced at the fact that human rights treaties are now not getting ratified at all. Senator Bricker's push for a constitutional amendment came largely out of an isolationist desire that the United States not ratify human rights treaties—a desire expressed at a time when those who favored racial integration saw human rights treaties as a means of ending segregation. Bricker indicated that 'the rights of the individual constitute a subject essentially within the domestic jurisdiction of his country.'[16] While he expressed a wish for the United States to 'play a leading part in advancing the cause of human rights all over the world,' he did not want any international influence on rights within the United States.[17] Ultimately, Bricker won a commitment from the Eisenhower Administration that it would promote human rights through 'persuasion, education, and example rather than formal undertakings' and would not seek to join human rights treaties.[18] The failure of the United States since 1995 to ratify any human

---

Hathaway, 'Treaties' End: The Past, Present, and Future of International Lawmaking in the United States' (2008) 117 Yale L J 1238, 1271–74.

[14] For a discussion of the various variants of the Bricker Amendment, and of the relative perspectives of Senator Bricker and his allies in the American Bar Association, see Rowland Brucken, *A Most Uncertain Crusade: The United States, the United Nations, and Human Rights 1941–1953* (NIU Press 2014) 214–53.

[15] Henkin, 'Editorial Comment, U.S. Ratification of Human Rights Conventions' (n 1) 349.

[16] 97 Cong Rec 11512 (18 September 1951).

[17] 97 Cong Rec 11514 (18 September 1951).

[18] Treaties and Executive Agreements: Hearings Before a Subcommittee on the Judiciary, 83rd Congr 825 (1953) (statement of Secretary of State Dulles).

rights treaties is in keeping with Bricker's philosophy that while the United States may promote human rights abroad, it should treat them as strictly domestic issues at home.

But there is a third piece to the experience of human rights treaties in the Senate since 1995. This is that there continues to be active pursuit of advice and consent of at least some of these treaties. While ICESCR and the American Convention have not received serious consideration since the Carter Administration, both CEDAW and CRPD have substantial support in the Senate.[19] In 2002, the Senate Foreign Relations Committee voted CEDAW forward to the full Senate, although it never received a floor vote, and in 2010 it was the subject of a hearing by the Senate Judiciary Committee's Subcommittee on Human Rights and the Law. In 2012, the Senate Foreign Relations Committee voted CRPD forward to a full Senate and it did receive a floor vote, although with a 61-38 vote it fell short of receiving the necessary two-thirds for advice and consent. The Committee held hearings again on CRPD in November 2013, although opposition from the ranking Republican on the Committee signaled that it would not go forward further in that session. It is unclear whether these treaties will ever get through the Senate, and CEDAW has now been before the Senate for thirty-four years since its transmission by the President in 1980. But its supporters continue to try.

2 Senator Proxmire and the Genocide Convention

The case of the unratified human rights treaties pending in the Senate might seem hopeless. Yet, the story of the Genocide Convention offers a powerful example otherwise.[20] The Genocide Convention was transmitted to the Senate in 1949, but it did not receive advice and consent until 1986—thirty-seven years later—and another two years would pass before the United States ratified it. Its ultimate approval owed much to Senator Proxmire, the Democrat from Wisconsin.

---

19   The details given below can mostly be found on the THOMAS Treaties database cited at n 6. See also Luisa Blanchfield, 'The U.N. Convention on the Elimination of All Forms of Discrimination Against Women (CEDAW): Issues in the U.S. Ratification Debate' (Congressional Research Services Report) (7 May 2013) 7–8, at <http://www.law.umaryland.edu/marshall/crsreports/crsdocuments/R40750_05072013.pdf> accessed 11 June 2014.

20   For a discussion of the provisions of the Genocide Convention, see Roger S Clark, 'State Obligations under the Genocide Convention in Light of the ICJ's Decision in the Case Concerning the Application of the Convention on the Prevention and Punishment of the Crime of Genocide' (2008) 61 Rutgers L Rev 75.

Senator Proxmire's views on human rights treaties were the antithesis of Senator Bricker's. To Senator Proxmire, '[t]he cause of human rights transcends national boundaries.'[21] He believed that as 'the foremost democratic nation in the world, the United States has a major role to play in promoting universal adherence to international law, based on concrete guarantees of freedom and justice.'[22] In his view, the U.S. failure to ratify human rights treaties was 'deplorable' and an 'embarrassment.'[23]

Beginning in 1967, Senator Proxmire took up the cause of the Genocide Convention in the Senate. His commitment was unswerving. As the Senate Majority leader, a Republican, admiringly observed in 1985:

> Senator Proxmire has set a record for persistence that may never be broken. *He has spoken on this subject every day the Senate has been in regular session since January 11, 1967.* He has made more than 2,900 speeches on the subject, all told, and he seems no less committed to the issue today than when he gave his first speech 17 years ago. [...] The Senator has not been deterred by the fact that this treaty and his efforts to ratify it have not received elaborate media attention. He has not been deterred by the fact that a legislative 'hold' was placed on this measure by the late Senator John Bricker and seems never to have been cleared. He has not been deterred by anything at all…[24] (emphasis added)

In 1970, the Senate held its first hearings on the Genocide Convention since the era of John Bricker. The Foreign Relations Committee or subcommittees thereafter held hearings in 1971, 1973, 1976, 1981, and 1984, but never received a floor vote despite being voted favorably forward out of committee in many of these years.[25] It was not until the Congressional session held in 1985–1986 when, with the support of President Reagan, the Genocide Convention successfully made it through committee and to a floor vote, where it was overwhelmingly approved with 83 votes in favor and 11 votes against.

---

21   122 Cong Rec 409 (1976).
22   122 Cong Rec 8279 (1976).
23   125 Cong Rec 3048 (1979).
24   131 Cong Rec 20013–14 (1985) (statement of Sen. Baker); see also Samantha Power, *'A Problem from Hell': American and the Age of Genocide* (HarperCollins 2002) ('Power, *A Problem from Hell*')166 (tallying 3211 speeches from 1967 to 1986).
25   For a full account of the Genocide Convention's time in the Senate, see Lawrence J LeBlanc, *The United States and the Genocide Convention* (Duke University Press 1991).

This approval came with a set of RUDs, although a less powerful packet than would accompany those human rights treaties which the Senate approved in the early 1990s. Senator Proxmire resisted at least some of these RUDs, but ultimately recognized that this was 'the only way that we could possibly do it.'[26] He had been forced to compromise, but with the compromise came the treaty's passage, at long last, and an example of persistence that offers hope for those seeking the ratification of other human rights treaties today.

3   Proxmire, Bricker, and the Glass Half-Full

Senator Proxmire's example inspires the continuing efforts to get human rights treaties through the Senate. In addition, at a higher level of generality, the internationalist vision he espoused has to some degree occurred through other means. For although it is very hard to get human rights treaties through the Senate, even unratified treaties can have direct effects on U.S. law. In other words, the integration of international human rights law into the United States that Senator Proxmire called for has come to pass in certain respects despite the inaction in the Senate. These developments have in turn led to objections that parallel the objections made to the ghost of Senator Bricker in interesting respects.

Human rights treaties influence U.S. law in myriad ways even when the United States has not ratified them. These influences appear in executive branch action, in legal decision-making by state and local governmental actors, and in federal judicial decisions. These influences are sporadic rather than comprehensive, and when they occur it is hard to assess how significant they are. Yet there is no denying the existence of these influences. Indeed, as Johanna Kalb has observed, in some ways the influence of unratified human

---

26   132 Cong Rec 2153 (1986); see also 131 Cong Rec 20875 (1985) (expressing disagreement with the two reservations attached by the Senate Foreign Relation Committee, one of which reserved out of the International Court of Justice (ICJ) jurisdiction and the other of which contained the unnecessary statement that nothing in the Convention authorized action by the United States that was prohibited by the Constitution); Power, *A Problem from Hell* (n 22) 167 (discussing the mixed feelings of Proxmire's staff on the Convention's passage with the RUDs). The resolution of advice and consent also included an understanding that the Convention not be ratified until implementing legislation was passed. This implementing legislation, which criminalized genocide under U.S. law, was known as the Proxmire Act; and after its passage the United States at last ratified the Genocide Convention (in Power, *A Problem from Hell* (n 22) 167–68).

rights treaties in U.S. law may be even stronger than the influence of those human rights treaties that have been ratified with RUDs.[27]

Unratified human rights treaties undoubtedly affect the engagement of the executive branch with other countries (such as at the Universal Periodic Review), but they can also have internal effects as well. For example, a 1995 Department of Justice guideline for asylum officers on dealing with gender-related asylum claims explained that the 'evaluation of gender-based claims must be viewed within the framework provided by existing international human rights instruments' and identified CEDAW as the 'most comprehensive' such instrument for women.[28] Internal effects of these unratified human rights treaties can also occur where state and local legislators, executive officials, or judges draw upon them. Perhaps the most famous example is the San Francisco ordinance implementing CEDAW within the city, but this is only one of many instances.[29]

While the most substantively significant uses of unratified human rights treaties may occur in the executive branch and in state and local governments, the uses that have attracted the most scholarly attention—and also popular attention—have occurred in the federal courts. One such use, which I will not otherwise discuss, is the role that unratified human rights treaties play in informing customary international law norms which in turn may be used by the

---

[27] Joanna Kalb, 'The Persistence of Dualism in Human Rights Treaty Implementation' (2011) 30 Yale L & Pol'y Rev 71, 73 (finding that although state and local 'engagement with [human rights] treaties is generally limited, it has occurred more frequently with respect to unratified human rights treaties than it has with those that have been ratified').

[28] Memorandum from Phyllis Coven, Office of International Affairs to All INS Asylum Officers re Considerations for Asylum Officers Adjudicating Asylum Claims for Women 2 (16 May 1995) at <http://www.refworld.org/docid/3ae6b31e7.html> accessed 11 June 2014; see also *Fisher v. INS* 79 F3d 955, 967 (9th Cir 1996) (Noonan, J, dissenting) (discussing this guideline). One possible justification from a legal perspective is the obligations stemming under international law from treaty signature (as opposed to ratification), but it is beyond the scope of this essay to analyze the reach of these obligations.

[29] For examples of state and local legislative and executive action, see Columbia Law School, Human Rights Project, 'Bringing Human Rights Home' 10–23 (2012), at <http://web.law.columbia.edu/sites/default/files/microsites/human-rights-institute/files/Bringing%20Human%20Rights%20Home.pdf> accessed 11 June 2014. For an example of the extensive scholarly literature on the subnational incorporation of international human rights treaties, see Catherine Powell, 'Dialogic Federalism: Constitutional Possibilities for Incorporation of Human Rights Law in the United States' (2001) 150 U Pa L Rev 245. For an example of a state supreme court drawing on an unratified human rights treaty in interpreting its own constitution, see *Diatchenko v. District Attorney for Suffolk Dist.* 1 NE 3d 270, 285 n6 (Mass 2013).

courts in contexts like cases brought under the Alien Tort Statute. Another use occurs in Supreme Court constitutional decisions where the Court references international norms embodied in unratified human rights treaties. There have been a handful of such uses in the last fifteen years, but I will focus on the 2005 decision in *Roper v. Simmons*.[30] *Roper* is perhaps the most prominent such use and it deals with an issue that Roger cares deeply about: the death penalty.

Specifically, *Roper* considered whether the Constitution bars the death penalty for persons who committed their crimes as juveniles. This is an issue as to which the United States has avoided treaty commitments: it entered a reservation with respect to this prohibition in Article 6(5) of the ICCPR and, as mentioned earlier, it has not ratified the CRC, which contains a similar prohibition.[31] Yet in holding that the Constitution does prohibit the death penalty for crimes committed by underage perpetrators, the Supreme Court cited these treaty provisions, as well as some other international and comparative law sources.[32] The Court did not claim to put much weight on these provisions, simply saying that they 'provide[d] respected and significant confirmation for our own conclusions,' but it nonetheless made a very deliberate choice to discuss them.[33]

The pushback against this use of unratified human rights treaties was immediate and emphatic. In dissent, Justice Scalia observed that '[u]nless the Court has added to its arsenal the power to join and ratify treaties on behalf of the United States, I cannot see how this evidence favors, rather than refutes' the Court's conclusion that the death penalty is unconstitutional as applied to juveniles.[34] His dissent was only the beginning of attacks on the Supreme Court's use of international and comparative law in constitutional interpretation. These attacks, which came from both scholars and politicians, argued that these uses were constitutionally impermissible, either because they involved non-originalist materials or because they reflected values that came from outside the U.S. democracy.[35]

---

30 543 U.S. 551 (2005). Other cases in which the Supreme Court has referenced international law in its constitutional decisions include *Graham v. Florida* 560 U.S. 48, 80–82 (2010) (dealing with life sentences without the possibility of parole for crimes that were not murders that were committed by juveniles); *Lawrence v. Texas* 539 U.S. 558, 573–577 (2003) (dealing with the criminalization of consensual same-sex intimate conduct within a home); *Atkins v. Virginia* 536 U.S. 304, 316–317 (2002) (dealing with the death penalty for the mentally disabled).

31 543 U.S. 576.

32 *Ibid*.

33 *Ibid* 578.

34 *Ibid* 622 (Scalia, J, dissenting).

35 See Jean Galbraith, 'International Law and the Domestic Separation of Powers' (2013) 99 Va L Rev 987, 989 n6 & 996 nn 18–19 (identifying sources).

I wish to suggest that there are interesting parallels between these objections and the objections raised by Professor Henkin and others to the Senate's attachment of RUDs to human rights treaties. The overarching parallel is that both types of objections employ formalist reasoning, but three more specific similarities can be observed as well.

First, for the objectors in both cases, the right outcome is a bright line. As Justice Scalia has explained in a speech, '[i]t is my view that modern foreign legal materials can *never* be relevant to an interpretation of—to the *meaning of*—the U.S. Constitution.'[36] Comparably, for Professor Henkin, human rights treaties should be embraced with few if any RUDs and be self-executing within the United States.[37]

Second, the objectors in both cases suggest that the actual outcome smacks of some kind of cheating. To Justice Scalia, if human rights treaties lack the votes to get through the Senate despite all the efforts of their Proxmire-like supporters, then it is unfair for these treaties to matter anyway. To Professor Henkin, it was problematic that while 'Senator Bricker lost his battle' for a constitutional amendment, 'his ghost is now enjoying victory in war' through the RUDs that 'achieve[] virtually what the Bricker Amendment sought, and more.'[38]

Third, and perhaps most significantly, these objections are linked to constitutional arguments that have a strongly originalist flavor. Justice Scalia's objection to the use of modern international and comparative materials is basically that these materials do not reflect the original understanding of the Constitution. He has observed that once judicial interpreters adopt a '"living Constitution" paradigm' ...then 'there is no reason foreign materials should not be used along with all others.'[39] For his part, Professor Henkin expressed particular disapproval of declarations of non-self-execution on the ground that the text of the Supremacy Clause makes treaties the 'law of the land' and 'there is no evidence of any intent, by the Framers...to allow the President or the Senate, by their ipse dixit, to prevent a treaty that by its character could be law of the land from becoming law of the land.'[40]

---

36 Antonin Scalia, 'Foreign Legal Authority in the Federal Courts' (2004) 98 Am Soc Int'l L Proc 305 ('Scalia, 'Foreign Legal Authority in the Federal Courts'') 307. For convenience, I focus here on Justice Scalia and Professor Henkin, although this analysis can apply to others with similar views.

37 Henkin, 'Editorial Comment, U.S. Ratification of Human Rights Conventions' (n 1) 349–50.

38 *Ibid* 349.

39 Scalia, 'Foreign Legal Authority in the Federal Courts' (n 36) 308.

40 Henkin, 'Editorial Comment, U.S. Ratification of Human Rights Conventions' (n 1) 346–47. Professor Henkin shows some equivocation on this point, in part because of his prior

To say that these arguments have parallels is by no means to equate their rightness or wrongness as a matter of legal doctrine or normative desirability. As a matter of positive experience, however, constitutional practice in foreign relation law has rarely favored bright lines or purely embodied originalist positions. Instead, history offers an account of complexity that lends itself to flexibility. In response to Professor Henkin, Professors Bradley and Goldsmith observed that the Senate has a long history with regard to RUDs and other devices for adding conditions to treaties.[41] Similarly, in response to the arguments of Justice Scalia and others, Sarah Cleveland and others have shown that the Supreme Court has long turned to international law in the course of constitutional interpretation.[42] In the past, in the present, and—we can expect—in the future, these patterns will continue.

The spirit of Senator Proxmire thus cannot claim complete victory. The cup does not overfloweth—but it is at least half full. If human rights treaties in the United States do not serve as powerful a role in the United States as they do in Europe, yet they do play far more of a role than Senator Bricker and his spiritual descendants would wish them too. Both ghosts can be heard as we pass by the billabong. Which one speaks louder depends on the choices of the living. So, drawing from Roger, '[s]tave off becoming immortal as long as you can—it can lead to too many regrets if you are no longer out there fighting the good fight!'[43]

---

defense of a 'special case' of non-self-execution in the 1950s. Scalia, 'Foreign Legal Authority in the Federal Courts' 347 & n26.

41   Bradley & Goldsmith, 'Treaties, Human Rights, and Conditional Consent' (n 9) 403–09.
42   Sarah H Cleveland, 'Our International Constitution' (2006) 31 Yale J Int'l L 1.
43   Clark, 'The International Criminal Law System' (n 5) 27 (quoting from his conversation with the statute of the late Peter Fraser).

CHAPTER 31

Judicial Review of Decision-Making Engaging Public Practices and Other Manifestations of Faith: Lessons from Roger Clark and *Beatty v. Gillbanks*

David Mullan

1   Introduction

In 1966, at the Victoria University of Wellington, I had the privilege of taking the course in Constitutional and Administrative Law taught by three of New Zealand's most distinguished public lawyers: Colin Aikman, then Dean of the Law Faculty, Ken Keith, until 2015 a judge a judge of the International Court of Justice, and Roger Clark. In many ways, it was the most significant event in my legal education as evidenced by my subsequent career as both an academic and practising public lawyer. I remain forever grateful to those giants in the field.

Roger Clark taught the component of the course devoted to civil liberties. I still recollect vividly the enthusiasm that he brought to our classroom discussion of the famous 1882 case of *Beatty v. Gillbanks*,[1] a case that pitted the marching members of the Weston-super-Mare 'soldiers' of the Salvation Army against both the antagonistic and challenging members of the Skeleton Army and ultimately the constabulary of that Somerset town. In this volume of essays celebrating Roger Clark's outstanding achievements, I use this case as a launching point for consideration of recent Canadian case law and controversy concerning the outward or public manifestations of religious beliefs and practice.

Of course, it goes without saying that the intersection of religious practice with the public domain and the exercise by others of their beliefs and freedoms is a much travelled road, and it is not my intention to engage in an elaboration of the various twists and turns that that very long road has taken

---

1   (1882) 9 QBD 308. I was interested to read in his obituary in The Telegraph, 30 September 2009, that *Beatty v. Gillbanks* also remained the favourite case of another distinguished public lawyer, Professor Sir David Williams: <http://www.telegraph.co.uk/news/obituaries/law-obituaries/6248213/Professor-Sir-David-Williams.html?fb> accessed 18 September 2014. Indeed, Sir David, in what must have been one of his last publications, wrote the entry on the case in Peter Cane & Joanne Conaghan (eds), *The New Oxford Companion to Law* (OUP 2008) 70.

since 1882. Rather, my objective is to describe briefly and analyse how the competing tensions have fared in the context of Canadian judicial review of administrative action which has placed restrictions on or responded to public manifestations of religious life and practices.

2   An Apparently Honourable History

The 1959 decision of the Supreme Court of Canada in *Roncarelli v. Duplessis* (and particularly the judgment of Rand J.)[2] remains one of the most celebrated Canadian public law decisions. It is one of a number of judicial responses to the Quebec government's sustained attempts to suppress Jehovah's Witnesses in the full and public practise of their faith.[3] The particular manifestation was a 1946 liquor police raid on a Montreal restaurant owned by Frank Roncarelli, a raid which led to the cancellation of Roncarelli's liquor licence. That cancellation ultimately ruined his business. It transpired that the impugned actions, while carried out under the formal direction of the General Manager of the Quebec Liquor Commission, were in reality dictated by the Premier of Quebec, Maurice Duplessis. The precipitating cause was that Roncarelli, a Jehovah's Witness had been standing bail for fellow Witnesses charged with various offences under both the *Criminal Code* and Quebec law restricting the activities of the Witnesses.

In terms of conventional judicial review law, the case epitomizes the application of several important common law principles: that administrative power should not be used at the dictation of someone on whom the relevant statutory regime has not bestowed any relevant authority; that administrative power should not be used for purposes alien to or not contemplated by the relevant statutory regimes; and, most importantly, at least for current purposes, that implicit in the grant of even broad or open-ended statutory discretion is the limitation that power should not be exercised in a way that supresses or is aimed at the exercise of common law rights and freedoms, and, in this instance, freedom of religion and expression and also the freedom to stand bail for someone charged with an offence.

As in *Beatty v. Gillbanks*, the majority of the Supreme Court was not convinced by arguments to the effect that there were public or societal order

---

2   [1959] SCR 121.
3   See also *Boucher v R* (1950) [1951] SCR 265, *Saumur v Quebec (City of)* [1953] 2 SCR 299, *Chaput v Romain* [1955] SCR 834, *Switzman v Elbling* [1957] SCR 285, and *Lamb v Benoit* [1959] SCR 321.

grounds on which the decision could be justified. Thus, for example, the majority rejected the contention that the Premier (who was also the Attorney General) was justified as a guardian of the public interest in instructing the General Manager to withdraw a privilege from someone who, by standing bail, was aiding and abetting the cause of a group responsible for fomenting public opinion against the Roman Catholic majority and the government of the day by means of aggressive proselytizing both in person and through scurrilous pamphleteering.[4] Common law constitutionalism, seen through the lens of freedoms such as those of religion, thought and expression, trumped any overriding state prerogatives to take action to preserve the existing order and to protect from disruption the exercise of religious freedoms and cultural norms of the majority. As Rod Macdonald argued in an article in a collection of papers marking the 50th anniversary of *Roncarelli v. Duplessis*, this amounted to preference for one form of 'social, political and legal theory' over another.[5]

However, it would be unwise to deduce from either *Roncarelli v. Duplessis* or *Beatty v. Gillbanks* that appeals to the preservation of public order and societal values in derogation from respect for religious practices are invariably irrelevant to the exercise of public power. In *Beatty v. Gillbanks*, after all, the Salvation Army assembly and parade were lawful in themselves. On the prior record, the objective of the Skeleton Army was the disruption of that assembly and parade, and, more generally, the instigation of mayhem. The legal setting in which the matter was adjudicated was a criminal prosecution, and an appeal from conviction and an order binding the Salvation Army over to keep the peace.

While *Roncarelli v. Duplessis* was an action in damages and not a criminal matter, it was in some senses an easier case as there was no suggestion that Roncarelli's posting of bail for Jehovah's Witnesses contributed directly to public disorder or the undermining of generally held societal values. There was also a disconnect between the motivations for the impugned actions of the Premier of Quebec and the General Manager, and the target of those actions, Roncarelli's liquor licence. At least this was so unless a reviewing court was prepared to read the open-ended discretion over the continuation of a liquor licence as importing into the statute a broad or general power to remove licences for reasons not specifically related to the sale of liquor. In short, justification of the motives of the government actors could have involved recognition of an implied statutory mandate to remove the licences of those whose conduct was seen as contrary to the values of the state as immediately embodied in the policies and objectives of the party in power. Alternatively, and of

---

4 *Roncarelli v Duplessis* (n 2) 144 (per Rand J).
5 See Roderick A Macdonald, 'Was Duplessis Right?' (2010) 55 McGill LJ 401, 432.

more transcendent application, would have been judicial acceptance of the proposition that the public law of Quebec was, irrespective of the current government, founded on principles of state protection that trumped either generally or in the particular circumstances the common law's recognition of freedom of religion and expression, and the right to stand bail for those charged with offences.

3   Fast Forward to 2003

The Jehovah's Witness faith did not become the predominant Christian group in Quebec, nor, however, did it disappear from the provincial landscape. Indeed, remarkably, the battle against door-to-door proselytizing by its adherents persisted in some communities. Startling testimony to this came in *Ville de Blainville v. Beauchemin.*[6] This involved a challenge by Jehovah's Witnesses to the application to members of their creed of a by-law adopted by the predominantly francophone community of Blainville. The by-law required a permit costing $100 to engage in door-to-door solicitation, and also barred any form of such solicitation except between 9 a.m. and 7:30 p.m. from Monday through Friday. The permit was for two months and could not be renewed earlier than a year after its initial issue. It was clearly aimed at Jehovah's Witnesses and their most intense periods of proselytizing: evenings and the weekends.

The Quebec Court of Appeal held that the by-law had no application to Jehovah's Witnesses and, reversing the first instance judge on this point, that the Witnesses had proved moral damages. Nonetheless, the Court did not award any such damages as the Witnesses had made the claim against the Mayor rather than the municipality itself.

Now is not the place to engage in a detailed critique of the Court of Appeal's judgment, but of particular significance is the extent to which the legal terrain had changed since *Roncarelli v. Duplessis* and the other Jehovah's Witness Supreme Court judgments of the Duplessis era. In holding that the by-law was inoperative to the extent that it applied to the door-to-door activities of Jehovah's Witnesses, the Court, as in *Roncarelli*, characterized its impact as 'a very serious infringement of their religious freedom.'[7] However, this freedom

---

6   (2003) 231 DLR. (4th) 706 (Qué CA), aff'g (2003), 202 DLR (4th) 147 (Qué SC). Interestingly, one of the counsel for the Jehovah's Witnesses was W Glen How, who had been involved in some of the Quebec Jehovah's Witnesses litigation in the 1950's though not directly Roncarelli v. Duplessis.

7   *Ville de Blainville v Beauchemin* (n 6) para 51.

was one that now had explicit constitutional recognition in Section 2(a) of the 1982 *Canadian Charter of Rights and Freedoms* and *quasi*-constitutional protection in Section 3 of the *Quebec Charter of human rights and freedoms*.[8] The same was true of the subsidiary freedoms relied on by the Witnesses: those of thought, belief, opinion and expression. These too were now explicitly guaranteed by Section 2(b) of the Canadian *Charter* and, in slightly different terms, by Section 3 of the Quebec *Charter*. In a very real sense, the constitutional protections relied on in *Roncarelli* had been elevated.

As against that, in an increasingly secular Quebec, justifications of the by-law on the basis of protecting the Roman Catholic majority and the government of the day against scurrilous attacks would have sounded hollow. Similarly, there was no basis at all for a claim, such as in *Beatty v. Gillbanks*, that the activities of the Jehovah's Witnesses were provoking civil disorder and public mayhem. Instead, the municipality was forced, in justifying the by-law on the basis of the protection of 'peace and public order in the territory of'[9] the municipality, to rely on protection of the privacy of its citizens.[10] While protection of privacy found explicit protection in Section 5 of the Quebec *Charter* and might also be an implicit component of provisions of the Canadian *Charter* and perhaps the Canadian common law constitution, it lacked the pedigree of the freedoms relied on by the Jehovah's Witnesses, and, for a wide variety of reasons, could not be set up as a justification of the violation of those freedoms by reference to Section 1 of the Canadian *Charter*: a reasonable limit that was 'demonstrably justified in a free and democratic society.' The by-law overreached in that its privacy objectives could have been achieved by the simple expedient of recognizing legislatively the right of citizens to post notices to the effect that the implicit consent given by citizens to others knocking on their doors had been withdrawn either totally or in part.[11]

4 The Impact of More Competitive Human Rights and Freedoms

Trinity Western University ('TWU') is a 'private' but publically accredited university[12] in the province of British Columbia. Its legal powers come from the

---

8 RSQ c C-12.
9 *Ville de Blainville v Beauchemin* (n 6) para 31.
10 *Ville de Blainville v Beauchemin* (n 6).
11 *Ville de Blainville v Beauchemin* (n 6) para 52.
12 Meaning in a Canadian setting that it did not depend on funding from the province but was an accredited degree granting institution.

Trinity Western University Act[13] and referentially the *Societies Act*,[14] under which it is incorporated. Section 3(2) of the TWU Act states that the objects of University

> ...shall be to provide for young people of any race, colour, or creed, university education in the arts and sciences with an underlying philosophy and viewpoint that is Christian.

TWU is also an accredited member of the Association of Universities and Colleges of Canada, the umbrella organization that represents both public and private universities, and the Council for Christian Colleges and Universities. It has a Community Covenant which its students are obliged to sign. In 1995, among the provisions of that Covenant (or Community Standards document, as it was then called) was a prohibition on the 'biblically condemned' practices of 'sexual sins including premarital sex, adultery, homosexual behaviour, and viewing of pornography.' Today, it has been softened calling for students to refrain from 'sexual expressions of intimacy' outside of the married state, marriage being defined as a state of union between 'one man and one woman.'

In 1996, the British Columbia College of Teachers declined to accredit fully[15] TWU's Teacher Education Program on the basis that the treatment of homosexual behaviour as sinful had the effect of excluding those who were gay or lesbian. Given the extent of the protection against discrimination on the basis of sexual orientation provided for in human rights codes and by Section 15 of the *Charter*, the College stated that it was not in the public interest to afford full certification to a teachers' training course which did not provide those protections to its students. This refusal provoked an application for judicial review which ultimately reached the Supreme Court of Canada.

The majority in *Trinity Western University v. British Columbia College of Teachers*[16] reiterated the position that the rights and freedoms guaranteed by the *Charter* were not hierarchically ordered and that the current case fell to be determined by the drawing of a line between the respective guarantees set up by the parties in justification of their positions.[17] However, there is no doubt

---

13   SBC 1969, c 44 (as amended) ('TWU Act').
14   Now Society Act, RSBC 1996, c 453.
15   At that time, students took only four of the five years of the education degree programme at TWU. The final year was taken at a public university, Simon Fraser University.
16   2001 SCC 31, [2001] 1 SCR 772, 31.
17   *Trinity Western University v British Columbia College of Teachers* (n 16) para 29 ('In our opinion, this is a case where any potential conflict should be resolved through the proper

that what was involved, at least for the majority, was a contest between Section 2(b)'s guarantee of freedom of religion and Section 15's promise of equality and freedom from discrimination on grounds such as sexual orientation. How should the College of Teachers have balanced TWU's assertion that freedom of religion protected its prohibition on homosexual behaviour, and the claim that a public accreditation body should not be approving degree programmes which condemned homosexual behaviour as sinful and demanded of those enrolling that they not engage in homosexual relations?

Ultimately, the Supreme Court majority resorted to administrative law grounds as the way through this thicket. The Court found that the College's limited justification of its decision had not taken sufficient account of the freedom of religion of the University and its members and the explicit recognition of religious public education rights in Section 93 of the *Constitution Act, 1867*. Also legally relevant was the place of private universities and colleges in Canada, universities and colleges which could lawfully give preferential treatment in their admissions policies to adherents to the relevant faith affiliation. By focussing primarily on the equality rights of homosexuals, the College had failed to address adequately the question that really mattered: Would graduates of the programme in a classroom setting not treat homosexuals fairly and respectfully? As there was no evidence that the existing programme (one in which students spent four years at TWU and a final year at one of the province's public universities) was producing other than competent, non-discriminating teachers, the Court held that there was no justification for denial of accreditation. Concentrating on the religious precepts of the TWU to the virtual exclusion of the actual impact of those precepts on the public school environment amounted to acting on the basis of irrelevant considerations.

As a consequence, the Court endorsed the first instance judge's issuance of an order in the nature of *mandamus* requiring the College to approve TWU's proposal on terms that the College's Teacher Education Programs Committee had recommended to it—five year interim approval subject to various conditions and forms of monitoring though, interestingly, not including assessment of the way in which its graduates conducted themselves in the classroom.[18]

While the fact situations are in many ways very different, there are echoes here of both *Beatty v. Gillbanks* and *Roncarelli v. Duplessis*. In all three, the justification for state action based on broad public interest considerations failed

---

delineation of the rights and values involved. In essence, properly defining the scope of the rights avoids a conflict in this case.').

18 (1997) 41 BCLR. (3d) 158 (S.C.), though the monitoring did include assessment of diversity in admissions to the programme.

in the face of the courts' evaluation of the impact of that action on freedom of religion. There is also an analogy that can be drawn between David Williams' support of the decision in *Beatty v. Gillbanks* as a refusal to countenance prior restraint in anticipation of public disorder[19] and the Supreme Court's demand in *Trinity Western University* that there be actual proof of a link between the relevant religious beliefs and practices, and the legitimate interests of the state, in that case, in ensuring that graduates of publicly accredited programmes do not bring the beliefs and practices on which their education was predicated to bear in ways which are detrimental to the rights and interests of those they are licensed to educate as part of a public school system. In terms of *Roncarelli*, there is a further parallel: that the refusal or withdrawal of state 'privileges' or licences cannot be predicated on religious beliefs and practices without ample proof of a connection between the exercise of the privilege or licence and the legitimate interests of the state: in *Trinity Western University*, the educational experience of those taught by graduates of the TWU education programme.[20]

Significantly, the dissenting judgment of L'Heureux-Dubé J. takes issue with the majority on evaluation of the evidential linkage. In a case where there was a potential threat to the right to equality guaranteed by Section 15 of the *Charter*, she was prepared to find justification of the College's decision in its fear that

> ...the particular world view held by Trinity Western University with reference to homosexual behaviour may have a detrimental effect in the learning environment of public schools.[21]

Where there was a much closer link than in *Roncarelli v. Duplessis* between what was at stake (accreditation) and the harm that was feared (discrimination on the basis of sexual orientation), and particularly where the harm is violation of an explicit constitutional guarantee (equality), the evidential requirements should not be as rigorous. As for Section 2(a) and freedom of religion, L'Heureux-Dubé J. minimized those claims to the point of non-existence,[22] though one suspects that her position on the evidential nexus was not

---

19   David Williams, *Keeping the Peace: The Police and Public Order* (Hutchinson 1967) 87–96.
20   Of course, it is also possible to characterize state interest in terms of not providing succour in the form of state recognition to those whose values differ from the values enshrined in the nation's constitutional norms and, in particular, the rights and freedoms protected by the Canadian Charter of Rights and Freedoms.
21   *Trinity Western University v British Columbia College of Teachers* (n 16) para 75, citing the College's decision.
22   *Trinity Western University v British Columbia College of Teachers* (n 16) paras 59–66.

dependent on that. Section 15 and protection of its guaranteed rights occupied a higher status in a hierarchical ordering of *Charter* rights and freedoms.

It is also worth recording that a variation on this contest is yet again before the courts,[23] this time involving accreditation decisions by the country's Law Societies and their umbrella organization, the Federated Law Societies of Canada of TWU's application for approval of a law degree programme. There have been conflicting decisions among the various accreditation bodies and litigation has already been commenced in which the same arguments have resurfaced albeit against the backdrop of the softened terms of the current TWU Community Covenant. What will be fascinating will be the nature of the factual record on which the courts will decide the various challenges and whether the *Trinity Western University* majority's insistence on clear proof of linkage between the religious practice or belief in question and violation of the rights of others will continue to prevail.

More generally, however, it is worth noting that in the world of competing constitutional rights, the Supreme Court has found comfort in an ability to treat the relevant evaluation as highly fact contingent. A prime example of this is *R. v. N.S.*[24] The case involved the competing rights of an accused on trial for sexual assault, and his accuser. Pitted against each other were the accused's right to a fair and open trial, and the accuser's religiously based claim to wear a *niqab* while testifying. Not surprisingly, the Supreme Court's response to the preliminary inquiry judge's order that the accuser remove her *niqab* was a remission back for reconsideration in accordance with a four question framework. This was aimed at achieving a satisfactory balance of the competing claims and very much located in terms of the particular factual context in which the claim was being adjudicated.[25]

5   The Relationship between Canada's Current Approach to Judicial Review of Administrative Action and Decisions Implicating Constitutional Rights and Freedoms

In *Roncarelli v. Duplessis*, the Supreme Court evaluated Roncarelli's claims within the dual framework of the then common law principles respecting

---

23   For a flavour of what has been going on, see Ian Mulgrew, 'Trinity Western dispute calls integrity of legal profession into question', *Vancouver Sun* (Vancouver, 15 July 2014).
24   2012 SCC 72, [2012] 3 SCR 726.
25   The ultimate outcome was a dropping of the sexual assault charges: 'Sex assault charges dropped against relatives of woman who fought for niqab', *Kingston Whig-Standard*, (Kingston, 18 July 2014).

judicial review of administrative action and the Quebec *Civil Code*'s provision with respect to the delictual liability of state authorities.[26] As seen already, in terms of the principles of judicial review, the analysis focussed principally on issues of jurisdiction, taking account of irrelevant factors, and acting for an impermissible purpose. In the particular context, those grounds were assessed partially through the lens of the implied constitutional rights that at least some members of the majority held were in play. From one perspective, the judgment of the majority in *Trinity Western University* also proceeds on the basis of those same mid-20th century conceptions of the grounds of judicial review, in that instance, principally a failure to take sufficient account of a constitutionally relevant factor: religious freedom.

However, there was another dimension to *Trinity Western University*, a dimension which produced an immediate disagreement between the majority judgment delivered by Iacobucci and Bastarache JJ., and the sole dissenter, L'Heureux-Dubé J. By 2001, the Supreme Court had accepted that establishing a standard of review was a necessary preliminary step in the adjudication of any judicial review application.[27] At that point, there were three accepted standards: non-deferential correctness and deferential unreasonableness and patent unreasonableness.[28] In *Trinity Western University*, the majority, after engaging in a standard of review analysis and emphasising the College's lack of expertise in the determination of questions of law involving human rights issues, applied a correctness or non-deferential standard in exercising its judicial review function.[29] L'Heureux-Dubé J. went to the other extreme and held that the standard of review was that of patent unreasonableness.[30] In doing so, she stated that the evaluation in issue was both fact-centred and at the core of the College's expertise, even to the extent that the College was obliged to take account of human rights values and *Charter* rights and freedoms.

Thereafter, the Supreme Court continued generally, though not invariably[31] to conduct judicial review of administrative decisions implicating *Charter*

---

26 What was then Article 1053 of the Quebec Civil Code.
27 At that time, the most complete and authoritative statement of the Court's position was *Pushpanathan v Canada (Minister of Citizenship and Immigration)* [1998] 1 SCR 982.
28 Save where statutorily designated as the standard of review, patent unreasonableness was eliminated by the Court in *Dunsmuir v New Brunswick* 2008 SCC 9, [2008] 1 SCR 190.
29 *Trinity Western University v British Columbia College of Teachers* (n 16) paras 15–19.
30 *Trinity Western University v British Columbia College of Teachers* (n 16) paras 51–66.
31 For an example of the Court exhibiting a willingness to defer to administrative judgment in decision-making implicating Charter rights and freedoms, see *Pinet v St. Thomas Psychiatric Hospital* 2004 SCC 21, [2004] 1 SCR 528. See also Chamberlain v. Surrey School District No. 36, 2002 SCC 86, [2002] 4 SCR 710.

rights and freedoms and also values on a correctness basis even to the extent of engaging in full evidential review of the decision under attack. This was nowhere more evident than in the 2006 judgment in *Multani v. Commission scolaire Marguerite-Bourgeoys*.[32] This involved an application for judicial review of a school board decision banning a Sikh pupil from wearing a *kirpan* at school except under what were claimed to be unduly restrictive conditions. In ultimately setting aside the school board's decision, the Supreme Court of Canada rejected the Quebec Court of Appeal's application of a deferential standard of reasonableness in reviewing the decision,[33] a review that had sustained the ban.[34] Emphasising that the decision engaged the freedom of religion of the pupil and his parents, the Court pronounced that administrative law standard of review analysis had no role to play and that, in such cases, the decision was to be evaluated by reference to the legal content of the constitutional right or freedom in issue, and, where there was a *prima facie* infringement, an assessment by reference to the standard test[35] of whether that violation was, by reference to Section 1, demonstrably justified in a free and democratic society. Moreover, to the extent that the Section 1 inquiry was itself highly fact-sensitive, this meant extensive non-deferential judicial assessment of the factual and mixed fact and law components of the Section 1 analysis. According to Charron J. (delivering the judgment of the majority), to apply administrative law standards and, in particular, to choose deferential reasonableness review

> ...could well reduce the fundamental rights and freedoms guaranteed by the *Canadian Charter* to mere administrative law standards or, at the very least, cause confusion between the two.[36]

In particular, this led the Court to scrutinize closely and reject the school board's assessment of the degree of danger posed by the pupil's wearing of a weapon to school. In the balancing exercise on the facts accepted by the Court, freedom of religion trumped any such perception of a possible threat to the personal safety of others, a right also protected by Section 7's guarantee of the right to life, liberty and security of the person.[37]

---

32   2006 SCC 6, [2006] 1 S.C.R. 256.
33   *Multani v Commission scolaire Marguerite-Bourgeoys* (n 32) para 15.
34   See [2004] RJQ 824, 241 DLR (4th) 336 (CA).
35   As developed in *R v Oakes* [1986] 1 SCR 103, in the context of the testing of the constitutional validity of legislation, as opposed to administrative action.
36   *Multani v Commission scolaire Marguerite-Bourgeoys* (n 32) para 16.
37   *Multani v Commission scolaire Marguerite-Bourgeoys* (n 32) paras 44–77.

However, within six years, the Court had abandoned the *Multani* approach. *Doré v. Barreau du Québec*,[38] arose out of Law Society disciplinary proceedings against a lawyer who had launched a highly critical attack on the integrity, behaviour, and qualifications of a Quebec Superior Court judge. In a challenge to the findings of the Barreau's Disciplinary Council (sustained on appeal to the Quebec Professions Tribunal) in which the lawyer had relied in justification of his conduct on Section 2(b) of the *Charter* and freedom of expression, the Court, now differently constituted, affirmed the pre-eminence of administrative law methodology.[39] It went on to apply the deferential standard of reasonableness to the assessment of the lawyer's conduct within the framework of his constitutional entitlement to freedom of expression. At the intersection between the legal rights and freedoms recognized by the *Charter* and the facts of the particular matter, the administrative decision-maker was entitled to considerable latitude. This led ultimately to the sustaining of the finding of conduct unbecoming and a reprimand.

It remains to be seen how far this new approach will extend. My sense is that it will not allow for deference to administrative decision-maker determination of pure questions of *Charter* law. There are also questions as to the range of decision-maker that will benefit from reasonableness review as the outcome of the initial administrative law standard of review analysis. Thus, for example, the majority in *TWU* held that the College of Teachers was not subject to either of the two existing deferential standards of review. Its functions were restricted to 'essentially educational matters';[40] it could not assert expertise or an entitlement to deference on questions of law concerned with human rights[41] or, for that matter, the reconciliation of 'competing rights.'[42] Does that analysis continue to represent the position of the Supreme Court in relation to administrative and executive decision-makers without the legal capacities or resources available to, for example, a law society disciplinary committee or other adjudicative tribunals or agencies? And, to what extent would the withholding of deference be appropriate given the Court's increasing tendency to, where appropriate, subject cases involving competing rights and freedoms to highly context-sensitive fact inquiries?

---

38 2012 SCC 12, [2012] 1 SCR 395.
39 *Doré v Barreau du Québec* (n 38) paras 22–57 (per Abella J, who had disagreed with the majority's approach in Multani).
40 *Trinity Western University v British Columbia College of Teachers* (n 16) para 18.
41 *Trinity Western University v British Columbia College of Teachers* (n 16) para 18.
42 *Trinity Western University v British Columbia College of Teachers* (n 16) para 17.

6   Conclusions

The societal and legal context in which issues involving state action affecting freedom of religion arise has changed dramatically and become much more complex and multi-faceted since *Beatty v. Gillbanks* in 1882. Indeed, despite comparatively recent manifestations of state attempts at suppressive regulation of Jehovah's Witnesses, there is a sense in which *Roncarelli v. Duplessis* concerns an issue that is largely of historical interest. The Salvation Army, Jehovah's Witnesses, and several other such non-conformist, proselytizing Christian religions are no longer seen as a threat to state order and public harmony. As a consequence, the state in its various manifestations is seldom roused to take action against them and provoke responses invoking freedom of religion.

However, it would clearly be folly to see the end of those particular contestations between religious freedom and the exercise of state power in the name of harmony and the interests of social order and majoritarian opinion as having evaporated, or, indeed, become any less significant.[43] Adherence to various forms of fundamentalist Christianity is increasing. Particularly where their influence on and engagement with the public institutions and policies of Canada is also increasing, the accommodation of the religious freedoms of those denominations and their members represents a particular challenge to the legal order. This is not so much the world of street marches and parades, of door-to-door solicitation (though they still occur) but that of sustained attention to influence on government policy and the inculcation of particular values through education at various levels. Perhaps even more significantly, and this is reflected by recent freedom of religion case law, the claims are those of religions other than Christian (Muslims, Sikhs, Hindus), and the extent to which many Canadians conceive of those claimants as an alien 'other' marks this as the most contentious domain for freedom of religion litigation, the modern day equivalent of the Salvation Army and the Jehovah's Witnesses.

However, extensive changes to the legal firmament even since 1959 mean that the context for such litigation, both in terms of the circumstances out of which it arises and applicable legal principles and doctrine, has also undergone a dramatic transformation. In particular, the advent of the *Charter* has afforded explicit constitutional protection to rights that previously were not legally recognized or operated only as implicit constitutional guarantees subject generally to legislative override. Now, many of society's most contentious

---

43   Indeed, there are many flashpoint issues that I have not canvassed in this essay such as restrictions on picketing at abortion clinics and withholding of consent to medical treatment especially for children on grounds of conscience.

debates pit freedom of religion against the 'new' rights and particularly those of equality. In particular, recognition of the rights of women, gays, lesbians, homosexuals, and transgendered persons, reproductive rights, and the right to privacy come into collision with the most firmly held religious beliefs and practices of many groups. Secularism, and preservation of cultural and social identity, rather than the rights of established and majority religions are now much more commonly the driving force in any move to curb religious freedoms. The prime example is the transformation of Quebec from the close-knit Roman Catholic community of the era of *Roncarelli v. Duplessis* to a largely secular state in which preservation of cultural and linguistic identity is the prevailing norm.

Recently, this was reflected most dramatically in the introduction by the then separatist government of Quebec of a *Charter of Quebec Values* Bill.[44] Among other things, this Bill would have placed significant restrictions on public sector workers wearing any form of religious symbol in the workplace. Interestingly, it had the public support of retired Supreme Court of Canada justice, Claire L'Heureux-Dubé,[45] who, in dissenting in *Trinity Western University*, had minimized the freedom of religion components of the competing claims and applied the highly deferential patent unreasonableness standard of review to the College of Teachers' assessment of the accreditation application. Ultimately, however, the defeat of the government at a general election, in part because of the Bill, spelled the end at least temporarily of this initiative.

The Supreme Court of Canada's record on freedom of religion has for the most part reflected a robust tolerance for the exercise of religious displays and practices in the face of challenges made in the name of overall state and societal interests. To that extent, it mirrors the position taken by the Court of Queen's Bench in *Beatty v. Gillbanks*. It is the principle of 'Show me the harm' in action. In the face of current challenges, it now remains to be seen whether this culture of minimal intrusion and respect will survive. More particularly, will the long-prevailing attitude yield to the force of other and sometimes competing rights and freedoms recognized in the *Charter*, the current willingness to accord considerable deference to official assessments of various threats posed by the exercise of religious freedom, and the increasing (though certainly not unopposed) pressures of secularism?

---

44   Bill 60, 1st Session, 40th Legislature, tabled on 7 November 2013.
45   See 'Former Supreme Court justices offer conflicting views of Quebec's secular charter', The Globe and Mail, 7 February 2014.

CHAPTER 32

The Alien Tort Statute, *Kiobel*, and the Struggle for Human Rights Accountability

Beth Stephens

Dedication

At an event honoring José Ramos-Horta, the first foreign minister and later president of the newly independent state of East Timor, Roger Clark remembered waking at the crack of dawn years earlier, on a snowy winter day, to travel with José to talk to a teachers' group. They spent hours in transit, on snowy roads and waiting for delayed flights, spoke to the small group that showed up, then turned around and traveled hours more on the return trip. A well-spent day, they agreed, because the cumulative impact of many such small events makes a movement. In my legal and political activism, when I become discouraged because our small victories are so often overshadowed by larger defeats, I often think of Roger and José, and I find the energy to move on, one step at a time.[1]

1   Introduction

From 1980 until 2013, victims and survivors of human rights abuses around the world filed civil lawsuits in the United States pursuant to the Alien Tort Statute ('ATS'),[2] seeking damages from the individuals or corporations responsible for their injuries. If the defendants were present in the United States, and the abuses violated core international human rights norms, federal courts asserted jurisdiction over the claims. Only a small number of lawsuits succeeded in holding defendants liable, and even fewer were able to collect money damages. Those involved nevertheless expressed satisfaction at the opportunity to tell their stories, make a record of what had happened to them, and force the defendants to respond to their claims. Human rights advocates welcomed the

---

1   Roger was speaking at the Rutgers-Camden Law School graduation in 2000, at which José Ramos Horta received an honorary degree.
2   28 USC s 1350.

litigation as a means to hold accountable a small number of perpetrators, set an example for others, and help develop substantive human rights norms.

In 2013, the Supreme Court in *Kiobel v Royal Dutch Petroleum* sharply limited the scope of the ATS. The full extent of the reduction is not yet clear, and many cases will continue to be litigated as common law claims or based on other, narrower statutes. Nevertheless, it seems likely that the decision will result in a significant decrease in US human rights litigation. The *Kiobel* decision was a product of a drumbeat of opposition to the ATS from corporate interests and government officials. But it is only the latest of many court decisions and legislative actions that have cut back on litigation as a tool to remedy societal wrongs. These restrictions have come in response to decades of concerted domestic and international resistance to the use of the courts to hold business and government actors accountable.

Restrictions on human rights litigation also reflect a decades-long struggle over the implementation of human rights norms. The human rights movement has long sought to establish mechanisms capable of holding accountable states, state officials, and private actors who violate those norms. The International Criminal Court is one tangible result of that effort. But vigorous opposition has blocked development of robust enforcement mechanisms and has undercut those that emerge. The rise and fall of ATS litigation is part of the larger struggle over whether government officials and corporations can be held accountable for their misdeeds.

2   The History of the Alien Tort Statute

The framers of the US Constitution were deeply concerned about the enforcement of international law. Before the ratification of the Constitution, when the Articles of Confederation granted the national government no power to punish those who violated international norms, leaders of the Confederation repeatedly expressed frustration about their inability to remedy international law violations. In two infamous incidents in the 1780s, the leaders of the national government were unable to respond to violations of the rights of foreign diplomats, and the governments of both France and the Netherlands threatened reprisals.[3] In the words of Edmund

---

3   *Sosa v Alvarez-Machain*, 542 US 692, 716–17 (2004); William R Casto, 'The Federal Courts' Protective Jurisdiction over Torts Committed in Violation of the Law of Nations' (1986) 18 Conn L Rev 467, 491–94.

Randolph, 'the Confederation might be doomed to be plunged into war, from its wretched impotency to check offenses against [international] law.'[4]

To remedy this deficiency, the Constitution granted control over foreign affairs to the federal government, including the power to define and punish offences against the law of nations.[5] In 1789, the first Congress enacted a Judiciary Act that granted federal courts jurisdiction over torts committed in violation of the law of nations, a statute now known as the Alien Tort Statute.[6] The one-sentence statute, which remains part of the US Code today, reads: 'The district courts shall have original jurisdiction of any civil action by an alien for a tort only, committed in violation of the law of nations or a treaty of the United States.' Although there is little explicit history about the statute, the general consensus holds that it was enacted to grant non-citizens the option of asking federal courts, rather than state courts, to decide cases involving some violations of international law.[7] Just a few years after the ATS was enacted, the US Attorney General observed that foreigners injured in an attack by US citizens in violation of the international rules governing neutrality could sue for damages under the ATS.[8]

The statute lay largely dormant until 1980, when a federal appellate court held in *Filártiga v Peña-Irala* that the ATS authorized claims by a non-US citizen for violations of modern international law norms.[9] In *Filártiga*, the family of a young man tortured to death in Paraguay sought damages from the torturer, a Paraguayan police officer, who had fled to the United States to avoid scrutiny in Paraguay. The US court held that torture constituted a violation of the law of nations, and allowed the lawsuit to proceed. As the court explained:

> [F]or purposes of civil liability, the torturer has become like the pirate and slave trader before him, *hostis humani generis*, an enemy of all mankind. Our holding today, giving effect to a jurisdictional provision enacted by our First Congress, is a small but important step in the fulfillment of the ageless dream to free all people from brutal violence.[10]

---

4   A Letter of His Excellency Edmund Randolph, Esquire, on the Federal Constitution (10 October 1787), in Herbert J. Storing (ed), 2 *The Complete Anti-Federalist* 86, 88 (University of Chicago Press 1981).

5   US Const, art I, s 8, cl 10.

6   Judiciary Act of 1789, ch 20, s 9, 1 Stat 73, 76–77.

7   For a full discussion of the history and modern application of the ATS, see Beth Stephens, 'The Curious History of the Alien Tort Statute' (2014) 89 Notre Dame L Rev 1467 ('Stephens, "The Curious History of the Alien Tort Statute"').

8   Breach of Neutrality, 1 Op Att'y Gen 57, 59 (1795) (William Bradford).

9   *Filártiga v Peña-Irala*, 630 F2d 876 (2d Cir 1980).

10   Ibid 890.

Filártiga was decided at a moment in which the international human rights movement was growing rapidly.[11] Around the world, newly formed and expanding local groups increasingly framed their struggles in the language of human rights. In the United States, the civil rights movement, the campaign to end the Vietnam War, and opposition to the foreign policy of President Richard M. Nixon spurred human rights organizing. President Jimmy Carter, who took office in 1977, made human rights advocacy a centerpiece of his foreign policy.

The *Filártiga* decision received a generally favourable response, and subsequent ATS cases were relatively non-controversial for almost two decades. Courts affirmed that victims and survivors of human rights abuses could sue those responsible for abuses such as torture, summary execution, disappearance, genocide, and crimes against humanity, if the perpetrator was subject to the jurisdiction of the US courts.[12] In *Kadic v Karadzic*, for example, survivors of abuses in Bosnia-Herzegovina sued Radovan Karadzic, leader of the Bosnian-Serbs, for genocide, war crimes, torture, and summary execution.[13]

In most of the early cases, the defendants left the United States at some point after the lawsuit was filed and declined to defend the allegations, leading to default judgments that usually could not be enforced. But plaintiffs, most of whom did not expect to collect damage awards, expressed satisfaction that the process had offered them the opportunity to tell their stories in a court of law and obtain judicial recognition of the human rights violations that they and their families had suffered. Dolly Filártiga, for example, described her family's lawsuit against the man who tortured her brother to death as 'an enormous victory' for human rights and the pursuit of justice.[14]

Civil human rights litigation was largely, although not entirely, confined to the United States. By comparison with the procedural rules in effect in much of the world, the US civil litigation system offers procedural advantages that made human rights litigation feasible, particularly in the 1980s and 1990s.[15] Criminal prosecutions for human rights violations have been very rare in the

---

11   Kenneth Cmiel, 'The Emergence of Human Rights Politics in the United States' (1999) 86 J Am Hist 1231.
12   Stephens, 'The Curious History of the Alien Tort Statute' (n 7) 1484–88.
13   *Kadic v Karadzic*, 70 F3d 232 (2d Cir 1995).
14   Dolly Filártiga, 'Foreword', in Beth Stephens and others, *Human Rights Litigation in US Courts* (2nd edn, Martinus Nijhoff 2008) xvii, xviii.
15   Beth Stephens, 'Translating Filártiga: A Comparative and International Law Analysis of Domestic Remedies for International Human Rights Violations' (2002) 27 Yale J Int'l L 1. However, as discussed in the next section, US procedure is now significantly less favorable

United States, however, both because of long delays in enacting the necessary criminal statutes[16] and because the US legal system does not permit private citizens to initiate criminal prosecutions. In Europe and parts of Latin America, by contrast, private campaigns to hold accountable human rights abusers more often led to criminal prosecutions, primarily against perpetrators who had fled their home countries and were found living in Europe.[17]

3 The Pushback against Civil Litigation in the United States

Most of the defendants in the few dozen ATS cases during the 1980s and 1990s were former government officials of repressive regimes with little political clout in the United States. In the late 1990s, a series of cases filed against US and foreign corporations and against officials of politically powerful governments triggered a backlash against human rights litigation. But this backlash was just one piece of a concerted attack on litigation as a means to provide redress for a range of violations of legal rights.

From the 1960s through the late 1980s, courts and legislatures significantly expanded access to the courts to challenge conduct that injured individual plaintiffs and also constituted a danger to society as a whole, including faulty and badly designed products, unfair contract terms, and civil rights violations.[18] These changes continued a process of legal reform that began in the early years of the twentieth century. Proponents argued that offering private parties enhanced access to judicial remedies helped to correct an imbalance that had permitted corporations and more privileged citizens to escape liability for injuries that they caused. Overall, the reforms during this time period

---

to plaintiffs than in the past, and the impact of the procedural changes on ATS litigation has been striking.

16 The United States criminalized torture committed outside the United States in 1995, 18 USC ss 2340, 2340A; the parallel statute criminalizing acts of genocide, 18 USC s 1091, was extended to acts committed abroad in 2007.

17 For an overview of current cases, see 'EU Update on International Crimes', Newsletter of the Universal Jurisdiction Network, Issue 12, 3 July 2014, at 8, available at http://www.redress.org/newsletters/eu-update-international-crimes. For a comparison of the accountability mechanisms available in the United States and those of other legal systems, see Stephens (n 15).

18 Jay M Feinman, *Un-Making Law: The Conservative Campaign to Roll Back the Common Law* 13–17 (Beacon Press 2004); James A Henderson, Jr & Theodore Eisenberg, 'The Quiet Revolution in Products Liability: An Empirical Study of Legal Change' (1990) 37 UCLA L Rev 479, 483–88.

reflected the widely shared view that litigation could play an important role 'in making America a safer, better place in which to live and work.'[19]

The growth of litigation seeking to enforce rights sparked a backlash that gained force in the 1980s. The campaign relied on unsubstantiated claims that tort litigation had exploded into an inefficient and unfair drain on the national economy. In a 1986 statement, for example, the chair of the National Association of Manufacturers characterized products liability lawyers and plaintiffs as a 'plague of locusts' who 'have brought a blood bath for US business and are distorting our traditional values.'[20] Others argued that damage awards had reached crisis proportions,[21] and that excessive tort liability had thrown the insurance industry into crisis. Although empirical studies demonstrated that the anti-litigation hysteria was unwarranted, the critics' inflated rhetoric succeeded in convincing large swaths of the country that an out-of-control legal system required major reform.[22]

Congress, state legislatures, and the judiciary responded with multiple new barriers to litigation. A range of statutory changes—some minor, others 'draconian'[23]—limited access to the courts, made litigation more difficult for plaintiffs, reduced the remedies available in successful litigation, and made it easier for businesses to impose one-sided contract terms on consumers. Newly enacted legislation imposed limits on damage awards, restricted the use of class actions, and created barriers to specific claims such as medical malpractice and products liability.

During the same time period, the Supreme Court engaged in a systematic reinterpretation of the rules governing federal litigation that significantly raised the barriers facing plaintiffs suing the government or corporations. From 1986–2005, under the leadership of Chief Justice William Rehnquist, the

---

19   Henderson & Eisenberg (n 18) 487.
20   Robert Dee, 'Blood Bath' (1986) 10 Enterprise 3 (statement by Chairman of the Board of the National Association of Manufacturers), quoted in Henderson & Eisenberg (n 18) 481.
21   Theodore Eisenberg, 'The empirical effects of tort reform' in Jennifer Arlen (ed), *Research Handbook on the Economics of Torts* 513, 520 (Edward Elgar Publishing 2013) (discussing allegations of a punitive damages crisis and concluding that the purported crisis was 'largely a social construct of entities like the US Chamber of Commerce', and reinforced by industry-funded, unfounded research).
22   'Using every technique of modern media-shaping, tort reform groups sought to assure that the public believed that products liability law was the cause of [a] threat to our way of life.' Theodore Eisenberg & James A Henderson, Jr, 'Inside the Quiet Revolution in Products Liability' (1992) 39 UCLA L Rev 731, 793. For a detailed response to the inflated critiques of the legal system, see Feinman (n 18).
23   Henderson & Eisenberg (n 18) 480.

Court's decisions betrayed a 'profound hostility to litigation',[24] which reflected its 'skepticism as to the ability of litigation to function as a mechanism for organizing social relations and collectively administering justice.'[25] This trend continued with the appointment of John Roberts as Chief Justice in 2005.[26] The barriers include multiple limits on litigants' power to bring suits, often through reinterpretations of congressional intent. For example, the Supreme Court adopted an increasingly strong presumption against recognizing a private right to sue to enforce a federal statute.[27] A private right to sue for a violation of a federal standard transforms that norm into a tool by which individuals can enforce the law. Limiting private enforcement leaves implementation of the norms to the overstretched, underfunded arms of the federal government.

Other changes have increased the pleading burden on plaintiffs seeking to bring federal claims; restricted discovery; encouraged judges to dismiss cases before trial; limited the role of expert witnesses; and enforced contracts requiring that disputes be settled by arbitration rather than litigation. Jay Feinman summarizes these changes as the result of a 'concerted effort by an array of business groups and conservative ideologues' to undermine legal protections for consumers, workers, small business people, homeowners, and the environment,[28] and as part of a broader campaign 'to reduce the ability of government to promote the common good.'[29]

4   The Pushback against Human Rights Litigation

Filártiga was decided in 1980, at a time of widespread support for litigation both as a tool of social change and a means for those injured by abuses of power to obtain redress for their injuries. Proponents sought to use human rights litigation to enforce human rights norms directly, without the need to

---

24   Andrew M Siegel, 'The Court Against the Courts: Hostility to Litigation as an Organizing Theme in the Rehnquist Court's Jurisprudence' (2006) 84 Tex L Rev 1097, 1107.
25   Ibid 1108.
26   'The Roberts Court has shown similar hostility to litigation as a means of vindicating legal rights.' Howard M Wasserman, 'The Roberts Court and the Civil Procedure Revival' (2012) 31 Rev Litig 313, 332.
27   Richard H Fallon Jr and others, *Hart and Wechsler's The Federal Courts and the Federal System* 705–07 (6th ed, Thomson Reuters/Foundation Press 2009) (tracing the Court's changing holdings on judicial power to recognize rights to sue for a statutory violation).
28   Feinman (n 18) 6, 172–89.
29   Ibid 4.

convince reluctant governments to take action to compensate victims and survivors and to punish perpetrators.

Despite the growing opposition to civil litigation, ATS cases were relatively noncontroversial until the late 1990s, largely because the small number of claims generally did not threaten business interests or others with significant political power within the United States. As of 1997, fewer than a dozen ATS lawsuits had produced judgments for plaintiffs, and most of those decisions were default judgments against defendants who moved out of the United States when the case was filed. Opposition increased rapidly, however, when cases were filed against corporations; against Chinese and Israeli officials; and, after the 11 September 2001 attacks, against US government officials accused of violating the rights of detainees in the United States and around the world.

Opponents of ATS litigation mounted a major challenge to the statute when the Supreme Court agreed to review the application of the ATS in *Sosa v Alvarez-Machain*, decided in 2004.[30] Although *Sosa* did not involve corporations, corporate advocates saw it as an opportunity to overturn the *Filártiga* line of cases. *Sosa* was filed by Humberto Alvarez-Machain, a Mexican citizen who was kidnapped in Mexico by agents hired by the US government and taken illegally across the border into the United States. In deciding *Sosa*, the Court reviewed for the first time the interpretation of the ATS that was adopted by the *Filártiga* court and had been accepted by every lower court to reach a decision on the issue in the intervening years.

The administration of President George W. Bush joined the opposition to the ATS with an additional motivation. At a time when the Bush administration was under international attack for violations of human rights committed as part of its so-called 'war on terrorism', administration officials feared that the ATS might support claims against the US government for human rights abuses committed by its officials and agents. The US government was joined on this issue by officials from other States who opposed efforts by private parties to hold officials accountable for actions taken while serving their governments. Despite strong rhetoric about individual accountability dating back to the Nuremberg tribunals, government officials continued to strongly resist efforts to hold them accountable for even the most egregious human rights violations. Bush administration concerns about accountability for torture and other human rights violations committed after 11 September 2001 heightened this resistance.

The challenge to the modern application of the ATS in *Sosa* relied on themes common to the broader attack on civil litigation. Sosa and his allies claimed

---

30   *Sosa v Alvarez-Machain* (n 3).

that the federal courts had no power to recognize a private right to sue for violations of international law, despite conceding that the eighteenth-century Congress that enacted the statute would have expected the courts to recognize such a right to sue. Opponents of ATS litigation thus asked the Court to apply a presumption about congressional intent retroactively, as the Court had done in other settings. Surprisingly, the six-justice Court majority opted instead to give effect to its understanding of the goals of the legislators who enacted the ATS. In so doing, the Court strongly affirmed judicial power to recognize a common law cause of action for violations of international law.

While affirming that the federal courts have the power to recognize a right to sue for violations of international law, the Court in *Sosa* rejected the claim of unlawful arrest and detention raised by Alvarez-Machain. The Court held that his abduction without warrant in Mexico, followed by a twenty-four-hour detention before his abductors turned him over to law enforcement officials in the United States, did not constitute a violation of a clearly defined, widely accepted international law norm. Thus, while upholding the *Filártiga* doctrine, the Court provided no model of what kind of claim would trigger a federal court's jurisdiction under the ATS. As discussed in the next section, opponents of human rights litigation successfully exploited this void nine years later, when the Supreme Court drastically limited the scope of the ATS in *Kiobel v Royal Dutch Petroleum Co*.[31]

ATS opponents mounted another unsuccessful Supreme Court challenge in 2010, in a case claiming that former foreign government officials were immune from civil tort claims in US courts.[32] The US Foreign Sovereign Immunities Act ('FSIA') protects foreign governments from most lawsuits alleging conduct outside the United States.[33] In *Samantar v Yousuf*, several Somali citizens had sued Mohamad Samantar, a former Somali government official who was living in the United States, for torture and other international law violations. Samantar claimed that foreign government officials were protected by the FSIA and thus immune to the same extent as foreign governments. He was joined in his appeal to the Supreme Court by immunity advocates concerned about ATS lawsuits filed against former Israeli government officials and other allies of the United States. The Supreme Court rejected the broad interpretation of the FSIA urged by Samantar and his supporters, but left unclear the scope of a possible common law immunity that might protect some foreign officials in future cases.

---

31 *Kiobel v Royal Dutch Petroleum Co*, 133 S Ct 1659 (2013).
32 *Samantar v Yousuf*, 560 US 305 (2010).
33 28 USC ss 1330, 1602–611.

The objections to US civil litigation against former foreign government officials resembled the campaign against criminal prosecutions of such officials in Europe and Latin America. Prosecutions of individuals found living in the forum state have proceeded.[34] However, efforts to use the concept of universal jurisdiction to support prosecutions of defendants who were not present in the forum state faced vehement opposition, particularly when focused on officials of politically powerful governments.[35] A Belgium statute authorizing universal jurisdiction prosecutions was sharply curtailed in 2003, after charges were filed against U.S. government officials.[36] A similar Spanish statute was narrowed in 2014 after an attempt to prosecute Chinese officials.[37]

Around the world, governments and corporations fought successfully to limit means by which private citizens could hold them accountable for human rights violations.

5 The Alien Tort Statute and the *Kiobel* Decision

In the late 1990s, human rights advocates filed several ATS lawsuits against corporations.[38] Several class action lawsuits filed by Holocaust survivors received widespread attention and, with the assistance of the US government, obtained large settlements. A handful of cases filed against corporations alleging abuses connected with their operations outside the United States initially had little success. In 2002, however, a district court in California ruled that ATS claims against Unocal Oil for human rights abuses in Burma could proceed.[39] In the

---

34   EU Update (n 17).
35   Luc Reydams, 'The Rise and Fall of Universal Jurisdiction' in William A Schabas & Nadia Bernaz (eds), *Routledge Handbook of International Criminal Law* 337 (Routledge 2010), available at <http://papers.ssrn.com/sol3/papers.cfm?abstract_id=1553734> accessed 4 August 2014.
36   Human Rights Watch, 'Belgium: Universal Jurisdiction Law Repealed' (2 Aug 2003), available at http://www.hrw.org/news/2003/08/01/belgium-universal-jurisdiction-law-repealed.
37   Andrés Cala, 'Spain: A human-rights avenger no longer?' The Christian Science Monitor (10 April 2014), available at <http://www.csmonitor.com/World/Europe/2014/0410/Spain-A-human-rights-avenger-no-longer> accessed 4 August 2014.
38   For an analysis of corporate-defendant ATS litigation, see Stephens, "The Curious History of the Alien Tort Statute" (n 7) 1512–13, 1517–23.
39   *Doe I v Unocal Corp, 395 F3d 932* (9th Cir 2002). The case settled in 2004 under undisclosed terms. Bloomberg News, 'Unocal Settles Rights Suit in Myanmar', N.Y. Times (14 Dec 2004), available at <http://www.nytimes.com/2004/12/14/business/14unocal.html> accessed 4 August 2014.

following decade, dozens of cases against corporations alleged human rights violations for abuses committed in countries around the world. Although many were dismissed quickly, approximately twenty led to protracted litigation, with at least three resolved through multi-million dollar settlements, including the Unocal litigation.

Opposition to the cases increased exponentially, with business associations arguing that the claims posed a serious threat to US businesses. Opponents challenged the standard by which corporations could be held liable for violations committed by government or private security forces working on behalf of the corporation, and obtained rulings limiting corporate liability unless the corporation assisted such forces with the purpose of committing human rights violations.[40]

In 2010, the Second Circuit Court of Appeals issued an unexpected decision in *Kiobel v Royal Dutch Petroleum Co* that threatened to halt all ATS corporate-defendant litigation. *Kiobel* involved claims that the corporation was responsible for summary executions, torture, and other human rights violations in Nigeria. In a 2–1 decision, the court held that corporations could not be sued under the ATS because international law does not recognize corporate liability for human rights violations.[41] The majority rejected the argument that international law binds corporations to the same extent as natural persons and held that there is no clearly defined, widely accepted norm of corporate accountability for violations of international law. Several appellate courts disagreed, however, holding that the ATS permits suits against corporations because international law binds all actors and makes no exception for corporations.[42]

The Supreme Court agreed to review the Second Circuit's *Kiobel* decision and to resolve the lower court split over corporate liability. The Court heard oral argument in 2012, but, instead of addressing that issue, asked for additional briefing on the more far-reaching question of whether the ATS applies to conduct that took place in the territory of a foreign state. The decision, issued in 2013, did not even address corporate liability under the ATS. Although the Court did not explain why it ducked the corporate accountability issue, it is possible that the five Supreme Court justices in the majority, all of whom had recently held that corporations have a constitutionally protected right to spend

---

40 Andrei Mamolea, 'The Future of Corporate Aiding and Abetting Liability under the Alien Tort Statute: A Roadmap' (2011) 51 Santa Clara L Rev 79.

41 *Kiobel v Royal Dutch Petroleum Co*, 621 F3d 111, 161 (2d Cir 2010), *aff'd on other grounds*, 133 S Ct 1659 (2013).

42 For example, *Flomo v Firestone Nat Rubber Co*, 643 F3d 1013 (2011).

money to influence elections,[43] may have been unwilling to issue a decision holding that those same corporations could not be sued when they participate in human rights violations such as genocide, torture, and summary executions.[44]

Whatever the explanation, the Court found an alternative basis on which to reject the claims. The *Kiobel* plaintiffs were non-citizens of the United States, who were suing a foreign corporation for events that took place solely outside of the United States. The Dutch corporate defendant's ties to the United States were limited to a small office in New York City. All nine justices agreed that such 'foreign-cubed' claims did not trigger ATS jurisdiction, but they disagreed about the reasoning behind their decision and the implications of the holding for future cases.

The five-justice majority opinion relied on a 2010 Supreme Court decision in which the Court had strengthened the traditional presumption that statutes do not apply outside the United States unless Congress intends that they govern extraterritorial conduct.[45] Critics pointed out that applying a heightened presumption to a previously enacted statute results in a statute that does not have the meaning intended by Congress. When new presumptions consistently restrict the enforceability of congressional norms, the cumulative impact is a dramatic, judicially imposed decrease in access to remedies for violations of statutory rights.

Applying the presumption against extraterritoriality in *Kiobel*, the Court concluded that nothing in the text, history, or purposes of the ATS indicated a congressional intent to apply the jurisdictional grant to claims arising in the territory of a foreign state. In so doing, the Court gave no weight to multiple indications that the Congress that enacted the statute would have expected extraterritorial application. For example, the text of the statute used the term 'tort', stating that it applies to a claim for 'a *tort*...committed in violation of the law of nations.' In the late-eighteenth century—and today as well—US law understood torts to be transitory, so that a person injured by a tort committed in the territory of a foreign state would have been able to sue in the United States if the defendant was found in the United States.

The contemporary history of the statute similarly supports extraterritorial application. US Attorney General William Bradford, who was familiar with the

---

43   *Citizens United v Fed Election Comm'n*, 558 US 310 (2010).
44   For a comparison of the *Citizens United v Fed Election Comm'n*, and *Kiobel* analyses of corporate rights and duties, see Beth Stephens, 'Are Corporations People? Corporate Personhood Under the Constitution and International Law' (2013) 44 Rutgers L J 1.
45   *Morrison v National Australia Bank*, 130 S Ct 2869 (2010).

Congress that enacted the ATS, relied on the statute in an opinion issued in the 1790s.[46] In his opinion, one of the few references to the statute in the decade after it was enacted, Bradford specifically stated that the ATS would apply to a civil suit by persons injured by a violation of international law committed within the territory of a foreign state, Sierra Leone. The opinion thus provides strong evidence that the statute was intended to apply to claims arising out of conduct in the territory of a foreign state, exactly the issue decided by *Kiobel*. The Court rejected this historical evidence, however, based largely on a false claim by the Bush administration that the events actually occurred on an international waterway, not in the territory of Sierra Leone.[47] Despite briefing that contradicted that claim, and evidence that Bradford himself knew, when he wrote his opinion, that the events took place in the territory of Sierra Leone,[48] the Court concluded that the facts were murky and gave no weight to the historical record.[49]

The concerns that animated the Congress that enacted the ATS also suggest that it intended to include at least some extraterritorial application of the statute. Commentators agree that, at a minimum, the statute was designed to provide remedies for international law violations for which the United States might be held liable. Violations committed by US citizens who are not subject to suit in the place where the violations occurred, for example, fall squarely within that category.

In addition, the extraterritorial application of the ATS was a background assumption in *Sosa*, a Supreme Court case decided just nine years earlier. Since the Court did not address the issue directly, the holding was not explicit. But the Bush administration had argued that the presumption against extraterritoriality should bar application of the ATS to the case, which was based on events that took place in Mexico.[50] The fact that the conduct occurred in Mexico was central to the Court's analysis in *Sosa*, so it cannot have ignored the issue. *Sosa* also cited the *Filártiga* decision with approval, along with the decisions in two other extraterritorial cases.[51] While this reasoning from *Sosa* is not decisive, it

---

46 Breach of Neutrality, 1 Op Att'y Gen 57 (1795) (William Bradford).
47 *Kiobel* (n 31) 1668.
48 Supplemental Brief of *Amici Curiae* Professors of Legal History 18–25, Kiobel v Royal Dutch Petroleum Co., 133 S Ct 1659 (2013) (No. 10–1491).
49 *Kiobel* (n 31) 1668.
50 Brief for the United States as Respondent Supporting Petitioner 46–50, Sosa v Alvarez-Machain, 542 US 692 (2004) (No. 03–339).
51 *Sosa v Alvarez-Machain* (n 3) 731.

certainly is relevant to the extraterritoritality analysis, yet the Court in *Kiobel* did not even address the impact of *Sosa* on the issue before it.

Finally, the US legal system has multiple doctrines to protect against the particular problems presented by the *Kiobel* case. If the defendant's ties to the United States are too attenuated, the case should be dismissed for lack of personal jurisdiction. And if the claims would be more efficiently tried in another place, the lawsuit can be dismissed under the doctrine of *forum non conveniens*. Rewriting the ATS was not a necessary means to respond to concerns about whether this particular case belonged in US courts.

These multiple flaws lend support to the view that the *Kiobel* decision is best understood as part of a campaign to limit litigation, rather than an effort to interpret the ATS. Aside from the holding that the ATS did not apply to the *Kiobel* facts, the significance of the case is both unclear and hotly contested. Presumably, *Kiobel* bars cases with similar facts: cases based only on events that occurred in the territory of a foreign state, and filed by non-US citizens against a foreign corporation with a minimal presence in the United States.

Beyond those facts, the majority opinion is unclear, and rendered even less definitive by the concurring opinion of Justice Kennedy, who provided the crucial fifth vote. After concluding that the presumption against extraterritoriality barred the *Kiobel* claims, the majority opinion stated that claims that 'touch and concern the territory of the United States...with sufficient force' will 'displace the presumption against extraterritoriality.' The subsequent sentence adds that 'mere corporate presence' will be insufficient to displace the presumption. But the majority opinion did not explain what connection with US territory would 'touch and concern' the United States 'with sufficient force.' The concurring opinions of both Justice Kennedy and Justice Alito suggest that this language is important. Justice Kennedy praised the majority for 'leav[ing] open a number of significant questions.' Justice Alito—joined by Justice Thomas—stated that he would have adopted a 'broader standard' that barred all claims alleging violations outside the United States, and criticized the majority's 'narrow approach.'

The 'narrow approach' bemoaned by Justices Alito and Thomas and praised by Justice Kennedy seems only to bar cases based on *Kiobel*-like facts, while leaving untouched ATS jurisdiction over claims that 'touch and concern' the United States with greater force. The lower courts have disagreed about the application of *Kiobel* to claims that have some connection to the United States. Some have read the opinion to bar *all* claims in which the violations occurred in a foreign state—the result preferred by Justices Alito and Thomas and apparently rejected by the majority.[52] Other courts, however, have applied the 'touch and concern' language to permit claims with some significant connection to the United States.[53]

The *Kiobel* decision joins a long line of decisions over the past 30 years in which an ever more assertive majority of the Supreme Court has limited access to judicial remedies as a means to protect individual rights. Despite these setbacks, decades of robust ATS litigation have contributed to strengthening the accountability movement in the United States and internationally. In addition to whatever categories of ATS claims manage to survive *Kiobel*, human rights litigation will continue under modern statutes enacted, in part, on the foundation built by the ATS. Claims of torture and extrajudicial killing, for example, can be filed against non-corporate defendants under the Torture Victim Protection Act.[54] Common law claims for wrongful death and assault and battery can be litigated against U.S. corporations in state courts.[55] Increasingly constrictive judicial and legislative rules will make such litigation more difficult, but the push for legal accountability will continue.

6   Conclusion

The international human rights movement has had considerable success in developing human rights standards. Enforcement of those norms, however, remains a formidable challenge. As victims and survivors of abuse forge new mechanisms to hold perpetrators accountable, they have encountered fierce resistance, particularly when they empower private parties to challenge powerful governmental and corporate interests. The history of the ATS reflects that common pattern. But ongoing efforts to develop new enforcement strategies demonstrate the accountability movement's commitment to the long, slow struggle to punish and deter gross violations of basic human rights.

---

52   For example, *Balintulo v Daimler AG*, 727 F3d 174 (2d Cir 2013) (stating that *Kiobel* 'expressly held that claims under the ATS cannot be brought for violations of the law of nations occurring within the territory of a sovereign other than the United States.').

53   For example, *Al Shimari v Caci Premier Technology, Inc*, 2014 WL 2922840 *5–13 (4th Cir June 30, 2014) (holding that the ATS affords jurisdiction over claims with substantial ties to the United States).

54   28 USC s 1350 (note).

55   Paul Hoffman & Beth Stephens, 'International Human Rights Cases Under State Law and in State Courts' (2013) 3 UC Irvine L Rev 9.

CHAPTER 33

Dynamics of International Legal Systems and State Regulatory Autonomy

Ari Afilalo

I met Roger fifteen years ago, as a candidate for a position on the international law faculty that he had joined 28 years before, and that remained his home base throughout a legendary journey. I got the job and, since then, I have been the midfielder whose locker is next to Pele's. If you make a right turn out of my door, you will walk immediately past the building crew's tiny headquarters, then an unimposing back stairway door, and to the left you will see the open door to Professor Clark's academic dwelling place. It is the last door in a long hallway lined with faculty offices, all the way away from the exit elevator, a mainstay in the heartland that is always open for business.

I have seen, walking past my door, thousands of Friends of Roger. Students, some discovering criminal law and some at the height of distinguished careers joined with long-legged joggers, important dignitaries from countries you mainly see on geography quizzes, judges whose names populate international law books, family, friends, and various mysterious characters I have not yet deconstructed. I could not always make out the languages they spoke, but I could always tell they were united in their fluent understanding of Roger's New Zealand drawl. Like the famed Biblical tent of Abraham, open on all sides to welcome travelers, Roger's office has always exuded a spirit of discussion, mixed with warmth and generosity, that has touched so many and that always leaves you with renewed trust in the inherent goodness of humanity. That is the spirit that I could feel from across the hall.

I am a teacher of international trade, a field that raises issues as fascinating as they come, but as to which only precious few jurists receive the gift of appreciation. When I was honored with an invitation to contribute to this wonderful book, I was humbled by the predictably star-studded table of contents and the breadth of the scholarship written in tribute to Roger. I accepted that my best chance at distinguishing myself was perhaps as a candidate for most arid and technically precise essay. The experience somehow evoked the first date with my wife and her look of disappointment when I admitted that I did not specialize in international human rights, or even in U.N. Resolutions, but that I knew a thing or two about customs duties.

But then, one bright day countless days past the final extended-again deadline, I had a moment of illumination. I understood that my view of Roger's cathedral gives me a unique angle into his spirit and what it stands for, and that my calling here is to humbly explain why it encapsulates what is best and hopeful about international law in the last 50 years. If you think that I went too quickly from customs duties to the sublime, consider this. I am French, and we in France have invented an extraordinary concept called *intime conviction*. That is an 'intimate belief' so close to you, intellectually but even more so viscerally, that it <u>must</u> be true universally. Something like, 'my gut feeling is so perfect it must be everyone's intuition.'

And I had an *intime conviction* moment *par excellence*, an unassailable understanding that in times when grand projects of the formidable legal thinkers of the 20th century come under attack as corrupted, unworkable, or obsolete, we should seek inspiration from Roger's spirit to learn how to carry through to this next Act of History the fundamental ideas that he was so instrumental to building into law in action. So here it is, together with some relevant gleanings about Roger as a teacher and colleague, and with no disclaimer whatsoever. I will let you in on a jealously guarded French secret: most *convictions intimes* turn out to be dead wrong. But this one, friends, is the real thing.

Roger, as a founding framer of the International Criminal Court ('ICC'), joined a group of epic jurists who contributed an astounding amount of transformative ideas to the international realm for decades. I am familiar with the heroes of trade, who were credited with successfully enabling another post-World War II transformative enterprise. The founding framers of trade law created a system that modern liberal democracies could join after World War II, rejecting protectionism in favor of liberalized trade, while remaining faithful to their foundational principles of domestic sovereignty. The legitimacy and practical acceptance of the international trade system rode on the success of the legal organic work. Free movement of goods, services or capital, would necessarily bring about a clash not only with protectionist measures that would become illegal overnight, but with domestic measures that involved health, labor, environmental or other measure, and could conflict with regulatory environments in the country of export. The job of the jurists was to create a system that would accommodate the competing imperatives.

The victors of World War II needed norms and institutions to carry out free trade while leaving enough regulatory space for domestic spending, regulating, counter-recession and other key measures etc. Legitimacy for the modern liberal democracies entailed a basic commitment by the State to protect its nationals' financial security and to support market conditions meeting public expectations of stability and growth. The GATT and its successors succeeded in liberalizing trade and introducing comparative advantage as the animating norm of international commerce, without overtly threatening redistributive justice choices. Sovereignty meant many things, but fundamentally it translated in the last century into a foundational principle that the default locus of power lies within the State. Unless the State relinquished power to an international institution, and even then with the caveat that the national government could always 'selectively' ignore international obligations, or operate international systems based on the 'rational choice' of government officials picking and choosing what to enforce, the State had virtually unfettered authority over the individuals, markets, businesses, assets, and land located within its boundaries.[1]

The first trade frameworks, with the notable exception of Europe (in a unique historical context), treaded lightly around the issue, and made it possible for States at the height of the development of administrative bureaucracies of powerful reach, to agreed to be bound by international trade law liberalizing commerce and endorsing comparative advantage.

While thinking about Roger, two scholars of trade and international constitutional law came to mind for their groundbreaking thinking: John Ruggie and Joseph Weiler. Both dealt with the issue of the line of demarcation between the international system and the domestic jurisdictions. John Ruggie famously defined the international trade system as reflecting 'embedded liberalism.'[2] Ruggie understood early on that the ethos of the modern liberal democratic State is to legislate and intervene on the market, acting for the welfare of its people. This commitment to being an *Etat-Providence*, a Provider State with welfare spending and interventionist needs, prompted the jurists of trade to ensure that the international system would 'embed' the right of States to follow taxation and redistribution. Each country could follow its own choices, and be free to discharge its essential, legitimating functions in its own way. Britain could go about 'cradle-to-grave' welfare, Japan could follow indicative planning policies, and each member of the State could generally apply and adjust the policies that make up the Administrative State free of international constraints.

---

1 For a thorough description of how international legal regimes applying the rational-choice theory and the process by which officials from different States select the disputed issues to press with their treaty partners, mindful of the need to balance enforcement norms with limiting the general reach of international law, see Jack L Goldsmith & Eric A Posner, *The Limits of International Law* (OUP 2005).

2 See John G Ruggie, 'Embedded Liberalism and the Postwar Economic Regimes' in his *Constructing the World Policy: Essays on International Institutionalization* (Routledge 1998).

The poets succeeded in writing this concept into the various provisions of normative law. This is what enabled a grand economic idea like comparative advantage to become the animating law of the land for approximately 150 States. Because it was born and raised in an incubator structure that signaled to States that their sovereignty, as it found expression at the time, would be preserved, liberalized trade could grow and open up markets at a pace acceptable to the States whose nations would do business in the globalizing marketplace. The key substantive doctrines shielding domestic legislation followed from the theoretical assumption that, as long as they rejected all protectionist or unjustifiably discriminatory policies, the States were free to legislate internally as they saw fit. If the poets had failed, the world could have remained mired in trade wars among liberal democracies unwilling to abandon their protectionist ways and to give up power to the collective of nations. The legal moves, again, enabled the trading world to move on to a system of trade compatible with the needs of international commerce and of the sovereign States that signed on to the transformed system.

Professor Weiler offered a theory of 'selective exit' that became an axiom of international law, and spoke to the same issues as Ruggie did.[3] Weiler's selective exit went beyond Ruggie's embedded liberalism in that it enabled a dynamic understanding of trade. Although he wrote in the context of Europe, Weiler understood and created a general theory allowing us to understand the balance between States and the collective of States at any given time. This was a major pillar of the theoretical construct of trade because international law and institutions can only evolve organically if they respect the proper balance of powers with the States. For the States, power meant specifically the ability to suspend their international obligations without risking a constitutional crisis or complete 'exit' from the international system. Selective exit was a pass given to States so that they could decide, as time passed and needs evolved, what domestic measure should displace international law out of an overriding concern for sovereignty, even though the State already accepted an international obligation that formally displaced sovereignty considerations. Too much closure of selective exit, like what happened in the 1960s European Community, when majority voting was scheduled to become effective at the same time as the European Court of Justice was engaged in its epic expansion of the reach of international law, would lead to a possible collapse of the system.

The 'selective exit' concept captured the essence of the make-up of international law, as well as of its evolution. The embedded liberalism of Ruggie described the state of the system in the modern liberal democratic age. The

---

3   Joseph H H Weiler, 'The Transformation of Europe' (1991) 100 Yale L J 2403.

selective exit axiom allowed us to understand the evolution of trade in relation to sovereignty, as the system moved to its next stage. Indeed, trade brought about a world where open borders meant not only more goods and services, but more integration of the business world. This is a natural process. A distributor in the United States that sources products in China may want to partner up with the Chinese supplier, and vice-versa. Product compatibilities create significant opportunities for joint ventures, acquisitions, licenses, or other business transactions. This is a process where global markets are created, with their own structures and norms for the various areas of industrial, commercial, financial and other activities.

Today, the international trade system has pushed back drastically the boundaries of State sovereignty. Individual actors can sue governments for disputes that would 50 years ago be the exclusive province of States, and their likely lack of appetite for challenging most violations. Investment treaties, covering the same subject matter as the WTO, have proliferated.[4]

WTO law has expanded to include side agreements, like TRIPS for intellectual property, requiring individual States to change their domestic law if it is not trade-compliant. (TRIPS, for example, mandates minimum levels of patent, trademark, and copyright protection under the domestic law of each participating States.) Remedies for violations now include large awards of damages enforceable in domestic courts (Philip Morris is challenging Australia's plain packaging legislation under the 1993 Agreement between the Government of Australia and the Government of Hong Kong for the Promotion and Protection of Investments. It is seeking billions of dollars, and if it prevails, the award would be enforceable in an Australian court),[5] instead of being limited to a

---

[4] The number of Bilateral Investment Treaties (BITS) increased from 385 at the end of the 1980s to approximately 3,000 by the end of 2014. For more about the overlap between BITS and the obligations assumed by WTO Members under the General Agreement on Trade in Services see Marie-France Houde & Katia Yannaca-Small, *'Relationships between International Investment Agreements'* (2004) OECD Working Papers on International Investment; Rudolf Adlung & Martín Molinuevo, 'Bilateralism in Services Trade: Is There Fire Behind the (Bit-) Smoke?' (2008) 11 J Int'l Econ L 365; and Ari Afilalo, *Failed Boundaries: The Near-Perfect Correlation between State-to- State WTO Claims and Private Party Investment Rights*, Jean Monnet Working Paper, 01/13.

[5] On 27 June 2011, Philip Morris Asia served Australia with a written notification of claim pursuant to Article 10 of the Hong Kong Agreement, at <http://www.ag.gov.au/Internationalrelations/InternationalLaw/Documents/Philip%20Morris%20Asia%20Limited%20 Notice%20of%20Claim%2027%20June%202011.pdf> accessed 29 January 2015. The Australian Government responded to the Notice of Arbitration on 21 December 2011, at <http://www. ag.gov.au/Internationalrelations/InternationalLaw/Documents/Australias%20Response%20

declaration of non-compliance by an international body. The degree of selective exit is closing down, as happened in Europe, and Professor Weiler gave us a barometer with which to understand this dyunamic evolution in time of the international system.

Professor Clark, as Professor deGuzman masterfully contextualized in her essay, also understood the supreme importance of the legal balancing of the international and national realms.[6] An international criminal court, with the power to prosecute and punish, had to respect the sovereignty concerns of its constituent States. Jurisdiction in the criminal context raises the same constitutional questions, laden with the potential existential crises, that trade experienced. The United States and other countries would not join the Statute of Rome ostensibly out of concern for the reach of the ICC and the potential for prosecutions that the U.S. is not yet ready to tolerate. Like trade, criminal law evolves, and the deeply nuanced view that Roger brings to the issue enables the system to evolve, along with transformations in social expectations and views.

Jurisdiction is an essential area, and Roger is one of the seminal thinkers of international criminal law that understood its significance beyond the narrow confines of a case. As Professor DeGuzman notes, Roger's position is that ICC norms that may sound substantive, like the requirement that a crime be committed in the context of an attack against a population should be understood as jurisdictional barriers. This frees the lawmakers and interpreters for the shackles of time. Today, the ICC can only prosecute crimes if they meet this jurisdictional requirement. It does not mean that the crime is not a crime against humanity, or never worthy of international prosecution. It merely reflects the experience of the States today, who have witnessed the Holocaust, the Armenian Genocide, and the Rwanda Genocide. That's what we know, and that is what the States are willing to transfer to the international realm at the moment. But it does not mean that, as the world evolved, this jurisdictional barrier always stays on the same line.

Consider the evolving strategic battles of the day. They raise squarely questions as to how we understood a population, an attack, in a world where there is no State, amorphous organizations, instant soldiers emerging from population that suspects their affiliation but lives a parallel life. Roger's tools allow the

---

to%20the%20Notice%20of%20Arbitration%2021%20December%202011.pdf> accessed 29 January 2015. The Australian plain packaging legislation was also challenged by numerous countries under the WTO: WT/DS434/1; WT/DS435/1; WT/DS441/R 'Australia—Tobacco Products and Packaging – Request for Consultations' (18 July 2012; 13 March 2012).

6 Margaret M DeGuzman, 'The Elusive Essence Of Crimes Against Humanity', in this *Festschrift*.

system to evolve, just like the trade system is slowly moving into the 21st century. If we considered the doctrines that he would classify as jurisdictional to be substantive, then the system would be stuck in the paradigm of the 20th century – just like embedded liberalism without the selective exit barometer takes too narrow a snapshot in time.

From across the hall, what strikes me is that Roger's big heart is reflected in his definition of humanity. For him, humanity is truly everyone. Either we all count, or nobody counts, as my favorite novel character would say.[7] I have no doubt that the world will accept Roger's view in time, and that the jurisdiction of the international criminal courts will in 50 years be as broad and uncontroversial as that of the local criminal court. Evil is evil is evil, and as a global society in the making we will come to fight it everywhere we see it. Roger's good heart infuses and comes in that vision, and they both are reflected in a view that leaves the system free to grow, at the pace that it can achieve, to reach this result. So thank you, Roger, for giving us scholarship and law as they should be. The ancient wisely said:

> Go and see which is the best trait for a person to acquire. Said Rabbi Eliezer: A good eye. Said Rabbi Joshua: A good friend. Said Rabbi Yossei: A good neighbor. Said Rabbi Shimon: To see what is born [out of ones actions]. Said Rabbi Elazar: A good heart. Said He [God] to them: I prefer the words of Elazar the son of Arach to yours, for his words include all of yours.

What comes out of the heart goes into the heart. I have been blessed with a good neighbor and a good friend, with a good eye, and the vision to see what will be born out of our actions, but above all a good heart. If you don't believe me, come feel it in the hallway.

---

7   Harry Bosch, the fictional detective created by Michael Connelly, coined the expression. It was appropriated by a politician in the last novel in the series, opening the door for me to 'borrow it' as well. *See* Michael Connelly, *The Burning Room* (Orion Books 2014).

CHAPTER 34

Practicing E-Legally: The United Nations Convention on the Use of Electronic Communications in International Commerce

Amelia H. Boss

I met Roger Clark my first day of law school: a dashing young Torts professor with a Kiwi accent who quickly inspired me to love the law and to use it in productive ways. Later, he became a good friend, a mentor, a confidant, a colleague, and, ultimately, my husband. We have shared a lot over the more than forty years that we have known each other, but the hardest obstacles we faced were in the mid 1980s when we decided to co-teach a course: International Business Transactions (with Roger teaching the international and I the business transactions). Roger was convinced that being in the classroom together for an entire semester would be the end of a beautiful relationship. It was quite the contrary: even after years together, we still had a lot to learn from each other. And, we also reaffirmed (teaching the course in Dublin, Paris or London to students amused by our differing accents and word usage) that we had a lot in common: that we view the law not just as an abstract system of rules but as an instrumental tool in addressing the needs of society. Indeed, while he has spent much of his time on international public law negotiations (particularly in the context of the International Criminal Court), I have become involved in private international law negotiations (particularly in the area of electronic commerce, a significant topic in our IBT course these last few years). Here is what we discuss with our students.

Increasingly, businesses are turning to new means of electronic technologies to improve their communications with customers, to access new worldwide markets, and to streamline their business practices. Many countries are attempting to revise their laws to accommodate new electronic commercial practices, and eliminate the barriers to increasing international trade. In so doing, they are increasingly considering ratification of the UN Convention on the Use of Electronic Communications in International Contracts ('Convention'),[1] and several have even enacted the provisions of the Convention as part of their domestic law.

---

1   United Nations Convention on the Use of Electronic Communications in International Contracts, UN Doc A/60/515 (adopted 23 November 2005, entered into force 3 January 2013)

An important question confronted by traders is how the Convention would affect their businesses, and the extent to which it may require changes to their established business practices. In other words, the concern is not what the Convention says technically, but its implications for the day-to-day functioning of international trade.

There are several key areas of concern for businesses moving from the traditional paper-based environment to the electronic environment. This article looks at the Convention through the eyes of a business utilizing electronic technologies as a part of their business plan to see what lessons may be learned from the Convention, and how several of their concerns are met: what law governs the transaction; can the transaction be carried out in electronic form; will the on-line process result in an enforceable contract; how will errors in communications be addressed; what information must be disclosed or exchanged before, during or after the transaction; is sufficient documentation of the transaction available; has a valid electronic signature been used that satisfies any formalities required of these types of transactions; have all applicable record-keeping requirements been satisfied.

1   What Law Will Govern My Transaction?

The Convention was drafted with the recognition that 'adoption of uniform rules to remove obstacles to the use of electronic communications in international contracts, including obstacles that might result from the operation of existing international trade law instruments, would enhance legal certainty and commercial predictability for international contracts and help States gain access to modern trade routes'.[2] Yet in order to obtain the benefits bestowed by the Convention, it is important for traders ensure at the front end that the Convention will apply to their transactions.

('Convention'). The Convention was published with an accompanying explanatory note. UN Convention On The Use Of Electronic Communications In International Contracts, at 13–100, UN Sales No. E.07.V.2 (2007) ('Explanatory Note'). The Convention is based on an early work produced by UNCITRAL, the UNCITRAL Model Law On Electronic Commerce, UN Doc A/Res/51/162/Annex, UN Sales No. E.99.V.4 (1999). For an in-depth discussion of the history and workings of the Convention, see Amelia H Boss & Wolfgang Kilian (eds), *The United Nations Convention On The Use Of Electronic Communications In International Contracts: An In-Depth Guide And Sourcebook* (Kluwer 2008). While Roger was off at International Criminal Court meetings around the world, the author served on the United States delegation to UNCITRAL during the negotiations leading to the creation of both the Convention and Model Law. She was often able to latch on to Roger's unique Antipodean network in New York and Vienna.

2   Convention (n 1) preamble, para 4.

The Convention applies to electronic communications that are made in connection with the formation and performance of a contract between parties whose places of business are in different States.[3] There is no need for both parties to have their places of business in Contracting States to the Convention, as long as the law of a Contracting State governs the contract. Whose law applies, which State's law? The governing law is determined by reference to the rules of private international law of the forum State (where the dispute is brought) if the parties had not chosen the governing law. If the governing law is that of a Contracting State, the Convention will then apply as the domestic governing law of the contract.

Determining the governing law under applicable rules of private international law is not an easy endeavour: the determination of what law applies often turns on where the lawsuit is brought, and that is not known until a dispute arises. Any trader wishing to ensure that it has the benefits of the Convention would be advised to choose the law of a State that is a party to the Convention.

Even if the applicable law is that of a Contracting State, the Convention requires that the parties to the transaction be in different States.[4] Since electronic communications occur relatively instantaneously across international borders without any physical or visual interaction, it is not always apparent if one is engaged in a transaction with a person in another country. If Party A knows that Party B has its place of business in another state, then Party A knows that it is likely that the Convention may apply, and may act accordingly.

What if Party A does not know where Party B is located? The Convention directly addresses this possibility: 'the fact that the parties have their businesses in different states is to be disregarded whenever this fact does not appear either from the contract or from the dealings between the parties or from information disclosed by the parties at any time before or at the conclusion of the contract'.[5] This creates a presumption that the contract is a domestic one unless there is contrary evidence putting the parties on notice that they are dealing with a person in a foreign country. Further, it provides that a party's place of business is 'presumed to be the location indicated by that party.'[6]

What is the implication of this for businesses? Because of presumption in favour of finding a domestic transaction, a trader wishing to achieve the advantages of the Convention is encouraged in its dealings with other parties to

---

3   *Ibid* art 1.
4   The key issue is whether the parties have their place of business in different states, and place of business is defined as 'any place where a party maintains a non-transitory establishment to pursue an economic activity....'. *ibid* art 4(h).
5   *Ibid* art 1.
6   *Ibid* art 6(1).

disclose its place of business at some point (during negotiations, in its communications, on its website, or elsewhere). If a trader fails to do so, and is ultimately sued in a foreign State, it will lose the advantages of the Convention and potentially be subject to the law of that foreign State.

In addition to disclosing one's own location, it would appear equally advisable for businesses to assure themselves of the location of the other party, to ascertain the international character of the transaction and the application of the Convention. Of course, such a business practice is advisable for a variety of other reasons (such as knowing where enforcement might be sought). In this way, the Convention reinforces what would otherwise be a good business practice: know who you are dealing with.

The Convention contains other key limitations. First, only business-to-business (B2B) transactions are covered. Contracts concluded with a consumer (i.e., a transaction made for personal, family or household purposes) are excluded.[7] This exclusion would include business-to-consumer, consumer-to-business, as well as consumer-to-consumer (although given the increasing technological sophistication—and buying habits—of many consumers, that exclusion may be questioned.) The Convention does not give any guidelines for determining whether a transaction is a consumer transaction, nor does it create any presumption that the international transaction is or is not a consumer transaction. In many cases, the nature of the transaction will be sufficient to make such a determination (compare the purchase of one baby crib shipped to a residential address to the purchase of 100 cribs or a turbine engine). In the absence of such external indicia, a prudent business would follow the fundamental maxim: know your customer.

Thus, traders wishing to take advantage of the Convention should consider (1) choosing the law of a Contracting State; (2) disclosing their principal place of business in communications with the other party; (3) requiring or otherwise ascertaining the principal place of business of the other party; and (4) knowing their customers.

2 Is the Transaction One Which Can be Carried Out in Electronic Form?

The threshold question for any type of transaction is whether it will be legally valid and enforceable if done in electronic form. In most cases this involves

---

[7] *Ibid* art 2(1)(a).

determining whether applicable law authorizes the transaction to be done in electronic form (or more appropriately, eliminates any legal barriers to doing the transaction electronically).

The question of 'is it real' has been the motivation behind extensive worldwide legislative efforts. The Convention deals with this issue in a straightforward manner reflecting the approach taken domestically in many countries: 'a communication or contract shall not be denied validity or enforceability on the sole ground that it is in the form of an electronic communication'.[8] Further, where a law requires the communication or contract to be in writing, an electronic communication may satisfy that requirement as long as the information it contains is accessible so as to be usable for subsequent reference.[9] If the law requires that a communication or contract be signed, that requirement is met if a method is used to identify the signing party and to indicate its intent to sign, and a method of signing is used that is as reliable as appropriate for that purpose.[10]

As a result of these provisions, a business need not fear that a court will hold a transaction unenforceable solely because it was conducted in electronic form; a business should be able to choose between conducting business electronically or on paper without fear that its choice will negatively impact the validity of the transaction. This is what the drafters of the Convention called the fundamental principle of technology neutrality.[11]

Businesses should be aware of two possibilities. First, a court may find that the transaction at issue is one that falls within the exceptions to the Convention: (1) transactions on a regulated exchange, (2) foreign exchange transactions, (3) inter-bank payment systems, interbank payment agreements or clearance and settlement systems relating to securities or other financial instruments, and (4) transfers of security rights in sale, loan or holding of or agreement to repurchase securities, or other financial assets held by an intermediary.[12] Second, while the principle of technology neutrality bars a court from refusing to enforce an electronic transaction solely because of its electronic form, courts may resort to other doctrines or defences to bar enforceability.

---

8   *Ibid* art 8.
9   *Ibid* art 9(2).
10   *Ibid* art 9 (3).
11   Explanatory Note (n 1) 47–49.
12   Convention (n 1) art 2.

Thus, it is fair to say that transactions *may* be conducted electronically, and contracts *may* be created in electronic form. The bigger question is *how* to conduct these transactions and form the contracts.

3 Is the Online Process Sufficient to Result in an Enforceable Contract?

Not all electronic transactions involve contracts. But for those that do, the process by which those contracts are created can be critical to enforceability. Requirements for the formation of enforceable contracts under domestic law may differ somewhat, but all require indications of assent often in the form of 'offer' and 'acceptance'. The questions of what constitute assent, offer and acceptance are questions that can arise whatever media is used to negotiate the transaction. The Convention largely leaves in place domestic contract law regimes, preferring to address only those situations in which the use of electronic communications poses unique legal issues. The drafters of the Convention made a deliberate decision to avoid undue interference with well established notions of contract law and to avoid creating specific rules for electronic transactions that might vary from rules applicable to other modes of negotiation.[13] The result is that domestic contract law regimes (or, in appropriate cases, the Convention on the International Sale of Goods)[14] will determine what constitutes an offer and acceptance, what is sufficient assent, whether one party had sufficient notice of applicable terms to be bound by them, etc.

The one area of substantive contract law that they did address involves two scenarios common in electronic commerce: goods or services advertised on websites, or communications sent to multiple recipients through bulk email invitations to make offers.[15] A proposal to conclude a contract made through one or more electronic communications which is not addressed to one or more specific parties, but is generally accessible to parties making use of information systems (including proposals that make use of interactive applications for the placement of orders through such information systems), is to be considered as an invitation to make an offer, unless it clearly indicates the intention

---

13 Explanatory Note (n 1) 147: 'UNCITRAL was mindful of the need to avoid undue interference with well established notions of contract law and to avoid creating specific rules for electronic transactions that might vary from rules that applied to other modes of negotiation'.
14 United Nations Convention on Contracts for the International Sale of Goods (1980) 1489 UNTS 3 ('CISG').
15 Convention (n 1) art 11.

of the party making the proposal to be bound in case of acceptance. The Convention reinforces the result in many domestic systems, where a general advertisement is often found lacking in demonstrating intent on the part of the merchant to be bound to any particular recipient.

Businesses should nonetheless exercise caution in making representations on websites or in mass emails. First, such statements may be used subsequently to establish the terms of a contract reached later in time. More importantly, from the perspective of contract formation, the Convention itself notes that the communication itself *may* demonstrate intent to be bound if it is specific enough. The configuration of many website shopping sites which are interactive in nature may arguably be sufficient to allow for the creation of an enforceable contract despite the operation of this Article.[16] While the website itself may not constitute the offer, the customer's order will generally be construed as a legal offer to contract. When the automated website issues a 'confirmation of order,' it would not be a far stretch to conclude that the 'confirmation of order' operated as an acceptance creating an enforceable deal. The Convention makes clear that a contract may be formed by the interaction between a natural person and an automated message system (or between two automated message systems) even though no human reviewed or intervened in the operation of that system.[17] The 'confirmation of order' would thus be treated the same as if sent from a natural person, and would be deemed an acceptance under most domestic regimes. Indeed, in most instances where the trader wants to enforce the order against the customer, it will argue an enforceable contract was created. If, however, the trader is unable to perform the contract (or decides it does not want to) because of limited quantities, increased prices, or unavailability of supplies, the trader might be exposed to contract damages for failure to perform.

Consequently, the protections afforded traders by Article 11 is of limited use when automated websites issue automatic confirmations. The trader needs to seek protections elsewhere. Some protections may be technological: an ordering system integrated with the inventory system, for example, will be able to determine whether the stock exists to fill orders received prior to the issuance of any confirmation by the ordering system. Others are found in sound business practices: assuring that all website information is correct and up-to-date. Some protection may be found in terms inserted by the trader in its confirmation

---

16   The Convention's presumption that a mass communication is only an invitation to offer operates 'unless it [the communication] clearly indicates the intention of the party making the proposal to be bound in case of acceptance'. *ibid.*
17   *Ibid* art 12.

('subject to availability,' for example). Traders should be careful, however, in insisting on 'protections' that delay the formation of the contract to the extent that the trader, when it performs, finds it cannot enforce the transaction against the customer.

4 What Information Must be Disclosed?

Because of the nature of electronic transactions, there is sometimes a concern that a party will not completely understand with whom he is dealing, what he is agreeing to, or generally what is happening. Thus, a prudent business practice may be to make certain information available to the other party to avoid the risk that a court may later find that the failure to disclose affects the enforceability of the transaction. Moreover, in some cases, applicable law requires the delivery of certain information from vendor to customer as a condition of enforceability. This is frequently (although not always) done as a consumer protection measure. In what way, if any, does the Convention affect these disclosure concerns?

The drafters of the Convention rejected the argument that the Convention should require special disclosures in an electronic environment, reasoning that to do so would create inequalities between paper based and electronic transactions. Nonetheless, the Convention does not displace disclosure requirements that would otherwise apply; indeed, the Convention explicitly recognizes (and upholds) disclosure requirements that may exist under national laws.[18]

Traders should therefore be aware of applicable disclosure requirements existing under national law, both with respect to the specific type of transactions in which its business may be engaged and more generally in the context of online or distance trading. For example, under the proposed Common Framework for a European Sales Law,[19] passed recently by the European Parliament, traders have a duty to disclose information about goods and related services to other traders, more particularly 'any information concern-

---

18   *Ibid* art 13 provides: 'Nothing in this Convention affects the application of any rule of law that may require a party that negotiates some or all of the terms of a contract through the exchange of electronic communications to make available to the other party those electronic communications which contain the contractual terms in a particular manner, or relieves a party from the legal consequences of its failure to do so'.

19   Text in Proposal for a Regulation on a Common European Sales Law COM (2011) 635 final. The European Council has yet to approve the proposal.

ing the main characteristics of the goods, digital content or related services to be supplied which the trader has or can be expected to have and which it would be contrary to good faith and fair dealing not to disclose to the other party'.[20] Moreover, in contracts concluded by electronic means, there are additional duties. The trader must make available the following information before a contract is formed: the technical steps to be taken in order to conclude the contract, whether or not a contract document will be filed with the trader and whether it will be accessible, the technical means for identifying input error, the language offered by the conclusion of the contract, and the contract terms.[21] Because the Convention does not affect the application of these disclosure laws, businesses should take steps to assure that these requirements are met.

5 How Will Errors in Communications be Addressed?

The use of automated messaging systems in the context of contract formation is recognized and validated by the Convention. The Convention makes it clear that the absence of human intervention does not by itself preclude contract formation.[22] In fact, the validity of a contract does not require human review of each of the actions carried by the automated message system or resulting contract.

The use of automated messaging systems also raises the possibility of errors, either as a result of human actions (striking the enter key multiple times or mis-entering a number) or as a result of the malfunctioning of the message system used. The potential of error exists in all communications, even between two human beings. A potential difference in the context of electronic commerce is that when an error does occur, there may not be a human being on the other end of the communication who might notice that error.

The Convention addresses the fear that, with the click of one button, a contract will be formed with no way to go back and correct a mistake, by supplementing (not supplanting) domestic doctrines such as mistake. To ease difficulties with 'input error' in transactions between a person and an automated message system, the Convention allows for a person to withdraw the erroneous part of the communication if the person: (1) notifies the other party immediately upon learning of the error; and (2) has not yet received any

---

20 Convention (n 1) art 23.
21 Ibid art 24.
22 Ibid art 24.

material benefit from the other party.[23] This approach to erroneous communications is of particular interest as it differs from the common law approach that often holds a party liable for the consequences of a unilateral mistake in a contract.

This provision is important because it gives protection to parties who are afraid to conduct business electronically because of the potential for error. But the protection is limited. First, the ability to claim an error is limited to communications between a natural person and an automated message system. The term 'natural person' is not defined in Convention but its meaning is readily discernible. Thus, the provision does not include mistakes made by an automated message system, even though that system is programmed by, and acts on behalf of, a human person. If a natural person makes a mistake and enters the quantity as '1,000' instead of '100', the provision may be triggered; if a system enters the wrong quantity term because it was programmed incorrectly, it is not. Second, the Article only covers 'input errors,' e.g. the placing two orders not one, or selecting the wrong date on an airline ticket. It does not cover transmission errors: where the message is garbled en route or the messaging system malfunctions. These transmission errors will continue to be governed by domestic law. Third, the party in error is given the right to 'withdraw'—but cannot correct—the erroneous communication. The reasoning may not be obvious, but take the situation where the wrong quantity is ordered: change in the quantity term may result in changes in other terms of the deal, and may require complete renegotiation of the transaction. Providing the party in error with the right to 'withdraw' gives that party the right to nullify the communication containing the error and potentially proceed with a new transaction.

Does any of this require a trader to reevaluate its business practices? How can a company using automated ordering or messaging systems protect itself under the Convention if the other party makes a mistake and attempts to avoid the entire transaction? The Convention provides a fool-proof way to protect against the errors of humans interacting with its technology: the error avoidance provisions apply *only if* 'the automated message system does not provide the person with an opportunity to prevent the error'.[24]

The implications of this last limitation should be obvious: the best business practice that exists to prevent errors allowing the other party to complete a transaction entered into with an automated system is to build an error-correction ability into the system. The customer should be given at least one—and preferably more—opportunities to review and correct information it inputs

---

23   *Ibid* art 14.
24   *Ibid* art 14.

before the communication is finally sent. Good business practices are a trader's best protection against unforeseen problems.

6 Accessibility—Are the Transaction Records Accessible to All Parties?

Another key requirement for the enforceability of electronic transactions under many national laws is that the documents that comprise the transaction be communicated in a form that can be retained and accurately reproduced by the receiving party. US law which validates the use of what it calls 'electronic records,' requiring that an electronic record be in a form that is 'capable of being retained and accurately reproduced for later reference by all parties or persons who are entitled to retain the contract or other record'.[25] The European Union Electronic Commerce Directive contains a similar requirement: 'contract terms and general conditions provided to the recipient must be made available in a way that allows him to store and reproduce them'.[26]

The Convention contains a similar notion requiring that transaction records of electronic communications be accessible to the parties, but it is 'hidden' in its definition of which electronic communications may satisfy writing requirements. In order for an electronic communication to be treated as the functional equivalent of a writing, the information contained in the communication must be 'accessible so as to be usable for subsequent reference'.[27] This requirement is explained as follows:

> The use of the word 'accessible' is meant to imply that information in the form of computer data should be readable and interpretable, and that the software that might be necessary to render such information readable should be retained. The word 'usable' is intended to cover both human use and computer processing. The notion of 'subsequent reference' was preferred to notions such as 'durability' or 'non-alterability', which would have established too harsh standards, and to notions such as 'readability' or 'intelligibility', which might constitute too subjective criteria.[28]

---

25 15 U.S.C. § 7001(e). See also UETA § 8(c) ('if a sender inhibits the ability of a recipient to store or print an electronic record, the electronic record is not enforceable against the recipient'.)
26 Directive 2000/31/EC (Electronic Commerce Directive), art 10(3).
27 *Ibid* art 9(2).
28 Explanatory Note (n 1) 146.

The Convention differs from some national laws that specifically require that, to enforce a record against a party, the party have the ability to store and print them. A business that affords the other party the ability to store, reproduce and print electronic communications does indeed meet the requirements of the Convention that the communications be 'accessible' so as to be 'usable' for future use. But the Convention, because it applies to all electronic communications in connection with the formation or performance of a contract (and not just the contract itself) recognizes that not all communications may be of the type susceptible to printing and reproduction. For example, an interactive website may allow the user to make certain choices by clicking and to signify its acceptance to the terms by clicking. The 'click' may not be printable, but under the convention as long as the information therein is 'accessible' so as to be 'usable' in the future, the click may be considered 'written'.

A further note about the Convention is that it does not require both parties to the transaction to possess the technological ability to access and use the information. Rather, the focus is on the ability of the party wishing to use the document to demonstrate that is accessible and usable. The fact that the recipient may choose not to reproduce or store a communication, or uses a device without such capabilities (for example, a hand-held device without a store or print capability), should not affect the enforceability of the transaction.

What is to be learned from this discussion of the Convention's definition of 'writing' and its requirement that information be accessible and usable? First, even though the Convention stops short of requiring that information in an electronic communication be capable of printing and storage by the recipient, providing information in that manner goes a long way towards satisfying the Convention. Second, and more important, businesses should examine their data storage policies to assure that information communicated electronically that may be subject to writing requirements be retained in a manner that it can be accessed and used in the future. This includes retaining the software necessary to access and manipulate the information. Moreover, while a simple 'keystroke' may not itself qualify as 'information,' prudent traders will structure and maintain their systems in a manner that allow them to demonstrate such a keystroke was indeed entered at the appropriate time.

7 Signature—Has a Valid Electronic Signature Been Used under Applicable Law?

Not all transactions require a signature. But in many cases a transaction is governed by a law or regulation that requires the presence of a signature before it will be considered legally effective. The common statute of frauds (which, in the United

States, requires contracts for the sale of goods in excess of $500 to be 'signed') is an example of such a law. While in the international context, the Convention on Contracts for the International Sale of Goods[29] does not require formalities such as a signed writing, it is not unusual to find the requirement of a signature sprinkled throughout domestic law. Even in cases where a signature is not required by law, a signature may be desirable to enhance enforceability, or to provide one party with additional assurance that the other party has agreed to the terms. In all such cases, the use of a legally valid and enforceable electronic signature is critical.

What is the electronic equivalent of a hand-written signature? There are innumerable and varying examples of the ways in which people attempt to 'sign' electronic communications; typical examples often cited include:

- a name typed at the end of an e-mail message by the sender;
- a digitized image of a handwritten signature that is attached to an electronic document;
- a password, PIN or secret code to identify the sender to the recipient (such as that used with ATM cards and credit cards);
- a unique biometrics-based identifier, such as a fingerprint, voice print, or a retinal scan;
- mouse click (such as on an 'I Accept' button);
- a sound (e.g., the sound created by pressing '9' on your phone to agree); and
- a 'digital signature' (created through the use of public key cryptography).

As technology and its applications develop, more signature variations occur. Today, 'tweets' from people are often identified by their 'handle,' just as on Facebook people who post messages are identified by their username. The advent of touch screens has enabled people to 'sign' electronic records simply by writing on a digital pad or touch screen.

Which of these 'electronic signatures' will satisfy the applicable writing requirements? At the outset, it should be noted that because of its fundamental belief in 'functional equivalence,' the Convention does not mandate that a signing occur in any fashion, but rather leaves it to the parties and the marketplace to decide what type signature to use. In order to satisfy any legal requirements for a signature, the Convention requires that:

- a method is used to identify the signer,
- the method is used to indicate the signer's intention in respect of the information contained in the electronic document, and

---

29   CISG (n 14).

- the method used is either (1) as reliable as appropriate to the purpose for which the electronic communication was generated, in light of all the relevant circumstances, or (2) proven in fact to have fulfilled the functions of identifying the signer and indicating the signer's intention.[30]

The first two elements are somewhat self explanatory. There must be a way of tying the alleged signature to a specific person; the dictionary definition of a signature is 'a distinctive mark, characteristic, or other thing that identifies somebody'. Second, there must be an appropriate relationship between the signature and the information with which it is associated; if a signature is required to demonstrate merely that a person had read a document, then the method must show that intention; if a signature is required to demonstrate a person's approval, then that intention must be shown.

The third requirement is more complicated, and this aspect of the Convention's signature requirements go beyond those that may exist under some domestic regimes. U.S. law, for example, only requires that the purported signer adopt the symbol or method with intent to sign the document.[31] The signature requirements of the Convention go further, and focus on the issue of security, by requiring the use of a method that is either 'as reliable as appropriate' or that in fact does identify the signer and its intention.

To explore the ramifications of this requirement, take two common examples of what may be asserted to be 'signatures:' a mouse click on an 'I agree' button, or a typewritten signature at the end of an email. While today these are seen as common occurrences, questions can be raised under the Convention as to whether these methods are as 'reliable as appropriate'.

The Explanatory Note makes it clear, however, that the Convention was intended to remove barriers to enforceability arising from signature requirements, not to create additional ones, and cautions that legal, technical and commercial factors must be taken into account in determining what is appropriate.[32] A 100€ purchase may not require same treatment as a 1,000,000€ trade.

More importantly, the Convention gives an alternative to the 'reliable as appropriate' test. While the mere clicking of a mouse may not appear too reliable, other indicia may demonstrate who clicked the button. If the actual identity of the party and its intent can be proved, then a party should not be able to repudiate its signature on the sole grounds that the 'click' was not as

---

30   Convention (n 1) art 9.
31   E-SIGN, 15 USC Section 7006(5) and UETA Section 2(8) (definitions of 'electronic signature').
32   Explanatory Note (n 1) 162.

reliable as appropriate. Thus, presumably even a mouse click could qualify as a signature under the U.N. Convention, but only when done in a way that allows the proponent to ultimately prove 'who' clicked, and to establish the intention behind the click. Indeed, in well-constructed on-line purchasing systems, the user must enter additional information to identify itself and its bona fides before getting to the point where it 'signs' a communication through a mere click.

It is important to note, however, that although clicking a mouse on an 'I Accept' button or typing a name on an e-mail message may qualify as legally enforceable signatures, they can be problematic. Without more, they offer no evidence as to 'who' clicked the mouse or typed the name that appears on the electronic document; to say that they are legally enforceable may be somewhat illusory, as a party's ability to authenticate a signature or use it to verify the integrity of a document may be very limited at best. While there may be technological ways of tying the key stroke to a particular computer, there is not necessarily any way of tying the keystroke to a particular individual. Thus, the document may be legally enforceable (i.e. signed) but the issue remains 'signed by whom'. This results in a proof problem of who is responsible for the communication, i.e., identifying the person who applied the symbol or executed the process. In many instances, there will be external evidence in the transaction (e.g. identifying information in the communications that point to the specific individual) but the fact remains that in doing business electronically, while the transaction may be legally enforceable, the problem is proving against whom it may be enforced. This risk is often mitigated by implementation of protective business measures, e.g. demanding payment before performance.

What are the implications of this aspect of the Convention for businesses? When transactions are automated, and conducted over significant distances using easily altered digital documents, the need for a way to ensure the identity of the sender/signer and the integrity of the document becomes pivotal. Thus, it is important to recognize that an electronic signature, by itself, may not provide the desired level of assurance of trustworthiness.

Trust, of course, plays a role in virtually all commercial transactions. Regardless of whether the deal is struck in cyberspace or in the more traditional paper-based world, each of the transacting parties must have some level of trust before they will be willing to proceed with the transaction. But how does one evaluate the trustworthiness of the transaction, of the electronic communications, between them? When vital business transactions depend on computer and network availability, the parties need to know that these will work properly and without interruption. When remote communications replace personal contact or a trusted medium such as the mail, the parties need to verify each other's identity. When easily copied and altered electronic records replace signed paper documents, the parties need assurance that these records are authentic and unaltered. And when sensitive data is stored electronically, the parties need assurances that the data is protected and accessible.

The Convention does not address these problems except in a very minimal way in its reliability test. Yet the trustworthiness of communications remains the pivotal issue in electronic transactions: proving authenticity and integrity. Not a pure legal, technology, or business question, addressing the issue of trustworthiness requires a coordinate approach involving legal, technological and business expertise.

8 Record Retention—Have Appropriate Electronic Records been Retained?

Record keeping is an essential part of business. In the event of a dispute, it is necessary to produce reliable evidence documenting the terms of the transaction and the agreement to the parties. Similar requirements also exist to satisfy regulatory requirements (e.g., regulations governing the insurance, securities, and banking industries or regulations issued by taxing authorities). For electronic transactions, the issue becomes a question of whether keeping electronic records will satisfy applicable statutes, regulations, or evidentiary rules, and if so, what requirements must be met for acceptable electronic records.

The Convention does not impose any record keeping requirements, but it does address domestic law requirements that a communication or contract be available or retained in its original form; in the context of electronic communications which can be infinitely duplicated during transmission, so it is difficult to define which message is the 'original'. The Convention[33] allows electronic communications to satisfy 'originality' requirements if

- there exists a reliable assurance as to the integrity of the information it contains from the time that it was first generated in its final form, as an electronic communication or otherwise, and

---

[33] The Convention utilized a 'functional equivalence' approach in determining what functions are served by the requirement of an original in paper-based communications, then articulating what requirements would allow electronic communications to fulfill those functions. Explanatory Note (n 1) 133–35, 167.

- when it is required to be made available, it is capable of being displayed to the person to whom it is to be made available.[34]

The key to the application of this article is the concept of data integrity: is the information contained in the electronic record both complete and accurate? That means ensuring that no unauthorized alterations are made to such data either intentionally or accidentally. Relevant questions include: Is the document the recipient received the same as the document that the sender sent? Is it complete? Has the document been altered either in transmission or storage?

Concerns regarding data integrity flow from the fact that electronic documents are easily altered in a manner that is not detectable. Moreover, because every copy of an electronic document is a perfect reproduction, there is no such thing as an original electronic document. Thus, unlike paper documents, electronic records come with no inherent attributes of integrity.

Under the Convention, the fact that the electronic document is a reproduction is not fatal: that electronic document (whether it be a copy, a scan into PDF, or a stored copy of a communication) will satisfy any legal requirement that the original be present. Thus, it is not necessary for a business to keep every piece of paper relating to transactions in the event that there is dispute and originals of the document are required. Under the Convention, documents and communications may be kept in electronic only form, and the electronic reproduction or stored message will satisfy the requirements of the originality.

The Convention does not dictate how the records may be stored, or when and how businesses may migrate from paper based to digital records. The challenge for the trader relying on these records is providing reliable assurance of the integrity of the document 'from the time it was first generated in its final form'. Under the Convention, the focus is on whether the information has remained complete and unaltered, apart from the addition of any endorsements and any change that arises in the normal course of communication, storage or display. The standard of reliability depends on the purpose for which the information was generated and all relevant circumstances. Thus, the Convention clarifies that businesses need not keep every paper and document in paper form; they may indeed move to paperless trading and paperless offices. But the Convention clarifies what is required of those businesses that do go paperless: when information is retained in electronic form, businesses should institute measures to guard against inadvertent (as well as intentional)

---

34 Convention (n 1) art 9(4).

alterations to the data. These measures may be technological (e.g. encrypting documents to preclude alteration). Alternatively, business practices may be implemented to guard against alteration (e.g. restricting access to servers, maintaining documentation of access, etc.). All of these measures are what would, in most cases, constitute good business practices.

9   Conclusion

How will the Convention affect business practices? In most respects, it will not. Traders who exercise reasonable commercial standards in their contracting practices, and act prudently in the conduct of their affairs when they utilize electronic communications will find that the Convention lends support by removing barriers to the validity and enforceability of their transactions. The Convention is supportive rather than regulatory: it does not tell businesses how to act, but supports them when they act rationally.

The key, however, is the exercise of reasonable commercial standards in contracting practices. The major impact of the Convention is that it moves the focus from the legality of a transaction to the reliability and trustworthiness of the underlying business practices. This puts the onus on businesses to carefully review the processes by which they conduct electronic transactions to gain a clear understanding of what will happen and how it will occur. This is critical for determining whether relevant electronic-specific requirements will be satisfied, identifying any new issues (legal or otherwise) that may be raised, and identifying those elements of the process that may need to be changed or restructured to ensure the validity and enforceability of the resulting transactions.

In undertaking an evaluation of the processes and practices employed within the business, traders should, at a minimum:

- Review the manner in which websites are structured to determine the manner in which contracts may be created, inadvertently as well as consciously.
- Assure that all the information required to be disclosed or available to the other party is accessible and meets domestic requirements of disclosure.
- Evaluate the manner in which electronic communications are signed, and the context in which the signing occurs.
- Apart from signing, evaluate the manner in which the system authenticates the identity of the other party in the event of dispute to avoid enforceability and admissibility problems.

Understanding the process—how it works—is essential in assuring that communications and contracts will be legally recognized and enforced. Traders who act prudently, understand their contracting practices, and observe reasonable commercial practices will find that the Convention supports the validity and enforceability of their transactions.

PART 7

Essays on New Zealand

∴

Maori wood carving known as the 'Ortiz Panels', reproduced with the kind permission of the Werner Forman Archives.

For the history surrounding these panels and their eventual return to New Zealand, see Chapter 35.

CHAPTER 35

Foreign Cultural Heritage Claims: *New Zealand v. Ortiz* Thirty Years Later

Robert K. Paterson and James A.R. Nafziger *

1   Introduction

Maori fishermen, according to Sir James Frazer, traditionally release the first fish caught in order to conciliate the other fish and tempt them, too, to be caught.[1] In resolving a dispute involving Maori cultural material, the English Court of Appeal (Civil Division) did the fishermen one better. It threw back a Maori object of questionable provenance into the sea of the international art market with pronouncements encouraging the judicial release of all such fish. Far from being a clever technique to lure lost cultural objects to the surface for appropriate reassignment of ownership, the Court's decision forestalled a movement, initiated more than a decade earlier, toward international cooperation to cleanse the art market of contraband objects. That movement has nevertheless proceeded apace.[2] This essay considers whether, more than three decades later, an English court would therefore reach a different if not opposite result.

At issue in *Attorney-General of New Zealand v. Ortiz*,[3] was the entry into the London auction market of five conjoined wooden panels (*epa*) carved by Maori craftsmen and forming the door of a Taranaki storehouse (*pataka*). The panels were recovered by a Maori man while cutting a track through a swamp. He then sold them to a London art dealer. Thereafter, the dealer

---

*   Professor Paterson would like to thank his colleagues Professors Elizabeth Edinger, Joost Blom and Craig Forrest for their helpful comments and Claire Hildebrand for her research assistance.

1   James G Frazer, *The Golden Bough: A Study in Magic and Religion* (Macmillan 1922, abridged ed Macmillan 1960) 611.

2   See John Henry Merryman & James AR Nafziger, 'The Private International Law of Cultural Property in the United States' (Supp 1994) Am J Comp L 221 ('Merryman & Nafziger, "The Private International Law of Cultural Property in the United States"') (analysis of the emerging regime of private international law in the context of developments in public international law as of the time of *Ortiz* and during the following decade).

3   [1982] 2 WLR 10 (Staughton J), [1982] 3 WLR 570 (CA) and [1983] 2 WLR 809 (HL).

sold the panels with the assurance of good title to defendant George Ortiz, a wealthy, Geneva-based collector of tribal art and antiquities.[4] Several years later Ortiz offered the panels for sale by Sotheby's in London.[5] Three days before a scheduled auction of the panels, however, the plaintiff, on behalf of the New Zealand government, sought a court injunction to restrain the sale and an order effecting a forfeiture of the objects to it. The plaintiff government claimed that the objects had been removed from New Zealand in violation of its antiquities and customs laws and were therefore subject to repatriation to it.

The trial judge in *Ortiz,* Staughton, J., held that insofar as the plaintiff's claim for a forfeiture of title to the Maori carvings was based on a violation of three New Zealand statutes—the *Historic Articles Act 1962,* and the *Customs Acts* 1913 and 1966—the judicial action amounted to enforcing rather than recognizing New Zealand law. In other words, the judge concluded that the trial court had been called upon not simply to recognize the statutes unexceptionably as governing law in a dispute or, less directly, to take account of them to supplement the governing law. Instead, the judge interpreted the Court's role to be the chosen means for directly enforcing the law, albeit extraterritorially. Under common law precedent its competence to do so was sustainable unless the statutes were deemed to be penal in nature. The trial judge ruled, however, that while certain provisions of the governing law provided for a fine and were, therefore, penal, the provisions regarding forfeiture were not. He then went on to considered whether the applicable statutes should be seen as public laws and unenforceable on that basis. He rejected the proposition that all public laws were unenforceable (as *jus imperii*), preferring to consider whether, on a case-by-case basis, there were public policy grounds for not enforcing the particular laws in question.[6] He then found that there were good reasons for the Court to enforce the New Zealand laws saying that '[c]omity requires that we should respect the national heritage of other countries, by according both recognition

---

4 See generally Kelvin Day, *Maori Wood Carving of the Taranaki Region* (Reed Books 2001) 38–39. None of the facts in the case were proven but were assumed for the purpose of legal argument. The scope of the Ortiz collection can be gauged from George Ortiz, *In Pursuit of the Absolute—Art of the Ancient World from the George Ortiz Collection* (Royal Academy of Arts 1994).

5 See *George Ortiz Collection of Primitive Works of Art* (Sotheby Parke Bennet & Co 1978), Lot 150; Robert Paterson, 'The Legal Dynamics of Cultural Property Export Controls: *Ortiz* Revisited' [Special Issue 1995] UBC Law Rev 241.

6 *Attorney-General of New Zealand v Ortiz* [1982] 2 WLR 10, 30.

and enforcement to their laws which affect the title to property while it is within their territory.'[7]

2   The Court of Appeal Decision in *Ortiz*

The defendant then appealed the judgment. In separate opinions, Lord Denning, Master of the Rolls, and Lord Justices Ackner and O'Connor concurred in allowing the appeal. The two principal issues were 1) whether, under New Zealand law, the Crown had become the owner of the panels and was therefore entitled to possession of them; and 2) whether the New Zealand law should be enforced by an English court. Rejecting the trial court's purposive or teleological methodology for interpreting the New Zealand statutes and adopting instead a plain-meaning approach, the Court of Appeal answered both questions negatively.

Lord Denning's lead opinion first rejected the plaintiff government's claim of 'automatic forfeiture', holding that it could not rely on the mere fact of an illegal export of the object to accomplish a forfeiture of title to it. Instead, the Court read the critical *Historic Articles Act* to provide, not for such automatic forfeiture, but merely for a liability to forfeiture. The key question was whether the New Zealand statutory law automatically 'affected' the door panels before they left the country because they had been within the country's national patrimony. After all, the objects were not just any old objects; arguably, they were specially protected. The Court seemed willing to enforce an automatic forfeiture, however, only on the basis of a trespass or trover action to recover objects affected by nationalization or actual sovereign possession. The Court thus found that, under New Zealand law, New Zealand had not become the owner of the panels.

The Court then assumed, arguendo, that the *Historical Articles Act* did provide for automatic forfeiture of an historic object from the time of its attempted export. If so, the question then became whether an English court should enforce that law. Noting that like New Zealand most countries prohibited the export of their historic articles without a license, the Court asked whether 'the law' (presumably English law) required or even permitted a court to enforce another country's automatic forfeiture law so as to require the repatriation of the door panels.

In denying such cooperation, Lord Denning took a profoundly territorialist approach of a sort that had been discarded elsewhere. Shortcutting any

---

[7]   *Ortiz* (n 6) 31.

choice-of-law analysis, he first turned to English law because 'New Zealand has inherited the common law of England; and also because its statutes and methods of interpretation are on much the same lines as our own.'[8] For Lord Denning, it was not only English law, however, but also international law, under which a national government has no right to exercise sovereign authority beyond its own territorial limits. His understanding of the international system was perhaps revealed in an apparently sincere, if quaint, apology: 'I hope our New Zealand friends will forgive me calling them a "foreign state".'[9] Later in his opinion, Lord Denning concluded that any act of a sovereign character, *jure imperii*, is unenforceable by other sovereign states. Quite simply, '[t]he courts of other countries will not allow [a foreign sovereign] to go beyond the [territorial] bounds.'[10] In line with this thinking, Lord Denning presumed that the New Zealand Parliament could never have intended to give its laws an extraterritorial reach. Thus, even if the Court were to have adopted a 'purposive' approach to statutory interpretation, as the trial court had done, it could not ascribe to the New Zealand Parliament an inappropriate purpose to effect an extraterritorial forfeiture of an object.

Lord Denning cited two well-known precedents for a refusal to enforce acts of a foreign sovereign: *Huntington v. Attrill*[11] and *Loucks v. Standard Oil Co. of New York*.[12] Because these precedents specifically involved penal and revenue laws, however, he then inquired whether they should be expanded to encompass the genus of *all* public acts. Not surprisingly, his answer was affirmative, thereby extending the precedents to other types of public laws, including the New Zealand statutes at issue should they not be considered as penal in nature. His doctrinal rejection of extraterritoriality was very much in line with traditional thinking at the time.[13]

In sum, Lord Denning wrote, '[if] any country should have legislation prohibiting the export of works of art, and providing for the automatic forfeiture of them to the state should they be exported, then that falls into the category of 'public laws' which will not be enforced by the courts of the country to which it is exported, or any other country, because it is an act done in the

---

8   *Attorney-General of New Zealand v Ortiz* [1982] 3 WLR 570 (CA), 576.
9   *Ortiz* (n 8) 581.
10 *Ortiz* (n 8) 582.
11 [1893] AC 150 (PC).
12 224 NY 99, 120 NE 198 (1918).
13 As applied to cultural material, see Paul M Bator, 'An Essay on the International Trade in Art' (1982) 34 Stan L Rev 275 (1982). This essay was largely completed in 1970, at the beginning of developments in modern cultural heritage law.

exercise of sovereign authority which will not be enforced outside its own territory.'[14] The other Court of Appeal judges did not agree with Lord Denning that there was such a broad category of unenforceable public laws. Instead, they viewed the New Zealand statutory law simply as penal legislation that was unenforceable on that narrower basis.

3   The House of Lords Decision in *Ortiz*

On further appeal to the House of Lords, the issue of enforceability of the New Zealand statutes was not discussed insofar as the Court thought the plaintiff had not established its entitlement to, or ownership of, the carvings prior to their departure from New Zealand. The House of Lords therefore upheld the Court of Appeal decision on the alternative basis that a precondition for an English court's enforcement of the pertinent New Zealand statutory law was actual seizure of the wood panels so as to vest title in the Crown, and, under New Zealand law, that had not occurred.[15] In a unanimous opinion, Lord Brightman said that the opinions of the Court of Appeal judges, as to the enforceability of the New Zealand laws, were *obiter dicta* and that the House of Lords did not wish to comment on their correctness.

4   A Trans-Atlantic Excursion

Lord Denning also ventured to predict the outcome if a United States court had decided the case.[16] He doubted that a United States court under the same circumstances would compel the return of a cultural object. His speculation to that effect was expressed so expansively as to rule out any international cooperation, even, for example, pursuant to the enforcement of criminal laws. Unfortunately, he failed to note groundbreaking decisions of federal courts in the United States in which violations of foreign antiquities laws had been deemed to define theft under the *National Stolen Property Act* ('NSPA')[17] so as to compel forfeiture of objects taken out of countries of origin in violation of their antiquities laws and brought into the United States.

---

14 *Ortiz* (n 8) 585.
15 *Attorney General of New Zealand v Ortiz* [1983] 2 WLR 809 (HL).
16 It is unclear why he hypothesized judicial action in the United States. Perhaps it was because of that country's status as a hub of the international art market.
17 18 USC §§2311, 2314, 2315 (2012).

The NSPA prohibits the sale, receipt or transportation of stolen goods that have moved in interstate or foreign commerce of any article with a value of $5000 or more that is known to have been stolen. Violations of the NSPA are punishable by a fine and/or imprisonment of up to ten years. Even though the NSPA itself does not specifically authorize seizure or forfeiture of cultural objects, it does provide a juridical basis for doing so when an object is brought into the United States 'contrary to law' and thereafter for returning the object to its country of origin. The NSPA also provides a basis for criminal prosecution of persons who have imported stolen material, according to either a United States or a foreign definition of theft, depending on the circumstances of a particular case.

Specifically, prior to *Ortiz,* federal courts in the *Hollinshead*[18] and *McClain I*[19] cases had established that the term 'stolen property' in the NSPA, to include cultural objects, may be defined by the law of the state of origin.[20] In *McClain I*, the prosecution was required to establish that pre-Columbian beads and ceramics that federal agents seized in the United States from the defendants had been 'stolen' from Mexico. Although the defendants argued that the Mexican statute was insufficient to characterize the removal of the objects from Mexico as 'theft' within the meaning of the NSPA, the court disagreed, and the defendants were convicted. In *McClain II*, however, the court ultimately reversed the substantive counts, though not a conspiracy count, because of the lower court's error in allowing the jury to decide a question of foreign law as to when the Mexican government had declared ownership of all such objects. That was not a factual issue; instead, it was a legal issue for the court to decide. As such, the court held that the prosecutor had failed to prove that the beads and ceramics had left Mexico after the effective date when the law which unquestionably established patrimonial ownership of such objects had come into force.[21]

---

18   *United States v Hollinshead*, 495 F 2d 1154 (9th Cir 1974).

19   *United States v McClain*, 545 F 2d 988 (5th Cir 1977) (McClain I); *United States v. McClain* 593 F 2d 658 (5th Cir 1979), *cert denied*, 444 U.S. 918 (1979) (McClain II).

20   For commentary, see Merryman & Nafziger, "The Private International Law of Cultural Property in the United States" (n 2) 228, 232–33.

21   593 F 2d 658 (McClain II). Later, a federal court in *Peru v. Johnson*, 720 F Supp 810 (CD Cal 1989), aff'd sub nom *Peru v Wendt*, 933 F 2d 1013 (9th Cir 1991), confronted with essentially the same issue as in McClain II, confirmed that a foreign state could not expect enforcement of its antiquities law in a federal court of the United States unless it had effectively declared patrimonial ownership over a controverted object or class of objects that included it, perhaps showing that it had applied its antiquities legislation to assert ownership domestically. The government of Peru, which sought to recover jewelry and ceramic

Thus, a foreign State must explicitly reduce to its ownership a particular cultural object or a class of objects that includes it in order to successfully seek the assistance of United States authorities to reclaim and repatriate the object under the NSPA. Even if a foreign state has not reduced an illegally exported object to its actual possession, however, it may validly seek the restitution of the object if it has previously declared ownership of the particular object or of a specific class of objects that includes it. The claimant state may then enlist United States cooperation in its return, including a request for prosecution of an illegal trafficker under the NSPA, so long as, prior to export, the foreign state has indicated with sufficient specificity that the object is part of its cultural patrimony and that its export would violate that state's law.[22] The court thereby confirmed the efficacy of the NSPA to effect a return of contraband cultural objects to their countries of origin. In the less important but earlier case of *Hollinshead*, which involved removal of a stela from a Mayan temple at Machiquila in Guatemala, the defendants apparently had made no serious attempt to argue the prior declaration rule; the court, without discussion, therefore simply treated removal in violation of the Guatemalan law as theft.

Although these were criminal cases that did not address the core issue in *Ortiz* of enforceability as a matter of private international law, they do call into question the breadth of Lord Denning's skepticism about *any* legal basis upon which the United States would compel the return of contraband objects to their countries of origin. Clearly, the patrimonial antiquities laws of foreign countries had established such a basis. Lord Denning's

---

objects from a Californian collector, lost its claim for three reasons. First, it was unable to prove that the objects in question came from Peru. Second, it was unable to prove that, even if they came from Peru, they were removed while the relevant Peruvian legislation was in force. The most interesting and potentially significant part of the decision, however, was based on uncontroverted evidence that Peru had not applied its patrimonial ownership law domestically. Nor had it ever explicitly declared patrimonial ownership over such items. Therefore, it could not validly claim that an illegally exported object had been 'stolen' within the meaning of the term in the NSPA.

22 Later, after *Ortiz*, a federal court extended this so-called 'prior declaration rule' to include objects over which Guatemala had claimed ownership effective only from the time of their illegal export, that is, only upon their *departure* from the state. The court held that 'while traveling in foreign commerce, the articles were stolen under the NSPA definitions in that they belonged to Guatemala, and not the person who unlawfully possessed the artifacts.' See *United States v Pre-Columbian Artifacts*, 845 F Supp 544 (ND Ill 1993). It is important to note, however, that the court was enforcing Guatemalan antiquity legislation, not its export law.

opinion, which was among his last decisions before retirement, is thus particularly interesting for both its emphatic rejection of legislative extraterritoriality and its insularity.

Later, in *United States v. Schultz*,[23] also a criminal case, the court confirmed the rule in *Hollinshead* and *McClain* that the NSPA applies to cultural material which is stolen in violation of a foreign patrimonial law where the foreign government had asserted ownership before the material left its soil. The court wrote as follows: 'We see no reason that property stolen from a foreign sovereign should be treated any differently from property stolen from a foreign museum or private home.'[24] In the same year as *Schultz* another federal court ordered the forfeiture of a moon rock to be returned to Honduras. What makes this decision particularly cogent in revisiting *Ortiz* was that it relied on Honduran patrimonial law in a *civil* forfeiture proceeding.[25]

5   The 1970 UNESCO Convention

Having denied New Zealand a judicial remedy, Lord Denning suggested that the retrieval of works of art exported in violation of foreign law 'must be achieved by diplomatic means. Best of all, there should be an international convention on the matter where individual countries can agree and pass the necessary legislation. It is a matter of such importance that I hope steps can be taken to this end.'[26] He seems to have been utterly unaware that, up to a point, there was such an agreement in force, and a highly visible and important one at that. As a U.S. federal judge in a famous cultural heritage case confirmed a few years after Ortiz, 'the judicial branch should certainly attempt to reflect in its decision making the spirit as well as the letter of an international agreement to which the United States is a party.'[27] The UNESCO *Convention on the Means of Prohibiting and Preventing the*

---

23   333 F 3d 393 (2d Cir 2003).
24   Schultz (n 23) 410.
25   *One Lucite Ball Containing Lunar Material*, 252 F Supp 2d 1367 (SD Fla 2003). See also *Turkey v OKS Partners*, 797 F Supp 64 (D Mass. 1992) (allowing Turkey to assert causes of action for return of a coin collection allegedly smuggled out of the country).
26   *Ortiz* (n 8) 585.
27   *Autocephalous Greek-Orthodox Church of Cyprus v Goldberg & Feldman Fine Arts, Inc.*, 917 F 2d 270, 296 (7th Cir 1990) (Cudahy J, concurring).

Illicit Import, Export and Transfer of Ownership of Cultural Property[28] already provided the means that might have compelled a different result in *Ortiz* had New Zealand and the United Kingdom been parties to it. Ironically, the States Parties to the agreement did include the United States, which for some reason Lord Denning had singled out (mistakenly) as a country whose courts would never order the return of objects to England pursuant to a patrimonial claim on the ground of forfeiture.

In particular, the UNESCO Convention contains, among other things, a provision, discussed below, by which States Parties are required to certify the exportability of cultural material as defined in the Convention and mutually deny the importation of uncertified material. A related provision establishes a basis for imposing penalties or administrative sanctions against persons responsible for infringing foreign export prohibitions. The Convention also provides for bilateral agreements on restitution of objects and for cooperation in response to requests of States Parties to bar the importation by other States Parties of particular objects within the cultural patrimony of the requesting States, on the basis that the objects or a class of objects that includes them are jeopardized as a result of pillage. Finally, States Parties agree to undertake, consistent with municipal laws, to facilitate recovery from their territories of stolen and inalienable foreign cultural 'property.'

Of particular relevance to *Ortiz* is Article 6 of the UNESCO Convention. It requires States Parties to introduce a certificate that authorizes the export of 'all items of cultural property exported in accordance with the regulations.' States Parties are then required 'to prohibit the exportation of cultural property from their territory unless accompanied by [the certificate]' and 'to publicize this prohibition by appropriate means, particularly among persons likely to export or import cultural property.' Article 6 therefore requires States Parties to mutually enforce each other's export controls over cultural 'property', as defined by the UNESCO Convention. Although the UNESCO Convention was not directly applicable in *Ortiz* because the United Kingdom was not then a party to it, Article 6 and perhaps other provisions in the Convention would have been of interest to Lord Denning had he been aware of it.[29]

---

28   Convention on the Means of Prohibiting and Preventing the Illicit Import, Export and Transfer of Ownership of Property (adopted 14 November 1970, entered into force 24 April 1972) 823 UNTS 231 ('UNESCO Convention').

29   While the United Kingdom accepted the UNESCO Convention in 2002, no specific legislation has been introduced to implement it besides the Dealing in Cultural Objects (Offences) Act, 2003 and earlier regulations concerning EU measures. See Kevin Chamberlain & Kristin Hausler, 'United Kingdom' in James AR Nafziger & Robert Kirkwood Paterson (eds),

6 Subsequent Developments in English and Commonwealth Law and Practice

As we have seen, the Court of Appeal in *Ortiz* was of the view that the New Zealand law was penal in character and could not be enforced in the courts of the United Kingdom. Lord Denning alone relied on a broader characterization of the New Zealand law as an unenforceable 'public' law. Though the rule against unenforceability of foreign penal laws is long-standing, there has always been uncertainty surrounding the issue of what foreign laws will be seen as penal in character. One policy justification advanced for the rule is that enforcement of foreign laws of a penal nature would represent an incursion by the judiciary into the realm of the executive branch of government. In *Attorney-General (UK) v. Heinemann Publishers Australia Pty. Ltd.* (often called the 'Spycatcher case'), a majority of the High Court of Australia thought the rule applied 'to claims enforcing the interests of a foreign sovereign which arise from the exercise of certain powers peculiar to government.'[30] *Heinemann* involved an attempt by the British government to prevent the publication in Australia of the confidential memoirs of a former British intelligence officer. The High Court of Australia dismissed the claim, characterizing it as an attempt to enforce foreign governmental interests. The claim was defined in terms of the interest sought to be enforced (governmental) rather than by the form of the action itself (an injunction to prevent publication).

In *Mbasogo v. Logo Ltd.* the English Court of Appeal also refused to accept as justiciable a claim for damages by the President of Equatorial Guinea against certain English residents for their alleged support of an insurrection in Equatorial Guinea.[31] The Court of Appeal accepted that a claim by a foreign state to enforce laws of a penal nature was an assertion of sovereign authority by that state in the courts of another and therefore represented an illegal extraterritorial assertion of such sovereignty (*jure imperii*). It approved of the following statement by Dr. F.A. Mann:

> Where the foreign State pursues a right that by its nature could equally well belong to an individual, no question of a prerogative claim arises and the State's access to the courts is unrestricted. Thus a State whose property is in the defendant's possession can recover it by an action in

---

Handbook on the Law of Cultural Heritage and International Trade (Edward Elgar 2014) 460, 493–496.
30   (1988) 78 ALR 449, 456.
31   [2007] QB 846.

detinue. A State which has a contractual claim against the defendant is at liberty to recover the money due to it. If a State's ship has been damaged in a collision, an action for damages undoubtedly lies. On the other hand a foreign State cannot enforce in England such rights as are founded upon its peculiar powers of prerogative. Claims for the payment of penalties, for the recovery of customs duties or the satisfaction of tax liabilities are, of course, the most firmly established examples of this principle.[32]

Claims that equally belong to states as to individuals, such as claims in conversion regarding stolen property, would not be affected by the rule regarding penal statutes, but those that were founded on the prerogative powers of states, such as the recovery of taxes, are seen as non-justiciable. The issue thus essentially becomes one of characterization. In *Mbasogo* the Court of Appeal thought that the alleged losses were the result of the actions of a foreign state to protect itself and its citizens (such as costs incurred in investigating the alleged conspiracy and in detaining suspects) and described them as instances of the 'paradigm function of government.'[33] The Court thought it impossible to characterize the losses claimed as property losses since they were the types of losses only a state could suffer. It was not seen as the proper role of a court to judge the reasonableness or propriety of the actions of foreign governments. While *Mbasogo* was not a case involving the enforcement of foreign penal legislation, it provided further justification for the inappropriateness of judicial encroachment on executive powers.

A Canadian decision provides an example of how the characterization of a claim can result in an opposite result to that reached in the above two cases. In *United States v. Ivey*, the plaintiff government sought to enforce in Ontario two default judgments obtained against the defendants pursuant to U.S. environmental legislation that facilitated the reimbursement of clean-up costs in relation to site contamination.[34] The Ontario Court of Appeal refused to characterize the U.S. statutory provisions as penal in nature, but instead found them to be restitutionary or remedial in character and not imposed with a view to punishing the party responsible for the loss.[35] Even though the claim-

---

32 FA Mann, 'Prerogative Rights of Foreign States and the Conflict of Laws' (1954) 40 Tr Gro Soc 25, 34.
33 *Mbasogo* (n 31) 874.
34 [1995] DLR 4th, 674.
35 Similar reasoning led to the enforcement in British Columbia of a foreign judgment to recover profits obtained by fraud in *United States Securities and Exchange Commission v Robert H Cosby and Global Action Investments Ltd.*, 2000 BCSC 338.

ant was the agency of a foreign state, this did not mean that the claim involved what the Court described as an 'illegitimate attempt to assert sovereignty beyond [its] borders.'[36] The Ontario Court of Appeal affirmed the trial court decision, saying that the action was best characterized as analogous to a common law claim in nuisance and was in substance of a commercial or private law nature. While it is somewhat unclear whether the public law category of unenforceable foreign laws exists in Canada, there have now been cases where comity and public policy, respectively, have been argued as grounds to reject the unenforceability of foreign law.[37]

Even United Kingdom courts have relaxed the characterization of foreign statutes as penal. In *United States Securities and Exchange Commission v. Manterfield*, for example, the Court of Appeal upheld an order freezing the UK assets of alleged fraudsters.[38] The Court emphasized that the claim could also have been brought in a civil action and should not therefore automatically be seen as penal in character. It relied on a New South Wales Court of Appeal decision[39] which had also upheld a claim on the basis that it sought compensation for victims of fraud, rather than the pursuit of a governmental interests such as national security as in the *Spycatcher* case.[40]

This line of Commonwealth jurisprudence illustrates various policy grounds for refusing to enforce foreign laws, whether of a penal or public nature. While the essence of these grounds is their direct connection to the acts of a foreign sovereign, an exception seems to have emerged when those acts are analogous to the exercise of private rights rather than purely governmental interests.

7   Iran v. Barakat Galleries Ltd.

The most significant English decision concerning illegally exported cultural material since *Ortiz* was the decision of the Court of Appeal in *Government of Iran v. Barakat Galleries Ltd.*[41] The case involved an action by Iran to recover

---

36   *Ivey* (n 34) 689.
37   See, eg, *Morguard Investments v DeSavoye* [1990] 3 SCR 1077.
38   [2009] 2 All ER 1009.
39   *Evans v European Bank Ltd.*, [2004] NSWCA 82. The plaintiff was the U.S. court-appointed receiver, on the application of the U.S. Federal Trade Commission, of a Vanuatu corporation party to a credit card fraud in the United States. The action was to recover proceeds of the fraud.
40   *Heinemann* (n 30).
41   [2007] EWCA Civ 1374. See Kevin Chamberlain, 'The Recognition and Enforcement of Foreign Cultural Heritage Laws: Iran v. Barakat' (2008) 13 Art, Antiquity & Law 161.

antiquities it claimed had both been illegally exported from Iran and were the property of that state. The judge at first instance, after hearing expert witnesses concerning Iranian law, had concluded that Iran had no title to the antiquities and that the relevant Iranian antiquities law was penal or public in character and therefore could not be given effect to in England. The Court of Appeal reversed both of these findings.

In its decision, the Court of Appeal concluded that under Iranian law the state was the owner of the antiquities in question. The Court also found that even if it was wrong in its conclusion as to title, Iran had 'an immediate right to possession of the antiquities that would vest ownership on [it] taking possession.'[42] Iranian law applied to both the determination of Iran's ownership and its right to possession, since the property was situated in Iran when both issues were subject to determination.[43]

As in *Ortiz*, Iran had never actually taken possession of the antiquities at issue, so that its title had never been perfected. This meant that the Court needed to consider whether Iran's claim involved a penal or public law that would not be recognized or enforced in England.

As to whether the Iranian law was to be characterized as penal, the Court of Appeal concluded that although the Iranian law contained provisions imposing various penalties, that did not render *all* of its provisions penal in nature. Instead it found that:

> The changes [the Iranian statute] made in relation to ownership of antiquities were not penal or confiscatory. They did not take effect retroactively. They did not deprive anyone who already owned antiquities of their title to them. They altered the law as to ownership of antiquities that had not yet been found, with the effect that these would all be owned by the State.... These were not penal provisions.[44]

Perhaps the most informative aspect of the decision in *Barakat* is its pronouncement regarding so-called 'public laws.' Rather than agreeing with the view of Lord Denning in *Ortiz*, that there was a general category of foreign public laws (like penal and revenue laws) that was unenforceable, the Court of Appeal in *Barakat* was of the view that there was a limited category of foreign

---

42 *Barakat* (n 41) para 84.
43 *Barakat* (n 41) para 86. This is also consistent with the reasoning in the well-known English case of *Winkworth v Christies* [1980] 1 Ch 496 that applied the law of the *lex situs* to determine title to movables.
44 *Barakat* (n 41) 111.

public laws which was categorically unenforceable and which involved the exercise or assertion of a sovereign right. In developing this analysis, the Court cited the *Mbasogo* and *Heinemann* cases for the principle that those cases, unlike *Barakat*, involved the vindication of government interests and the exercise of certain powers peculiar to governments.[45] The Court thought that (currency) exchange control legislation and possibly, 'but by no means [certainly]' also export restrictions, would fall within this category.[46] As well as referring to Lord Denning in *Ortiz*, the Court cited *King of Italy v. de Medici*,[47] which also suggests that export controls are unenforceable, but described it as being 'not fully reported and...of little assistance.'[48]

In any case, the Court in *Barakat* determined that Iran was not attempting to enforce foreign export restrictions, but rather was simply asserting rights of ownership.[49] It concluded that even if the case did involve an attempt to enforce a public law, it should not be decided on the basis of a general principle that no public laws would be enforceable under English law.[50] While founding its own conclusions on orthodox principles of conflict of laws regarding choice-of-law rules applicable to issues of property ownership, the Court of Appeal seemed to suggest that there should now be some 'degree of flexibility in dealing with claims to enforce public laws' and made extensive reference to an emerging body of international instruments addressing illicit trade in cultural material—such as the 1970 UNESCO Convention, the 1995 *UNIDROIT Convention on Stolen or Illegally Exported Cultural Objects* and the Commonwealth Scheme.[51]

Finally, the Court considered whether the claim by Iran was maintainable insofar as Iran had not taken possession of the antiquities it claimed. It is accepted law that where a state acquires title to property by confiscation or a compulsory process from a former owner, its title will only be recognized if the property has been reduced to possession.[52] Without possession, the state is forced to rely on the law that legitimizes its claim to ownership, which will be

---

45 *Barakat* (n 41) para 117.
46 *Barakat* (n 41) paras 127–28.
47 (1918) 34 TLR 623.
48 *Barakat* (n 41) para 128.
49 *Barakat* (n 41) para 131.
50 *Barakat* (n 41) para 151.
51 *Barakat* (n 41) para 154. For the text of the Convention, see (1995) 34 ILM 1322 ('UNIDROIT Convention'). The Commonwealth Scheme on the Protection of the Material Cultural Heritage was agreed to at a meeting of Commonwealth law ministers in Mauritius in 1993.
52 *Barakat* (n 41) para 143.

unenforceable as an 'exercise (of) its sovereign authority.'[53] The Court of Appeal then said:

> But in these proceedings Iran does not assert a claim based on its compulsory acquisition from private owners. It asserts a claim based upon title to antiquities which form part of Iran's national heritage, title conferred by legislation that is nearly 30 years old. This is a patrimonial claim, not a claim to enforce a public law or to assert sovereign rights. We do not consider that this is within the category of case where recognition of title or the right to possess under the foreign law depends on the State having taken possession.[54]

Thus, the Court rejected Barakat's argument that the Iranian laws were unenforceable because they were in substance both penal and public.

As we have seen, a similar line of reasoning had been adopted earlier by the U.S. Court of Appeals for the Second Circuit in *United States v. Shultz*, where the defendant was convicted of conspiracy to receive stolen property (Egyptian antiquities).[55] The Court in *Shultz* decided that an Egyptian cultural patrimony law declaring that all antiquities found in Egypt after 1983 were State property vested ownership in the Egyptian government for the purpose of prosecution under the U.S. *National Stolen Property Act*. As in *Barakat*, the Egyptian antiquities law was recognized in *Shultz* on the basis that it created sovereign patrimonial rights that were recognizable irrespective of whether the State had taken actual possession of the objects involved. This was in contrast to *Ortiz*, where the claim was not patrimonial since the only source for New Zealand's claim to title made was forfeiture pursuant to its export control laws.

8 Summary and Conclusion

It is now over 40 years since the events that led to the decisions of the English courts in *Ortiz* occurred. George Ortiz himself died in October, 2013[56] and the whereabouts of the Maori panels that were once in contention remained undisclosed—until a surprising recent development.[57] Nevertheless, the case

---

53   *Barakat* (n 41) para 148.
54   *Barakat* (n 41) para 149.
55   *Barakat* (n 41) para 23.
56   See Hermione Waterfield, 'In Tribute: George Ortiz' (2014) 18 Tribal Art 157.
57   See, *infra*, text accompanying note 69.

has long resonated amongst cultural heritage specialists as a symbol of the legal complexities surrounding the global movement of cultural objects.

In the aftermath of *Ortiz,* New Zealand, which became party to both the UNESCO and UNIDROIT Conventions in 2007, has implemented significant changes to its cultural property legislation.[58] These include new rules about the ownership of newly discovered Maori artifacts (*taonga tuturu*).[59] If these and other provisions had been in place when the Ortiz panels had been discovered, the outcome in that case might well have been different.

While the common law principles about the enforcement of foreign cultural property export controls remain unaltered, many states have implemented their own versions of their obligations under the UNESCO Convention to facilitate efforts by source countries to recover illegally exported cultural material. In Canada, for example, a foreign state that is party to the UNESCO Convention can request the Federal Minister of Canadian Heritage to assist in the recovery and return of cultural property that has been illegally exported from a foreign state.[60] The Attorney-General of Canada can then bring an action for recovery on behalf of the requesting state. It is clear that it is not a prerequisite to such a claim that the claimant establish title to the property in question. A similar procedure is now in place under New Zealand law.[61]

The English Court of Appeal in *Barakat* ended its reasoning with a discussion of public policy. It noted that the UNESCO Convention had been ratified by the United Kingdom in 2003 and executed by the United States in its *Convention on Cultural Property Implementation Act of 1983*. The point of this discussion seemed to be to illustrate 'the international acceptance of the

---

58 See Piers Davies & Paul Myburgh, 'New Zealand' in *Handbook on the Law of Cultural Heritage and International Trade* (n 29) 286.

59 See Robert Paterson, 'Taonga Maori Renaissance: Protecting the Cultural Heritage of Aotearoa/New Zealand', in James AR Nafziger & Ann M Nicgorski (eds), *Cultural Heritage Issues: The Legacy of Conquest, Colonization and Commerce* (Martinus Nijhoff 2009) 114–15. Australia also introduced legislation in 1986 (The Protection of Movable Cultural Heritage Act 1986), Section 9 of which provides for automatic forfeiture of a protected object upon its export without a permit. It is questionable if such forfeiture would be enforced by an English court given the comments by the Court in Barakat (n 53). For a survey of Australian law, see Craig Forrest, 'Australia' in *Handbook on the Law of Cultural Heritage and International Trade* (n 29) 44.

60 See Robert Paterson, 'Canada' in *Handbook on the Law of Cultural Heritage and International Trade* (n 29) 74, 88–89.

61 See Davies & Myburgh (n 58) 291. Since New Zealand is also party to the UNIDROIT Convention, the remedy also extends to state parties to that convention.

desirability of protection of the national heritage' and the compatibility of the Court's finding with such public policy.[62]

What remains unresolved is whether, if the sole basis for a foreign state's attempt to claim the return of cultural heritage removed from its territory is a violation of its export restrictions, a claim for its return could now be successful. There is no reported case that upholds a claim of this kind in the absence of proof of title or a right to possession. The Court of Appeal in *Barakat* expressed the view that there were positive policy reasons why such a claim 'which otherwise complies with the requirements of private international law' should not be dismissed merely because to do so would enforce foreign public laws.[63] Earlier, the Court referred to export restrictions as possibly, but by no means certainly, within the category of laws that would not be enforced because they represented the assertion or exercise of a sovereign right.[64] In *Ortiz* itself, it seems clear enough that the defendant had acquired good title to the panels. An order requiring him to return them to New Zealand would have amounted to a confiscation, seemingly incompatible with the opinion of the Court in *Barakat* that such appropriation is unenforceable unless the state already had legal possession of the property involved.[65] This situation is distinguishable from the circumstances in the *Manterfield* case where the action was seen as comparable to a civil action restoring losses due to fraud.[66] A different outcome in *Ortiz* would have deprived someone of their property and vested it in a government that otherwise had no claim to ownership or possession.

If an English court were to revisit the issue unanswered by the House of Lords in *Ortiz*—are restrictions on the export of cultural material enforceable by a state outside its borders?—it would need to develop a principled basis for doing so and, in particular, one that differentiated these kinds of foreign public laws from others that would presumably remain unenforceable such as taxation and other revenue laws. Another challenge would be whether a new approach to export controls would be indiscriminate or subject to some criteria as to which laws were reasonable and thus enforceable.[67] One attraction of the decisions in *Barakat* and *Shultz* is that they both involved the recognition

---

62   *Barakat* (n 41) para 163.
63   *Barakat* (n 41) para 154.
64   *Barakat* (n 41) paras 125–128.
65   See *supra*, text accompanying note 52.
66   *United States Securities and Exchange Commission v Manterfield* (n 38).
67   This is the approach taken in art 5 of the UNIDROIT Convention which places the onus on the requesting state to prove that the illegal export has impaired certain state interests, such as the integrity of a complex object or its traditional or ritual use by a tribal or indigenous community.

of comprehensive cultural patrimony laws that vested title to newly discovered cultural material in states with long histories of vulnerability to the vicissitudes of colonialism and looting of sites. This scenario is absent when an already privately-owned object is sold to a foreign purchaser who then fails to obtain proper export clearances. Perhaps this less fraught scenario is best dealt with by selective intergovernmental agreement, as is the case in the United States.[68]

The question posed at the start of this essay was whether an English court would likely decide *Ortiz* differently were a case with identical facts to now arise. Our answer, assuming an absence of any legitimate basis for New Zealand to claim ownership or a right of possession of the object in question, is 'no.' *Plus ça change, plus c'est la même chose*. Despite significant evidence of judicial support for international legal initiatives surrounding the return of illegally exported cultural material, there has been no clear indication that English law, along with that of other Commonwealth countries and the United States, would not continue to regard foreign export controls over cultural material to be penal or public in character and thus unenforceable. *Ortiz* and *Barakat* support the view that in order to secure the return of illegally exported cultural objects, source states must establish title according to the laws applicable to the objects while located in the territory of the source state. Relying on comity or public policy in isolation is not enough.

9   The Panels Return

In early July, 2014, it was announced that the carved Maori panels that had been the subject of the English court decisions in *Ortiz* had arrived back in New Zealand. After the death of George Ortiz in 2013, representatives of the New Zealand government entered into negotiations with the Ortiz family which resulted in an agreement to purchase the panels for approximately $US 4 million. The panels are now at the Puke Ariki Museum in New Plymouth under a trust (guardianship) arrangement between the Maori Te Atiawa people, the museum and the New Zealand Crown.[69]

---

68   See James AR Nafziger, 'United States' in *Handbook on the Law of Cultural Heritage and International Trade* (n 29) 506, 524–25. See also Robert Paterson, 'Moving Culture: The Future of National Cultural Property Export Controls' (2012) 12 Sw J Int'l L 287.

69   See Helen Harvey, 'Motunui panels returned to Taranaki' at <http://www.stuff.co.nz/taranaki-daily-news/67462225/motunui-panels-returned-to-taranaki> accessed 17 April 2015.

PART 8

Essays from the Field

∴

CHAPTER 36

Reform of UN Inquiries

*Geoffrey Palmer**

1   Introduction

I have known Roger Clark for more than 50 years, going back to the time we were both law students at the Victoria University of Wellington, he a couple of years ahead of me. I was instrumental in ensuring he came to the University of Iowa in 1971 where we both taught torts and he taught criminal law. He never returned New Zealand permanently, about which I feel twinges of guilt. We were joint authors of a New Zealand book of cases and material on torts,[1] he helped me with reforming the criminal law when I was Minister of Justice.[2] I have visited him at Rutgers on several occasions over the years and spoken to his classes. His contribution to international law, criminal law, international criminal law and international human rights law has been outstanding both in a practical sense and in his research contributions. He has never forgotten his New Zealand origins to which his fabulous parties in New Jersey on Waitangi Day are a continuing testament. In 2014 his New Zealand alma mater honoured him with an Honorary LLD. I salute you, Roger.

The subject of my contribution to this *Festschrift* looks at the United Nations ('UN') inquiry, a mechanism which was also the subject of Roger's attentions over two decades ago, and in which many of Roger's longstanding professional interests in human rights, international criminal law and institutions, justice and accountability, and foreign relations converge. The area is not without controversy.[3] In a

---

*   The author wishes to acknowledge excellent research assistance and editing from Rachel Opie.
1   Peter D McKenzie, Geoffrey W R Palmer & Roger S Clark, *Tort in Transition: A New Zealand Collection in the Accident Compensation Era* (Fourth Estate Books Limited 1976). For a review, see Peter Handford, 'Reviews: Tort in Transition' (1977) 40 MLR 608.
2   Geoffrey Palmer, *Reform: A Memoir* (Victoria University Press 2013) 331.
3   For example, the controversy surrounding the competence of Human Rights Council-mandated commissions of inquiry or fact-finding missions to make findings of international crimes. See Lyal S. Sunga, 'How can UN human rights special procedures sharpen ICC fact-finding?' (2011) 15(2) Int'l J Hum Rts 187; Théo Boutruche, 'Credible Fact-Finding and Allegations of International Humanitarian Law Violations: Challenges in Law and Practice' (2011) 16(1) J Conflict & Sec L 10; Catherine Harwood, 'The Competence of UN Human Rights Council Commissions of Inquiry to Make Findings of International Crimes' at <http://ssrn.com/abstract=2330808> and <http://dx.doi.org/10.2139/ssrn.2330808> accessed March 2014.

piece he contributed to a volume on international law and fact-finding in the field of human rights,[4] Roger examined the issue of legal representation in fact-finding inquiries, and he concluded after an exhaustive analysis of the international practice on the topic that '...it might be valuable for fact-finding bodies to consider ways and means of drawing upon legal expertise in the examination of witnesses or in the marshalling of evidence.'[5] While UN inquiries have evolved somewhat, Roger's conclusion still stands and it is one with which I strongly agree. Fact-finding should follow the principles of due process and all fact finding at the international level remains replete with difficulties.[6]

2 Making Sense of UN Inquiries

The issues exist now in a more acute form than when Roger wrote about them. UN inquiries of many types have been an expanding feature of the legal landscape for more than 30 years. As long ago as 1980, it was suggested fact-finding is 'potentially, a significant weapon in the armory of world order.'[7] There is ample indication that within the corridors of the UN itself fact-finding inquiries are increasingly regarded 'as effective tools to draw out facts necessary for wider accountability efforts.'[8]

The trend appears to be an increasing one since the Agenda for Peace was launched by the Secretary-General in 1992, in which it was stressed that timely and accurate knowledge of the facts was necessary to make preventive diplomacy work. He said:

---

4   Roger S Clark, 'Legal Representation' in Bertrand G Ramcharan (ed), *International Law and Fact-Finding in the Field of Human Rights* (Martinus Nijhoff 1982) 104.

5   *Ibid* 130.

6   Shabtai Rosenne, *Essays on International Law and Practice* (Koninklijke Brill NV 2007) Ch 14 'Fact Finding Before the international Court of Justice' 235; Anna Riddell & Brenden Plant, *Evidence before the International Court of Justice* (British Institute of International and Comparative Law 2009); Simon Halink 'All Things considered: How the International Court of Justice Delegated its Fact-Assessment to the United Nations in the *Armed Activities Case* '(2008) 40 NYU J Int'L L & Pol (Special Issue) 13.

7   Thomas M Franck & H Scott Fairley 'Procedural Due Process in Human Rights Fact-finding by International Agencies' (1980) 74 AJIL 308.

8   UNSC, 'Report of the Secretary-General on the Rule of Law and Transitional Justice in Conflict and Post-Conflict Societies' (2011) UN Doc S/2011/634, para 25; UNCHR, 'Report of the Secretary-General on Impunity' (2006) UN Doc E/CN.4/2006/89.

An increased resort to fact-finding is needed, in accordance with the Charter, initiated either by the Secretary-General, to enable him to meet his responsibilities under the Charter, including Article 99, or by the Security Council or the General Assembly. Various forms may be employed selectively as the situation requires. A request by a State for the sending of a United Nations fact-finding mission to its territory should be considered without undue delay.[9]

We may be witnessing a proliferation of fact-finding inquiries, but they have been with us as long as the UN itself. An enormous of array of inquiries have been established, dispatched, and undertaken by its various organs. In addition to fact-finding as we understand it today, from 1946, the use of inquiry in the forms of observation, verification, fact-finding, monitoring, reporting, and political engagement have been used as ways of seeking to address any conceivable matter of concern to the international community: border infringements, aggression, conflict, self-determination, holding of elections, political assassinations, violations of embargoes and sanctions regimes, implementation of peace agreements, deployment of peace operations, and violations of international humanitarian law and international human rights law, to name a few.[10]

---

9 UNGA/UNSC, 'Report of the Secretary-General on Agenda for Peace' (1992) UN Doc A/47/277, S/24111.

10 For example, the Security Council established, in 1946, the Commission of Investigation concerning Greek Frontier incidents (UNSC, 'Report on the Commission of Investigation concerning Greek Frontier Incidents' (1946) UN Doc S/339), and it has dispatched 'Special Missions' for decades. For a selection of early Special Missions, see UNSC Res 189 (4 June 1964) UN Doc S/RES/189; UNSC Res 289 (23 November 1970) UN Doc S/RES/289; UNSC Res 294 (15 July 1971) UN Doc S/RES/294; UNSC Res 446 (22 March 1979) UN Doc S/RES/446; UNSC Res 496 (15 December 1981) UN Doc S/RES/496; UNSC Res 571 (20 September 1985) UN Doc S/RES/571; UNSC Res 819 (16 April 1993) UN Doc S/RES/819.

The General Assembly mandated groups of experts to address specific matters. See, for example, UNGA Res 39/98D (13 December 1992) UN Doc A/RES/39/98D; UNGA Res 42/37C (30 November 1987) UN Doc A/RES/42/37C. It also established as subsidiary organs a number of committees, ad hoc committees, advisory committees, special committees, a high-level committee and working groups that may be considered to have inquiry functions in relation to issues relevant to its work, for example, UNGA Sub-Committee on the Situation in Angola, UNGA Res 1603 (XV) (20 April 1961) UN Doc A/RES/1603 (XV); Special Committee on the Situation with regard to the Implementation of the Declaration on the Granting of Independence to Colonial Countries and Peoples, UNGA Res 1654 (XVI) (27 November 1961), UN Doc A/RES/1654 (XVI); Special Committee on Israeli Practices, UNGA Res 2443 (XXIII) (19 December 1968) UN Doc A/RES/2443 (XXIII); Committee on the Exercise of the Inalienable Rights of the Palestinian People, UNGA Res 3376 (XXX) (10 November 1975) UN Doc A/RES/3376 (XXX).

The enormous range of inquiries presents a definitional problem. UN inquiries take on almost any conceivable form, go by different names, have a huge range of tasks, roles and hoped for outcomes, and are working in all corners of the UN. Attempting to make an exhaustive statement about all of them is sure to fail. For the purposes of this contribution, I wish to narrow down the field somewhat. My primary concern relates to the quasi-judicial ad hoc bodies that continue to be established under an often broad mandate to undertake fact-finding and reporting, as well as legal evaluation of the facts, in relation to a particular set of events.

TABLE: NUMBERS OF UN INQUIRIES

UN entity	Inquiries mandated or established
Security Council since 1992	9
General Assembly since 1992	1
Human Rights Council since 2006	12
Secretary-General since 1992	11

United Nations inquiries are now frequently mandated by the Human Rights Council,[11] the most recent example being the inquiry chaired by

---

The Secretary-General has dispatched inspection, observation or verification teams, groups of experts, missions of inquiry, and special envoys. By brief example see, Letter of the Secretary-General, UN Doc S/16227 and S/16628 (14–15 June 1984); UNSC, 'Reports of the Specialists appointed by the Secretary-General to investigate allegations concerning the use of chemical weapons S/16433 and S/20060' (1984, 1988) UN Doc S/S/16433, S/20060; UNSC, 'Report of a mission dispatched by the Secretary-General on prisoners of war in Iraq and Iran' (1985) UN Doc S/16962; UNSC 'Presidential Note regarding goodwill mission to Abkhazia' (10 September 1992) UN Doc S/24542; UNSC 'Presidential Statement regarding mission to Georgia (8 October 1992) UN Doc S/24637; UNSC 'Presidential Statement regarding goodwill mission to Tajikistan and Central Asia' (30 October 1992) UN Doc S/24742.

11 Pursuant to General Assembly resolution 60/251 (2006), the Human Rights Council has established numerous commissions of inquiry or fact-finding missions: Commission of Inquiry on Lebanon, UNHRC Res S-2/1 (13 November 2006) UN Doc A/HRC/RES/S-2/1; High Level Fact-Finding Mission to Beit Hanoun, UNHRC Res S-3/1 (15 November 2006) UN Doc A/HRC/RES/S-3/1; High Level Mission on the Situation of Human Rights in Darfur, UNHRC Decision S-4/101 (13 December 2006) UN Doc A/HRC/DEC/S-4/101; OHCHR Mission on the Situation of Human Rights in Honduras, UNHRC Res 12/14 (12 October 2009) UN Doc A/HRC/RES/12/14; United Nations Fact-Finding Mission on the Gaza Conflict, UNHRC Res S-9/1 (12 January 2009), UN Doc A/HRC/RES/S-9/1; Committee of Independent Experts [regarding Gaza conflict], UNHRC Res

retired Australian High Court Judge Michael Kirby on human rights in North Korea.[12] They have also been, and continue to be, established by the

13/9 (14 April 2010) UN Doc A/HRC/RES/13/9 and UNHRC Res 15/6 (6 October 2010) UN Doc A/HRC/RES/15/6; International Fact-Finding Mission to Investigate Violations of International Law [regarding 31 May 2010 Flotilla incident], UNHRC Res 14/1 (23 June 2010) UN Doc A/HRC/RES/14/1; Independent, International Commission of Inquiry on Côte d'Ivoire, UNHRC Res 16/25 (13 April 2011) UN Doc A/HRC/RES/16/25; International Commission of Inquiry on Libya, UNHRC Res S-15/1 (3 March 2011) UN Doc A/HRC/RES/S-15/1 and UNHRC Res 17/17 (14 July 2011) UN Doc A/HRC/RES/17/17; OHCHR Fact-Finding Mission on Syria, UNHRC Res S-16/1 (4 May 2011) UN Doc A/HRC/RES/S-16/1; International Commission of Inquiry on Syria, UNHRC Res S-17/1 (23 August 2011) UN Doc A/HRC/RES/S-17/1, UNHRC Res 19/22 (10 April 2012) UN Doc A/HRC/RES19/22, UNHRC Res 21/26 (17 October 2012) UN Doc A/HRC/RES/21/26 and UNHRC Res 22/24 (12 April 2013) UN Doc A/HRC/RES/22/24. The Human Rights Council's predecessor, the Commission on Human Rights, also authorised a number of inquiry mechanisms. See, for example, UNCHR Res 2 (XXV) (6 March 1967); UNCHR Res 20 (XXXVI) (29 February 1980); UNCHR Res 1997/58 (1997) UN Doc E/CN.4/1997/58; UNCHR Res S-5/1 (2000) UN Doc E/CN.4/RES/S-5/1.

[12] UNHRC Res 22/13 (9 April 2013) UN Doc A/HRC/RES/22/13; UNHRC 'Report of the International Commission of Inquiry on Human Rights in the Democratic Peoples' Republic of Korea' (7 February 2014) UN Doc A/HRC/25/63 and A/HRC/25/CRP.1. Note also that the Human Rights Council Special Procedures (currently, 37 thematic and 14 country mandates) are mandated to undertake country visits, conduct thematic studies and convene expert consultations, work through the communications procedure (individual complaints and communications with States), and report annually to the Human Rights Council and the General Assembly. In addition, Special Rapporteurs have been requested to carry out ad hoc inquiries falling within their areas of expertise, see for example, UNHRC, 'Reports of the Special Rapporteur on the human rights situation in the Palestinian territories occupied since 1967 pursuant to resolution 3/1 of the Human Rights Council' (2006, 2007), UN Doc A/HRC/4/116 and A/HRC/5/11; UNHRC, 'Combined report of seven thematic procedures on technical assistance to the Government of the Democratic Republic of the Congo and urgent examination of the situation in the east of the country' (5 March 2009) UN Doc A/HRC/10/59.

UN treaty bodies also carry out fact-finding through, for example, conduct of country visits, consideration of individual complaints and state reports. Some treaty bodies have a specific inquiry function: the Committee against Torture, Committee on the Elimination of Discrimination against Women, Committee on the Rights of Persons with Disabilities, Committee on Enforced Disappearances, Committee on Economic Social and Cultural Rights and Committee on the Rights of the Child.

The UN High Commissioner for Human Rights dispatches fact-finding missions pursuant to UNGA Res resolution 48/141 (1993), UN Doc A/RES/48/141. For example, fact-finding and/or assessment missions to Uzbekistan (2005), Kenya (2007), Tunisia (2011), Egypt (2011), Libya (2011), Bahrain (2011), Yemen (2011), Mali (2013), Central African Republic (2013), and on Syria (2011, 2012, 2013). The High Commissioner has also sent fact-finding teams to areas upon request from UN offices or peace missions.

Security Council, and the Secretary-General, and to a much lesser extent, the General Assembly.[13] As this contribution is being written, the International Commission of Inquiry for the Central African Republic is beginning its work following its establishment by the Security Council.[14] Since 1992, the Security Council has also set up inquiries to examine events in the Federal Republic of Yugoslavia,[15] Somalia,[16] Rwanda,[17] Burundi,[18] Côte d'Ivoire,[19] Sudan (Darfur)[20] and Lebanon.[21]

The Secretary-General has established inquiries upon the request of States, the Security Council and international or regional organisations. In May 2008, he was asked by the Government of Pakistan to establish an international commission for the purpose of investigating the assassination of Ms. Benazir Bhutto[22] More recently, upon the request of a number of States, the Secretary-General established an investigation into the use of chemical weapons in the Syrian Arab Republic.[23] In 2010, he set up a panel to examine the matters rele-

---

Other UN entities have also set up inquiries on occasion. For example, the Commission of Enquiry on the effects of chewing coca leaf, UN Economic and Social Council Res 1948/123 (2 March 1948) UN Doc E/RES/1948/123/(VI)C and UN Economic and Social Council Res 1948/159 (10 August 1950, UN Doc E/RES/1948/159(VII)IV; the International Commission against Impunity in Guatemala (CICIG), Agreement to Establish the CICIG between the United Nations and Guatemala, ratified by the Congress of the Republic of Guatemala on 1 August 2007.

13 In 1998, the General Assembly resolved to appoint a Group of Experts for Cambodia to bring about reconciliation and strengthen democracy and address accountability. See UNGA Res 52/135 (27 February 1998) UN Doc A/RES/52/135; UNGA, 'Report of the Group of Experts for Cambodia established pursuant to General Assembly Resolution 52/135' (18 February 1999).
14 UNSC Res 2127 (5 December 2013) UN Doc S/RES/2127.
15 UNSC Res 780 (6 October 1992) UN Doc S/RES/780.
16 UNSC Res 885 (16 November 1993) UN Doc S/RES/885.
17 UNSC Res 935 (1 July 1994) UN Doc S/RES/935; UNSC Res 1013 (7 September 1995) UN Doc S/RES/1013; UNSC Res 1161 (9 April 1998) UN Doc S/RES/1161.
18 UNSC Res 1012 (28 August 1995) UN Doc S/RES/1012.
19 UNSC Presidential Statement 2004/17 (25 May 2004) UN Doc S/PRST/2004/17.
20 UNSC Res 1564 (18 September 2004) UN Doc S/RES/1564; International Commission of Inquiry on Darfur, 'Report to the United Nations Secretary-General' (25 January 2005).
21 UNSC Res 1595 (7 April 2005) UN Doc S/RES/1595.
22 Letter from the Secretary-General to the President of the Security Council (3 February 2009) UN Doc S/2009/67; United Nations Commission of Inquiry, 'Report into the Facts and Circumstances of the Assassination of the Former Pakistani Prime Minister Mohtarma Benazir Bhutto' (31 March 2011).
23 Letter from the Secretary-General to the President of the Security Council (25 March 2013) UN Doc S/2013/184; UNSC/UNGA, United Nations Mission to Investigate Allegations

vant to an accountability process in Sri Lanka in light of the human rights and international humanitarian law violations arising out of the end of the civil war in that country.[24] The Secretary-General may also establish inquiries acting on his inherent authority under what is termed his 'good offices', which has developed to see the Secretary-General undertaking a growing role in international conflict resolution.[25] The Panel of Inquiry into the 31 May 2010 Flotilla incident, in which nine people lost their lives, and of which I was the Chair,[26] was of this class, although in June 2010 the Security Council took note 'of the statement of the UN Secretary-General on the need to have a full investigation

---

of the Use of Chemical Weapons in the Syrian Arab Republic 'Report on the Alleged Use of Chemical Weapons in the Ghouta Area of Damascus on 21 August 2013' (16 September 2013) UN Doc A/67/997—S/2013/553.

24 Press Statement, 'Secretary-General Names Panel of Experts to Advise on Accountability for Possible Rights Violations during Sri Lanka Conflict' (22 June 2010) UN Doc SG/SM/12967; Report of Secretary General's Panel of Experts on Accountability in Sri Lanka (31 March 2011). For additional examples, see UNSC, 'Report of the Fact-Finding Mission to Investigate Human rights Violations in Abkhazia, Republic of Georgia' (17 November 1993) UN Doc S/26795; Note by the Secretary-General on the International Commission for Togo (29 July 2000) UN Doc E/CN.4/Sub.2/2000/8; Press Release, 'Acting High Commissioner for Human Rights Establishes Independent Commission of Inquiry for Côte d'Ivoire' (8 April 2004) UN Doc AFR/896, HR/4731; UNSC, Report of the Independent Commission of Experts to Review the Prosecution of Serious Violations of Human Rights in Timor Leste (15 July 2005) UN Doc S/2005/458; UNSC, Record of Meeting (13 June 2006) UN Doc S/PV.5457; UNSC, 'Twenty-first Report of the Secretary-General on United Nations Organization Mission in Democratic Republic of Congo' (13 June 2006) UN Doc S/2006/390, para 54; Letter from the Secretary-General to the President of the Security Council on Establishment of International Commission of Inquiry for Guinea (28 October 2009) UN Doc S/2009/556.

25 The term 'good offices' has its origins in the 1899 and 1907 Hague Conventions. The Secretary-General also acts pursuant to Article 99 of the United Nations Charter, which provides, '[t]he Secretary-General may bring to the attention of the Security Council any matter which in his opinion may threaten the maintenance of international peace and security.' See, for example, Christiane Bourloyannis, 'Fact-Finding by the Secretary-General of the United Nations' (1989–1990) 22 NYU J Int'l L and Pol 641; Bertrand G Ramcharan, *Humanitarian Good Offices in International Law* (Martinus Nijhoff Publishers 1983) 55; Axel Berg, 'The 1991 Declaration on Fact-Finding by the United Nations' (1993) 4 EJIL 107; Thomas Franck, 'The Secretary-General's Role in Conflict Resolution: Past, Present, Conjecture' (1995) 6 EJIL 360.

26 Press Statement from Secretary-General on Panel of Inquiry on 31 May 2010 Flotilla Incident (2 August 2010) UN Doc SG/SM/13032; Report of the Secretary-General's Panel of Inquiry on the 31 May 2010 Flotilla Incident (September 2011).

into the matter and it calls for a prompt, impartial credible and transparent investigation conforming to international standards.'[27]

I became interested in the issues surrounding United Nations inquiries as a result of chairing the Flotilla Panel ('Panel'). The Panel was asked in its Terms of Reference to examine and identify the facts, circumstances and context of the incident that took place on 31 May 2010, and to consider and recommend ways of avoiding similar incidents in the future. The Panel included a member from both of the States centrally involved, namely, Turkey and Israel, which agreed the Terms of Reference and membership; the Terms of Reference were to a substantial extent the result of negotiations. The Panel was to operate by consensus. In the event that was not possible, the Chair (myself) and Vice-Chair (President Alvaro Uribe from Colombia) were empowered to decide the finding or recommendation. The Terms of Reference also laid down to a substantial degree the methods of work by which the Panel was to receive and review reports from the Turkish and Israeli national investigations into the incident and request clarifications and information that it may require. Representatives of Turkey and Israel appeared before the Panel in New York and were questioned.[28] The Flotilla incident was concurrently the subject of another inquiry, mandated by the Human Rights Council to look into the international humanitarian law and international human rights law implications of the incident, which Israel would not co-operate with.[29] It is strange to think that different parts of the UN can set up different inquiries into the same matters. It should be avoided.

I recite these matters to indicate the reasons that caused me to think about such inquiries and their complications. I do not wish in this essay to deal with the matters of substance in the two inquiries mentioned above, but rather I will explore the following issues that can be stated in a series of questions:

- What are the fundamental features of such inquiries? What do they aim to achieve?
- What are their limitations or shortcomings?

---

[27] UNSC Presidential Statement (1 June 2010) UN Doc S/PRST/2010/9.

[28] For my views on this inquiry see Geoffrey Palmer, *Reform: A Memoir* (Victoria University Press 2013) 662–79.

[29] UNHRC Res 14/1 (23 June 2010) UN Doc A/HRC/RES/14/1; UNHRC, 'Report of the International Fact-finding mission to investigate violations of international law including international humanitarian and human rights law result of Israeli attacks on the Flotilla of Ships carrying humanitarian assistance' (27 September 2010) UN Doc A/HRC/15/21.

- Given the increasing use of inquiries within the UN system, what could be done to provide greater clarity and coherence in respect to inquiries and thus increase their effectiveness?

3   Purposes of Inquiries

Many reasons exist as to why inquiries are established, and there are striking parallels between the purposes and roles of national and international inquiries. Setting up an inquiry is often done in common law countries, where inquiries are usually established by the executive government. There are two categories of inquiry, the first being those where policy analysis is the main requirement and the government desires an impartial report examining the approaches that could be taken on a new, controversial or difficult topic. This kind of inquiry allows for the range of views on a topic as contained in public submissions to the inquiry to be gathered and analysed, and identification of preferred policy options in the inquiry's recommendations. The second category of inquiry examines the conduct of individuals and organisations and may make adverse findings about their behaviour.[30] This category usually does not encompass alleged criminal offending, which is not a matter to be properly pursued by an inquiry but by prosecution in a court. Nevertheless, the inquiry may reveal evidence for launching such a prosecution.

In 2005, the British House of Commons Public Administration Select Committee summarised the views of submitters to it as to why inquiries were set up by the United Kingdom Government:

- Establishing the facts: providing a full and fair account of what happened especially in circumstances where the facts are disputed, or the course and causation of events is not clear;
- Learning from events, and so helping to prevent their recurrence by synthesising and distilling lessons which can be used to change practice;
- Catharsis or therapeutic exposure: providing an opportunity for reconciliation and resolution, by bringing protagonists face to face with each other's perspectives and problems;

---

30   See New Zealand Law Commission, A New Inquiries Act (NZLC R102, 2008); New Zealand Law Commission, The Role of Public Inquiries (NZLC IP1, 2007). UNHRC, 'Report of the Special Rapporteur on extrajudicial, summary or arbitrary executions, Philip Alston' (2 May 2008) UN Doc A/HRC/8/3, paras 12–58.

- Reassurance: rebuilding public confidence after a major failure by showing the government is making sure it is fully investigated and dealt with;
- Accountability, blame, and retribution: holding people and organisations to account, and sometimes indirectly contributing to the assignations of blame and to mechanisms for retribution;
- Political considerations: serving a wider political agenda for government in demonstrating that 'something is being done' or in providing leverage for change.[31]

These reasons may be similarly applied to inquiries established at the international level. UN inquiries operate in a particular political reality. As noted by M. Cherif Bassiouni, the organ that establishes the inquiry determines its subject matter, scope, political authority and influence over the bureaucracy. The mandate determines its mission, duration and authority. He says that: 'Because the values of truth and justice have become part of the *realpolitik*, nothing can be done to contradict these values.'[32] Based on my experience, this is a conclusion with which I agree.

Yet, UN inquiries have considerable advantages even in fraught and highly politicised situations. When established, as most are, by an inter-state body, they are the result of a majority decision. They are made up of independent experts. They are not dependent on the individual states involved in the matter at issue. UN inquiries are comparatively cost-effective, can be mobilised relatively quickly, and can be flexible in design. In the fulfilment of their mandates, UN inquiries can cast light on events, clarify issues and produce a narrative of what actually happened which may be helpful both with respect to victims and/or for resolving the dispute. They can identify wrongdoing, hold nations to account for their actions and suggest where State and individual responsibility lies. Inquiries can also lay the groundwork for future accountability processes, including international prosecutions through the International Criminal Court.[33] Inquiries frequently make recommendations aimed at preventing the recurrence of the particular event and/or for broader UN engagement. Their reporting may also be highly significant for galvanising state and public action as happened as a result of, for example, the work of the Commission of Experts

---

[31] House of Commons Public Administration Select Committee *Government by Inquiry* (2003–04, HC 51-I).

[32] M Cherif Bassiouni, 'Appraising UN Justice-Related Fact-Finding Missions' (2001) 5(35) Wash U J L & Pol'y 35, 39.

[33] See, for example, Lyal S. Sunga, 'How Can UN Human Rights Special Procedures Sharpen ICC Fact-Finding?' (2011) 15(2) Intl J Hum Rts 187.

on Yugoslavia, which saw the creation of the International Criminal Tribunal for the former Yugoslavia, and the International Commission of Inquiry on Darfur, following which the Security Council referred the situation in that region to the International Criminal Court. Inquiries can also advance the norms and values of international law and provide a means for affected persons and groups to be heard.[34]

The considerable expansion in the use of inquiries indicates that their advantages have made them an attractive tool for States and the United Nations. This may especially be true today where global instability and threats pose severe challenges to the international community, and where defining concepts such as the rule of law, accountability and human rights have taken centre stage.

4 Shortcomings of Inquiries

The growing use of inquiries, and their potential, demands that they are looked at with a critical eye. There is a need to develop a better understanding of the challenges confronting these inquiries and their shortcomings, and to identify how they can be made most effective. Professor Philip Alston has remarked that UN inquiries are a subject 'for sustained exploration, critique, and refinement.'[35] Yet, as he noted:

> there have been few efforts to collect best practices, to provide resources to facilitate the creation of effective missions in the future, or to guide and assist those carrying out different functions within the context of such missions. This stands in contrast to the detailed studies undertaken of a great many dimensions of the activities of the international criminal courts and tribunals.[36]

---

34   See generally Philip Alston, 'Commissions of Inquiry as Human Rights Fact-Finding Tools' (2011) ASIL Proceedings: Commissions of Inquiry into Armed Conflict 81; Antonio Cassese, 'Fostering Increased Conformity with International Standards: Monitoring and Institutional Fact-Finding' in Antonio Cassese (ed), *Realizing Utopia: the Future of International Law* (Oxford University Press 2012) 295, 303; Rob Grace & Claude Bruderlein, 'Building Effective Monitoring, Reporting, and Fact-Finding Mechanisms' (2012) Program on Humanitarian Policy and Conflict Research Working Paper, at <http://www.hpcrresearch.org/publications/applied-research/hpcr-research-and-working-papers> accessed 12 March 2014.

35   Philip Alston, 'Commissions of Inquiry as Human Rights Fact-Finding Tools' (2011) ASIL Proceedings: Commissions of Inquiry into Armed Conflict 81.

36   *Ibid*, 84–85.

Some effort has been made more recently to remedy the relative paucity of scholarship in this area; the Harvard University's programme on Humanitarian Policy and Conflict Resolution has produced a series of helpful analyses of the design and planning of monitoring, reporting and fact finding missions and associated matters.[37] However, it is apparent that more could be done.

In observations below, I highlight two aspects of UN inquiries that, in my experience, could benefit from further reflection: (i) the issue of State consent, or rather lack of consent, that plagues many inquiries; (ii) the absence of an ability on the part of inquiries to require the production of evidence.

(1)   *State Consent*

It is inconceivable that an inquiry would be established in a domestic setting without the consent of the State. Indeed, where sufficient political will exists for an inquiry, consent is inherent in the act of the executive government that then establishes it.

The analogy is imperfect for UN inquiries. There is no executive government within the UN. Inquiries are often not established at the behest of a State, but instead by an inter-state body or a high-level UN official. There has long been a requirement that the State that will be the subject of investigation must consent to it. This requirement is a corollary of State sovereignty and the principle of non-intervention, where Chapter VII is not in play, and was explicitly provided for in the 1991 General Assembly Declaration on Fact-Finding by the United Nations

---

37   Rob Grace & Claude Bruderleirn, 'Building Effective Monitoring, Reporting, and Fact-Finding Mechanisms' (2012) Program on Humanitarian Policy and Conflict Research Working Paper <http://www.hpcrresearch.org/publications/applied-research/hpcr-research-and-working-papers>, accessed on 12 March 2014; Théo Boutruche, 'Selecting and Applying Legal Lenses in Monitoring, Reporting, and Fact-Finding Missions' (2013) Program on Humanitarian Policy and Conflict Research Working Paper, at <http://www.hpcrresearch.org/publications/applied-research/hpcr-research-and-working-papers> accessed 8 March 2014; Rob Grace, 'The Design and Planning of Monitoring, Reporting, and Fact-Finding Missions' (2013) Program on Humanitarian Policy and Conflict Research Working Paper, at <http://www.hpcrresearch.org/publications/applied-research/hpcr-research-and-working-papers> accessed 4 March 2014; Cynthia Petrigh, 'Protection of Witnesses, Victims and Staff in Monitoring, Reporting, and Fact-Finding Missions' (2014) Program on Humanitarian Policy and Conflict Research Working Paper, at <http://www.hpcrresearch.org/publications/applied-research/hpcr-research-and-working-papers> accessed 14 March 2014; Stephen Wilkinson, 'Finding the Facts: Standards of Proof and Information Handling in Monitoring, Reporting, and Fact-Finding Missions' (2014) Program on Humanitarian Policy and Conflict Research Working Paper, at <http://www.hpcrresearch.org/publications/applied-research/hpcr-research-and-working-papers> accessed 12 March 2014.

in the Field of the Maintenance of International Peace and Security.[38] The Declaration clearly states that the affected State must consent to the dispatch of a fact-finding mission to its territory, although it also requests States to endeavour to follow a policy of admitting fact-finding missions to their territory.[39]

In more recent times, however, UN inquiries have been established without the agreement of the affected State. Furthermore, consent has not been forthcoming following the establishment of a multitude of inquiries. One need only to think of the Human Rights Council-mandated in international commissions of inquiry on Syria and the Democratic Peoples' Republic of Korea, not to mention the Human Rights Council Fact-Finding Mission on Israeli Settlements or the Secretary-General's Panel of Experts on Sri Lanka. In fact, the Flotilla Panel, established by the Secretary-General, was unusual in securing the consent of both nations whose conduct was under investigation, although Government representatives were members of the Panel.

Lack of consent by a State has not prevented inquiries from being established, or carrying out their functions. Yet, the question needs to be asked whether undertaking fact-finding in the absence of State consent has the effect of rendering an inquiry dead before it has begun.

The answer must surely be 'it depends'. Although it seems highly preferable that a recalcitrant State should not be able to prevent an inquiry taking place simply through the refusal of its consent, the necessity for consent should depend upon the circumstances of each inquiry. The purpose, mandate and outcomes of an inquiry that is required to examine allegations of violations of

---

38 Declaration on Fact-Finding by the United Nations in the Field of the Maintenance of International Peace and Security, UNGA Res 46/59 (9 December 1991) UN Doc A/RES/46/59. See also Axel Berg, 'The 1991 Declaration on Fact-Finding by the United Nations' (1993) 4 EJIL 107. The reluctance of States to consent to fact-finding inquiries is demonstrated by the history of the International Humanitarian Fact Finding Commission set up under the First Protocol of the Geneva Conventions to investigate 'grave breaches' of IHL.

The consent of the State party whose conduct is being investigated is required. Just over 75 of the 173 State parties to the Protocol have made general declarations expressing consent to the IHFC and the low uptake may be a contributing factor to the fact that the Commission has never been called upon to act. See the lament from the IHFFC in its 2012 statement to the UNGA Sixth Committee, where it queries why States have chosen to use ad hoc fact finding missions rather than the 'established body': <http://www.ihffc.org/Files/en/news/statement_unga_2012.pdf> accessed 8 April 2014.

39 Declaration on Fact-Finding by the United Nations in the Field of the Maintenance of International Peace and Security, UNGA Res 46/59 (9 December 1991) UN Doc A/RES/46/59, Annex, paras 6 and 21.

international humanitarian law and international human rights law violations may be quite different from one established by the Secretary-General in the exercise of his 'good offices'. It is worth recalling that in human rights fact-finding, the lack of consent of the State is nothing new; States have traditionally been unwilling to open up their human rights record to scrutiny and fact-finding approaches have been developed to respond to this reality. This does not, however, lessen the need for any inquiry of this type to ensure the State has been given reasonable opportunity to be heard, or it risks delegitimisation. With inquiries established for preventive diplomacy objectives, the absence of consent may bring into question the utility of having an inquiry at all.

Most inquiries are now tasked with making recommendations. It is apparent that a State that has not consented to an inquiry is unlikely to consider seriously an inquiry's recommendations to put its house in order, no matter how well devised. Moreover, an inquiry is neither an adjudication nor an arbitration, although it has some elements of both. While the law can be canvassed, it cannot be authoritatively determined and the legal findings made by inquiries have the same legal force as a legal opinion and may be highly contestable. Again, a state that has withheld its consent is unlikely to accept the legal position presented. Looked at it in this way, consent may not be a prerequisite for the establishment and conduct of some inquiries, but it is relevant in deciding whether to go ahead. The consent of the State to a human rights investigation may be viewed sceptically and seen to be detrimental to the independence of an investigation. Careful analysis of the likely difficulties is required before it is decided to proceed.

(2)   *Lack of Coercive Powers*

An even greater incapacity for UN inquiries flows from the absence of coercive powers. In order to find out what happened and secure the relevant information, domestic inquiries have coercive powers that are provided for by statutes regulating public inquiries.[40] Such an inquiry should be able to receive any information that may assist it regardless of whether such evidence would be admissible in a court of law. It needs to have to power to summon witnesses, to require any person to produce documents in their possession, and ensure that evidence is not destroyed, procedural orders are followed and misleading information is not supplied, including through the availability of criminal

---

40   Inquiries Act 2013 (New Zealand); Inquiries Act 2005 (UK); Royal Commissions Act 1902 (Australia); Inquiries Act, 1985 (Canada).

sanction. The members of an inquiry need immunity against liability for anything done, reported, stated or omitted in the exercise of their powers. There also needs to be provision for the protection of the members against being compelled to give evidence in a court in relation to an inquiry. Witnesses and other participants in the inquiry also require similar privileges and immunities.

Obviously such an array of legal powers is not available to UN inquiries, and it is not likely that the improvements can be made within the foreseeable future. Similar to the international courts and tribunals, UN inquiries are dependent upon the co-operation of States, including those State or States that are the subject of investigation. However, in many situations with which UN inquiries are dealing the incentives on States not to co-operate are high and the UN Charter provides no powers to secure evidence that a sovereign State wishes to hide or protect. The UN enjoys no coercive powers to compel witnesses or evidence to be brought before it under pain of punishment, although the United Nations Convention on Privileges and Immunities 1946 does apply to protect inquiry members and staff. It is difficult to see how such enforcement powers could be conferred as the law now stands without the consent of affected nations in the inquiry. On its face, it is hard to escape the conclusion that UN inquiries are relatively impotent when co-operation is not forthcoming. Moreover, the absence of the State in the fact-finding process leaves the validity of an inquiry's findings more vulnerable to attack than one established under domestic law.

It is necessary to discriminate between the various types of UN inquiries. A lack of State co-operation could well scuttle any possibility of a positive outcome for an inquiry established to contribute to resolving a dispute between two States. But, a surprising amount has been achieved by UN inquiries investigating violations of human rights and/or international humanitarian law. In such instances, inquiries generally look well beyond the State to other sources of information; indeed the nature of the investigation demands it. For instance, interviews and public hearings can be held in person with victims and witnesses located outside the State concerned and multiple forms of communication enable information to be shared by those on the territory of the State. Video, photography and satellite imagery are also important sources of information, as are the United Nations, its agencies, and other organisations. There is no question that everything should be done to ensure all interested parties, including the State, are heard. However, co-operation of State may not be imperative to an inquiry, and the non-cooperation of a State should not necessarily bar the launching of an inquiry.

5   Enhancing Efficacy

Inquiries have proliferated in the UN over the past ten years or so, and especially from the Human Rights Council. Can they be improved in shining light on events, helping to resolve disputes or provide findings that materially assist the international community and the UN in furtherance of their objectives? The inherent shortcomings of UN inquiries argue for their organisation, coordination and methodology to be as soundly based as it can be in the circumstances. Such is not currently the case, despite the repeated calls over many years for common procedures to be put in place.[41] The need remains in a heightened form.

The UN Office of the High Commissioner for Human Rights has methodologies for commissions of inquiry and fact-finding missions, undertaken 'lessons learned' exercises and, most recently, produced a publication containing guidance on and practice in international commissions of inquiry and fact-finding missions.[42] The relevant documents are not publicly available and analysis of them is impossible. Transparency and credibility suggests they should be available. Work of a similar kind does not appear to be underway in other parts of the UN. For those working in many UN inquiries, then, there is no principled operational guidance and each inquiry has to figure out for itself what to do and how to do it.

Professor M. Cherif Bassiouni, who has led a number of fact-finding missions, wrote in 2001:

> After fifty years there is no standard operating procedure for fact-finding missions. Admittedly, any standard operating procedure needs to be

---

41   See, for example, Stephen B Kaufman, 'The Necessity for Rules of Procedure in *Ad Hoc* United Nations Investigations' (1969) 18 Am U L Rev 739; Thomas M Franck & H Scott Fairley 'Procedural Due Process in Human Rights Fact-finding by International Agencies' (1980) 74 AJIL 308; Bertrand G Ramcharan (ed) 'Substantive Law Applicable' in *International Law and Fact-Finding in the Field of Human Rights* (Martinus Nijhoff Publishers 1982) 26, 38; M Cherif Bassiouni, 'Appraising UN Justice-Related Fact-Finding Missions' (2001) 5(35) Wash U J L & Pol'y 35 ('Bassiouni, 'Appraising UN Justice-Related Fact-Finding Missions'") 40–41; Antonio Cassese, 'Fostering Increased Conformity with International Standards: Monitoring and Institutional Fact-Finding' in Antonio Cassese (ed), *Realizing Utopia: the Future of International Law* (OUP 2012) 295, 303.

42   See, for example, UNHRC, 'Annual Report of the United Nations High Commissioner for Human Rights Report to the Human Rights Council' (18 December 2013) UN Doc A/HRC/25/19, para 73; OHCHR, 'Annual Report of the Office of the High Commissioner for Human Rights 2012', 43; OHCHR, 'Annual Report of the Office of the High Commissioner for Human Rights 2011', 61.

tailored to the situation. But no manual exists to describe how an investigation should be conducted and there is no standard, though adaptable, computer program to input collected data. Worse of all, there is no continuity. In short, there is nothing to guide, instruct, or assist the heads and appointees to these missions of how to better carry out their mandates. It strains one's belief that in fifty years the most elementary aspects of standardized organisation, planning and documentation have not been developed.[43]

A 'standard operating procedure' must embody the fundamental principles of due process, such as independence, fairness, impartiality and objectivity, transparency and 'do no harm'.[44] These requirements are no different from inquiries established in the domestic system.[45] The degree to which inquiries adhere to these principles determines the integrity of the process and, ultimately, their credibility. Given the plain difficulties of securing jurisdiction for international litigation or arbitration without State consent, these inquiries function as a proxy for such legal activity to some degree. Often they are the only analysis or assessment of a situation that is ever made. This reinforces the notion that they should be conducted as rigorously and as fairly as possible.

In 1980, Professor Thomas Franck made clear his view that the prospects for fact-finding 'rest upon a fragile assumption of 'fairness' and 'credibility' that only conscious vigilance can sustain.'[46] It is crucial, therefore, to 'develop uni-

---

[43] Bassiouni, 'Appraising UN Justice-Related Fact-Finding Missions' (n 41) 40–41.

[44] Declaration on Fact-Finding by the United Nations in the Field of the Maintenance of International Peace and Security, UNGA Res 46/59 (9 December 1991) UN Doc A/RES/46/59, para 3. Fundamental principles guiding the work of UN inquiries have been explicitly set out in the terms of reference/methods of work of some inquiries, eg Terms of Reference for the International Fact-Finding Mission on Israeli Settlements (2012), at <http://www.ohchr.org/Documents/HRBodies/HRCouncil/RegularSession/Session19/FFM/FFMSettlementTOR.pdf> accessed 14 March 2014; Report of the International Commission of Inquiry on Human Rights in Democratic Peoples' Republic of North Korea (7 February 2104) UN Doc A/HRC/25/CRP.1, para 29, and website of the International Commission of Inquiry on Human Rights in Democratic Peoples' Republic of North Korea (2013–2014), at <http://www.ohchr.org/EN/HRBodies/HRC/CoIDPRK/Pages/Callforsubmissions.aspx > accessed 14 March 2014.

[45] See for example New Zealand Law Commission, New Zealand Law Commission, A New Inquiries Act (NZLC R102, 2008), paras 3.17–3.18, 4.30–4.33, 4.75; 'Report of the Special Rapporteur on extrajudicial, summary or arbitrary executions, Philip Alston' (2 May 2008) UN Doc A/HRC/8/3, para 25.

[46] Thomas M Franck & H Scott Fairley 'Procedural Due Process in Human Rights Fact-finding by International Agencies' (1980) 74 AJIL 308, 309.

versally applicable minimal standards of due process to control both the way the facts are established and what is done with them afterwards.'[47]

It would be no easy task to devise and agree such a standardized set of procedures applicable across UN inquiries. To argue for one format is to argue for a set of procedures that would be too simplified and general to be of much practical use. One difficulty lies in the angle of narration. Catastrophe wears many cloaks when it comes to the UN, and it matters whether the issues revolve around disputes between States, armed conflict, violations of human rights or humanitarian disasters. Maintaining peace and security is not the same thing as humanitarian concerns and human rights, although they clearly do shade into one another in a number of instances. The approach taken by an inquiry is likely to vary depending upon its purpose and whether it is primarily concerned with security issues, human rights issues or international humanitarian law.

Furthermore, throughout the life of an inquiry and often in very short time frames, determinations must be made about all facets of the inquiry's operation. There is not space to elaborate here, but the following brief discussion gives a small sense of range and complexity of the issues inquiries confront.

What will be the methodology for ascertaining the facts in light of the nature of the inquiry? The differences between the common law and the civil law approaches that permeate attitudes to international law, and also resonate in the field of inquiries, may not be straightforward to resolve. Furthermore, what are the sources to be used, and how will their credibility be tested and their information be corroborated? Frequently, the events will be highly contested by affected parties or nations. What can be done to overcome the absence of coercive powers to summon, and examine witnesses, and require the presentation of documents? Furthermore, international law issues will hang like shadow over the inquiry, and will inevitably influence the fact-finding and the evaluation of the facts. What methodology should be applied to ensure the necessary separation of the facts from the legal context?

Another contentious area relates to the burden of proof. Is the balance of probabilities sufficient? Does this need to be articulated and applied consistently by all UN inquiries? What impact does the level of proof, and the consequent approach to information gathering, have on possible future accountability processes such as national or international prosecutions? Moreover, not only are the facts difficult to establish but in many instances the application of the law to the facts is complicated by the uncertain nature of many of the norms of international law, particularly customary law.

---

47   Ibid.

Propaganda from governments and deliberate misinformation can occur in publicity concerning highly politically charged inquiries. States with strong agendas and political determination over particular issues they regard as fundamental to them will attack the inquiry.[48] Preserving independence of appointment and action in this environment is both difficult and critical.

Complexity and the circumstance-specific nature of inquiries, pose particular challenges to the formulation of a set of procedures to guide them. That does not mean that they should remain rudderless. All inquiries have the same stages of operation: the establishment of the mandate, the design and planning of the mission, the examination or fact-finding and evaluation of the facts, and the report. Within those stages, members of inquiries will be confronted with a range of identical or similar issues. A set of procedures would usefully draw out the general considerations that must be accounted for and navigated through to ensure proper process and best practice. These should not be purchased at the cost of the flexibility. In addition to a general set of procedures, consideration by the different entities of the UN involved in inquiries should be given to developing separate sets of procedures to instruct and guide inquiries depending on their purpose, and the subject matter with which they are primarily concerned.

The efficacy of UN inquiries will not be enhanced solely by a clear procedural framework. There is much that can be done outside the operation of the inquiries themselves. In most instances, UN inquiries are mandated to make recommendations and they do so after a full consideration and evaluation of the facts. Tailored to the specific situation at hand, recommendations have the potential to influence positive changes in law and practice. Generally speaking, there is a failure by those empowered to do so to take steps to implement these recommendations. This seriously limits the impact and the potential of inquiries.[49] Some follow-up mechanisms need to be developed.

---

48   Bassiouni, 'Appraising UN Justice-Related Fact-Finding Missions' Missions' (n 41), 40–41.

49   Instances in which recommendations have been implemented include the Security Council referral under the Rome Statute of the International Criminal Court following the recommendation for referral made by the International Commission of Inquiry on Darfur, see UNSC Res 1593 (31 March 2005), UN Doc S/RES/1593; the establishment of a country office by the Office of the High Commissioner for Human Rights with a mandate to monitor the human rights situation and assist with recommended reform of the judicial sector, following the recommendation made by the Secretary-General's Commission of Inquiry for Guinea; the creation of the Extraordinary Chambers in the Courts of Cambodia, following the Secretary-General's Group of Experts for Cambodia recommendation for an *ad hoc* tribunal.

6   Conclusion

Understanding the UN in all its component parts, its agencies and the rich variety of special offices poses challenges to diplomats. Its networks are vast, complex and almost Byzantine. The relationships within are often competitive and not everyone is marching to the beat of the same drum.

Despite the accelerating use of UN inquiries, they suffer from inherent weaknesses. Those weaknesses cannot all be overcome, but steps can be taken to improve their processes. Such action will enhance the credibility of UN inquiries and give their findings more weight. The UN is a complex set of structures inhabited by a massive bureaucracy, and is difficult to manage. Elements of the UN sometimes find themselves in competition or least at odds with one another. In such circumstances, rigorous attention to high quality independent appointments and fair systematic methods of working should enhance the credibility of inquiries, and therefore advance the purposes for which they are established. There should also be greater coordination so various elements of the UN do not work at odds with one another. In addition to a generally applicable set of procedures, each part of the UN that conducts inquiries should develop a publicly available manual that sets out the inquiry-specific requirements concerning the qualifications of appointees, the framing of the terms of reference, the fair methods and procedure that can be employed and the levels of support available. All attempts should be made to ensure consistency, where possible, between these various inquiry-specific manuals. This should not impair the flexibility that is a valuable feature of such inquiries, but it will prevent the waste of time and resources involved in re-inventing the wheel on each occasion an inquiry is established. Where an inquiry will receive no co-operation or is doomed in its prospects of arriving at the truth it may be better not to establish it. The coin of inquiry must not be debased if it is to fulfil its function of promoting accountability and exposing the activities of international malefactors. Such machinery as is available to UN to conduct inquiries needs to be carefully calibrated, prudently managed and conducted upon the basis of processes that are transparent and clear to everyone. UN inquiries are proxy for courts in important ways. Courts depend upon independence, procedural fairness, efficiency and public confidence for their place within municipal governments.[50] Those are the qualities that UN inquiries need to exhibit. There are too many gaps as matters stand.

---

50   See Shimon Shetreet, 'Judicial Independence and Accountability: Core Values in Liberal Democracies' in Hoong Phun Lee (ed), *Judiciaries in Comparative Perspective* (Cambridge University Press 2011) 3.

CHAPTER 37

'Knocked over by a Pile of Bombs. Hasn't Felt Well since': Nuclear Test Veterans and the UK Ministry of Defence Pensions System

Sue Rabbitt Roff

I met Roger in 1976 when I was the fledgling Information Officer to the Petitioning Delegation to the United Nations of the Democratic Republic of East Timor. Roger was advising José Ramos-Horta as he fought the long diplomatic campaign to support the armed struggle that saw the emergence of independent Timor-Leste a quarter century later.

In 1980, I became the New York officer of the London-based Minority Rights Group and its Non-Governmental Representative to the United Nations. Roger was a frequent petitioner in the Decolonisation Committee and other fora of the UN for the International League of Human Rights with his closely argued, erudite legal analyses of small-state sovereignty issues in territories such as East Timor and New Caledonia. As a distinguished international lawyer, his submissions were treated with the highest respect and often (eventually) became the *dicta* on the legal issues.

Although I had grown up downwind of atomic weapons testing in Australia, it was Roger who educated me about the wider issues as he worked with the Marshall Islanders and other Micronesians to address the legacy of US nuclear testing. And the French were still testing in the Pacific, which led to a lot of work for Roger. In 1986, we (and Amy Boss, together with Elsa Hammerich and David Wright) went to Palau as part of an International Observer Mission for the December 1986 Referendum on nuclear-free sovereignty.

Through Roger, I met several Marshall Islanders who were passing through New York to the US radiobiological testing laboratory on Long Island. Most of them had scars from thyroid operations, which gave me pause for thought. In 1991, life's twists and turns found me working as a social scientist in a Scottish medical school. With the indulgence of the lateral-minded, my Director permitted me to conduct research into the long-term health effects of radiation exposure from atomic and nuclear weapons testing.

I was able to get small travel grants to US archives to study the almost verbatim records of the Atomic Bomb Casualty Commission, and published a study of the medical research conducted in Hiroshima and Nagasaki on the

50th anniversary of the bombings. The book *Hotspots: The Legacy of Hiroshima and Nagasaki*[1] was used by several US, UK and Australian veterans of the Allied occupation of post-war Japan to secure war pensions for radiogenic injury.

As a result, I was approached by the British Nuclear Tests Veterans Association ('BNTVA') to study the self-reported morbidity and mortality in their membership which they feared was attributable to their participation in atomic and nuclear weapons testing. It seemed to me that if we could evidence radiation injury in the men who were required (often as National Servicemen) to work with the weaponeers at the test sites it might be some contribution to the non-proliferation campaign (in which, Roger was of course very active in the treaty debates).

According to the UK Ministry of Defence:

> Between 1952 and 1958 the UK conducted a total of 21 atmospheric nuclear tests in Australia and at islands in the Pacific Ocean. In addition, a number of minor trials were also conducted in Australia between 1953 and 1963. UK personnel also participated in US nuclear weapons tests based at Christmas Island in 1962. Over 20,000 UK service personnel and civilian scientists were involved in the tests.[2]

The indomitable Secretary of the BNTVA, Sheila Gray—widow of a Monte Bello veteran—and I undertook a simple audit study of the ex-servicemen members that provoked a decade of disputation that the UK Ministry of Defence ('MOD') was trying to lay the issues to rest with a vastly expensive data-linkage epidemiological study ('the NRPB studies'). We were able to show with our case data that the NRPB studies under-ascertained the incidence of at least one marker condition, multiple myeloma.

By the late 1990s, we had accumulated considerable archival material about the Australian and Christmas Island tests. Veterans would give us documents from their personal files; we went to the Australian and UK public records depositories. At the same time, there were important developments in radiobiology, including the official adoption by the international regulatory agencies that there was 'no threshold' below which

---

1 Sue Rabbit Roff, *Hotspots: The Legacy of Hiroshima and Nagasaki* (Cassell 1995).
2 UK Ministry of Defence Guidance Note, 'Nuclear: emergency planning and atmospheric testing programme', last updated 19 February 2013, at <https://www.gov.uk/nuclear-emergency-planning-and-atmospheric-testing-programme> accessed 25 September 2014.

exposure to radiation was safe. Despite this, veterans of the atomic and nuclear tests were usually denied war pensions for possibly radiogenic illnesses by the UK Ministry of Defence.

Although the great majority of pensions applications were rejected by the Ministry of Defence in the early 1990s some pensions were being awarded by the MOD's War Pensions Agency and some were awarded on appeal by the independent Pensions Appeals Tribunal as listed below:

1990

- The WPA awarded a pension to a veteran who had served in Operation *Grapple*, for **myeloma**.
- The Department of Social Security ('DSS') reversed its earlier decision and granted a war widow's pension to the widow of a veteran who had died from **multiple myeloma**, which he attributed to his participation in the cleanup at Christmas Island. It was noted that 'The NRPB Report of 28 January 1988 makes no distinction between test participants who were present at the detonations and others like [this veteran] who were involved in subsequent operations at the test site.'

1991

- An Operation *Grapple* veteran was awarded a pension by the WPA for **duodenal ulcer and lumbar spondylosis**.
- The widow of a veteran who had died from **carcinoma of the left kidney** after service during Operation *Grapple*, was awarded a War Widow's Pension. The Decision states simply that 'The Tribunal finds that the death of the above-named (deceased) was substantially hastened by (a) an injury, wound or disease namely EXPOSURE TO IONISING RADIATION DURING SERVICE.' (Emphasis in original).
- A veteran's widow was awarded a pension because her husband's **amyloidosis** was attributed to service which included service in Operation *Grapple*.
- A veteran of Operation *Grapple* was awarded a pension by the PAT for his **multiple myeloma**.
- Another Operation *Grapple* veteran was awarded a pension by the PAT for his **endobronchial amyloidosis**.

1992

- A veteran of Operation *Grapple* was awarded a pension by the WPA for his **multiple myeloma**.
- The widow of a veteran who had died of **disseminated lymphoma**, was awarded a War Widow's Pension by the Pensions Appeals Tribunal, but the WPA appealed this decision to the High Court of Justice Queen's Bench Division. In his decision in October 1993, Mr Justice Drake confirmed the PAT decision finding *inter alia* that the veteran

> frequently made visits on service to Christmas Island and stayed for short periods: perhaps only a few days at a time, perhaps for a little bit longer. During those periods there he also swam in the waters of Christmas Island and ate fish which had been caught there. He was discharged in 1969 in good health but he subsequently suffered from, and ultimately died of, Hodgkin's disease. The basis of [the widow's] claim for a pension was that her husband's death had been hastened by his exposure to radiation resulting from the nuclear testing which had taken place on Christmas Island in 1957, 1958 and again in 1962.

Mr Justice Drake commented of the first NRPB Report,

> I have not seen a copy of that report and there seems nothing to indicate that it was in fact before the Pensions Appeal Tribunal. I do not know the numbers of persons considered who were present on Christmas Island at the relevant time, or the comparable sample of control numbers in the United Kingdom. Nor do I know the precise basis on which they were compared, or whether it took into account, for example, possible exposure to radiation by eating fish contaminated by radiation ... I take into account—as I think I am entitled to—that the correlation between radiation and subsequent symptoms shown in a person exposed to it are not yet settled beyond all doubt. Knowledge is still advancing and it is clear in this case that the tribunal, in giving their reasons and decision, were influenced by that very fact. They took account of the evidence of the medical opinion, but they also took into account [this veteran's] periods of service on Christmas Island. Clearly they took the view that at the very least he may well have been exposed to a measure of radiation and the precise measure would not be known; that he had been exposed to water in the lagoon and fish from the lagoon and clearly they took the view that

the water and fish may have been contaminated and exposed him further to radiation.

1994

- The PAT granted a war pension to a veteran who had served during Operation *Grapple*, and was suffering from **non-Hodgkin's lymphoma**. However, it was noted that the Department claimed

(a) 'The detonation of the nuclear device was based upon it taking place at an altitude where there fireball would be clear of the surface, and only in weather conditions which would guarantee only negligible fall out or rain out from the nuclear cloud around Christmas Island. On the spot monitoring had not shown significant radioactive contamination.
(b) There had been some monitoring of lagoon water and the fish therein. There had been no need to prohibit service personnel from using the lagoon for fishing or swimming.
(c) There was, in the Department's view, a comprehensive Health Physics arrangement at Christmas Island.
(d) There was no need for all the personnel on Christmas Island to have radiation film badges: of these (sic) who had badges, only three persons were recorded as receiving exposure.'

The Tribunal gave weight to the following in finding that the appellant had raised a reasonable doubt in his favour:

(a) 'In spite of the Department's assertion that a fundamental basis of the test was that weather conditions should not produce fall out on the island, their own statement now accepted showers and the possibility could not be excluded that some of these might have been heavy.
(b) The Department while denying possible radiation consequences, did not accept that fishing and swimming the lagoon in the aftermath of the test had in fact been permitted.
(c) The Department's own recent admission that in at least three cases men issued with dosimeters had suffered radiation, and the accepted fact that [the veteran], although present at the test, had not been issued with any dosimeter.

(d) The straightforward and reliable presentation of the appellant and his assertion that he had not received radiation treatment as suggested by the Department.
(e) The line of the High Court judgement in the Titmus case (another Christmas Island radiation case) that radiation knowledge is ongoing: the safety parameters of thirty years ago may no longer be adequate guide.'

1995

- The widow of a veteran who died from **Oat Cell Carcinoma Left Main Bronchus**, which he attributed to his Operation *Grapple* service, was awarded a pension by the PAT.

1997

- An Operation *Grapple* veteran was awarded a pension for **malignant melanoma**.
- Another Operation *Grapple* veteran, was awarded a pension by the PAT for **adenocarcinoma of the stomach** for the following stated reasons:

(1) 'Despite the contention of the Secretary of State that the Appellant was not in the contaminated area, the Appellant has given clear evidence that in his capacity as a Movement Controller he moved all around the Island and into affected areas.
(2) The Appellant has given clear evidence of being issued with a personal film badge which changed colour. This was removed from him. The Tribunal notes that the Secretary of State has no comment to make on this statement.
(3) The Tribunal are satisfied that the emergence of this cancer is attributable to the services of the Appellant in the R.A.F. on Christmas Island.'

Having reviewed these decisions, Sheila and I began to help veterans prepare their appeals using the documentary evidence that was accumulating about the contamination of the test sites. We used this in combination with information about the more than 20 conditions that the US authorities considered to be potentially radiogenic, and for which veterans and 'down-winders' in the US and Marshall Islands were being awarded pensions and compensation. We also relied on the increasing acceptance of the 'no threshold' view of dangerous levels of radiation exposure. We teamed up with Ian Greenhalgh, a lawyer whom I had met during filming of a television documentary about the case he had won for a veteran of the British Commonwealth Occupation Forces in Hiroshima using information found in a public library copy of my *Hotspots: the Legacy of Hiroshima and Nagasaki*.

The reasoning of the PAT decisions in our favour became progressively more concerned with the probability rather than the possibility ('reasonable doubt') that various aspects of the participants' work and life at the test sites had led to sufficient exposure to induce radiogenic injury, often manifesting itself decades after their service. The PAT consists of a legally trained Chair, a senior medical adviser and a representative of the branch of the armed services in which the appellant served.

1997

- A veteran who had served in Operation *Grapple*, and who already had a pension for **cancer of the skin and solar keratosis** that were attributed by the PAT to exposure to sunlight on Christmas Island, was also awarded a pension for **dental caries and damage to salivary glands** which the PAT attributed to his work as a clerk in air movements and as a quartermaster:

  > On one occasion very shortly after an H Bomb test, [this veteran] formed part of the crew of a Dakota flight to Fiji to collect samples. The mushroom cloud was still evident and their aeroplane flew through it. The samples were loaded into the cabin and the flight returned to Christmas Island.
  >   On this evidence it is the Tribunal's view that this episode and possibly others was the source of the high radiation levels which have led to [this veteran's] skin cancer, rather than a mere seven months of exposure to tropical sunshine. We also find the medical evidence and opinions provided by specialists on behalf of [this veteran] to be most persuasive. These are clearly eminent people in their field and they describe a link between high radiation levels (usually in X-rays) and damage to salivary glands leading to dental caries.

- A veteran who had served in Maralinga, was awarded a pension by the WPA for his **generalised anxiety disorder**.
- The PAT awarded a pension to a veteran who had served in the vicinity of Hiroshima in 1950, for his condition of **polycythemia rubra vera**.
- A veteran who had served during Operation *Brigadoon*, was awarded a pension by the PAT for his **carcinoma of the thyroid**. The PAT found that

[The veteran] served in Xmas island from 16th February 1962 to 26th July 1963. During this time the Brigadoon series of nuclear tests were carried out and in all 25 explosions took place between April and July 1962. Some tests were carried out outside normal working hours but [the veteran] would have been in the open for a majority. The troops were issued with dosimeter badges only for the duration of the test, and from [the veteran's] evidence there appears to have been no procedure for identifying which badge belonged to which serviceman.

It is [this veteran's] case that the measured levels of radiation exposure are unreliable, firstly because the badges have proved to be defective and secondly because he was exposed to further radiation subsequent to the tests from residual fallout, swimming in contaminated sea and eating contaminated fish. We agree that the records produced by the War Pensions Agency are inherently unreliable per se, for the reasons put forward by [the veteran]. We also find that there is a likelihood that [the veteran] continued to receive radiation exposure subsequent to the tests from the sources suggested.

[The veteran] suffers from a form of cancer which is known to be linked to radiation exposure although we accept that there can be other causes as well. It is also clear that [the veteran] had not been exposed to any other significant level of radiation save his period of service on Xmas Island. The onset of the condition is known to occur some 30 or more years after such exposure so that in terms of timing there does appear to be a connection. Since no reliance can be given to the recorded exposure levels and as scientific opinion is now that any degree of exposure, however small, is harmful, we believe that a reasonable doubt has been raised that [the veteran] was exposed to levels of radiation which caused the Carcinoma of the Thyroid from which he now suffers.

There has been considerable debate over the findings of the NRPB report. For the purpose of this particular case we have placed very little reliance on these findings for the following reasons:

1. The Brigadoon test veterans form a very small proportion of the total sample.
2. These tests were the last and largest carried out and any development of cancer as a result would be correspondingly later than the earlier *Grapple* series.
3. The data underlying the NRPB study was collected in 1988 and 1990 when many Brigadoon veterans were still healthy; as indeed was [the veteran] at that time.

1999

- A veteran who had served in the RAF at both Maralinga and on Operation *Grapple*, was awarded a war pension by the PAT for **multiple sclerosis**.
- The widow of a veteran who had served with Operation *Brigadoon* was awarded a pension for his **carcinoma of the stomach**.
- A veteran who had served during Operation *Grapple* was awarded a pension by the PAT for **cataracts**.
- A veteran who had served in Maralinga and during Operation *Grapple* was awarded a pension by the WPA for his **multiple myeloma**.

2000

- In January, 2000 the PAT awarded a veteran who served in Operation *Grapple* a pension for **Lymphoma and Carcinoma of the Rectum**.
- The widow of a veteran who had served in Operation *Grapple*, was awarded a pension by the PAT in respect of his death from **sarcoma**. The PAT stated *inter alia* that:

We note that:

(1) The Oxford Text Book of Oncology indicates at p. 1438 that Sarcomas tend to occur in areas previously exposed to radiation.
(2) The Radiological Safety Regulations for Christmas Island indicates that the effects of excessive exposure to radiation may become apparent only after a period of years;
(3) Dr Edward Paul Radford, a physician with considerable experience in radiation biology, gave evidence at the 'Deverall' hearing that in 1994 it was accepted that any cancer can be produced by radiation if the other factors were rigid.
(4) The incidence of the primary cancer—Condition (2)—is so rare that there has been no possibility of epidemiological research into the condition.

We find, having taken account of the matters set out above that all the conditions could have been caused by radiation.
We then went on to consider whether [this veteran] was exposed to more radiation at Christmas Island than 'background' radiation to which the general public is and was exposed.

> We accept that his posting was 43 kms from the test site. However, we note that he was the Chief Signals man and had ample opportunity to travel around the Island. Furthermore, we accepted [his widow's] evidence that her husband told her about bicycling round the Island and his diet of coconut milk. We consider that [the veteran] did not always remain at the base camp and could have and did venture much closer to the test site. Furthermore, we took particularly note that the readings of radiation levels at P.33 of the Safety Division Technical Note No.16/52 show that it was extrapolated, that on 22 August 1958 the day of the first test, there was a level of radiation at the base camp where [the veteran] was stationed, <u>above</u> the recommended limit for continuous occupation for members of the public.
>
> We find, bearing in mind the matter set out above, that [the veteran] was exposed to radiation in excess of that to which (sic) he would have encountered if he had not served in the Royal Navy and Christmas Island. (Emphasis in original)

- The widow of a veteran who had served in Maralinga and during Operation *Grapple*, was awarded a pension by the PAT for **psychiatric conditions.**
- The PAT awarded the widow of a Maralinga veteran a pension in respect of his death from **pharyngeal cancer** giving as one of its reasons

> Although the N.R.P.B. Report did not find primary pharyngeal carcinoma to be associated with the nuclear tests veterans the British cohort was small compared with the American and Marshall Islands cohorts in whom the condition has been recognised and accepted.

The PAT also 'considered that [the veteran] was exposed to considerably higher levels of radiation than suggested by the Atomic Weapons Establishment [...].'

- The widow of a Monte Bello veteran was awarded a pension in respect of his death from **carcinoma of the prostate and carcinoma of the bladder.**

2001

- The widow of another Monte Bello and Maralinga veteran was awarded a widow's pension in respect of his death from **cancer of the parotid/salivary gland.**

- The WPA awarded a veteran who had participated in the clean-up at Christmas Island, a pension for **rectal carcinoma**.
- The WPA awarded the widow of a veteran who had served in Operation *Grapple*, a pension following his death from **multiple myeloma**.
- Although the PAT had rejected the appeal of a veteran in relation to **bilateral cataracts** following service at Christmas Island in 1964, this decision was reversed in 2001 because of technical inaccuracies on the medical facts in the Decision.
- The PAT awarded the widow of an Operation *Grapple I* veteran a pension in respect of his death from **carcinoma of pancreas**. The Tribunal stated *inter alia*

> The Secretary of State relies largely on a Report from the AWE dated 11.7.2000 which contends that at the time of the test (sic) the late [veteran] was at least 30kms, probably 35 kms, from the point of detonation of each test and that the 'effective dose equivalent received by [the veteran] consequent upon his participation in Operations Grappple Y and Z was not indistinguishable from zero.' The Report went on to contend that 'Since [the veteran's] exposure to ionising radiation arising from participation in Operations *Grapple* Y and Z was insignificant, it is not credible that such exposure could have posed any hazard to his health'. It is noted that in one quotation it is stated that his exposure to ionising radiation was not indistinguishable from zero whilst the other quotation refers to his exposure being insignificant.
> [...]
> It is accepted that there is a universal exposure to ionising radiation but having read the recorded evidence presented to it and having listened to the cogent arguments presented by Mr Greenhalgh the Tribunal finds that Christmas Island was exposed to ionising radiation in excess of the natural background radiation by reason of the nuclear tests. The Tribunal does not have to consider the extent of such excess radiation as it is accepted that 'There is no threshold level below which no carcinogenic effect is produced'.
> The Tribunal accepts [the veteran's widow's] evidence that her late husband had a lot of free time whilst he was on Christmas Island and that he did travel around the Island and swam in the vicinity of the Island. The Tribunal further accepts that Christmas Island is a dusty place. Apart from stating that the late [veteran] was at least 30-35 km distant from the point of detonation, the Secretary of State has no information as to his

whereabouts on the Island at other times. [The veteran] was not issued with a dosimeter and accordingly no measurement of his external radiation was taken and there is no way in which any ingestion of radiation, particularly alpha radiation, could be measured.

It was contended on behalf of the Appellant that it was possible that the late [veteran] could have ingested alpha particles through dust on his travel around the Island, through swimming or through the food chain, noting particularly his liking for fish. The Tribunal found that the early onset of loss of hair and teeth could indicate exposure to excess radiation. Whilst the Tribunal notes that the Secretary of State states that the first symptoms of [the veteran's] Carcinoma of the Pancreas were in April 99, the Tribunal finds on considering all the evidence presented to it that there is reasonable doubt that there could be a very considerable latent period between exposure to ionising radiation and the recognition of symptoms and in this respect the Tribunal notes that the Appendix on Cancer of Pancreas states that 'Psychiatric abnormalities are common' and the recorded evidence indicates such anomalies as early as the 1960's....

Having considered all the evidence presented to it the Tribunal finds the following facts:

1. Christmas Island was exposed to excess ionising radiation.
2. The late [veteran] would have been exposed to such radiation either during the actual test or as a result of fall-out.

The Legal Chairman of this Tribunal was Mr Warriner, the Deputy President of the Pensions Appeals Tribunals of England and Wales.

- the PAT awarded the widow of a veteran a pension in respect of his death from **left cerebellar haemangioblstoma** arising out of his service in Nagasaki in 1945, noting *inter alia* that

    There is no threshold in relation to the dangers of exposure to radiation.

- The WPA awarded an Operation *Grapple* veteran a pension for **basal cell carcinoma of the skin and solar keratoses of the skin.**
- The widow of an Operation *Grapple* and Maralinga veteran was awarded a pension by the PAT in respect of her death from **multiple myeloma.**
- The widow of a Monte Bello veteran was awarded a pension by the PAT in respect of his death from **multiple myeloma.**

- An Operation *Grapple* veteran, was awarded a pension from the WPA for **post traumatic stress syndrome**.
- The PAT (Scotland) allowed an appeal under Section 1 of the Pensions Appeal Tribunals Act 1943 against a Decision of the Secretary of State in respect of the entitlement of a veteran to a pension for the **Non-Hodgkin's Lymphoma** he attributed to service during Operation *Grapple*. The decision reveals 'the present policy of the WPA' as being the following

> In general an award of War Pension will be considered in any case where reliable evidence of service exposure to Ionising Radiation and there is a recognised causal link between the claimed condition and such exposure.

It went on to state that

> It is accepted there is a recognised causal link between NHL and exposure to radiation. The only question accordingly was whether there was reliable evidence of service exposure. We note that the policy does not require evidence of excessive exposure but just service exposure. This change of policy no doubt arises because of the present medical view that there is little basis for saying that low radiation doses have no associated cancer risk. (Emphasis in original)

The Decision also notes that

> While accepting the general proposition that each case must be considered on its own facts, it gives us some confidence that we are reaching a decision consistent with that reached in other such cases… We consider that there should be consistency of decision making. The only party who has full details of the other claims is the Department. If they wish to argue that the other decisions are of no relevance then it seems to us that they should be putting the full details of these claims before the Tribunal.

2002

- The PAT awarded the widow of an Operation *Grapple*, veteran a pension in respect of his death from **chronic myelomonocytic leukaemia**.
- In February 2002 the WPA awarded another Operation *Grapple* veteran a pension for his **post-traumatic stress syndrome**.

- In March, 2002, the PAT awarded the widow of an Operation *Grapple* veteran a pension in respect of his death from **carcinoma of head of pancreas**. The Tribunal found *inter alia*

  > The Secretary of State relies largely on a report from the AWE dated 2.8.00 which contends that at the time of the test the late [veteran] was at least 30 km, probably 35 km, from the point of detonation of each test and that the 'effective dose equivalent received by [the veteran] consequent upon his participation in Operations *Grapple* Y and Z was not distinguishable from zero'. The Report went on to contend that 'Since [the veteran's] exposure to ionising radiation arising from participation in Operations *Grapple* Y and Z was insignificant, it is not credible that such exposure could have posed any hazard to his health.' It is noted that in the first passage quoted above it is stated that his exposure to ionising radiation was not distinguishable from zero whilst the other passage refers to his exposure being insignificant.
  >
  > ... It is accepted that there is a universal exposure to ionising radiation but having read the recorded evidence presented to it and having listened to the arguments presented by Mr Greenhalgh the Tribunal finds that Christmas Island was exposed to ionising radiation in excess of the natural background radiation by reason of the nuclear tests. The Tribunal does not have to consider the extent of such excess radiation as it is accepted that 'There is no threshold level below which no carcinogenic effect is produced'.

  The Tribunal also found that letters this veteran wrote during his time on Christmas Island

  > provide reliable evidence that [he] was close enough to the explosions to be directly affected by them physically at the time in the way described in the letters. In particular he was knocked over by the blast wave from the bomb that was exploded on 23.9.58.
  >
  > The Tribunal accepts [his widow's] evidence that her late husband did not have a lot to do while he was on Christmas Island. It is a reasonable inference that he is likely to have travelled around the island in his free time. The Tribunal also accepts [the widow's] evidence that her husband swam in the vicinity of the island. The Tribunal further accepts that Christmas Island is a dusty place. The Secretary of State maintains that [the veteran] was at least 30–35 km distant from the point of detonation, but he has no information as to [the veteran's] whereabouts on the island

at other times. [The veteran] was not issued with a dosimeter and accordingly no measurement of his external radiation was taken and there is no way in which any ingestion of radiation, particularly alpha radiation, could be measured.

It was contended on behalf of the appellant that it was possible that [the veteran] could have ingested alpha particles through dust on his travels around the island, through swimming or through the food chain. Whilst the Tribunal notes that the Secretary of State states that the first symptoms of [the veteran's] carcinoma of the pancreas were in 1999, the Tribunal finds on considering all the evidence presented to it that there is a reasonable doubt that there could be a very considerable latent period between exposure to ionising radiation and the recognition of symptoms.

… Having considered all the evidence presented to it the Tribunal finds the following facts:

1. Christmas Island was exposed to excess ionising radiation.
2. The late [veteran] would have been exposed to such radiation either during the actual tests or as a result of fall-out.

Although this Tribunal sat in Manchester rather than London, the language of the Decision closely follows that in an earlier case.

- In April, 2002 the PAT awarded a veteran who had served in Maralinga, a pension for **cancer of the colon.**

Early in the new millennium, the BNTVA developed severe factionalism, as some members decided to work with no win/no fee (except the mounting expenses) lawyers to pursue personal injury compensation claims in the UK courts. A decade and several millions pounds later, those claims were struck out because it was held that the veterans had no real prospect of success in proving a causal link between their participation in atomic and nuclear weapons tests and their subsequent illnesses.[3] The fact that the same Ministry of Defence had awarded or been overruled in not awarding the above—and probably more—pensions was not raised in the compensation litigation by either side.

Veterans of the UK atomic tests continue to win pensions and appeals, as do their *confreres* in Australia and New Zealand, and even France where the same

---

[3] Ministry of Defence (Respondent) v AB and others (appellants) [2012] UKSC 9.

approach has begun to prove successful. Inasmuch as pensions pass to widows and can amount to £10,000 or more a year, many veterans feel that they are a fair form of compensation although the decision-making process is still too protracted and far from transparent. The BNTVA is now campaigning for a Benevolent Fund to be established to match the support provided by the US, Canada and Australia to their atomic and nuclear test veterans.

CHAPTER 38

Overcoming Implementation Issues of the Victims' Law in Colombia

Ashley Clark

1   Introduction

My father was a consultant to the United Nations Secretariat in the drafting of the 1985 Declaration of Basic Principles of Justice for Victims of Crime and Abuse of Power ('Declaration').[1] The Declaration insists that the needs of victims should be met by four modalities: access to justice and fair treatment; restitution (from the guilty parties); compensation (from the government when the offender cannot be made accountable); and access to assistance, in the form of material, medical, psychological or social assistance, as needed. Over the past decade, the Government of Colombia has been engaged in an effort to provide justice for victims of ongoing civil strife in the country. That programme is in the spirit of the Declaration. In what follows, I describe the valiant efforts to give operational effect to the abstract principles of the Declaration in Colombia and describe some of the successes and failures.[2]

Colombia has been ravaged by internal armed conflicts since independence, although the intensity, locations, and actors have morphed through the decades. This has led to roughly 674,000 homicides, 94,000 of which were

---

1 Declaration of Basic Principles of Justice for Victims of Crime and Abuse of Power, UNGA Res 40/34 (Annex) (29 November 1985) ('Victims Declaration'). For more, see Roger S Clark, *The United Nations Crime Prevention and Criminal Justice Program: formulation of standards and efforts at their implementation* (University of Pennsylvania Press 1994) ('Clark, *The United Nations Crime Prevention and Criminal Justice Program*') ch 7.

2 This report is a condensed version of a longer report by the author commissioned by USAID/Colombia which first explored successful implementations of a variety of laws from around the world in post-conflict, post-disaster and extreme poverty contexts. It then created a framework through which to identify major issues with implementation and potential alternatives to overcome those issues, and applied this structure to Colombia. Most of the material on Colombia itself was gleaned from interviews the author conducted with practitioners implementing a USAID victims project in Colombia, agencies outsourced to deal with implementation, government officials, non-governmental organisations (NGOs) and victims who work beside them.

attributed directly to the internal conflict, in the period 1964–2007.[3] During that time, roughly 51,500 were kidnapped, 6,000 were forcibly disappeared, and 11,000 were tortured.[4] All told, estimates indicate that at least 5.7 million people have been forcibly displaced.[5] Since the early 2000s, the government of Colombia has enacted various laws in order not only to end the on-going conflicts, but also to establish comprehensive victims' rights.[6] The government of Colombia held several unsuccessful peace talks with guerilla groups while also pursuing legislation to end the cycle of violence. Earlier legislation in the 1990s was aimed at acknowledging internally displaced persons' rights, but failed to establish mechanisms that would result in empowerment. For example, Law 387 of 1997 established the principle of caring for internally displaced people and affirmed many of their rights, but did not explicitly provide reparations or any process through which the victims could petition the government.[7] The National Development Plans for 2002–2010 (Law 812 (2003) and Law 1151 (2007)) created subsidies for the purchasing of land; however, due to the laws' inability to guarantee rights and ownership, the law actually led to an increase in displacements.[8]

By 2005, a series of actions by the Colombian Congress and Constitutional Court marked a change in the commitment to enact comprehensive victims' rights.[9] In 2004, the Constitutional Court declared in decision T-025 that the current situation of internally displaced persons in Colombia constituted 'an

---

3 All figures can be found in Jemima Garcia-Godos & Knut Andreas O Lid, 'Transitional Justice and Victims' Rights before the End of a Conflict: The Unusual Case of Colombia' (2010) 42 J Lat Amer Stud 487 ('Garcia-Godos & Lid, 'Transitional Justice and Victims' Rights before the End of a Conflict: The Unusual Case of Colombia").

4 *Ibid.*

5 Center for Internal Displacement, Monitoring, 'Internal Displacement.' Global Overview of Trends and Developments (2014) 39, at <http://www.internal-displacement.org/assets/publications/2014/201405-global-overview-2014-en.pdf> accessed 2 February 2015.

6 Nicole Summers, 'Colombia's Victims' Law: Transitional Justice in a Time of Violent Conflict?' (2012) 25 Harv Hum Rts J 219 ('Summers, 'Colombia's Victims' Law: Transitional Justice in a Time of Violent Conflict?") 224.

7 At <http://www.brookings.edu/~/media/Projects/idp/Colombia_Law387_1997_Eng.pdf> accessed 2 February 2015.

8 Morten Bergsmo et al (eds), *Distributive Justice in Transitions* (Torkel Opsahl 2010) 319, available at <http://www.fichl.org/fileadmin/fichl/documents/FICHL_6_web.pdf> accessed 2 February 2015.

9 Summers, 'Colombia's Victims' Law: Transitional Justice in a Time of Violent Conflict?' (n 6) 224.

unconstitutional state of affairs' and demanded the adoption of urgent and special measures for assuring rights.[10]

In response, the Colombian Congress passed the 2005 Law of Peace and Justice, which attempted to aid demobilization[11] and increase victims' access to reparations.[12] However, the law did not include state responsibility to protect victims from future abuses or provide state-financed reparations, instead declaring that perpetrators were responsible for reparations.[13] In addition, the law put a heavy burden on the victims themselves, who, in order to receive reparations, had to report the crime and then go through a legal proceeding to establish the culpability of that particular crime's perpetrator. Only after this was completed could a victim seek damages from the guilty party. The requirement of formally reporting a crime meant many victims did not report due to fear of retaliation.[14] The process was also overly complicated and the institutional mechanisms were weak. An investigation by the Social Foundation (a European non-governmental organization) found that implementing institutions did not have the infrastructure, physical resources, technical resources and human resources to care properly for the victims.[15] As a result, barely 235,000 victims came forward by 2008, only 24 of whom received any damages.[16]

In June of 2011, President Juan Manuel Santos Calderón and the Colombian Congress passed the Victims and Land Restitution Law ('Victims' Law').[17] This declares the state's responsibility in the crimes since 1985[18] through its failure

---

10   Colombian Constitutional Court, Decision T-025 of 2004, at <http://www.brookings.edu/~/media/Projects/idp/Colombia_T%20025_2004.PDF> accessed 2 February 2015, III.2.1.3.
11   One of the ways this was accomplished was by granting broad amnesty from criminal prosecution, see Garcia-Godos & Lid, 'Transitional Justice and Victims' Rights before the End of a Conflict: The Unusual Case of Colombia' (n 3) 497.
12   L 975 D O art 1.
13   Ibid arts 29, 42, 44, 70.
14   Garcia-Godos & Lid, 'Transitional Justice and Victims' Rights before the End of a Conflict: The Unusual Case of Colombia' (n 3) 509.
15   IM Ortiz, M Bleeker, Fundación Social, J Ciurlizza, A Milena B Vargas, Los retos de la justicia transicional en Colombia. Percepciones, opiniones y experiencias 2008. Panorama cualitativo y cuantitativo nacional con énfasis en cuatro regiones: Antioquia, Valle del Cauca, Montes de María y Meta (Fundación Social y Comisión Europea 2010) 117.
16   Summers, 'Colombia's Victims' Law: Transitional Justice in a Time of Violent Conflict?' (n 6) 224.
17   Ley de Víctimas y Restitución de Tierras, Law 1448 ('Victims' Law') L 1448 D O.
18   People who have suffered injuries prior to 1985 may be considered victims for the purposes of seeking rights to truth and justice, but are not entitled to damages or restitution. Victims' Law (n 17) art 3, para 4.

to protect citizens and establishes a system of reparations funded by seized land and property from the conflict.[19] The Law defines 'victims' as anyone who has suffered violations of international humanitarian law or serious and flagrant violations of international standards of human rights.[20]

The Victims' Law is a major expansion of the 2005 Law of Peace and Justice in terms of access to reparations for victims in Colombia. It accomplishes five major goals. First, it expands the definition of 'victim' from internally displaced people to encompass those who have been disappeared, murdered, or suffered other serious violations of human rights.[21] In addition, it declares that victimhood is acquired independently from the identification, apprehension, prosecution or conviction of a specific perpetrator.[22] Third, it shifts the legal burden of proof regarding land ownership distinctly in favour of victims. Fourth, it creates an institutional structure to manage, administer, and adjudicate claims to restitution of land.[23] Finally, it expands the number of services (such as psychological and other health services) available to beneficiaries.[24]

This paper looks at the journey between a seemingly well-written law and its successful implementation. It finds that the Victims' Law suffers from government-response issues, mainly a degraded infrastructure, lack of local capacity, and serious operational issues stemming from an overly cumbersome 'declaration form' through which victims apply for relief. Given the time constraints built into the Victims' Law, the report gives some short-term and long-term recommendations.

2   Implementation Issues with the Victims' Law

The 2011 Victims' Law created the Special Administrative Unit for Victim Support and Reparations (Victims Unit) to oversee the operations, coordination, and implementation of the Law.[25] The Unit is also responsible for creat-

---

19   Victims' Law (n 17) art 1, art 19.
20   *Ibid* art 3.
21   *Ibid* art 3.
22   *Ibid* para 28(4), 49, 51–54. This is consistent with the Victims Declaration (n 1) para 2.
23   Victims' Law (n 17) art 76–78.
24   *Ibid* arts 35, 38. This too is consistent with the Victims Declaration (n 1) paras 14 and 15.
25   *Ibid* art 168. The finances for the Victims Unit were established later in the year through the government's Financial Plan, which projected a cost of 54 billion Colombian pesos (COP) over a 10 year period. Documento CONPES 3712/2011, 'Plan de financiación para la sostenibilidad de la ley 1448 de 2011', Consejo Nacional de Política Económica y Social, Departamento Nacional de Planeación.

ing the National Plan for reparations, including psychosocial assistance, an integrated health plan, and a program of collective reparation for the victims. The Victims Unit spent the entire first year of the program establishing regional units, allocating resources, and building technical platforms (such as computer systems that could be used across different coordinating agencies) to enroll and track victims. Only approved and enrolled beneficiaries could access the host of services provided by the Victims Unit and other agencies. Implementation of the law has been substantially decentralised, especially collection of claims and some distribution of funds, but the most important eligibility decisions are made at the national level. The Victims Unit is currently working with departments and municipalities to implement the various benefits of the Victims' Law, such as access to psychosocial services, legal services, and education, as well as ongoing applications from individual municipalities for central government funding.[26] 'Administrative reparation', which is a cash transfer from the government to victims, is only part of a larger reparations goal. Part of this reparations goal is formal recognition of victim status from the government and individualized pathways to services (such as psychosocial and educational) designed by governmental actors for victims.[27] The Victims Unit is being aided particularly by partners at an intergovernmental body, the International Organization for Migration ('IOM').

In order to receive the benefits, victims must 'declare', or enroll with the government onto a national registry. A victim must go to a person within a public ministry or, in most cases, a local ombudsman or *personero* to 'declare', making a formal statement of what happened as well as answer questions from a form furnished by the government. Declarations are therefore conducted in person and not completed without a representative of the government, local or national, present. The forms and statement are then sent to a central bureaucrat at the Victims Unit to evaluate the declaration. The applicant is given one of three designations: to be 'included', thereby put on the registry and gain access to a bundle of governmental services; 'not included', where they are allowed to re-submit the declaration and have their case re-evaluated; or 'excluded', where the central authorities have determined that the individual is trying illicitly to become a 'victim' and is barred from reapplication.

---

26 Interview with Poveda Heiby, Victims Institutional Strengthening Program (VISP) Component 1: Technology, Government of Colombia Response (International Organization for Migration (IOM), Bogota, Colombia 7 May 2013) (notes of interview on file with the author) ('Interview with Poveda Heiby').

27 International Organization for Migration (IOM), *VISP Context, Programs at a Glance* (IOM Headquarters Bogota, Colombia 6 May 2013) ('*VISP Context, Programs at a Glance*').

A broad overview of the situation indicates a strong initial demand by beneficiaries for inclusion in the programme and access to benefits. From the beginning of the programme until April 2013, the Victims Unit was able to provide administrative reparations and/or other services to 156,000 people.[28] To put this number into context, one must examine how many people potentially qualify for the programme and how many have been able to apply to date. Internal Mercy Corps data indicate that an estimated 5–6 million people qualify for the Victims' Law in Colombia as it is written.[29] There is high demand for enrollment in the Victims' Law; in 2012 alone, there were over 200,000 statements given. However, as only 7,000 of those were given directly online, the vast majority had to be re-typed at the central location in order to be placed in the computer database. According to the IOM, 81% of applicants, the vast majority, are approved initially,[30] and the majority of people who appeal their decision are later given 'status', meaning they were declared victims and allowed to access program benefits. Although the database for enrollment was originally set-up from the 2005 Peace and Justice Act, 60% of the current list of victims is in response to the 2011 Victims' Law.[31] This may indicate that the Victims' Law is better promoted than its predecessor, has a larger definition for beneficiaries, and/or has purported to provide benefits sought by applicants.

The major problem of the implementation of the Victims' Law is government response, as witnessed by the lengthy waiting lists and long waits for those seeking enrollment. Many municipalities report lengthy waiting lists of victims who tried to declare but were turned away for a multitude of reasons, such as lack of personnel or forms.[32] Furthermore, although the Law states that those seeking status will not wait longer than 3 months for a declaration, most applicants end up waiting 7–9 months.[33] Issues both at the local level and at the centralized agency cause these delays,[34] such as economic

---

28 Interview with Hido Redrass, National Victims Unit Main Headquarters (Bogota, Colombia, May 8, 2012) (notes of interview on file with author) ('Interview with Hido Redrass').

29 Interview with Diana Roa on Mercy Corps Implementation Strategy (Mercy Corps Bogota, Colombia. 7 May 2013) (notes of interview on file with the author) ('Interview with Diana Roa'). Mercy Corps is an international non-governmental development organization.

30 *VISP Context, Programs at a Glance* (n 27).

31 Interview with Poveda Heiby (n 26).

32 S Amaya, *Women and the Victims Law* (Pan-American Development Foundation 2013) ('Amaya, *Women and the Victims Law*').

33 Center of Attention for Victims, 'Visit to Field Projects' (Centro Dignificar 9 May 2013).

34 Interview with Diana Roa (n 29).

constraints, infrastructural problems and personnel and operational issues. In addition to overwhelming demand faced by the Victims Unit, local officials, implementing agencies and coordinating agencies (Mercy Corps, Chemonics, IOM, Ministry of Health, and the Pan American Development Foundation), all reported that the system was overwhelmed by demand for inclusion in the national registry.[35]

Although the Victims' Law is an exceptional legal instrument aimed at providing victims an ambitious range of governmental services,[36] some argue that its implementation has led to serious degradation of governmental services to all citizens across the board as it has diverted resources from other projects.[37] Scrutiny of the current situation reveals that the implementation of the Victims' Law is occurring within the context of economic constraints and an inadequate infrastructure, as will be discussed in the following paragraphs. However, the biggest problem to targeting and enrolling victims stems from weaknesses in administration, mainly personnel and operational issues.

Economic Constraints

In order to understand the economic constraints, first we must examine how the Victims' Law is funded. This turns out to be a very complicated endeavor. Under Article 134, the Victims Unit will implement a program to promote accompanying adequate investment of resources that the victim receives as compensation. The law then creates the four institutions to help with the implementation of these various reparations, including the National Information Network for the Care and Reparation of Victims (*Red Nacional de Información para la Atención y Reparación a las Víctimas*), the National System of Care and Comprehensive Reparation of the Victims (*Sistema Nacional de Atención y Reparación Integral a las Víctimas*), the National Plan of Attention and Integral

---

35 Interview with Fernando Calado of the international development company Chemonics, on Chemonics Implementation Efforts (Chemonics International, 8 May 2013) (notes of interview on file with the author) ('Interview with Fernando Calado'); Poveda Heiby, Victims Institutional Strengthening Program (VISP) Component 1: Technology, Government of Colombia Response (International Organization for Migration (IOM), Bogota, Colombia 7 May 2013) (notes of interview on file with the author); VISP Component 2: Health Care and Integrative Services. Ministry of Health, 'VISP Component 2: Health Care and Integrative Services' (Bogota, Colombia 7 May 2013) (notes of interview on file with the author); Amaya, *Women and the Victims Law* (n 32).

36 Summers, 'Colombia's Victims' Law: Transitional Justice in a Time of Violent Conflict?' (n 6) 225–26.

37 Interview with Fernando Calado (n 35).

Reparation to Victims (*Plan Nacional de Atención y Reparación Integral a las Víctimas*), and the Reparation Fund for Victims of Violence (*Fondo para la Reparación de las Victimas*)[38] Article 177 of the Victims' Law states that the funds will come from the following: (1) fines imposed on individuals or armed groups outside the law through judicial and administrative proceedings; (2) voluntary contributions from governments, international organisations, individuals and other entities, (3) voluntary contributions by financial institutions as a result of voluntary donation option at the end of ATM and Internet transactions; (4) voluntary contributions by large chain stores and supermarkets; (5) economic forfeitures from those who have been convicted of conspiracy for organizing, promoting, arming or financing armed groups; (6) amounts in judicial decisions due to the support provided by companies that have funded armed groups; and (7) proceeds of forfeiture (*Extincion de Dominio*).

In addition to the formation of the institutions (specifically the Fund), the Victims' Law states that the Victims Unit, along with the municipalities, districts and governors shall have 'the duty to ensure the necessary technical, logistical and budgetary means to ensure the creation and maintenance' of participation of victims.[39] The government of Colombia approved the Financial Plan for the Victims' Law in December 2011, which states that all entities of the State must appropriate sufficient resources to care properly for all victims. In 2012, it was reported that the central government also approved 6.1 billion pesos for the implementation, 2.3 billion pesos for education and health of victims and 3.8 trillion for health care programs.[40] Furthermore, international agencies, such as the European Union and USAID/Colombia have donated significant funds to aid in the implementation of the Law. In 2012, the European Union pledged 3 million euros.[41] The US government, through USAID, has also provided $50 million in funds over 3 years (from FY2012–2015) to 'provide technical assistance to the GOC for the first three years of the implementation of the Victims' Law to ensure that effective institutions, policies and systems at all levels—national, departmental and municipal—are established

---

38   It is important to note that the Reparation Fund for Victims of Violence was created by the Justice and Peace Law (art 54 of Law 975 of 2005). Under this article, The Fund consists of all the assets or resources in any capacity delivered by the persons or illegal armed groups referred to in the Act.
39   Victims' Law (n 17) art 168, para 5 and 10.
40   See: Xiomara Cecilia Balanta Moreno, 'Reparations: Limitations and Challenges of Colombia Victims Law (Act 1448 of 2011)' (2014) Vol. 4 No. 5(1) JHSS 152, 159, at <http://www.ijhssnet.com/journals/Vol_4_No_5_1_March_2014/19.pdf> accessed 2 February 2015.
41   *Ibid.*

and operational'.[42] In essence, the central government provides funds to departments and local municipalities, but those local governments must apply for the funding.[43] Therefore, there are a lot of potential sources of funding for implementation of the law that must be funneled through various levels of government and working units.

However, despite the potential inflows of cash both domestically and internationally, the actual use of funds has been delayed. Domestically, the procurement process for the funds from the national government for implementation has been slow and piecemeal. Coupled with a flawed procurement system, domestic funds are often ill disbursed. According to the Victims' Law, all municipalities by law must have a budget to implement the Law. Unfortunately, this is not happening due to lack of coordination. The vision set out in the Law is that a committee for a municipality, composed of victims groups and organizations, should design a budget for the municipality to implement the Law. However, this budget is rarely incorporated into the budget the municipality submits to the central government.[44]

In principle, domestic efforts at victim services are supplemented by the funding and services of assorted international governmental and non-governmental agencies. In practice, however, international donor funding runs the risk of being misallocated, as with domestic funds. The issue is not a lack of funds, but misallocation of existing grants. International donors have divided the country into different municipalities in which they work, and they are doing different work within those areas.[45] In theory, this could lead to testing of different approaches and ultimately better use of funds. However, the agencies do not talk to one another or share their successes or failures. In addition, the piece-meal approach has led to confusion about enrollment by the victims.

International donors are also funding flagship programs that do not address the underlying issues of implementation of the Victims' Law and may well represent the priorities of the organization rather than those of the Colombian

---

42   See USAID/Colombia 'Colombia Program At-A-Glance' (8 August 2013) at <http://www.usaid.gov/sites/default/files/Colombia%20Country%20Fact%20Sheet%20Augst%202013_USAID_at_a_Glance.pdf> accessed 2 February 2015.

43   Interview with Hido Redrass (n 28).

44   Interview with Nathalie Mendez and Paula Ila, VISP Component 3: Historical Memory and Transitional Justice (Bogota, Colombia, 7 May 2013) (n 28) (notes of interview on file with author) ('Interview with Nathalie Mendez and Paula Ila').

45   Interview with Diana Parra on USAID/AECOM Public Policy Program in Banking (AECOM Bogota, Colombia, 8 May 2013) (notes of interview on file with author).

Government. They are funding programs offering such items as 'free housing' or 'free prosthetics' to victims, without training or capacity building. Valuable as these services are to individual victims, instead of repairing or strengthening the social welfare systems to cope with victims, they are creating unsustainable parallel structures.

Infrastructural Issues

Poor roads, lack of governmental buildings and intermittent access to telecommunications have resulted in backlogs and long delays in the receiving of victim's declarations and approval of their status. The Victims' Law requires that all declarations be sent to the centralized Victims Unit for processing; however implementation is being delayed by the faulty infrastructure.

Many parts of Colombia also lack permanent structures for governmental operations, both local and national. For example, in Quidbo, the capital of Chocó, there has been an effort to provide comprehensive victim services since the passage of the 2005 Peace and Justice Law. However, the regional department or *departamento*, one of 32 such units in the country, is among the poorest; as such, governmental agents (especially *personeros*) designated to take statements and offer services have met with internally displaced persons and then eventually a broader category of victims in a building that doubles as a boxing ring.[46] Due to lack of physical facilities for both declaration and other services related with the Victims' Law, there have been numerous reported cases of victims traveling to urban facilities to access these services rather than doing so locally.[47] The major transportation issues caused by the lack of road infrastructure mean that this journey is difficult for those who take it and a huge hindrance for others who opt not to.

Finally, there is a serious dearth of telecommunications in the rural and often most conflict-affected parts of the country. Landlines cover only about 15% of the country.[48] The Internet is used on a regular basis by roughly half of the country.[49] This is slightly below the South American regional average, although Colombia's fixed broadband penetration is higher than would be

---

46 Site visit by the author to Choco, Colombia, accompanied by Angela Suarez Alvarez, Program Manager, USAID/Colombia, 10 May 2013 (notes of visit on file with author).

47 Ministry of Health, 'VISP Component 2: Health Care and Integrative Services' (Bogota, Colombia 7 May 2013).

48 Lucia Bibolini, 'Colombia—Telecoms, Mobile, Broadband and Forecasts' (July 2012), at <http://www.budde.com.au/Research/Colombia-Telecoms-Mobile-Broadband-and-Forecasts.html#overview> accessed 11 November 2014 ('Biblioni, 'Colombia—Telecoms, Mobile, Broadband and Forecasts'').

49 *Ibid*: between 38% and 55%, depending on the data.

expected given the country's low economic indicators.[50] Government facilities, such as those where *personeros* take statements from victims, routinely lack Internet access.[51] However, mobile penetration within the country is at 100%.[52]

This has contributed significantly to the backlog. Where there is internet access, online forms can be entered and quickly sent to the centralized Victims Unit for processing. However, in situations without internet, hard copies are compiled then sent in batches to Bogota or the department capital for processing, slowing down the process.[53] There are also situations, such as in Chocó, where there is intermittent access to internet. A conversation with a government agent taking declarations explained that sometimes during a declaration the internet gets overloaded and shuts down. This means that they have to begin the entire process again, as all the information is lost.[54] This is not an isolated problem, and has been reported in other parts of the country.[55]

Personnel and Operational Issues

Compounding serious infrastructural problems within Colombia are a multitude of issues with personnel and their operations. Local ombudsmen, or *personeros,* are legally in charge of statement taking at a local level. However, they are physically overwhelmed by the demand for statements as well as their other tasks. Secondly, *personeros* may not always be the best people to take statements from victims. Finally, the physical forms that many *personeros* are in charge of are cumbersome and add to delays.

Personeros have the general task of protecting citizens in their dealings with local government. *Personeros* are often overwhelmed. They have over 1,200 legal obligations with which to comply, only one of which is to take statements from victims and help them declare.[56] Many *personeros* only attend to victims 1–2 days a week, creating long delays and their schedules are utterly unpredictable. As a result, many victims, lacking the ability to communicate in advance to obtain a firm appointment, have to travel long distances, often two or three

---

50 Ibid.
51 Skype interview with Natalie Baal and Ivan Cardona (Geneva, Switzerland 23 April 2013), Joint IDP Profiling Service, (notes of interview on file with author) ('Skype interview with Natalie Baal and Ivan Cardona').
52 Biblioni, 'Colombia—Telecoms, Mobile, Broadband and Forecasts' (n 48).
53 Skype interview with Natalie Baal and Ivan Cardona (n 51).
54 Conversation with local officials during site visit, Chocó, Colombia (10 May 2013) (n 46) (notes of conversations on file with author).
55 Skype interview with Natalie Baal and Ivan Cardona (n 51).
56 Interview with Fernando Calado (n 35).

times, to get a meeting with the *personero*.[57] There is also confusion, both among *personeros* and victims, of the exact role and responsibilities of the *personero*.[58]

Some feel that *personeros* are not always the best people to take statements from victims. First, the majority of them are not trained in appropriate methods to deal with victims.[59] Secondly, their familiarity may be a hindrance in situations of sensitive crimes. For example, some women who have faced sexual violence claimed they did not declare themselves to their local *personero* due to the smallness of their town. They feared that the *personero,* who knew their attacker, would divulge confidential information or tell others within the community of the attack.[60] Finally, *personeros* are appointed by the local municipality, and may be there due to cronyism and not merit.[61]

It is also claimed that *personeros* do not always understand the importance of their work and how it fits into a larger framework. Even before the Victims' Law, the government did provide for victims. However, the Victims' Law brought with it not just more benefits to victims, but also the idea of transitional justice. Some local staff within the *departamentos*, not surprisingly, do not understand how transitional justice differs from traditional justice, thereby undermining the regular legal process.[62] Furthermore, this extends beyond *personeros*;[63] as funding for the implementation of the Victims Law comes from municipalities, departments and local governors, as well as the central government, there needs to be buy-in from local mayors and other civil servants for the program's sustainability.[64]

---

57   Amaya, *Women and the Victims Law* (n 32).
58   Interview with Nathalie Mendez & Paula Ila (n 44).
59   Interview with Soraya Mesa on children, youth and ex-combatants (Instituto Colombiano de Bienestar Familiar (ICBF) Bogota, Colombia, 8 May 2013) (notes of interview on file with author).
60   Amaya, *Women and the Victims Law* (n 32).
61   *Ibid.*
62   Interview with Nathalie Mendez & Paula Ila (n 44). The 2011 Law is underpinned by an instinct that victims of violations of human rights and humanitarian law have special claims on the state because of the state's failure to protect them. For some questions about what kinds of victims are 'special' and how best limited resources are to be allocated, see Clark, *The United Nations Crime Prevention and Criminal Justice Program* (n 1) 184, 194.
63   Amaya, *Women and the Victims Law* (n 32).
64   Interview with Reed Carly, Colombian Context (Berkeley, California, USA, 18 April 2013) (notes of interview on file with author).

Finally, the forms that the *personeros* use create delays from the local and central government. The forms suffer from insufficient quantity, non-adaptability, and cumbersome design. As mentioned before, the vast majority of declarations are made using paper forms, which have to be retyped by the central office to be put into the computer database. They are often very difficult to get to and from the rural areas.

The forms do not adapt to the needs of a victim and require an unnecessarily lengthy process.

The forms are the same for every victim, despite the different traumas they have undergone.[65] Secondly, the forms are lengthy. They can take 2–3 hours for each victim to share their entire history.[66] This means that a *personero* can only register 7–8 victims per day, without the necessary mental breaks.[67] The main form itself has 12 annexes, 11 for each particular violation and one for group declarations. Each annex must be filled and stapled to the main form. The form, therefore, requires a strong competency to complete the legal forms.[68]

The idea is that the forms will provide the Victims Unit with the information it needs to design a unique reparations and rehabilitation plan for each victim.[69] The Victims Unit designed this form to be a one-stop procedure; victims only have to talk about their traumas once and get all of their needs designed through one form. However, only 60% of victims explicitly ask to be included in the reparations program.[70] This indicates that the combination of declaration with statement-taking might not be what the victims want and they should be split. When the Victims Unit created the form, they combined the process of registration with more general statement-taking. Registration arguably differs from other kinds of statement-taking, as the goal is not a detailed picture of the crime, but rather merely proof for qualification into a program. During the initial enrollment period, there was apparently little to no clarity around the criteria for inclusion and burden of proof for the form.[71]

The paper form has also led to backlogs at the central agency, which processes claims. The vast majority of the statements are taken on paper forms, and those at the headquarters of the Victims Unit are in charge of re-typing all of the claims into the computer. Due to the length of the forms, this is a

---

65 VISP Context, Programs at a Glance (n 27).
66 Interview with Hido Redrass (n 28).
67 Interview with Fernando Calado (n 35).
68 Skype interview with Natalie Baal and Ivan Cardona (n 51).
69 Interview with Hido Redrass (n 28).
70 Ibid.
71 Skype interview with Natalie Baal and Ivan Cardona (n 51).

time-consuming process[72] and the Government simply lacks a sufficient number of data entry people. Since the registry and national records is the main tool of assessing varying demand, backlogs at this agency have led to a delayed public policy response.[73] This is compounded by the lack of understanding around the inclusion criteria for each type of declaration. Furthermore, processing occurs at the national level, which may not be able to access local knowledge. The communication between the central and local governments is extremely limited.

The Victims' Law suffers from under-enrollment due to a number of factors, the most important of which are personnel and operational issues. The policy was designed from the top-down, but designated implementation to the local level without taking into account the competencies and limitations.[74] This has caused massive delays, which are starting to discourage constituents from declaring.

Other Constraints

Compounding the issue of the inadequate government response are temporal restrictions in the Victims' Law. The Law only allows a 2-year period for enrollment of internally displaced people and a 4-year period for people who have had human rights crimes committed against them since 1985. After those dates, only ongoing victims can declare.[75] Given the weak dissemination of information about the Law and the lack of local capacity to handle claims, the time constraint is a serious issue and could potentially disenfranchise the majority of victims.

3 Conclusion

Turning an abstract idea such as victim reparation into an operational programme is always a challenge, even in a society with a highly-developed infrastructure. As I hope the previous discussion has indicated, the challenge is even greater without such 'givens'.

What modest steps, short of a vast increase in the size of the relevant bureaucracy, massive road-building and development of communication systems, might Colombia take to at least ameliorate some of the current

---

72   Interview with Poveda Heiby (n 26).
73   *Ibid.*
74   Interview with Nathalie Mendez and Paula Ila (n 44).
75   *VISP Context, Programs at a Glance* (n 27).

difficulties? Notably, the Victims Coordination Unit, created by the Victims' Law, should probably try harder to coordinate amongst those working in the field, including the assorted aid agencies which sometimes seem to be working on their own agenda, without necessarily contributing to the overall goal of post-conflict justice. In particular, it would be helpful to encourage such bodies to contribute to infrastructure development rather than engaging in random acts of charity. Perhaps a structural way can be found to relieve the pressure on the *personeros*, the local ombudsmen who have many other tasks than assisting in filling in registration forms. In this respect, careful attention and evaluation should be given to trials that have been conducted by two NGOs, the Pan-American Development Association and Chemonics International, of mobile victim teams or MVTs, using mobile communications platforms for text-messaging.[76] The teams travel in a van to selected locations and assist both in the enrollment of victims and in the provisions of other services such as legal representation and health care. This seems intuitively like a good idea and it ought to be possible to assess empirically how well these innovations work.

Furthermore, the forms themselves can probably be simplified with an understanding that 'one size fits all' is seldom a good solution. Finally, gains have been made in the area of mobile-technology, which can be used to create forms compatible with any smart-phone that can be directly submitted to the central agency over data networks.

Victim services, moreover, do not operate in a vacuum. Colombia, and others similarly situated, need ultimately to ensure that capacity gains be across

---

[76] There are two main types of mobile platforms: SMS-based and adaptive questionnaire-based. RapidSMS and FrontlineSMS, for example, are open platform tools that can post data to web-based servers via text messaging (SMS). RapidSMS, for example, is a free and open-source framework for dynamic data collection, logistics coordination and communication developed by UNICEF. However, SMS based programs are limited in their user interface flexibility and more practical with simple text information and short forms. SMS based technology can be used with any mobile phone without installation of special on-phone software, and require low hardware overhead. They are ideal for projects with many field workers with fewer questions. On the other hand, projects that involve many questions but fewer field workers, as well as variety of data types (i.e. GPS, Photos, etc) are better with more adaptive technologies, such as EpiSurveyor or Open Data Kit (ODK). For more on these technologies, see Sarah Underwood. 'Improving Disaster Management' (2010) 53 Communications of the ACM 18 (doi:10.1145/1646353.1646362); and Frances Jeffrey-Coker et al., 'Open Data Kit: Implications for the Use of Smartphone Software Technology for Questionnaire Studies in International Development' (2010) (sel.columbia.edu/wp-content/uploads/2).

the board for all government services, not just victim services. Victims-only governmental approach is not a sustainable structural model in a country where like Colombia victims, though large in number, still represent only about ten percent of the population. Agencies, national and local, should not be designed only for victims. They should be facilities for all citizens but facilities that understand different and specific needs for victims.

Curriculum Vitae of Roger S. Clark

Roger S. Clark
Board of Governors Professor, Rutgers University School of Law,
217 North Fifth Street, Camden, New Jersey 08102–1203
(856) 225-6390 (phone) 225-6516 (fax)
rsclark@camden.rutgers.edu

Education

B.A. (1964), LL.B. (1964), LL.M. (First Class Honors) (1967), LL.D. (1997), LL.D. honoris causa (2014) Victoria University of Wellington, New Zealand
LL.M. (1968), J.S.D. (1972) Columbia University, New York
Admitted as Barrister and Solicitor of the High Court of New Zealand (1964)

Professional Experience

1998–present: Board of Governors Professor, Rutgers University School of Law
1982–1998: Distinguished Professor, Rutgers University School of Law
1973–1982: Professor of Law, Rutgers University School of Law
1972–1973: Associate Professor of Law, Rutgers University School of Law
1985–1986: Visiting Professor of Law, University of Miami Law School
1971–1972: Visiting Associate Professor, College of Law, University of Iowa
1969–1971: Senior Lecturer in Law, Victoria University
1968–1969: Doctoral Fellow, Columbia University School of Law
August 1968: United Nations Student Intern, Human Rights Division
1967–1968: American Council of Learned Societies Fellow, Columbia University School of Law
1964–1967: Junior Lecturer and Lecturer in Law, Victoria University
1962–1963: Legal Officer, New Zealand Ministry of Foreign Affairs
1960–1962: Law Clerk, New Zealand Justice Department
June–July 2014: University of San Diego Summer Program, London
July–August 2013: University of San Diego Summer Program, Paris
June–July 2010: University of San Diego Summer Program, London
February–May 2005: Visiting Professor, Temple Law School Graduate Program, at Tsinghua University, Beijing
September–December 2004: Visiting Professor, Victoria University of Wellington, New Zealand
April–June 2001: Guest Professor, Faculty of Law, University of Graz, Austria

1999–present: Faculty, Salzburg Summer School on International Criminal Law
June 1998: Temple University Summer Program, Athens
January–May 1994: Temple University Semester Abroad Program, Tokyo
August–Dec. 1990: Adjunct Professor of International Law, University of Pennsylvania
June–August 1989: University of San Diego Summer Program, Paris
June–August 1987: University of San Diego Summer Program, Trinity College, Dublin
May–June 1984: Guest Professor, Faculty of Law, University of Graz, Austria
August 1970: Visiting Senior Lecturer, University of the South Pacific, Fiji

Areas of Teaching Interest and Experience

International Law; International Protection of Human Rights (offered variously as a Seminar, a Course or a Clinic); International Organizations; International Criminal Law and Criminal Justice Policy; United States Foreign Relations and National Security Law; Criminal Law. (Periodically, with Professor Amelia H. Boss: International Business Transactions).

Publications

Books

International Criminal Law: Cases and Materials (LexisNexis, Newark, 3rd ed., 2009) (with Edward M. Wise & Ellen S. Podgor) (2nd ed., 2004, Teacher's Manual to same, 2005, 2011) (Supplements, 2006, 2008)

Understanding International Criminal Law (LexisNexis, Newark, 3rd ed., 2013, 2nd ed., 2008) (with Ellen S. Podgor)

International and National Law in Russia and Eastern Europe: Essays in Honor of George Ginsburgs (Martinus Nijhoff, The Hague, 2001) (editor & contributor) (with Ferdinand Feldbrugge & Stanislaw Pomorski)

The Case against the Bomb: Marshall Islands, Samoa, and Solomon Islands before the International Court of Justice in Advisory Proceedings on the Legality of the Threat or Use of Nuclear Weapons (Rutgers Law School, Camden, New York, London, 1996) (editor & contributor) (with Madeleine Sann)

The Prosecution of International Crimes: A Critical Study of the International Tribunal for the Former Yugoslavia (Transaction, New Brunswick, N.J., 1996) (editor) (with Madeleine Sann)

The United Nations Crime Prevention and Criminal Justice Program: Formulation of Standards and Efforts at Their Implementation (University of Pennsylvania Press for Procedural Aspects of International Law Institute, Philadelphia, 1994)

Human Rights Sourcebook (Paragon House, New York, 1987) (with A. Blaustein & J. Sigler)

No-Fault Automobile Insurance in Action (Oceana, Dobbs Ferry, N.Y., 1977) (with A. Widiss, J. Little & T. Jones)

Tort in Transition: A New Zealand Collection of Cases and Materials on Tort in the Accident Compensation Era (Fourth Estate Publishing, Wellington, 1976) (with P. McKenzie & G. Palmer)

The Development of the New Zealand Constitution (N.Z. Dept. of Education, Wellington, 1975)

A United Nations High Commissioner for Human Rights (Martinus Nijhoff, The Hague, 1972)

Essays on Criminal Law in New Zealand (Sweet & Maxwell, Wellington, 1971) (editor & contributor)

Articles, Book Chapters and Forewords

Jurisdiction Over Transnational Crime, in Neil Boister & Robert Currie eds., *Routledge Handbook of Transnational Criminal Law* 91 (2015)

Is The Butter Battle Book's *Bitsy Big Boy Boomeroo Banned? What Has International Law to Say about Weapons of Mass Destruction?* 58 *New York L. Sch. L. Rev.* 507 (2014)

Alleged Aggression in Utopia: An International Criminal Law Exam Question for 2020, in William A. Schabas, Yvonne McDermott & Niamh Hayes eds., *The Ashgate Research Companion to International Criminal Law: Critical Perspectives* 63 (Ashgate, Aldershot, 2013)

The Crime of Aggression: From the Trial of Takashi Sakai, August 1946, to the Kampala Review Conference on the ICC in 2010, in Kevin Jon Heller & Gerry Simpson eds., *The Hidden Histories of War Crimes Trials* 387 (Oxford University Press, Oxford, 2013)

Concluding Thoughts, in Suzannah Linton ed., *Hong Kong's War Crimes Trials* 199 (Oxford University Press, Oxford, 2013)

Epilogue, in Mohamed Elewa Badar, *The Concept of* Mens Rea *in International Criminal Law* 433 (Hart, Oxford and Portland, 2013)

Peacekeeping Forces, Jurisdiction and Immunity: A Tribute to George Barton, 43 *Victoria U. of Wellington L. Rev.* 77 (2012)

Foreword, in Sarah Finnin, *Elements of Accessorial Liability: Article 25(3)(b) and (c) of the Rome Statute of the International Criminal Court* (Martinus Nijhoff, Leiden, 2012)

Some Aspects of the Concept of International Criminal Law: Suppression Conventions, Jurisdiction, Submarine Cables and The Lotus, 22 *Criminal Law Forum* 519 (2011) (contribution to Symposium in honor of Professor Otto Triffterer's 80th birthday), expanded version in *Jurisdiction in International Law: Reflections on* The Lotus, *Submarine Cables, Counterfeiters and Hijackers*, United Nations Audiovisual Library of International Law, available at: legal.un.org/avl/ls/Clark_S.html (2012)

Complementarity and the Crime of Aggression, in Carsten Stahn & Mohammed M. El Zeidy eds., *The International Criminal Court and Complementarity: From Theory to Practice* 721 (Cambridge University Press, Cambridge, 2011)

History of Efforts to Codify Crimes against Humanity: From the Charter of Nuremberg to the Statute of Rome, in Leila Nadya Sadat ed., *Forging a Convention for Crimes against Humanity* 8 (Cambridge University Press, Cambridge, 2011)

Amendments to the Rome Statute of the International Criminal Court Considered at the First Review Conference on the Court, Kampala, 31 May–11 June 2010, 2 Goettingen J. Int'l L. 689 (2010)

The Development of International Criminal Law, in Chile Eboe-Osuji ed., *Protecting Humanity: Essays in International Law and Policy in Honour of Navanethem Pillay* (Martinus Nijhoff, Leiden, 2010)

The Role of the United Nations, in Mangai Natarajan ed., *International Crime and Justice* 337 (Cambridge University Press, Cambridge, 2010)

The Attrition of Capital Punishment Worldwide as the American Law Institute Withdraws Its Model Penal Code Provision Recommending How to Do It, 21 Criminal Law Forum 511 (2010) (review essay)

Aggression in International and in New Zealand Law, in Brian Lynch ed., *Celebrating 75 Years of New Zealand Institute of International Affairs* 49 (NZIIA, Wellington, 2010)

The International Criminal Law System, 8 New Zealand J. Pub. & Int'l L. 27 (2010)

Effecting Amendments to the Rome Statute that May Be Decided upon at the First Review Conference in 2010, 81 Int'l Rev. Penal L. 65 (2010)

The 'Weapons Provision' and Its Annex: The Belgian Proposals, in Roberto Bellilli ed., *International Criminal Justice: Law and Practice from the Rome Statute to Its Review* 489 (Ashgate, Farnham & Burlington, 2010)

Negotiating Provisions Defining the Crime of Aggression, Its Elements and the Conditions for ICC Exercise of Jurisdiction Over It, 20 European J. Int'l L. 1103 (2009)

The Review Conference on the Rome Statute of the International Criminal Court, Kampala, Uganda, 31 May–11 June 2010, 16 Australian International Law Journal 9 (2009)

Building on Article 8(2)(b)(xx) of the Rome Statute of the International Criminal Court: Weapons and Methods of Warfare, 12 New Criminal Law Rev. 366 (2009)

The Crime of Aggression, in Carsten Stahn & Göran Sluiter eds., *The Emerging Practice of the International Criminal Court* 709 (Brill, The Netherlands, 2009)

Ambiguities in Articles 5(2), 121 and 123 of the Rome Statute, 41 Case Western Reserve J. Int'l Law 413 (2009)

The International League for Human Rights, in David P. Forsythe ed., 3 *Encyclopedia of Human Rights* (Oxford University Press, Oxford, 2009)

In General, Should Excuses Be Broadly or Narrowly Construed? 42 Texas Tech Law Rev. 327 (2009)

Elements of Crimes in Early Confirmation Decisions of the Pre-trial Chambers of the International Criminal Court, 6 New Zealand Y.B. Int'l L. 209 (2008)

Drafting a General Part to a Penal Code: Some Thoughts Inspired by the Negotiations on the Rome Statute of the International Criminal Court and by the Court's First Substantive Law Discussion in the Lubanga Dyilo Confirmation Proceedings, 19 Criminal Law Forum 519 (2008)

The Military Commissions Act of 2006: An Abject Abdication by Congress, 6 Rutgers J. Law & Pub. Pol'y 78 (2008)

State Obligations under the Genocide Convention in Light of the ICJ's Decision in the Case Concerning the Application of the Convention on the Prevention and Punishment of the Crime of Genocide, 61 Rutgers L. Rev. 75 (2008)

Several entries, in Otto Triffterer ed., *Commentary on the Rome Statute of the International Criminal Court, Observers' Notes, Article by Article* (C.H. Beck, Hart, Nomos, Munich, Oxford, Baden-Baden, 2nd ed., 2008)

The Crime of Aggression and the International Criminal Court, in M. Cherif Bassiouni ed., *International Criminal Law* 243 (3rd ed., 2008), also in José Doria, Hans-Peter Gasser & M. Cherif Bassiouni eds., *The Legal Regime of the International Criminal Court: Essays in Honor of Professor Igor Pavlovich Blishchenko* (2009)

Apartheid, in M. Cherif Bassiouni ed., *International Criminal Law* 599 (3rd ed., 2008)

Creating and Explaining the International Criminal Court, 19 Criminal Law Forum 589 (2008) (book essay)

Nuremberg and the Crime against Peace, 6 Wash. U. Global Studies Law Review 527 (2007)

Western Sahara and the United Nations Norms on Self-determination and Aggression, in *International Law and the Question of Western Sahara* (Karin Arts & Pedro Pinto Leite ed., IPJET, Oporto, 2007)

Possible Amendments for the First ICC Review Conference in 2009, 2007 New Zealand Yearbook of International Law 103

The International Criminal Court and the Crime of Aggression, 2007 China Review of International Criminal Law 213 (in Chinese, Wang Xiumei trans.)

Aggression: A Crime under Domestic Law? 2006 New Zealand Law Journal 349

Some Challenges Facing the Assembly of States Parties of the International Criminal Court, in Eduardo Vetere & Pedro David eds., *Victims of Crime and Abuse of Power: Festschrift in Honour of Irene Melup* 141 (United Nations, Bangkok, 2005)

The Role of the United Nations, in Mangai Natarajan ed., *Introduction to International Criminal Justice* 117 (McGraw Hill, New York, 2005)

Nuclear Weapons and *Weapons of Mass Destruction*, in Dinah L. Shelton Editor-in-Chief, *Encyclopedia of Genocide and Crimes against Humanity* 754 and 1151 (Thomson Gale, Detroit, 2005)

The United Nations Convention against Transnational Organized Crime, 50 Wayne L. Rev. 161 (2004)

The Rome Statute of the International Criminal Court and Weapons of a Nature to Cause Superfluous Injury or Unnecessary Suffering, or Which Are Inherently Indiscriminate, in John Carey, William V. Dunlap & R. John Pritchard eds., *International Humanitarian Law: Challenges* 259 (Transnational Publishers, New York, 2004)

Justice without Borders: The International Criminal Court (Panel Discussion), 17 Temple Int'l & Comp. L. J. 90 (2003)

Rethinking Aggression as a Crime and Formulating Its Elements: The Final Work-Product of the Preparatory Commission for the International Criminal Court, 15 Leiden J. Int'l L. 859 (2002)

The Interrogation of Karl Hermann Frank & the Kristallnacht Documents, 4 Rutgers J. L. & Relig. 2 (2002)

Foreword to Bertrand G. Ramcharan, *The United Nations High Commissioner for Human Rights: The Challenges of International Protection* IX (Martinus, Nijhoff, The Hague, 2002)

The Mental Element in International Criminal Law: The Rome Statute of the International Criminal Court and the Elements of Offences, 12 Crim. L.F. 291 (2001), German translation, *Subjektive Merkmale im Völkerstrafrecht: Das Römische Statute des Internationalen Strafgerichtshofs und die Verbrechenselemente*, 114 Zeitschrift Für Die Gesamte Strafrechtswissenschaft 372 (2002) (Thomas Weigend trans.)

Crimes against Humanity and the International Criminal Court, in Roger Clark, Ferdinand Feldbrugge and Stanislaw Pomorski eds., *International and National Law in Russia and Eastern Europe: Essays in Honor of George Ginsburgs* 139 (Martinus Nijhoff, The Hague, 2001), reprinted in Mauro Politi & Guiseppe Nesi eds., *The Rome Statute of the International Criminal Court: A Challenge to Impunity* 75 (Ashgate/ Dartmouth, Aldershot, 2001)

Foreword to Angie Zelter ed., *Trident on Trial: The Case for People's Disarmament* (Luath Press, Edinburgh, 2001)

The ICC Statute: Protecting the Sovereign Rights of Non-parties, in Dinah Shelton ed., *International Crimes, Peace and Human Rights: The Role of the International Criminal Court* (Transnational Publishers, Ardsley, New York, 2000)

How International Human Rights Law Affects Domestic Law, in Adamantia Pollis & Peter Schwab eds., *Human Rights: New Perspectives, New Realities* 185 (Reinner, Boulder & London, 2000)

East Timor, Indonesia and the International Community, 14 Temple Int'l & Comp. L. J. 75 (2000)

Creating a Statute for the International Criminal Court: A Jurisdictional Quandary, 22 Suffolk Transnat'l L. Rev. 461 (1999)

Several entries, in Otto Triffterer ed., *Commentary on the Rome Statute of the International Criminal Court, Observers' Notes, Article by Article* (Nomos Verlagsgesellschaft, Baden-Baden, Germany, 1999)

Steven Spielberg's "Amistad" and Other Things I Have Thought about in the Past Forty Years: International (Criminal) Law, Conflict of Laws, Insurance and Slavery, 30 Rutgers L. J. 371 (1999)

Preamble and Final Clauses, in Roy Lee ed., *The International Criminal Court: The Making of the Rome Statute, Issues, Negotiations, Results* 421 (Kluwer, The Hague, 1999) (with Tuiloma Neroni Slade)

Apartheid, in M. Cherif Bassiouni ed., *International Criminal Law (Crimes)* 643 (Transnational Publishers, Ardsley, 2nd ed., New York, 1999)

Human Rights Strategies of the 1960s within the United Nations: A Tribute to the Late Kamleshwar Das, 21 Human Rights Q. 308 (1999)

Treaty and Custom, in Laurence Boisson de Chazournes & Philippe Sands eds., *International Law, The International Court of Justice and Nuclear Weapons* 171 (Cambridge, England, 1999)

Obligations of Third States in the Face of Illegality: Ruminations Inspired by the Weeramantry Dissent in the Case Concerning East Timor, in Antony Anghie & Garry Sturgess eds., *Legal Visions of the 21st Century: Essays in Honour of Judge Christopher Weeramantry* 631 (Kluwer, The Hague, 1998)

East Timor and An International Criminal Court, in Pedro Pinto Leite ed., *The East Timor Problem and the Role of Europe* 95 (IPJET, Lisbon, 1998)

Toward an International Criminal Court, in Yael Danieli, Elsa Stamatopoulou & Clarence Dias eds., *The Universal Declaration of Human Rights: Fifty Years and Beyond* 99 (Baywood, Amityville, 1998) (with David Tolbert)

Countering Transnational and International Crime: Defining the Agenda, in Peter J. Cullen & William C. Gilmore ed., *Crime Sans Frontières: International and European Legal Approaches* 20, Hume Papers on Public Policy, Vol. 6, Nos. 1 & 2 (1998)

Methods of Warfare that Cause Unnecessary Suffering or Are Inherently Indiscriminate: A Memorial Tribute to Howard Berman, 28 Cal. West. Int'l L. J. 379 (1998)

The Proposed International Criminal Court: Its Establishment and Its Relationship with the United Nations, 8 Crim. L.Forum 411 (1997), reprinted in 2 Mediterranean J. Hum. Rts 127 (1998)

The Case Concerning Oil Platforms (Islamic Republic of Iran v. United States of America): Preliminary Objection, 10 Leiden J. Int'l L. 541 (1997)

Nuremberg and Tokyo in Contemporary Perspective, in Tim McCormack & Gerry Simpson eds., *The Law of War Crimes: A Synthesis of National and International Approaches* 171 (Martinus Nijhoff, The Hague, 1997)

Public International Law and Private Enterprise: Damages for a Killing in East Timor, 3 Australian J. Human Rights 21 (1996), shorter version in Paddy Ireland & Per Laleng, *The Critical Lawyers' Handbook* 2 (Pluto, London, 1997)

The Laws of Armed Conflict and the Use or Threat of Use of Nuclear Weapons, 7 Crim. L. Forum 265 (1996)

Coping with Ultimate Evil through the Criminal Law, 7 Crim. L. Forum 1 (1996) (with Madeleine Sann)

The 1985 United Nations Declaration of Basic Principles of Justice for Victims of Crime and Abuse of Power, in G. Alfredsson & P. Macalister-Smith eds., *The Living Law of Nations, Essays on Refugees, Minorities, Indigenous Peoples and the Human Rights of Other Vulnerable Groups in Memory of Atle Grahl-Madsen* (N.P. Engel, Kehl am Rhein, 1996)

Issues of Implementation and Coordination, in Yael Danieli, Nigel S. Rodley & Lars Weisaeth eds., *International Responses to Traumatic Stress* 425 (Baywood, New York, 1996) (with Daniel Nsereko)

The 'Decolonization' of East Timor and The United Nations Norms on Self-determination and Aggression, and *The Substance of the East Timor Case in the ICJ*, Chapters in *International Law and the Question of East Timor* (CIIR & IPJET, London, 1995)

United Nations Standards and Norms in Crime Prevention and Criminal Justice, 5 J. Transnat'l L. & Contemp. Prob. 287 (1995)

Introduction to Symposium on International Criminal Law (with Ved P. Nanda), 5 J. Transnat'l L. & Contemp. Prob. i (1995)

Foreword, Toward a Right to Peace: Selected Papers of John H.E. Fried VII (Altheia Press, Northampton, Mass., 1994)

Stocktaking after Two Sessions of the Commission on Crime Prevention and Criminal Justice, 4 Crim. Law Forum 471 (1993), reprinted in M. Cherif Bassiouni ed., *The Contributions of Specialized Institutes and Non-Governmental Organizations to the United Nations Criminal Justice Program. In Honor of Adolfo Beria di Argentine* (Kluwer, The Hague, 1995)

Timor Gap: The Legality of the "Treaty on the Zone of Cooperation in an Area between the Indonesian Province of East Timor and Northern Australia," [1992] Pace YB Int'l L. 69, reprinted in Peter Carey & G. Carter Bentley eds., *East Timor at the Crossroads. Forging of a Nation* (Cassell, London, 1995)

Some International Law Aspects of the East Timor Affair, 5 Leiden J. Int'l L. 265 (1992), reprinted as *The East Timor Affair in International Law*, 4 Camões Center Quarterly 25 (1992–93)

United Nations Model Treaties on Cooperation in the Criminal Process, 18 Commonwealth L. Bull. 1544 (1992)

Criminal Code Reform in New Zealand? A Martian's View of the Erewhon Crimes Act 1961 with Some Footnotes to the 1989 Bill, 21 Vict. U. Wellington L. Rev. 1 (1991)

Crime: The UN Agenda on International Cooperation in the Criminal Process, 15 Nova L. Rev. 475 (1991)

Crimes against Humanity at Nuremberg, and *Codification of the Principles of the Nuremberg Trial and the Subsequent Development of International Law*, in G. Ginsburgs & V. Kudriavtsev eds., *The Nuremberg Trial and International Law* 177 & 249 (Kluwer, The Hague, 1990)

The Eighth United Nations Congress on the Prevention of Crime and the Treatment of Offenders, Havana, Cuba August 27–September 7, 1990, 1 Crim. L. Forum 513 (1990)
Foreword and *Constitutionalism and Palau's Self-determination: A Lawyer's Perspective*, in B. Aldridge & C. Myers, *Resisting the Serpent: Palau's Struggle for Self-determination* XIII & 197 (Fortkamp, Baltimore, 1990)
Human Rights and the U.N. Committee on Crime Prevention and Control, 506 The Annals 68 (1989)
State Terrorism: Some Lessons From the Sinking of the "Rainbow Warrior," 20 Rutgers L. J. 393 (1989)
Free Association—A Critical View, in P. Leary ed., *Proceedings: Conference on the Future Status of the United States Virgin Islands, University of the Virgin Islands* (1989)
The Committee on the Rights of the Child: Who Pays? in C. Cohen ed., *Independent Commentary: United Nations Convention on the Rights of the Child* 59 (Defense for Children International, New York, 1988) (with F. Gaer), updated version in 7 N.Y. L. S. J. Human Rights 123 (1989).
Offenses of International Concern: Multilateral State Treaty Practice in the Forty Years Since Nuremberg, 57 Nordic J. Int'l L. 49 (1988)
"Termination" of the Pacific Islands Trust, 81 American J. Int'l L. 927 (1987) (Letter to Editor)
International Human Rights Law, in R. Janosik ed., *Encyclopedia of the American Judicial System* 334 (Scribner's, New York, 1987)
The Crime of Apartheid, in M. Bassiouni ed., *International Criminal Law* 299 (Transnational Publishers, Dobbs Ferry, N.Y., 1986)
Preventing and Combating Intolerance of Religion or Belief, World Order, Winter 1985–86, 19
East Timor and International Law, 2 Mennesker og Rettigheter (Norway) 32 (1984)
Approaching a No-Fault or Uninsured Motorist Claim, and *Statutory Basis of No-Fault and Uninsured Motorist Systems*, Chapters 1 and 2 of *No-Fault/Uninsured Automobile Insurance* (Matthew Bender, New York, 1984)
Models of National or Local Action to Prevent or Combat Intolerance of Religion or Belief, Background Paper for United Nations Seminar on the Encouragement of Understanding, Tolerance and Respect in Matters Relating to Religion or Belief, Geneva, December 1984, U.N. Doc. HR/GENEVA/1984/BP.3 (1984)
Transnational Legal Problems of Refugees, 17 Vanderbilt J. Transnat'l L. 179 (1984) (review essay on 1982 Michigan Yearbook of International Legal Studies)
Humanitarian Intervention, Help to Your Friends and State Practice, 13 Ga. J. Int'l & Comp. L. 211 (1983)
The United Nations Declaration on the Elimination of All Forms of Intolerance and of Discrimination Based on Religion or Belief, 31 Chitty's L. J. 23 (1983)
Human Rights and the United Nations High Commissioner for Refugees, 10 Int'l J. Legal Info. 287 (1982)

State Terrorism: Disappearances, 13 *Rutgers L. J. 531* (1982) (with Maureen R. Berman)

International Human Rights Fact-Finding: The Role of Legal Representation, in B. G. Ramcharan ed., *International Law and Fact-Finding in the Field of Human Rights* (Martinus Nijhoff, The Hague, 1982)

Does the Genocide Convention Go Far Enough? (Symposium on Genocide and Humanicide), 8 *Ohio Northern L. J.* 321 (1981)

The International League for Human Rights and South West Africa 1947–1957—The Human Rights NGO as Catalyst in the International Legal Process, 3(4) *Human Rights Q.* 101 (1981)

The "Decolonization" of East Timor and the United Nations Norms on Self-determination and Aggression, 7 *Yale J. World Pub. Order* 2 (1980)

Self-determination and Free Association: Should the United Nations Terminate the Pacific Islands Trust? 21 *Harv. Int'l. L. J.* 1 (1980)

Legal Principles of Non-socialist Economic Integration as Exemplified by the European Economic Community, 8 *Syracuse J. Int'l L. & Commerce* 1 (1980)

Enforcement of International Human Rights Law: The Role of Lawyers, 28 *Chitty's L. J.* 4 (1980)

The United Nations and Religious Freedom, 11 *N.Y.U. J. Int'l L. & Pol.* 197 (1978)

Some Developments in New Jersey Criminal Law, in Proceedings of the Prosecutors' Institute (Delaware Law School, Widener College, Wilmington, Del., 1977) mimeo

Measures to Protect Religious Freedom, in L. Sohn & M. Galey eds., *New Aspects of the International Protection of Human Rights, Twenty-Fifth Report of the Commission to Study the Organization of Peace* 36 (Stanley Foundation, N.Y., 1977) (summary of working paper prepared for Commission, mimeo, 1976)

No-Fault in Delaware, 6 *Rutgers-Camden L. J.* 225 (1974), updated version in Widiss, Little, Clark, Jones, *No-Fault Automobile Insurance in Action* (Oceana, Dobbs Ferry, N.Y., 1977) (with G. Waterson)

The First Twenty-Five Years of the Universal Declaration of Human Rights—and the Next, 48 *Conn. Bar J.* 111 (1974) (originally published in English and French as working paper for World Peace Through World Law Conference, Abidjan, 1973) (with Leo Nevas)

The U.N. and Human Rights: Some Modest Proposals, 59 *A.B.A.J.* 1393 (1973) (with Leo Nevas)

Some Jurisprudential Questions on Economic, Social and Cultural Rights, in Report of the Human Rights Committee, Conference on Non-Governmental Organizations in Observance of the 25th Anniversary of the Universal Declaration of Human Rights (N.Y., 1973)

Medina: An Essay on the Principles of Criminal Liability for Homicide, 5 *Rutgers-Camden L. J.* 59 (1973)

Disorderly Behavior, in S. Webb & J. Collette eds., *New Zealand Society: Contemporary Perspectives* 361 (Wellington, 1973)

The Trust Territory of the Pacific Islands: Some Perspectives, 1973 *Proc. Am. Soc'y Int'l L.* 17
Meetings, Processions, Symbolic Speech and the Law, N.Z. L. J. 209, 249 [1972]
A Jurisprude Looks at the Road Toll, 2 *Otago L. Rev.* 441 (1972)
Overmastering Physical Force, 14 *Crim. L. Q.* (Canada) 413 (1972)
Accident: Or What Became of Kilbride v. Lake? in R. Clark ed., *Essays on Criminal Law in New Zealand* 47 (1971)
Police Powers to Seize and Detain Goods and Documents, N.Z. L. J. 153 [1971]
Police Power to Arrest without Warrant, N.Z. L. J. 176 [1970]
Hans Kelsen's Pure Theory of Law, 22 *J. Legal Ed.* 170 (1970)
The Defence of Impossibility and Offences of Strict Liability, 11 *Crim. L. Q.* (Canada) 154 (1969)
Broadcasting and Private Enterprise: The Proposed Broadcasting Authority, 30 *N.Z. J. Pub. Admin.* 29 (1968)
Automatism and Strict Liability, 5 *Vict. U. Wellington L. Rev.* 12 (1968)
Chapters 1, 2, 4 & 5 of J. Robson ed., *New Zealand: The Development of Its Laws and Constitution* (Stevens, London, 1967) (with C.C. Aikman & K.J. Keith)
Strict Liability Offences of Possession, N.Z. L. J. 182 [1967]
Some Developments in Administrative Law, 29 *N.Z. J. Pub. Admin.* 48 (1967) (with C.C. Aikman)
The Narcotics Act 1965, 2 *N.Z. U. L. Rev.* 92 (1966)
Some Developments in Administrative Law, 28 *N.Z. J. Pub. Admin.* 96 (1966) (with C.C. Aikman)
Some Developments in Administrative Law, 27 *N.Z. J. Pub. Admin.* 45 (1965) (with C.C. Aikman)
The Geneva Accords and the Two Vietnams, in M. Bassett ed., *New Zealand and South East Asia* 12 (Auckland, 1965)
French Tests and International Law, New Zealand Monthly Review, No. 52, 5 (1964–5)

Reports
Report of the Commission of Experts on Reforming Internal Justice at the United Nations (with Geoffrey Robertson and Ousmane Kane) (New York, 2006)
Report of the International Observer Mission, Palau Referendum, December 1986 (with A. Boss, E. Hammerich, S. Roff & D. Wright) (International League for Human Rights & Minority Rights Group, New York, 1987)

Compiled and Edited
Symposium, International Criminal Law, 5(2), *Transnat'l L. & Contemp. Prob.* (Iowa City, Iowa, 1995) (with Ved Nanda)
Democracy in South Korea: A Promise Unfulfilled (A Report on Human Rights 1980–1985) (New York, 1985, for the International League for Human Rights and the International Human Rights Law Group) (general editor & contributor)

Micronesia: The Problem of Palau, Minority Rights Group Report No. 63 (New York, 1984, rev. ed. 1987) (with S. Roff)

Constitutions of Dependencies and Special Sovereignties: The Trust Territory of the Pacific Islands, in A. Blaustein & E. Blaustein eds. (Oceana, Dobbs Ferry, N.Y., 1982) (successor volumes on the Commonwealth of the Northern Mariana Islands, the Federated States of Micronesia, the Marshall Islands and Palau, 1988)

Constitutions of the Countries of the World: New Zealand, in A. Blaustein & G. Flanz eds. (Oceana, Dobbs Ferry, N.Y., 1985)

Constitutions of Dependencies and Special Sovereignties: New Zealand Territories, in A. Blaustein & E. Blaustein eds. (Oceana, Dobbs Ferry, N.Y., 1985)

Book Reviews

Boas, G., W.A. Schabas & M.P. Scharf, *International Criminal Justice: Legitimacy and Coherence* (2012), Criminal Law and Criminal Justice Books, January 2014, available at: http://clcjbooks.rutgers.edu/books/international-criminal-justice.html

Ambos, K., *Treatise on International Criminal Law. Vol. 1: Foundations and General Part* (2013), 24 Criminal Law Forum 561 (2013)

Braithwaite, J., H. Charlesworth & A. Soares, *Networked Governance of Freedom and Tyranny: Peace in Timor-Leste* (2012), 35 Human Rights Quarterly 241 (2013)

Hagan, J. & W. Rymond-Richmond, *Darfur and the Crime of Genocide* (2009), 22 Criminal Law Forum 445 (2011)

Glasius, M., *The International Criminal Court: A Global Civil Society Achievement* (2006), 19 Criminal Law Forum 589 (2008)

Olusanya, O., *Identifying an Aggressor under International Law: A Principles Approach* (2006), 19 Criminal Law Forum 303 (2008)

Weeramantry, C.G., *Universalising International Law* (2004), 99 American Journal of International Law 298 (2005)

Kolodzeij, E.A., ed., *A Force Profonde: The Power, Politics and Promise of Human Rights* (2003), Human Rights Review October/December 2005, 135

Ambos, K. & M. Othman eds., *New Approaches in International Criminal Justice: Kosovo, East Timor, Sierra Leone and Cambodia* (2003), 15 Criminal Law Forum 467 (2005)

Maguire, P., *Law and War: An American Story* (2000), Society May/June 2002, 89

Kauzlarich, D. & R.C. Kramer, *Crimes of the American Nuclear State at Home and Abroad* (1998), 10 Social and Legal Studies 428 (2001)

Beigbeder, Y., *Judging War Criminals: The Politics of International Justice* (1999), 22 Human Rights Quarterly 302 (2000)

Nanda, V.P. & D. Krieger, *Nuclear Weapons and the World Court* (1998), 14 Emory International Law Review 199 (2000)

Stith, K. & J.A. Cabranes, *Fear of Judging: Sentencing Guidelines in the Federal Courts* (1998), 11 Criminal Law Forum 249 (2000)

Weeramantry, C.G., *Justice without Frontiers. Vol. 1: Furthering Human Rights* (1997), *Vol. 2: Protecting Human Rights in the Age of Technology* (1998), and *The Lord's Prayer: Bridge to a Better World* (1998), 94 *American Journal of International Law* 232 (2000)

Bassiouni, M.C. & E.M. Wise, *Aut Dedere Aut Judicare: The Duty to Extradite or Prosecute in International Law* (1995), 91 *American Journal of International Law* 204 (1997)

Reicher, H., ed., *Australian International Law Cases and Materials* (1995), [1996] *Canadian Yearbook of International Law* 518

Nadelmann, E.A., *Cops across Borders: The Internationalization of U.S. Criminal Law Enforcement* (1993), 6 *Criminal Law Forum* 249 (1995)

Weeramantry, C.G., *Nauru: Environmental Damage under International Trusteeship* (1992), 28 *The International Lawyer* 186 (1994)

Schabas, W.A., *The Abolition of the Death Penalty in International Law* (1991), *Canadian Yearbook of International Law* 433 [1993]

Paton, A., *Cry the Beloved Country* (1948), 14 *Human Rights Quarterly* 653 (1992)

Tolley, H., *The U.N. Commission on Human Rights* (1987), 83 *American Journal of International Law* 190 (1989)

Humphrey, J.A., *Human Rights and the United Nations: A Great Adventure* (1984), 79 *American Journal of International Law* 195 (1985)

Hannum, H. ed., *Guide to International Human Rights Practice* (1984), 12 *International Journal of legal Information* 271 (1984)

Australian Senate Standing Committee on Foreign Affairs and Defence, *The Human Rights Conditions of the People of East Timor* (1983), 12 *International Journal of legal Information* 68 (1984)

Dunn, J., *Timor: A People Betrayed* (1983), 12 *International Journal of legal Information* 66 (1984)

Ramcharan, B.G., *Humanitarian Good Offices in International Law: The Good Offices of the United Nations Secretary-General in the Field of Human Rights* (1983), 12 *International Journal of legal Information* 64 (1984)

Tay, A.E.-S. ed., *Teaching Human Rights* (1981), 77 *American Journal of International Law* 349 (1983)

International Commission of Jurists, *States of Emergency: Their Impact on Human Rights* (1983), 11 *International Journal of legal Information* 308 (1983)

Elkind, J.B., *Interim Protection—A Functional Approach* (1981), 11 *International Journal of legal Information* 58 (1983)

Zartman, I.W. & M. Berman, *The Practical Negotiator* (1982), 10 *International Journal of legal Information* 271 (1982)

Morrisson, C., *The Dynamics of Development in the European Human Rights Convention System* (1981), 10 *International Journal of legal Information* 261 (1982)

Ball, M., *The Promise of American Law: A Theological, Humanistic View of Legal Process* (1981), 10 *International Journal of legal Information* 80 (1982)

Williams, P. ed., *The International Bill of Rights* (1981), 10 *International Journal of Legal Information* 74 (1982)

McDougal, M.S., H.D. Lasswell & L. Chen, *Human Rights and World Public Order: The Basic Politics of an International Law of Human Rights* (1980), 76 *American Journal of International Law* 184 (1982)

Bedard, R. ed., *Human Rights and Europe: A Study of the Machinery of Human Rights Protection of the Council of Europe* (2nd ed., 1980), 9 *International Journal of Law Libraries* 229 (1981)

Dominguez, J.I, N.S. Rodley, B.Wood & R. Falk, *Enhancing Global Human Rights* (1979), 74 *American Journal of International Law* 226 (1980)

Auerbach, J.R., *Unequal Justice: Lawyers and Social Change in Modern America* (1976), 9 *Victoria University of Wellington Law Review* 208 (1977–78)

Hill, L.B., *The Model Ombudsman: Institutionalizing New Zealand's Democratic Experiment* (1976), 92 *Political Science Quarterly* 354 (1977)

New Zealand Department of Justice, *Crime in New Zealand* (1968), 5 *Victoria University of Wellington Law Review* 268 (1968–70)

Harding, A., *A Social History of English Law* (1966), 5 *Victoria University of Wellington Law Review* 115 (1968–70)

Rubinstein, A., *Jurisdiction and Illegality* (1965), 1 *New Zealand Universities Law Review* 593 (1965)

Wheare, K.C., *Legislatures* (1963), 1 *New Zealand Universities Law Review* 368 (1964)

Membership in Professional Associations

American Civil Liberties Union
American Law Institute (Life member)
American Society of International Law
International Commission of Jurists, American Section
International Law Association, American Branch
New Zealand Council for Civil Liberties
International Society for the Reform of Criminal Law
Society of American Law Teachers

Professional and Public Service

General Editor: *Procedural Aspects of International Law* ("PAIL") monographs (2004–present)

Editorial Board: *Criminal Law Forum: An International Journal* (1998–present) (Editor-in-Chief 1989–1998)

Editorial Board: *Human Rights Review* (1999–present)
Editorial Advisory Board: *The International Lawyer* (1997–present)
Editorial Board: *Journal of South Pacific Law* (2013–present)
Editorial Advisory Board: *New Zealand Yearbook of International Law* (2003–present)
Editorial Advisory Board: *Istanbul Journal of Human Rights Law* (2012–present)
Board: International Centre for Criminal Law Reform and Criminal Justice Policy, Vancouver, B.C. (2007–present)
Board: International Platform of Jurists for East Timor (1998–present)
Board: International Society for the Reform of Criminal law (1998–present)
Board: New Zealand Centre for Global Studies (2013–)
Board: U.S. Friends of Victoria University of Wellington (President 2008–2013)

Involvement with United Nations and International Criminal Court

Counsel to Republic of Marshall Islands, Nuclear Weapons Cases, International Court of Justice (2014-present)

Representative of Government of Samoa to Review Conference on International Criminal Court, Kampala (2010)

Representative of Government of Samoa to Assembly of States Parties for the International Criminal Court and to the Assembly's Special Working Group on the Crime of Aggression (2002–2010)

Representative of Government of Samoa to Preparatory Commission for the International Criminal Court (1999–2002)

Representative of Government of Samoa at United Nations Diplomatic Conference of Plenipotentiaries on the Establishment of an International Criminal Court, Rome, (1998)

Representative of Government of Samoa to Preparatory Committee on the Establishment of an International Criminal Court, New York, 1996–1998

Counsel to Samoa, Illegality of Nuclear Weapons Case, International Court of Justice, 1995–96 (one of team that argued case)

Member, New Zealand delegation, Ninth United Nations Congress on the Prevention of Crime and the Treatment of Offenders, Cairo, Egypt, 1995

Member, New Zealand observer delegation to United Nations Commission on Crime Prevention and Criminal Justice, Vienna, 1992, 1993, 1996

Observer of New Zealand to Intergovernmental Working Group on the Creation of an Effective International Crime and Justice Programme, Vienna, 1991

Special Guest, Regional Seminars in Observance of the Thirtieth Anniversary of the Declaration on the Granting of Independence to Colonial Countries and Peoples, held in Port Vila, Vanuatu, and Bridgetown, Barbados, 1990

Member, New Zealand delegation, Eighth United Nations Congress on the Prevention of Crime and the Treatment of Offenders, Havana, Cuba, 1990

Member, United Nations Committee on Crime Prevention and Control, 1987–1990 (The Committee, now replaced by the Commission on Crime Prevention and Criminal Justice, supervised the work of the United Nations in the criminal justice area and was the preparatory committee for the five-yearly Congresses on the Prevention of Crime and the Treatment of Offenders)

Crime Prevention and Criminal Justice Branch, Consultant on Victims of Crime and of Abuse of Power, 1983–85 (report-writing and drafting in preparation for and at Seventh United Nations Congress on the Prevention of Crime and the Treatment of Offenders)

Centre for Human Rights, 1984 (author of Background Paper for United Nations Seminar on the Encouragement of Understanding, Tolerance and Respect in Matters Relating to Religion or Belief, Geneva, December 1984)

Index

Aaland Islands Report   267
abduction   171, 541
Ackner, Desmond   579
act of aggression   24, 40, 41, 43, 44, 45, 46, 48, 62, 65, 67, 263, 269, 286, 293, 413, 414, 415, 416, 417, 418, 426, 427
Act of Free Choice   237, 240, 243, 244, 245, 257, 272
Act of State doctrine   185, 499
active personality principle   306, 487, 493
Additional Protocol I
    Article 51(5)(b)   343, 346
    Article 52(1)   343
    Article 57 (2)(a)(iii)   346
    Article 57(2)(b)   346
    Article 57(2)(iii)(b)   343
Additional Protocol II
    Article 13 (2)   342
    Article 14, 350   453
    Article 4(2)(c)   348
    Article 85   340
Adenauer, Konrad   36
administrative sanctions   452, 585
advice and consent   507, 508, 509, 510, 512, 514
Afilalo, Ari   552
African Charter of Human and Peoples' Rights   137, 180, 279
African Commission on Human and Peoples' Rights   137, 262
African Union   82, 91, 94, 96, 102, 103, 269, 272, 273, 274
Agenda for Peace   598, 599
aggravating circumstances   92, 388, 463, 466
Ahmadou Dadio Diallo (Guinea v. Democratic Republic of the Congo)   191
Aikman, Colin   14, 519
Al Bashir   91, 93, 94, 95, 96
Al Bashir, Assan Ahmad   94, 95, 96
al-Assad, Bashar   231
Alien Tort Statute   164, 169, 474, 494, 496, 498, 499, 503, 504, 516, 533, 534, 535, 536, 537, 539, 541, 542, 543, 545, 547
Alito, Samuel A.   165, 546
Allott, Phillip   113, 114
Alston, Philip   605, 607, 613

Ambos, Kai   50, 307, 324, 358, 361, 382, 383, 395, 397, 398, 400, 402, 403, 406
American Bar Association
    ABA   325, 511
American Convention on Human Rights   136, 137, 179, 509
    Article 5 (2)   137
    Article 5(1)   137
American Law Institute (ALI)
    Model Penal Code
        Advisory Committee   463
        Section 210.6   464
    Restatements of the Law   462
    Sentencing Project   462, 464, 465, 466, 467, 468, 472
American Society of International Law
    ASIL   27
Amnesty International   3, 14, 135, 144, 385, 471
Anaya, James   248, 254
Annan, Kofi   83, 96, 97, 99, 110
annexation   40, 42, 43, 414
antiquities laws   582, 589, 591
arbitrary detention   171, 500
Armenian Genocide   553
Articles of Confederation   534
Arts, Karin   260, 270
Ashhurst, William H.   429, 443
Ashworth, Andrew   196, 392, 393, 397, 404, 408
Asian Human Rights Commission   243, 249, 250, 257
Assembly of States Parties   334
assistance to rebels   231, 232
Atomic Bomb Casualty Commission   617
attacks on civilian objects   343, 344
attacks on undefended towns and villages   344
Attorney-General (UK) v. Heinemann Publishers Australia Pty. Ltd   104, 586, 588, 590
Attorney-General of New Zealand v. Ortiz   482, 575, 577, 578, 579, 580, 581, 582, 583, 584, 585, 586, 588, 589, 590, 591, 592, 593, 594, 635
Australian Criminal Code
    Division   268, 195
aut dedere aut judicare   170, 330, 331
automated message system   561, 563, 564
Ayala Lasso, José   160, 161

Baldwin, Clive   376, 377, 390
Ballard, Chris   240, 246, 247, 248, 249
Banivanua-Mar, Tracey   242, 256, 258
Barbie, Klaus   315
Barcelona Traction, Light and Power Company, Limited (Belgium v. *Spain)*   183, 191, 192, 193, 194, 500
Barriga, Stefan   39, 41, 43, 44, 45, 47, 49, 283, 284, 286, 287, 288, 289, 290, 291, 292, 293, 294, 296, 418
Barton, George   14, 473
Basic Principles and Guidelines on the Right to a Remedy and Reparation for Victims of Gross Violations of International Human Rights Law and Serious Violations of International Humanitarian Law   182
Basic Principles on the Role of Lawyers   147
Basic Principles on the Use of Force and Firearms by Law Enforcement Officials   144
Bassiouni, M. Cherif   10, 305, 308, 316, 318, 319, 326, 327, 329, 376, 606, 612
Bastarache, Michel   528
Beatty v. Gillbanks   519, 520, 521, 523, 525, 526, 531, 532
Bemba   99, 379, 380, 382, 383, 385, 386, 387
Bentham, Jeremy   208, 429
Blackmum, Harry A.   466
Blackstone, William   429
Body of Principles for the Protection of all Persons under any Form of Detention or Imprisonment   145
bombing campaign   229, 231
Bork, Robert   499
Bosnia v. Serbia   321
Buchanan, Allen   268, 269

Boss, Amy   617
Boutros-Ghali, Boutros   160, 214
Bradford, William   535, 544, 545
Bradley, Curtis   494, 495, 499, 501, 504, 510, 518
Breyer, Stephen G.   166, 167, 484
Bricker, John W.   507, 508, 511, 512, 513, 514, 517, 518
British Nuclear Tests Veterans Association BNTVA   618, 631, 632

Brownlie, Ian   213, 273, 317, 442, 490, 492
Burroughs, John   121
Bush, George H.W.   225, 226, 228
Bush, George W.   58, 226, 377, 540, 545

Callins v. Collins   466
Camarena-Salazar, Enrique   170
Canada
    Constitution Act
        Section 93   525
    Crimes against Humanity and War Crimes Act
        Section 2(2)   195
    Criminal Code
        Section 2   195
    Criminal Code (criminal liability of organizations) Amendment Act
        Section 1   195
Canadian Charter of Rights and Freedoms
    Section 2(a)   523
    Section 2(b)   523
capital punishment. *See* death penalty
Capital Punishment Report   470
Carter, Jimmy   260, 479, 512, 536
Case 2/2   319
Case Concerning the Factory at Chorzów   177
Cassese, Antonio   181, 383, 438, 607, 612
chain of command   375, 378, 379, 380, 385
Chemical Weapons Convention   130, 511
Choice of Law   474, 475, 476, 478, 479, 480
Chomsky, Noam   3, 255
Christmas Island   618, 619, 620, 621, 622, 623, 625, 626, 627, 628, 630, 631
Churchill, Winston   222, 223, 230
Claeys, Gregory   211
Clark, Roger S.
    'Alleged Aggression in Utopia: An International Criminal Law Exam Question for 2020'   62, 69
    'Amendments to the Rome Statute of the International Criminal Court Considered at the First Review Conference on the Court, Kampala, 31 May–11 June 2010'   344
    'Crimes Against Humanity at Nuremberg'   299, 311, 312, 313, 314
    'East Timor, Indonesia and the International Community'   237

INDEX

'Criminal Code Reform in New Zealand? A Martian's view of the Erewhon Crimes Act 1961 with some footnotes to the 1989 Bill'   17, 444
  'Drafting a General Part to a Penal Code: Some Thoughts Inspired by the Negotiations on the Rome Statute of the International Criminal Court and by the Court's First Substantive Law Discussion in the Lubanga Dyilo Confirmation Proceeding'   357, 384
  'East Timor and an International Criminal Court'   260
  'Foreword' to The United Nations High Commissioner for Human Rights: the Challenges of International Protection   159
  'French Tests and International Law'   12
  'History of Efforts to Codify Crimes Against Humanity: From the Charter of Nuremberg to the Statute of Rome'   299, 327
  'Human Rights Strategies of the 1960s Within the United Nations: A Tribute to the Late Kamleshwar Das'   15, 28
  'Is The Butter Battle Book's Bitsy Big Boy Boomeroo Banned? What Has International Law to Say About Weapons of Mass Destruction?'   12, 26, 52, 54, 55, 56, 57, 120, 123, 130, 132
  'Negotiating Provisions Defining the Crime of Aggression, its Elements and the Conditions for ICC Exercise of Jurisdiction Over It'   283, 389
  'No-Fault in Delaware'   22
  'Nuremberg and the Crime against Peace'   412
  'Offenses of International Concern: Multilateral State Treaty Practice in the Forty Years Since Nuremberg'   18, 445
  'Rethinking Aggression as a Crime and Formulating Its Elements: The Final Work-Product of the Preparatory Commission for the International Criminal Court'   283, 389
  'Self-Determination and Free Association: Should the United Nations Terminate the Pacific Islands Trust?'   16
  'Some International Law Aspects of the East Timor Affair'   260
  'State Obligations Under the Genocide Convention in Light of the ICJ's Decision in the Case Concerning 'Strict Liability Offences of Possession'   391
  'Timor Gap: The Legality of the 'Treaty on the Zone of Cooperation in an Area Between Indonesian Province of East Timor and Northern Australia"   25, 260
  'The International League for Human Rights and South West Africa 1947–1957 – The Human Rights NGO as Catalyst in the International Legal Process'   16
  'The Crime of Aggression: From the Trial of Takashi Sakai, August 1946, to the Kampala Review Conference on the ICC in 2010'   22
  'The Crime of Aggression and the International Criminal Court'   283
  'The 'Decolonization' of East Timor and the United Nations Norms on Self-Determination and Aggression'   260
  'Obligations of Third States in the Face of Illegality: Ruminations inspired by the Weeramantry Dissent in the Case Concerning East Timor'   260
  'Peacekeeping forces, jurisdiction and immunity: A tribute to George Barton'   14, 473
  'State Obligations under the Genocide Convention in Light of the icj's Decision in the Case Concerning the Application of the Convention on the Prevention and Punishment of the Crime of Genocide'   12
  'Steven Spielberg's "Amistad" and Other Things I have Thought About in the Past Forty Years: International (Criminal) Law, Conflict of Laws, Insurance and Slavery'   7, 15, 20
  'The Attrition of Capital Punishment Worldwide as the American Law Institute Withdraws its Model Penal Code Provision Recommending How to Do It'   471

Criminal Code Reform (cont.)
    'The Laws of Armed Conflict and the Use or Threat of Use of Nuclear Weapons' 52, 53, 56
    'The Mental Element in International Criminal Law: The Rome Statute of the International Criminal Court and the Elements of Offences' 384, 473
    'Western Sahara and the United Nations Norms on Self-Determination and Aggression' 260, 263
    A United Nations High Commissioner for Human Rights 10, 15, 73, 158, 159, 174
    Human Rights Sourcebook 473
    International Criminal Law: Cases and Materials 461
    International and National Law in Russia and Eastern Europe: Essays in Honor of George Ginsburgs 299
    The Case against the Bomb: Marshall Islands, Samoa, and Solomon Islands before the International Court of Justice in Advisory Proceedings on the Legality of the Threat or Use of Nuclear Weapons 8, 12, 125
    Report of the Commission of Experts on Reforming Internal Justice at the United Nations 473
    Report of the International Observer Mission, Palau Referendum, December 1986 473
    The United Nations Crime Prevention and Criminal Justice Program: Formulation of Standards and Efforts at their Implementation 18, 73, 633
    Tort in Transition: A New Zealand Collection of Cases and Materials on Tort in the Accident Compensation Era 597
    Understanding International Criminal Law 461
Clark-Podgor Motion 464, 465, 466, 472
clash of civilizations 105
Clinton, William J. 226, 227, 228, 229, 230, 232, 511
Colombian Constitutional Court T025 634
Commission on Crime Prevention and Criminal Justice 137, 138, 150, 151
Committee of 24. See Special Committee on the Situation with regard to the Implementation of the Declaration on the Granting of Independence to Colonial Countries and Peoples
Common Framework for a European Sales Law 562
common law principles 520, 527, 592
common plan 366, 368, 369, 412, 435, 436
compensation 22, 162, 178, 179, 180, 181, 182, 222, 480, 588, 622, 631, 632, 633, 639
complementarity principle 50, 69, 88, 96, 176, 184, 196, 197, 287
complicity 3, 71, 162, 170, 172, 187, 201, 254, 255, 308, 358, 372
Congress of Vienna 72, 73, 74, 75, 77, 78, 79, 80
consensus 37, 47, 53, 61, 62, 65, 150, 155, 283, 291, 292, 293, 294, 296, 297, 309, 424, 480, 482, 503, 535, 604
conspiracy 364, 412, 413, 435, 436, 437, 582, 587, 591, 640
Control Council Law No. 10 187, 188, 318, 381
    Article II (2) 443
control theory 363
Convention Against Transnational Organised Crime 446
Convention for the Protection of Submarine Telegraph Cables 431
Convention on Cultural Property Implementation Act 592
Convention on Privileges and Immunities 611
Convention on the Elimination of All Forms of Discrimination against Women 509, 510, 512, 515
Convention on the Law of the Sea 278
Convention on the Rights of Persons with Disabilities 509, 510, 512
Convention on the Rights of the Child 197, 215, 509
Convention on the Use of Electronic Communications in International Contracts 555
Convention on the Use of Electronic Communications in International Contracts 555
Convention On The Use Of Electronic Communications In International Contracts 556
co-perpetrator 321, 368, 369
corporate civil liability 191

INDEX 669

corporate criminal responsibility 89, 194, 195
Correll, Hans 261, 262, 264, 277, 278
Cottier, Michael 351
Crawford, James 264, 273, 274, 277, 442
crime of aggression 20, 22, 27, 31, 32, 38, 39, 40, 41, 42, 44, 45, 46, 47, 48, 49, 50, 51, 53, 55, 56, 61, 62, 66, 67, 69, 89, 90, 112, 155, 275, 283, 284, 285, 286, 287, 288, 291, 292, 293, 294, 295, 297, 336, 389, 390, 409, 410, 411, 412, 413, 415, 416, 426
    leadership character 40, 49
    leadership requirement 416, 418
    threshold clause 44, 45, 47, 416
    Understandings 47
Crimes Against Humanity Initiative 326, 332
crimes against peace 34, 87, 112, 313, 314, 315, 317, 331, 412, 413, 423, 434, 491, 500
    Sadao Araki 423
Criminal Law Forum 18
cultural heritage 266, 580, 584, 592, 593
Currie, Brainerd 476
Curtiss-Wright 503, 507
customary international law 39, 43, 44, 45, 90, 96, 131, 171, 175, 177, 186, 187, 188, 189, 190, 191, 263, 302, 312, 315, 316, 317, 318, 320, 321, 323, 324, 327, 340, 344, 347, 364, 365, 390, 435, 494, 495, 496, 497, 498, 500, 502, 503, 504, 505, 506, 515

damage to neutral states 121, 126
Danner, Allison 309
Das, Kamleshwar 15, 28
Dayton Accord 229
death penalty 461, 463, 464, 465, 466, 467, 468, 469, 470, 471, 472, 516
    abolition 468, 469
Death Penalty Information Center 470, 471
Declaration of Basic Principles of Justice for Victims of Crime and Abuse of Power 633
Declaration on Fact-Finding by the United Nations in the field of the Maintenance of International Peace and Security 603, 608, 609, 613
Declaration on Principles of International Law and Friendly Relations among States 86, 87, 216, 262, 263, 265, 279
Declaration on the Rights of Indigenous Peoples 250, 254

decolonisation 16, 21, 238, 239, 253, 269, 273
DeGuzman, Margaret M. 553
Democratic Republic of the Congo 99, 337, 344, 345, 352
Democratic Republic of the Congo v. Uganda 352
departamento 642, 644
deterrent effect 67
Dieter, Richard C. 471
disproportionate attack 345, 346
disproportionate harm 121, 126
Dobson, Andrew 209
Drake, Rowan 620
Drew, Caitriona 270
Drooglever, Pieter 237, 240, 243, 244, 253, 257, 272
drone strikes 58
dual-use objects 392, 394, 408
Dumbarton Oaks Conference 222
Dutch New Guinea 237, 240, 272
duty to investigate 145

earned sovereignty 268, 272
East Timor 3, 10, 16, 21, 22, 23, 24, 25, 233, 237, 238, 241, 254, 256, 258, 260, 263, 271, 272, 274, 333, 533, 617
effective control 141, 379, 380, 381, 382, 388, 402
effective remedy 176, 177, 178, 179, 181, 182
Eichmann, Adolf 315
Eisenhower, Dwight D. 243, 511
electronic commerce 555, 560, 563
electronic communications 556, 557, 560, 562, 565, 566, 567, 570, 572
electronic signature 556, 567, 569
electronic transaction 559
El-Masri 161
erga omnes obligation 184, 263, 278, 321
eternal values 105
European Anti-Fraud Office (OLAF) 447, 452, 456
European Commission of Human Rights 137
European Convention on Human Rights 35, 38, 136, 179, 440
European Court of Human Rights 137, 161
European Court of Justice 551
European Prison Rules
    Rule 52(2) 141
European Union 102, 180, 261, 266, 275, 276, 277, 278, 447, 565, 640

European Union Electronic Commerce Directive   565
extradition   14, 320, 321, 324, 328, 455, 489, 504
Extraordinary Chambers in the Courts of Cambodia
  ECCC   319
extraterritorial jurisdiction   169, 453

fair trial   88, 454, 504
fairness   157, 201, 406, 454, 466, 486, 613, 616
federal common law   166, 494, 498
Federated Law Societies of Canada   527
Feinman, Jay   539
Filártiga v. Peña-Irala   163, 473, 493, 494, 495, 496, 498, 499, 501, 503, 535, 536, 539, 540, 541, 545
Finnis, John   105
First World War   31, 32, 33, 50, 75, 349, 383
Fisheries Partnership Agreement   275
Five Point Plan for Nuclear Disarmament   131
Flomo v. Firestone Natural Rubber Co llc   164, 174, 176
Flotilla incident   601, 603, 604
Flotilla Panel   604, 609
Focal Point for consultations   47
Foreign Sovereign Immunities Act   474, 484, 488, 496, 497, 541
Forest Peoples Programme   250
forum non conveniens   167, 499, 546
Fourth Chautauqua Declaration   329
Franck, Thomas   90, 603, 613
Frazer, James   577
free, prior, and informed consent   143, 250, 258
freedom of religion   520, 522, 525, 526, 528, 529, 531, 532
Freeport-McMoRan   246
French Code of Penal Procedure
  Article 689-11   195
French Penal Code
  article 131-38   195
  article 131-39   195
  article 213-3   195
French Polynesia   123, 125, 254
Friendly, Henry J.   496
Fyfe, David M.   423

Gardner, Richard   159
Gaza   349, 600

Gbagbo, Laurent   99, 304, 305
General Agreement on Tariffs and Trade (GATT)   549
general principles of law   177, 189, 190, 191, 193, 194, 212, 215, 317
Geneva Convention III
  Article 23   348
Geneva Convention IV
  Article 28   348
Geneva Conventions
  Common Article 3   339, 341
genocide   27, 38, 49, 59, 60, 87, 95, 103, 108, 112, 127, 130, 160, 161, 166, 169, 176, 183, 184, 195, 216, 224, 225, 227, 228, 239, 255, 256, 257, 258, 259, 284, 298, 312, 318, 319, 320, 321, 322, 324, 326, 336, 389, 419, 420, 421, 424, 426, 427, 428, 432, 441, 442, 500, 514, 536, 537, 544
Genocide Convention   257, 315, 319, 320, 321, 322, 508, 512, 513
Germany
  Code of Crimes under International Law   49
Ginsburg, Ruth B.   166
Gless, Sabine   445, 446, 447, 448, 450, 454
global community   103, 114, 118, 449, 495
global issues   101, 108
global society   103, 104, 118
global values   106
Goldsmith, Jack   494, 495, 500, 501, 510, 518, 550
Government of Iran v. Barakat Galleries Ltd   588, 589, 590, 591, 592, 593, 594
Grall, Jane A.   463
grave breaches of the Geneva Conventions   336, 338, 339, 340, 341, 439, 441, 442, 609
Gray, Sheila   618
Green, Joyce H.   498
Grewe, Wilhelm   36
Griffiths, Samuel   430
gross human rights violations   172, 184, 185, 198
Grotius, Hugo   105, 273, 384, 411
group crime   361, 367, 368, 370
Guiding Principles on Business and Human Rights
  Implementing the United Nations "Protect, Respect and Remedy" Framework'   199, 202

INDEX

Habermas, Jürgen 105
Hague Agreement 242, 243
Hague Regulations
    Article 46 187
    Article 47 187
    Article 48 187
Hamas 349
Hamdan v. Rumsfeld 436
Hammarskjöld, Dag 110, 113, 114
Hammerich, Elsa 617
harm principle 395
Hashimoto, Kingoro 423
Heller, Kevin Jon 22, 66
Henkin, Louis 507, 508, 509, 511, 517, 518
Hess, Rudolf 423
Hessbruegge, Jan 153, 162, 175
High Command 381, 438
High Commissioner for Refugees
    UNHCR 228
high level panel to inquire, report and
    recommend on reparation for
    victims of sexual violence in armed
    conflicts 181
Hirsi 161
Hissene-Habre Case 170
Historic Articles Act 578, 579
Holbrook, Richard 229
Holocaust 542, 553
Hudson, Manley 190
    1503 procedure' 16
Human Rights Council Fact-Finding Mission
    on Israeli Settlements 609
human shields 229, 347, 348, 349
humanitarian assistance 226, 342,
    343, 604
humanitarian intervention 21, 24, 60
Huntington v. Attrill 580
Hutus 227, 421

I.G. Farben 187, 188
Iacobucci, Frank 528
immunity 14, 67, 90, 91, 92, 93, 94, 95, 96,
    163, 184, 194, 376, 473, 496, 497, 498,
    499, 503, 504, 541, 611
    sitting heads of State 91
impunity 56, 61, 69, 83, 84, 88, 89, 90, 93, 99,
    100, 172, 176, 183, 184, 185, 186, 305, 309,
    311, 322, 326
inchoate crime 393, 419, 426, 427

incitement 216, 233, 314, 409, 410, 411, 417,
    418, 419, 420, 421, 422, 423, 424, 425, 426,
    427, 428
    war council incitement 423, 424
    'warmongering' incitement 423, 410, 428
indigenous peoples 146, 237, 248, 250, 258
indiscriminate harm 121, 126
individual criminal responsibility 33, 38, 89,
    90, 184, 185, 186, 328, 413, 415, 416, 426,
    429
Indonesia 16, 23, 25, 124, 237, 238, 239, 241,
    242, 243, 244, 245, 246, 247, 248, 249,
    250, 251, 252, 253, 254, 258
Interahamwe militia 421
Inter-American Court of Human Rights 137
internally displaced persons 634, 636, 642, 646
international armed conflict 337, 338, 339,
    340, 341, 342, 343, 344, 346, 347, 349,
    350, 351, 352, 353, 355
International Commission of Inquiry for the
    Central African Republic 602
International Committee of the Red
    Cross(ICRC) 343, 344, 348, 349, 350, 390
    Customary International Humanitarian
    Law Study 348
international constitutional law 204, 205,
    212, 213, 214, 215, 217, 218
International Court of Justice,(ICJ) 8, 10, 12,
    15, 26, 73, 87, 112, 119, 120, 121, 122, 123,
    125, 127, 128, 129, 224, 260, 317, 352, 434,
    471, 514, 598
International Court of Justice Statute
    Article 38(1)(a) 317
    Article 38(1)(c) 189
    Article 38(1)(c) 190
International Covenant on Civil and Political
    Rights 136, 140, 178, 212, 214, 215, 217, 219,
    224, 425, 509, 516
    Article 10(1) 136, 140
    Article 2(2) 178
    Article 2(3) 178
    Article 20 425
    Article 20(1) 425
    Article 6(5) 516
International Covenant on Economic, Social
    and Cultural Rights 142, 212, 214, 509, 512
international crimes 49, 83, 88, 89, 96, 99,
    176, 185, 300, 301, 309, 318, 321, 336, 356,
    374, 386, 389, 390, 447, 502

International Criminal Court
  activation of jurisdiction
    State referrals   289, 290, 292, 295
    Security Council referrals   64, 94, 95, 96, 288, 289, 295
  Assembly of States Parties   83, 98, 153, 284, 343, 354, 355, 390, 415
  Elements of Crimes   20, 309, 416, 426
  exercise of Jurisdiction   67, 69, 283, 290, 389
  obligation to cooperate with the Court   145
  Pre-Trial Division   64, 65, 66, 70, 294
  Preparatory Commission   41, 283, 285, 286, 389, 409
    2000 German Discussion Paper   43
    2002 Coordinator's Paper   43
  Prosecutor
    proprio motu investigation   39, 46, 64, 65, 70, 286, 288, 289, 290, 292, 295
  Rome Statute
    Article (8(2)(b)(iv)   342
    Article 121   91
    Article 121(5)   291, 292
    Article 15 ter   45, 293, 294
    Article 15 ter   293
    Article 25   387, 416
    Article 25 (3)   44, 356, 358, 365
    Article 25 (3)bis   416
    Article 25(3)(a)   369, 370, 371, 372
    Article 25(3)(d)   359, 361
    Article 25(3)(e)   427
    Article 25(3)(f)   426
    Article 75(1)   180
    Article 8 bis   415
    Article 8(2)(a)   336, 338, 355
    Article 8(2)(b)   129, 336
    Article 8(2)(b)(ii)   342, 344
    Article 8(2)(b)(v)   342
    Article 8(2)(b)(xxv)   348
    Article 8(2)(b)(xxvi)   351, 352, 353
    Article 8(2)(e)(i)   341, 342, 344, 345, 347
    Article 8(2)(e)(iii)   342, 343
    Article 8(2)(e)(iv)   352
    Article 8(2)(e)(vii)   337, 351
  Rules of Procedure and Evidence
    Rule 145 (1)(c)   361, 362

International Criminal Tribunal for Rwanda   91, 161, 181, 202, 303, 318, 319, 341, 378, 379, 387, 389, 420, 421
  Statute
    Article 4   341, 348, 414, 457
International Criminal Tribunal for the former Yugoslavia   91, 181, 229, 302, 303, 318, 319, 323, 338, 339, 340, 341, 344, 355, 376, 378, 379, 380, 381, 387, 388, 389, 440
  Statute
    Article 2   338, 341
    Article 3   338, 339, 341, 355
    Article 7(1)   387, 388, 439, 440, 441, 442
    Article 7(3)   387, 388
international human rights law   15, 22, 136, 140, 141, 159, 164, 174, 182, 196, 197, 199, 203, 212, 213, 215, 218, 499, 514, 597, 599, 604, 610
International Law Assciation (ILA)
  Declaration of International Law Principles on Reparation for Victims of Armed Conflict   181
International Law Commission   36, 40, 83, 87, 178, 182, 275, 301, 302, 311, 314, 316, 317, 328, 330, 331, 332, 333, 413, 435, 436
  Articles on the Responsibility of States for Internationally Wrongful Acts (2001)   182
  Draft Code of Offenses Against the Peace and Security of Mankind   301
International Lawyers for West Papua   255
International League for Human Rights   16, 28, 473
International Military Tribunal   38, 87, 89, 91, 185, 187, 285, 300, 312, 314, 375, 382, 412, 422, 435, 491
International Military Tribunal for the Far East   413, 418, 423
International Organization for Migration   637
International Parliamentarians for West Papua   255
International Platform of Jurists for East Timor   333
International Society for the Reform of Criminal Law   18
inter-State mutual legal assistance convention   325

INDEX

intifadah 351
invasion 23, 24, 89, 237, 262, 274, 275, 414
Iraq 24, 26, 48, 54, 56, 57, 61, 89, 222, 226, 231, 232, 377, 390, 423, 491, 600
Ireland
  Geneva Conventions Act 376
Israel 58, 125, 131, 231, 232, 264, 278, 315, 335, 349, 422, 491, 604
Ituri 337, 352, 353, 354

Jackson, Robert 34, 38, 39, 51, 52, 54, 223, 285, 313, 375, 423, 483, 488, 493, 507
Jacobs, Dov 337
Jalloh, Charles Chernor 305, 307
Janki, Melinda 255
Jehovah's Witnesses 520, 521, 522, 523, 531
John Doe viii et al. v. Exxon Mobil Corporation et al. 164
Johnston, Douglas 115, 213
joint criminal enterprise 440, 442, 443, 444
joint perpetration 365, 366, 369
judicial review 520, 524, 528
jus cogens 215, 216, 219, 500, 501
jus imperii 578
Just War 56, 59, 411

Kaddafi, Muammar 230, 231
Kadi 277
Kadic v. Karadzic 501, 502, 536
Kagan, Elena 166
Kaiser Wilhelm II 112, 376
Kalb, Johanna 514
Kampala amendments 48, 49, 50, 69, 283, 355
  Explanatory Memorandum to the German Bill of Ratification 47
Kampala Review Conference 20, 22, 45, 47, 343, 354, 415
  abs proposal 288, 289
  Belgian proposal 343, 344
  cabs paper 290, 291
Karadžić, Radovan 376
Karma, Filep 252, 253, 411
Katanga and Ngudjulo 347
Kaufman, Irving 479, 498, 499, 612
Kaul, Hans-Peter 37, 39, 41, 285, 304
Kearney, Michael 409, 423, 425
Keitel, Wilhelm 423
Keith, Kenneth 14, 15, 519

Kellogg-Briand Pact 335, 412
Kennedy, Anthony 164, 165, 546
Khmer Rouge 319, 320
Kigali Declaration of the Fifth Colloquium of Prosecutors of the International Criminal Tribunals 329
King of Italy v. de Medici 590
Kiobel 161, 162, 163, 164, 165, 166, 168, 169, 170, 172, 173, 174, 177, 185, 186, 188, 189, 190, 194, 199, 202, 203, 473, 487, 489, 533, 534, 535, 537, 539, 541, 542, 543, 544, 545, 546, 547
Kirby, Michael 601
kirpan 529
Koh, Harold 175, 295
Kosovo 48, 57, 60, 61, 125, 228, 229, 230, 231, 234, 256, 265, 266, 267, 268, 271, 274, 278
Kouchner, Bernard 220, 221
Kreß, Claus 31, 32, 39, 47, 48, 49, 50, 53, 306
Krupp 187
Kuwait 24, 89

Lauterpacht, Hersch 14, 273, 313
law enforcement 83, 447, 450, 455, 456, 457, 458, 541
Law of Peace and Justice 636
League of Nations 72, 74, 75, 76, 109, 116, 136, 265, 335, 411, 433
  Covenant (of the) 335
Leflar, Robert 476
Legge, JD 242
Leite, Pedro Pinto 260, 270
l'Heureux-Dubé, Claire 526, 528, 532
Libya 26, 97, 99, 230, 231, 232, 234, 474, 489, 497, 498, 501, 503, 601
Liechtenstein Institute on Self-Determination 43, 286
life imprisonment 19, 393
like-minded states 37, 471
Lloyd George, David 32
Locarno Treaties 412
Lockyer v. Gibb 404
London Charter 313, 314
  Article 6(c) 313
Lord Wright 444
Lotus 8, 127, 170, 432, 488
Loucks v. Standard Oil Co. of New York 580
Luban, David 300, 306

INDEX

Macdonald, Ronald St J   115, 213, 521
Maori   577, 578, 591, 592, 594
Marshall Islands   8, 10, 12, 13, 19, 52, 123, 125, 131, 622, 626
Martens Clause   329
Masterplan for the Acceleration and Expansion of Indonesia's Economic Development   249
Mazower, Mark   207, 208, 209
Mbarushimana   304, 344, 345, 346, 347, 362
Mbasogo v. Logo Ltd   586
McClain I   582
McClain II   582
McDougall, Carrie   417
McNair, Arnold   190
Medina, Ernest   383, 385
meetings of the intergovernmental expert group   137, 138, 139, 140, 141, 142, 143, 144, 145, 146, 147, 148, 149, 150
Meltzer Report   467, 468
Meltzer, Daniel   467
Merauke Integrated Food and Energy Estate   249
Mexico   124, 128, 170, 171, 172, 483, 491, 494, 503, 504, 505, 540, 541, 545, 582
military necessity   126
Mill, John S.   17, 419
Millennium Declaration   106, 216
Milošević, Slobodan   376
Ministry of Defence (UK) War Pensions Agency   619
mitigating circumstances   463, 466
Model Nuclear Weapons Convention   130
Monte Bello   618, 626, 628
Morel de Letelier v. Chile   498, 499
Morning Star   243, 252, 253
Morocco   23, 74, 261, 262, 263, 264, 265, 267, 268, 269, 270, 271, 272, 274, 275, 276, 277
Morris, Ian   205, 206
Morris, Norval   465, 467
Moscow Conference   222
Multani v. Commission scolaire Marguerite-Bourgeoys   529
Murphy, Frank   374
Murphy, Sean   330
My Lai massacre   383, 385

Namibia   16, 25, 124, 20, 261, 263, 264, 271
Namibia Advisory Opinion   124, 260, 261, 263, 264, 271

Narasimhan, Chakravarthi   244
National Plan for reparations   637
National Stolen Property Act (NSPA)   581, 591
nationalization   579
natural law   104, 105
ne bis in idem   452, 454
necessity (principle of)   59, 143
necessity (requirement of)   57
negligence   383, 384, 385, 386, 407, 431
neoterritorialist approach   475, 479, 480, 482
Neroni Slade, Tuiloma   6, 8, 11, 12, 19
Netherlands   33, 162, 175, 240, 242, 320, 534
New York Agreement   243, 244
New Zealand   6, 8, 10, 11, 12, 13, 14, 15, 17, 26, 110, 119, 120, 123, 124, 128, 129, 130, 135, 156, 157, 237, 238, 254, 255, 391, 430, 444, 482, 507, 519, 548, 574, 575, 577, 578, 579, 580, 581, 584, 585, 586, 591, 592, 593, 594, 597, 605, 610, 613, 631
Nickerson, Eugene   498
Nicolson, Harold   72, 73, 74, 75, 76, 77, 78, 79, 80, 81
Nigeria   153, 154, 156, 157, 162, 430, 543
niqab   527
Nixon, Richard M.   536
Non-Aligned Movement   41
Non-Aligned States   17
non-international armed conflict   38
non-proliferation campaign   618
Non-proliferation Treaty Review Conference   127
non-recognition   263, 277
non-self-governing territory   237, 254, 262, 269, 274, 276
Norms on the Responsibilities of Transnational Corporations and Other Business Enterprises with Regard to Human Rights   199
North Atlantic Treaty Organization   57, 58, 60, 61, 128, 223, 229, 231
nrpb Report   619, 620
Ntaganda   99, 305, 379, 383, 386, 387
nuclear disarmament   123, 126, 127, 131
Nuclear Non-Proliferation Treaty (NPT)   122
nuclear tests   12, 17, 26, 123, 125, 618, 619, 624, 626, 627, 630
nuclear weapons   7, 10, 12, 17, 19, 26, 27, 52, 53, 54, 56, 108, 119, 120, 121, 122, 123, 124, 125, 126, 127, 128, 129, 130, 617, 618

INDEX

Nuclear Weapons Advisory Opinion 8, 10, 12, 26, 52, 73, 119, 120, 121, 122, 124, 125, 126, 127, 128, 129, 130
nuclear-armed vessels 124
nullum crimen sine lege 34, 35, 36, 399
Nuremberg precedent 34, 35, 36, 38, 318
Nuremberg Principles 87, 315, 331
Nuremberg trials 18, 186, 311
Nworgu, Angela 154

O'Connor, Patrick 478, 579
Obama, Barack 58, 230, 231, 232, 380, 509, 511
obligation to respect human rights 164, 169, 174, 175
occupation 22, 23, 40, 42, 43, 187, 231, 237, 239, 241, 257, 258, 261, 262, 274, 275, 279, 348, 352, 353, 354, 414, 618, 626
Oertley, Paul 162
Ogoni 162
Ogoniland 162
Operation *Brigadoon* 623, 625
Operation *Grapple* 619, 620, 622, 623, 625, 627, 628, 629, 630
opt-out approach 290, 291, 292
Oxford Martin Commission for Future Generations 209

Palestine 125, 262, 263, 264, 271, 274, 275, 349, 430, 474, 496
Palmer, Geoffrey 15, 17, 597, 604
PanAmerican Development Association and Chemonics International 647
Papua New Guinea 17, 124, 239, 249
Papua Presidium Council 253
Papuan People's Council (the) 253
Paris Peace Conference 72, 73, 74, 75, 77, 81
Partial Test Ban Treaty 123
passive personality principle 485, 489, 493
pataka 577
Paton, Alan 13
patrimonial claim 585, 591
patrimonial ownership 582, 583
penal law of Danzig 433
Pensions Appeals Tribunal 619, 620
Permanent Court of International Justice 177, 190, 432
personal data (protection of) 455
personero 637, 644, 645
Philip Morris 451, 452, 479, 552
Phillips, Nicholas 85

pillage 187, 188, 585
Pinochet 321, 492, 501
Pinochet III (House of Lords) 321
Plan Nacional de Atención y Reparación Integral a las Víctimas 640
Ploeg, Anton 240
policy element 20, 299, 300, 304, 306, 308, 310, 323
Polisario 262, 269, 271, 272, 273
political prisoners 137
positive law 104, 105, 411
possession offences 391, 393, 394, 395, 396, 397, 399, 400, 405, 406, 407
Pot, Pol 320
Poulgrain, Greg 240, 242, 245
Preparatory Committee 317, 334
President Wilson's Fourteen Points 75, 76
Princeton Process 43, 286, 287, 418
principle of complementarity. *See* complementarity principle
Principle of culpability 383, 386, 388, 406
principle of equality 215
principle of legality 302, 317, 369, 429, 438
Principles and Guidelines on Access to Legal Aid in Criminal Justice Systems 147
Principles of International Law Recognized in the Charter of the Nuremberg Tribunal 83, 87, 88, 90, 96, 413
Principles on the Effective Investigation and Documentation of Torture and other Cruel, Inhuman or Degrading Treatment or Punishment 145
Principles on the Effective Prevention and Investigation of Extra-legal, Summary and Arbitrary Executions 144
privacy 143, 457, 523, 532
private international law 481, 509, 555, 557, 577, 583, 593
prohibition against causing unnecessary suffering to non-combatants 121, 126
propaganda 221, 314, 423, 425
Proposed International Convention for the Prevention and Punishment of Crimes Against Humanity 326
Prosecutor v. Abdullah Al-Senussi 97
Prosecutor v. Akayesu 88, 419, 420, 421
Prosecutor v. Bikindi 420, 421, 422
Prosecutor v. Kambanda 419, 421
Prosecutor v. Karadžić 376

Prosecutor v. Katanga   97, 99, 304, 347, 358, 362, 363, 365, 366, 369, 370, 371, 372, 398
Prosecutor v. Ruto and Sang   97
Prosecutor v. Thomas Lubanga Dyilo   99, 337, 338, 352, 353, 354, 356, 357, 358, 359, 361, 362, 363, 364, 365, 366, 367, 368, 369, 384
Prosecutor v. Uhuru Muigai Kenyatta   93, 97, 156, 233
protective principle   485, 490, 491
Protocol on the Illicit Trade in Tobacco Products   446, 447, 449, 450, 451, 452, 453, 454, 455, 456, 457, 458
  Article 1(14)   456
  Article 16 (3)   450
  Article 26(2)(a)   453
  Article 29(11)   455
  Article 30(10)   455
  Article 4(e)   456
  Article 8(1)   456
  Article 8(12)   457
  Article 8(13)   457
  Article 8(5)   456
  Article 8(6)   456
Proxmire, Edward W   507, 508, 512, 513, 514, 517, 518
Quebec   268, 520, 521, 522, 523, 528, 529, 530, 532
Quebec Seccession (Supreme Court of Canada) 267, 269
Quebec Charter of human rights and freedoms   523

Ra'ad Zeid Al-Hussein, Zeid   288, 289
Radford, Edward P.   625
Radiological Safety Regulations for Christmas Island   625
Rainbow Warrior   4, 12, 17
Ramos-Horta, José   3, 10, 16, 17, 533, 617
Randolph, Edmund   535
Reagan, Ronald   119, 120, 487, 500, 501, 513
reasonableness   167, 529, 530, 587
Rechtsgut   392, 395, 396, 400
recklessness   367, 384, 407
Red Nacional de Información para la Atención y Reparación a las Víctimas   639
Reese, Willis   476
regional citizenship   102, 103
rehabilitation   179, 180, 182, 645
Rehnquist, William   481, 538, 539

Reitz, Kevin   464, 467
reparation   177, 178, 179, 180, 181, 182, 183, 189, 190, 195, 637, 646
reservations   329, 507, 514
Responsibility to Protect doctrine   111, 215, 219, 225, 233, 319, 320, 325, 327
responsible choice   23
restitution   177, 635
right to life   215, 218, 224, 529
rights to lands and territories   258
risk to harm   396
Roberts, John G.   165, 480, 489, 505, 539
Robinson, Darryl   303, 304, 307, 334, 339, 383, 386
Robinson, Jennifer   238, 239
Robinson, Paul H.   463
Rodham Clinton, Hilary D.   175
Rodley, Nigel   135, 136, 137, 139, 145
Röling, Bernard V.A.   382
Rome Conference   19, 31, 39, 83, 284, 323, 334, 341
Rome Statute. *See* ICC Statute
Roncarelli v. Duplessis   520, 521, 522, 525, 526, 527, 531, 532
Roosevelt, Eleanor   198, 223
Roosevelt, Franklin D.   110, 222, 223
Roosevelt, Theodore   507
Root, Elihu   86
Rosenberg, Alfred   423
Roth, Alvin   204
Royal Dutch Petroleum Company   162, 175
Ruggie Report   199, 201, 202
Ruggie, John   199, 200, 550
rule of law   8, 35, 38, 83, 84, 85, 86, 87, 93, 98, 99, 100, 176, 177, 183, 197, 198, 204, 216, 433, 450, 451, 453, 454, 455, 474, 477, 502, 562, 607
Rutherford, Danilyn   237, 242, 243, 244, 253
Rwanda   37, 88, 99, 108, 112, 124, 160, 161, 181, 225, 227, 228, 229, 234, 303, 318, 341, 344, 375, 378, 419, 435, 553, 602
Rwanda Genocide   553

safety and personal security of prisoners   141
Sakai   22
Salvation Army   519, 521, 531
Saltford, John   240, 241, 243, 244
Samantar v. Yousuf   473, 541

INDEX 677

Samoa   7, 8, 10, 11, 12, 19, 20, 26, 31, 52, 53, 83, 124, 125, 128, 254, 283, 323, 333, 334, 391, 409, 471
Santa Clara Law School   175
Sarawi Arabic Democratic Republic (SADR)   269, 272, 273, 274, 276, 279
Sarei v. Rio Tinto (v)   164, 176
Saro-Wiwa, Ken   162
Sayadi and others v. Belgium   217
Scalia, Antonin   165, 173, 481, 482, 516, 517, 518
Schabas, William   12, 305, 326
secession   21, 254, 256, 267, 268, 269
Second World War   53, 56, 67, 78, 87, 187, 217, 223, 241, 376, 377, 382, 389, 412
self-defence   24, 60, 126, 129
  pre-emptive self-defence   58
self-determination   3, 10, 22, 23, 27, 76, 107, 111, 238, 239, 240, 242, 244, 245, 248, 253, 254, 255, 256, 258, 259, 261, 262, 263, 264, 265, 266, 267, 269, 270, 271, 272, 274, 277, 278, 279, 599
self-executing   224, 511, 517
Senate Foreign Relations Committee   510, 512
Serbs   229, 439, 536
serious violations of international humanitarian law   321, 336, 341, 441
Seuss Geisel, Theodor   119
Shell Petroleum Development Company (Nigeria)   162
Shell Transport & Trading Company, plc   162, 175
Shiller, Robert   205
Shukri, Muhammed Aziz   418
Simpson, Gerry   22, 333
Sinclair, Ian   155, 156, 501
Singla, Parvesh   425, 426
Sistema Nacional de Atención y Reparación Integral a las Víctimas   639
Skeleton Army   519, 521
Sloss, David   175
Somalia   225, 226, 227, 228, 229, 473, 602
Sosa v. Alvarez-Machain   163, 166, 167, 170, 171, 172, 173, 174, 484, 494, 502, 504, 505, 534, 540, 541, 545, 546
Sotomayor, Sonia M.   166
sources of international law   86, 189, 215
South Africa   5, 13, 15, 17, 89, 124, 136, 261, 264, 272
Southern Sudan Referendum Act   273
Southern Sudan Referendum Commission   272
sovereign possession   579
Spain   74, 106, 183, 191, 192, 261, 262, 264, 267, 269, 271, 321, 377, 497, 500, 542
Special Administrative Unit for Victim   636
Special Autonomy   252, 253, 255
Special Autonomy Law   252
Special Committee on the Situation with regard to the Implementation of the Declaration on the Granting of Independence to Colonial Countries and Peoples   16
Special Court for Sierra Leone   91, 92, 93, 307, 309, 319, 375, 378
Special Rapporteur on Torture   139, 141, 144
Special Working Group on the Crime of Aggression   20, 43, 44, 45, 46, 47, 62, 154, 284, 286, 409, 418
Spycatcher case. *See* Attorney-General (UK) v. Heinemann Publishers Australia Pty. Ltd
Srebrenica   230, 322
Standard Minimum Rules for the Treatment of Prisoners   135, 136, 139, 145, 149
  Rules 22–26   151
  Rule 27   143, 151
  Rule 30   143, 147
  Rule 33   144
  Rule 35(1)   147
  Rule 36   147
  Rule 37   147, 344
  Rule 44   145, 151
  Rule 54   144, 151
  Rule 55   148, 152
  Rule 58   140
  Rule 6   140, 146, 151, 152
  Rule 6(1)   151
  Rule 7   149, 151, 344
  Rule 93   147
  Rule 95   136
starvation of civilians   347, 349, 350
State conduct element   40, 41, 42, 44, 45
state consent   288, 291, 608
Staughton, J.   577, 578
Steiker, Carol S.   469
Steiker, Jordan M.   469
Steinbach, Armin   277, 278
Stephens, James Fitzjames   430

Stewart, James G.   358
Streicher, Julius   314
subsequent conduct   395
Sudan People's Liberation Movement   273
Suharto   244, 245, 246, 247, 248, 252
Sukarno   241, 242, 243, 244, 247
superior responsibility   374, 375, 377, 378, 379, 380, 381, 383, 384, 387, 388, 389, 390
supply chain control   446
suppression conventions   445, 449, 450, 451, 452, 453, 454, 455, 458
Syria   230, 231, 232, 234, 601, 609

Tadić   37, 88, 338, 340, 341, 353, 435, 439, 443, 444
Taylor, Charles   92, 376
Taylor, Telford   385
technology neutrality (principle of)   559
Tehran Conference   222
territorial principle   485
terrorism   18, 218, 231, 297, 318, 320, 327, 432, 436, 437, 443, 474, 488, 492, 497, 499, 504, 540
Thomas, Clarence   546
Titmus   622
torture   128, 136, 137, 138, 140, 141, 143, 144, 145, 148, 149, 151, 169, 170, 172, 179, 215, 218, 222, 224, 315, 316, 318, 320, 321, 473, 498, 499, 500, 535, 536, 537, 540, 541, 543, 544, 547
Torture Victim Protection Act   502, 547
tracking and tracing regime   446, 456, 457
transnational crime   447, 448, 449
transnational criminal law   445, 446, 447, 448, 449, 450, 453, 454, 457, 458
Traynor, Michael   464, 466, 467
Trinity Western University Act   524
Trinity Western University v. British Columbia College of Teachers   524, 526, 528, 530
TRIPS   552
Truman, Harry S.   222, 223, 508
Trust Territory of the Pacific Islands   17
Trusteeship Council   4, 16, 17
Tutsis   420, 421
Tutu, Desmond   99, 255

Uganda   82, 85, 90, 93, 98, 99, 124, 227, 342, 353, 415, 474

UNAMIR   227
UNESCO Convention on the Means of Prohibiting and Preventing the Illicit Import, Export and   584, 585, 590, 592
UNIDROIT Convention on Stolen or Illegally Exported Cultural Objects   590
Union des Patriotiques Congolais   353
United Kingdom   10, 13, 17, 35, 37, 124, 127, 131, 137, 377, 390, 412, 443, 585, 586, 588, 592, 605, 620
United Nations
    Charter   40, 43, 44, 54, 56, 57, 59, 86, 95, 96, 111, 115, 116, 199, 213, 215, 216, 221, 222, 223, 263, 264, 277, 285, 293, 295, 335, 413, 414, 415, 416, 417, 611
        Article 1   413
        Article 2 (4)   43
        Article 2(4)   24, 335, 414
        Article 28(b)   116
        Article 73   277
        Articles 1   2, 55 and 56, 199
        manifest violation requirement   42, 43, 44, 70, 415, 416, 417
    Committee on Crime Prevention and Control   4
    Economic and Social Council   135, 182, 602
        Resolution 1237 (XLII)   159
    General Assembly
        Fourth Committee   16
        Sixth Committee   35, 330, 331, 333, 609
        Resolution 1541   23, 263
        Resolution 3314 (XXIX)   44, 63, 262, 263, 269, 413, 414, 415
            Article 1   414
            Article 3   40, 43, 44
        Resolution 48/141   160, 161, 601
        Resolution 48/46   276
        Resolution 49/40   276
        Resolution 51/45M   130
        Resolution 65/230   137
    Global Education First Initiative   109
    High Commissioner for Human Rights   10, 73, 158, 159, 174
    Human Rights Committee   16, 17, 136, 217, 218
    Human Rights Council   138, 157, 199, 216, 597, 600, 601, 604, 609, 612

INDEX

Human Rights Commission   199
Human Rights Programme   15
Panel of Experts on Sri Lanka   609
Permanent Forum on Indigenous Issues   255
Security Council   46, 165
Temporary Executive Authority   243
UNPROFOR   228, 230
United States of America   33, 47, 51, 58, 263, 381, 437
    Agency for International Development   640, 641, 642
    federal law   173
    Senate Judiciary Committee   512
    Supreme Court   161, 163, 164, 170, 171, 173, 174, 175, 185, 374, 390, 436, 483, 486, 487
United States Securities and Exchange Commission v. Manterfield   588, 593
United States v. Ivey   587
United States v. Schultz   584
Universal Declaration of Human Rights   82, 198, 200, 201, 222, 223, 432, 440
universal jurisdiction   39, 49, 69, 184, 319, 320, 321, 327, 376, 377, 492, 542
Universal Periodic Review   212, 216, 515
universalism   101, 104, 117
universality principle. *See* Universal jurisidction
Unocal Oil   542

van Boven, Theo   178
Van den Wyngaert, Christine   326, 362, 363, 365, 366, 369, 371, 372
Vattel, Emmerich de   153, 197
Verdachtsstrafe   394
Versailles Treaty
    Art. 227   33
    Article 231   33
Vervaele, John A.E.   445, 447, 448, 454
'vested rights' approach   475, 477, 479, 480, 482, 493
Victims and Land Restitution Law (or Victims' Law)   633, 634, 635, 636, 637, 638, 639, 640, 641, 642, 644, 646, 647
    Article 177   640
Victims and Land Restitution Law (or Victims' Law)   639

Victoria University of Wellington   6, 13, 158, 519, 597
Vienna Convention of Consular Rights   471
Vienna Declaration and Programme of Action   160
Vienna World Conference on Human Rights   216
Ville de Blainville v. Beauchemin   522, 523
von Schirach, Baldur   314
vulnerable groups   89, 138, 142, 146, 152

Wall Advisory Opinion   264, 278
war of aggression   33, 34, 36, 42, 48, 52, 56, 71, 412, 413, 436
Wechsler, Herbert   463, 539
Weeramantry, Christopher   121, 124, 260
Weiler, Joseph   550
Weissbrodt, David S.   199
Wenaweser, Christian   44, 283
Werle, Gerhard   49, 360, 361, 362, 369
West New Guinea   239, 240, 241, 242, 245
West Papua   237, 238, 239, 240, 241, 242, 243, 244, 245, 246, 248, 249, 250, 251, 252, 253, 254, 255, 256, 257, 258, 259, 272
Western Sahara   7, 21, 23, 260, 261, 262, 263, 264, 265, 266, 267, 268, 269, 270, 271, 272, 273, 274, 275, 276, 277, 278, 279
Whitney R. Harris World Law Institute   326
widespread or systematic attack against any civilian population   130, 299, 301, 302, 303, 319, 440
Williams, David   519, 526
Williams, Glanville   419
World Court Project   124
World Federalist Movement   109
World Health Organisation Framework Convention on Tobacco Control FCTC   446
World Health Organization   125, 139
Wright, David   617
Yamashita   374, 377, 378, 382, 383, 385, 390, 491, 495
Youngstown   507
Yowied Village   251
Yusuf and Al Barakaat   277

Zimring, Frank   464

Printed in the United States
By Bookmasters